Lecture Notes in Computer Science 1538

Edited by G. Goos, J. Hartmanis and J. van Leeuwen

Springer
Berlin
Heidelberg
New York
Barcelona
Hong Kong
London
Milan
Paris
Singapore
Tokyo

Jieh Hsiang Atsushi Ohori (Eds.)

Advances in Computing Science – ASIAN'98

4th Asian Computing Science Conference
Manila, The Philippines, December 8-10, 1998
Proceedings

Springer

Series Editors

Gerhard Goos, Karlsruhe University, Germany
Juris Hartmanis, Cornell University, NY, USA
Jan van Leeuwen, Utrecht University, The Netherlands

Volume Editors

Jieh Hsiang
National Chi-Nan University, College of Science and Technology
Puli, Nantou, Taiwan
E-mail: hsiang@csie.ntu.edu.tw

Atsushi Ohori
Kyoto University
Research Institute for Mathematical Sciences
Sakyo-ku, Kyoto 606-8502, Japan
E-mail: ohori@kurims.kyoto-u.ac.jp

Cataloging-in-Publication data applied for

Die Deutsche Bibliothek - CIP-Einheitsaufnahme

Advances in computing science : proceedings / ASIAN '98, 4th Asian Computing Science Conference, Manila, The Philippines, December 8 - 10, 1998. Jieh Hsiang ; Atsushi Ohori (ed.). - Berlin ; Heidelberg ; New York ; Barcelona ; Hong Kong ; London ; Milan ; Paris ; Singapore ; Tokyo : Springer, 1998
(Lecture notes in computer science ; Vol. 1538)
ISBN 3-540-65388-0

CR Subject Classification (1998): F, I.2.3, D.3

ISSN 0302-9743
ISBN 3-540-65388-0 Springer-Verlag Berlin Heidelberg New York

Typesetting: Camera-ready by author
SPIN 10692998 06/3142 – 5 4 3 2 1 0 Printed on acid-free paper

Preface

This volume contains the proceedings of the *Fourth Asian Computing Science Conference* (ASIAN98), held December 8–10, 1998, in Manila, the Philippines. The previous three ASIAN conferences were also published as Lecture Notes in Computer Science, Volumes 1023 (Bangkok, 1995), 1179 (Singapore, 1996), and 1345 (Kathmandu, 1997).

Initiated in 1995 by the Asian Institute of Technology in partnership with INRIA and UNU, the ASIAN conference series aims at providing a forum in Asia for the exchange of the most recent research ideas and results in computer science and information technology. While each year features several emphasized themes, the 1998 conference focuses on the research areas of (1) formal reasoning and verification, (2) programming languages, (3) data and knowledge representation, and (4) networking and Web computing.

There were 43 submissions to the conference, out of which 17 were chosen for presentation and inclusion in this proceedings. The papers were submitted from Australia, Brazil, China, France, Germany, India, Italy, Japan, Korea, New Zealand, the Philippines, Russia, Singapore, Spain, Switzerland, Taiwan, Thailand, the United Kindom, and the United States of America. The program committee meeting was held virtually over the Internet. The selection was finalized after a fifteen-day period of lively discussion. Each paper was carefully reviewed and received at least three reports.

In addition to 17 highly selective papers, this year's conference also features a keynote speech by Jeannette M. Wing (Carnegie Mellon University) on *Formal Methods: Past, Present, and Future*, two invited talks by Susumu Hayashi (Kobe University) on *Testing Proofs by Examples* and Claude Kirchner (INRIA) on *The Rewriting Calculus as a Semantics of ELAN*, and two tutorials by Tomasz Janowski (UNU/IIST) on *Semantics and Logic for Provable Fault-Tolerance* and R.K. Shyamasundar (TIFR) on *Mobile Computation: Calculus and Languages*.

We would like to take this opportunity to thank our sponsors, the steering committee for the organization, the program committee and the reviewers for the excellent and conscientious job in evaluating the papers, the local committee for the local arrangements, Bill McCune and Claude Kirchner for generously providing the package for Web PC management and technical help in setting it up, and assistants Camel Dai and Takeomi Kato for managing the website. Without the collective work of everyone this conference would not have been possible.

September 1998

Jieh Hsiang, Atsushi Ohori
Program Co-Chair
ASIAN'98

Steering Committee

Zhou Chaochen (UNU/IIST, Macau)
Shigeki Goto (Waseda U., Japan)
Joxan Jaffar (NUS, Singapore)
Gilles Kahn (INRIA, France)
Kanchana Kanchanasut (AIT, Thailand)
Jean-Jacques Levy (INRIA, France)
R.K. Shyamasundar (TIFR Bombay, India)
Kazunori Ueda (Waseda U., Japan)

Program Committee

Eliezer A. Albacea (UP, Philippines)
Juergen Avenhaus (U. Kaiserslautern, Germany)
Arbee L.P. Chen (NTHU, Taiwan)
Hubert Comon (ENS Cachan, France)
Nachum Dershowitz (UI, USA)
Xiaoshan Gao (CAS, China)
Georges Gonthier (INRIA, France)
Jieh Hsiang *Co-Chair* (NTU, Taiwan)
Kohei Honda (U. Edinburgh, UK)
Oscar Ibarra (UCSB, USA)
Tomasz Janowski (UNU/IIST, Macau)
Deepak Kapur (SUNY Albany, USA)
Claude Kirchner (INRIA, France)
Chidchanok Lursinsap (Chula/AIT, Thailand)
Michael Maher (Griffith U., Australia)
Greg Morrisett (Cornell U., USA)
Bobby Achirul Awal Nazief (UI, Indonesia)
Tobias Nipkow (TU München, Germany)
Atsushi Ohori *Co-Chair* (Kyoto U., Japan)
Beng Chin Ooi (NUS, Singapore)
H.N. Phien (AIT, Thailand)
G. Sivakumar (IIT Bombay, India)
John Slaney (ANU, Australia)
Scott Smolka (SUNY Stony Brook, USA)
P.S. Thiagarajan (SMI,Chennai,India)
Yoshito Toyama (JAIST, Japan)
Roland H. C. Yap (NUS, Singapore)
Hsu-Chun Yen (NTU, Taiwan)
Jerome Yen (HKU, HK)
Kwangkeun Yi (KAIST, Korea)

Local Arrangements

Jonathan Dayao (DLSU, Philipines)

Additional Referees

Walter Burkhard
Murilo Camargo
Michael Codish
Thomas Deiss
Xiaoqun Du
Maribel Fernandez
L. Fribourg
Maurizio Gabbrielli
Isabelle Gnaedig
Masahito Hasegawa
Xin He
Wu Hui
Stan Jarzabek
Y. Jurski
Jyrki Katajainen
F. Laroussinie
H. Lin
Xinxin Liu
Bernd Löchner
Irina Lomazova
Paul S. Miner
Olaf Müller
Susumu Nishimura
Catuscia Palamidessi
Giridhar Pemmasani
Andreas Podelski
Xu Qiwen
Denis Roegel
Peter Scholz
Peter Stuckey
Jianwen Su
Taro Suzuki
Dang Van Hung
Willy Zwaenepoel

Sponsoring Institutions

Asian Institute of Technology
Institut national de la recherche en informatique et en automatisme
National University of Singapore
Tata Institute of Fundamental Research
Waseda University
United Nations University International Institute for Software Technology

Contents

Testing Proofs by Examples

Susumu Hayashi[1*] and Ryosuke Sumitomo[2]

[1] Department of Computer and Systems Engineering,
Faculty of Engineering, Kobe University,
1-1 Rokko-dai, Nada, Kobe, Japan,
shayashi@kobe-u.ac.jp
[2] Graduate School of Science and Technology
Kobe University, 1-1 Rokko-dai, Nada, Kobe, Japan,
sumitomo@pascal.seg.kobe-u.ac.jp

Abstract. We will present the project of *proof animation*, which started last April. The motivations, aims, and problems of the proof animation will be presented. We will also make a demo of ProofWorks, a small prototype tool for proof animation.

Proof animation means to execute formal proofs to *find* incorrectness in them. A methodology of executing formal proofs as programs is known as "proofs as programs" or "constructive programming." "Proofs as programs" is a means to *exclude* incorrectness from programs by the aid of formal proof checking. Although proof animation resembles proof as programs and in fact it is a contrapositive of proofs as programs, it seems to provide an entirely new area of research of proof construction.

In spite of wide suspicions and criticisms, formal proof developments are becoming a reality. We have already had some large formal proofs like Shanker's proof of Gödel's incompleteness theorem and proof libraries of mathematics and computer science are being built by some teams aided by advanced proof checkers such as Coq, HOL, Mizar, etc.

However, construction of big formal proofs is still very costly. The construction of formal proofs are achieved only through dedicated labors by human beings. Formal proof developments are much more time-consuming and so costly activities than program developments.

Why is it so?

A reason would be lack of means of *testing proofs*. Testing programs by examples is less reliable than verifying programs formally. It is practically impossible to exclude all bugs of complicated software only by testing. Verification is superior to testing for achieving "pure-water correctness," a correctness at the degree of purity of pure water.

However, testing is much easier and more efficient to find 80% or 90% of bugs in programs. Since the majority of softwares need correctness only at the degree

* Supported by No. 10480063, Monbusyo, Kaken-hi (the aid of Scientific Research, The Ministry of Education)

Jieh Hsiang, Atsushi Ohori (Eds.): ASIAN'98, LNCS 1538, pp. 1–3, 1998.

of purity of tap water, the most standard way of debugging is still testing rather than verification. Furthermore, the majority of people seem to find that testing programs is more enjoyable than verification.

For software developments, we have two options. However, we have only one option for formal proof developments. Obviously checking formal proofs by formal inference rules corresponds to verification. (In fact, the activity of verifications is a "subset" of formal proofs by formal proof checking.) Thus, we may set an equation

$$\frac{X}{\text{formal checking of proofs}} = \frac{\text{testing programs}}{\text{formal verification of programs}}$$

A solution X would be a means to find errors in formal proofs quickly and easily, although it cannot certify pure-water correctness.

By Curry-Howard isomorphism, a mathematical theory bridging functional programs and proofs, the solution of this equation is

$$X = \text{testing proofs by } \textit{execution of proofs},$$

Since it resembles and shares aims with "animation of formal specifications" in formal methods, we call it proof animation. We often call it "testing of proofs" as well.

A plausible reaction to proof animation may be as follows:

> How can bugs exist in formal proofs? Formally checked proofs must be correct by definition!

Bugs can exist in completely formalized proofs, since *correctness of formalization cannot not be formally certified.* This is an issue noticed in the researches of formal methods, e.g. Viper processor verification project [1] and, even earlier, by some logicians and philosophers, e.g., L. Wittgenstein and S. Kripke [3]!

We will discuss that this difficulty is a source of inefficiency of formal proof developments and proof animation may ease it. A proof animation tool ProofWorks, figure 1, is still under construction and case studies are yet to be performed. Nonetheless, the experiences with proof-program developments in PX projects [?] shows such a methodology can eliminate bugs of some kind of constructive proofs very quickly and easily.

In the talk, we will discuss the theoretical and technical problems to be solved to apply proof animation to actual proof development.

We will also give demos of ProofWorks, if facilities are available. The current version of ProofWorks is a JAVA applet proof checker. Figure 1 represents ProofWorks running on a Web browser. Formal proofs under development is represented in the left box by Mizar-like formal language. Clicking "Extract" button, it extracts a computational content of the proof, which appears in the right box. The computational content is pure functional programs in the current version of ProofWorks. ProofWorks associates the proof text with program text. Positioning a cursor in one of the boxes and clicking one of >> or << buttons,

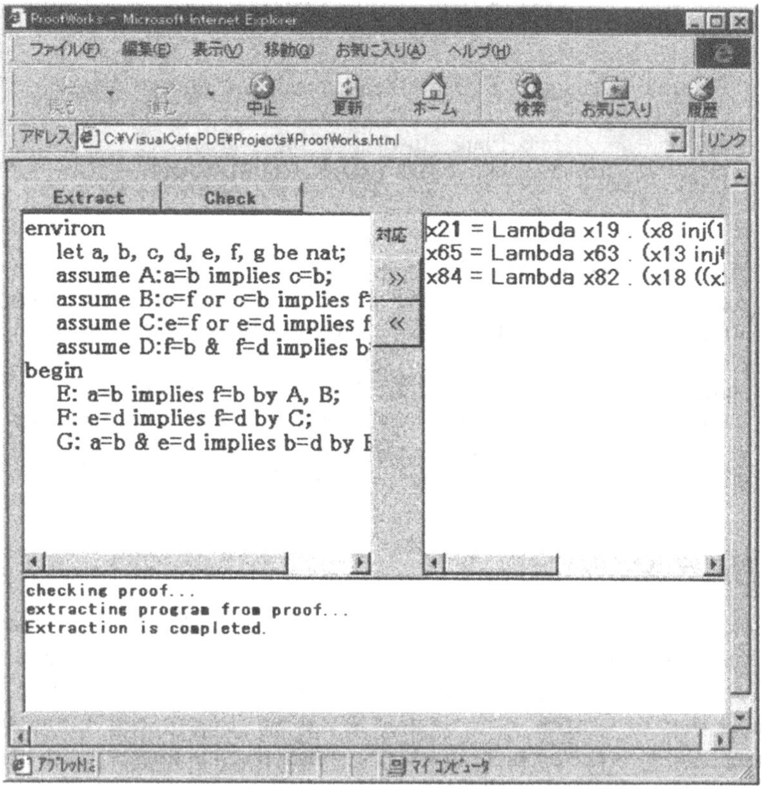

Fig. 1. ProofWorks

it shows the corresponding places in the other box. Thus, by finding a bug in a program in the right box, ProofWorks can show the corresponding points of in the proof in the left box, where a bug likely sits.

A full paper and other informations on proof animation will be available at

`http://pascal.seg.kobe-u.ac.jp/~hayashi`

References

1. Cohn, A.: The Notion of Proof in Hardware Verification, *Journal of Automated Reasoning*, Vol.5, 127-139, 1989.
2. Hayashi, S. and Nakano, H.: *PX: A Computational Logic*, The MIT Press, 1988
3. Kripke, S.: *Wittgenstein on Rules and Private Language*, Harvard University Press, Cambridge, Massachusetts, 1982
4. Sumitomo, R.: *ProofWorks: An Environment for Animation of Proofs*, Master thesis, Graduate School of Science and Technology, Kobe University, 1997.

Rigid Reachability*

Harald Ganzinger, Florent Jacquemard, and Margus Veanes

Max-Planck-Institut für Informatik
Im Stadtwald, 66123 Saarbrücken, Germany

Abstract. We show that rigid reachability, the non-symmetric form of rigid E-unification, is undecidable already in the case of a single constraint. From this we infer the undecidability of a new rather restricted kind of second-order unification. We also show that certain decidable subclasses of the problem which are $\mathcal{P}$-complete in the equational case become EXPTIME-complete when symmetry is absent. By applying automata-theoretic methods, simultaneous monadic rigid reachability with ground rules is shown to be in EXPTIME.

1 Introduction

Rigid reachability is the problem, given a rewrite system R and two terms s and t, whether there exists a ground substitution σ such that $s\sigma$ rewrites in some number of steps via $R\sigma$ into $t\sigma$. The term "rigid" stems from the fact that for no rule more than one instance can be used in the rewriting process. Simultaneous rigid reachability is the problem in which a substitution is sought which simultaneously solves each member of a system of reachability constraints (R_i, s_i, t_i). A special case of [simultaneous] rigid reachability arises when the R_i are symmetric, containing for each rule $l \to r$ also its converse $r \to l$. The latter problem was introduced in [14] as "simultaneous rigid E-unification". (Symmetric systems R arise, for instance, from orienting a given set of equations E in both directions.) It has been shown in [8] that simultaneous rigid E-unification is undecidable, whereas the non-simultaneous case with just one rigid equation to solve is NP-complete [13]. The main result in this paper is that for non-symmetric rigid reachability already the case of a single reachability constraint is undecidable, even when the rule set is ground. From this we infer undecidability of a rather restricted form of second-order unification for problems which contain just a single second-order variable which, in addition, occurs at most twice in the unification problem. The latter result contrasts a statement in [19] to the opposite.

The absence of symmetry makes the problem much more difficult. This phenomenon is also observed in decidable cases which we investigate in the second part of the paper. For instance we prove that a certain class of rigid problems which is $\mathcal{P}$-complete in the equational case becomes EXPTIME-complete when symmetry is absent. Our results demonstrate a very thin borderline between the decidable and the undecidable fragments of rigid reachability with respect to several syntactical criteria. In particular, for ground R and variable-disjoint s and

* A full version of this paper is available as MPI-I Research Report MPI-I-98-2-013.

Jieh Hsiang, Atsushi Ohori (Eds.): ASIAN'98, LNCS 1538, pp. 4–21, 1998.

t, the problem is undecidable, whereas it becomes *decidable* when, in addition, either s or t is linear.

In the Section 6 we will apply automata-theoretic methods to the monadic case and establish an EXPTIME upper bound for monadic simultaneous rigid reachability for ground rewrite systems. This generalizes the analogous result of [17] for simultaneous rigid E-unification. Also, our proof is more direct and provides a better upper bound, closer to the PSPACE lower bound given in [17]. A PSPACE upper bound for this problem has been proved more recently in a joint work with Cortier [4].

2 Preliminaries

A *signature* Σ is a collection of *function symbols* with fixed arities ≥ 0 and, unless otherwise stated, Σ is assumed to contain at least one *constant*, that is, one function symbol with arity 0. The set of all constants in Σ is denoted by $Con(\Sigma)$. We use $a, b, c, d, a_1, \ldots$ for constants and $f, g, f_1, \ldots$ for function symbols in general. A designated constant in Σ is denoted by c_Σ.

A *term language* or simply *language* is a triple $L = (\Sigma_L, \mathcal{X}_L, \mathcal{F}_L)$ where (i) Σ_L is a signature, (ii) $\mathcal{X}_L$ $(x, y, x_1, y_1, \ldots)$ is a collection of first-order variables, and (iii) $\mathcal{F}_L$ $(F, G, F_1, F', \ldots)$ is a collection of symbols with fixed arities ≥ 1, called *second-order variables*. The various sets of symbols are assumed to be pairwise disjoint. Let L be a language. L is *first-order*, if $\mathcal{F}_L$ is empty; L is *second-order*, otherwise. L is *monadic* if all function symbols in Σ_L have arity ≤ 1. The set of all terms in a language L, or *L-terms*, is denoted by $\mathcal{T}_L$. We use $s, t, l, r, s_1, \ldots$ for terms. We usually omit mentioning L when it is clear from the context. The set of first-order variables of a term t is denoted by $Var(t)$. A *ground* term is one that contains no variables. The set of all ground terms in a language L is denoted by $\mathcal{T}_{\Sigma_L}$. A term is called *shallow* if all variables in it occur at depth ≤ 1. The size $\|t\|$ of a term t is defined recursively by: $\|t\| = 1$ if $t \in \mathcal{X}_L \cup Con(\Sigma_L)$ and $\|f(t_1, \ldots, t_n)\| = \|t_1\| + \ldots + \|t_n\| + 1$ when $f \in \Sigma_L \cup \mathcal{F}_L$.

We assume that the reader is familiar with the basic concepts in term rewriting [9,1]. We write $u[s]$ when s occurs as a subterm of u. In that case $u[t]$ denotes the replacement of the indicated occurrence of s by t. An *equation in L* is an unordered pair of L-terms, denoted by $s \approx t$. A *rule in L* is an ordered pair of L-terms, denoted by $s \rightarrow t$. An equation or a rule is *ground* if the terms in it are ground. A *system* is a finite set. Let R be a system of ground rules, and s and t two ground terms. Then s *rewrites* in R to t, denoted by $s \xrightarrow[R]{} t$, if t is obtained from s by replacing an occurrence of a term l in s by a term r for some rule $l \rightarrow r$ in R. The term s *reduces* in R to t, denoted by $s \xrightarrow[R]{*} t$, if either $s = t$ or s rewrites to a term that reduces to t. R is called *symmetric* if, with any rule $l \rightarrow r$ in R, R also contains its converse $r \rightarrow l$. Below we shall not distinguish between systems of equations and symmetric systems of rewrite rules. The *size* of a system R is the sum of the sizes of its components: $\|R\| = \sum_{l \rightarrow r \in R}(\|l\| + \|r\|)$.

Rigid Reachability. Let L be a first-order language. A *reachability constraint*, or simply a constraint in L is a triple (R, s, t) where R is a set of rules in L, and s and

t are terms in L. We refer to R, s and t as the *rule set*, the *source term* and the *target term*, respectively, of the constraint. A substitution θ in L *solves* (R, s, t) (in L) if θ is grounding for R, s and t, and $s\theta \xrightarrow[R\theta]{*} t\theta$. The problem of solving constraints (in L) is called *rigid reachability* (for L). A system of constraints is *solvable* if there exists a substitution that solves all constraints in that system. *Simultaneous rigid reachability* or *SRR* is the problem of solving systems of constraints. *Monadic* (simultaneous) rigid reachability is (simultaneous) rigid reachability for monadic languages.

Rigid E-unification is rigid reachability for constraints (E, s, t) with sets of equations E. *Simultaneous Rigid E-unification* or *SREU* is defined accordingly.

Finite Tree Automata. Finite bottom-up tree automata, or simply, tree automata, from here on, are a generalization of classical automata [10,22]. Using a rewrite rule based definition [3,5], a *tree automaton* (or *TA*) A is a quadruple $(Q_A, \Sigma_A, R_A, F_A)$, where (i) Q_A is a finite set of constants called *states*, (ii) Σ_A is a *signature* that is disjoint from Q_A, (iii) R_A is a system of *rules* of the form $f(q_1, \ldots, q_n) \to q$, where $f \in \Sigma_A$ has arity $n \geq 0$ and $q, q_1, \ldots, q_n \in Q_A$, and (iv) $F_A \subseteq Q_A$ is the set of *final states*. The *size* of a TA A is $\|A\| = |Q_A| + \|R_A\|$.

We denote by $T(A, q)$ the set $\{t \in \mathcal{T}_{\Sigma_A} \mid t \xrightarrow[R_A]{*} q\}$ of ground terms *accepted* by A in state q. The set of terms *recognized* by the TA A is the set $\bigcup_{q \in F_A} T(A, q)$. A set of terms is called *recognizable* or *regular* if it is recognized by some TA.

Word automata. In monadic signatures, every function symbol has an arity at most 1, thus terms are words. For monadic signatures, we thus use the traditional, equivalent concepts of alphabets, words, finite automata, and regular expressions. A word with a variable $a_1 \ldots a_n x$ corresponds to the term $a_1(a_2(\ldots a_n(x))) \in \mathcal{T}_\Sigma$. The substitution of x by a term u is the same as the concatenation of the respective words. A finite (word) automaton A is a tuple $(Q_A, \Sigma_A, R_A, q_A^{\mathrm{i}}, F_A)$ where the components Q_A, Σ_A, R_A, F_A have the same form and meaning as the corresponding components of a tree automaton over a monadic signature, and where, additionally, q_A^{i} is the initial state. A transition $a(q) \to q'$ of R_A ($a \in \Sigma_A$, $q, q' \in Q_A$) is denoted $q \xrightarrow{a} q'$.

Second-Order Unification. Second-order unification is unification for second-order terms. For representing unifiers, we need expressions representing functions which, when applied, produce instances of a term in the given language L. Following Goldfarb [15] and Farmer [11], we, therefore, introduce the concept of an *expansion* L^* of L. Let $\{z_i\}_{i \geq 1}$ be an infinite collection of new symbols not in L. The language L^* differs from L by having $\{z_i\}_{i \geq 1}$ as additional first-order variables, called *bound variables*. The *rank* of a term t in L^*, is either 0 if t contains no bound variables (*i.e.*, $t \in \mathcal{T}_L$), or the largest n such that z_n occurs in t. Given terms t and $t_1, t_2, \ldots, t_n$ in L^*, we write $t[t_1, t_2, \ldots, t_n]$ for the term that results from t by simultaneously replacing z_i in t by t_i for $1 \leq i \leq n$. An L^*-term is called *closed* if it contains no variables other than bound variables. Note that closed L^*-terms of rank 0 are ground L-terms.

A *substitution in* L is a function θ with finite domain $\mathrm{dom}(\theta) \subseteq \mathcal{X}_L \cup \mathcal{F}_L$ that maps first-order variables to L-terms, and n-ary second-order variables to L^*-terms of rank $\leq n$. The result of applying a substitution θ to an L-term s, denoted by $s\theta$, is defined by induction on s:

1. If $s = x$ and $x \in \mathrm{dom}(\theta)$ then $s\theta = \theta(x)$.
2. If $s = x$ and $x \notin \mathrm{dom}(\theta)$ then $s\theta = x$.
3. If $s = F(t_1, \ldots, t_n)$ and $F \in \mathrm{dom}(\theta)$ then $s\theta = \theta(F)[t_1\theta, \ldots, t_n\theta]$.
4. If $s = F(t_1, \ldots, t_n)$ and $F \notin \mathrm{dom}(\theta)$ then $s\theta = F(t_1\theta, \ldots, t_n\theta)$.
5. If $s = f(t_1, \ldots, t_n)$ then $s\theta = f(t_1\theta, \ldots, t_n\theta)$.

We also write $F\theta$ for $\theta(F)$, where F is a second-order variable. A substitution is called *closed*, if its range is a set of closed terms. Given a term t, a substitution θ is said to be *grounding for* t if $t\theta$ is ground, similarly for other L-expressions. Given a sequence $\boldsymbol{t} = t_1, \ldots, t_n$ of terms, we write $\boldsymbol{t}\theta$ for $t_1\theta, \ldots, t_n\theta$.

Let E be a system of equations in L. A *unifier* of E is a substitution θ (in L) such that $s\theta = t\theta$ for all equations $s \approx t$ in E. E is *unifiable* if there exists a unifier of E. Note that if E is unifiable then it has a closed unifier that is grounding for E, since $\mathcal{T}_{\Sigma_L}$ is nonempty. The *unification problem for* L is the problem of deciding whether a given equation system in L is unifiable. In general, the *second-order unification* problem or *SOU* is the unification problem for arbitrary second-order languages. *Monadic* SOU is SOU for monadic second-order languages. By SOU *with one second-order variable* we mean the unification problem for second-order languages L such that $|\mathcal{F}_L| = 1$.

Following common practice, by an *exponential* function we mean an integer function of the form $f(n) = 2^{P(n)}$ where P is a polynomial. The complexity class EXPTIME is defined accordingly.

3 Rigid Reachability Is Undecidable

We prove that rigid reachability is undecidable. The undecidability holds already for constraints with some fixed ground rule set which is, moreover, terminating. Our main tool in proving the undecidability result is the following statement.

Lemma 1 ([16]). *One can effectively construct two tree automata* $A_{\mathrm{mv}} = (Q_{\mathrm{mv}}, \Sigma_{\mathrm{mv}}, R_{\mathrm{mv}}, \{q_{\mathrm{mv}}\})$, $A_{\mathrm{id}} = (Q_{\mathrm{id}}, \Sigma_{\mathrm{id}}, R_{\mathrm{id}}, \{q_{\mathrm{id}}\})$, *and two canonical systems of ground rules* $\Pi_1, \Pi_2 \subseteq \mathcal{T}_{\Sigma_{\mathrm{mv}}} \times \mathcal{T}_{\Sigma_{\mathrm{id}}}$, *where the only common symbol in* A_{mv} *and* A_{id} *is a binary function symbol* $\bullet$,[1] *such that, it is undecidable whether, given* $t_{\mathrm{id}} \in \mathcal{T}_{\Sigma_{\mathrm{id}}}$, *there exists* $s \in T(A_{\mathrm{mv}})$ *and* $t \in T(A_{\mathrm{id}})$ *such that* $s \xrightarrow[\Pi_1]{*} t$ *and* $t_{\mathrm{id}} \bullet s \xrightarrow[\Pi_2]{*} t$.

The main idea behind the proof of Lemma 1 is illustrated in Figure 1. In the rest of this section, we consider fixed A_{mv}, A_{id}, Π_1 and Π_2 given by Lemma 1.

Undecidability of simultaneous rigid E-unification follows from this lemma by viewing the rules R_{mv} and R_{id} of the automata A_{mv} and A_{id}, respectively, as

---

[1] We write $\bullet$ ("dot") as an infix operator.

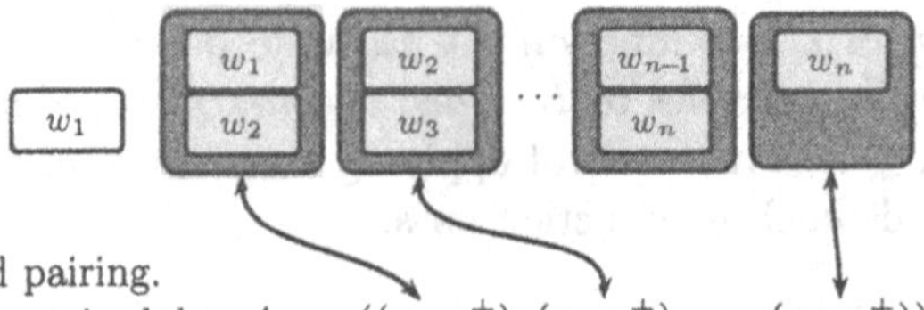

Figure 1: Shifted pairing.

The terms recognized by A_{mv}, $((v_1, v_1^+), (v_2, v_2^+), \ldots, (v_n, v_n^+))$, represent a sequence of moves of a given Turing machine, where v_i^+ is the successor of v_i according to the transition function of the TM.

Each term t recognized by A_{id} represents a sequence of IDs of the TM $(w_1, w_2, \ldots, w_n)$.

The two rewrite systems Π_1 and Π_2 are such that s reduces in Π_1 to t if and only if $v_i = w_i$ for $1 \leq i \leq k = n$, and $t_{\text{id}} \cdot s$ reduces in Π_2 to t if and only if t_{id} represents w_1, $v_i^+ = w_{i+1}$ for $1 \leq i < n$, and w_n is the final ID of the TM. It follows that such s and t exist if and only if the TM accepts the input string represented by t_{id}.

---

well as the rewrite systems Π_1 and Π_2, as sets of equations, and by formulating the reachability constraints between s and t as a system of rigid equations. It is *not* possible, though, to achieve the same effect by a *single* rigid E-unification constraint for a combined system of equations. The interference between the component systems cannot be controlled due to the symmetry of equality. This is different for reachability where rewrite rules are only applied from left to right. In fact, our main idea in the undecidability proof is to combine the four rewrite systems R_{mv}, R_{id}, Π_1, and Π_2 into a single system and achieve mutual non-overlapping of rewrite rules by renaming the constants in the respective signatures.

3.1 Renaming of Constants

For any integer m and a signature Σ we write $\Sigma^{(m)}$ for the constant-disjoint copy of Σ where each constant c has been replaced with a new constant $c^{(m)}$, we say that $c^{(m)}$ *has label* m. Note that non-constant symbols are not renamed. For a ground term t and a set of ground rules R over Σ, we define $t^{(m)}$ and $R^{(m)}$ over $\Sigma^{(m)}$ accordingly.

Given a signature Σ and two different integers m and n, we write $\Sigma^{(m,n)}$ for the following set of rules that simply replaces each label m with label n:

$$\Sigma^{(m,n)} = \{ c^{(m)} \to c^{(n)} \mid c \in Con(\Sigma) \}.$$

We write $\Pi^{(m,n)}$, where Π is either Π_1 or Π_2, for the following set of rules:

$$\Pi^{(m,n)} = \{ l^{(m)} \to r^{(n)} \mid l \to r \in \Pi \}.$$

Lemma 2. *Let m, n, k and l be distinct integers. The statements (i) and (ii) are equivalent for all all $s \in T_{\Sigma_{\text{mv}}}$ and $t_{\text{id}}, t \in T_{\Sigma_{\text{id}}}$.*

(i) $s \xrightarrow[\Pi_1]{*} t$ *and* $t_{\text{id}} \centerdot s \xrightarrow[\Pi_2]{*} t$.
(ii) $s^{(m)} \xrightarrow[\Pi_1{}^{(m,n)}]{*} t^{(n)}$ *and* $t_{\text{id}}^{(l)} \centerdot s^{(k)} \xrightarrow[\Pi_2{}^{(k,l)}]{*} t^{(l)}$.

Proof. The left-hand sides of the rules in Π_1 and Π_2 are terms in $\mathcal{T}_{\Sigma_{\text{mv}}}$ and the right-hand sides of the rules in Π_1 and Π_2 are terms in $\mathcal{T}_{\Sigma_{\text{id}}}$. But Σ_{mv} and Σ_{id} are constant-disjoint. ⊠

3.2 The Main Construction

Let R_{u} be the following system of ground rules:

$$R_{\text{u}} = R_{\text{mv}}^{(0)} \cup R_{\text{mv}}^{(2)} \cup \Sigma_{\text{mv}}{}^{(0,1)} \cup \Sigma_{\text{mv}}{}^{(2,1)} \cup R_{\text{id}}^{(4)} \cup R_{\text{id}}^{(6)} \cup \Sigma_{\text{id}}{}^{(4,3)} \cup \Sigma_{\text{id}}{}^{(6,3)} \cup \Sigma_{\text{id}}{}^{(4,5)} \cup \Pi_1{}^{(0,5)} \cup \Sigma_{\text{id}}{}^{(6,7)} \cup \Pi_2{}^{(2,7)}$$

Note that constants with odd labels occur only in the right-hand sides of rules and can, once introduced, subsequently not be removed by R_{u}. Let f_{u} be a new function symbol with arity 12. We consider the following constraint:

$$\begin{pmatrix} R_{\text{u}}, f_{\text{u}}(\ x_0,\ x_2,\ x_0, x_2,\ y_4,\ y_6,\ y_4, y_6, y_4, x_0, y_6, t_{\text{id}}^{(7)} \centerdot x_2\ ), \\ f_{\text{u}}(\ q_{\text{mv}}^{(0)}, q_{\text{mv}}^{(2)}, x_1, x_1, q_{\text{id}}^{(4)}, q_{\text{id}}^{(6)}, y_3, y_3, y_5, y_5, y_7,\ y_7\ ) \end{pmatrix} \tag{1}$$

Our goal is to show that solvability of (1), for a given $t_{\text{id}} \in \Sigma_{\text{id}}$, is equivalent to the existence of s and t satisfying the condition in Lemma 1. Note that, for all ground terms t_i and s_i, for $1 \leq i \leq 12$,

$$f_{\text{u}}(t_1, \ldots, t_{12}) \xrightarrow[R_{\text{u}}]{*} f_{\text{u}}(s_1, \ldots, s_{12}) \quad \Leftrightarrow \quad t_i \xrightarrow[R_{\text{u}}]{*} s_i \text{ (for } 1 \leq i \leq 12).$$

As a first step, we prove a lemma that allows us to separate the different subsystems of R_{u} that are relevant for the reductions between the corresponding arguments of f_{u} in the source term and the target term of (1).

Lemma 3. *For every substitution θ, θ solves the constraint (1) if and only if θ solves the system (2)–(5) of constraints.*

$$\left.\begin{array}{lll} (\ R_{\text{mv}}^{(0)}, & x_0, & q_{\text{mv}}^{(0)}\ ) \\ (\ R_{\text{mv}}^{(2)}, & x_2, & q_{\text{mv}}^{(2)}\ ) \\ (\ \Sigma_{\text{mv}}{}^{(0,1)}, & x_0, & x_1\ ) \\ (\ \Sigma_{\text{mv}}{}^{(2,1)}, & x_2, & x_1\ ) \end{array}\right\} \tag{2}$$

$$\left.\begin{array}{lll} (\ R_{\text{id}}^{(4)}, & y_4, & q_{\text{id}}^{(4)}\ ) \\ (\ R_{\text{id}}^{(6)}, & y_6, & q_{\text{id}}^{(6)}\ ) \\ (\ \Sigma_{\text{id}}{}^{(4,3)}, & y_4, & y_3\ ) \\ (\ \Sigma_{\text{id}}{}^{(6,3)}, & y_6, & y_3\ ) \end{array}\right\} \tag{3}$$

$$\left.\begin{array}{lll} (\ \Sigma_{\text{id}}{}^{(4,5)}, & y_4, & y_5\ ) \\ (\ \Pi_1{}^{(0,5)}, & x_0, & y_5\ ) \end{array}\right\} \tag{4}$$

$$\left.\begin{array}{lll} (\ \Sigma_{\text{id}}{}^{(6,7)}, & y_6, & y_7\ ) \\ (\ \Pi_2{}^{(2,7)}, & t_{\text{id}}^{(7)} \centerdot x_2, & y_7\ ) \end{array}\right\} \tag{5}$$

Proof. The direction '$\Leftarrow$' is immediate, since if θ solves a constraint (R, s, t) then obviously it solves any constraint (R', s, t) where $R \subseteq R'$.
The direction '$\Rightarrow$' can be proved by case analysis, many cases being symmetrical. For instance, we show that if θ solves (1), then θ solves the two first constraints of (2), namely $x_i\theta \xrightarrow[R^{(i)}_{\mathrm{mv}}]{*} q^{(i)}_{\mathrm{mv}}$ for $i = 0, 2$. We give the proof for $i = 0$, which, by symmetry, also proves the case $i = 2$. We know that $x_0\theta \xrightarrow[R_{\mathrm{u}}]{*} q^{(0)}_{\mathrm{mv}}$. We prove by induction on the length of reductions that, for all t, if $t \xrightarrow[R_{\mathrm{u}}]{*} q^{(0)}_{\mathrm{mv}}$ then $t \xrightarrow[R^{(0)}_{\mathrm{mv}}]{*} q^{(0)}_{\mathrm{mv}}$. The base case (reduction is empty) holds trivially. If the reduction is nonempty, then we have for some $l \to r \in R_{\mathrm{u}}$, and by using the induction hypothesis, that $t \xrightarrow[l \to r]{} s \xrightarrow[R^{(0)}_{\mathrm{mv}}]{*} q^{(0)}_{\mathrm{mv}}$. Therefore all constants in r have label 0, since r is a subterm of s and $s \in \mathcal{T}_{\Sigma^{(0)}_{\mathrm{mv}} \cup Q^{(0)}_{\mathrm{mv}}}$. Hence $l \to r \in R^{(0)}_{\mathrm{mv}}$, and consequently $t \xrightarrow[R^{(0)}_{\mathrm{mv}}]{*} q^{(0)}_{\mathrm{mv}}$. ⊠

The following lemma relates the solvability of (1) to Lemma 1.

Lemma 4. *For $t_{\mathrm{id}} \in \mathcal{T}_{\Sigma_{\mathrm{id}}}$, the constraint (1) is solvable if and only if there exists $s \in T(A_{\mathrm{mv}})$ and $t \in T(A_{\mathrm{id}})$ such that $s \xrightarrow[\Pi_1]{*} t$ and $t_{\mathrm{id}} \bullet s \xrightarrow[\Pi_2]{*} t$.*

Proof. ($\Leftarrow$) Assuming that given s and t exist, define $x_i\theta = s^{(i)}$ for $i \in \{0, 1, 2\}$ and $y_i\theta = t^{(i)}$ for $i \in \{3, 4, 5, 6, 7\}$. It follows easily from Lemma 2 and Lemma 3 that θ solves (1).

($\Rightarrow$) Assume that θ solves (1). By Lemma 3, θ solves (2)–(5). First we observe the following facts.
(i) From θ solving (2), it follows that there exists $s \in T(A_{\mathrm{mv}})$ such that $x_0\theta = s^{(0)}$ and $x_2\theta = s^{(2)}$.
(ii) From θ solving (3), it follows that there exists $t \in T(A_{\mathrm{id}})$ such that $y_4\theta = t^{(4)}$ and $y_6\theta = t^{(6)}$.
From θ solving (4) and by using (ii), it follows that $y_5\theta = t^{(5)}$. Now, due to the second component of (4) and by using (i), we get that: $s^{(0)} \xrightarrow[\Pi_1{}^{(0,5)}]{*} t^{(5)}$.
From θ solving (5) and by using (ii), it follows that $y_7\theta = t^{(7)}$. Now, due to the second component of (5) and by using (i), we get that: $t^{(7)}_{\mathrm{id}} \bullet s^{(2)} \xrightarrow[\Pi_2{}^{(2,7)}]{*} t^{(7)}$.
Finally, use Lemma 2. ⊠

We conclude with the following result.

Theorem 1. *Rigid reachability is undecidable. Specifically, it is undecidable already under the following restrictions:*

- *the rule set is some fixed ground terminating rewrite system;*
- *there are at most eight variables;*
- *each variable occurs at most three times;*
- *the source term and the target term do not share variables.*

Proof. The undecidability follows from Lemma 1 and Lemma 4. The system R_{u} is easily seen to be terminating, by simply examining the subsystems. The other restrictions follow immediately as properties of (1). ⊠

We have not attempted to minimize the number of variables in (1). Observe also that all but one of the occurrences of variables are shallow (the target term is shallow).

4 A New Undecidability Result for SOU

We prove that SOU is undecidable already when unification problems contain just a single second-order variable which, in addition, occurs twice. This result contrasts a claim to the opposite in [19]. Let Σ_{u} be the signature consisting of the symbols in R_{u} and the symbol f_{u}. Let $R_{\mathrm{u}} = \{\, l_i \to r_i \mid 1 \leq i \leq m \,\}$. Let $\boldsymbol{l}_{\mathrm{u}}$ denote the sequence $l_1, l_2, \ldots, l_m$ and $\boldsymbol{r}_{\mathrm{u}}$ the sequence $r_1, r_2, \ldots, r_m$. Let L_{u} be the following language:

$$L_{\mathrm{u}} = (\Sigma_{\mathrm{u}}, \{x_0, x_1, x_2, y_3, y_4, y_5, y_6, y_7\})$$

Let F_{u} be a new second-order variable with arity $m+1$. Let $\underline{\mathrm{cons}}$ be a new binary function symbol and $\underline{\mathrm{nil}}$ a new constant. The language L_1 is defined as the following expansion of L_{u}:

$$L_1 = (\Sigma_{\mathrm{u}} \cup \{\underline{\mathrm{cons}}, \underline{\mathrm{nil}}\}, \mathcal{X}_{L_{\mathrm{u}}}, \{F_{\mathrm{u}}\}).$$

We can show that, given $t_{\mathrm{id}} \in \mathcal{T}_{\Sigma_{\mathrm{id}}}$, the following second-order equation in L_1 is solvable if and only if the constraint (1) is solvable:

$$\begin{aligned} &F_{\mathrm{u}}(\boldsymbol{l}_{\mathrm{u}}, \underline{\mathrm{cons}}(f_{\mathrm{u}}(q_{\mathrm{mv}}^{(0)}, q_{\mathrm{mv}}^{(2)}, x_1, x_1, q_{\mathrm{id}}^{(4)}, q_{\mathrm{id}}^{(6)}, y_3, y_3, y_5, y_5, y_7, y_7), \underline{\mathrm{nil}})) \approx \\ &\quad \underline{\mathrm{cons}}(f_{\mathrm{u}}(x_0, x_2, x_0, x_2, y_4, y_6, y_4, y_6, y_4, x_0, y_6, t_{\mathrm{id}}^{(7)} \cdot x_2), F_{\mathrm{u}}(\boldsymbol{r}_{\mathrm{u}}, \underline{\mathrm{nil}})) \end{aligned} \tag{6}$$

Lemma 5. *Given $t_{\mathrm{id}} \in \mathcal{T}_{\Sigma_{\mathrm{id}}}$, (1) is solvable if and only if (6) is solvable.*

Proof. The direction '⇒' follows from [23, Lemma 2] and the observation that if θ solves (1) then $x\theta \in \mathcal{T}_{\Sigma_{\mathrm{u}}}$ for all $x \in \mathcal{X}_{L_{\mathrm{u}}}$. In particular, it is not possible that $\underline{\mathrm{cons}}$ or $\underline{\mathrm{nil}}$ appear in the terms that are substituted for $\mathcal{X}_{L_{\mathrm{u}}}$.

We prove the other direction. Assume that θ solves (6). We show that θ solves (1). A straightforward inductive argument shows that $F_{\mathrm{u}}\theta$ is an L_1^*-term of rank $m+1$ of the following form: (recall that z_i is the i'th bound variable)

$$F_{\mathrm{u}}\theta = \underline{\mathrm{cons}}(s_1, \underline{\mathrm{cons}}(s_2, \ldots, \underline{\mathrm{cons}}(s_k, z_{m+1}) \cdots)),$$

for some $k \geq 1$, by using that R_{u} is ground and that $\underline{\mathrm{cons}} \notin \Sigma_{\mathrm{u}}$ (see [23, Lemma 1]). Hence, since θ solves (6), it follows that

$$\begin{aligned} &\underline{\mathrm{cons}}(s_1[\boldsymbol{l}_{\mathrm{u}}, t'], \ldots \underline{\mathrm{cons}}(s_{i+1}[\boldsymbol{l}_{\mathrm{u}}, t'], \ldots \underline{\mathrm{cons}}(t\theta, \qquad \underline{\mathrm{nil}}) \cdots) \cdots) = \\ &\underline{\mathrm{cons}}(s\theta, \qquad \ldots \underline{\mathrm{cons}}(s_i[\boldsymbol{r}_{\mathrm{u}}, \underline{\mathrm{nil}}], \ldots \underline{\mathrm{cons}}(s_k[\boldsymbol{r}_{\mathrm{u}}, \underline{\mathrm{nil}}], \underline{\mathrm{nil}}) \cdots) \cdots), \end{aligned} \tag{7}$$

where s is the source term of (1), t is the target term of (1), and $t' = \underline{\mathrm{cons}}(t\theta, \underline{\mathrm{nil}})$. So there exists a reduction in $R_{\mathrm{u}} \cup \{t' \to \underline{\mathrm{nil}}\}$ of the following form:

$$\begin{array}{ccccccc} s_1[\boldsymbol{l}_{\mathrm{u}}, t'] & & s_2[\boldsymbol{l}_{\mathrm{u}}, t'] & & s_k[\boldsymbol{l}_{\mathrm{u}}, t'] & & t\theta \\ \parallel & \searrow^{*} & \parallel & \cdots & \parallel & \searrow^{*} & \parallel \\ s\theta & & s_1[\boldsymbol{r}_{\mathrm{u}}, \underline{\mathrm{nil}}] & & s_{k-1}[\boldsymbol{r}_{\mathrm{u}}, \underline{\mathrm{nil}}] & & s_k[\boldsymbol{r}_{\mathrm{u}}, \underline{\mathrm{nil}}] \end{array}$$

This means that $s\theta \xrightarrow[R_{\mathrm{u}}\cup\{t'\to\underline{\mathrm{nil}}\}]{*} t\theta$, *i.e.*,

$$\begin{array}{l} f_{\mathrm{u}}(\, x_0,\ x_2,\ x_0, x_2,\ y_4,\ \ y_6,\ y_4, y_6, y_4, x_0, y_6, t_{\mathrm{id}}^{(7)} \cdot x_2\,)\theta \\ \qquad\qquad\qquad \xrightarrow[R_{\mathrm{u}}\cup\{t'\to\underline{\mathrm{nil}}\}]{*} \\ f_{\mathrm{u}}(\, q_{\mathrm{mv}}^{(0)}, q_{\mathrm{mv}}^{(2)}, x_1, x_1, q_{\mathrm{id}}^{(4)}, q_{\mathrm{id}}^{(6)}, y_3, y_3, y_5, y_5, y_7, \quad y_7 \quad)\theta \end{array}$$

It is sufficient to show that $x_0\theta, x_2\theta, y_4\theta, y_6\theta \in \mathcal{T}_{\Sigma_{\mathrm{u}}}$. Because then $s\theta \in \mathcal{T}_{\Sigma_{\mathrm{u}}}$ and the rule $t' \to \underline{\mathrm{nil}}$ can not be used in the reduction of $s\theta$ to $t\theta$, since $\underline{\mathrm{nil}}$ does not occur in Σ_{u}. To begin with, we observe that

$$x_i\theta \xrightarrow[R_{\mathrm{u}}\cup\{t'\to\underline{\mathrm{nil}}\}]{*} q_{\mathrm{mv}}^{(i)} \quad (i=0,2) \quad \text{and that} \quad y_i\theta \xrightarrow[R_{\mathrm{u}}\cup\{t'\to\underline{\mathrm{nil}}\}]{*} q_{\mathrm{id}}^{(i)} \quad (i=4,6).$$

It follows by easy induction on the length of reductions that $t' \to \underline{\mathrm{nil}}$ can not be used in these reductions, since $\underline{\mathrm{nil}}$ does not not occur in R_{u}. Hence, $x_0\theta, x_2\theta, y_4\theta, y_6\theta \in \mathcal{T}_{\Sigma_{\mathrm{u}}}$, as needed. ⊠

We conclude with the following result, that follows from Lemma 1, Lemma 4, and Lemma 5.

Theorem 2. *Second-order unification is undecidable with one second-order variable that occurs at most twice.*

The role of first-order variables in the above undecidability result is important. Without first-order variables, and if there is only one second-order variable that occurs at most twice, second-order unification reduces to *ground reachability*, [20], and is thus decidable.

5 Decidable Cases

We show that rigid reachability and simultaneous rigid reachability is decidable when the rules are all ground, either the source s or the target t of any constraint is linear, and the source s and the target t are *variable-disjoint*, that is, $\mathit{Var}(s) \cap \mathit{Var}(t) = \emptyset$. The non-simultaneous case then turns out to be EXPTIME-complete. EXPTIME-hardness holds already with just a single variable. This contrasts with the fact that rigid E-unification with one variable is $\mathcal{P}$-complete [7]. When additionally both the source and target terms are linear, then rigid reachability and simultaneous rigid reachability are both $\mathcal{P}$-complete.

Note that the only difference between the conditions for undecidability of rigid reachability in Theorem 1 and the condition for decidability in Theorems 4, 5, and 6 is the linearity of source and (or) target terms. In the rest of the section, we assume fixed a signature Σ.

5.1 Decidable Cases of Rigid Reachability

We begin with defining a reduction from rigid reachability to the emptiness problem of the intersection of n regular languages recognized by tree automata

$A_1, \ldots, A_n$. This intersection emptiness problem is known to be EXPTIME-complete, see [12], [21] and [24]. We may assume the states sets of the $A_1, \ldots, A_n$ to be disjoint and that each of these tree automata has only one final state. We call these final states, respectively, $q^{\mathrm{f}}_{A_1}, \ldots, q^{\mathrm{f}}_{A_n}$. For stating the following lemma, we extend the signature Σ by a new symbol f of arity n, and assume that $n > 1$.

Lemma 6. *$T(A_1) \cap \ldots \cap T(A_n) \neq \emptyset$ iff the following constraint has a solution:*

$$(R_{A_1} \cup \ldots \cup R_{A_n},\ f(x, \ldots, x),\ f(q^{\mathrm{f}}_{A_1}, \ldots, q^{\mathrm{f}}_{A_n}))$$

Proof. ($\Rightarrow$) is obvious. For ($\Leftarrow$) we use the fact that the new symbol does not occur in any transition rule of the $A_1, \ldots, A_n$. Therefore, and since the state sets are disjoint, any reduction in $f(x, \ldots, x)\theta \xrightarrow[R_{A_1} \cup \ldots \cup R_{A_n}]{*} f(q^{\mathrm{f}}_{A_1}, \ldots, q^{\mathrm{f}}_{A_n})$ (where θ is a solution) takes place in one of the arguments of $f(x, \ldots, x)\theta$. Moreover, if the reduction is in the i-th subterm, it corresponds to the application of a rule in R_{A_i}. (It is possible, though, to apply a start rule in R_{A_j} within the i-th subterm, with $i \neq j$.) But any reduction of this form blocks in that the final state $q^{\mathrm{f}}_{A_i}$ can not be reached from the reduct.) The fact than $n > 1$ prohibits states of the automata to appear in $x\theta$. ⊠

Theorem 3. *Rigid reachability is* EXPTIME*-hard even when the rules and the target are ground and the source contains only a single variable.*

For obtaining also an EXPTIME upper bound for a somewhat less restrictive case of rigid reachability we will apply tree automata techniques. In particular, we will exploit the following fact of preservation of recognizability under rewriting, which is a direct consequence of results in [6].

Proposition 1 ([2])**.** *Let R be a ground rewrite system and t a linear term. The set $\{u \in \mathcal{T}_\Sigma \mid u \xrightarrow[R]{*} t\sigma, t\sigma \text{ ground}\}$ is recognizable by a tree automaton A the size of which is in $O(\|t\| * \|R\|^2)$.*

Proposition 2. *The subset of $\mathcal{T}_\Sigma$ of ground instances of a given linear term s is recognizable by a tree automaton A_s the size of which is linear in the size of s.*

Theorem 4. *Rigid reachability, when rules are ground, the target is linear and the source and the target are variable-disjoint, can be decided in times $O(n^{3k+4})$, where n is the size of the constraint, and k is the total number of occurrences of non-linear variables in the source term.*

Observe that the time upper bound becomes $O(n^4)$ when s is linear, since $k = 0$ in this case.

Proof. Assume to be given a reachability constraint (R, s, t) of the required form. We first construct a tree automaton A from t and R with the properties as provided by Proposition 1, that is, recognizing the predecessors with respect to R of the ground instances of t. The size $\|A\|$ of A is in $O(n^3)$.

If the source s is linear, then there is a solution for (R, s, t) iff $T(A) \cap T(A_s) \neq \emptyset$, where A_s is the tree automaton of Proposition 2. Since the intersection of recognizable languages is recognizable by a tree automaton the size of which is the product of the original tree automata, the solvability of the given constraint can be decided in time $O(\|s\| * n^3) \subseteq O(n^4)$.

If the source s is not linear, we reduce our rigid reachability problem to $|Q_A|^k$ problems of the above type. We assume wlog that A has only one final state q^{f}. Let (s_i) be the finite sequence of terms which can be obtained from the source s by the following replacements: for every variable x which occurs $j \geq 2$ times in s, we choose a tuple $(q_1, \ldots, q_j)$ of states of A such that[2] $\cap_{i \leq j} T(A, q_i) \neq \emptyset$, and we replace the ith occurrence of x with q_i for $i \leq j$ in s.

Then the two following statements are equivalent:

(i) the constraint (R, s, t) has a solution.
(ii) one of the constraints $(R_A, s_i, q^{\mathrm{f}})$ has a solution.

(i) ⇒ (ii): Assume that σ is a solution of the constraint (R, s, t). This means in particular that $s\sigma \in T(A)$ *i.e.* $s\sigma \xrightarrow[A]{*} q^{\mathrm{f}}$. Let τ be the restriction of σ to the set of linear variables of s and θ be its restriction to the set of non-linear variables of s. We have $s\theta \xrightarrow[R_A]{*} s_i$ by construction and τ is a solution of the constraint $(R_A, s_i, q^{\mathrm{f}})$.

(ii) ⇒ (i): Assume $s_i\tau \xrightarrow[R_A]{*} q^{\mathrm{f}}$ for some i and some grounding substitution τ. To each non-linear variable x of s, we associate a term $s_x \in \cap_{i \leq j} T(A, q_i)$ (it exists by construction) where $q_1, \ldots, q_j$ are the states occurring in s_i at positions corresponding to x in s. This defines a substitution θ on the non-linear variables of s (by $x\theta = s_x$) such that $s\tau\theta \in T(A)$. Hence $s\tau\theta \xrightarrow[R]{*} t\sigma$ for some grounding substitution σ which is only defined on the variables of t. Since $Var(s) \cap Var(t) = \emptyset$, the domains of θ, τ and σ are pairwise disjoint and $\tau \cup \theta \cup \sigma$ is indeed a solution to the constraint (R, s, t).

Complexity: The number of possible s_i is smaller than $|Q_A|^k$ *i.e.* it is in $O(n^{3k})$. Rigid reachability for one constraint (A, s_i, q^{f}) can be decided in time $O(n^4)$, according to the first part of this proof. Altogether, this gives a decision time in $O(n^{3k+4})$. ⊠

By symmetry, rigid reachability is also decidable when rules are ground, the source is linear and the source and the target are variable-disjoint, with the same complexities as in Theorem 4 according to the (non)-linearity of the target.

As a consequence we obtain these two theorems:

Theorem 5. *Rigid reachability is* EXPTIME*-complete when rules are ground, the source and the target are variable-disjoint, and either the source or the target is linear.*

[2] One can decide this property in time $\|A\|^k \in O(n^{3k})$.

Theorem 6. *Rigid reachability is $\mathcal{P}$-complete when the rules are ground, the source and the target are variable-disjoint, one of the source or the target is linear, and the number of occurrences of non-linear variables in the other is bounded by some fixed constant k independent from the problem.*

Note that the linear case corresponds to $k = 0$.

Proof. For obtaining the lower bound, one may reduce the $\mathcal{P}$-complete uniform ground word problem (see [18]) to rigid reachability where rules, source and target are ground. The upper bound has been proved in Theorem 4. ⊠

5.2 Decidable Cases of Simultaneous Rigid Reachability

We now generalize Theorem 6 to the simultaneous case of rigid reachability.

Theorem 7. *Simultaneous rigid reachability is $\mathcal{P}$-complete for systems of pairwise variable-disjoint constraints with ground rules, and sources and targets that are variable-disjoint and linear.*

Proof. Apply Theorem 6 separately to each constraint of the system. ⊠

Similarly, we can prove:

Theorem 8. *Simultaneous rigid reachability is* EXPTIME*-complete for systems of pairwise variable-disjoint constraints with ground rules, and sources and targets that are variable-disjoint and such that at least one of them is linear for each constraint.*

The problem remains in $\mathcal{P}$ (see Theorem 6) if there is a constant k independent from the problem and for each s_i (resp. t_i) which is non-linear, the total number of occurrences of non-linear variable in s_i (resp. t_i) is smaller than k.

We can relax the conditions in the above Theorem 8 by allowing some common variables between the s_i.

Theorem 9. *Simultaneous rigid reachability is in* EXPTIME *when all the rules of a system of constraints $\big((R_1, s_1, t_1), \ldots, (R_m, s_m, t_m)\big)$ are ground, either every t_i is linear or every s_i is linear, and for all $i, j \leq n$, the terms s_i and t_j and respectively the terms t_i and t_j (when $i \neq j$) are variable-disjoint.*

Proof. We prove for the case where every t_i is linear, the other case follows by symmetry. We reduce this problem to an exponential number of problems of the type of Theorem 8.

We associate a TA A_i to each pair (t_i, R_i) which recognizes the language $\{u \in \mathcal{T}_\Sigma \mid u \xrightarrow[R_i]{*} t_i\sigma, t_i\sigma \text{ ground}\}$ (see Proposition 1). The size of each A_i is in $O(\|t_i\| * \|R_i\|^2)$. We assume wlog that the states sets of the A_i are pairwise disjoint and that the final states sets of the A_i are singletons, namely $F_{A_i} = \{q_i^{\mathrm{f}}\}$. We construct for each $i \leq m$ a sequence of terms $(s_{i,j})$ obtained by replacement of variables occurrences in s_i (regardless of linearity) by states of A_i. To each m-tuple $(s_{1,j_1}, \ldots, s_{m,j_m})$, we associate a system which contains the constraints:

1. $(R_{A_1}, s_{1,j_1}, q_1^{\mathrm{f}}), \ldots, (R_{A_m}, s_{1,j_m}, q_m^{\mathrm{f}})$
2. for every variable x which occurs k times in $\{s_1, \ldots, s_n\}$, with $k \geq 2$, $(R_{A_1} \uplus \ldots \uplus R_{A_m}, f_{\mathrm{u}}^k(x, \ldots, x), f_{\mathrm{u}}^k(q_1, \ldots, q_k))$, where f_{u}^k is a new function symbol of arity k and $q_1, \ldots, q_k$ are the states occurring in $s_{1,j_1}, \ldots, s_{1,j_m}$ at the positions corresponding to x in $s_1, \ldots, s_m$.

Then the system $((R_1, s_1, t_1), \ldots, (R_n, s_n, t_n))$ has a solution iff one of the above systems has a solution. Each of these systems has a size which is polynomial in the size of the original system and moreover, each fulfills the hypothesis of Theorem 8 and can thus be decided in EXPTIME. Since the number of the above systems is exponential (in the size of the initial problem), we have an EXPTIME upper bound for the decision problem. ⊠

6 Monadic Simultaneous Rigid Reachability

Our second main decidability result generalizes the decidability proof of Monadic SREU for ground rules [17]. Moreover, our proof gives an EXPTIME upper bound to monadic SREU for ground rules. Although, the lower bound is known to be PSPACE [17], no interesting upper bound has been known before for this problem. We shall use basic automata theory for obtaining our result. More recently, and using different techniques, monadic rigid reachability with ground rules was found to be decidable also in PSPACE [4]. The presentation in this section will be in terms of words rather than monadic terms.

Recognizing Substitution Instances. We will first show that n-tuples of substitution instances of monadic terms are recognizable. For this purpose we let automata compute on $((\Sigma \cup \{\bot\})^n)^*$, where $\bot$ is a new symbol. The representation of a pair of words of Σ^* as a word $((\Sigma \cup \{\bot\})^2)^*$ is given by the product $\otimes$ defined as follows:

$$
\begin{aligned}
a_1 \ldots a_n \otimes b_1 \ldots b_m &= \langle a_1, b_1\rangle, \ldots, \langle a_n, b_n\rangle, \langle \bot, b_{n+1}\rangle, \ldots, \langle \bot, b_m\rangle \quad \text{if } n < m \\
a_1 \ldots a_n \otimes b_1 \ldots b_m &= \langle a_1, b_1\rangle, \ldots, \langle a_m, b_m\rangle, \langle a_{m+1}, \bot\rangle, \ldots, \langle a_n, \bot\rangle \quad \text{if } n \geq m
\end{aligned}
$$

We extend this definition of $\otimes$ associatively to tuples of arbitrary length in the obvious way.

Lemma 7. *Let L_1, …, L_n be recognizable subsets of Σ^*. Then $L_1 \otimes \ldots \otimes L_n$ is recognizable (in $((\Sigma \cup \{\bot\})^n)^*$). The size of the product automaton can be bounded by the product of the sizes of its factor automata.*

When constructing an automaton for $\Sigma^* \otimes L$ from an automaton A for L, the size of the product automaton can be bounded by $c * \|A\|$, for some (small) constant c if the alphabet Σ is assumed to be fixed.

Theorem 10. *Given p monadic Σ-terms s_i, the set of tuples of their ground instances $\{s_1\theta \otimes \ldots \otimes s_p\theta \mid \theta \text{ ground }\}$ is recognizable by an automaton with size exponential in $\sum_{j=1}^{p} |s_j|$.*

The proof of Theorem 10 will be based on three technical lemmas.

Lemma 8. *Let L be a language of tuples of the form $a_1 \otimes \ldots \otimes a_n$ that is recognized by A. Then, for any permutation π, the language*

$$L_\pi = \{a_{\pi 1} \otimes \ldots \otimes a_{\pi n} \mid a_1 \otimes \ldots \otimes a_n \in L\}$$

can be recognized by an automaton of the same size as A.

Proof. We apply the permutation π to the tuples of symbols appearing in the rules of R_A. ⊠

Lemma 9. *Given $s, t \in \Sigma^*$, the set $\{su \otimes tu \mid u \in \Sigma^*\}$ is recognizable by an automaton with size exponential in $|s| + |t|$.*

Proof. The automaton reads words $s'u \otimes t'v$, checking that $s' = s$ and $t' = t$ and that $u = v$. For the latter test, the automaton has to memorize (in states) the last $\big||t| - |s|\big|$ symbols of Σ read in $s'u$. This is the reason of the exponential number of states. An example of the construction for $\Sigma = \{0, 1\}$, $s = 0$ and $t = 101$, is given in figure 2. ⊠

The construction underlying the proof of Lemma 9 cannot be generalized to the case of non-monadic signatures. However, one can generalize it (in the monadic case) to the product of an arbitrary number p of words.

Lemma 10. *Given $p \geq 1$, the set $\{s_1 u \otimes \ldots \otimes s_p u \mid u \in \Sigma^*\}$ is recognizable by an automaton with size exponential in $\sum_{j=1}^{p} |s_j|$.*

Proof. By induction on p. The base case $p = 1$ is trivial, and the case $p = 2$ is proved in Lemma 9. Assume that $p \geq 2$ and that we have an automaton A with $T(A) = \{s_1 u \otimes \ldots \otimes s_p u \mid u \in \Sigma^*\}$ and one more word s_{p+1}. Let A'' be an automaton such that $T(A'') = \{s_p u \otimes s_{p+1} u \mid u \in \Sigma^*\}$. A'' may be obtained by applying Lemma 9 again. Clearly,

$$(T(A) \otimes \Sigma^*) \cap (\underbrace{\Sigma^* \otimes \ldots \otimes \Sigma^*}_{p-1} \otimes T(A'')) = \{s_1 u \otimes \ldots \otimes s_{p+1} u \mid u \in \Sigma^*\}.$$

According to Lemma 7, this language is recognizable by an automaton A', and, by Lemmas 7 and 9, $\|A'\|$ is of the order $2^{\sum_{j=1}^{p} |s_j|} * 2^{|s_p| + |s_{p+1}|}$. ⊠

Now we are ready to prove Theorem 10.

Proof. The terms s_i are either ground or have the form $s_i(x_i)$ with one occurrence of a variable x_i "at the end". Let, for any variable x occurring in any of the terms, $s_{i_1}, \ldots, s_{i_n}$ be those terms among the s_i which contain x. According to Lemma 10, the language

$$L_1^x = \{s_{i_1}\theta \otimes \ldots \otimes s_{i_n}\theta \mid \theta \text{ ground }\}$$

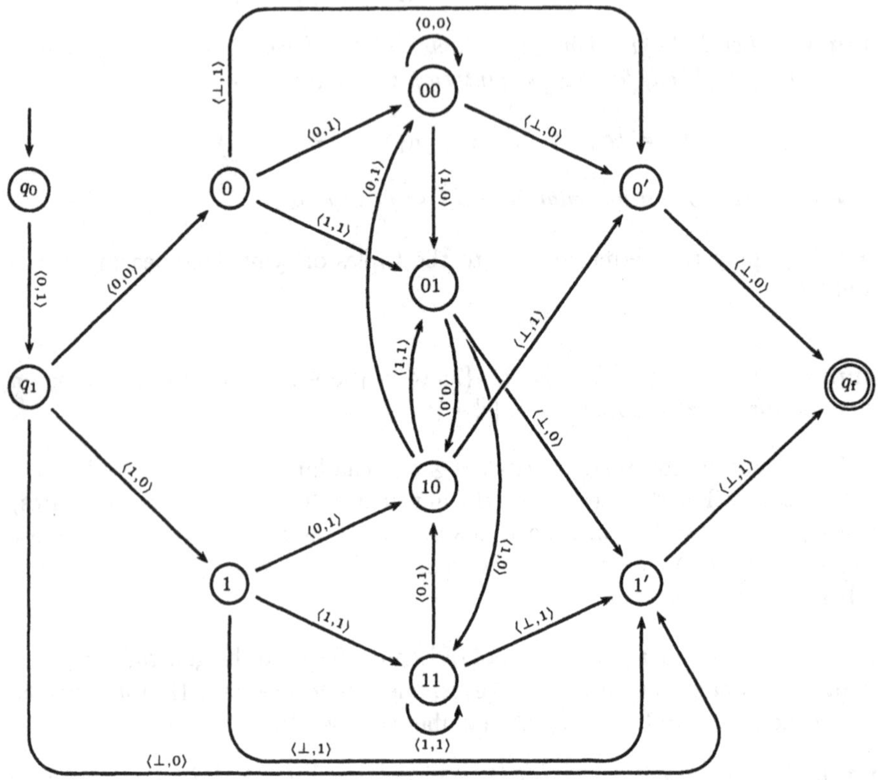

Figure 2: An example illustrating the proof of Lemma 9.

is recognizable by an automaton of size exponential in $\sum_j |s_{i_j}|$. From the Lem -ma 7 we infer that $L_2^x = L_1^x \otimes \Sigma^* \otimes \ldots \otimes \Sigma^*$, with $p-n$ factors of Σ^*, is recognizable by an automaton with size exponential in $\sum_j |s_{i_j}|$. Finally, $L^x = (L_2^x)_\pi$, with π a permutation which maps the first n indices j to i_j, that is, puts the s_{i_j} into their right place in the sequence $1\ldots p$, is also recognizable by an automaton of the same size, see Lemma 8. Moreover, it is not difficult to see that

$$L_g = \{t_1 \otimes \ldots \otimes t_p \mid t_i = s_i \text{ if } s_i \text{ ground, and } t_i \in \Sigma^*, \text{ otherwise}\}$$

is recognizable by an automaton with size polynomial in $\max|s_i|$. The desired language arises as the intersection of the languages L^x and L_g so that recognizability with the stated complexity bound follows. ⊠

For solving reachability constraints, we also need to recognize rewriting relations.

Theorem 11 **([6]).** *Given a ground rewrite system R on Σ^*, the set $\{u \otimes v \mid u \xrightarrow[R]{*} v\}$ is recognizable by an automaton the size of which is polynomial in the size of R.*

Theorem 12. *Rigid reachability in monadic signatures is in* EXPTIME *when the rules are ground.*

Proof. Let (R, s, t) be a constraint over the monadic signature Σ. We show that the set of "solutions" $\mathcal{S} = \{s\theta \otimes t\theta \mid s\theta \xrightarrow[R]{*} t\theta\}$ is recognizable. s and t may contain at most one variable which we denote by x and y, respectively. These two variables may or may not be identical. Applying Theorem 10, we may infer that $\{s\theta \otimes t\theta \mid x\theta \text{ and } y\theta \text{ ground }\}$ is recognizable by an automaton A with size exponential in $|s| + |t|$. By Theorem 11, the set $\{u \otimes v \mid u, v \in \Sigma^*, u \xrightarrow[R]{*} v\}$ is recognizable by an automaton A' with size polynomial in the size of R. Clearly $\mathcal{S} = T(A) \cap T(A')$, and emptiness is decidable in time linear in the size of the corresponding intersection automaton (which is exponential in $|s| + |t|$ and polynomial in the size of R). ⊠

The extension to the simultaneous case of Theorem 12 generalizes and improves a result of [17].

Theorem 13. *Simultaneous rigid reachability in monadic signatures is decidable in* EXPTIME *when the rules are ground.*

Proof. The construction is a generalization of the one for Theorem 12. Suppose we are given the system of constraints (R_i, s_i, t_i), $1 \leq i \leq n$. We first construct an automaton A_i for each $i \leq n$ such that $T(A_i) = \{u \otimes v \mid u, v \in \Sigma^*, u \xrightarrow[R_i]{*} v\}$. Then $A = \bigotimes_{i=1}^{n} A_i$ (see Lemma 7) recognizes the language:

$$T(A) = \{u_1 \otimes v_1 \otimes u_2 \otimes \ldots \otimes u_n \otimes v_n \mid \text{ for all } i \leq n, u_i, v_i \in \Sigma^*, u_i \xrightarrow[R_i]{*} v_i\}.$$

The size of A is the product of the sizes of the A_i, hence of order M^n where M is the maximum of the sizes of the A_i. In Theorem 10 we have shown that the language

$$L^G = \{s_1\theta \otimes t_1\theta \otimes \ldots \otimes s_n\theta \otimes t_n\theta \mid \theta \text{ ground}\}$$

is recognizable by an automaton A^G of size exponential in $\sum_i |s_i| + |t_i|$. The simultaneous reachability constraint is solvable if and only the intersection $L^G \cap T(A)$ is non-empty. According to the respective sizes of the automata in the above intersection, this gives an EXPTIME upper-bound for deciding simultaneous rigid reachability. ⊠

7 Conclusion

We have shown that absence of symmetry makes the solving of rigid reachability constraints in general much harder. In the non-simultaneous case one jumps from decidability to undecidability. In the case of ground rewrite rules, source terms with just a single variable, and ground target terms, the complexity increases from $\mathcal{P}$-completeness to EXPTIME-completeness. The undecidability of rigid reachability implies a new undecidability result for second-order unification problems with just a single second-order variable that occurs twice. We have also seen that automata-theoretic methods provide us with rather simple proofs of upper bounds in the monadic case.

Acknowledgments

The authors wish to thank the referees for their useful remarks and suggestions, which led to significant improvements of the results presented in this paper.

References

1. F. Baader and T. Nipkow. *Term Rewriting and All That.* Cambridge University Press, 1998.
2. J.-L. Coquidé and R. Gilleron. Proofs and reachability problem for ground rewrite systems. In *Proc. of the 6th International Meeting of Young Computer Scientists*, volume 464 of *LNCS*, pages 120–129, 1990.
3. J.L. Coquidé, M. Dauchet, R. Gilleron, and S. Vágvölgyi. Bottom-up tree pushdown automata: classification and connection with rewrite systems. *Theoretical Computer Science*, 127:69–98, 1994.
4. V. Cortier. PSPACE-completeness of monadic simultaneous rigid reachability. Unpublished manuscript, july 1998.
5. M. Dauchet. Rewriting and tree automata. In H. Comon and J.P. Jouannaud, editors, *Term Rewriting (French Spring School of Theoretical Computer Science)*, volume 909 of *Lecture Notes in Computer Science*, pages 95–113. Springer Verlag, Font Romeux, France, 1993.
6. Max Dauchet, Thierry Heuillard, Pierre Lescanne, and Sophie Tison. The confluence of ground term rewriting systems is decidable. In *Proc. 3rd IEEE Symp. Logic in Computer Science, Edinburgh*, 1988.
7. A. Degtyarev, Yu. Gurevich, P. Narendran, M. Veanes, and A. Voronkov. The decidability of simultaneous rigid E-unification with one variable. In T. Nipkow, editor, *Rewriting Techniques and Applications*, volume 1379 of *Lecture Notes in Computer Science*, pages 181–195. Springer Verlag, 1998.
8. A. Degtyarev and A. Voronkov. Simultaneous rigid E-unification is undecidable. UPMAIL Technical Report 105, Uppsala University, Computing Science Department, May 1995.
9. N. Dershowitz and J.-P. Jouannaud. Rewrite systems. In J. Van Leeuwen, editor, *Handbook of Theoretical Computer Science*, volume B: Formal Methods and Semantics, chapter 6, pages 243–309. North Holland, Amsterdam, 1990.
10. J. Doner. Tree acceptors and some of their applications. *Journal of Computer and System Sciences*, 4:406–451, 1970.
11. W.M. Farmer. Simple second-order languages for which unification is undecidable. *Theoretical Computer Science*, 87:25–41, 1991.
12. Thom Frühwirth, Ehud Shapiro, Moshe Y. Vardi, and Eyal Yardemi. Logic programs as types for logic programs. In *6th IEEE Symp. Logic In Computer Science*, pages 300–309, 1991.

13. J.H. Gallier, P. Narendran, D. Plaisted, and W. Snyder. Rigid E-unification is NP-complete. In *Proc. IEEE Conference on Logic in Computer Science (LICS)*, pages 338–346. IEEE Computer Society Press, July 1988.
14. J.H. Gallier, S. Raatz, and W. Snyder. Theorem proving using rigid E-unification: Equational matings. In *Proc. IEEE Conference on Logic in Computer Science (LICS)*, pages 338–346. IEEE Computer Society Press, 1987.
15. W.D. Goldfarb. The undecidability of the second-order unification problem. *Theoretical Computer Science*, 13:225–230, 1981.
16. Y. Gurevich and M. Veanes. Partisan corroboration, and shifted pairing. Research Report MPI-I-98-2-014, Max-Planck-Institut für Informatik, September 1998.
17. Y. Gurevich and A. Voronkov. Monadic simultaneous rigid E-unification and related problems. In P. Degano, R. Corrieri, and A. Marchetti-Spaccamella, editors, *Automata, Languages and Programming, 24th International Colloquium, ICALP'97*, volume 1256 of *Lecture Notes in Computer Science*, pages 154–165. Springer Verlag, 1997.
18. D. Kozen. Complexity of finitely presented algebras. In *Proc. 9th STOC*, pages 164–177, 1977.
19. J. Levy. Decidable and undecidable second-order unification problems. In T. Nipkow, editor, *Rewriting Techniques and Applications, 9th International Conference, RTA-98, Tsukuba, Japan, March/April 1998, Proceedings*, volume 1379 of *Lecture Notes in Computer Science*, pages 47–60. Springer Verlag, 1998.
20. J. Levy and M. Veanes. On the undecidability of second-order unification. Submitted to *Information and Computation*, 1998.
21. Helmut Seidl. Haskell overloading is dexptime-complete. *Inf. Process. Letters*, 52:57–60, 1994.
22. J.W. Thatcher and J.B. Wright. Generalized finite automata theory with an application to a decision problem of second-order logic. *Mathematical Systems Theory*, 2(1):57–81, 1968.
23. M. Veanes. The relation between second-order unification and simultaneous rigid E-unification. In *Proc. Thirteenth Annual IEEE Symposium on Logic in Computer Science, June 21–24, 1998, Indianapolis, Indiana (LICS'98)*, pages 264–275. IEEE Computer Society Press, 1998.
24. Margus Veanes. On computational complexity of basic decision problems of finite tree automata. Technical Report 133, Computing Science Department, Uppsala University, 1997.

Mechanizing Reasoning about Large Finite Tables in a Rewrite Based Theorem Prover *

Deepak Kapur and M. Subramaniam

Computer Science Department, State University of New York, Albany, NY
kapur@cs.albany.edu subu@cs.albany.edu

Abstract. Finite tables are commonly used in many hardware and software applications. In most theorem provers, tables are typically axiomatized using predicates over the table indices. For proving conjectures expressed using such tables, provers often have to resort to brute force case analysis, usually based on indices of a table. Resulting proofs can be unnecessarily complicated and lengthy. They are often inefficient to generate as well as difficult to understand. Large tables are often manually abstracted using predicates, which is error-prone; furthermore, the correctness of abstractions must be ensured. An approach for modeling finite tables as a special data structure is proposed for use in *Rewrite Rule Laboratory* (*RRL*), a theorem prover for mechanizing equational reasoning and induction based on rewrite techniques. Dontcare entries in tables can be handled explicitly. This approach allows tables to be handled directly without having to resort to any abstraction mechanism. For efficiently processing large tables, concepts of a *sparse* and *weakly sparse* tables are introduced based on how frequently particular values appear as table entries. Sparsity in the tables is exploited in correctness proofs by *doing case analyses on the table entries rather on the indices.* The generated cases are used to deduce constraints on the table indices. Additional domain information about table indices can then be used to further simplify constraints on indices and check them. The methodology is illustrated using a nontrivial correctness proof of the hardware SRT division circuit performed in *RRL.* 1536 cases originally needed in the correctness proof are reduced to 12 top level cases by using the proposed approach. Each individual top level case generated is much simpler, even though it may have additional subcases. The proposed approach is likely to provide similar gains for applications such as hardware circuits for square root and other arithmetic functions, in which much larger and multiple lookup tables, having structure similar to the sparse structure of the SRT table, are used.

1 Introduction

With the declining memory costs and for faster speed, lookup tables are being widely used in high performance hardware applications. Recent hardware implementations of complex arithmetic functions such as division, square root and

* Partially supported by the National Science Foundation Grant no. CCR-9712366.

Jieh Hsiang, Atsushi Ohori (Eds.): ASIAN'98, LNCS 1538, pp. 22–42, 1998.

other arithmetic functions are based on large finite lookup tables with preprogrammed values [3,2]. As an example, the hardware implementation of the radix 4 SRT division algorithm, the source of the now notorious Intel Pentium bug, uses a large finite lookup table for quotient digit selection. This paper is motivated by our recent work in which SRT division algorithm was automatically verified using the theorem prover *Rewrite Rule Laboratory* (*RRL*) using several different formulations of the quotient digit selection lookup table[8,10][0].

Our experience in these verification efforts suggests that most theorem provers for mechanizing induction including our own theorem prover *RRL* do not provide adequate support for reasoning about finite tables. Tables used in applications typically have structure. Many lookup tables have only a few distinct entries. Many of the entries are *dont-cares* either because those portions of a table are not expected to be accessed, or the way such a table is being used, the behavior does not depend upon the entry value for those indices. Further, indices may be ordered; in many cases indices are subranges over numbers, finite bit vectors etc. A typical approach for specifying lookup tables in a prover is by a case expression (conditional expression) over the table indices (using *if then else* like expressions, for examples, in PVS, ACL2). Such descriptions are too general, and do not bring forth the structure in finite lookup tables.

A prover would typically resort to brute force case analyses based on the table indices regardless of the table structure. This may get prohibitively expensive for large tables. A hardware implementation of the SRT division algorithm, for instance, uses a table with up to 800 entries [13]. Implementations of arithmetic functions such as the square root are based on much larger lookup tables [15,16,17] and many of these implementations use multiple lookup tables[15,16]. In order for the verification to scale up to these applications, it is necessary that the underlying structure in tables be better exploited by theorem provers.

The main goal of this paper is to propose an approach for facilitating mechanized reasoning about finite lookup tables in theorem provers such as *RRL*. We propose modeling finite lookup tables as a special data type, much like numbers and booleans. Viewing a finite table as a special data type instead of a predicate or a finite subset of a Cartesian product results in a compact and direct axiomatization, without having to bother about index values for which the table is not defined. *Sparse* and *weakly sparse* tables are defined based on how frequently particular values appear as table entries. A mechanism for considering the dont-care entries is discussed.

The above concepts are exploited to mechanize reasoning about properties of algorithms using finite tables. It is shown that for sparse and weakly sparse tables, case analyses performed based on the table entries rather than the table indices, results in fewer top level cases in a proof attempt, thus producing compact and elegant proofs. For each table entry, from the instance of a given property, simpler constraints on the table indices can be deduced by projec-

[0] In [8] the correctness of the SRT division algorithm was established in *RRL* using a predicate based formulation of a lookup table whereas [10] describes a more direct verification strategy using a function based specification of the lookup table.

tion using quantifier elimination techniques such that testing them suffices to establish the given property. Structure and properties of the table indices can be further exploited to reduce the number of index values for which the constraints over the indices need to be checked.

Directly considering tables used in circuit implementations instead of manually abstracting them using predicates has a distinct advantage, and is likely to be preferred by hardware designers. Firstly, abstractions can be error-prone. Secondly, their correctness must be established separately. Thirdly, there can be a significant abstraction gap between a concrete circuit implementation and its description using abstractions, depending upon the nature and complexity of the abstraction process. The main argument for abstracting tables is that large tables can lead to unsurmountable number of cases, which can be difficult to manage as well as there can be considerable redundancy. The proposed approach addresses these concerns by firstly avoiding abstractions by directly considering tables as they are, and secondly by exploiting the structure of tables–their entries as well as indices.

The power of the proposed approach is especially evident from the radix 4 SRT division algorithm that employs a large lookup table for quotient digit selection with unspecified entries. The main invariant establishing the convergence of this algorithm is proved by the proposed approach in section 5. The number of cases in the proof reduce from the 1536 required in [10], based on traditional modeling of tables with case analyses being performed on table indices, to 12 top level cases using the proposed approach. The individual cases generated by the proposed approach are also much simpler than those generated by case analyses over table indices.

An integration of tables into the theorem prover PVS is described in [14]. The aim there is to provide a special syntactic notation for describing different more general types of tables to aid user specification and to analyze tables for disjointness, coverage and consistency using PVS. Unlike our approach, table construct in [14] translates into regular PVS constructs (*cond,case*) that perform case analyses on the table indices. The notion of *dontcare* in this paper is similar to *blank entry* described there. A specification of the SRT division quotient digit selection table is also given there. However, this description uses higher order features of PVS such as dependent types and no attempt is made there to exploit the structure of the table besides the dontcare entries in proving properties. Support for specifying and analyzing tables is provided by tools such as *Tablewise* [6], *SCR** [5] and consistency checker for RSML [4]. However, these tools are aimed at developing consistent and complete table specifications, and do not address the use of structure in tables while proving properties involving tables as done in this paper.

2 Formalizing Finite Lookup Tables in RRL

A finite n-dimensional table is a data structure indexed by an n-tuple; for every legal n-tuple of index values, it has an entry value. Some of the table entries may be unspecified or dont cares. Figure 1 below has examples of two tables: a matrix and a table implementing a finite function. Without the proposed extension, there are at least two ways to define a finite table in *RRL*.

1. Define a table as a function with the Cartesian product of index types as its domain and the entry type as its range. Each index tuple for which the table has an entry, the function is defined to be the entry. Otherwise, the function is partially specified. In that case, to use the cover-set induction method to generate cases in proofs [20], it is necessary to relativize the original formula using a formula specifying the subdomain on which the function is defined.
2. Define a table as a predicate that is a subset of the Cartesian product of the index types and the entry type. Both index values for which there is a table entry as well as those index values for which there is no table entry would have to be given. Further, a lack of functional notational is likely to lead to cumbersome expression of properties involving a table.

dm	0	1	2	3
0	1	0	0	0
1	0	2	0	0
2	0	0	3	0
3	0	0	0	4

gcd	0	1	2	3
0	-	1	2	3
1	1	1	1	1
2	2	1	2	1
3	3	1	1	3

Fig. 1. Diagonal and GCD4 Tables

To avoid having to specify the index tuples to be excluded from a table specification, we define a table as a special data type with a functional notation for accessing table entries. Ideally, we would like a table to be input graphically to *RRL* as given in Figure 1. In the absence of that, we propose a simple mechanism using finite enumerated types for indices.

A finite enumerated data type is a finite set of distinct values, typically denoted by a finite set of distinct free constructor symbols, i.e., every two distinct constructors are not equal. Such a data type `en` can be specified by listing its constructors as nullary constants of types `en` and declaring them to be *free*. Since finite subranges of natural numbers are often used for indices, a finite enumerated data type can also be specified as a subrange: `enum en: [lo ... hi: nat]` where `lo` and `hi` are natural numbers with `lo <= hi`. Subranges over integers can also be used as shown below for the quotient digit selection table for SRT division.

If the constructors of an enumerated type are given using numbers, then an implicit conversion from the values of the enumerated type to numbers is done so that the usual operations on numbers supported by *RRL* as a part of the quantifier-free theory of Presburger arithmetic can be used [9]. As will be evident below, for SRT division, such an implicit conversion is quite useful. In this sense, the constructor names used for enumerated types can be overloaded.

Using enumerated types, a parameterized data type construct `table` is introduced. Each instance of this construct gives a specific data type `table`. A `table` instance is specified by the name of the table, followed by a list of *index* types, each assumed to be an enumerated type, and a *value* type for table entries. This is followed by a list of all table entries; no order among the table entries is assumed.

A parameterized (generic) function `lookup` is associated with `table` to access the entries of a specific table given the index values. We slightly abuse the notation and write `lookup(t, i1, j1)` to mean the entry associated with the index values `i1, j1` in the table `t`. For convenience, we introduce the syntactic sugar for `lookup(t, i1, j1)` and write it as `t(i1, j1)`. A table can then be specified by enumerating its entries as: `t(i1, j1) := v1, t(i2, j2) := v2, ...` . For example, the diagonal matrix dm can be specified as follows. Numbers $0, 1, 2, 3$ are free constructors of the enumerated type $n03$. The value type of the table is natural numbers, but only the subrange $0 - 4$ is being used.

```
[0, 1, 2, 3 : -> n03]
table [ dm : n03, n03 -> nat ]
dm(0, 0) := 1,   dm(0, 1) := 0,   dm(0, 2) := 0,  dm(0, 3) := 0,
dm(1, 0) := 0,   dm(1, 1) := 2,   dm(1, 2) := 0,  dm(1, 3) := 0,
dm(2, 0) := 0,   dm(2, 1) := 0,   dm(2, 2) := 3,  dm(2, 3) := 0,
dm(3, 0) := 0,   dm(3, 1) := 0,   dm(3, 2) := 0,  dm(3, 3) := 4.
```

2.1 Specifying Tables with Dontcare Entries

Many lookup tables in practice have dontcare entries, i.e., for certain index values, it does not really matter what the table entry is. This may be so either because table is not meant to be used for such index values, or the properties of interest involving the table do not depend upon the entry value for such index values. A table with dontcare entries is supported similar to a table without dontcare entries, with the difference that a special constant value `dontcare` is used as an entry value. Constant `dontcare` is the only value of a built-in sort called *Dtcare*, and the value type of such a table is a union of *Dtcare* and *er*, the type of other table entries.

For example, in Figure 1, the table *gcd*, denoting the greatest common divisor function for the modular 4, is deliberately made for illustrative purpose to have a dontcare value (indicated by $-$ in the table) when both of its arguments are 0. The specification of this table is given below.

```
table [gcd : n03, n03 -> nat U Dtcare ]
gcd(0, 0) := dontcare,   gcd(0, 1) := 1,  gcd(0, 2) := 2,  gcd(0, 3) := 3,
gcd(1, 0) := 1,          gcd(1, 1) := 1,  gcd(1, 2) := 1,  gcd(1, 3) := 1,
gcd(2, 0) := 2,          gcd(2, 1) := 1,  gcd(2, 2) := 2,  gcd(2, 3) := 1,
gcd(3, 0) := 3,          gcd(3, 1) := 1,  gcd(3, 2) := 1,  gcd(3, 3) := 3.
```

3 Mechanizing Reasoning about Finite Tables

We now illustrate using a simple example how properties about tables are proved in the theorem prover *RRL* in the absence of the proposed approach.

Consider proving a simple property about dm.

$$(C1): \; dm(x,y) \; * \; z \; \leq \; (y+1)*z,$$

where x and y are variables of the enumerated type n03, z is a natural number, $*$ denotes multiplication over numbers.

Without using the table data type, dm would have been partially specified as a binary function from natural numbers to natural numbers. So the above formula would not be meaningful without the conditions $0 \leq x, y \leq 3$. The conjecture $(C1)$ will have to be relativized as:

$$(C1)': \; dm(x,y) \; * \; z \; \leq \; (y+1)*z \;\; if \;\; (0 \leq x \leq 3) \wedge (0 \leq y \leq 3).$$

The proof of $(C1)$ is attempted by exhaustive case analysis over the possibles values of x and y (4 each) leading to 16 cases. Each of the 16 cases can be easily proved by simplification (invoking the decision procedure for quantifier-free Presburger arithmetic in *RRL* for instance). For example, for $x = 0, y = 1$, we have:

$$dm(0,1)*z \; \leq \; (1+1)*z \;\; if \;\; (0 \leq 0 \leq 3) \; \wedge (0 \leq 1 \leq 3)$$

The formula simplifies to true using the definitions of dm and $*$ to $0 \; \leq \; 2*z$.

The reader would notice that the case generated for the table entry $dm(0,2)$ is similar. As a matter of fact, all the cases generated corresponding to the table entry 0 would be established in the same way, irrespective of the values of the indices x and y.

We introduce the notion of a *sparse* table in the next section following the terminology from matrix algebra. We show how sparsity in the tables (e.g. dm) can be exploited to identify common structure among different cases.

3.1 Sparse Tables

Definition 1 *A table t is sparse iff there is at least one table entry $t(i_1, \cdots, i_n)$ such that the number of index tuples with that entry is at least $\geq |t|/2$, where $|t|$ is the size of t.*

In a sparse table, thus, the majority of the entries have the same value. This entry value is called the *most frequent entry value.* The table dm is sparse with the most frequent entry value being 0. Similarly, the table gcd is also sparse with the most frequent entry value being 1.

Mechanizing Reasoning about Sparse Tables In many applications, while reasoning about sparse tables, the cases generated corresponding to the most frequent entry value are often proved in a similar fashion. The proofs usually follow due to the special properties of the most frequent entry value regardless of the corresponding values of the indices. This information can be exploited while attempting proofs.

From the conjecture and the most frequent entry value, properties that indices must satisfy can be generated. And such properties are often easier to prove than the original conjecture. As a result, it is not only easy to mechanically prove such a conjecture by case analysis on table entries instead of case analysis on indices, but even a hand-proof is likely to be simplified using this approach.

Consider the above conjecture $(C1)$ about the diagonal matrix dm.

$$(C1): \quad dm(x,y) \ * \ z \ \leq \ (y+1) * z.$$

Let us attempt to prove based on the table entries in dm instead of index values x, y. There are 5 cases, instead of 16 cases due to different index values x and y. First, we attempt a proof for index tuples for which the table entry is the most frequent entry value 0. $(C1)$ reduces to $(C1.0): \ 0 \ * \ z \ \leq \ (y+1) * z$, with the implicit assumption that only those values of x and y for which $dm(x,y) = 0$ must be considered. This formula simplifies to $(C1.0): \ 0 \ \leq \ (y+1) * z$, which is true for natural numbers. Notice that different values of x and y for which the table entry is 0 need not be considered.

Now consider the remaining entry values. For $dm(x,y) = 1$, $(C1)$ reduces to $(C1.1): \ 1 \ * \ z \ \leq \ (y+1) * z$, which simplifies to $(C1.1): \ z \ \leq \ (y+1) * z$, which reduces to true no matter what y is.

For $dm(x,y) = 2$, $(C1)$ reduces to $(C1.2): \ 2 \ * \ z \ \leq \ (y+1) * z$, which simplifies to $(C1.2): \ z \ \leq \ y * z$. This formula is not true unless $y \geq 1$. Since $dm(x,y) = 2$ implies that $x = 1, y = 1$. So, this case also follows.

The other two cases also follow as they constrain y to be 2 and 3.

As this simple example illustrates, case analysis based on indices would have resulted in 16 cases for the above formula, whereas case analysis based on table entry values results in only 5 cases. 12 cases corresponding to the entry value 0 are handled as one single case, thus recognizing a common proof structure.

3.2 Deducing Constraints over Indices for Table Entries

As suggested above, case analysis on table entry values often leads to a simpler version of the conjecture. For each table entry v, a proof of the simplified conjecture can be attempted exhaustively, by substituting only those index values with the table entry v. Redundancy and duplication in proofs for different cases can be avoided this way.

Another promising approach is to generate from the simplified conjecture, a constraint on index values that must be satisfied for the conjecture to be valid for a particular table entry v. It can then be checked whether the index values corresponding to v indeed satisfy the constraint.

In the above example, for $dm(x,y) = 2$, the formula simplifies to $\forall z \ \ z \leq y * z$. One possibility is to exhaustively check the conjecture for values of y for which $dm(x,y) = 2$. In case there are many values of x, y for which the table entry is 2, another way is to eliminate z from the above formula by quantifier elimination, which gives the constraint $1 \leq y$ on y, which is indeed true.

The main idea in deriving constraints on index variables from a given conjecture for a particular table entry value is that of *projection* of the values of index variables. This can be obtained by eliminating non-index variables from the negation of the simplified formula by quantifier elimination. This is described below.

Consider a universally quantified conjecture $\phi(x_1, \cdots, x_n, y_1, \cdots, y_m)$ where $x_1, \cdots, x_n$ are the index variables and $y_1, \cdots, y_m$ are the nonindex variables, and ϕ has occurrences of table terms indexed by $x_1, \cdots, x_n$. Without any loss of generality and for simplicity, we assume a single table term $t(x_1, \cdots, x_n)$. Consider a particular entry value, say v of $t(x_1, \cdots, x_n)$; let I be the finite set of index tuples (values of $x_1, \cdots, x_n$) for which the table t has entry value v.

When ϕ is attempted for the case $t(x_1, \cdots, x_n) = v$, a formula ϕ_1 with $t(x_1, \cdots, x_n)$ replaced by v is obtained from ϕ. Typically ϕ_1 is simpler than ϕ. If it can be proved, we are done. In general, ϕ_1 need not be valid, in which case, the goal is to find an equivalent quantifier-free formula $\psi(x_1, \cdots, x_n)$ without any nonindex variables such that for each index tuple satisfying ψ, ϕ_1 is true for every value of the nonindex variables. And, this can be achieved by quantifier-elimination methods.

Let $\theta(x_1, \cdots, x_n)$ be $\neg\forall \ y_1, \cdots y_m \ \ \phi_1(x_1, \cdots, x_n, y_1, \cdots, y_m)$. The formula θ characterizes the index tuples for which there is at least a tuple of values for nonindex variables that falsifies ϕ_1. The corresponding index tuples constitute the complement of I. Let $\psi_1(x_1, \cdots, x_n)$ be a quantifier-free formula equivalent to $\neg\forall \ y_1, \cdots y_m \ \ \phi_1(x_1, \cdots, x_n, y_1, \cdots, y_m)$. Then $\psi = \neg\psi_1$ characterizes the set of index tuples such that for all values of nonindex variables, ϕ_1 is true. The formula $\psi(x_1, \cdots, x_n)$ is the constraint on index variables for ϕ to be valid if $t(x_1, \cdots, x_n) = v$. If for every tuple in I, ψ is true, then ϕ is valid for the case when $t(x_1, \cdots, x_n) = v$.

The above discussion gives an algorithm as well as sketches a correctness proof of the proposed algorithm. For eliminating nonindex variables, different techniques can be used. If the nonindex variables range over numbers, then Fourier's elimination algorithm in *RRL* can be used.

The above algorithm is illustrated on $(C1)$:

$$(C1): \ \ dm(x, y) \ * \ z \ \leq \ (y + 1) * z.$$

For $dm(x, y) = 3$, $(C1)$ simplifies to $(C1.3): \ \ 3 \ * \ z \ \leq \ (y+1)*z$, which reduces to: $(C1.3): \ \ 2 \ * \ z \ \leq \ y * z$. It must be shown that $(C1.3)$ is true for every z on values of y for which $dm(x, y) = 3$. The variable z is the nonindex variable. Negating $(C1.3)$ gives: $\exists z, \ \ 2 \ * \ z \ > \ y * z$. Using $z = 1$, the quantifier can be eliminated giving $2 \ > \ y$. The negation of the above formula $2 \leq y$ is the constraint on y, which is indeed the case for y such that $dm(x, y) = 2$.

3.3 Tables with Dontcare Entries

A `dontcare` entry in a table either denotes portions of the table that are not supposed to be accessed or a dontcare entry may be used like a *wild-card* in which case the validity of a conjecture involving the table does not depend on the particular entry value. In both these situations, for a dontcare entry value, it must be ensured the index values for which the table entry is dontcare, the conjecture is valid independent of the table entry. This particular case is handled separately without replacing the table term by the dontcare value. This is illustrated using the property ($C2$) about the *gcd* function.

$$(C2): \quad odd(gcd(x,y)) \;\; if \;\; odd(x) \vee odd(y).$$

The case analysis is done based on different values of $gcd(x, y)$. The case corresponding to the dontcare value in the *gcd* table is when $x = 0, y = 0$. For that case, ($C2$) simplifies to:

$$(C2.d): \quad odd(gcd(0,0)) \;\; if \;\; odd(0) \vee odd(0),$$

which is true as *odd*(0) reduces to false by the definition of *odd*.

The other cases are proved by case analyses on entries as done before. Three cases are generated, corresponding to the entry values 1, 2 and 3 respectively.

The reader should compare the simplicity, compactness and elegance of the above proof of ($C2$) with a proof based on exhaustive case analysis on x and y.

3.4 Weakly Sparse Tables

Lookup tables used in applications such as the SRT division and square root [13] have a different structure than sparse tables. There is no one single entry that is occurring most frequently in a table. Instead, the table entry is either the dontcare value or from a small subset of values. For example, the large quotient digit table in the SRT division algorithm has only 6 distinct values corresponding to the quotient digit that can arise in any iteration of the division algorithm: $\{-2, -1, 0, 1, 2\}$ and a dontcare value. The notion of a *weakly sparse* table is introduced to characterize such tables.

Definition 2 *A table* `t, table [t:e1, e2→er]`, *is weakly sparse iff* $|entries(t)| \leq minimum(|e1|, |e2|)$, *where* $entries(t)$ *is the set of all table entries including the dontcare value, if used.*

The rationale behind this definition is that performing case analysis on entry values for a weakly sparse table does not result in more cases than would arise if the case analysis is done on any of the index variables.

Even if a table is neither sparse nor weakly sparse, mechanizing proofs of properties involving tables based on entries may lead to fewer cases with simpler proofs. If the number of distinct table entries is much less than the total number of distinct index tuples, proof attempts using case analysis based on table entries can be helpful. Sometimes, it is also possible to use properties of index types as well for testing constraints on indices deduced from an instantiation of a given conjecture based on a particular table entry value. This is illustrated in the verification of the main invariant of the SRT division algorithm in the next section.

In the next section, we illustrate the proposed approach using the SRT division circuit. We first describe in detail the algorithm realized by the circuit, with a focus on the P-D plot and quotient digit selection table. This is followed by a brief review of the circuit. The specification of SRT division in *RRL* is partially reviewed, focusing on the quotient digit selection table. Finally, a correctness proof of the main invariant of the circuit is discussed based on the proposed approach.

4 SRT Division

The SRT division algorithm[19,12,13] is an iterative algorithm for dividing a normalized dividend by a normalized divisor in which the quotient is computed digit by digit by repeatedly subtracting the multiples of the divisor from the dividend. The algorithm can be formalized in terms of the following recurrences about division in base (radix) r.

$$\begin{aligned} P_0 &:= dividend/r, \quad Q_0 := 0, \\ P_{j+1} &:= r * P_j - q_{j+1} * D, \quad for\ j = 0, \cdots, n-1, \\ Q_{j+1} &:= r * Q_j + q_{j+1}, \quad for\ j = 0, \cdots, n-1, \end{aligned}$$

where D is the positive divisor, P_j is the partial remainder at the beginning of the j-th iteration, and $0 \leq P_j < D$, for all j, Q_j is the quotient at the beginning of the iteration j, q_j is the quotient digit at iteration j, n is the number of digits in the quotient, and r is radix used for representing numbers. The bounds on the successive partial remainder $0 \leq P_j < D$ guarantee the convergence of the algorithm.

SRT dividers used in practice incorporate several performance enhancing techniques while realizing the above recurrences. In particular, it is necessary to minimize the number of iterations and efficiently *i*) compute the quotient digit in each iteration, *ii*) multiply divisor by the quotient digit, as well as partial remainders and quotients by radix, and *iii*) perform subtraction/addition.

The SRT division algorithm in this paper uses the radix 4, and the quotient digits are represented by a *redundant signed-digit* representation with digits in the range $[-2, 2]$. Tradeoffs between speed, radix choice and redundancy of quotient digits are discussed in [13]. Because of the redundancy, the bounds on the successive partial remainders for the convergence of the algorithm can be looser:

$$-D * 2/3 \leq P_j \leq D * 2/3.$$

By substituting the recurrence for the successive partial remainders, the range of shifted partial remainders, $4 * P_j$, that allow a quotient digit k to be chosen is:

$$[(k - 2/3) * D, (k + 2/3) * D].$$

The above relation between the shifted partial remainder range P and divisor D is diagrammatically plotted as a *P-D plot* given in Figure 2. The plot

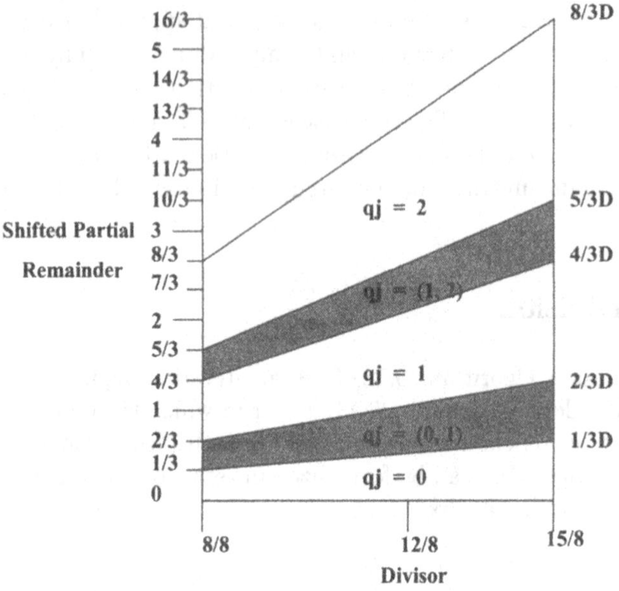

Fig. 2. P-D Plot for Radix 4

gives the shifted partial remainder ranges in which a quotient digit can be selected, without violating the bounds on the next partial remainder. For example, when the partial remainder is in the range $[5/3D, 8/3D]$, the quotient digit 2 is selected. The shaded regions represent quotient digits overlaps where more than one quotient digits selection is feasible. So if the partial remainder is in the range $[4/3D, 5/3D]$, either 2 or 1 can be used. Due to the overlap between the lower bound for the P/D ratio for quotient digit k and the upper bound for the quotient digit $k-1$, P/D ratio can be approximated in choosing quotient digits.

Redundancy in quotient digits allows the quotient digit to be selected based on only a few significant bits of the partial remainder and the divisor. As explained in [13], for a radix 4 SRT divider with the partial remainders and divisor of arbitrary width n, $n > 8$, it suffices to consider partial remainders up to 7 bits of accuracy and a divisor up to 4 bits of accuracy. This reduces the complexity of the quotient selection process, as it can be implemented as a finite table. and the partial remainder computation can be overlapped with the quotient digit selection computation.

The quotient digit selection table implementing the *P-D* plot for radix 4 is reproduced above from [13]. Rows are indexed by the shifted truncated partial remainder $g7g6g5g4.g3g2g1$ (represented in 2's complement); columns are indexed by the truncated divisor $f1.f2f3f4$; table entries are the quotient digits. The table is compressed by considering only row indices up to 5 bits since only a few entries in the table depend upon the 2 least significant bits $g2g1$ of the shifted partial remainder. For those cases, the table entries are symbolic values A, B, C, D, E are:

parrem	Divisor f1.f2f3f4							
g7g6g5g4.g3g2g1	1.000	1.001	1.010	1.011	1.100	1.101	1.110	1.111
1010.0	–	–	–	–	–	–	–	–
1010.1	–	–	–	–	–	–	-2	-2
1011.0	–	–	–	–	–	-2	-2	-2
1011.1	–	–	–	-2	-2	-2	-2	-2
1100.0	–	–	-2	-2	-2	-2	-2	-2
1100.1	-2	-2	-2	-2	-2	-2	-2	-2
1101.0	-2	-2	-2	-2	-2	-2	B	-1
1101.1	-2	-2	-2	B	-1	-1	-1	-1
1110.0	A	B	-1	-1	-1	-1	-1	-1
1110.1	-1	-1	-1	-1	-1	-1	-1	-1
1111.0	-1	-1	D	D	0	0	0	0
1111.1	0	0	0	0	0	0	0	0
0000.0	0	0	0	0	0	0	0	0
0000.1	1	1	1	1	E	0	0	0
0001.0	1	1	1	1	1	1	1	1
0001.1	2	C	1	1	1	1	1	1
0010.0	2	2	2	2	C	1	1	1
0010.1	2	2	2	2	2	2	2	1
0011.0	–	2	2	2	2	2	2	2
0011.1	–	–	2	2	2	2	2	2
0100.0	–	–	–	–	2	2	2	2
0100.1	–	–	–	–	–	2	2	2
0101.0	–	–	–	–	–	–	–	2
0101.1	–	–	–	–	–	–	–	–

Table 1. Quotient Digit Selection Table

$A = -(2 - g2 * g1)$, $B = -(2 - g2)$, $C = 1 + g2$, $D = -1 + g2$, $E = g2$.

Every entry in the table is thus for four remainder estimates. The - entries in the table are the *dontcare* entries.

In the above recurrence relations, q_{j+1} is replaced by `qtable(up, ud)`, where `qtable` is the quotient selection table, `up, ud` are, respectively, the truncated partial remainder and divisor.

4.1 SRT Divider Circuit

A radix 4 SRT divider circuit based on the above quotient digit selection table is described in Figure 3. The registers *divisor*, *remainder* in the circuit hold the value of the divisor and the successive partial remainders respectively. The register q holds the selected quotient digit along with its sign; the registers *QPOS* and *QNEG* hold the positive and negative quotient digits of the quotient. A multiplexor *MUX* is used to generate the correct multiple of the divisor based on the selected quotient digit by appropriately shifting the divisor. The hardware component *QUO LOGIC* stands for the quotient selection table, and it is typically implemented using an array of preprogrammed read-only-memory. The hardware component *DALU* is a full width ALU that computes the partial remainder at each iteration. The component *GALU* (the guess ALU [13]) is an 8-bit ALU that computes the approximate 8-bit partial remainder to be used for quotient selection. The components $<<2$ perform left shift by 4.

The circuit is initialized by loading dividend/4 (by right shifting the dividend by 2 bits) and the divisor into the remainder and divisor registers. The quotient is initialized to be zero by setting the registers *QPOS* and *QNEG* to be zero. The quotient digit register q is initialized by the appropriate alignment of the dividend and the divisor. At each iteration, the correct multiple of the quotient digit and the divisor is output by *MUX*. This output and the partial remainder in the remainder register are input to *DALU* to compute the next partial remainder. An 8 bit estimate of the partial remainder in the remainder register and an 8 bit estimate of the output of the MUX are input to the *GALU*.

GALU computes an 8 bit estimate of the next partial remainder which is left shifted by 4, and then used with the truncated divisor ($d1$) to index into *QUO LOGIC* to select the quotient digit for the next iteration. Note that *GALU* and the quotient digit selection are done in parallel with the full width *DALU* so that the correct quotient digit value is already available in the register q at the beginning of each iteration.

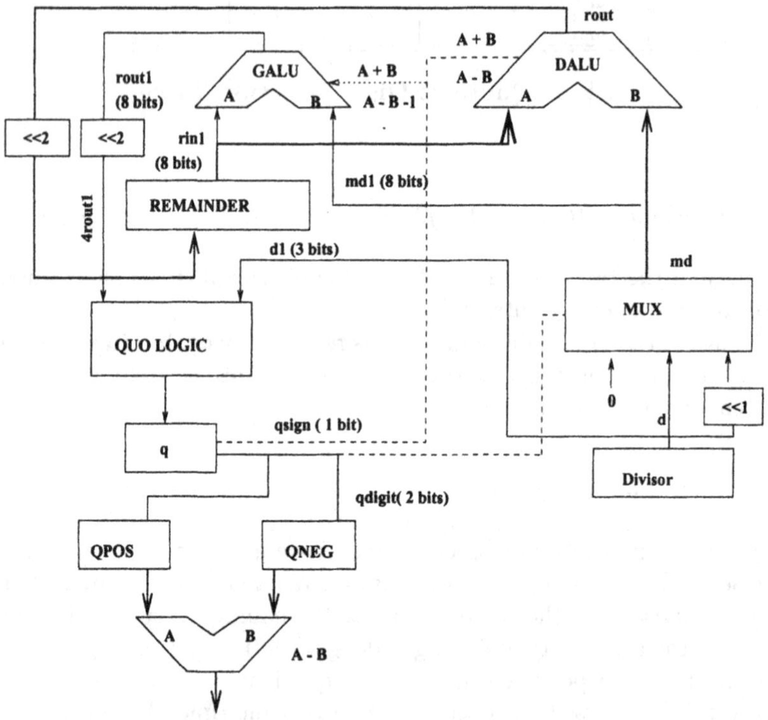

Fig. 3. SRT Division Circuit using Radix 4

4.2 Specifying Quotient Digit Selection Table in RRL

The quotient digit selection table is specified in *RRL* by `qtable` as an instance of the parameterized table type. The table indices are given by the integer subranges `column` and `row`. The entry type of `qtable` is the union of integers and `Dtcare`, but only the subrange `[m(2)...2]` is used. The unary function `m` is the minus operation on integers [1]. As the table is too big to be included here, we give a partial specification of one of the rows–the eighth row.

The eighth row corresponds to four shifted truncated remainder estimates: $\{-17/8, -9/4, -19/8, -5/2\}$ depending upon the values of $g2g1$; they are scaled up by multiplying by 8, to $\{-17, -18, -19, -20\}$ (2's complement is used in Table 1 for row indices). Below, the table entries for row index 20 are given.

```
[8...15 : column]                [m(48)...47: row]
table [qtable : row, column -> integer U Dtcare]
qtable(m(20),8)  := m(2),  qtable(m(20),9)  := m(2),
qtable(m(20),10) := m(2),  qtable(m(20),11) := m(2),
qtable(m(20),12) := m(1),  qtable(m(20),13) := m(1),
qtable(m(20),14) := m(1),  qtable(m(20),15) := m(1).
```

The table entry for the eighth row and the column index 1.011 (11) is B, where $B = -(2-g2)$. For all other column indices, the entries do not depend upon $g2g1$. So for all column indices other than 11, the table value is the same irrespective of whether the row index is $-20, -19, -18$ or -17.

For the column index 11, the table entries are however different: it is -2 if the row index is -20 or -19, since in that case $g2$ is 0; if the row index is -18 or -17, then the table entry is -1.

```
qtable(m(19),11) := m(2) qtable(m(18),11) := m(1) qtable(m(17),11) := m(1)
```

Other rows are similarly specified, with each row defining 32 table entries.

4.3 Verifying Boundedness of Partial Remainders

The main invariant of SRT division is specified in *RRL* using `qtable` as:

```
(C3): m(2) * divsr <=
      12 * parrem - 3 * qtable(up, ud) * divsr <= 2 * divsr if
      m(2) * divsr  <= 3 * parrem  <= 2 * divsr and
      ud  <= 8 * divsr < ud  + 1 and up <=  32 * parrem < up + 1.
```

The above formula states that if the partial remainder `parrem` in the previous iteration is within bounds of the divisor `divsr` (the absolute value of the partial remainder is within two-thirds of the divisor) and if the table indices `up`, `ud` correctly approximate the divisor and the partial remainder within certain bounds, then the partial remainder computed in the next iteration `4 * parrem - qtable(up, ud) * divsr` would continue being appropriately bounded by the divisor.

In [8,10], we reported two different methods for proving this invariant. In [10], $(C3)$ was automatically proved in *RRL* by modeling quotient selection table as

[1] Instead of using fractional numbers for indices, it is more convenient and faster for *RRL* to use their scaled integer versions as indices to the table. So all row and column indices are scaled up by 8. Scaling up effectively leads to using number representations of bit vectors of the shifted truncated partial remainder estimate and the truncated divisor estimate by dropping the decimal point.

a function over integers, and by performing case analysis on the table indices *up* and *ud*. This leads to 1536 cases, 768 cases each for proving the upper bound and lower bound, respectively. Dontcare entries are modeled by out-of-bound integers, and the intermediate cases generated are extremely cumbersome. In [8], the proof was done using an intensional formulation of the quotient table by abstracting table entries in terms of boundary value predicates proposed in [1]. This approach requires user guidance in terms of additional lemmas besides the manual abstraction of the table. Establishing the correctness of this manual abstraction is nontrivial.

We discuss below how a simple correctness proof of ($C3$) can be done based on the proposed approach that avoids many of these problems.

4.4 Correctness Proof

The correctness proof of ($C3$) is done by case analyses on table entry values rather on the indices. For the lower bound, this leads to 6 top level cases–5 corresponding to the entry values in the subrange `[m(2)...2]`, and one case is generated for the dontcare entry value. Six cases are generated for the upper bound as well.

The Case of Quotient Digit 0 For *qtable(up, ud)* = *0*, ($C3$) simplifies to

```
(C3.0): (-divsr) <= (6 *  parrem) <= divsr if
        (-2 * divsr) <= (3 * parrem) <= (2 * divsr) and
        (ud <=  (8 * divsr) < (ud + 1)) and
        (up <=  (32 * parrem) < (up + 1)).
```

Consider the subcase of this simplified formula to show `- divsr <= 6 * parrem`. This formula could have been verified using different values of up and ud for which the `qtable` gives 0. Instead, we illustrate how quantifier elimination can be used to derive a simple constraint on up and ud based on the algorithm discussed in subsection 3.2. This constraint can be checked more easily.

The negated formula is:

```
(Exists. parrem, divsr)[
(6 * parrem < -divsr) and (-2 * divsr <= 3 * parrem) and
(3 * parrem <= 2 * divsr) and
(ud <=  (8 * divsr) and (8 * divsr < ud + 1) and
(up <=  32 * parrem) and (32 * parrem < up + 1)]
```

The non-index variable `parrem` can be eliminated by one Fourier elimination step [9] by cross-multiplying the coefficients of `parrem`. The resulting formula is `6 * up <= -32 * divsr`. One more Fourier step on this formula using `ud <= 8 * divsr` eliminates the remaining nonindex variable `divsr` to give `48 * up < -32 * ud`. The constraint on indices is generated by negating and simplifying this formula:

```
(0, Lowerbound):        up >= -2/3 ud.                    (I)
```

For second subcase corresponding to the the upper bound `6 * parrem <= divsr`, the nonindex variables `divsr, parrem` are eliminated from the negated formula using Fourier steps, leading to the constraint

```
(0, Upperbound):        up + 1 <= 2/3 ud.                    (II)
```

Constraints on Indices for Other Quotient Digits The constraints for *qtable (up, ud) = 1* and *qtable (up, ud) = 2* are similarly derived. They are given below.

```
(1, Lowerbound):        up      >=  1/3 (ud + 1)             (III)
(1, Upperbound):        up + 1 <= 5/3 * ud                   (IV)
(2, Lowerbound):        up >= 4/3 (ud + 1)                   (V)
```

The constraints on the indices for the lower and upper bounds for the table entries $m(2)$ and $m(1)$ can be similarly calculated. These lead to 3 additional constraints on the indices. One additional case is generated for the table entry *dontcare*. All of these 9 cases can then be established by case analyses over the index values.

Note that there is no constraint on indices deduced from the upper bound subcase for the entry value 2. Thus the upper bound holds for all values of *up* and *ud*. This is evident from the *P-D Plot* which shows that the maximum value of *up* is `8/3 ud` for choosing the quotient digit 2 and the hypothesis in $(C3)$ ensure that this is always the case.

The validity of the invariant $(C3)$ is reduced to showing that the above 9 constraints on indices `up, ud` are satisfied for different quotient digit values. These constraints can be checked exhaustively by explicitly plugging in various values of `up, ud` which give rise to each of quotient digits. Below, we show how structure about the indices can be exploited further to check these constraints without having to explicitly substitute values of `up` and `ud`.

Since the above constraints are simple inequalities, and indices are subranges over numbers, this information can be used to simplify this check as illustrated below.

Consider constraint `(I): up >= - 2/3 ud`. For `qtable(up, ud) = 0`, `ud` ranges over [8...15], meaning `-2 * ud` is in the range `[m(30), m(16)]`. The constraint is satisfied for all values of `up` greater than or equal to `m(5)`. The remaining values of `up, ud` to be considered are:

```
[(m(6), 10),..., (m(6), 15),(m(7), 12),..., (m(7), 15),...,
(m(8), 12),..., (m(8), 15).]
```

For `up = m(6)`, `ud` is between 10 and 15, so `9 <= ud` as per the constraint. Similarly, when `up = m(7)` or `up = m(8)`, `ud` is between 12 and 15; the constraint is satisfied in both cases. So all cases are considered. The index domain structure can thus be exploited for further simplifying the checking these constraints.

A similar analysis works for constraint `(II)` and other quotient digits, including the dontcare entry.

5 Implementation Status

The proposed approach has been integrated into the theorem prover *RRL*. The prover provides support for specifying and reasoning about finite tables as a special data type. Sparsity information about the input tables is automatically computed by *RRL* based on the table dimensions and the frequency of occurrence of the entries. This analysis is integrated with *RRL*'s heuristics to reason about conjectures expressed using tables.

If a table-expression appears in a conjecture, and the associated table is sparse, case analyses based on table entries is invoked. Otherwise, induction based on table indices is done in a usual way. A table definition is preprocessed by *RRL* to generate a `table cover set`, which is a map from table entries to a set of index tuples. For each table entry, there is a top level case generated by replacing the table-expression in the conjecture by the table entry. The resulting formula is simplified using rewriting and the decision procedures of *RRL*. If the validity of the case does not depend upon indices, such as the main invariant ($C3$) of SRT division for the dontcare values, simplification would typically prove it. Disproving any top level case leads to the conjecture being disproved. Otherwise, projection is attempted to eliminate the nonindex variables from the formula. If projection is unsuccessful for a top level case, i.e, it is not possible to generate a formula all of whose variables are table indices only, then entry based case analyses is abandoned with *RRL* attempting induction based on indices.

Projection is currently implemented only for tables with numeric indices and entries. We have modified the linear arithmetic decision procedure implemented in *RRL* to do projection. The procedure has been changed to be invoked with a set of variables to be eliminated from the input formula. Variables are eliminated one at a time using Fourier's elimination procedure.

Case analysis based on table entry values for attempting a conjecture reduces, in the worst case, to case analysis based on index values. So there is not much additional overhead, but advantages can be significant in case of sparse and weakly sparse tables. However, the current implementation, does not reuse any part of a failed proof attempt based on case analyses of entries. An entry based case analyses might succeed in establishing the conjecture for most of the entry values and may fail only for a few entry values. In such cases, it suffices to consider the indices corresponding to these failing entry values and perform explicit case analyses based on indices. As of now we perform the case analyses for all index values.

The preliminary implementation has been successfully used to prove the main invariant of SRT division and other examples. These experiments have led us to focus on several interesting performance enhancements in RRL. Currently, the intermediate coefficients generated by projection can become very large, and this adversely affects the performance of entry based case analyses, especially since numbers are represented in unary in *RRL*. A substantial speed-up in performance will result if arithmetic calculations are directly supported in *RRL*. Other optimizations to keep the numbers smaller, such as dividing structure of tables–their entries as well as indices.

6 Explicit vs. Abstracted Quotient Digit Selection Tables

SRT division has also been mechanically verified using *Analytica* [1] and *PVS* [18,7]. A major difference between these verification efforts and the proposed approach is in the representation of the quotient digit selection table. These approaches use an abstracted version of the table whereas an explicit and exhaustive quotient digit selection table is used by the proposed approach.

The main feature of the radix 4 SRT divider proof in [1] was an abstraction of the quotient selection table using boundary value predicates. From the quotient selection table in [13], an intensional specification of the table is developed that only considers the minimum and maximum values of a partial remainder for every quotient digit. Nothing is specified about other intermediate partial remainder values for a quotient digit and the invariant is not checked for these values. It is, therefore, possible to certify erroneous quotient digit selection tables correct using this approach unless the abstraction is proved correct. As stated in [1], the primary reason for using an abstracted table is to reduce the number of cases in the correctness proof.

A radix 4 SRT divider based on an abstract table similar to the one used in [1] was automatically verified using *RRL* [8]. This was primarily an exercise in determining how much of the correctness proof in [1] could be automated in *RRL* without using any symbolic computation algorithms of computer algebra systems used in [1]. Much to our pleasant surprise, we found that no extensions had to be made to *RRL*. *RRL* was able to find proofs of all the formulas automatically, without any interaction.

In order to avoid the potential gaps in the correctness proofs due to an abstract table, we subsequently formalized the SRT divider using an explicit and exhaustive representation of the quotient digit selection table with 768 entries [10]. Such a table can be obtained by a direct translation of a hardware PLA (programmable logic array), realizing the quotient selection logic of a commercial SRT divider. The SRT divider based on this explicit table was fully automatically verified in a push-button mode in *RRL*. Furthermore, the proofs could be done easily and quickly using *RRL* compared to the proofs based on the intensional specification of the table, even though a lot more cases had to be considered; the instantiated conjectures could be easily established by *RRL*. Details of these proofs can be found in [10].

The proofs of most of the subcases generated by *RRL* based on the explicit quotient digit selection table share a common structure. In this paper, we have shown how this commonality in proofs can be automatically detected by the theorem prover *RRL*, and used to further simplify the correctness proofs. The proof described in this paper is based on an explicit representation of quotient digit selection table unlike those in [1,8]. No manual abstraction is done. The entry based case analyses considers all possible values of partial remainders while verifying the invariant, and not just the boundary values as done in [1,8]. It is encouraging that by exploiting simple characteristics of tables such as sparsity, a comprehensive correctness proof simpler than the one based on manual abstraction [1,8] can be automatically obtained, while eliminating the scope of errors introduced by manual abstraction.

The proofs reported in [18] using the PVS system are more general. The specification and the proof are organized manually using sophisticated mechanisms of the *PVS* language which supports higher-order logic, dependent types, overloading, module facility, a special data type *table* [18]. Miner and Leathrum's work [7] is a further generalization of the proof in [18]. Their paper mentions analysis of three different SRT lookup tables using PVS. The URL (`ftp://air16.larc.nasa.gov/ pub/fm/ larc/fp_div/ dump_ieee_srt_divide`) has the PVS proof dump of a radix 4 SRT divider. The quotient selection table used there is based on [13]. The table specification uses dependent subtypes to constrain the index values. Not all possible values of the table indices are explicitly enumerated in the table. Only those values of the partial remainder are considered for which there is at least one divider value for which a legal quotient digit can be chosen, i.e., the first and the last rows of Table 1 in this paper are not enumerated. Further, the table is not explicit in that it uses 5 bits to approximate the partial remainder in most of the cases, and uses 7 bits only for certain boundary cases as described in [13]. Each entry of this table is expanded into 4 entries of the explicit table as described in this paper.

The PVS dump has 54 top level cases. 33 additional proof obligations are generated to discharge the assumptions associated with the dependent types. Unlike the correctness proofs in [1,?] all possible values of the partial remainder and divisor are considered. However, the specification is developed with considerable human ingenuity, and the resulting proof is manually driven, even though parts of the proof can be done automatically using previously developed PVS tactics.

In contrast, we have focussed on an explicit table specification that can be easily generated from commonly used representations of the quotient tables in practice. We have then described how simple heuristics can be built into the prover to eliminate unnecessary and tedious aspects of correctness proofs based on the explicit representation.

7 Concluding Remarks

The idea of performing case analysis based on table entries when the number of such entries is much smaller than the table size, seems pretty obvious. But somehow, it has not been emphasized in the automated deduction literature. No special heuristics for reasoning about tables implementing finite functions have been studied.

In this paper, we have emphasized exploiting the entries in a table for doing case analysis in mechanizing proof attempts of conjecture involving the table. The number of cases generated by the proposed approach is the same as that based on case analyses on indices in the worst case. Given, indices drawn from domains with cardinality d_1 and d_2, the total number of cases generated by index based case analyses is $d_1 * d_2$. In the proposed approach, for any entry v, even when the index values need to be explicitly enumerated, only those values of the indices i and j are considered where $table(i, j) = v$. Thus, in the worst case, the overall cases considered is no worse that done by index based case analyses.

The effectiveness of the proposed approach is demonstrated on a nontrivial example of the radix 4 SRT division circuit which uses a weakly sparse quotient digit selection table. We believe that other aspects of table structure can be effectively exploited as well for attempting a conjecture about a table, particularly ordering and relationship between indices as well as any possible functional relationship among indices and the table entries. This was demonstrated for verifying constraints on indices deduced by quantifier elimination from simplified conjectures for particular table entries.

We plan on attempting proofs of properties of other circuits implemented using large tables using *RRL* which is likely to be helpful in developing better and additional heuristics for reasoning about finite tables. Digit-serial arithmetic circuits including square root and elementary functions such as exponential, logarithms also use lookup tables. The tables used for the square root function exhibit sparsity much like division.

The digit-serial realizations of elementary functions are also specified by recurrences similar to the used for division ([11] pp. 378-434.) The lookup tables typically used in realizing these functions contain precomputed values of terms in the recurrence that cannot be directly realized in hardware. These tables do not exhibit sparsity, but, the entries in such a table are typically related by a constant additive or multiplicative factor, which can be used to simplify the proofs.

These recurrences specify how the partial result should extended at each step by a bit based on the range of values to which the partial result computed so far belongs. The convergence of these algorithms is established based on the partial result always being within certain bounds at each step. The choice of the bit at each step is done by having a lookup table with only a few leading bits of the partial result. Sparsity considerations appear to be applicable to such lookup tables.

The use of simple heuristics for handling large tables facilitates direct and explicit specification of tables used in circuit implementations, instead of manually abstracting them using predicates. The use of direct and explicit tables has several advantages. It avoids the errors that may be introduced by abstractions. Additional proof obligations for proving abstractions correct are avoided. Moreover, the gap between implementation and verification models of circuits is reduced. The main drawback of using explicit tables however, is the large number of cases that are generated in the correctness proofs. implementation and the verification The proposed approach addresses these concerns by firstly avoiding abstractions by directly considering tables as they are, and secondly by exploiting the structure of tables–their entries as well as indices.

References

1. E.M. Clarke, S.M. German and X. Zhao, "Verifying the SRT division algorithm using theorem proving techniques," Proc. *Computer Aided Verification, 8th Intl. Conf.* Brunswick, August 1996, Springer LNCS 1102, 111-122.
2. *Proc. of the IEEE International Symposium on Computer Arithmetic,*, IEEE Computer Society 1995.
3. *Proc. of the IEEE International Symposium on Computer Arithmetic,*, IEEE Computer Society 1997.
4. M.P. Heimdahl and N. Leveson, "Consistency and completeness analyses of state-based requirements," *17th Intl. Conf. on Software Eng.*, IEEE, 1995.
5. C. Heitmeyer, A. Bull, C. Gasarch, B. Labaw, "SCR*: A toolset for specifying and analyzing requirements," *In Proc. of COMPASS'95*, IEEE 1995.
6. D.N. Hoover and Z. Chen, "Tablewise, a decision table tool", *In Proc. of COMPASS'95*, IEEE 1995.
7. P.S. Miner and J.F. Leathrum Jr., "Verification of IEEE compliant subtractive division algorithm," Proc. *FMCAD'96*, LNCS 1166, Palo Alto, CA, 1996.
8. D. Kapur, "Rewriting, decision procedures and lemma speculation for automated hardware verification," Proc. *10th Intl. Conf. Theorem Proving in Higher Order Logics,* LNCS 1275, 1997.
9. D. Kapur and X. Nie, "Reasoning about numbers in Tecton," Proc. *8th Intl. Symp. Methodologies for Intelligent Systems, (ISMIS'94)*, October 1994.
10. D. Kapur, M. Subramaniam "Mechanizing Reasoning About Arithmetic Circuits: SRT Division," *In Proc. of 17th FSTTCS,* LNCS (eds. Sivakumar and Ramesh), 1997.
11. A.R. Omondi, *Computer Arithmetic Systems: Algorithms, Architecture and Implementations,* Prentice Hall 1994.
12. K.D. Tocher, "Techniques of multiplication and division for automatic binary computers," *Quarterly Journal of Mechanics and Applied Mathematics,* 11(3), 1958.
13. G.S. Taylor, "Compatible hardware for division and square root," Proc. *5th IEEE Symp. on Computer Architecture,* May 1981.
14. S. Owre, J.R. Rushby, N. Shankar, "Integration in PVS: Tables, Types, and Model Checking," *Proc. of TACAS,*, LNCS 1217, Springer Verlag, April 1997.
15. M.D.Ercegovac, T. Lang, "Radix-4 Square Root Without Initial PLA," *IEEE Trans. on Computers,* Vol. 39. No. 8, Aug. 1990.
16. J.H.Zurawski, J.B. Gosling, "Design of a high speed square root multiply and divide unit", *IEEE Trans. on Computers*, vol. C-36, 1987.
17. D.D. Sarma and D.Matula, "Measuring the Accuracy of ROM Reciprocal Tables", *IEEE Int. Symp. on Comput. Arithmetic,* IEEE Computer Society, 1993.
18. H. Ruess, N. Shankar and M.K. Srivas, "Modular verification of SRT division," Proc. *Computer Aided Verification, 8th Intl. Conf. - CAV'96,* New Brunswick, 1996, Springer LNCS 1102 (eds. Alur and Henzinger).
19. J.E. Robertson, "A new class of digital division methods," *IRE Trans. on Electronic Computers,* 1958, 218-222.
20. H. Zhang, D. Kapur, and M.S. Krishnamoorthy, "A mechanizable induction principle for equational specifications," Proc. *9th (CADE),* Springer LNCS 310, 1988.

A Polymorphic Language Which Is Typable and Poly-step

Luca Roversi

Institute de Mathématiques de Luminy
UPR 9016 – 163, avenue de Luminy – Case 907
13288 Marseille Cedex 9 – France
rover@iml.univ-mrs.fr
http://www.iml.univ-mrs.fr

Abstract. A functional language Λ_{LA} is given. A sub-set $\Lambda^{\mathrm{T}}_{\mathrm{LA}}$ of Λ_{LA} is automatically typable. The types are formulas of Intuitionistic Light Affine Logic with polymorphism *à la* ML. Every term of $\Lambda^{\mathrm{T}}_{\mathrm{LA}}$ can reduce to its normal form in, at most, poly-steps. $\Lambda^{\mathrm{T}}_{\mathrm{LA}}$ can be used as a prototype of programming language for **P-TIME** algorithms.

1 Introduction

In [3], Girard introduced Light Linear Logic which *captures* **P-TIME**. This means that the cut-elimination process of Light Linear Logic terminates in polynomial time with respect to the dimension of any given derivation, and, vice versa, all **P-TIME** Turing machines can be encoded as data-types in Light Linear Logic.

Girard left as an open problem to find a concrete syntax for **ILLL**, namely for Intuitionistic Light Linear Logic. This paper introduces an untyped functional language Λ_{LA} which has a typable sub-set $\Lambda^{\mathrm{T}}_{\mathrm{LA}}$. The types for $\Lambda^{\mathrm{T}}_{\mathrm{LA}}$ are formulas of **ILLL** with a polymorphism *à la ML*. The types can be inferred automatically.

Before introducing $\Lambda^{\mathrm{T}}_{\mathrm{LA}}$, it is worth recalling the main mechanism of **ILLL** to bound the cut-elimination complexity. The key point is avoiding the proliferation of the contraction rule

$$(Contraction)\frac{\Gamma, A, A \vdash B}{\Gamma, A \vdash B}\ ,$$

that can take place when eliminating the cuts in a derivation of Intuitionistic Logic. For example, let C_n be the *typable* λ-term $\overline{2}\overline{2}\ldots$, which has $n \geq 2$ Church Numerals $\overline{2} \stackrel{\mathrm{def}}{\equiv} \lambda xy.x(xy)$ in it. The length of the left-most reduction of C_n to its normal form growths exponentially in n. This happens essentially because there are redexes that, once reduced, yield two residual redexes each, thus developing a reduction space with the form of a tree. Logically, this means that there are contraction rules that duplicate other contraction rules as effect of the cut-elimination. Figure 1 gives an intuitive pictorial representation of this.

The non-exponential proliferation of the c-nodes in **ILLL** is a consequence of two main aspects. First, in **ILLL**, a derivation can be duplicated only if enclosed

Jieh Hsiang, Atsushi Ohori (Eds.): ASIAN'98, LNCS 1538, pp. 43–60, 1998.

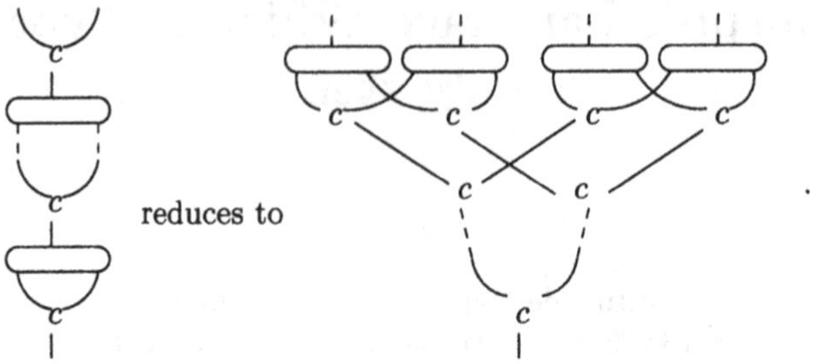

Fig. 1. From lists to trees of contractions

into a *region*, called !-box. Second, any !-box can derive a formula, from *at most a single assumption*. For example, let Π be a derivation of **ILLL**, proving B from *the single* assumption A. Then, the !-box $!\Pi$, built on Π is:

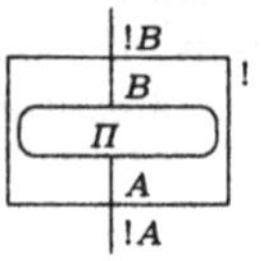

A cut-elimination step duplicating $!\Pi$ is such that:

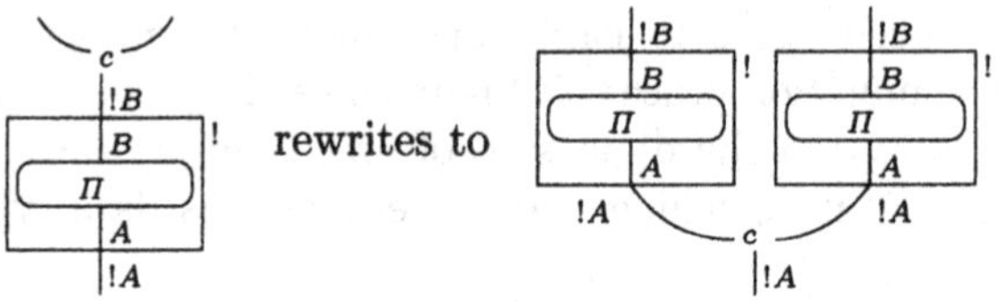

The !-box divides the space in two parts: one inside, and the one outside it. This means that, unlike Intuitionistic Logic, the c-node here above, which contracts $!A$, does not trivially extend any tree of c-nodes inside the !-box: there is the !-box border in between. In first approximation, this means that any exponentially growing tree of c-nodes, in a derivation Π of **ILLL**, is an (exponential) function of the maximal number of nested !-boxes of Π. But, this is a detail...

The second feature of **ILLL** is that any !-box has at most one assumption. This means that, if at some stage of the cut-elimination process, a !-box has a tree of c-nodes in it, then every c-node was present somewhere, in the same !-box, since the beginning of the cut-elimination. In this way, the non-exponential proliferation of c-nodes holds when composing the deductions of **ILLL**.

We complete the description of the novel part of **ILLL** by describing the behavior of a second region in it. If Π is a deduction proving B from two, possibly empty, sets of assumptions $A_1 \ldots A_n$ and $A'_1 \ldots A'_m$, then, the §-box $\S\Pi$ with Π in it, is:

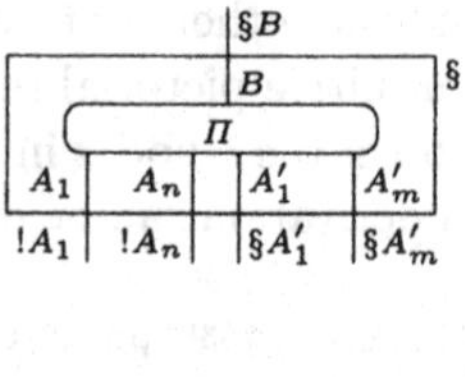

The §-boxes increase the expressiveness of **ILLL**. Without §-boxes, Church Numerals could not be encoded in **ILLL**. The presence of an arbitrary number of assumptions of a §-box that can be contracted should not worry. The non-exponential proliferation of c-nodes is preserved because §-boxes themselves can not be duplicated. Hence, the creation of trees with too many c-nodes below any §-box is forbidden.

The computational behavior of the language $\Lambda^{\mathrm{T}}_{\mathrm{LA}}$ incorporates the features here above of the cut-elimination of **ILLL**. The language $\Lambda^{\mathrm{T}}_{\mathrm{LA}}$, however, is the functional counterpart of a natural deduction for the sequent calculus that Asperti introduced in [1], where the original sequent calculus in [3] has greatly simplified. The point of [1] is to move from **ILLL** to its *affine* version **ILAL**, where unrestricted weakening is allowed.

Contributions. This work introduces an *untyped* functional language Λ_{LA}. It has a sub-set $\Lambda^{\mathrm{T}}_{\mathrm{LA}}$ of *typable* elements. The types for $\Lambda^{\mathrm{T}}_{\mathrm{LA}}$ are the formulas of a natural deduction that we introduce. The natural deduction proves a sub-set of the formulas derived by Asperti's sequent calculus for Intuitionistic Light Affine Logic **ILAL** [1]. The types have a polymorphism *à la* ML [8]: only external quantifiers are allowed. The types for the elements of $\Lambda^{\mathrm{T}}_{\mathrm{LA}}$ can be automatically inferred by a type inference algorithm. In particular, the type τ inferred for any $M \in \Lambda^{\mathrm{T}}_{\mathrm{LA}}$ is *principal.*

In spite Asperti's sequent calculus for **ILAL** greatly simplifies the original system for Light Linear Logic in [3], the natural deduction it induces still has enough rules to make a concrete functional syntax quite heavy. Following a methodological hint already in [1], the following simplification is introduced: contraction is left as an implicit structural rule of the natural deduction. This choice influences the design of $\Lambda^{\mathrm{T}}_{\mathrm{LA}}$ as follows: $\Lambda^{\mathrm{T}}_{\mathrm{LA}}$ must be defined on two disjoint sets of variables names: one contains the names for the terms that can be duplicated during the computations. The other set contains the names for linearly used terms. This makes $\Lambda^{\mathrm{T}}_{\mathrm{LA}}$ a sort of *call by value* language: the two kinds of variables "decide" what can be duplicated, and when.

The language $\Lambda^{\mathrm{T}}_{\mathrm{LA}}$ is *strongly normalizable* and *Church-Rosser.* It is also *correct* with respect to **P-TIME**. Namely, if $M \in \Lambda^{\mathrm{T}}_{\mathrm{LA}}$, then M represents an algorithm in **P-TIME**. Moreover, $\Lambda^{\mathrm{T}}_{\mathrm{LA}}$ admits a poly-step reduction strategy. This means that any term M of $\Lambda^{\mathrm{T}}_{\mathrm{LA}}$ can be reduced to its normal form in, at most, a number of steps polynomial in the dimension of M.

The completeness of $\Lambda^{\mathrm{T}}_{\mathrm{LA}}$ with respect to **P-TIME** is left open.

"Index". Section 2 introduces the untyped language Λ_{LA}. Section 3 defines the natural deduction for **ILAL**, decorated with the terms of $\Lambda^{\mathrm{T}}_{\mathrm{LA}}$. Section 4 is about the correctness of Λ_{LA} with respect to **P-TIME**. Section 5 recalls the expressiveness of $\Lambda^{\mathrm{T}}_{\mathrm{LA}}$ and shows some encodings of usual λ-Calculus terms in it. When reading Section 2, and 3, we suggest to refer to Section 5 for having programming examples on $\Lambda^{\mathrm{T}}_{\mathrm{LA}}$. Section 6 introduces the poly-step strategy. Section 7 defines the type inference algorithm in natural deduction style. Section 8 concludes the

paper with some reference to related, and future work. Appendix A introduces some of the details about $\mathtt{G}_{\mathrm{LA}}$ that Asperti skipped in [1].

Acknowledgments. This work has been developed also with some useful discussions with Andrea Asperti, Stefano Guerrini, Tom Kranz, Yves Lafont. The work has been supported by a TMR-Marie Curie Grant, contract n. ERBFM-BICT961411.

2 The Functional Language

The Syntax. Let `Term-Variables` be a set of identifiers ranged over by x, y, w, z, and `!-Term-Variables` be another set of identifiers ranged over by X, Y, W, Z. Moreover, let χ be ranging over `Term-Variables` $\cup$ `!-Term-Variables`. The set Λ of the functional terms is given by:

$$\begin{aligned} M,N,P,Q ::= \texttt{Term-Variables} \mid \texttt{!-Term-Variables} \mid \lambda\chi.M \mid (MN) \mid\ !M \mid \\ !(M)[^{N}/_{\chi}] \mid \S M \mid \S(M)[^{M_1}/_{\chi_1} \cdots {}^{M_n}/_{\chi_n}] \mid \texttt{let}\ X = M\ \texttt{in}\ N \end{aligned}$$

The term constructors $\lambda, !, \S$, and `let` bind free variables. As usual, λ is such that, if χ is in the free variable set $\mathtt{FV}(M)$ of M, then it can not be in $\mathtt{FV}(\lambda\chi.M)$. The term constructor ! can be applied either to a closed term M, yielding the closed !-box $!M$, or to an open term M with a *single* variable χ. In this case, the free variables of the !-box obtained are in $\mathtt{FV}(N)$. In particular, N is called the *interface* of the !-box just built, and M is its *body*. The operator § builds §-boxes. It can be applied to a term M with free variables $\chi_1, \cdots, \chi_n$, being $n \geq 1$. All $\chi_1, \cdots, \chi_n$ get bounded, and the free variables of the obtained §-boxes are in $\cup_{i=1}^{n}\mathtt{FV}(M_i)$. Again, all M_is are the interface of the §-box just built, and M is its *body*. Finally, if $X \in \mathtt{FV}(N)$, then `let` binds X. The square brackets in ! and §-boxes belong to the syntax, and delimit the interface of the boxes themselves.

The substitution of M for χ in N is denoted by $N\{^{M}\downarrow_{\chi}\}$. It is defined as a partial function. Namely, it behaves like the usual variable-clash free substitution only in one of the two following cases:

- M is either a !-box, or in `!-Term-Variables`, and χ is in `!-Term-Variables`,
- M is any term, and χ belongs to `Term-Variables`,

Otherwise, the substitution is undefined.

The elements of Λ are considered up to α-equivalence. For example, $!(M)[^{N}/_{\chi}]$ is α-equivalent to $!(M\{^{\chi'}\downarrow_{\chi}\})[^{N}/_{\chi'}]$. Parenthesis will be omitted when writing terms, if no ambiguity exists.

The Dynamics. The rewriting system $\rightsquigarrow$ on Λ is the contextual closure of the relation $\triangleright$ on $\Lambda_{\mathrm{LA}} \times \Lambda_{\mathrm{LA}}$ here below:

- β-group

$$\begin{aligned} (\lambda x.M)N &\triangleright_1 M\{^{N}\downarrow_{x}\} \\ (\lambda X.M)Y &\triangleright_2 M\{^{Y}\downarrow_{X}\} \\ (\lambda X.M)!N &\triangleright_3 M\{^{!N}\downarrow_{X}\} \\ (\lambda X.M)!(N)[^{Y}/_{\chi}] &\triangleright_4 M\{^{!(N)[^{Y}/_{\chi}]}\downarrow_{X}\} \\ (\lambda X.M)!(N)[^{P}/_{\chi}] &\triangleright_5 (\lambda Y.M\{^{!(N)[^{Y}/_{\chi}]}\downarrow_{X}\})P \quad \texttt{if}\ P \notin \texttt{!-Term-Variables} \end{aligned}$$

- !!-group

$$
\begin{aligned}
!(M)[{}^{!N}/_{x}] &\rhd_1 !M\{{}^{N}\!\downarrow_{x}\}\\
!(M)[{}^{!(N)[{}^{P}/_{\mathsf{x}}]}/_{x}] &\rhd_2 !(M\{{}^{N}\!\downarrow_{x}\})[{}^{P}/_{\mathsf{x}}]\\
!(M)[{}^{!(Y)[{}^{P}/_{\mathsf{Y}}]}/_{\mathsf{X}}] &\rhd_3 !(M\{{}^{Y}\!\downarrow_{\mathsf{X}}\})[{}^{P}/_{\mathsf{Y}}]\\
!(M)[{}^{!!N}/_{\mathsf{X}}] &\rhd_4 !(M\{{}^{!N}\!\downarrow_{\mathsf{X}}\})\\
!(M)[{}^{!!(N)[{}^{P}/_{\mathsf{x}}]}/_{\mathsf{X}}] &\rhd_5 !(M\{{}^{!(N)[{}^{Y}/_{\mathsf{x}}]}\!\downarrow_{\mathsf{X}}\})[{}^{!P}/_{\mathsf{Y}}]\\
!(M)[{}^{!(!(N)[{}^{P}/_{\mathsf{x}}])[{}^{Q}/_{\mathsf{x}'}]}/_{\mathsf{X}}] &\rhd_6 !(M\{{}^{!(N)[{}^{Y}/_{\mathsf{x}}]}\!\downarrow_{\mathsf{X}}\})[{}^{!(P)[{}^{Q}/_{\mathsf{x}'}]}/_{\mathsf{Y}}]
\end{aligned}
$$

- §!-group

$$
\begin{aligned}
\S(M)[\cdots{}^{!N}/_{x_i}\cdots] &\rhd_1 \S(M\{{}^{N}\!\downarrow_{x_i}\})[\cdots\ \cdots]\\
\S(M)[\cdots{}^{!(N)[{}^{P}/_{\mathsf{x}}]}/_{x_i}\cdots] &\rhd_2 \S(M\{{}^{N}\!\downarrow_{x_i}\})[\cdots{}^{P}/_{\mathsf{x}}\cdots]\\
\S(M)[\cdots{}^{!(Y)[{}^{P}/_{\mathsf{Y}}]}/_{\mathsf{X}_i}\cdots] &\rhd_3 \S(M\{{}^{Y}\!\downarrow_{\mathsf{X}_i}\})[\cdots{}^{P}/_{\mathsf{Y}}\cdots]\\
\S(M)[\cdots{}^{!!N}/_{\mathsf{X}_i}\cdots] &\rhd_4 \S(M\{{}^{!N}\!\downarrow_{\mathsf{X}_i}\})[\cdots\ \cdots]\\
\S(M)[\cdots{}^{!!(N)[{}^{P}/_{\mathsf{x}}]}/_{\mathsf{X}_i}\cdots] &\rhd_5 \S(M\{{}^{!(N)[{}^{Y}/_{\mathsf{x}}]}\!\downarrow_{\mathsf{X}_i}\})[\cdots{}^{!P}/_{\mathsf{Y}}\cdots]\\
\S(M)[\cdots{}^{!(!(N)[{}^{P}/_{\mathsf{x}}])[{}^{Q}/_{\mathsf{x}'}]}/_{\mathsf{X}_i}\cdots] &\rhd_6 \S(M\{{}^{!(N)[{}^{Y}/_{\mathsf{x}}]}\!\downarrow_{\mathsf{X}_i}\})[\cdots{}^{!(P)[{}^{Q}/_{\mathsf{x}'}]}/_{\mathsf{Y}}\cdots]
\end{aligned}
$$

- §§-group

$$
\begin{aligned}
\S(M)[\cdots{}^{\S N}/_{x_i}\cdots] &\rhd_1 \S(M\{{}^{N}\!\downarrow_{x_i}\})[\cdots\ \cdots]\\
\S(M)[\cdots{}^{\S(N)[\cdots{}^{P}/_{\mathsf{x}}\cdots]}/_{x_i}\cdots] &\rhd_2 \S(M\{{}^{N}\!\downarrow_{x_i}\})[\cdots\ \cdots{}^{P}/_{\mathsf{x}}\cdots\ \cdots]\\
\S(M)[\cdots{}^{\S(Y)[{}^{P}/_{\mathsf{Y}}]}/_{\mathsf{X}_i}\cdots] &\rhd_3 \S(M\{{}^{Y}\!\downarrow_{\mathsf{X}_i}\})[\cdots{}^{P}/_{\mathsf{Y}}\cdots]\\
\S(M)[\cdots{}^{\S!N}/_{\mathsf{X}_i}\cdots] &\rhd_4 \S(M\{{}^{!N}\!\downarrow_{\mathsf{X}_i}\})[\cdots\ \cdots]\\
\S(M)[\cdots{}^{\S!(N)[{}^{P}/_{\mathsf{x}}]}/_{\mathsf{X}_i}\cdots] &\rhd_5 \S(M\{{}^{!(N)[{}^{Y}/_{\mathsf{x}}]}\!\downarrow_{\mathsf{X}_i}\})[\cdots{}^{\S P}/_{\mathsf{Y}}\cdots]\\
\S(M)[\cdots{}^{\S(!(N)[{}^{P}/_{\mathsf{x}}])[\cdots{}^{Q}/_{\mathsf{x}'}\cdots]}/_{\mathsf{X}_i}\cdots] &\rhd_6\\
&\S(M\{{}^{!(N)[{}^{Y}/_{\mathsf{x}}]}\!\downarrow_{\mathsf{X}_i}\})[\cdots\ \cdots{}^{\S(P)[\cdots{}^{Q}/_{\mathsf{x}'}\cdots]}/_{\mathsf{Y}}\cdots\ \cdots]
\end{aligned}
$$

- `let` -group

$$
\begin{aligned}
\texttt{let}\ X = Y\ \texttt{in}\ P &\rhd_1 P\{{}^{Y}\!\downarrow_{\mathsf{X}}\}\\
\texttt{let}\ X = !M\ \texttt{in}\ P &\rhd_2 P\{{}^{!M}\!\downarrow_{\mathsf{X}}\}\\
\texttt{let}\ X = !(M)[{}^{N}/_{\mathsf{x}}]\ \texttt{in}\ P &\rhd_3 \texttt{let}\ Y = N\ \texttt{in}\ P\{{}^{!(M)[{}^{Y}/_{\mathsf{x}}]}\!\downarrow_{\mathsf{X}}\}
\end{aligned}
$$

Of course, the α-equivalence must be used to avoid variable clashes when rewriting terms. As usual, $\rightsquigarrow^*$ is the reflexive, and transitive closure of $\rightsquigarrow$ on Λ. The functional language Λ_{LA}, subject of this work, is $\langle\Lambda,\rightsquigarrow\rangle$.

Discussion. It is worth giving some intuition about the meaning of the dynamics.

Λ_{LA} is a kind of restriction of the untyped call-by-value λ-Calculus[9], which rewriting rule is:

$$(\lambda x.M)N \rightarrow_{\beta_v} M\{{}^{N}\!\downarrow_{x}\} \text{ if } N \text{ is a value },$$

where the variables, and the λ-abstractions are values. Namely, only the terms with a specific form can be substituted for the variables. The rewriting system $\rightsquigarrow$ behaves analogously to $\rightarrow_{\beta_v}$. Following the definition of the *partial* substitution of terms for variables, given above, no constraints exist when replacing

$x \in$ `Term-Variables` by *any* term. The idea is that, in the typable sub-set $\Lambda^{\mathrm{T}}_{\mathrm{LA}}$, x stands for any non duplicable, or *linear*, entity. Consequently, replacing M for x can not result in the duplication of M. On the contrary, only the !-boxes and the elements of !-`Term-Variables` can be substituted for a variable $X \in$!-`Term-Variables`. This because, in the typable sub-set $\Lambda^{\mathrm{T}}_{\mathrm{LA}}$, X represents duplicable, or *non linear*, resources. In the usual call-by-value terminology, any term is a value, with respect to the linear variables. On the other side, only the !-boxes, and the !-`Term-Variables`, which represent the duplicable regions of **ILLL**, are values for the non linear variables.

Take the β-group, for example. The first four axioms follow what just said here above. The axiom $\rhd_5$ needs a side condition to take it apart from $\rhd_4$. In particular, $\rhd_5$ serves to avoid the substitution for X of the interface P, as it could also not be a !-box.

As a second example, consider the !!-group. The relation defined by the !!-rules makes two terms communicating, when such two terms are contained in two distinct !-boxes. The communication takes place by substituting the term contained in one !-box for the free variables of the term contained in the other !-box. The rule $\rhd_1$ deals with the case where one term N is in a !-box which constitutes the interface of another !-box, whose content is M. The communication between N and M can take place independently from the form of N, accordingly to what said above. Otherwise, N must reduce to a further, deeper !-box, before the substitution takes place: see the rule $\rhd_4$. The remaining !!-rules cover all the possible *disjoint* cases, according to the form of the !-box in the interface.

All the other groups preserve the definition of the substitution, and are defined to cover all *disjoint* cases, according to the form of the term being substituted.

3 The Type Assignment

The Types. Let assume to have a set `Type-Variables`, ranged over by α, β, γ, and δ. The *types* are defined by the grammar: $\tau, \rho, \mu, \nu ::=$ `Type-Variables` $\mid \tau \multimap \rho \mid\ !\tau \mid \S\tau$. The *type schemes* originate from the grammar: $\sigma ::= \forall\alpha_1 \ldots \alpha_n.\tau$, with $n \geq 0$. As usual, $\forall$ is a binder: the free variables of $\forall\alpha_1 \ldots \alpha_n.\tau$ are $\mathtt{FV}(\tau) \setminus \{\alpha_1 \ldots \alpha_n\}$. We say that τ is *!-exponential*, and we write !-exp(τ), if there is a type τ' such that $\tau = \forall\alpha_1 \ldots \alpha_n.!\tau'$, with $n \geq 0$.

A *set of assumptions* takes the form $\{\chi_1 : \sigma_1, \ldots, \chi_n : \sigma_n\}$, where every σ_i is a *type scheme*, and every χ_i belongs to `Term-Variables` $\cup$!-`Term-Variables`. A set of assumptions $\Gamma = \{\chi_1 : \sigma_1, \ldots, \chi_n : \sigma_n\}$ is *well formed* if it satisfies two constraints: *(i)* χ_i belongs to !-`Term-Variables` if, and only if, !-exp(σ_i) holds with $n \geq i \geq 0$; *(ii)* Γ can be thought of as a function with finite domain $\{\chi_1, \ldots, \chi_n\}$. Namely, $\chi : \sigma_1$, and $\chi : \sigma_2$ can not belong to Γ, if $\sigma_1 \neq \sigma_2$, up to the obvious α-equivalence on types.

The statement !-exp(Γ) holds on a well formed set of assumptions Γ if all types in the co-domain of Γ are !-exponential or, equivalently, if the domain of Γ is a sub-set of !-`Term-Variables`. Consequently, a well formed set of assumptions, whose domain is contained in `Term-Variables`, is *linear*. We take Γ as a meta-variable for ranging over generic well formed sets of assumptions, Θ for denoting !-exponential sets of well formed assumptions, and, Δ, Φ, Ψ, and Υ for dealing with the linear sets of well formed assumptions.

The *type substitutions* are functions from `Type-Variables` to *types*. The notation: $\{^{\tau_1}\!\downarrow_{\alpha_1} \cdots {}^{\tau_n}\!\downarrow_{\alpha_n}\}$, stands for a type substitution that simultaneously replaces every τ_i for α_i, and which is the identity on all the type variables different from $\alpha_1, \ldots, \alpha_n$. The type substitutions are ranged over by S, R, T, and U. Moreover, for any type σ and any set Γ of assumptions, $S\sigma$, and $S\Gamma$ denote the application of the obvious extensions of S to type schemes and sets of assumptions. In general, the substitutions do not preserve well formed sets of assumptions. For example, $\Delta = \{x : \alpha\}$ is well formed, but $S\Delta$ is not, if $S = \{^{!\tau}\!\downarrow_\alpha\}$. So, for any *well formed* set of assumptions Γ, and substitution S, the *compatibility* predicate S-compatible with-Γ holds exactly when $S\Gamma$ is well formed. Moreover, it holds:

Lemma 1. *If S is $S_1 S_2$, and S*-compatible with-Γ, *then so it is S_2.*

The type schemes can be ordered: $\forall\beta_1 \ldots \beta_n.\tau \geq \forall\alpha_1 \ldots \alpha_m.S\tau$ if both $\mathtt{FV}(\tau) \supseteq \{\beta_1, \ldots, \beta_n\}$, and $\mathtt{FV}(S\tau) \supseteq \{\alpha_1, \ldots, \alpha_m\}$, for a given S.

The Typing Rules. For any well formed set of assumptions Γ, any functional term M, and any type scheme σ, we write the judgment: $\Gamma \vdash_{\mathrm{T}} M : \sigma$ if it is a conclusion of a deduction in the following system:

$$(Ax)\frac{}{\Gamma, \chi : \sigma \vdash_{\mathrm{T}} \chi : \sigma}$$

$$(\forall_E)\frac{\Gamma \vdash_{\mathrm{T}} M : \forall\alpha.\sigma}{\Gamma \vdash_{\mathrm{T}} M : \{^{\tau}\!\downarrow_\alpha\}\sigma} \qquad (\forall_I)\frac{\Gamma \vdash_{\mathrm{T}} M : \sigma \quad \alpha \notin \Gamma}{\Gamma \vdash_{\mathrm{T}} M : \forall\alpha.\sigma}$$

$$(\multimap_E)\frac{\Theta, \Delta_1 \vdash_{\mathrm{T}} M : \tau' \multimap \tau \qquad \Theta, \Delta_2 \vdash_{\mathrm{T}} N : \tau'}{\Theta, \Delta_1, \Delta_2 \vdash_{\mathrm{T}} MN : \tau} \qquad (\multimap_I)\frac{\Gamma, \chi : \tau \vdash_{\mathrm{T}} M : \tau'}{\Gamma \vdash_{\mathrm{T}} \lambda\chi.M : \tau \multimap \tau'}$$

$$(!)\frac{\Gamma \vdash_{\mathrm{T}} N :!\tau' \qquad \chi : \tau' \vdash_{\mathrm{T}} M : \tau}{\Gamma \vdash_{\mathrm{T}} !(M)[^{N}/_{x}] :!\tau} \qquad (!_\emptyset)\frac{\vdash_{\mathrm{T}} M : \tau}{\Gamma \vdash_{\mathrm{T}} !M :!\tau}$$

$$(\S)\frac{\begin{array}{ll} m+n+p+q \geq 1 & \\ \Theta, \Delta_i \vdash_{\mathrm{T}} M_i : \tau_i & (1 \leq i \leq m) \\ \Theta, \Phi_j \vdash_{\mathrm{T}} N_j :!!\rho_j & (1 \leq j \leq n) \\ \Theta, \Psi_k \vdash_{\mathrm{T}} P_k : \S\mu_k & (1 \leq k \leq p) \\ \Theta, \Upsilon_l \vdash_{\mathrm{T}} Q_l : \S!\nu_l & (1 \leq l \leq q) \\ x_1 : \tau_1 \ldots x_m : \tau_m, X_1 :!\rho_1 \ldots X_n :!\rho_n, & \\ y_1 : \mu_1 \ldots y_p : \mu_p, Y_1 :!\nu_1 \ldots Y_q :!\nu_q \quad \vdash_{\mathrm{T}} M : \tau & \end{array}}{\begin{array}{l} \Theta \ldots \Delta_i \ldots \Phi_j \ldots \Psi_k \ldots \Upsilon_l \ldots \vdash_{\mathrm{T}} \S(M)[\,^{M_1}/_{x_1} \cdots {}^{M_m}/_{x_m}\;, \\ \qquad\qquad\qquad\qquad\qquad\qquad {}^{N_1}/_{X_1} \cdots {}^{N_n}/_{X_n}\;, \\ \qquad\qquad\qquad\qquad\qquad\qquad {}^{P_1}/_{y_1} \cdots {}^{P_p}/_{y_p}\;, \\ \qquad\qquad\qquad\qquad\qquad\qquad {}^{Q_1}/_{Y_1} \cdots {}^{Q_q}/_{Y_q}\;] : \S\tau \end{array}}$$

$$(\S_\emptyset)\frac{\vdash_{\mathrm{T}} M:\tau}{\Gamma\vdash_{\mathrm{T}} \S M:\S\tau} \qquad (\mathtt{let}\ )\frac{\Theta,\Delta_1\vdash_{\mathrm{T}} M:\sigma \qquad X:\sigma,\Theta,\Delta_2\vdash_{\mathrm{T}} N:\tau}{\Theta,\Delta_1,\Delta_2\vdash_{\mathrm{T}} \mathtt{let}\ X=M\ \mathtt{in}\ N:\tau}$$

Observe that (Ax), $(!_\emptyset)$, and $(\S_\emptyset)$ have implicit weakening, while $(\multimap_E)$, $(\S)$, and $(\mathtt{let}\ )$ have implicit contraction.

Definition 1. *$\Lambda^{\mathrm{T}}_{\mathrm{LA}}$ is the sub-set of Λ_{LA}* typable *by $\vdash_{\mathrm{T}}$, namely, $M\in\Lambda^{\mathrm{T}}_{\mathrm{LA}}$, if, and only if, there are Γ, and σ such that $\Gamma\vdash_{\mathrm{T}} M:\sigma$.*

Lemma 2. *The following rules are admissible in $\vdash_{\mathrm{T}}$:*

$$(\geq)\frac{\chi:\sigma',\Gamma\vdash_{\mathrm{T}} M:\sigma'' \qquad \sigma\geq\sigma'}{\chi:\sigma,\Gamma\vdash_{\mathrm{T}} M:\sigma''}$$

$$(WR)\frac{\Gamma\vdash_{\mathrm{T}} M:\sigma \qquad \mathrm{domain}(\Gamma')\cap\mathrm{domain}(\Gamma)=\emptyset \qquad \mathtt{FV}(M)\subseteq\mathtt{V}\subseteq\mathrm{domain}(\Gamma)}{\{\chi:\Gamma(\chi)\mid\chi\in\mathtt{V}\},\Gamma'\vdash_{\mathrm{T}} M:\tau}$$

Proof. By structural induction on M.

Clearly, rule (WR) simultaneously weakens, and extends Γ.

Lemma 3 (Substitution).

1. *Let $\Theta,x:\sigma,\Delta\vdash_{\mathrm{T}} M:\sigma'$. Then, $\Theta,\Phi,\Delta\vdash_{\mathrm{T}} M\{^N\!\downarrow_x\}:\sigma'$, for any $\Theta,\Phi\vdash_{\mathrm{T}} N:\sigma$.*
2. *Let $\Theta,X:!\tau,\Delta\vdash_{\mathrm{T}} M:\sigma$. Then, $\Theta,\Phi,\Delta\vdash_{\mathrm{T}} M\{^N\!\downarrow_X\}:\sigma$, for any $\Theta,\Phi\vdash_{\mathrm{T}} N:!\tau$ such that N is a !-box or it belongs to* `!-Term-Variables`.

Proof. By induction on M.

Theorem 1 (Subject Reduction). *If $\Gamma\vdash_{\mathrm{T}} M:\sigma$, and $M\leadsto N$, then $\Gamma\vdash_{\mathrm{T}} N:\sigma$.*

Proof. By induction on M, using Substitution Lemma here above.

4 Correctness

A possible statement of correctness for $\Lambda^{\mathrm{T}}_{\mathrm{LA}}$ states: any $M\in\Lambda^{\mathrm{T}}_{\mathrm{LA}}$ represents an algorithm in **P-TIME**.

The proof of such a statement is very simple. First, we consider a language $\mathtt{G}_{\mathrm{LA}}$ of graphs. A strategy that reduces any graph G in a time at most polynomial in the dimension of G exists. Second, $\mathtt{G}_{\mathrm{LA}}$ is proved to be a model of $\Lambda^{\mathrm{T}}_{\mathrm{LA}}$. So, $\Lambda^{\mathrm{T}}_{\mathrm{LA}}$ becomes a functional notation for dealing with **P-TIME**.

The language $\mathtt{G}_{\mathrm{LA}}$ is explicitly introduced in Appendix A. It is the graph version of the sequent calculus of Intuitionistic Light Affine Logic **ILAL** in [1].

Let use $\mathtt{G}_{\mathrm{LA}}$ as a model for $\Lambda^{\mathrm{T}}_{\mathrm{LA}}$. First, let $>$ be the reduction relation on $\mathtt{G}_{\mathrm{LA}}$, which we recall in Appendix A. The intuition about $>$ says that, up to some irrelevant details, it mimics the cut-elimination steps of **ILAL** on $\mathtt{G}_{\mathrm{LA}}$. Then, take $\Leftrightarrow$ as the equational theory of $>$ on $\mathtt{G}_{\mathrm{LA}}$, namely, its reflexive, transitive, and symmetric closure.

Theorem 2 (Correctness). *There exists an embedding* $(.)^\bullet$ *of* $\Lambda^{\mathrm{T}}_{\mathrm{LA}}$ *into* $\mathtt{G}_{\mathrm{LA}}$ *such that, if* $M \rightsquigarrow^* N$*, then* $M^\bullet \diamond N^\bullet$.

$(.)^\bullet$ is the obvious adaptation to $\Lambda^{\mathrm{T}}_{\mathrm{LA}}$ of the embedding of the natural deduction of Intuitionistic Logic into its sequent calculus, where $(\mathtt{let}\ X = N\ \mathtt{in}\ M)^\bullet \stackrel{\mathrm{def}}{\equiv} ((\lambda X.M)N)^\bullet$. Then, the correctness of $\Lambda^{\mathrm{T}}_{\mathrm{LA}}$ is implied by the *confluence* of $\gtrdot$.

Theorem 3 (Confluence). *The rewriting system* $\rightsquigarrow$ *is confluent.*

This theorem is implied by the *strong normalizability*, and the *local confluence* of $\Lambda^{\mathrm{T}}_{\mathrm{LA}}$. In particular, $\Lambda^{\mathrm{T}}_{\mathrm{LA}}$ is *strongly normalizing* because, following Girard in [3], we can embed it into System F [4]. The local confluence comes from verifying that $\rightsquigarrow$ has not critical pairs.

5 Expressiveness

Any polynomial $f(x_1, \ldots, x_n)$ of arity $n \geq 0$, either linear, or not, can be represented as a term $\langle f(x_1, \ldots, x_n)\rangle$ of $\Lambda^{\mathrm{T}}_{\mathrm{LA}}$. In particular, the `let` constructor is required when $f(x_1, \ldots, x_n)$ is not linear.

Following also a referee's suggestion, we do not introduce the whole encoding of the polynomials. Only the Church Numerals and some operation on them are given, together with some further intuition about how the reduction complexity is controlled. Those interested to more details about the encoding of polynomials are referred to [10], where also the predecessor is introduced.

The Church Numerals. Let $\mathbf{int}_\tau$ be an abbreviation for $!(\tau \multimap \tau) \multimap \S(\tau \multimap \tau)$. For any $n \geq 1$, define:

$$\overline{0} \stackrel{\mathrm{def}}{\equiv} \lambda X.\S\lambda y.y : \mathbf{int}_\tau$$
$$\overline{n+1} \stackrel{\mathrm{def}}{\equiv} \lambda X.\S(\lambda y.y_1(\ldots(y_n y)\ldots)))[^X/_{y_1} \cdots {}^X/_{y_n}] : \mathbf{int}_\tau \ .$$

Now, define an *erasure* function on $\Lambda^{\mathrm{T}}_{\mathrm{LA}}$ as follows: from a given M, delete all the occurrences of !, and §. Then, for any $[\cdots {}^N/_\chi \cdots]$ of any box, substitute N for χ in the body, no matter the forms of N and χ are. Finally, erase all the interfaces, and collapse `Term-Variables` and `!-Term-Variables` into a single set. Of course, the substitutions must avoid variable clash. Applying this erasure to any term of Λ_{LA} would yield a term of the usual λ-Calculus. In particular, the terms here above, would be mapped into the usual Church Numerals. Some combinators on them:

$$succ \stackrel{\mathrm{def}}{\equiv} \lambda zX.\S(\lambda y.y_1(y_2 y))[^X/_{y_1}{}^{(zX)}/_{y_2}] : \mathbf{int}_\tau \multimap \mathbf{int}_\tau$$
$$sum \stackrel{\mathrm{def}}{\equiv} \lambda wzX.\S(\lambda y.y_1(y_2 y))[^{(wX)}/_{y_1}{}^{(zX)}/_{y_2}] : \mathbf{int}_\tau \multimap \mathbf{int}_\tau \multimap \mathbf{int}_\tau$$
$$iter \stackrel{\mathrm{def}}{\equiv} \lambda x_n X_s x_b.\S(yw)[^{(x_n X_s)}/_y{}^{x_b}/_w] : \mathbf{int}_\tau \multimap !(\tau \multimap \tau) \multimap \S\tau \multimap \S\tau$$
$$mult \stackrel{\mathrm{def}}{\equiv} \lambda xY.iter\ x\ !(\lambda w.sum\ zw)[^Y/_z]\ \S\overline{0} : \mathbf{int}_{\mathbf{int}_\tau} \multimap !\mathbf{int}_\tau \multimap \S\mathbf{int}_\tau \ .$$

The successor *succ* , the *sum* , and the multiplication *mult* do the obvious thing. The iteration *iter* takes as arguments a numeral, a *step function*, and a *base* where to start the iteration from.

Observe that *iter* $\overline{2}$ $(!\overline{2})$ $(\S\overline{0})$ can not have type, for $\overline{2}$, and any numeral here above, can not be used as a step function. This because the step function is required to have identical domain and co-domain. This should not surprise. In the introduction we pointed out that the application of $\overline{2}$ to $\overline{2}$ is the starting point to yield exponentially growing computations.

Notice, however, that there are variations of $\overline{0}$, and $\overline{1}$ that we can use as step function for *iter* :

$$\begin{aligned}
\overline{0}' &\stackrel{\text{def}}{\equiv} \lambda x.\S\lambda y.y : \S(\alpha \multimap \alpha) \multimap \S(\alpha \multimap \alpha)\\
\overline{0}'' &\stackrel{\text{def}}{\equiv} \lambda X.!\lambda y.y :!(\alpha \multimap \alpha) \multimap !(\alpha \multimap \alpha)\\
\overline{1}' &\stackrel{\text{def}}{\equiv} \lambda x.\S(\lambda y.y_1 y)[^x/_{y_1}] : \S(\alpha \multimap \alpha) \multimap \S(\alpha \multimap \alpha)\\
\overline{1}'' &\stackrel{\text{def}}{\equiv} \lambda X.!(\lambda y.y_1 y)[^X/_{y_1}] :!(\alpha \multimap \alpha) \multimap !(\alpha \multimap \alpha) \ .
\end{aligned}$$

We conclude with an example about reduction:

$$\begin{aligned}
&sum\ \overline{1}\overline{1}\\
&\rightsquigarrow^{\beta}_{1,1} \lambda X.\S(\lambda y.y_1(y_2 y))[^{\overline{1}X}/_{y_1}\ ^{\overline{1}X}/_{y_2}]\\
&\rightsquigarrow^{\beta}_{2,2} \lambda X.\S(\lambda y.y_1(y_2 y))[^{\S(\lambda z.z_1 z)[^X/_{z_1}]}/_{y_1}\ ^{\S(\lambda w.w_1 w)[^X/_{w_1}]}/_{y_2}]\\
&\rightsquigarrow^{\S\S}_{2,2} \lambda X.\S(\lambda y.(\lambda z.z_1 z)((\lambda w.w_1 w)y))[^X/_{z_1}\ ^X/_{w_1}]\\
&\rightsquigarrow^{\beta}_{1,1} \lambda X.\S(\lambda y.z_1(w_1 y))[^X/_{z_1}\ ^X/_{w_1}]\\
&\stackrel{\text{def}}{\equiv} \overline{2}\ .
\end{aligned}$$

For example, the notation $\rightsquigarrow^{\S\S}_{2,2}$ stands for a sequence of two contextual applications of $\rhd_2$, belonging to the §§-group.

6 Poly-step Reduction Strategy

$\Lambda^{\mathrm{T}}_{\mathrm{LA}}$ can be proved to have a *poly-step* normalization process. This means that, given a term M, there is a *normal strategy* such that M rewrites to a normal term N with no more $\rightsquigarrow$-steps than the dimension $|M|$ of M. Notice that, for a term M, being poly-step in the above sense, is not exactly as having a **P-TIME** normalization process in $|M|$. Counting the time would mean to consider at least the cost of the renaming operations, and of the substitution of the terms for the variables. But this is not an issue, as Λ_{LA} is only an abstract language to program with, and not an implementation language.

The proof that $\Lambda^{\mathrm{T}}_{\mathrm{LA}}$ is poly-step split in two parts.

First, we show that the rewriting relation $\gg$ of the language of graphs G_{LA}, is computationally adequate with respect to the rewriting relation $\rightsquigarrow$ of Λ_{LA}. This means showing:

Theorem 4 (Adequacy). *There exists an embedding* $(.)^p$ *from* Λ_{LA} *to* G_{LA} *such that, if* $M \leadsto^* N$*, then* $M^p \gg^* N^p$.

Second, we define a *canonical* reduction strategy $\leadsto_p^*$ on $\leadsto$. Then, the existence of a poly-time reduction strategy $\gg_p^*$ for G_{LA}, allows to prove:

Theorem 5 (Poly-step Adequacy). *For any term* M *of* $\Lambda_{\mathrm{LA}}^{\mathrm{T}}$*, if* $M \leadsto_p^* N$*, then* $M^p \gg_p^* N^p$.

Proving Adequacy. The embedding $(.)^p$ can not be as simple as $(.)^\bullet$, otherwise we could only prove Correctness, as we did in Section 4.

Here, we want more: any reduction step of $\Lambda_{\mathrm{LA}}^{\mathrm{T}}$, in fact, has to stand for a reduction sequence of G_{LA} (Appendix A.) The problem for showing this is that Λ_{LA} does not have explicit contraction, unlike G_{LA}. Recall that any contraction node of G_{LA} determines whether a graph can be duplicated, or not; in Λ_{LA}, the same effect is obtained with two distinguished sets of variables. The result is that the situations where a contraction node of G_{LA} gets stuck, correspond to pairs of term *constructors* of $\Lambda_{\mathrm{LA}}^{\mathrm{T}}$ that can not annihilate each other. For example, consider the following one-step reduction of a term to its normal form:

$$P \stackrel{\text{def}}{\equiv} (\lambda X.xXX)!(M)[^{yz}/_X] \leadsto (\lambda Y.x!(M)[^Y/_X]!(M)[^Y/_X])(yz) \stackrel{\text{def}}{\equiv} Q \ .$$

Taking $(.)^p$ as $(.)^\bullet$, the graph P^p would be the one expected:

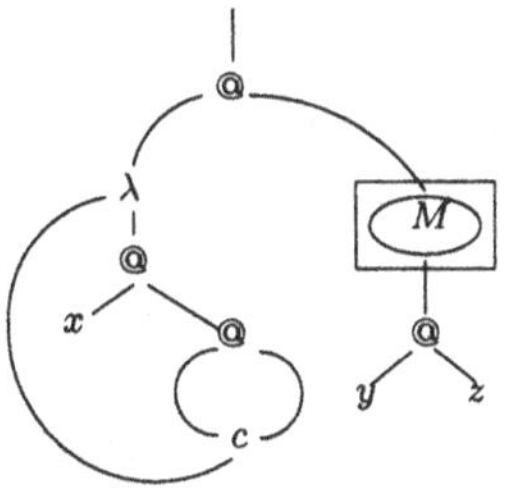

On the contrary, Q^p would be:

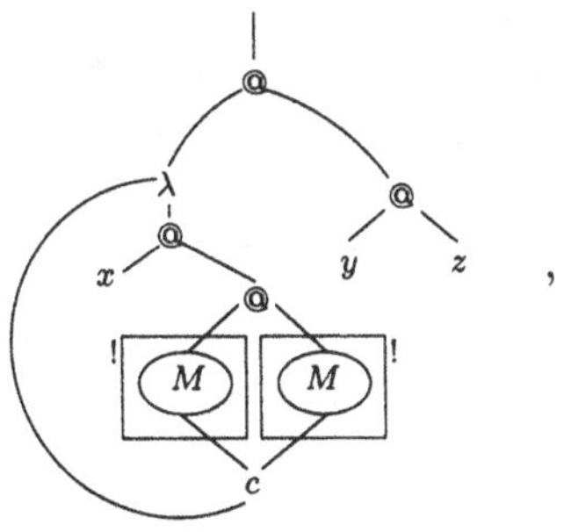

which is not quite what we want: Q^p would not be the graph that P^p reduces to. The difference between $(.)^\bullet$ and $(.)^p$ must be the ability to detect when a configuration in a term of $\Lambda_{\mathrm{LA}}^{\mathrm{T}}$ must be translated in the obvious way, as for P, or if it must be simplified, as for Q. Situations like the one here above involve pair of boxes as well. For example, let $P \stackrel{\text{def}}{\equiv} \lambda xyz.xyz$. Then, take the terms:

$$!(PXX)[^{!!(M)[^N/_x]}/_X]$$
$$!(PXX)[^{!(!(M)[^N/_x])[^Q/_{x'}]}/_X]$$
$$\S(PXX)[^{!!(M)[^N/_x]}/_X]$$
$$\S(PXX)[^{!(!(M)[^N/_x])[^Q/_{x'}]}/_X]$$
$$\S(PXX)[^{\S!(M)[^N/_x]}/_X]$$
$$\S(PXX)[^{\S(!(M)[^N/_x])[\cdots^Q/_{x'}\cdots]}/_X]$$

and reduce them: $(.)^\bullet$ would not allow to prove adequacy. Summing up, $(.)^p$ must be sensitive to the "history" of some pair of term constructors in a given term.

This need is accomplished by taking a labeling function which maps the term constructors λ, !-box, §-box, and the application of Λ_{LA} to natural numbers. Then, for any M, $(M)^p$ consists of two main steps. The first yields the same result, say G_M, as $(M)^\bullet$. The second step operates on G_M by reducing it with $\gg$. These reductions eliminate *only* those pairs of nodes of G_M which are images of two term constructors with the same label.

Of course something has to correctly set the labeling. This can be done by $\rightsquigarrow$, when yielding the right-hand side of: $\rhd^{\beta}_{5}$, $\rhd^{!!}_{5,6}$, $\rhd^{\S!}_{5,6}$, and $\rhd^{\S\S}_{5,6}$.

Proving $\Lambda^{\text{T}}_{\text{LA}}$ being Poly-step. Let M be given. We say that N is at depth $i \geq 0$, and we write N^i, if it is in the body of i nested boxes of M. The notion of depth can obviously be used also for the redexes, which are the left-hand side terms of the rewriting relation $\rhd$ in Section 2. Let us classify the redexes in two sets. The β-redexes belong to the β-group or to the `let` -group. The box-redexes are all the others. Now, assume M having at most d nested boxes. For any $0 \leq i \leq d$, the ith *reduction round* reduces all the β-redexes N^i and all the box-redexes N^{i-1}, in any order. Finally, the *poly-step reduction strategy* $\rightsquigarrow^*_p$ is the sequence of reduction rounds which starts from the 1st and stops (at most) at the dth.

$\Lambda^{\text{T}}_{\text{LA}}$ is poly-step because the strategy $\rightsquigarrow^*_p$ is the the obvious adaptation of the poly-time strategy $\gg^*_p$ on G_{LA}. To get $\gg_p$ as in [1], just replace $\gg$ for $\rightsquigarrow$, and let the β-redexes be the left-hand graphs of $\rhd_{1,3,4,5,6,7,8,9,10}$ in Appendix A, while the box-redexes be all the other ones.

7 The Type Inference

This section is essentially technical. It defines the adaptation to Λ_{LA} of the Damas-Milner type inference for ML [2]. For a less verbose presentation it is worth introducing some notations.

Never before used type variables are called *fresh*.

For any sub-set $\mathtt{V}$ of $\mathtt{Term\text{-}Variables} \cup \mathtt{!\text{-}Term\text{-}Variables}$, and for any well formed set of assumptions Γ, $\Gamma^{\mathtt{V}}$ stands for Γ restricted to $\chi \in \mathtt{V}$, while $\Gamma_{\mathtt{V}}$ is Γ restricted to $\chi \notin \mathtt{V}$.

Let $\tau_1, \ldots, \tau_n, \tau'_1, \ldots, \tau'_n$ be any tuple of types. Then, $\vdash_{\mathrm{U}} \{\tau_1 = \tau'_1, \ldots, \tau_n = \tau'_n\} \Rightarrow U$, denotes the obvious algorithm that yields the *most general unifier* U, of the pairs $\tau_1 = \tau'_1, \ldots, \tau_n = \tau'_n$, if any. Otherwise, $\vdash_{\mathrm{U}} \{\tau_1 = \tau'_1, \ldots, \tau_n = \tau'_n\} \Rightarrow \mathtt{failure}$.

The identity substitution on types is $\mathcal{I}$.

For any set of assumptions Γ, and any type τ, the notation $\forall\Gamma.\tau$ stands for the type $\forall\alpha_1 \ldots \alpha_n.\tau$, where $\{\alpha_1 \ldots \alpha_n\}$ is $\mathtt{FV}(\tau) \setminus \mathtt{FV}(\Gamma)$.

The Algorithm For any well formed set of assumptions Γ, any functional term M, any substitution S, and any type τ, the algorithm for the type inference derives two kinds of judgments: either $\vdash_{\mathrm{TI}} \Gamma; M \Rightarrow S; \tau$ or $\vdash_{\mathrm{TI}} \Gamma; M \Rightarrow \mathtt{failure}$. The first corresponds to the success of the algorithm, while, the second to its failure.

The following rules in Natural Semantics[5] define $\vdash_{\mathrm{TI}}$ to derive judgments of the first kind. The rules for the second kind of judgment are omitted, because obvious. The rules of the algorithm are:

$$(Ax)\,\frac{\begin{array}{l} n \geq 0 \\ \gamma_1, \ldots, \gamma_n \text{ fresh} \\ S = \{{}^{\gamma_1}\!\downarrow_{\alpha_1} \cdots {}^{\gamma_n}\!\downarrow_{\alpha_n}\} \end{array}}{\vdash_{\mathrm{TI}} \Gamma, \chi : \forall\alpha_1 \ldots \alpha_n.\tau; \chi \Rightarrow \mathcal{I}; S\tau}$$

$$(\mathtt{let})\,\frac{\begin{array}{l} \vdash_{\mathrm{TI}} \Gamma; M \Rightarrow S_M; \tau_M \\ \gamma \text{ fresh} \\ \vdash_{\mathrm{U}} \{\tau_M = !\gamma\} \Rightarrow U \\ \vdash_{\mathrm{TI}} X : (\forall S_M\Gamma.!U\gamma), S_M\Gamma_{\{X\}}; N \Rightarrow S_N; \tau_N \\ S_N S_M \text{-compatible with-} \Gamma \end{array}}{\vdash_{\mathrm{TI}} \Gamma; \mathtt{let}\ X = M\ \mathtt{in}\ N \Rightarrow S_N S_M; \tau_N}$$

$$(\multimap_E)\,\frac{\begin{array}{l} \vdash_{\mathrm{TI}} \Gamma; M \Rightarrow S_M; \tau_M \\ \vdash_{\mathrm{TI}} S_M\Gamma; N \Rightarrow S_N; \tau_N \\ \gamma \text{ fresh} \\ \vdash_{\mathrm{U}} \{S_N\tau_M = \tau_N \multimap \gamma\} \Rightarrow U \\ US_N S_M \text{-compatible with-} \Gamma \end{array}}{\vdash_{\mathrm{TI}} \Gamma; MN \Rightarrow US_N S_M; U\gamma}$$

$$(\multimap_{I_x})\,\frac{\begin{array}{l} \gamma \text{ fresh} \\ \vdash_{\mathrm{TI}} \Gamma_{\{x\}}, x : \gamma; M \Rightarrow S; \tau \\ S \text{-compatible with-} (\Gamma_{\{x\}}, x : \gamma) \\ S \text{-compatible with-} \Gamma^{\{x\}} \end{array}}{\vdash_{\mathrm{TI}} \Gamma; \lambda x.M \Rightarrow S; S\gamma \multimap \tau}$$

$$(\multimap_{I_X})\,\frac{\begin{array}{l} \gamma \text{ fresh} \\ \vdash_{\mathrm{TI}} \Gamma_{\{X\}}, X : !\gamma; M \Rightarrow S; \tau \\ S \text{-compatible with-} (\Gamma_{\{X\}}, X : !\gamma) \\ S \text{-compatible with-} \Gamma^{\{X\}} \end{array}}{\vdash_{\mathrm{TI}} \Gamma; \lambda X.M \Rightarrow S; (!S\gamma) \multimap \tau}$$

$$(!_x)\,\frac{\begin{array}{l} \vdash_{\mathrm{TI}} \Gamma; N \Rightarrow S_N; \tau_N \\ \gamma \text{ fresh} \\ \vdash_{\mathrm{U}} \{\tau_N = !\gamma\} \Rightarrow U \\ \text{not}(!\text{-exp}(U\gamma)) \\ \vdash_{\mathrm{TI}} x : U\gamma, US_N\Gamma_{\{x\}}; M \Rightarrow S_M; \tau_M \\ S_M U S_N \text{-compatible with-} \Gamma \end{array}}{\vdash_{\mathrm{TI}} \Gamma; !(M)[{}^N/_x] \Rightarrow S_M U S_N; !\tau_M}$$

$$(!_X)\,\frac{\begin{array}{l} \vdash_{\mathrm{TI}} \Gamma; N \Rightarrow S_N; \tau_N \\ \gamma \text{ fresh} \\ \vdash_{\mathrm{U}} \{\tau_N = !!\gamma\} \Rightarrow U \\ \vdash_{\mathrm{TI}} X : !U\gamma, US_N\Gamma_{\{X\}}; M \Rightarrow S_M; \tau_M \\ S_M U S_N \text{-compatible with-} \Gamma \end{array}}{\vdash_{\mathrm{TI}} \Gamma; !(M)[{}^N/_X] \Rightarrow S_M U S_N; !\tau_M}$$

$$(!_\emptyset)\,\frac{\begin{array}{l} \vdash_{\mathrm{TI}} \emptyset; M \Rightarrow S; \tau \\ S \text{-compatible with-} \Gamma \end{array}}{\vdash_{\mathrm{TI}} \Gamma; !M \Rightarrow S; !\tau}
\qquad
(\S_\emptyset)\,\frac{\begin{array}{l} \vdash_{\mathrm{TI}} \emptyset; M \Rightarrow S; \tau \\ S \text{-compatible with-} \Gamma \end{array}}{\vdash_{\mathrm{TI}} \Gamma; \S M \Rightarrow S; \S\tau}$$

$$
\begin{array}{ll}
\vdash_{\mathrm{TI}} S_{i-1}\cdots S_1\Gamma; M_i \Rightarrow S_i;\tau_i & (1\le i\le m)\\
\vdash_{\mathrm{TI}} R_{j-1}\cdots R_1 S_m\cdots S_1\Gamma; N_j \Rightarrow R_j;\rho_j & (1\le j\le n)\\
\vdash_{\mathrm{TI}} T_{k-1}\cdots T_1 R_n\cdots R_1 S_m\cdots S_1\Gamma; P_k \Rightarrow T_k;\mu_k & (1\le k\le p)\\
\vdash_{\mathrm{TI}} U_{l-1}\cdots U_1 T_p\cdots T_1 R_n\cdots R_1 S_m\cdots S_1\Gamma; Q_l \Rightarrow U_l;\nu_l & (1\le l\le q)\\
\gamma_1\ldots\gamma_m,\alpha_1\ldots\alpha_n,\beta_1\ldots\beta_p,\delta_1\ldots\delta_q \text{ fresh} & \\
\vdash_{\mathrm{U}} \bigcup_{1\le i\le m}\{U_q\cdots U_1 T_p\cdots T_1 R_n\cdots R_1 S_m\cdots S_{i+1}\tau_i = !\gamma_i\} \cup & \\
\quad \bigcup_{1\le j\le n}\{U_q\cdots U_1 T_p\cdots T_1 R_n\cdots R_{j+1}\rho_j = !!\alpha_j\} \cup & \\
\quad \bigcup_{1\le k\le p}\{U_q\cdots U_1 T_p\cdots T_{k+1}\mu_k = \S\beta_k\} \cup & \\
\quad \bigcup_{1\le l\le q}\{U_q\cdots U_{l+1}\nu_l = \S!\delta_l\} \Rightarrow U & \\
\mathrm{not}(!\text{-}\mathrm{exp}(U\gamma_i)) & (1\le i\le n)\\
\mathrm{not}(!\text{-}\mathrm{exp}(U\beta_k)) & (1\le k\le p)\\
\Gamma_1 = \{x_1:\gamma_1,\ldots,x_m:\gamma_m,\ X_1 :!\alpha_1,\ldots,X_n :!\alpha_n, & \\
\qquad y_1:\beta_1,\ldots,y_p:\beta_p, Y_1 :!\delta_1,\ldots,Y_q :!\delta_q\ \} & \\
\Gamma_2 = U_q\cdots U_1 T_p\cdots T_1 R_n\cdots R_1 S_m\cdots S_1\Gamma_{\{x_1\ldots x_m,X_1\ldots X_n,y_1\ldots y_p,Y_1\ldots Y_q\}} & \\
\vdash_{\mathrm{TI}} U\Gamma_1, U\Gamma_2; M \Rightarrow S_M;\tau_M & \\
SUU_q\cdots U_1 T_p\cdots T_1 R_n\cdots R_1 S_m\cdots S_1 \text{-compatible with-} \Gamma & \\
\hline
\vdash_{\mathrm{TI}} \Gamma; \S(M)[{}^{M_1}/_{x_1}\cdots{}^{M_m}/_{x_m}, & \\
\qquad {}^{N_1}/_{X_1}\cdots{}^{N_n}/_{X_n}, & \\
\qquad {}^{P_1}/_{y_1}\cdots{}^{P_p}/_{y_p}, & \\
\qquad {}^{Q_1}/_{Y_1}\cdots{}^{Q_q}/_{Y_q}\ ] \Rightarrow S_M UU_q\cdots U_1 T_p\cdots T_1 R_n\cdots R_1 S_m\cdots S_1;\S\tau_M &
\end{array}\ (\S)
$$

The last rule is a "nightmare" because of the complexity of the type assignment rule for the §-box. For example, the line:

$$\vdash_{\mathrm{TI}} S_{i-1}\cdots S_1\Gamma; M_i \Rightarrow S_i;\tau_i\ (1\le i\le m)$$

stands for the statements:

$$
\begin{array}{l}
\vdash_{\mathrm{TI}} \Gamma; M_1 \Rightarrow S_1;\tau_1\\
\vdash_{\mathrm{TI}} S_1\Gamma; M_2 \Rightarrow S_2;\tau_2\\
\vdots\\
\vdash_{\mathrm{TI}} S_{m-1}\cdots S_1\Gamma; M_m \Rightarrow S_m;\tau_m
\end{array}
$$

Theorem 6 (Correctness). *Let Γ be well formed. If $\vdash_{\mathrm{TI}} \Gamma; M \Rightarrow S;\tau$, then $S\Gamma \vdash_{\mathrm{T}} M:\tau$. In particular, S-compatible with-Γ.*

Proof. Induction on the calls to $\vdash_{\mathrm{TI}}$, using Lemma 2.

Theorem 7 (Completeness). *Let Γ, and $S\Gamma$ be well formed. If $S\Gamma\vdash_{\mathrm{T}} M:\sigma$, then $\vdash_{\mathrm{TI}}\Gamma;M\Rightarrow S_M;\tau_M$, and there is $\bar{S}$ such that $S=\bar{S}S_M$, and $\bar{S}(\forall S_M\Gamma.\tau_M)\geq \sigma$.*

Proof. Induction on the length of the derivation of $S\Gamma \vdash_{\mathrm{T}} M:\tau$, using Lemma 1, and 2.

Completeness states that any type assigned by $\vdash_{\mathrm{T}}$ to M can be obtained as an instance of the type τ that $\vdash_{\mathrm{TI}}$ infers for M. So, τ is *principal* for M.

8 Conclusions

This work has presented an untyped functional language Λ_{LA} which has a sub-set $\Lambda^{\mathrm{T}}_{\mathrm{LA}}$ that can be typed automatically by a type inference algorithm. The types for the terms of $\Lambda^{\mathrm{T}}_{\mathrm{LA}}$ are polymorphic formulas of Intuitionistic Light Affine Logic.

The main properties of $\Lambda^{\mathrm{T}}_{\mathrm{LA}}$ are related to the functions it can represent, and to the complexity of its rewriting system. Every term of $\Lambda^{\mathrm{T}}_{\mathrm{LA}}$ represents a **P-TIME** algorithm. Moreover, there is a poly-step reduction strategy: it gets to the normal form of any term M in, at most, a polynomial number of steps, with respect to the dimension of M. Finally, $\Lambda^{\mathrm{T}}_{\mathrm{LA}}$ is Church-Rosser. So, we can think of it as a programming language to deal with algorithms with a computational complexity which is predictable and, at least in principle, reasonably low.

However, Λ_{LA} still needs improvements. Its syntax is still quite heavy. The main goal, like also a referee suggested, is to eliminate the interfaces from boxes.

The completeness of $\Lambda^{\mathrm{T}}_{\mathrm{LA}}$ is still open.

There are other languages to program algorithms in **P-TIME** [6, 7]. The weakness of $\Lambda^{\mathrm{T}}_{\mathrm{LA}}$, with respect to them, is that completeness is still open. Its strength come from its clean logical base.

References

[1] A. Asperti. Light Affine Logic. In *Proceedings of Symposium on Logic in Computer Science LICS'98*, 1998.

[2] L. Damas and R. Milner. Principal type-schemes for functional programs. In *Proceedings of Symposium on Logic in Computer Science LICS'82*, January 1982.

[3] J.-Y. Girard. Light Linear Logic. *Information and Computation*, 143:175 – 204, 1998.

[4] J.-Y. Girard, Y. Lafont, and P. Taylor. *Proofs and Types.* Cambridge University Press, 1989.

[5] C.A. Gunter. *Semantics of Programming Languages: Structures and Techniques.* Foundations of Computing. The MIT Press, 1992.

[6] M. Hoffmann. A mixed modal/linear lambda calculus with applications to Bellantoni-Cook safe recursion. In *Proceedings of Computer Science Logic 1997 (CSL'97), Aarhus, Denmark*, volume To appear, 1997.

[7] D. Leivant and J.-Y. Marion. Lambda calculus characterizations of poly-time. *Fundamenta Informaticae*, 19:167 – 184, 1993.

[8] R. Milner, M. Tofte, and R. Harper. *The Definition of Standard ML.* The MIT Press, 1990.

[9] G. Plotkin. Call-by-name, call-by-value and the λ-calculus. *Theoretical Computer Science*, 1:125 – 159, 1975.

[10] L. Roversi. Concrete syntax for intuitionistic light affine logic with polymorphic type assignment. In *Theoretical Computer Science: Proceedings of the Sixth Italian Conference (Prato).* World Scientific (TO APPEAR), 9 – 11 November 1998.

A The Language of Graphs

This section introduces $\mathtt{G}_{\mathrm{LA}}$. The language $\mathtt{G}_{\mathrm{LA}}$ is the graph language Asperti refers to in [1] to prove that the sequent calculus for **ILAL** captures **P-TIME**.

The language $\mathtt{G}_{\mathrm{LA}}$ is the least set of graphs containing the wires: 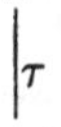 which correspond to the axioms, and such that, if G, and G' are in $\mathtt{G}_{\mathrm{LA}}$, then the following graphs belong to $\mathtt{G}_{\mathrm{LA}}$ as well:

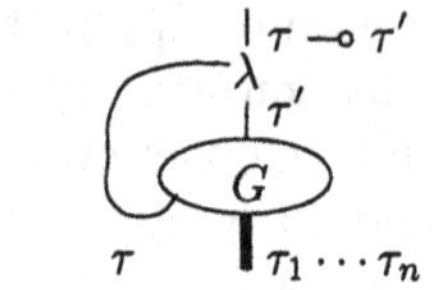

⊸–introduction on the right

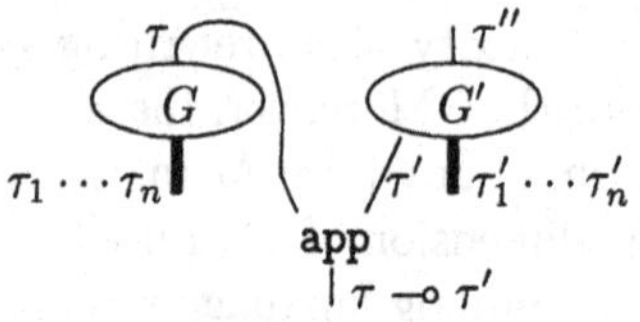

⊸–introduction on the left.

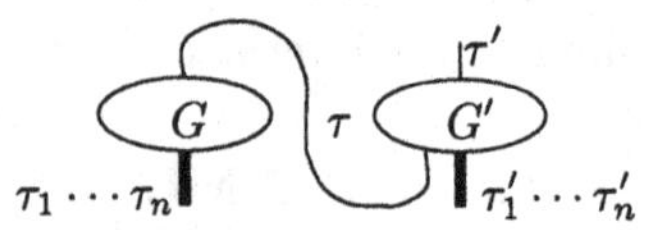

Cutting two derivations.

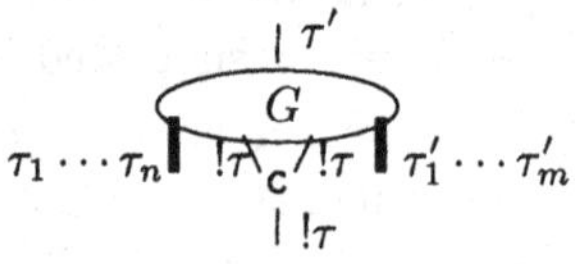

Contraction.

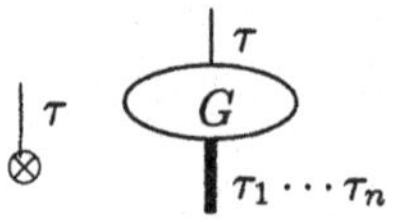

Weakening.

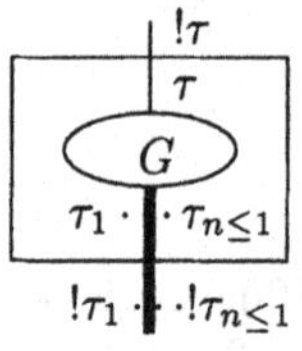

!-box.

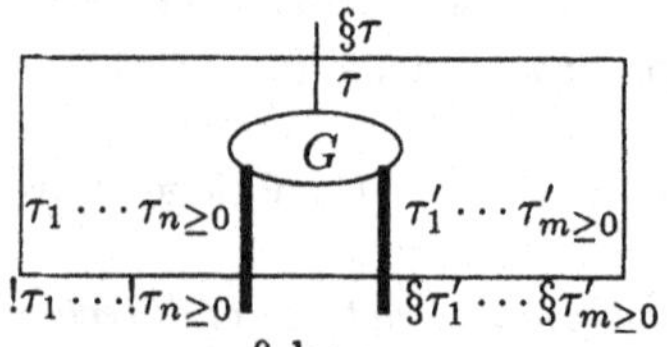

§-box.

The elements of $\mathtt{G}_{\mathrm{LA}}$ have a single upward link: the *root.* They have also a, possibly empty, set of sticking down links: the *inputs.* Multiple inputs are denoted by thick lines.

The rewriting system $\gg$ is the least relation on $\mathtt{G}_{\mathrm{LA}} \times \mathtt{G}_{\mathrm{LA}}$ containing the *contextual closure* of a relation $\triangleright$ between *parts* of graphs. The relation $\triangleright$ is:

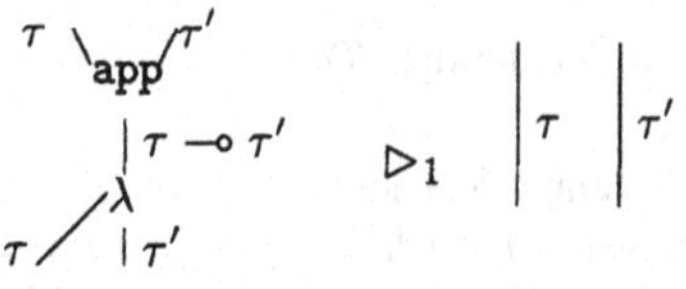

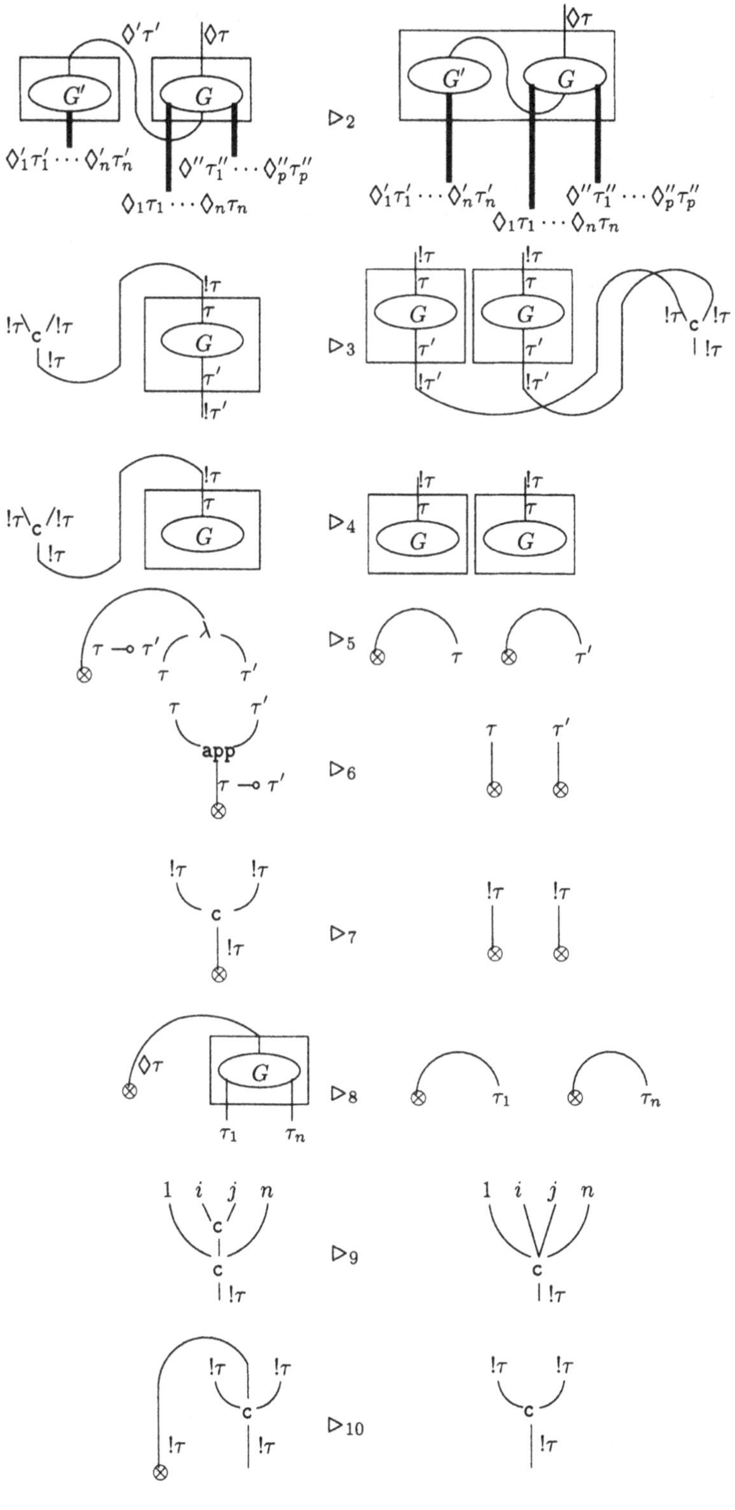
▷2
▷3
▷4
▷5
▷6
▷7
▷8
▷9
▷10
app

The rule $\triangleright_2$ is defined with the following proviso: if $\lozenge \equiv \S$, then $\lozenge' \in \{!, \S\}$. Otherwise, if $\lozenge \equiv !$, then $\lozenge'$ can only be !. Of course, the bounds for n, p, and q are consistent with these two cases. Moreover, every $\lozenge_i, \lozenge'_j, \lozenge''_k$ range over the set $\{!, \S\}$. Rule $\triangleright_8$ applies to both cases $\lozenge =!$, and $\lozenge = \S$. The rules $\triangleright_9$, and $\triangleright_{10}$ are a sort of garbage-collection.

We insist recalling that both G_{LA} and its rewriting relation $\gtrdot$ are the language effectively used by Asperti to capture **P-TIME**[1].

The reflexive, and transitive closure $\gtrdot^*$ of the rewriting system here above is *locally confluent*, and *strongly normalizing*. Hence, it is also *Church-Rosser*. The strategy able to reduce to any graph G in poly-time, with respect to its dimension, is recalled in Section 6.

Cut Elimination for Classical Proofs as Continuation Passing Style Computation

Ichiro Ogata

Electrotechnical Laboratory
1-1-4 Umezono Tsukuba 305-8568 JAPAN
ogata@etl.go.jp http://www.etl.go.jp/~ogata

Abstract. We show that the one can consider proof of the Gentzen's **LK** as the continuation passing style(CPS) programs; and the cut-elimination procedure for **LK** as computation. To be more precise, we observe that Strongly Normalizable(SN) and Church-Rosser(CR) cut-elimination procedure for (intuitionistic decoration of) **LKT** and **LKQ**, as presented in Danos et al.(1993), precisely corresponds to call-by-name(CBN) and call-by-value(CBV) CPS calculi, respectively. This can also be seen as an extension to classical logic of Zucker-Pottinger-Mints investigation of the relations between cut-elimination and normalization.

1 Introduction

Continuation Passing Style(CPS): Since Griffin's influential work [12] on the Curry-Howard correspondence between classical proofs and CPS programs, there has been a lot of interest on programming in classical proofs. It is because these classical calculi relate to important programming concepts such as non-local exit or exception handling. In Griffin's result, Plotkin's call-by-name (CBN) CPS translation on simply-typed λ-calculus induces a Gödel's double-negation translation on their types.

Proof theory: There is a long line of proof theoretical approaches to understanding "deconstructive" classical logic. That is, classical logic that has Strongly Normalizing (SN) and confluent (Church-Rosser or CR) cut-elimination procedure. This thread began with Girard's linear logic(**LL**)[8], followed by **LC** [9] and the logic of unity (**LU**) [10]. It reaches to **LKT** and **LKQ** [3] and more general $\mathrm{LK}^{\mathrm{tq}}$ [4] through Danos, Joinet and Schellinx (DJS). These works are all based on logic in Gentzen-style sequent calculus [7].

We unify the proof theoretical approach (i.e. SN and CR cut-elimination procedure) and the reduction system approach (CPS). Otherwise said, we found new, strict Curry-Howard isomorphism between Gentzen-style classical logic and programs. As a slogan, it can be said as "classical proofs as programs and cut elimination as computation". Particularly Classical Natural Deduction (**CND**)[20] style programs and its computation are interpreted by **LKT** and **LKQ** proofs and cut-elimination. We also show that Plotkin's CPS translation, in fact, can be understood as the translation from **ND** terms to **CND** terms.

Jieh Hsiang, Atsushi Ohori (Eds.): ASIAN'98, LNCS 1538, pp. 61–78, 1998.

LKT and **LKQ** are variations of Gentzen's original system **LK**. Confluency is recovered by adding some restrictions on logical rules to **LK**, though soundness and completeness w.r.t. classical provability is still retained. DJS proved the confluency of cut-elimination procedure for **LKT** and **LKQ** by using a beautiful relation with the multiplicative exponential part of classical linear logic (**MELL**), called **inductive linear decoration** and **taking skeleton**. Decoration is a kind of sound and faithful embedding between two logical system. The key is, computational properties are preserved between the original system and the decorated system. From this property, one can see that confluency of cut elimination procedure for **LKT** and **LKQ** is an immediate corollary to confluency for **MELL**[2].

In this paper, we focus on the intuitionistic version of decoration which is analogue of linear one. Our method can be seen as "yet another proof" of SN and CR property of cut-elimination for **LKT** and **LKQ**, since typed λ-calculus is also proven to be SN and CR [11]. Our contribution is to the notion how (intuitionistic decoration of) **LKT** and **LKQ** relate to the typed λ-term assignments, hence **LK**; and to the observation that this is identical to CPS programs through the consideration on **CND** interpreted by **LK**. To our knowledge, this is the first paper that shows the direct Curry-Howard correspondence between Gentzen style classical logic and CPS programs. Historically, CPS programs are studied under natural deduction style — i.e. term of the form of abstraction($\rightarrow$ introduction) and application($\rightarrow$ elimination).

Related Works: However at least CBN part of these frameworks should be considered as folklore. Girard already suggest the relation between λ-calculus and **ILU** in [10]. Also DJS themselves gave a guess in the final remark of [3] and in there introduction of [4] about the relation between **LKT**, negative fragment of **LC** and Parigot's **CND**. DeGroote revealed the relation between CBN CPS and Parigot's $\lambda\mu$-calculus which is an computational interpretation of **CND** [5]. Moreover there is a detailed work of Herbelin[13] about term calculus on **LJT** which is an intuitionistic fragment of **LKT**. He interpret **LJT** proofs as programs ($\overline{\lambda}$-calculus) and cut-elimination steps as reduction steps, as we do. We show that $\overline{\lambda}$-calculus is completely included as an intuitionistic case of our CBN CPS calculus.

We also have to mention to the pioneering work of Murthy[15]. He shows that one can interpret the proof of Girard's **LC** (of which negative fragment is **LKT**, positive fragment is **LKQ**) by CPS programs through the method called "intuitionistic extract". This is quite similar to our intuitionistic decoration method. However he can't give an answer to the question "appropriateness of this term extraction method for LC". It is because he didn't consider the relation between the computation and cut-elimination. By the way, Murthy's paper includes good references for classical control calculi which we omit in this paper.

The idea of assigning typed λ-terms to Gentzen style logical system, itself, is not new. As there are an early proof theoretical works on **LJ** by Prawitz[24], Zucker[26], Pottinger[23] and Mints[14]. Their method is essentially CBN because of the intrinsic cut orientation of **LJ**. However, our term assignment is far more precise, because we consider more general classical case. We *simulate* cut-elimination step for classical **LK** proofs through normalization. As a result SN and CR cut-elimination procedure on **LK** are simulated by normalization. This detailed analysis results in two different simulation (CBN and CBV) if we restrict **LK** to **LJ**.

Throughout this paper, we only handle propositional logic. We also put emphasis on CBV case, as the CBN case is the obvious analogue to CBV case. Some tables for CBN systems are given in appendix. We only employ implication ($\rightarrow$) as logical connectives, since this will be sufficient for us to explain our subject. However it can be extended to second order (system F polymorphism [8]).

$$\frac{}{A \Rightarrow\ ;\ A}\ (\mathrm{Ax}) \qquad \frac{\Gamma \Rightarrow \Delta\ ;\ A}{\Gamma \Rightarrow \Delta, A\ ;}\ (\mathrm{D})$$

$$\frac{\Gamma_0 \Rightarrow \Delta_0\ ;\ A \quad \Gamma_1, A \Rightarrow \Delta_1\ ;\ \Pi}{\Gamma_0, \Gamma_1 \Rightarrow \Delta_0, \Delta_1\ ;\ \Pi}\ (\text{t-cut}) \qquad \frac{\Gamma_0 \Rightarrow \Delta_0, A\ ;\ \Pi \quad \Gamma_1, A \Rightarrow \Delta_1\ ;}{\Gamma_0, \Gamma_1 \Rightarrow \Delta_0, \Delta_1\ ;\ \Pi}\ (\text{m-cut})$$

$$\frac{\Gamma \Rightarrow \Delta\ ;\ \Pi}{\Gamma, A \Rightarrow \Delta\ ;\ \Pi}\ (\mathrm{LW}) \qquad \frac{\Gamma, A, A \Rightarrow \Delta\ ;\ \Pi}{\Gamma, A \Rightarrow \Delta\ ;\ \Pi}\ (\mathrm{LC}) \qquad \frac{\Gamma \Rightarrow \Delta\ ;\ \Pi}{\Gamma \Rightarrow \Delta, A\ ;\ \Pi}\ (\mathrm{RW}) \qquad \frac{\Gamma \Rightarrow \Delta, A, A\ ;\ \Pi}{\Gamma \Rightarrow \Delta, A\ ;\ \Pi}\ (\mathrm{RC})$$

$$\frac{\Gamma_0 \Rightarrow \Delta_0\ ;\ A \quad \Gamma_1, B \Rightarrow \Delta_1\ ;}{\Gamma_0, \Gamma_1, A \rightarrow B \Rightarrow \Delta_0, \Delta_1\ ;}\ (\mathrm{L} \rightarrow) \qquad \frac{\Gamma, A \Rightarrow \Delta, B\ ;}{\Gamma \Rightarrow \Delta\ ;\ A \rightarrow B}\ (\mathrm{R} \rightarrow)$$

Table 1. Original Derivation Rules for **LKQ**

2 Decoration

2.1 Notations

In this paper, we entirely use the indexed formula version of logical system. We use six logical systems. **LK** and **LJ** by Gentzen [7], and **LKT** and **LKQ** by DJS [3]. We choose our notation to adapt that of DJS [4]. **CND** is an extension to classical logic of natural deduction (in sequent style representation) by Parigot [19, 20, 21]. It has several conclusions on left-hand-side of sequents. We also add **ND** as an intuitionistic case of **CND**.

Formulas are that of propositional logic constructed from $\rightarrow$. We use same implication symbol between logical systems. **Indexed formula** is an ordered pair of a formula and an index. We assume there are denumerably many **λ-indices** (resp. **μ-indices**) ranged over $x, y, z \dots$ (resp. $\alpha, \beta, \gamma, \dots$). We write an indexed formula (A, x) as A^x and (A, α) as A^α.

Sequents of each logical systems are of the form as follows:

$$\begin{aligned}\textbf{LJ}: &\quad \Gamma \Rightarrow A\\ \textbf{LK}: &\quad \Gamma \Rightarrow \Delta\\ \textbf{LKT}: &\quad \Pi^h\,;\, \Gamma \Rightarrow \Delta\\ \textbf{LKQ}: &\quad \Gamma \Rightarrow \Delta;\, \Pi\\ \textbf{ND}: &\quad \Gamma \Rightarrow A\\ \textbf{CND}: &\quad \Gamma \Rightarrow \Delta\end{aligned}$$

where $\Rightarrow$ is the **entailment sign** of the calculus. We use **rhs** and **lhs** for the right-hand-side and left-hand-side of the entailment sign, respectively. Γ is a λ-context which is a set of λ-indexed formula. Δ is a μ-context which is also a set of μ-indexed formula. Comma means taking union as sets. Thus the set $\Gamma_0 \cup \Gamma_1$ is denoted by "Γ_0, Γ_1". $\{A^x\} \cup \Gamma$ by "A^x, Γ."

The rhs of the sequent of **LJ** and **ND** is an unindexed formula which may be a fixed arbitrary atomic formula ϕ. We define intuitionistic negation $\neg A$ as $A \to \phi$.

In **LKT**, Π^h denotes at most one λ-indexed formula. In **LKQ**, Π denotes at most one unindexed formula. The place on the left of semi-colon where Π^h is located in **LKT** is called **stoup** according to Girard[9]. We also call this specially placed λ-index as head-index and always denote by h. We also call the place on the right of semi-colon as stoup in **LKQ**.

In our version of **CND**, there is no unindexed formula in lhs. This is contrast to Parigot's original system, where the rhs of **CND** has exactly one unindexed formula (called *current formula*).

If φ maps indexed formulas to indexed formulas, then if $\Gamma = {A_1}^{x_1}, \dots, {A_n}^{x_n}$, we write $\varphi\Gamma$ for the set $\varphi({A_1}^{x_1}), \dots, \varphi({A_n}^{x_n})$. For example, $\neg\neg\Gamma^t$ for $(\neg\neg A_1^t)^{x_1}$, $\dots, (\neg\neg A_n^t)^{x_n}$, where "t" maps an **LKT** formula to an **LJ** formula.

The following conventions are used in distinguishing between occurrences of indexed formulas in a given logical rule, e.g. (L $\to$) of **LK**:

$$\frac{\Gamma_0 \Rightarrow \Delta_0, A^\alpha \quad \Gamma_1, B^y \Rightarrow \Delta_1}{(A \to B)^x, \Gamma_0, \Gamma_1 \Rightarrow \Delta_0, \Delta_1}\ (\mathrm{L} \to)\ .$$

The indexed formula $(A \to B)^x$ is called the **main** formula of the rule with main connective $\to$; the occurrences of A^α and B^y in the premises will be referred to as the **active** formula. All other occurrences are said to be **passive** and will be referred to as the **context**. In the special case of cut, active formula occurrences are also termed cut-formulas.

We only handle **multiplicative** rules in every logical system. That is, λ-contexts (and μ-contexts) in the conclusion are the union of λ-contexts (and μ-contexts) in the premises.

Hereafter, in order to improve readability, we only write active and main formula, and omit context as follows:

$$\frac{\Rightarrow A^{\alpha} \quad B^{y} \Rightarrow}{(A \to B)^{x} \Rightarrow} \ (\mathrm{L} \to).$$

In our logical system, **structural rules** are implicit. As we interpret contexts as sets, occurrences of a formula with the same index are automatically contracted. One can interpret this that binary rules are always followed by appropriate explicit **contractions**, which is *renaming* of index to the same name. We also interpret axiom rules contains appropriate **weakenings** as contexts. Notice that in **LKT** and **LKQ**, application of structural rules are restricted within Γ and Δ. Specifically Π^{h} and Π (i.e. formulas in the stoup) is not the subject of weakening.

Initial index is an index which appears for the first time in whole proof. We assume all initial indices are distinct unless they are truly related(i.e. subject of further implicit contraction). This is possible, by introducing the "concatenation" to indexes on every binary rules. See for Zucker[26] for detail of this method.

We quote the original derivation rules for **LKQ** from [3] in Table 1. Notice that there is a difference in the definition for structural rules and contexts, as we mentioned above. In the original definition, contexts are interpreted as multisets, and structural rules are explicit.

We here explain abbreviations which appears in names of derivation rules. The letter L/R stands for **Left** and **Right** introduction, D for **Dereliction**, C for **Contraction** and W for **Weakenings**. Notice that we use the different name of cut rules from DJS. We use **h-cut** instead of "head", **m-cut** instead of "mid" and **t-cut** instead of "tail". This is needed to avoid confusion because these are too common word to refer as technical term.

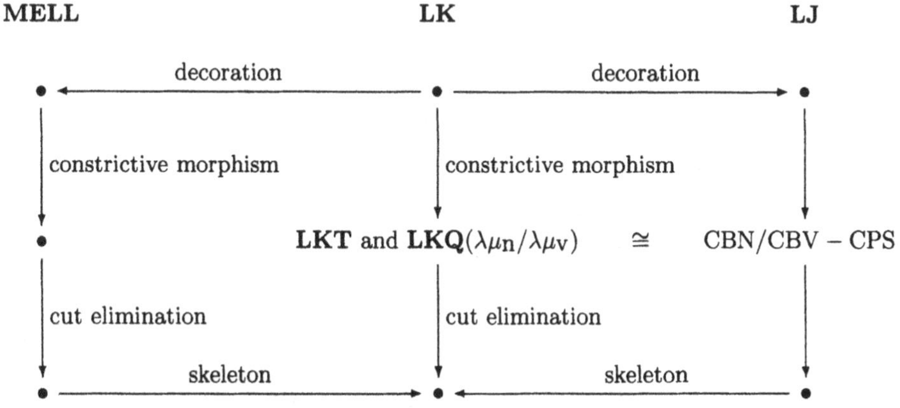

Table 2. Reduction Preserving Properties

2.2 Decorating LKT and LKQ

In this subsection, we briefly introduce **LKT** and **LKQ** and (linear and intuitionistic) decoration method[3, 4], on which our method is based. We shall assume the basics of multiplicative exponential part of classical linear logic(**MELL**), and the cut elimination procedure(linear procedure) for **MELL**; See e.g. [25] for introduction.

LKT and **LKQ** are embeddable into the **MELL** by means of **linear decoration** of DJS [4]. Under linear decoration, cut elimination for **LKT/LKQ** becomes an immediate corollary to cut-elimination for (second order) **MELL**, as reductions of the linear or intuitionistic decoration of a derivation π become reductions of the **LKT/LKQ**. "(Taking) skeleton" is the reverse operation of decoration. It means "simply forget about exponentials $(!, ?)$" from derivation.

They also are embeddable into **LJ** by means of **intuitionistic negation decoration** (or simply **intuitionistic decoration**) which is analogue of linear decoration.

Definition 1 (DJS). *Decoration on formulas are defined as follows:*

$$A^t, A^q := A \quad (\textit{for } A \textit{ atomic})$$

LKT/LKQ *to* **LJ**

$$(A \to B)^t := (\neg\neg A^t) \to (\neg\neg B^t)$$
$$(A \to B)^q := A^q \to (\neg\neg B^q)$$

LKT/LKQ *to* **MELL**

$$(A \to B)^t := !?\, A^t \multimap ?\, B^t$$
$$(A \to B)^q := !\, A^q \multimap ?!\, B^q.$$

Proposition 1 (DJS). *Decoration on sequents: following embeddings are both sound and faithful.*

$$\mathbf{MELL} \vdash \Pi^t, !?\,\Gamma^t \Rightarrow ?\,\Delta^t \qquad \textit{iff}$$
$$\mathbf{LKT} \vdash \Pi;\ \Gamma \Rightarrow \Delta \qquad \textit{iff}$$
$$\mathbf{LJ} \vdash \Pi^t, \neg\neg\Gamma^t, \neg\Delta^t \Rightarrow \phi$$

$$\mathbf{MELL} \vdash !\,\Gamma^q \Rightarrow ?!\,\Delta^q, \Pi^q \qquad \textit{iff}$$
$$\mathbf{LKQ} \vdash \Gamma \Rightarrow \Delta;\ \Pi \qquad \textit{iff}$$
$$\mathbf{LJ} \vdash \Gamma^q, \neg\Delta^q \Rightarrow \Pi^q$$

Remark 1. DJS describes the intuitionistic q-translation on formulas as $(A \to B)^q := (\neg B^q) \to (\neg A^q)$ in [4]. However it is not so different from our definition. This only affects to the order of λ-abstraction and application for term assignment in L $\to$ and R $\to$ (See next section). We obey the traditional CBV translation.

Proposition 2 (DJS). *reduction preserving properties: Cut elimination step for* **LKT** *and* **LKQ** *is one-to-one to the cut elimination for its linear decoration.*

Proposition 3 (DJS). *Cut-elimination procedure for* **LKT/LKQ** *is Strongly Normalizing (SN) and Church-Rosser (CR).*

Because Cut-elimination procedure of **MELL** is proven to be SN and CR [2]. All properties above for linear decoration also holds for intuitionistic decoration.

Proposition 4 (DJS). **LKT** *and* **LKQ** *is sound and complete w.r.t. classical provability.*

Soundness is easy, as ignoring semicolon in **LKT** and **LKQ** derivation induce **LK** derivation. For completeness, DJS shows a concrete method (**constrictive morphism**) through which one can convert any **LK** derivation into **LKT** and **LKQ** derivation.

We display above facts as diagram in Table 2.

3 Continuation Passing Style(CPS) Calculus

3.1 Typed λ-Calculus

Raw λ-term Raw λ-terms are defined as follows:

$$\begin{array}{rll} s,t := & x & \textbf{λ-variable} \\ \mid & \lambda x^A.t & \textbf{λ-abstraction} \\ \mid & st & \textbf{application}. \end{array}$$

Application associates to left, i.e. we write "stu" instead of "$(st)u$". We identify the set of λ-variables with the set of λ-index of formula. We use the set of **free variables** in term t denoted as $\mathrm{FV}(t)$ in usual sense. Otherwise said, in the term assignment judgment, each type of λ-variables that occur free in λ-terms are identified with the formula which is λ-indexed of the same name. We let v range over **values** which are λ-abstraction or λ-variable.

Substitution $t\,[x^A := s]$ means the standard substitution as meta-operation. It is the result of substituting s for the free occurrences of x (of the same type as s) in t which is defined as follows:

$$\begin{aligned} x\,[x^A := s] &= s \\ y\,[x^A := s] &= y, \qquad \text{if} \quad x \neq y \\ (\lambda y^B.t_1)\,[x^A := s] &= \lambda y^B.(t_1\,[x^A := s]) \\ (t_1\,t_2)\,[x^A := s] &= (t_1\,[x^A := s])(t_2\,[x^A := s]), \end{aligned}$$

In the third clause it is not needed to say "provided that $y \neq x$ and y is not free in s", by our assumption on initial indices.

β-Contraction $\triangleright$ denotes one step **β-contraction** and $\overset{*}{\triangleright}$ denotes its reflexive transitive closure, as usual:

$$(\beta) \qquad (\lambda x^A.t)s \triangleright t\,[x^A := s]$$

We often omit to indicate the type of λ-variable in λ-abstraction in case it is clear from the context. The λ-term of the form $(\lambda x.t)s$ is called **β-redex.** t is **normal** iff no subterm of t is a β-redex. The result of β-contraction on β-redex is called **β-contractum.**

$$\frac{}{x:\ A^x \Rightarrow A}\ (\mathrm{Ax}) \qquad \frac{v:\ \Rightarrow A}{kv:\ (\neg A)^k \Rightarrow \phi}\ (\mathrm{D})$$

$$\frac{v:\ \Rightarrow A \quad t:\ A^x \Rightarrow C}{(\lambda x.t)v:\ \Rightarrow C}\ (\text{t-cut}) \qquad \frac{s:\ (\neg A)^k \Rightarrow C \quad t:\ A^x \Rightarrow \phi}{(\lambda k.s)(\lambda x.t):\ \Rightarrow C}\ (\text{m-cut})$$

$$\frac{t:\ B^y \Rightarrow \phi \quad v:\ \Rightarrow A}{mv(\lambda y.t):\ (A \to \neg\neg B)^m \Rightarrow \phi}\ (\mathrm{L}\to) \qquad \frac{t:\ A^x, (\neg B)^l \Rightarrow \phi}{\lambda x.\lambda l.t:\ \Rightarrow A \to \neg\neg B}\ (\mathrm{R}\to)$$

Table 3. CBV CPS term assignment to intuitionistic decoration of **LKQ**

3.2 Definitions

Term assignment judgment (or simply judgment) is an ordered pair of λ-term and LJ sequent. We write a judgment $(s, \Gamma \Rightarrow C)$ as $s:\ \ \Gamma \Rightarrow C$. **Derivation rules** define the term assignment judgment. **Derivation**) is a tree of derivation rules of which leaves are axioms, of which nodes are derivation rules other than axiom.

We use π for the derivation. **End judgment** $s:\ \ \Gamma \Rightarrow C$ is the judgment which appears as root of the derivation tree π. We call the sequent $\Gamma \Rightarrow C$ as **proved sequent** of derivation π. We call the term s as a assigned term to the derivation π, and refer to it by the notion of TermOf(π). We say the term TermOf(π) is **typable** by proved sequent. Two derivations are **equal** if they differ only by the index of formula in the proved sequent. We say that the derivation is **cut-free** if it contains neither m-cut nor t-cut.

Let π be the derivation of which last inference rule is m-cut. We call the TermOf(π), which is a β-redex, as **m-cut redex. t-cut redex** is defined in the same way.

3.3 Term Assignment to LKQ

We categorize λ-variables into 2 groups — object and continuation variable. We use $x, y, z, \ldots$ for **object-variables** and identify with λ-indices. We use $m, n, l, \ldots$ (instead of $\alpha, \beta, \gamma, \ldots$) for **continuation-variables**, according to the standard notion of CPS; and identify with μ-indices.

To determine the term assignment, we interpret the Gentzen-style **LJ** derivations by translating them into **ND** derivation. As an example, we display L $\rightarrow$ rule interpreted by **ND** as follows:

$$\dfrac{\dfrac{m:\ (A \rightarrow \neg\neg B)^m \Rightarrow A \rightarrow \neg\neg B \quad v:\ \Rightarrow A}{mv:\ (A \rightarrow \neg\neg B)^m \Rightarrow \neg\neg B}(\rightarrow \mathrm{E}) \quad \dfrac{t:\ B^y \Rightarrow \phi}{\lambda y.t:\ \Rightarrow \neg B}(\rightarrow \mathrm{I})}{mv(\lambda y.t):\ (A \rightarrow \neg\neg B)^m \Rightarrow \phi}(\rightarrow \mathrm{E})\,.$$

For the name of natural deduction style rules, we use (E) for **elimination** and (I) for **introduction**.

Our term assignment to **LJ**, which is the intuitionistic decoration of **LKQ**, is displayed in Table 3. We call this term assignment system as **call-by-value continuation-passing style** (CBV CPS) calculus.

3.4 Cut-Elimination and Normalization

In this subsection, we prove that the cut-elimination step for **LKQ** is one-to-one to the normalization, thus can be simulated by β-contraction on typed λ-term. We prove this by showing that both m-cut and t-cut satisfies this property.

Our term assignment faithfully reflects the structure of sequent calculus. Thus inductive definition of substitution on terms agrees with induction on the length of derivation for sequent calculus. We can state this formally as follows:

Proposition 5. *(subterm property) In every derivation rule, all terms of premises are included as subterm in the term of conclusion.*

Proof. Mechanical checking of term assignment for each derivation rules.

Proposition 6. *The derivation π is cut-free iff TermOf(π) is normal.*

Proof. ($\Rightarrow$) By induction on the length of derivation. E.g. for L $\rightarrow$; by induction hypothesis v and t are normal, hence $mv(\lambda x.t)$ is normal. ($\Leftarrow$) Obvious as term of conclusion of t-cut and m-cut themselves are β-redexes.

To relate the permutation of premise of the cut (during cut elimination step) to the conversion of the term, it is good to introduce the notion of **explicit substitution**[1].

Definition 2. *(explicit substitution)* **Explicit substitution** *is of the form $t\ \langle x^A := s\rangle$. In this framework, β-contraction divided into two phases. One is "syntactic" β-contraction, and the other is explicit rules for substitution— i.e.*

we consider each inductive definition of substitution as computational step, instead of meta-operation. The syntactic β-contraction is defined as follows:

$$(\lambda k^{\neg A}.s)(\lambda x.t) \rhd s\,\langle k^{\neg A} := \lambda x.t\rangle.$$

Thanks to the subterm property, each one-step permutation of premise corresponds to few steps of explicit substitution. Now we start the technical matter.

Proposition 7. *(m-cut elimination) The derivation π converts to π' by one m-cut elimination step iff TermOf(π) $\rhd$ TermOf(π') by contracting the m-cut redex associated to the m-cut.*

Proof. Cut elimination step for **LKT** and **LKQ** is the obvious analogue of the linear procedure[3, 8]. Thus *right* premise of the m-cut is going to be duplicated/erased according to the contraction/weakening on $(\neg A)^k$.

The m-cut shall change into (zero, one, or many) t-cut rule(s). We assume this m-cut redex is of the form $(\lambda k.s)(\lambda x.t)$. By using explicit substitution, this syntactically contracts to $s\,\langle k := \lambda x.t\rangle$.

case 1. implicit structural rules We take (t-cut) as an example for binary rules. We display how m-cut permute right premise (i.e. $t\colon\ A^x \Rightarrow \phi$) with (t-cut) with implicit contraction in Table 9 in appendix. By the definition of substitution implicit contraction duplicates $\lambda x.t$, as is expected. As is the case of implicit weakenings, it erases $\lambda x.t$.

case 2. dereliction If the rule is (D), assigned (sub) term is of the form of kv. This term is contracted to $(\lambda x.t)v$, which represents another t-cut. See Table 10.

Proposition 8. *(t-cut elimination) The derivation π converts to π' by one t-cut elimination step, iff TermOf(π) $\rhd$ TermOf(π') by contracting the t-cut redex.*

Proof. Elimination of t-cut means that *left* premise of the t-cut is going to be duplicated/erased according to contraction/weakening on A^x. T-cut is then eliminated at the point where object variable is introduced — i.e. axiom or (L $\rightarrow$) rule. We assume this t-cut is of the form of $(\lambda x.t)v$. This contracts to $t\,\langle x := v\rangle$. Cut-formula is A^x.

case 1. implicit structural rules it is almost the same with the previous discussion on m-cut. v will be duplicated/erased according to the number of occurrences of x.

case 2. producer of initial index In this case, the β contraction on the t-cut redex corresponds to the elimination of the t-cut. Explicit substitution step corresponds to permutation of the left premise of t-cut.

case 2.1 (Ax) In this case, $\lambda x.t = \lambda x.x$. The t-cut contractum is v. This contraction corresponds to elimination of t-cut together with axiom which appears as right premise of t-cut.

case 2.2 (L $\rightarrow$) In this case, $\lambda x.t = \lambda m.mv'(\lambda y.t')$. Thus t-cut contractum is $vv'(\lambda y.t')$. Now we will go into sub-cases according to the derivation rule that introduced value v.

case 2.2.1 (Ax) In this case, $v = m'$ and the t-cut contractum is $m'v'(\lambda y.t')$. This only means renaming of variable from m to m'. This corresponds to elimination of axiom which occurs as left premise of t-cut. Recall that, by definition, derivations that differs only by the index of formula is *equal* derivation.

case 2.2.2 (R $\rightarrow$) In this case, $v = (\lambda x.\lambda l.t)$ and the t-cut contractum is $(\lambda x.\lambda l.t)v'(\lambda y.t')$. If this newly created β-redex represents the combination of t-cut and m-cut redex, then the proof is done. See. Table 11

It remains to check whether $(\lambda x.\lambda l.t)v'(\lambda y.t')$ is equal to $(\lambda x.(\lambda l.t)(\lambda y.t'))v'$ or not. However, from our assumption on initial indexes, x, l does not appear in neither v' nor t'. Thus we can always exchange the order of two explicit substitution: $\langle x := v' \rangle$, $\langle l := \lambda y.t' \rangle$. This means that these substitutions are essentially parallel. In fact, this is exactly how restrictions on **LKT** and **LKQ** works to avoid so called q/t dilemma, and to recover confluency[3, 4].

Remark 2. We choose q-decoration $A^q \rightarrow (\neg\neg B^q)$ instead of DJS's $(\neg B^q) \rightarrow (\neg A^q)$. This only affects on the order of abstraction (such as $\lambda l.\lambda x.t$) and application (such as $m(\lambda y.t)v$).

$$\frac{}{kx:\quad A^x, (\neg A)^k \Rightarrow \phi}\ (\mathrm{Ax}_v) \qquad \frac{t:\quad A^x, (\neg B)^l \Rightarrow \phi}{m(\lambda x.\lambda l.t):\quad \neg(A \rightarrow \neg\neg B)^m \Rightarrow \phi}\ (\mathrm{R} \rightarrow_v)$$

$$\frac{s:\quad (\neg A)^k \Rightarrow \phi \quad t:\quad A^x \Rightarrow \phi}{(\lambda k.s)(\lambda x.t):\quad \Rightarrow \phi}\ (\mathrm{cut}_v) \qquad \frac{t:\quad B^y \Rightarrow \phi \quad s:\quad (\neg A)^{k'} \Rightarrow \phi}{(\lambda k'.s)(\lambda n.mn(\lambda y.t)):\quad (A \rightarrow \neg\neg B)^m \Rightarrow \phi}\ (\mathrm{L} \rightarrow_v)$$

Table 4. CBV CPS term assignment to intuitionistic decoration of **LK**

3.5 Term Assignment to LK

Lemma 1. *(completeness)* **LKQ** *is complete w.r.t classical provability.*

Proof. We show one can convert any (intuitionistic decoration of) **LK** derivation into (intuitionistic decoration of) **LKQ** derivation by induction on the length of derivation. The only interesting case is (L $\rightarrow$). We have "$t:\quad B^y \Rightarrow \phi$" and "$s:\quad (\neg A)^{k'} \Rightarrow \phi$" as induction hypothesis. We calculate this as follows:

$$\dfrac{s:\ (\neg A)^{k'} \Rightarrow \phi \quad \dfrac{\dfrac{}{n:\ A^n \Rightarrow A}\,(\mathrm{Ax}) \quad t:\ B^y \Rightarrow \phi}{mn(\lambda y.t):\ (A \to \neg\neg B)^m, A^n \Rightarrow \phi}\,(\mathrm{L}\to)}{(\lambda k'.s)(\lambda n.mn(\lambda y.t)):\ (A \to \neg\neg B)^m \Rightarrow \phi}\,(\text{m-cut})$$

Constructive proof above automatically generates the CBV term assignment to (intuitionistic decoration of) **LK**.

Theorem 1. *Typed λ-term assignment shown in Table 4 defines the SN and CR cut elimination procedure for* **LK**.

Proof. All of the propositions in this section and the fact that typed λ-calculus is proven to be SN and CR [11].

Cut-free **LK** derivation does not always mean cut-free **LKQ** derivation, since (L $\to$) in **LK** derivation converts into **LKQ** derivation including one "additional" m-cut. This m-cut is called **correction cut**. Eliminating of this m-cut (i.e. contracting m-cut redex) exactly means **constrictive morphism**[3].

We also display CBN term assignment in Table 7(for **LKT**) and Table 8(for **LK**) in appendix.

$$\dfrac{}{xk:\ (\neg\neg A)^x, (\neg A)^k \Rightarrow \phi}\,(\mathrm{Ax}) \qquad \dfrac{t:\ (\neg\neg A)^x, \neg\neg\Gamma, (\neg B)^{k'}, \neg\Delta \Rightarrow \phi}{k(\lambda x.\lambda k'.t):\ \neg\neg\Gamma, \neg(\neg\neg A \to \neg\neg B)^k, \neg\Delta \Rightarrow \phi}\,(\to \mathrm{I})$$

$$\dfrac{u:\ \neg\neg\Gamma_0, \neg(\neg\neg A \to \neg\neg B)^{k''}, \neg\Delta_0 \Rightarrow \phi \quad s:\ \neg\neg\Gamma_1, (\neg A)^{k'}, \neg\Delta_1 \Rightarrow \phi}{(\lambda k''.u)(\lambda m.m(\lambda k'.s)k):\ \neg\neg\Gamma_0, \neg\neg\Gamma_1, (\neg B)^k, \neg\Delta_0, \neg\Delta_1 \Rightarrow \phi}\,(\to \mathrm{E})$$

Table 5. CBN CPS Term Assignment to intuitionistic decoration of **CND**

$$\dfrac{}{kx:\ A^x, (\neg A)^k \Rightarrow \phi}\,(\mathrm{Ax}) \qquad \dfrac{t:\ A^x, \Gamma, (\neg B)^{k'}, \neg\Delta \Rightarrow \phi}{k(\lambda x.\lambda k'.t):\ \Gamma, \neg(A \to \neg\neg B)^k, \neg\Delta \Rightarrow \phi}\,(\to \mathrm{I})$$

$$\dfrac{u:\ \Gamma_0, \neg(A \to \neg\neg B)^{k''}, \neg\Delta_0 \Rightarrow \phi \quad s:\ \Gamma_1, (\neg A)^{k'}, \neg\Delta_1 \Rightarrow \phi}{(\lambda k''.u)(\lambda m.(\lambda k'.s)(\lambda n.mnk)):\ \Gamma_0, \Gamma_1, (\neg B)^k, \neg\Delta_0, \neg\Delta_1 \Rightarrow \phi}\,(\to \mathrm{E})$$

Table 6. CBV CPS Term Assignment to intuitionistic decoration of **CND**

3.6 Term Assignment to CND

Our term assignment can be extended to (intuitionistic decoration of) **CND**. Namely, **CND** derivations are interpreted by **LK** derivation, and normalization is interpreted by cut elimination. This interpretation enables us to compare our CPS calculi with standard CPS calculi of which logical base is natural deduction(in the next section). The only interesting case, in interpretation, is application(i.e. (→ E)) rule, since abstraction (i.e. (→ I)) is directly read off as (R →). (→ E) is interpreted by the combination of (L →) and cut rule.

$$\dfrac{u:\ (\neg D)^{k''} \Rightarrow \phi \quad \dfrac{s:\ (\neg A)^{k'} \Rightarrow \phi \quad \dfrac{}{kh:\ B^h, (\neg B)^k \Rightarrow \phi}\,(\mathrm{Ax})}{m(\lambda k'.s)(\lambda h.kh):\ (\neg\neg A \to \neg\neg B)^m, (\neg B)^k \Rightarrow \phi}\,(\mathrm{L} \to)}{(\lambda k''.u)(\lambda m.m(\lambda k'.s)(\lambda h.kh)):\ (\neg B)^k \Rightarrow \phi}\,(\mathrm{h\text{-}cut})$$

$$\dfrac{u:\ (\neg E)^{k''} \Rightarrow \phi \quad \dfrac{s:\ (\neg A)^{k'} \Rightarrow \phi \quad \dfrac{}{ky:\ B^y, (\neg B)^k \Rightarrow \phi}\,(\mathrm{Ax}_v)}{(\lambda k'.s)(\lambda n.mn(\lambda y.ky)):\ (A \to \neg\neg B)^m, (\neg B)^k \Rightarrow \phi}\,(\mathrm{L} \to_v)}{(\lambda k''.u)(\lambda m.(\lambda k'.s)(\lambda n.mn(\lambda y.ky))):\ (\neg B)^k \Rightarrow \phi}\,(\mathrm{cut}_v)\ ,$$

where $D = \neg\neg A \to \neg\neg B$ and $E = A \to \neg\neg B$. Finally we get typed λ-term assignments for (intuitionistic decoration of) **CND**. We display them in Table 5 and 6.

4 Related Works

4.1 Plotkin's CPS Translation

We quote the Plotkin's CPS translation[22]. For CBN:

$$\begin{aligned} \underline{x} &= \lambda k.xk \\ \underline{\lambda x.L} &= \lambda k.k(\lambda k.\underline{L}) \\ \underline{MN} &= \lambda k.\underline{M}(\lambda m.m\underline{N}k) \end{aligned}$$

For CBV:

$$\begin{aligned} \underline{x} &= \lambda k.xk \\ \underline{\lambda x.L} &= \lambda k.k(\lambda x.\underline{L}) \\ \underline{MN} &= \lambda k.\underline{M}(\lambda m.\underline{N}(\lambda n.mnk)). \end{aligned}$$

Proposition 9. *Plotkin's CPS translation is exactly the one that translates* **ND** *terms into* **CND** *terms.*

Proof. In intuitionistic case of **CND**, μ-context Δ always contains only one continuation variable. We name this as k. In order to see the relation, we only need some renaming; $\lambda k'.t = \underline{L}$, $\lambda k''.u = \underline{M}$, $\lambda k'.s = \underline{N}$. With this renaming, they are identical to the terms of our typed λ-term assignment to **CND**(See, again, Table 5 and 6).

Plotkin shows that CPS translated λ-term *simulates* CBN/CBV reduction strategy of original λ-term. This precise relation justifies our claim — CBN/CBV precisely corresponds to t/q colouring of the formula. He also pointed out, among these reductions, there are two kind of reductions. One is **proper** reduction and the other is **administrative** one. We can state this precisely(in CBV case)—elimination of t-cut is the proper one and represents intuitionistic computation; and elimination of m-cut is administrative one and represents classical computation. Among the administrative reductions, some of them are constrictive morphisms and others are classical(e.g. continuation) calculations.

4.2 Felleisen's $\lambda\mathcal{C}$ Operator

In our CPS calculus, Felleisen's $\mathcal{C}$ operator[6] is a cut-free derivation of peirce's law. We mechanically calculate them as follows:

$$\text{CBN: } \mathcal{C} = \lambda y.\lambda k.y(\lambda h.h(\lambda k'.k'(\lambda x.\lambda l.xk))(\lambda h.kh))$$
$$\text{CBV: } \mathcal{C} = \lambda y.\lambda k.y(\lambda x.\lambda l.kx)(\lambda x.kx),$$

where type of k is $\neg A$. Type of y is $\neg\neg((A \to B) \to A)^t$ (CBN),$((A \to B) \to A)^q$ (CBV) respectively.

Remark 3. In CBN, Felleisen uses identity function "I" (i.e. top-level continuation) of type $A \to A$, instead of our $\lambda h.kh$ of type $\neg A$. That is, he fix ϕ to A. Felleisen also use "I" instead of $\lambda x.kx$ in CBV.

4.3 Herbelin's $\overline{\lambda}$-Calculus

In Herbelin's work[13], $\overline{\lambda}$-terms are assigned to **LJT** which can be regarded as intuitionistic version of **LKT**. Thus our "classical" CBN CPS calculus includes "intuitionistic" $\overline{\lambda}$-calculus, naturally. We define inductive translation $()^*$ as follows:

$$
\begin{array}{lr}
(\text{Ax}) & (.\ [\,])^* = (k\ h) \\
(\text{D}) & (x\ l)^* = (x\ \lambda h.(.\ l)^*) \\
(\text{L}\to) & (.\ [u\ ::\ l])^* = ((h\ \lambda k.u^*)\ \lambda h.(.\ l)^*) \\
(\text{R}\to) & \lambda x.u^* = (k\ \lambda x.\lambda k.u^*) \\
(\text{h-cut}) & (.\ (l@l'))^* = ((\lambda k.(.\ l)^*)\ \lambda h.(.\ l')^*) \\
(\text{h-cut}) & (u\ l)^* = ((\lambda k.u^*)\ \lambda h.(.\ l)^*) \\
(\text{m-cut}) & (.\ l[x := u])^* = ((\lambda x.(.\ l)^*)\ u^*) \\
(\text{m-cut}) & (v[x := u])^* = ((\lambda x.v^*)\ u^*),
\end{array}
$$

where k is the only continuation variable in the sequent. The fifth(first h-cut) clause shows that substitution for continuation variable: k by another argument list means concatenation of argument list.

5 Conclusions and Further Directions

We revealed that the CBN/CBV reduction scheme for "classical proofs as programs" precisely corresponds to the Gentzen-style cut elimination procedure for **LKT** and **LKQ**. Our approach, cut elimination to be simulated by normalization, can be seen a new approach to Gentzen-style type theory. This merges Gentzen-style and natural deduction style, which means explicit substitutions are naturally included in our calculus as a computational step corresponding to permutation of cut.

Besides CPS, on the line of "classical proofs as programs" approach, Parigot's $\lambda\mu$-calculus [18, 19, 20, 21] is also considered as a standard. DeGroote revealed the relation between CBN CPS and $\lambda\mu$-calculus [5]. Moreover, Ong and Stewart (OS) introduce a call-by-value (CBV) version of $\lambda\mu$-calculus in [17] in which they introduce a new reduction rule (ζ_{arg}). Parigot proves the computational properties (such as SN and CR) of CBN versions of $\lambda\mu$-calculus individually. OS also does the same in CBV case. This seems to be enough circumstantial evidence that reduction system for CPS calculus and $\lambda\mu$-calculus are isomorphic on both CBN and CBV case. $\lambda\mu$-calculus can be presented as a term calculus directly on **LKT** and **LKQ**. Isomorphisms w.r.t reduction systems are direct consequence of decoration method and its reduction preserving properties. We are now working for the draft[16] to show the precise relation between them.

References

[1] Martín Abadi, Luca Cardelli, P.-L. Curien, and Jean-Jacques Lévy. Explicit substitutions. In *Conference Record of the Seventeenth Annual ACM Symposium on Principles of Programming Languages*, pages 31–46, San Francisco, California, January 1990.

[2] Vincent Danos. *La Logique Linéaire Appliquée à l'étude de Divers Processus de Normalisation (Principalement du λ-Calcul)*. PhD thesis, University of Paris VII, June 1990.

[3] Vincent Danos, Jean-Baptiste Joinet, and Harold Schellinx. Sequent calculi for second order logic. In J.-Y. Girard, Y. Lafont, and L. Regnier, editors, *Advances in Linear Logic*, pages 211–224. Cambridge University Press, 1995. Proceedings of the Workshop on Linear Logic, Ithaca, New York, June 1993.

[4] Vincent Danos, Jean-Baptiste Joinet, and Harold Schellinx. A new deconstructive logic: linear logic. *Journal of Symbolic Logic*, 62(3), September 1997.

[5] Phillipe de Groote. A cps-translation of the $\lambda\mu$-calculus. In *Proceedings Trees in Algebra and Programming - CAAP'94*, pages 85–99. Springer-Verlag LNCS 787, April 1994.

[6] Matthias Felleisen, Daniel P. Friedman, Eugene Kohlbecker, and Bruce Duba. Reasoning with continuations. In *Proceedings, Symposium on Logic in Computer*

Science, pages 131–141, Cambridge, Massachusetts, 16–18 June 1986. IEEE Computer Society.

[7] G. Gentzen. Untersuchungen über das logische schließen. *Mathematische Zeitschrift*, 39:176–210,405–431, 1935.

[8] Jean-Yves Girard. Linear logic. *Theoretical Computer Science*, 50:1–102, 1987.

[9] Jean-Yves Girard. A new constructive logic: Classical logic. *Mathematical Structures in Computer Science*, 1:255–296, 1991.

[10] Jean-Yves Girard. On the unity of logic. *Annals of Pure and Applied Logic*, 59:201–217, 1993.

[11] Jean-Yves Girard, Yves Lafont, and P. Taylor. *Proofs and Types.* Cambridge Tracts in Theoretical Computer Science 7. Cambridge University Press, 1988.

[12] Timothy G. Griffin. A formulae-as-types notion of control. In *Conference Record of the Seventeenth Annual ACM Symposium on Principles of Programming Languages*, pages 47–58, San Francisco, California, January 1990.

[13] Hugo Herbelin. A λ-calculus structure ismorphic to gentzen-style sequent calculus structure. In L. Pacholski and J. Tiuryn, editors, *Proceedings of the 1994 Annual Conference of the European Association for Computer Science Logic*, Kazimierz, Poland, September 1994. Springer Verlag, LNCS 933.

[14] Grigori Mints. Normal forms for sequent derivations. In Piergiorgio Odifreddi, editor, *Kreiseliana - About and Around George Kreisel.* A K Peters Ltd., March 1996.

[15] Chetan R. Murthy. A computational analysis of Girard's translation and LC. In *Proceedings, Seventh Annual IEEE Symposium on Logic in Computer Science*, pages 90–101, Santa Cruz, California, 22–25 June 1992. IEEE Computer Society Press.

[16] Ichiro Ogata. Classical proofs as programs, cut elimination as computation. Manuscript, June 1998.

[17] C.-H. L. Ong and C. A. Stewart. A curry-howard foundation for functional computation with control. In *Proceedings of ACM SIGPLAN-SIGACT Symposium on Principle of Programming Languages, Paris, January 1997.* ACM Press, 1997.

[18] Michel Parigot. Free deduction: An analysis of "computations" in classical logic. In *RCLP 1990/1991*, pages 361–380, 1991.

[19] Michel Parigot. Lambda-mu-calculus: An algorithmic interpretation of classical natural deduction. In *LPAR 1992*, pages 190–201, 1992.

[20] Michel Parigot. Classical proofs as programs. In *3rd Kurt Gödel Colloquium*, pages 263–276. Springer-Verlag LNCS 713, 1993.

[21] Michel Parigot. Strong normalization for second order classical natural deduction. In *Proceedings, Eighth Annual IEEE Symposium on Logic in Computer Science*, pages 39–46, Montreal, Canada, 19–23 June 1993. IEEE Computer Society Press.

[22] G. D. Plotkin. Call-by-name, call-by-value and the λ-calculus. *Theoretical Computer Science*, 1(2):125–159, December 1975.

[23] G. Pottinger. Normalization as a homomorphic image of cut-elimination. *Annals of Mathematical Logic*, 12:323–357, 1977.

[24] D. Prawitz. *Natural Deduction, a Poof-Theoretical Study.* Almquist and Wiksell, Stockholm, 1965.

[25] Anne S. Troelstra. *Lectures on Linear Logic.* CSLI Lecture Notes 29, Center for the Study of Language and Information, Stanford, California, 1992.

[26] J. I. Zucker. Correspondence between cut-elimination and normalization, part i and ii. *Annals of Mathematical Logic*, 7:1–156, 1974.

Appendix

$$\frac{}{kh:\quad A^h, (\neg A)^k \Rightarrow \phi}\ (\mathrm{Ax}) \qquad \frac{t:\quad A^h \Rightarrow \phi}{x(\lambda h.t):\quad (\neg\neg A)^x \Rightarrow \phi}\ (\mathrm{D})$$

$$\frac{s:\quad (\neg A)^k \Rightarrow \phi \quad t:\quad A^h \Rightarrow \phi}{(\lambda k.s)(\lambda h.t):\quad \Rightarrow \phi}\ (\text{h-cut}) \qquad \frac{s:\quad (\neg A)^k \Rightarrow \phi \quad t:\quad (\neg\neg A)^x \Rightarrow \phi}{(\lambda x.t)(\lambda k.s):\quad \Rightarrow \phi}\ (\text{m-cut})$$

$$\frac{t:\quad B^h \Rightarrow \phi \quad s:\quad (\neg A)^k \Rightarrow \phi}{m(\lambda k.s)(\lambda h.t):\quad (\neg\neg A \to \neg\neg B)^m \Rightarrow \phi}\ (\mathrm{L} \to) \qquad \frac{t:\quad (\neg\neg A)^x, (\neg B)^l \Rightarrow \phi}{k(\lambda x.\lambda l.t):\quad \neg(\neg\neg A \to \neg\neg B)^k \Rightarrow \phi}\ (\mathrm{R} \to)$$

Table 7. CBN CPS term assignment to intuitionistic decoration of **LKT**

$$\frac{}{x(\lambda h.kh):\quad (\neg\neg A)^x, (\neg A)^k \Rightarrow \phi}\ (\mathrm{Ax}_n) \qquad \frac{s:\quad (\neg A)^k \Rightarrow \phi \quad t:\quad (\neg\neg A)^x \Rightarrow \phi}{(\lambda x.t)(\lambda k.s):\quad \Rightarrow \phi}\ (\mathrm{cut}_n)$$

$$\frac{t:\quad (\neg\neg A)^x, (\neg B)^l \Rightarrow \phi}{m(\lambda x.\lambda l.t):\quad \neg(\neg\neg A \to \neg\neg B)^m \Rightarrow \phi}\ (\mathrm{R} \to_n)$$

$$\frac{t:\quad (\neg\neg B)^y \Rightarrow \phi \quad s:\quad (\neg A)^{k'} \Rightarrow \phi}{(\lambda y.t)(\lambda l.x(\lambda m.m(\lambda k'.s)l)):\quad \neg\neg(\neg\neg A \to \neg\neg B)^x \Rightarrow \phi}\ (\mathrm{L} \to_n)$$

Table 8. CBN CPS term assignment to intuitionistic decoration of **LK**

$$\dfrac{\dfrac{v:\ (\neg A)^k \Rightarrow B \quad s:\ B^y, (\neg A)^k \Rightarrow C}{(\lambda y.s)v:\ (\neg A)^k \Rightarrow C}\,(\text{t-cut}) \qquad t:\ A^x \Rightarrow \phi}{((\lambda y.s)v)\,\langle k := \lambda x.t\rangle:\ \Rightarrow C}\,(\text{m-cut}) .$$

converts to:

$$\dfrac{\dfrac{v:\ (\neg A)^k \Rightarrow B \quad t:\ A^x \Rightarrow \phi}{v\,\langle k := \lambda x.t\rangle:\ \Rightarrow B}\,(\text{m-cut}) \qquad \dfrac{s:\ B^y, (\neg A)^k \Rightarrow C \quad t:\ A^x \Rightarrow \phi}{s\,\langle k := \lambda x.t\rangle:\ B^y \Rightarrow C}\,(\text{m-cut})}{(\lambda y.s\,\langle k := \lambda x.t\rangle)(v\,\langle k := \lambda x.t\rangle):\ \Rightarrow C}\,(\text{t-cut})$$

Table 9. Permutation of right premise of m-cut over t-cut with Implicit Contraction

---

$$\dfrac{\dfrac{v:\ \Rightarrow A}{kv:\ (\neg A)^k \Rightarrow \phi}\,(\text{D}) \qquad t:\ A^x \Rightarrow \phi}{kv\,\langle k := \lambda x.t\rangle:\ \Rightarrow \phi}\,(\text{m-cut}) \quad \text{converts to:} \quad \dfrac{v:\ \Rightarrow A \quad t:\ A^x \Rightarrow \phi}{(\lambda x.t)v:\ \Rightarrow}\,(\text{t-cut})$$

Table 10. Permutation of right premise of m-cut over (D)

$$\dfrac{\dfrac{t:\ A^x, (\neg B)^l \Rightarrow \phi}{\lambda x.\lambda l.t:\ \Rightarrow A \to \neg\neg B}\,(\text{R}\to) \qquad \dfrac{t':\ B^y \Rightarrow \phi \quad v':\ \Rightarrow A}{mv'(\lambda y.t'):\ (A \to \neg\neg B)^m \Rightarrow \phi}\,(\text{L}\to)}{(mv'(\lambda y.t'))\,\langle m := \lambda x.\lambda l.t\rangle:\ \Rightarrow \phi}\,(\text{t-cut})$$

converts to:

$$\dfrac{v':\ \Rightarrow A \qquad \dfrac{t:\ A^x, (\neg B)^l \Rightarrow \phi \quad t':\ B^y \Rightarrow \phi}{(\lambda l.t)(\lambda y.t'):\ A^x \Rightarrow \phi}\,(\text{m-cut})}{(\lambda x.(\lambda l.t)(\lambda y.t'))v':\ \Rightarrow \phi}\,(\text{t-cut})$$

Table 11. Permutation of left premise of t-cut over (L $\to$) and (R $\to$)

Semantics and Logic for Provable Fault-Tolerance, A Tutorial

Tomasz Janowski

The United Nations University
International Institute for Software Technology
P.O. Box 3058, Macau
tj@iist.unu.edu

Abstract. This tutorial is about design and proof of design of reliable systems from unreliable components. It teaches the concept and techniques of fault-tolerance, at the same time building a formal theory where this property can be specified and verified. The theory eventually supports a range of useful design techniques, especially for multiple faults. We extend CCS, its bisimulation equivalence and modal logic, under the driving principle that any claim about fault-tolerance should be invariant under the removal of faults from the assumptions (faults are unpredictable); this principle rejects the reduction of fault-tolerance to "correctness under all anticipated faults". The theory is applied to the range of examples and eventually extended to include considerations of fault-tolerance and timing, under scheduling on the limited resources. This document describes the motivation and the contents of the tutorial.

1 Motivation

1.1 Why Fault-Tolerance?

With growing complexity of computer systems and despite the progress in the technology of the basic components (software or hardware), the possibility that such systems are affected by faults is ever present. Some faults (design faults) could in theory be discovered off-line but even applying formal methods we cannot responsibly claim, except for the simplest of cases, to have discovered all. Other faults (hardware physical faults) are not even amenable to formal analysis as they can only manifest themselves on-line. This uncertainly as to the presence of faults calls for redundancy becoming part of a system.

1.2 Why Prove Fault-Tolerance?

With full verification of realistic systems being practically infeasible, we emphasise the importance of verifying those parts of a system that are directly responsible for the management of redundancy: (1) More promise more risk – redundancy often leads to intricate management problems and may introduce design faults itself. (2) Critical parts – after a fault occurs it is crucial that

Jieh Hsiang, Atsushi Ohori (Eds.): ASIAN'98, LNCS 1538, pp. 79–83, 1998.

mechanisms to prevent a failure of an already impaired system are "correct". (3) Faults are unpredictable – fault-tolerance implies "correctness under all anticipated faults" but is the converse true?

Finally, fault-tolerance is not without cost, it asks for more redundancy while performance asks for less. For given set of computing resources it is useful to capture this tradeoff (reliability versus performance) formally and study, even optimise, the effect of design decisions without actually building the system.

1.3 Why Provable Fault-Tolerance?

A common approach is to reduce provable fault-tolerance to provable correctness. When we claim fault-tolerance for a given implementation $Impl$ relative to a fault assumption $Faults$ and a specification $Spec$, we only proceed to prove correctness of an implementation $\mathcal{T}(Impl, Faults)$ which represents syntactically how $Impl$ behaves in the presence of $Faults$ [15,16,8]; this reduction is most common without introducing the transformation $\mathcal{T}$ explicitly [4,2,12,22,18,19,21,14,1,23]. Although attractive for many reasons, e.g. reuse of a variety of tools and techniques already available for proving correctness, the method also raises some questions about its feasibility and applicability.

Feasibility. Correctness under all anticipated faults is necessary for provable fault-tolerance but is it sufficient? After all, faults are unpredictable and even if we assume their presence they may never actually occur. Our claim should therefore be invariant under some, perhaps even all of such faults being removed from the assumptions. Consider a preorder $<$ on the fault assumptions which represents the relative severity of faults: $Fault_1 < Fault_2$. This represents that $Fault_1$ is less severe than $Fault_2$; say $Fault_2$ represents that a communication medium may both omit and permute messages and $Fault_1$ represents only omission. Then we would expect that verifying $Impl$ as tolerant of $Fault_2$ would immediately imply that it is tolerant of $Fault_1$ alone. We may also invent $NoFault$ representing the strongest assumption (no faults) and expect that $Impl$, if tolerant of any $Fault$, would also be tolerant of $NoFault$: $NoFault < Fault$ for any $Fault$; tolerance with respect to $NoFault$ could reasonably coincide with 'plain' correctness. Claims about fault-tolerance based on the implicit verification must be justified with respect to fault-monotonicity [9]!

Applicability. Formal reasoning can be (should be) considered as a means to analyse as well as support design of 'correct' systems. How to support design of systems tolerant of faults? There are many issues in this case that do not appear in the broader context: design of a system which is correct with respect to its specification, without taking faults into account. A theory for provable fault-tolerance which is based on reducing fault-tolerance to correctness in the presence of all faults, may not bring effective help into such design issues. Among the issues is the growing complexity of a system for an increasing number of tolerated faults, along the chain $NoFault < Fault_1 < \ldots < Fault_n$. We may like to have design techniques which support this dimension.

2 Contents

The tutorial consists of five parts. They are: fault-tolerance, provable correctness, provable fault-tolerance, design for provable fault-tolerance and real-time and provable fault-tolerance.

2.1 Fault-Tolerance

We introduce the concept of fault-tolerance informally, placed in the broader context of system dependability and the means to achieve it: fault-avoidance, fault-prevention, fault-forecasting and fault-tolerance. We explain in general how to build systems with this property, why proving this property is important, and the ways we could approach the proof, first by reduction to provable correctness.

2.2 Provable Correctness

The basic framework includes process algebra (CCS, [18]), its bisimulation semantics [17,20] and associated modal logic [6], all built on the domain of labelled transition systems [13].

Here proving correctness of a fault-affected systems is insufficient by itself to imply that the original system is provably fault-tolerant. We show this by example: a version of the alternating bit protocol which is correct in the presence of faults but incorrect in the absence of faults. We also show a protocol which receives two proofs, in the absence of faults and in the presence of all faults, but fails the proof in the presence of some of the faults. The reduction does not work: fault-tolerance needs a proper semantic definition to be provably preserved under the removal of faults from the assumptions (they are unpredictable).

2.3 Provable Fault-Tolerance

We present ways to model faults semantically, by additional transitions introduced into the semantics of a process, all labelled by an internal action. A fault-description language is defined to describe and combine such fault assumptions (representing the presence of multiple faults). This will use additional declarations for process constants and induce different fault-affected semantics of the process language, one for every fault-description term (a corresponding equivalence is introduced). Fault-tolerant bisimilarity is defined, stronger than bisimilarity but fault-monotonic. Its properties are investigated, among them is reduction to original bisimulations with some additional properties, and fault decomposition: proving fault-tolerance for multiple faults by proving properties of bisimulations for every fault separately [10]. Finally, a logic is introduced with asymmetric modal operators, shown to provide a characterisation of the fault-tolerant bisimilarity and able to support reasoning about fault-tolerance itself: the logic is fault-monotonic (the original modal logic is not). We use many examples to illustrate the relation and its properties.

2.4 Design for Provable Fault-Tolerance

The relation enjoys many properties that help verification, as above. It also enjoys properties to help design for provable fault-tolerance. We derive a number of well-founded techniques, especially to alleviate complexity of the design for an increasing number of tolerated faults [8], as follows:

1. **Preserving fault-tolerance.**
   Preservation rules that allow to modify design of a system while preserving (provably) the set of tolerated faults. Given *Impl* which is tolerant of *Fault* relative to *Spec*, it should be possible to modify *Impl* into *Impl'*, following the rules, and still be able to claim this property. This may help to simplify design, for given level of fault-tolerance, as well as tolerate more faults.
2. **Increasing fault-tolerance.**
   Incremental refinement towards an increasing number of tolerated faults. We start with a system which is only correct with respect to its specification, then introduce faults incrementally, say given $Fault_1 < Fault_2$ and $Impl_1$, tolerant of $Fault_1$ with respect to *Spec*, we refine $Impl_1$ into $Impl_2$, following the preservation rules, which also becomes tolerant of $Fault_2$.
3. **Deducing fault-tolerance.**
   Separate development: deducing fault-tolerance of an overall system from fault-tolerance of its components. Suppose $|$ is an operator of the language and $Fault_1 \vee Fault_2$ is the least upper bound of $Fault_i$ $(i = 1,2)$ with respect to $<$. If $Impl_i$ is tolerant of $Fault \vee Fault_i$ with respect to $Spec_i$, if neither $Impl_1$ is affected by $Fault_2$ nor $Impl_2$ by $Fault_1$, then $Impl_1|Impl_2$ is tolerant of $Fault \vee \bigvee_{i=1,2} Fault_i$ with respect to $Spec_1|Spec_2$.

We apply those techniques to the stepwise design of a distributed database, supporting atomic transactions despite failures of the underlying hardware. The development proceeds compositionally, separating the issues of concurrency and failures (both threaten atomicity) and given sequential, concurrent and distributed transactions. The solutions include: stable storage, mutual exclusion, and two- and three-phase commit with reliable communication [9].

2.5 Real-Time and Provable Fault-Tolerance

The framework is extended to include consideration of fault-tolerance and timing [11]. The extension includes the proper semantic definition of time [24], with algebra, logic and the model of faults then readily applied, and the sequence of increasingly realistic architectures for considering limited resources: processors, memory, clocks and network. These allow definitions of tasks that are: independent; communicate using the shared memory; are partitioned between the nodes of a distributed system, all connected by the multiple-access network and each providing local resources. We exemplify techniques for mapping tasks onto fault-free (static) or fault-affected (dynamic) resources, and how such techniques could be verified (schedulability) or synthesised for given timing requirements.

References

1. G. Bruns. Applying process refinement to a safety-relevant system. Technical report, Lab. for Foundations of Computer Science, University of Edinburgh, 1994.
2. K.M. Chandy and J. Misra. *Parallel Program Design*. Addison-Wesley, 1988.
3. R. Cleaveland, J. Parrow, and B. Steffen. The Concurrency Workbench: A semantics-based tool for the verification of concurrent systems. *ACM Transactions on Programming Languages and Systems*, 15(1):36–72, 1993.
4. F. Cristian. A rigorous approach to fault-tolerant programming. *IEEE Transactions on Software Engineering*, 11(1):23–31, 1985.
5. J. Fitzgerald, C. Jones, and P. Lucas, editors. *FME'97: Industrial Applications and Strengthened Foundations of Formal Methods*, volume 1313 of *LNCS*, 1997.
6. M. Hennessy and R. Milner. Algebraic laws for nondeterminism and concurrency. *Journal of the ACM*, 32(1):137–161, 1985.
7. T. Janowski. Fault-tolerant bisimulation and process transformations. In *Proc. 3rd Int. Symposium on Formal Techniques in Real-Time and Fault-Tolerant Systems*, volume 863 of *LNCS*, pages 373–392, 1994.
8. T. Janowski. Stepwise transformations for fault-tolerant design of CCS processes. In *Proc. 7th Int. Conference on Formal Description Techniques*, pages 505–520. Chapman and Hall, 1994.
9. T. Janowski. *Bisimulation and Fault-Tolerance*. PhD thesis, Department of Computer Science, University of Warwick, 1995.
10. T. Janowski. On bisimulation, fault-monotonicity and provable fault-tolerance. In *Proc. 6th Int. Conference on Algebraic Methodology and Software Technology*, LNCS, 1997.
11. T. Janowski and M. Joseph. Dynamic scheduling in the presence of faults: Specification and verification. In *Proc. 4rd Int. Symposium on Formal Techniques in Real-Time and Fault-Tolerant Systems*, volume 1135 of *LNCS*, pages 279–297, 1996.
12. He Jifeng and C.A.R. Hoare. Algebraic specification and proof of a distributed recovery algorithm. *Distributed Computing*, 2:1–12, 1987.
13. R. Keller. Formal verification of parallel programs. *Communications of ACM*, 19(7):561–572, 1976.
14. K.G. Larsen and R. Milner. A compositional protocol verification using relativized bisimulation. *Information and Computation*, 99:80–108, 1992.
15. Z. Liu. *Fault-Tolerant Programming by Transformations*. PhD thesis, University of Warwick, 1991.
16. Z. Liu and M. Joseph. Transformations of programs for fault-tolerance. *Formal Aspects of Computing*, 4:442–469, 1992.
17. R. Milner. A Calculus of Communicating Systems. *LNCS*, 92, 1980.
18. R. Milner. *Communication and Concurrency*. Prentice-Hall International, 1989.
19. K. Paliwoda and J.W. Sanders. An incremental specification of the sliding-window protocol. *Distributed Computing*, 5:83–94, 1991.
20. D. Park. Concurrency and automata on infinite sequences. *LNCS*, 104, 81.
21. J. Peleska. Design and verification of fault tolerant systems with CSP. *Distributed Computing*, 5:95–106, 1991.
22. K.V.S. Prasad. *Combinators and Bisimulation Proofs for Restartable Systems*. PhD thesis, Department of Computer Science, University of Edinburgh, 1987.
23. H. Schepers. *Fault Tolerance and Timing of Distributed Systems*. PhD thesis, Eindhoven University of Technology, 1994.
24. W. Yi. *A Calculus of Real Time Systems*. PhD thesis, Department of Computer Science, Chalmers University of Technology, 1991.

The Rewriting Calculus as a Semantics of ELAN

Horatiu Cirstea and Claude Kirchner

LORIA - INRIA, 615, rue du Jardin Botanique, 54600 Villers-lès-Nancy, FRANCE
{Horatiu.Cirstea,Claude.Kirchner}@loria.fr,
http://www.loria.fr/~{cirstea, ckirchne}

Rewriting techniques are now recognized as a fundamental concept in many areas of computer science including mechanized theorem proving and operational semantics of programming languages.

From a conceptual as well as operational point of view, the notion of rewrite rule application is crucial. It leads immediately to the concept of rewriting strategy which fully defines the way several rules are applied.

The combined concepts of rewrite rules and strategies are the first class objects of the programming language ELAN [BKK+98][1]. In this language, the actions to be performed are described using first-order conditional rewrite rules and the control is itself specified using strategies that can be non-deterministic. The use of these strategies is permitted directly in the rules via where statements. This provides a very natural way to describe e.g. theorem provers, constraint solvers, knowledge based reasoning techniques. Moreover such specifications can be executed very efficiently via new compilation techniques implemented in the ELAN compiler [MK98,Vit96]. In the first part of our talk we will present these concepts and provide running examples of their use.

Making the rule application an explicit object is the first step in the elaboration of the recently introduced rewriting calculus [CK98]. The ρ-calculus, as we call it, provides abstraction through the rewriting arrow and explicit rule application. It also embeds the notion of sets of results to deal with non-deterministic computations. Furthermore, the calculus is parameterized by the matching algorithm used in order to fire the rules. In its simplest instance, ρ-calculus embeds standard first-order rewriting as well as λ-calculus. In the second part of the talk, we will introduce the ρ-calculus and show how it provides a simple semantics for ELAN programs.

References

[BKK+98] Peter Borovanský, Claude Kirchner, Hélène Kirchner, Pierre-Etienne Moreau, and Christophe Ringeissen. An overview of ELAN. In Claude Kirchner and Hélène Kirchner, editors, *Proceedings of the second International Workshop on Rewriting Logic and Applications*, volume 15, http://www.elsevier.nl/locate/entcs/volume16.html, Pont-à-Mousson (France), September 1998. Electronic Notes in Theoretical Computer Science.

[1] http://www.loria.fr/equipes/protheo/PROJECTS/ELAN/elan.html

Jieh Hsiang, Atsushi Ohori (Eds.): ASIAN'98, LNCS 1538, pp. 84–85, 1998.

[CK98] Horatiu Cirstea and Claude Kirchner. ρ-calculus. Its syntax and basic properties. Research report 98-R-218, LORIA, August 1998.

[MK98] P.E. Moreau and H. Kirchner. A compiler for rewrite programs in associative-commutative theories. In C. Palamidessi, H. Glaser, and K. Meinke, editors, *Principles of Declarative Programming*, number 1490 in Lecture Notes in Computer Science, pages 230–249. Springer-Verlag, September 1998.

[Vit96] Marian Vittek. A compiler for nondeterministic term rewriting systems. In Harald Ganzinger, editor, *Proceedings of RTA'96*, volume 1103 of *Lecture Notes in Computer Science*, pages 154–168, New Brunswick (New Jersey), July 1996. Springer-Verlag.

Tried Linear Hashing

C.H. Ang, S.T. Tan, and T.C. Tan

School of Computing
National University of Singapore
Republic of Singapore, 119260
{angch, tanst, tantc}@comp.nus.edu.sg

Abstract. Tried linear hashing is a combination of linear hashing and trie hashing. It expands the file gracefully as linear hashing, and organizes each chain of overflow buckets with the use of a trie to ensure that any bucket can be retrieved in one disk access.

1 Introduction

When a large volume of data is stored in a disk file, to retrieve the relevant data quickly for a given key, a hashing method which is able to compute the disk address of the record from the given key is needed. There are many hashing methods proposed in the past 2 decades.

The easiest way to devise a hash function associated with a file, called the *primary file*, is to make use of modulo arithmetic. We regard a primary file as a table with T entries. The required hash function h is defined as $h(k) = k \ mod\ T$ where k is a given key, and k is inserted into bucket (or *node*) $h(k)$. When a node is full, subsequent insertions will cause the node to overflow.

The overflow problem can be resolved by either keeping all items in excess in an area for temporary holding, or they can be stored in separate chains, one for each node that overflows. The block in the primary file is called the *home block* of the chain, and those overflow blocks are grouped together in a file called the *overflow file*, or the *secondary file.* Both solutions have increasing access cost as the overflow area or the overflow chains are ever growing. The performance will deteriorate as the volume of data increases. In order to keep the response time within a certain reasonable limit, the data stored in the primary and secondary files are to be unloaded and restored into a new primary file of bigger size. This is a rather expensive housekeeping routine that has to be carried out periodically and thus it discourages the use of hashing method in commercial applications.

To handle the file expansion gracefully, more sophisticated methods are needed. The general 2-prong approach is to increase the file size a little at a time and to maintain the disk block addresses separately in a directory. When overflow occurs, a new block will be appended and items affected will be redistributed whereas unrelated items in other blocks will not be moved. The *grid file* [14] and the *extendible hashing* [5] are two such schemes. Both schemes require that the directories with entries containing pointers to the relevant disk blocks be maintained.

Jieh Hsiang, Atsushi Ohori (Eds.): ASIAN'98, LNCS 1538, pp. 86–94, 1998.

When the directory is small enough to reside in the memory, both methods guarantee the retrieval of any item in 1 disk access. If the directory is large, 2 disk accesses will be required: one for reading the directory block that contains the pointer, and another to read in the data block by following the pointer. It is clear that when the volume of data is large, the size of directory will be large too. When data are clustered, it will cause excessive node splitting and the directory will be doubled very often with many entries being duplicated. This is a very serious weakness.

Linear hashing [10] and *spiral hashing* [13] can be used to get rid of the directory so that the data file will grow gracefully, but these methods have their weaknesses. Since our interest is on linear hashing and its variants, we will exclude spiral hashing from our discussion. Linear hashing can be improved in several ways. For example, it can be modified to expand partially so as to increase the storage utilization [9] [15], to make it order preserving [6], employing interpolation-based index [4], to optimize its performance for key-sequential access [6], and to generalize it to multidimensional space [7]. These variants of linear hashing use separate chaining to resolve the key collision problem. Only the *recursive linear hashing* [16] proposed by Ramamohanarao and Sacks uses a predetermined number of linear hashing files to organize the overflow blocks.

On the other hand, Ilsoo Ahn [1] proposed the use of *filter buffer* to describe all the overflow blocks. Torn [17] proposed *Overflow Indexing (OVI)* to describe every overflowed key. Litwin [11] proposed *trie hashing* in which only one trie was used, and other enhancements such as [12] to include controlled load. All these methods rely on the additional memory structure to ensure that given a key, the required record can always be retrieved in one read.

In this paper, we propose *tried linear hashing*, which is a combination of linear hashing and trie hashing. We discuss linear hashing and trie hashing in sections 2 and 3. In section 4, the tried linear hashing method is described. We present some empirical results for comparison in section 5 and conclude our presentation in section 6.

2 Linear Hashing

Linear hashing is a hashing method applied to data files that grow or shrink dynamically as data are being inserted or deleted, with high space utilization and no significant deterioration in access time when the files become very big. It requires a family of hash functions $\{h_d\}$ such that most of the time 2 consecutive functions h_d and h_{d+1} are used. Each h_d is defined as $h_d : k \rightarrow k \ mod \ N * 2^d$ where N is the number of buckets in the file at the beginning and d ($d >= 0$) the depth of the file.

Initially, $d = 0$, and $h_0(k) = k \ mod \ N$ is used. All incoming keys are inserted into the buckets according to the address computed. When the file is so densely populated that it exceeds certain limit L, the *load factor*, the file is expanded by appending a block for redistribution of data at the end of the file. This will lower the storage utilization u, reduce the number of overflow blocks, and hence maintain the cost of accessing the overflow chains at a reasonably low level. For the first overflow encountered, all keys in bucket 0 will be rehashed into either bucket 0 or bucket N according to the hashing function h_1 instead of h_0. The *split pointer* sp is used to point to the block to be split and it is initialized to 0. After the block sp is split, sp will be incremented by 1. Thus all blocks will take turn to split. When block $N-1$ is split, the size of the file will have been doubled to $2N$, sp will be reset to 0 and the depth d will be incremented by 1.

Below is the algorithm used to insert a new key into a primary file of depth d using linear hashing. Note that $u = n/t$ where n is the number of items (keys, records) inserted so far and t is the total number of slots provided. If the bucket capacity is b and the files (primary and secondary) have s buckets, then $t = b*s$.

Linear Hashing Insertion (Key *k*)

BucketAddress p, $p1$
StorageUtilization u
$p \leftarrow h_d(k)$
If $p \geq sp$
then $p = h_{d+1}(k)$
Insert k into bucket p, or an overflow bucket when it is full
Compute u
If $u > L$
then
  $p_1 \leftarrow 2^d * N + sp$
  Redistribute all keys in bucket p, its overflow buckets if any, and the new key k into buckets p and p_1 according to h_{d+1}
  $sp \leftarrow sp + 1$
  If $sp \geq 2^d * N$
  then $sp \leftarrow 0$; $d \leftarrow d + 1$

As the roving split pointer sp gives blindly each block a chance to split, very often a block will overflow before it is split. When this occurs, a block in the overflow file will be allocated to store the overflowed keys and linked to the home block. When a chain of overflow buckets becomes very long, the time to retrieve an item on it also gets longer.

3 Trie Hashing

Trie hashing is one of the fastest access methods for dynamic and ordered files. Its efficiency lies in the use of a trie. It starts out with a bucket in which all keys will be stored. When an overflow occurs, another bucket will be appended at the end of the primary file. All keys will then be redistributed into the overflow bucket and the new bucket just allocated by comparing the value of the first character of each key with a discriminator, which is a suitable value that will usually divide the keys evenly. A key having the first character smaller than or equal to the discriminator will go into the original bucket, otherwise it will go into the new bucket. No secondary file is needed.

The result of splitting the buckets is described in a trie with the discriminator and its associated position within the key stored in each internal node, and the bucket addresses stored in the leaf nodes.

When the keys are numbers, a bit is used for comparison instead of using the whole character. As a result, the discriminators are not required to be stored in the internal nodes. During the search, each bit of the given key will be examined. If it is zero, proceed to the left subtree, otherwise go to the right subtree. This is the *digital searching* [8].

We may describe the bit checking by a family of functions $\{s_d\}$ where $s_d(k) = (k/2^d)\ mod\ 2$, d is the depth of the node in which s_d is being used. Below is the algorithm used to insert a new key k.

Trie Hashing Insertion (Key k)

TrieNode p
integer d
$p \leftarrow$ the root of the trie;
$d \leftarrow 0$;
While (p is an internal node)
    If $s_d(k) = 0$
    then $p \leftarrow p.left$
    else $p \leftarrow p.right$
    $d \leftarrow d + 1$
Read in *p.bucket*
If (*p.bucket* is not full) insert k
else
    Allocate one more bucket
    Perform bucket splitting and update the trie

It is possible that after redistribution, all keys go into the same bucket and overflow again. This may result in multiple empty buckets being allocated and the depth of the trie will be increased by more than one. If the keys are uniformly distributed, these empty buckets will be filled subsequently.

4 Tried Linear Hashing

Although linear hashing allows the data file to grow gracefully, the existence of some long overflow chains will make the retrieval of items in these chains slow. On the other hand, although trie hashing allows us to access the overflow blocks through a trie, the number of nodes to visit is large when many keys are stored in the file.

Intuitively, the combination of these two methods should give us a hashing algorithm in which the primary file can expand gracefully while the tries, used to describe the chains of overflow buckets, one trie for each home bucket with overflow buckets, are usually very small and require the visit of one or two nodes most of the time. Whenever the primary file expands, the overflow blocks described in the trie affected may be lifted from the overflow file back into the primary file, and hence the height of the tries will not grow without bound.

What is needed in maintaining many tries is an array *trie*[ ] of pointers to the roots of the tries. This array should be large enough for the primary file used. Below is the insertion algorithm of the tried linear hashing method.

Tried Linear Hashing Insertion (Key k)

BucketAddress p, p_1
StorageUtilization u
TriePointer *trie*[ ]
integer d
$p \leftarrow h_d(k)$
If $p \geq sp$
then $p = h_{d+1}(k)$
If (!*trie*[*p*])
then
    Insert k into bucket p
    Handle bucket overflow and the creation of trie accordingly.
else
    Follow the trie structure *trie*[*p*]
    Insert k into the bucket found
    Handle bucket overflow and the updating of trie accordingly.
Compute u
If $u > L$
then
    $p_1 \leftarrow 2^d * N + sp$
    Redistribute all keys in bucket p, all of its overflow buckets, and the new key k into buckets p and p_1 according to h_{d+1}
    $sp \leftarrow sp + 1$
    If $sp \geq 2^d * N$
    then $sp \leftarrow 0$; $d \leftarrow d + 1$

5 Empirical Results

Several experiments have been conducted to find out how much saving in disk accesses can be achieved when tried linear hashing is used as compared to the original linear hashing. In the experiments, the node capacity is set to 30, the initial hash file size is 5 buckets and the load factor limit L is set at 0.6, 0.7, 0.8, and 0.9. We created several files containing different number of items and measure the total number of node accesses during file creation. The statistics are listed in the following tables.

From the tables, it is noticed that the number of disk accesses has been reduced by 5% for L = 0.6 to 62% for L = 0.9. This is quite a substantial improvement over the original linear hashing during file creation. When the load factor is increased, more overflow blocks are allocated and accessed. Since

Number of Items	Linear (a)	Tried Linear (b)	b/a (%)
1000	2237	2176	97
2000	4556	4362	96
3000	7071	6629	94
4000	9264	8787	95
5000	11579	10922	94
6000	14095	13272	94
7000	16256	15423	95
8000	18454	17549	95
9000	20739	19644	95
10000	23181	21848	94

Table 1. Hash file creation cost. Load factor = 0.6

Number of Items	Linear (a)	Trie Linear (b)	b/a (%)
1000	2516	2185	87
2000	5188	4393	85
3000	7748	6649	83
4000	10516	8837	84
5000	12880	10899	85
6000	15574	12948	83
7000	18753	15560	83
8000	20920	17636	84
9000	23226	19696	85
10000	25674	21751	85

Table 2. Hash file creation cost. Load factor = 0.7

Number of Items	Linear (a)	Trie Linear (b)	b/a (%)
1000	3142	2049	65
2000	6741	4098	61
3000	10078	6154	61
4000	13861	8179	59
5000	17021	10247	60
6000	20593	12299	60
7000	24494	14326	58
8000	28385	16370	58
9000	31551	18429	58
10000	34865	20487	59

Table 3. Hash file creation cost. Load factor = 0.8

Number of Items	Linear (a)	Tried Linear (b)	b/a (%)
1000	4099	2047	50
2000	9746	4096	42
3000	14964	6152	41
4000	20292	10245	40
5000	25759	10245	40
6000	31365	12297	39
7000	37231	14324	38
8000	43067	16368	38
9000	49331	18427	37
10000	55109	20485	37

Table 4. Hash file creation cost. Load factor = 0.9

the accesses of the overflow blocks have been diverted to the associated tries in memory, the reduction in the number of accesses to the overflow blocks is expected to be greater as the load factor increases. This is confirmed by the outcomes of the experiments.

The use of the split functions $\{s_d\}$ effectively turns the files into a structure created by a general bucket method of degree 2 [3], in which each full bucket is split into 2 when it overflows. The storage utilization) of this kind of structure is about 0.69. As a result, the load factor of tried linear hashing is about 0.7 even when the load factor limit is set at 0.9.

To have a fairer comparison on the retrieval cost, we use $L = 0.7$. The saving in file creation cost is 15% using our algorithm. As for the retrieval cost, it is always one with tried linear hashing. Based on the file with 10000 keys, the average retrieval cost for linear hashing is 1.09 and the maximum cost is 2. When L is 0.8 (0.9), the corresponding figures are 1.51 (2.62) and 3 (5) respectively.

Note that when $L = 0.7$, the cost in retrieving a key from a file created through linear hashing or tried linear hashing are comparable when the keys are uniformly distributed. When the distribution of the keys are skewed or clustered, there will be many long chains of overflow buckets. The performance of tried linear hashing remains unchanged whereas that of linear hashing is greatly affected.

6 Conclusion

In this paper, we study linear hashing and trie hashing. Although linear hashing allows the data file to expand gradually online without the need to do an offline file expansion, it fails to organize its overflow buckets for quick retrieval. On the other hand, trie hashing imposes a trie structure onto the overflow buckets for efficient handling, but it requires many nodes of the trie to be visited.

We propose to combine the two algorithms into one and call it tried linear hashing. The new hashing method has the best of both worlds. It expands the file gradually as in linear hashing, and it organizes the overflow file through many small tries, one for each chain of overflow buckets as in trie hashing. In fact, the original trie hashing is a special case of our tried linear hashing in which only one bucket is used in the primary file and only one trie is used for the overflow buckets.

An experiment is carried out to measure the cost involved in terms of number of disk accesses to insert various number of keys using linear hashing and tried linear hashing. It is noted that when the file is moderately loaded at 70%, the cost of file creation is reduced by about 15% and the retrieval cost is guaranteed to be 1 whereas linear hashing requires 1.09. The cost saving is greater when the load factor is higher.

In another paper [2], we describe a new hashing method *Filtered linear hashing* in which linear hashing is being combined with filtered hashing. Both tried linear hashing and filtered linear hashing are equally efficient in terms of the file creation and key retrieval cost. In view of the complexity of merging the empty buckets when substantial deletions are performed in filtered linear hashing, the use of tried linear hashing is preferred.

References

1. Ilsoo Ahn: Filtered Hashing. LNCS 730, 85-96.
2. C.H. Ang, S.T. Tan, and T.C. Tan, Filtered linear hashing, in preparation.
3. C.H. Ang and H. Samet, Approximate average storage utilization of bucket methods with arbitrary fanout, Nordic Journal of Computing 3(1996), 280-291.
4. Walter A. Burkhard, Interpolation-Based Index Maintenance, BIT 23(1983), 274-294.
5. R. Fagin, J. Nievergelt, N. Pippenger, and H. R. Strong, Extendible hashing – a fast access method for dynamic files, ACM Transactions on Database Systems 4, 3(September 1979), 315-344.
6. N. I. Hachem and P. B. Berra, Key-sequential access methods for very large files derived from linear hashing, Proceedings of the Fifth IEEE International Conference on Data Engineering, Los Angeles, February 1989, 305-312.
7. Andreas Hutflesz, Hans-Werner Six, and Peter Widmayer, Globally order preserving multidimensional linear hashing, Proceedings of the fourth IEEE International Conference on Data Engineering, Los Angeles, February 1988, 572-579.
8. D. E. Knuth, The art of computer programming, Vol. 3, Addison-Wesley, 1973.
9. P.A. Larson, Linear hashing with partial expansions, Proceedings of the Sixth International Conference on Very Large Data Bases, Montreal, October 1980, 224-232.
10. W. Litwin, Linear hashing: a new tool for file and table addressing, Proceedings of the sixth International Conference on Very Large Data Bases, Montreal, October 1980, 212-223.
11. W. Litwin, Trie hashing: further properties and performance, Proceedings of the international conference on Foundation of Data Organization, May 21-24, 1985, Kyoto, Japan, 51-60.
12. W. Litwin, N. Roussopoulos, G. Levy, and W. Hong, Trie Hashing With Controlled Load, IEEE Transactions on Software Engineering, Vol. 17, No. 7, July 1991, 678-691.

13. G. N. N. Martin, spiral storage: incrementally augmentable hash addressed storage, Theory of computation Report No. 27, Department of Computer Science, University of Warwick, Coverntry, Great Britain, March 1979.
14. J. Nievergelt, H. Hinterberger, and K. C. Sevcik, The grid file: an adaptable, symmetric multikey file structure, ACM Transactions on Database Systems 9, 1(March 1984), 38-71.
15. K. Ramamohanarao and J. W. Lloyd, Dynamic hashing schemes, Computer Journal 25, 4(November 1982), 478-485.
16. K. Ramamohanarao and R. Sacks-Davis, Recursive linear hashing, ACM Transactions on Database Systems 9, 3(September 1984), 369-391.
17. Aimo A. Torn, Hashing with overflow indexing, BIT 24(1984), 317-332.

A New Factoring Algorithm for Magic Predicates

Xiaoyong Du, Zhibin Liu, and Naohiro Ishii

Department of Intelligence and Computer Science,
Nagoya Institute of Technology, Japan
{duyong,zhibin,ishii}@egg.ics.nitech.ac.jp

Abstract. The magic-sets method is a basic query optimization method in the deductive database systems. However, the original magic-sets method may generate large magic predicates for recursive queries. In this case, the evaluation of the magic predicates dominate the whole evaluation cost. Factorized magic sets can limit the sizes of generated magic predicates by splitting some magic predicates. However, it suffers from a new "over-splitting" problem. In this paper, we focus on a problem: what is the best splitting schema for a magic predicate, given a magic program. We propose a hypergraph model to represent the magic program as well as its naive evaluation procedure. An intuition is a magic predicate whose arguments belong to different connected components in infinite number of its generated graphs is considered to be a big one. It thus should be split. Based on the hypergraph model, we propose a new concept, called c-partition, as the best splitting of a magic predicate. Although we still do not know how to construct a c-partition, we define a serial of d[k]-partitions to approximate the c-partition. We prove that d[k]-partition is better then the existing splitting algorithm. Our method is a global splitting strategy for magic predicates, in the sense that it decides whether or not to split a magic predicate by considering the whole program.
keywords: deductive databases, query optimization, magic sets, factoring

1 Introduction

The magic-sets is an efficient algorithm for optimizing recursive as well as non-recursive queries in deductive databases and rule-based systems, and implemented as a standard facility in many prototype systems [3,4]. The magic-sets is a technique that allows us to rewrite the rules for each query form so that the advantages of top-down and bottom-up methods are combined. The method is effective (optimal) in the sense that it generates no unnecessary facts.

However, the magic-sets method assumes that the size of each magic predicate is usually smaller than the corresponding recursive predicate. Therefore, the magic-sets method generates magic predicates as many as possible, and maximizes the arity of each magic predicate. This strategy may result in generating large magic predicates

Jieh Hsiang, Atsushi Ohori (Eds.): ASIAN'98, LNCS 1538, pp. 95–112, 1998.

Example 1. Consider the following program Γ. It is a typical same-generation program.

$$sg(X,Y) : -flat(X,Y).$$
$$sg(X,Y) : -up(X,U)down(Y,V)sg(U,V).$$

Assume that the given query is $sg(1,1)$, that is, both the first and second arguments are bound. Then a typical magic-sets transformation of the program, denoted as Γ^{mg}, would be

$$sg^{bb}(X,Y) : -m\_sg^{bb}(X,Y)flat(X,Y).$$
$$sg^{bb}(X,Y) : -m\_sg^{bb}(X,Y)up(X,U)down(Y,V)sg^{bb}(U,V).$$
$$m\_sg^{bb}(U,V) : -m\_sg^{bb}(X,Y)up(X,U)down(Y,V).$$
$$m\_sg^{bb}(1,1).$$

where, $m\_sg^{bb}(U,V)$ is magic predicate. Its definition rules (the third and fourth ones in the program) are called magic rules. The set of magic rules is called magic program. □

In Γ^{mg}, the magic predicate m_sg^{bb} acts as a filter to restrict the computing space of a bottom-up evaluation of the recursive predicate sg^{bb}. The superior letter *bb* is called adornment of the corresponding predicate, which represents the bound information for that predicate. *bb* means two arguments of the predicate *sg* are bounded by the query constant.

Experience from relation databases showed that set-at-a-time operations are very important for database application. Hence, to answer a query $p(\bar{c},\bar{X})$, where $\bar{c}$ is a vector of bound arguments, to a program P, a bottom-up semi-naive evaluation is usually employed in database application. However, for a recursive query, it may contain many temporary results in its evaluation which have no contribution to the final query results. In order to reduce the computing space of the semi-naive evaluation, the original program is modified by the magic-sets method[1,8,7]. The basic idea of the magic-sets method is to convey the bound information of the query to rule definitions so as to reduce the relative facts set of the bottom-up semi-naive evaluation. The magic-sets method constructs one magic predicate, denoted as m_p, for every IDB predicate p in each rule in the original program. The original rules to define p are modified by inserting m_p in the body of the rule. That is, the modified rule has the form $p : -m\_p, body(p)$, where $body(p)$ represents the body of the original rule. m_p thus acts as a filter to evaluate the p. Those tuples that are in $body(p)$ but not in m_p are excluded in the evaluation. Clearly, the smaller the relation m_p, the more efficient the bottom-up semi-naive evaluation. We denote the magic-set program of P by P^{mg}.

Ullman[9] and Seki[6] showed that the size of search space represented by the stored relation sg^{bb} is equal to the search space of the top-down evaluation. Hence, magic-set program is optimal in the sense that it does not generate unnecessary facts. Unfortunately, the size of m_sg^{bb} is possibly very large. Let us consider an EDB in Example 1 as follows: $up = \{(1,2),(2,3),\cdots,(n-1,n),(n,1)\}$, $down = \{(1,2),(2,3),\cdots,(n-2,n-1),(n-1,1)\}$. Then magic predicate m_sg^{bb}

is the set $\{(i,j)|i=1,\cdots,n;j=1,\ldots,n-1\}$, which size is bounded by $O(n^2)$. In this case, the magic-sets processing actually computes the Cartesian product of relations *up* and *down*.

For overcoming this problem, a way of factoring magic predicates is proposed [5,7], called factorized magic-sets. Magic predicates are repeatedly split until every magic rules (rule whose head is a magic predicate) satisfies the following conditions:

(1) The non-magic predicates in the body constitute a connected set.
(2) Every variable in the head of a magic rule appears in some non-magic predicate or the body contains only magic predicate.

In other words, a magic predicate $m\_p(\bar{X},\bar{Y})$ should be partitioned if there is a rule to define $m\_p(\bar{X},\bar{Y})$, which contains at least two connected components in the body, each contains $\bar{X}$ and $\bar{Y}$ respectively, or $\bar{X}$ belongs to a magic predicate and does not appear in any non-magic predicates, where $\bar{X}$ and $\bar{Y}$ are two vectors of arguments of p.

Example 2. The magic predicate m_sg^{bb} in Example 1 is defined by a rule in which body there are two disconnected base predicates *up* and *down*, thus it should be partitioned into two smaller magic predicates, $bf\_m\_sg^{bb}$ and $fb\_m\_sg^{bb}$, as follows.

$$\begin{array}{l} bf\_m\_sg^{bb}(U) : -bf\_m\_sg^{bb}(X)up(X,U). \\ fb\_m\_sg^{bb}(V) : -fb\_m\_sg^{bb}(Y)down(Y,V). \\ bf\_m\_sg^{bb}(1). \\ fb\_m\_sg^{bb}(1). \end{array}$$

Every magic predicate is unary now. So, they do not produce big relations obviously. □

Sippu and Soisalon-Soininen[7] proved that the size of a factorized magic predicate is linear in the size of the largest temporary result that is the join of a set of connected non-magic predicates in the definition of the magic predicate. However, as being pointed out by themselves, factoring may result in worse behavior as compared to original magic predicates. That is, the original magic predicates may be a stronger filter for basic (semi-)naive evaluation than the factorized one. Intuitively, if $m\_p(X,Y)$ is not a big one, we should compute it explicitly, because the size of $m\_p(X,Y)$ is less than that of $m\_p(X)\times m\_p(Y)$, where $m\_p(X)$ and $m\_p(Y)$ are the project of $m\_p(X,Y)$ respectively. However, if $m\_p(X,Y)$ is a big one. Constructing $m\_p(X,Y)$ explicitly may dominate the cost of whole evaluation. Hence the key is to estimate the size of magic predicates.

Sippu and Soisalon-Soininen's strategy [7] decides the size of a magic predicate according to the property of each definition rule. We thus call it as a local splitting algorithm. This strategy may split some magic predicate too small. We call this problem "over-splitting". It means the factored magic predicates may weaken the filtering effect in the bottom-up evaluation. Let us see the following example.

Example 3. Consider the following magic rules

$$m\_q^{bb}(U,V) : -m\_p^{bbf}(X,Y)d(X,Y,U,V).$$
$$m\_p^{bbf}(U,V) : -m\_q^{bb}(X,Y)a(X,U)b(Y,V).$$
$$m\_q^{bb}(1,1).$$

By the factorized magic-sets method, $m\_p^{bbf}(X,Y)$ will be split to two smaller unary magic predicates:

$$m\_q^{bb}(U,V) : -fbf\_m\_p^{bbf}(X)bff\_m\_p^{bbf}(Y)d(X,Y,U,V).$$
$$fbf\_m\_p^{bbf}(U) : -m\_q^{bb}(X,Y)a(X,U).$$
$$bff\_m\_p^{bbf}(V) : -m\_q^{bb}(X,Y)b(Y,V).$$
$$m\_q^{bb}(1,1).$$

If we transform the above magic program to the following equivalent form, both magic predicates are defined by rules in which body all base predicates are connected. By Sippu and Soisalon-Soininen's splitting criterion, both of them need not to be split.

$$m\_q^{bb}(U,V) : -m\_q^{bb}(S,T)a(S,X)b(T,Y)d(X,Y,U,V),$$
$$m\_p^{bbf}(U,V) : -m\_p^{bbf}(S,T)d(S,T,X,Y)a(X,U)b(Y,V),$$
$$m\_p^{bbf}(U,V) : -a(1,U)b(1,V),$$
$$m\_q^{bb}(1,1).$$

□

This example give us a hint that if we consider the global property of all rules that define the magic predicate, we are possible to overcome the "over-splitting" problem. In this paper, we focus on such a problem: what is the best splitting schema for magic predicates in a magic program.

The remainder is organized as follows: Section 2 introduces some basic concepts as well as Sippu and Soisalon-Soininen's factorized magic-sets method. Section 3 proposes a hypergraph model to represent the magic program as well as its naive evaluation procedure. We then propose a new criterion for splitting: a magic predicate whose arguments belong to different connected components in infinite number of its generated graphs should be split. We summarize it as a concept called c-partition. Section 4 defines a concept, called d-partition, to approximate the optimal splitting schema. We prove that the d-partitions is better than Sippu and Soisalon-Soininen's factoring. This result enhances the availability of the factorized magic-sets method. Section 5 concludes this paper.

2 Recursive Queries, Magic-Sets, and Factorization

We first briefly introduce the basic concepts of recursive queries, magic-sets in Datalog language, and Sippu and Soisalon-Soininen's factorized magic-sets method. The details of Datalog language refers to Ullman [8]. The details of the factorized method refers to [7].

Assume that there is an underlying first-order language without function symbols. A *(Datalog) program*[8] is a finite set of clauses called rules of the form:

$$R : p(\bar{X}) : -p_1(\bar{X}_1) \cdots p_m(\bar{X}_m).$$

where $m \geq 0$; $p(\bar{X})$, called the *head*, is an atom of an ordinary predicate, and $p_1(\bar{X}_1) \cdots p_m(\bar{X}_m)$, called the *body*, stands for the conjunction $p_1(\bar{X}_1) \wedge \ldots \wedge p_m(\bar{X}_m)$; each $p_i(\bar{X}_i)$ is called the subgoal (predicate) and is an atom of either an ordinary predicate or a built-in predicate. A rule with an empty body is a *fact*, which contains no variables. A query is a rule without a head, with some of its variables possibly bound to constants. A predicate is called *base predicate* (or EDB predicate) if it is not a head in the program. Otherwise it is called *derived predicate* (or IDB predicate). A derived predicate is called *recursive* if it is contained in a cycle in the *dependency graph* of a program, which has all predicates of the program as the nodes and has an edge from *p* to *q* if p is found in the body and *q* is found in the head of the same rule in the program. The IDB predicates in the same cycle are called mutually recursive predicates. A rule is *recursive* if it contains some recursive predicates. Nonrecursive rules are called *exit rules*, and the corresponding base predicate is called *exit predicate.*

Definition 1. *Let C be the set of predicates. Two variables, X and Y, are connected in C if they appear in a predicate in C or there is another variable Z such that X and Z are in a predicate in C and both Z and Y are connected in C. Two predicates are connected if they each contain one of a pair of connected variables.*

Let C be the set of all EDB predicates of a rule. Connectivity among both variables and predicates in C is an equivalence relation. It splits all predicates in C into some connected components. We say a rule is a single-connected-component rule if all EDB predicates are connected, otherwise the rule is a multiple-connected-component rule.

Example 4. In Example 1, Let $C = \{up, down\}$ be the set of base predicates of the second rule. C contains two connected components. So the second rule is a two-connected-component rule. □

Although a rule is possibly a multiple-connected-component rule, we require that the rule become single-connected-component one if we add the IDB predicates into the predicate set C. Furthermore, we require that all IDB predicates are rectified. That is, its variables are distinct.Otherwise, we can replace them by different variables and introduce an equal predicate between them. We also require that the rules are safe, that is, all variables in the head of a rule should appear in the body of that rule also.

Two important concepts in magic-sets transformation are adornments and sideways information passing strategy (sips for short)[1,8,7]. An *adornment* is an annotation on a predicate that gives information about how the predicate is used. The typical adornment system contains only bound (b for short) and free(f

for short) adornments. For example, the adornment of the query in Example 1 sg^{bb} means that the first and second arguments of sg are bound. A sips is a decision on how to pass the boundings available in the body of a rule while evaluating the rule. However, the choice of the best sips for a magic program is beyond this paper. We simply choice a full sips, which propagates all the binding information from the rules' head to the rule's body and between the subgoals, and reorder all predicates in the body from left to right that obeys the partial order defined by the sips.

The details of the typical magic-sets method is omitted here. Our purpose is to overcome the problem of the existing factorized magic-set method that we mentioned in previous section. Factoring magic predicates is done over the magic program generated by the typical magic-set method. Hence, in this paper, we assume that we have had a magic program without concerning how to generate. Hence, we only introduce Sippu and Soisalon-Soininen's factorized magic-sets algorithm[7] here.

The kernel of the algorithm is a factoring algorithm. It replaces the magic predicate, which variables are not connected in the set of EDB predicates of the rule, by its b-factors. At first, we define the concept of b-factoring of an adornment and their product operation.

Definition 2. *Let α and β be adornments for an n-ary predicate p, which are considered as bit vectors with $b = 1$ and $f = 0$. The disjunction of α and β, denoted as $\alpha \vee \beta$, is the bitwise "or" of α and β; the conjunction of α and β, denoted as $\alpha \wedge \beta$ is the bitwise "and" of α and β; and the negation of α, denoted as $\neg\alpha$, is the bitwise "not" of α.*

Definition 3. *$\alpha \leq \beta$ if $\alpha \vee \beta = \beta$; $\alpha < \beta$ if $\alpha \leq \beta$ and $\alpha \neq \beta$.*

Definition 4. *A set of $\{ \alpha_1, \cdots, \alpha_m \}$ of adornments for a k-ary predicate p is a b-factoring of an adornment α for p, if $\alpha_1 \vee \cdots \vee \alpha_m = \alpha$ and, for all $i \neq j$, $\alpha_i \wedge \alpha_j = f^k$, where f^k represents f written k times. Each α_i is called a b-factor of α.*

Definition 5. *Let $F = \{\alpha_1, \cdots, \alpha_m\}$ and $G = \{\beta_1, \cdots, \beta_n\}$ be b-factorings of an adornment α of a k-ary predicate. The product of these factorings, denoted by $F \times G$, is defined as $\{\alpha_i \wedge \beta_j | i = 1, \cdots, m, j = 1, \cdots, n\} \backslash \{f^k\}$*

Obviously, the product of two b-factorings of α is always a b-factoring of α.

Example 5. Consider the adornment $\alpha = bb$ of the IDB predicate m_sg in the second rule of Example 1. $\{bf, fb\}$ is a b-factoring of α, because $bf \vee fb = bb$, and $bf \wedge fb = ff$. □

Definition 6. *Let F and G be two b-factoring of α. G is a refinement of F, denoted by $G \leq F$, if for every factor $\beta \in F$ there are factors $\gamma_1, \cdots, \gamma_n \in G$ such that $\beta = \gamma_1 \vee \cdots \vee \gamma_n$, that is, $\{\gamma_1, \cdots, \gamma_n\}$ is a b-factoring of β.*

Next, we introduce factoring algorithm. It takes as input a magic-sets transformed program P^{mg} of a safe datalog program P with rectified rule heads and rectified IDB subgoals. The algorithm produces, for each adorned IDB predicate p^α, a b-factoring $B_{p,\alpha}$ of the adornment α.

Algorithm 1 : *(Factoring)*
Input: P^{mg}
Output: $B_{p,\alpha}$, *for all derived predicates* p *in* P^{mg}
Method:

(1). $B_{p,\alpha} = \{\alpha\}$ *for each adorned IDB predicate* p^α.
(2). For each magic rule

$$R : m\_r^\beta(\bar{V}) : -m\_p^\alpha(\bar{U})p_1(\bar{X}_1)\cdots p_k(\bar{X}_k)$$

in P^{mg}, *let* C *be the set of the non-magic subgoals of* R, *which is partitioned into a set of connected components, say* $C_1, \cdots, C_m, m \geq 1$.
(2.1) [splitting those arguments whose variables appear in EDB predicates] *Replace* $B_{r,\beta}$ *by* $B_{r,\beta} \times \{\beta_1, \cdots, \beta_m, \delta\}$, *where* $\beta_i \leq \beta$ $(i = 1, \cdots, m)$ *be the adornment for the predicate* r *that designates as bound exactly those arguments in* $m\_r^\beta(\bar{V})$ *that appear in some subgoal in* C_i; $\delta = \beta \wedge \neg(\beta_1 \vee \cdots \vee \beta_m)$. $\{\beta_1, \cdots, \beta_m, \delta\}$ *is a b-factoring of* β.
(2.2)[splitting those arguments whose variables appear only in the magic predicate in the body]
If $\bar{V}$ *contains two variables that appear only in* $\bar{U}$ *in the body of* R *and that belong to different factors in* $B_{p,\alpha}$, *then the* $B_{r,\beta}$ *must be refined further by replaced with* $B_{r,\beta} \times (\{\hat{\beta}\} \cup \{\beta_\gamma | \gamma \in B_{p,\alpha}\})$, *where* $\hat{\beta} \leq \beta$ *is the adornment for* r *that designates as bound exactly those variables in* $m\_r^\beta(\bar{V})$ *that appear in* $\bar{X}_1, \cdots, \bar{X}_k$; $\beta_\gamma \leq \beta$ $(\gamma \in B_{p,\alpha})$ *is the adornment for* r *that designates as bound exactly those variables* V *in* $m\_r^\beta(\bar{V})$ *that satisfy the following conditions:*
- V *does not appear in* $\bar{X}_1 \cdots \bar{X}_k$, *and*
- V *appears in* $m\_p^\alpha(\bar{U})$ *in a position that is also designated as bound by* γ.

Clearly, $\{\hat{\beta}\} \cup \{\beta_\gamma | \gamma \in B_{p,\alpha}\}$ *is a b-factoring of* β.
This step should be repeated until no change occurs. □

Example 6. Consider the magic predicate mg_sg in Example 1.There is only one rule to define this magic predicate. $C = \{up(X, U), down(Y, V)\}$, which is partitioned into two connected components. Hence the adornment $\{bb\}$ of mg_sg is replaced by its b-factoring $\{bf, fb\}$.

Based on this factoring algorithm, the original magic program can be revised by splitting those magic predicates which corresponding adornment set contains more than two elements. [7].

Algorithm 2 *(Factorized magic program)*
Input: $B_{p,\alpha}$, P^{mg}
Output: P^{fmg}
Method:

(1) For each factor $\hat{\gamma} \in B_{q,\gamma}$, there is a seed

$$\hat{\gamma}\_m\_q^{\gamma}(\bar{Y}_b)$$

where $\bar{Y}_b$ consists of the bound arguments from $q^{\hat{\gamma}}(\bar{Y})$

(2) For each magic rule

$$m\_r^{\beta}(\bar{V}) : -m\_p^{\alpha}(\bar{U})p_1(\bar{X}_1)\cdots p_k(\bar{X}_k).$$

in P^{mg} and for each factor $\hat{\beta} \in B_{r,\beta}$, there is a factored magic rule. The head of the factorized magic rule is $\hat{\beta}\_m\_r^{\beta}(\bar{W})$, where $\bar{W}$ consists of those arguments from $\bar{V}$ that are designated as bound by $\hat{\beta}$. The body of the factorized magic rule is constructed as follows. If $\bar{W}$ is contained in $\bar{U}$, then the body consists of the subgoal $\alpha_j\_m\_p^{\alpha}(\bar{U}_j)$, where $\alpha_j \in B_{p,\alpha}$, and $\bar{U}_j \subseteq \bar{U}$ that are designed as bound by α_j $(1 \leq j \leq m)$. If $\bar{W}$ is contained in $\bar{X}_1, \cdots, \bar{X}_k$, then the body contains every subgoal $p_l(\bar{X}_l)$, where $\bar{X}_l \cap \bar{W} \neq \phi$, and all those subgoals that are connected to $p_l(\bar{X}_l)$ via a path not going through any subgoal $p_i(\bar{X}_i), i > l$.

(3) For each modified rule

$$p^{\alpha}(\bar{X}) : -m\_p^{\alpha}(\bar{X}^b)p_1(\bar{X}_1)\cdots p_n(\bar{X}_n)$$

in P^{mg}, there is a modified rule

$$p^{\alpha}(\bar{X}) : -\alpha_1\_m\_p^{\alpha}(\bar{U}_1)\cdots\alpha_m\_m\_p^{\alpha}(\bar{U}_m)p_1(\bar{X}_1),\cdots p_n(\bar{X}_n)$$

where $B_{p,\alpha} = \{\alpha_1, \cdots, \alpha_m\}$ and $\bar{U}_i\,(i = 1, \cdots, m)$ consists of those arguments in $m\_p^{\alpha}(\bar{X}^b)$ that are designated as bound by α_i. □

Example 7. The adornment set of the magic predicate m_sg in Example 1 contains two b-factors. Hence m_sg should be split. The result magic program is the one listed in Example 2. □

3 A Hypergraph Model for Magic Programs

The above factoring algorithm decides splitting of a magic predicate according to the connectivity in the set of the non-magic predicates of each definition rule. That is, the factoring is based on the local property of the rule. This is the reason that the factoring algorithm suffers the "over-splitting" problem we mentioned in Introduction. To tackle the optimal splitting problem, we need a power tool to represent the global property of the magic program easily. In this section, we propose a hypergraph model to represent the magic program as well as its naive evaluation procedure. Corresponding to a magic predicate, there are a set of generated graphs. We see that a magic predicate may produce a big relation if its arguments belong to different connected components in infinite generated graphs. Thus this kind of magic predicate should be split.

According to the magic-sets method, we know that the magic predicates may be mutually recursive with some IDB predicates. For evaluating a nonlinear multiple-rule mutually-recursive query, its (semi-)naive algorithm can be viewed as a loop of two steps until there is no change occur:

(1) evaluating all magic predicates by fixing all IDB predicates (their initial values are empty);
(2) evaluating all IDB predicates by using the obtained magic predicates.

In this research, we pay attention to the sizes of magic predicates. Hence, IDB predicates in evaluating magic predicates can be treated as same as EDB predicates in one iterative step. That is, we can assume the size of any IDB predicate is not big in each iteration. Furthermore, each magic rule contains exact one magic predicate in its body. All rules are safe and all subgoals in the body of a rule, including those magic subgoals, are connected. As the result, the magic programs of a Datalog program is a safe, rectified, multiple-rule, linearly-recursive program.

Therefore, in the following discussion, we consider a multiple-rule linearly-recursive program. The magic rules are safe and rectified. Furthermore, for simplicity, we omit the adornmentations of the magic predicates as well as the prefix "$m\_$" of the magic predicates. The other predicates in the body, including IDB predicates and EDB predicates, are called non-magic predicates.

Definition 7. *Let*

$$R : p(\bar{U}) : -r(\bar{V})p_1(\bar{X}_1) \cdots p_m(\bar{X}_m)$$

be a rule. A labeled hypergraph, denoted by $G(R) = (V, E, L^+, L^-)$, is defined for R as follows.

(1) V is a finite, nonempty set of nodes. A node is defined by a variable in the rule. Furthermore, a node is labeled by X itself if X is a variable appearing only in some non-magic predicate of the rule; a node is labeled by p_i^+ if the corresponding variable appears in the i-th position of the magic predicate p (head of the rule); a node is labeled by r_i^- if the corresponding variable appears in the i-th position of the magic predicate r (in the body of the rule). We call a node with mark "+" a positive node, and that with mark "-" a negative node. For convenience, we call the label X v-label (variable-label), and the label like p_i^+, r_i^- a-label (argument-label).

(2) E is a finite, nonempty set of undirected hyperedges such that a hyperedge is defined and labeled by q among nodes corresponding to variables $\bar{X}$ if $q(\bar{X})$ is a non-magic predicate in the rule.

(3) L^+ is the set of all a-labels of positive nodes

(4) L^- is the set of all a-labels of negative nodes

If $L^-(G) = \phi$, the graph is called E-graph, otherwise I-graph. If $L^+(G) = L^-(G)$ except the "+" and "-" mark, the graph is called self-recursive graph. The node not appearing in any hyperedge is called dangling node.

Example 8. The graph representation of the magic rules in Example 3 is showed in Fig. 1. The first rule consists of a unique hyperedge, and the second rule contains two separated components. The third rule can be viewed as a rule as $q(X,Y) : -e(X,Y)$, where $e(x,Y)$ contains only one tuple (1,1). □

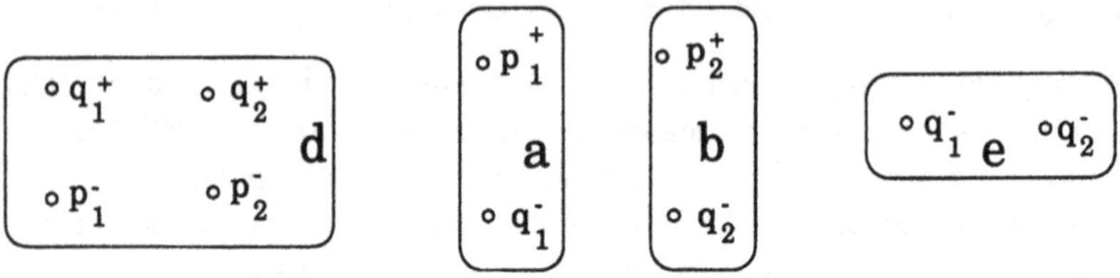

(a) (b) (c)

Fig. 1. Hypergraph representation for a magic program, (a) and (b) are I-graphs, (c) is E-graph

Two edges a and b are connected if they contains at least one common node, or a is connected with a hyperedge c and c contains at least one common node with b. Two nodes are connected if there appear in a set of connected hyperedges. A graph $G(R)$ is called connected if all of its positive nodes are connected.

Definition 8. *(Definition Graph) Let $P = \{R_1, \cdots, R_m\}$ be a program, where R_i are rules. Then P can be represented by a set of graphs $G(P) = \{G(R_1), \cdots, G(R_m)\}$, which are divided into two parts: $G_i(P) = \{S \in G(P) | S$ is an I-graph$\}$; $G_e(P) = \{S \in G(P) | S$ is an E-graph$\}$; $G(P) = (G_i(P), G_e(P))$ is called definition graph of P.*

Definition 9. *(Gluing) Let $S = G(R_1)$ and $T = G(R_2)$ be two graphs defined for two rules R_1 and R_2, respectively. Gluing S and T, denoted by $S * T$, is a graph if the negative nodes of S and positive nodes of T has the same a-labels except $+$ and $-$. The corresponding nodes are combined in the new graph, and are assigned with new v-labels, Their previous a-labels are deleted. Otherwise, it is an empty graph (incompatible). If G and H are two sets of graphs, $G * H = \{S * T | S \in G, T \in H\}$.*

Gluing operation is similar to the resolution operation in logic programming or join operation in relational databases. When we use the second rule to resolve m_p in the first one, we obtain a new rule which corresponding graph is exactly the one obtained by gluing the graph of the first rule and that of the second rule.

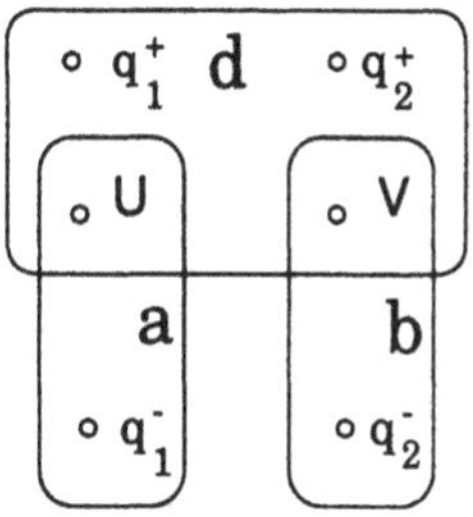

Fig. 2. Gluing the graph (a) with (b) in Fig. 1

Hence, the naive evaluation of a program P can be represented by gluings of the graphs in $G(P)$ each other.

Definition 10. *(k-th I-graph) Let $G_i(P)$ and $G_e(P)$ be a pair of I-graph and E-graph for a program P. The k-th (order) I-graphs of $G_i(P)$, denoted by $G_i^k(P)$, are defined iteratively as follows:*

$$G_i^1(P) = G_i(P);$$
$$G_i^k(P) = G_i^{k-1}(P) * G_i(P)$$

Definition 11. *(k-th E-graph) Let $G_i(P)$ and $G_e(P)$ be a pair of I-graph and E-graph for a program P. The k-th (order) E-graphs, denoted by $R^k(P)$, are defined as follows:*

$$R^0(P) = G_e(P);$$
$$R^k(P) = G_i^k(P) * G_e(P)$$

We denote $G^*(P) = \cup_{k=1}^{\infty}(G_i^k(P))$, $R^*(P) = \cup_{k=1}^{\infty}(R^k(P))$, and $Gen(P) = \cup_{k=1}^{\infty}(G_i^k(P) \cup R^k(P)) = G^*(P) \cup R^*(P)$. $G^*(P)$, $R^*(P)$, and $Gen(P)$ are called generated I-graph, generated E-graph, and generated graph, respectively. Similarly, for a magic predicate p, we denote $G^*(p)$, $R^*(p)$ and $Gen(p)$ as the subset of graphs in $G^*(P)$, $R^*(P)$ and $Gen(P)$, respectively, whose positive nodes are marked as p_i^+.

Lemma 1. *Let P be a program. then*

$$\begin{aligned} &(1) \quad G_i^m(P) = (G_i(P))^m \\ &(2) \quad R^{m+n}(P) = G_i^m(P) * R^n(P) \end{aligned}$$

where $(G_i(P))^m$ is a shorthand for $G_i(P) * \cdots * G_i(P)$ ($m-1$ gluing operations)

Proof. (1). It is proved by induction on m. At first, $G_i^1(P) = G_i(P)$ from the definition. Next, we have $G_i^m(P) = G_i^{m-1}(P) * G_i(P) = (G_i(P))^{m-1} * G_i(P) = (G_i(P))^m$.

(2). By the definition and (1), we have

$$\begin{aligned} G_i^m(P) * R^n(P) &= G_i^m(P) * G_i^n(P) * G_e(P) && ; R^n(P) = G_i^n(P) * G_e(P) \\ &= (G_i(P))^m * (G_i(P))^n * G_e(P) && ; (1) \\ &= (G_i(P))^{m+n} * G_e(P) && ; definition \\ &= G_i^{m+n}(P) * G_e(P) && ; (1) \\ &= R^{m+n}(P) && ; definition. \end{aligned}$$

□

Next, we prove an important theorem.

Theorem 1. *(Transformation Theorem) Let $(G_i^k(P), \cup_{j=0}^{k-1} R^j(P))$ be a hypergraph defining a new program, say Q, where $G_i^k(P)$ is the k-th I-graph and $R^j(P)(j = 0, \cdots, k-1)$ are j-th E-graphs of P. Then $R^*(P) = R^*(Q)$.*

Proof. (1) For an arbitrary graph $S \in R^*(P)$, assume it is in $R^l(P)$, that is, it is an l-th E-graph. If $l \le k$ then $R^l(P) \subseteq G_e(Q) \subseteq R^*(Q)$. If $l > k$, assume $l = a * k + b$, we have $R^l(P) = R^{a*k+b}(P) = G_i^{a*k}(P) * R^b(P) = (G_i^k(P))^a * R^b(P) = G_i^a(Q) * R^b(P) \subseteq G_i^a(Q) * G_e(Q)$, hence $R^l(P) \subseteq R^a(Q) \subseteq R^*(Q)$. Hence, $S \in R^*(Q)$, $R^*(P) \subseteq R^*(Q)$.

(2) For an arbitrary $S \in R^*(Q)$, assume it is in $R^l(Q)$. Since $R^l(Q) = G_i^l(Q) * G_e(Q) = (G_i(Q))^l * G_e(Q) = (G_i^k(P))^l * (\cup_{j=0}^{k-1} R^j(P)) = G_i^{k*l}(P) * (\cup_{j=0}^{k-1} R^j(P))$, we have $R^l(Q) \subseteq R^*(P)$. Hence, $S \in R*(P)$, $R^*(Q) \subseteq R^*(P)$ □

In relational database theory, we usually assume that the size of predicate which is defined by a connected nonrecursive relation expression is not very big. In our graph model natation, The predicate defined by an E-graph is not a big one, because any E-graph is a single-connected-component graph. Hence, for a magic predicate p, if there are only finite number of I-graphs in $G^*(p)$ whose positive nodes belong to different connected components, p is not a big relation. Because those connected components will become connected in a new program, according to Theorem 1. Assume k is the largest order of those I-graphs whose positive nodes belong to different connected components, then $(G_i^k(P), \cup_{j=0}^{k-1} R^j(P))$ is a new program Q which is equal to the original program but contains no more then two connected components in its $G_i^*(Q)$. Hence, magic predicate p will not produce big relation in Q.

However, if there are infinite number of such I-graph in $G_i^*(p)$, the corresponding magic predicate may form a big relation very easily. Since each connected component forms at lease one cycle in data independently with the other connected components. Let the largest length cycle in each connected component be $c_1, \cdots, c_k$, respectively. If all of cycles c_i are relatively prime, the size of the result relation of the magic predicate is $c_1 c_2 \cdots c_k$. Hence, the magic predicate produce a big one in this case.

From this intuition, we need only to identify and factor those magic predicates p whose $G^*(p)$ contains infinite number of I-graphs which contain more then 2 connected components. In the next section, we propose an algorithm to identify such magic predicates.

4 Arguments Partitioning

In this section, we tackle the optimal splitting problem based on the proposed graph model. From the analysis of previous sections, we know that those arguments which are not connected in finite number of generated graphs should be split. Otherwise, they should be remained in a same predicate. We summarize it as the following definition.

Definition 12. *(c-partition) Given a set of graphs Gen(p). A partition* $c^{(p)} = \{c_1^{(p)}, \cdots, c_k^{(p)}\}$ *of the positive nodes in each graph in Gen(p) is called a c-partition of the magic predicate p if*

(1) For any given positive integer K*, there are* $k > K$ *graphs in Gen(p) in which* $p_s \in c_i^{(p)}$ *and* $p_t \in c_j^{(p)} (i \neq j)$ *are not connected.*

(2) There are at most finite number of graphs in Gen(p) in which $p_s \in c_i^{(p)}$ *and* $p_t \in c_i^{(p)}$ *are not connected.*

$c_i^{(p)}$ *is called a c-block of the c-partition* $c^{(p)}$*. Brackets are used to represent a block of the c-partition.*

c-partition is the optimal splitting schema for magic predicates.

Theorem 2. *Let* $c^{(p)} = \{c_1^{(p)}, \cdots, c_k^{(p)}\}$ *be a c-partition of the magic predicate p. Assume* $p_s \in c_i^{(p)}$ *and* $p_t \in c_i^{(p)}$ $(s \neq t)$ *are two positive nodes in the same block. Then there exist a finite integer, such that* p_s *and* p_t *are connected in all generated graphs of the graph* $G(Q) = (G_i^K(p), \cup_{j=0}^{k-1} R^j(p))$

Proof. According to the definition of the c-partition, there are only finite number of graphs in $Gen(p)$ in which p_s^+ and p_t^+ are not connected. Let K be the largest order of the I-graphs in these graphs. Consider the graph $(G_i^K(p), \cup_{j=0}^{K-1} R^j(p))$. In the graph, p_s^+ and p_t^+ are connected in all E-graphs $R^j(p)(j = 0, \cdots, K-1)$, because those I-graphs in $Gen(p)$ in which p_s^+ and p_t^+ are not connected become connected R-graphs in $G(Q)$. p_s^+ and p_t^+ are connected in all I-graphs of $G(Q)$. □

This theorem says if the arguments in the same c-block are defined as a new predicate, this predicate will not produce a big relation.

Theorem 3. *c-partition is unique for a given Gen(p). That means if* $c^{(p)}$ *and* $d^{(p)}$ *are two c-partitions of Gen(p), then* $c^{(p)} = d^{(p)}$.

Proof. Let $c^{(p)} = \{c_1^{(p)}, \cdots, c_k^{(p)}\}$ and $d^{(p)} = \{d_1^{(p)}, \cdots, d_l^{(p)}\}$ be two different c-partitions of the magic predicate p. Without loss of generality, assume $p_s \in c_1^{(p)}$ and $p_s \in d_1^{(p)}$, but $c_1^{(p)} \neq d_1^{(p)}$. According to the definition of c-partition, there exist an integer k_c, such that all arguments in $c_1^{(p)}$ become connected in all generated graph of $(G_i^{k_c}(p), \cup_{j=0}^{k_c-1} R^j(p))$. Similarly, there exist an integer k_d, such that all arguments in $d_1^{(p)}$ become connected in all generated graphs of $(G_i^{k_d}, \cup_{j=0}^{k_d-1} R^j(p))$. Let $k = max(k_c, k_d)$. Then in all generated graphs $(G_i^k(p), \cup_{j=0}^{k-1} R^j(p))$, the arguments in $c_1^{(p)}$ and $d_1^{(p)}$ become connected, since both contain p_s. By the definition of c-partition, $c_1^{(p)}$ should be as the same as $d_1^{(p)}$. It is a contradiction with the assumption. □

This theorem says that the optimal splitting schema for a specific magic predicate is unique. Hence, we need only an algorithm to construct a c-partition without concerning if it is the best. Unfortunately, we have no an algorithm to construct the c-partition recently. Instead, we propose a concept to approximate the c-partition in the sequel,

Definition 13. *Given a set of graphs Gen(p). A partition* $d[k]^{(p)} = \{d_1^{(p)}, \cdots, d_k^{(p)}\}$ *of the positive nodes in the graphs Gen(p) is called a d[k]-partition (or d-partition when we need not to emphasize the order) of the magic predicate p if there are at most finite number of graphs in Gen(p) which order is less than and equal to k that* $p_s \in d_i^{(p)}$ *and* $p_t \in d_i^{(p)}$ *are not connected.* $d_i^{(p)}$ *is called a d-block of the d[k]-partition Similarly, brackets are used to represent a block of the d-partition.*

Different with c-partition, we do not care if two nodes in different blocks are not connected. We just require that the nodes in the same block should be connected except in some finite number of graphs.

Definition 14. *Let* $c^{(p)}$ *and* $d^{(p)}$ *be two c-partition or d-partition. We say* $c^{(p)} \leq d^{(p)}$ *if for each block* $c_i^{(p)} \in c^{(p)}$*, there exist a block* $d_j^{(p)} \in d^{(p)}$*, such that* $c_i^{(p)} \subseteq d_j^{(p)}$.

From the definition of c-partition and d-partition, we have the following property.

Theorem 4. *Given a set of graphs Gen(p), and two integer* $k \leq l$. *Let* $c^{(p)}$ *be a c-partition of p, and* $d[k]^{(p)}$ *and* $d[l]^{(p)}$ *be d[k]-partition and d[l]-partition of p, respectively. Then*
(1). $d[k]^{(p)} \leq c^{(p)}$
(2). $d[k]^{(p)} \leq d[l]^{(p)}$

This theorem says that we have $d[1]^{(p)} \leq d[2]^{(p)} \leq \cdots \leq c^{(p)}$. Hence, c-partition is the upper bound of all d[k]-partitions. We can use d-partition to approximate the optimal c-partition.

Next, we give an algorithm to evaluate d-partitions.

Definition 15. *Let* $c^{(p)} = \{c_1^{(p)}, \cdots, c_k^{(p)}\}$ *and* $d^{(p)} = \{d_1^{(p)}, \cdots, d_l^{(p)}\}$ *be two partitions of the magic predicate p.* $c^{(p)} \times d^{(p)} = \{c_i^{(p)} \cap d_j^{(p)} | i = 1, \cdots, k; j = 1, \cdots, l\}$, *called product of two partition.*

Obviously, product $c^{(p)} \times d^{(p)}$ is still a partition of p, and $c^{(p)} \times d^{(p)} \leq c^{(p)}$, $c^{(p)} \times d^{(p)} \leq d^{(p)}$.

Algorithm 3 *(Constructing the d[k]-partition for magic predicates)* [1]
Input: $G(P), k$
Output: d[k]-partition of each magic predicate
Method:

(1) If $k = 1$, *construct a partition* $d^{(p)}$ *for p as follows. Let* $R \in Gen(p))$, C *the set of no-magic predicates in R. Construct an initial partition* $d[1]^{(p,R)}$ *for every rule* $R \in Gen(p)$. *Each block consists of all positive nodes of a connected components in C. In this step, we do not consider the existence of magic predicate in the body.* $d[1]^{(p)} = \times_{R \in Gen(p)}(d[1]^{(p,R)})$.
(2) If $k > 1$, *we first transform the program P and then construct the partition.*
  (2.1) Construct a new hypergraph $G(Q) = (G_i^k(P), \cup_{j=0}^{k-1} R^j(P))$
  (2.2) Construct a d[1]-partition for p in the new hypergraph $G(Q)$. *Then, it is the d[k]-partition of p in the hypergraph* $G(P)$.

Example 9. Consider the magic program in Example 3. We construct d-partitions as follows. (1) $d[1]^{(q)} = \{[q_1^+, q_2^+]\}$, and $d[1]^{(p)} = \{[p_1^+], [p_2^+]\}$. (2) By doing graph transformation $(G_i^2(P), R^0(P) \cup R^1(P))$, and constructing d[1]-partition in the new graph, we get $d[2]^{(q)} = \{[q_1^+, q_2^+]\}$, $d[2]^{(p)} = \{[p_1^+, p_2^+]\}$. Please note, although the two arguments of mg_p belong to different connected components in the second rule, they belong to the same block in the d[2]-partition. As the result, we have two single block d-partitions. Since $d[2]^{(p)} \leq d[k]^{(p)} (k \geq 2)$, and $d[2]^{(p)}$ is already a single-block partition, $d[k]^{(p)} = d[2]^{(p)}, (k \geq 2)$. □

The following is a more complex example. It consists of two self-recursive rules.

Example 10. A program is defined as follows:

$$\begin{cases} r_0 : p(X,Y,Z,U,V,W) :- e(X,Y,Z,U,V,W). \\ r_1 : p(X,Y,Z,U,V,W) :- a_1(X,W)a_2(Y,X_1)a_3(Z,Y_1)a_4(U,Z_1) \\ \qquad\qquad a_5(U_1,V_1)a_6(V,W_1)p(X_1,Y_1,Z_1,U_1,V_1,W_1). \\ r_2 : p(X,Y,Z,U,V,W) :- b_1(X,Y,X_1)b_2(Z,Z_1,Y_1,U_1)b_3(U,V_1), \\ \qquad\qquad b_4(V,W_1,W)p(X_1,Y_1,Z_1,U_1,V_1,W_1). \end{cases}$$

The initial partitions for rule r_1 and r_2 are

$$d[1]^{(p,r_1)} = \{[p_1^+, p_6^+][p_2^+, p_1^-][p_3^+, p_2^-][p_4^+, p_3^-][p_5^+, p_6^-][p_4^-, p_5^-]\}$$
$$d[1]^{(p,r_2)} = \{[p_1^+, p_2^+, p_1^-][p_3^+, p_2^-, p_3^-, p_4^-][p_4^+, p_5^-][p_5^+, p_6^+, p_6^-]\}$$

[1] In the following algorithm, we do not concern dangling nodes in I-graphs. They can be processed in the same way in [7].

Hence the d[1]-partition is

$$\begin{aligned} d[1]^{(p)} &= \{[p_1^+, p_6^+][p_2^+][p_3^+][p_4^+][p_5^+]\} \times \{[p_1^+, p_2^+][p_3^+][p_4^+][p_5^+, p_6^+]\} \\ &= \{[p_1^+][p_2^+][p_3^+][p_4^+][p_5^+][p_6^+]\} \end{aligned}$$

That is, it consists of a set of single node blocks.

For d[2]-partition, after generating the 2-th I-graphs, we have their initial partitions as

$$\begin{aligned} d[2]^{(p,r_1r_1)} &= \{[p_1^+, p_6^+][p_2^+, p_5^+][p_3^+, p_1^-][p_4^+, p_2^-][p_3^-, p_6^-][p_4^-, p_5^-]\} \\ d[2]^{(p,r_1r_2)} &= \{[p_1^+, p_6^+][p_2^+, p_3^+, p_1^-][p_4^+, p_2^-, p_3^-, p_4^-][p_5^+, p_5^-, p_6^-]\} \\ d[2]^{(p,r_2r_1)} &= \{[p_1^+, p_2^+, p_5^+, p_6^+][p_3^+, p_1^-, p_2^-, p_3^-][p_4^+, p_6^-][p_4^-, p_5^-]\} \\ d[2]^{(p,r_2)r_2} &= \{[p_1^+, p_2^+, p_3^+, p_1^-, p_2^-, p_3^-, p_4^-, p_5^-][, p_4^+, p_5^+, p_6^+, p_6^-]\} \end{aligned}$$

After deleting negative nodes, and computing products of them, we obtain

$$d[2]^{(p)} = \{[p_1^+][p_2^+][p_3^+][p_4^+][p_5^+][p_6^+]\}$$

Similarly, we can get $d[3]^{(p)} = \{[p_1^+, p_6^+][p_2^+][p_3^+][p_4^+][p_5^+]\}$. The node p_1^+ and p_6^+ become connected in $d[3]^{(p)}$.

□

Theorem 5. *The partition obtained by Algorithm 1 is a d-partition.*

Proof. We first prove the case of k=1. Since the nodes are in a same block should be connected by a hyperedge in its I-graphs, they are connected in all generated I-graphs with higher order. Hence it is d[1]-partition.

We then prove the case of k Comparing the graph $(G_i^1(P), R^0(P))$ with the graph $(G_i^k(P), \cup_{j=0}^{k-1} R^j(P))$, The different part are those graphs with order less than and equal k. The I-graph with an order $\leq k$ in $(G_i^1(P), R^0(P))$ has been transformed to an E-graph in $(G_i^k(P), \cup_{j=0}^{k-1} R^j(P))$. Hence the nodes in a block of the generated d-partition are connected each other in all I-graphs with order great then k. Only in those I-graphs with order $\leq k$, these nodes may belong to different blocks. □

By comparing the two algorithms, it is easy to see that Sippu and Soisalon-Soininen's factoring algorithm is exactly our d[1]-partition, except processing of dangling nodes in I-graphs. In the current version of the d-partition algorithm, we do not concern the processing of dangling nodes. that is, those nodes corresponding to the variables in the magic predicates in the head that do not appear in any EDB predicates in the body of the rule. Hence, we have the following result

Theorem 6. *Let $s^{(p)}$ be the partition for a magic predicate p that obtained by Sippu and Soisalon-Soininen's factoring algorithm 1, and $d^{(p)}$ be a d-partition. Then $s^{(p)} \leq d^{(p)}$.*

It means our algorithm can generate a better splitting schema. It thus solves the "over-splitting" problem partially. In the following, we give out the revised factoring algorithm in our graph model notation. It can also process dangling nodes. In order to capture more information, the a-labeled nodes should be attached with v-labels also.

Algorithm 4 : *(Revised Factoring)*
Input: $G(P), k \geq 1$
Output: $d^{(p)}$
Method:

(1). The initial partition $d^{(p)}$ is a one-block partition. That is, it consists of all arguments of magic predicate p.
(2). Constructing $G(Q) = (G_i^k(P), \cup_{j=0}^{k-1} R^j(P))$ from $G(P)$.
(3). For each I-graph $R \in G(Q)$, which positive nodes are marked by p^+ and negative nodes are marked by q^-, let C be the set of the non-magic subgoals of R, which is partitioned into a set of connected components, say $C_1, \cdots, C_m, m \geq 1$. Replace $d^{(p)}$ by $d^{(p)} \times d^{(p,R)}$, where $d^{(p,R)} = \{\delta_1^{(p,R)}, \cdots, \delta_m^{(p,R)}, \delta^{(p,R)}\}$ is the d[1]-partition of R, $\delta_i^{(p,R)}$ consists exactly of those arguments which appear in some subgoal in C_i. $\delta^{(p,R)} = d^{(p)} - \cup_{j=1}^{m}(\delta_j^{(p,R)})$.
(4). If graph R contains two dangling positive nodes and their corresponding dangling negative nodes (that is, they have the same v-labels) belong to different blocks in $d^{(q)}$, then the $d^{(p)}$ must be replaced by $d^{(p)} \times \bar{d}^{(q)}$, where $\bar{d}^{(q)}$ is obtained from $d^{(q)}$ as follows.
  - *remain those blocks that consists of exactly dangling nodes.*
  - *combine all the other blocks that containing no dangling node.*

This step should be repeated until no change occurs. □

5 Conclusions and Further Research

The concepts of factorization proposed firstly by Sagiv[5], and revised by Sippu and Soisalon-Soininen [7]. Its primary purpose is to guarantee that the magic-set algorithm does not generate big temporary relations. A common assumption is that a predicate defined by a set of EDB predicates which are connected each other has a reasonable size. However, although their strategy can guarantee that the generated magic predicates are defined by single-connected-component rules, it suffers from the "over-splitting" problem. That is, some original magic predicates that do not produce bid relations will be split. In this paper, we focused on the problem: what is the best splitting schema for a recursively-defined magic predicate under the same assumption? We proposed the concept of c-partition as the solution. Unfortunately, we have not found an appropriate algorithm to construct this best splitting schema. As an approximate solution, we proposed d[k]-partition concept, and proved that d[k]-partition is better than d[l]-partition if $k \geq l$. We also proved that all d-partitions are better than Sippu and Soisalon-Soininen's factoring. All of these results are based on a proposed hypergraph model to represent a magic program as well as its naive evaluation procedure.

There are still some open problems. At first, In the current version of the algorithm of constructing d-partition, we generating higer order I-graphs explicitly. From Example 9 and Example 10, we see that it is possible to generate d-partition directly from the pattern of initial partitions. Hence, developing a more efficient algorithm to construct d-partition is still interesting. Next, we know that $d[1]^{(p)} \leq d[2]^{(p)} \leq \cdots \leq c^{(p)}$, where $d[k]^{(p)}$ is d[k]-partition and $c^{(p)}$ is c-partition. That means $c^{(p)}$ is an upper bound of d-partitions. We further hope that the following proposition is true.

Proposition 1. *For a given program P, there exist a finite integer k such that the d[k]-partition is exactly the c-partition.*

Moreover, the existence of an efficient algorithm to construct c-partition directly is also interesting.

Acknowledgment

The authors thank anonymous referees for their helpful comments and suggestions.

References

1. Bancilhon, F., Maier, D., Sagiv, Y., Ullman, J.D. : "Magic Set and Other Strange Ways to Implement Logic Programs". *Proc. ACM SIGACT-SIGMOD-SIGART Symposium on Principles of Database Systems(PODS)*, (1986).
2. Siebes, A. etc.: "Deductive Databases: Challenges, Opportunities and Future Directions (panel discussion)" *Proc. Int'l Workshop Logic in Databases*, pp.225–230 (1996)
3. Ramakrishnan, R., and Ullman, J.D.: "A Survey of Deductive Database Systems", JLP Vol.23, No.2, 1995.
4. Minker,J.: "Logic and Databases: A 20 Year Retrospective" *Proc. Int'l Workshop Logic in Databases*, pp. 3–57 (1996)
5. Sagiv, Y.:"Is There Anything Better Than Magic?", *Proc. North American Conference on Logic Programming*, pp.235–254 (1990).
6. Seki, H: On the Power of Alexander Templates. *Proc. ACM SIGACT-SIGMOD-SIGART Symp. Principles of Database Systems(PODS)*, pp.150-159 (1989)
7. Sippu, S., Soisalon-Soininen, E.: "An Analysis of Magic Sets and Related Optimization Strategies for Logic Queries", *JACM* Vol.43, No.6, pp. 1046–1088, (Nov 1996)
8. Ullman, J.D.: "Principles of Database and Knowledge-Based Systems", Vol. 1 and 2, Computer Science Press, New York, (1989).
9. Ullman, J.D.: "Bottom-up Beats Top-down", *Proc. ACM SIGACT-SIGMOD-SIGART Symp. Principles of Database Systems(PODS)*, pp.140–149 (1990)

An Optimal Parallel Algorithm for the Perfect Dominating Set Problem on Distance-Hereditary Graphs

Sun-Yuan Hsieh[1], Gen-Huey Chen[1], and Chin-Wen Ho[2]

[1] Department of Computer Science and Information Engineering, National Taiwan University, Taipei, Taiwan
[2] Department of Computer Science and Information Engineering, National Central University, Chung-Li, Taiwan

Abstract. In the literature, there are quite a few sequential and parallel algorithms for solving problems on distance-hereditary graphs. With an n-vertex distance-hereditary graph G, we show that the perfect dominating set problem on G can be solved in $O(\log^2 n)$ time using $O(n+m)$ processors on a CREW PRAM.

1 Introduction

A graph is *distance-hereditary* [2,18] if the distance stays the same between any of two vertices in every connected induced subgraph containing both (where the *distance* between two vertices is the length of a shortest path connecting them). Distance-hereditary graphs form a subclass of perfect graphs [11,14,18] that are graphs G in which the maximum clique size equals the chromatic number for every induced subgraph of G [13]. Two well-known classes of graphs, trees and cographs, both belong to distance-hereditary graphs. Properties of distance-hereditary graphs are studied by many researchers [2,5,8,9,10,11,12,14,18,19,20], [21,22] which resulted in sequential or parallel algorithms to solve quite a few interesting graph-theoretical problems on this special class of graphs.

Previous parallel algorithms designing on distance hereditary graphs are briefly summaried as follows. In [10], Dahlhaus presented an algorithm to recognize the distance-hereditary graph in $O(\log^2 n)$ time using $O(n + m)$ processors on a CREW PRAM, where n and m are the number of vertices and edges of a given graph. In [9], all-to-all vertices distance of a distance-hereditary graph were computed. In [19], Hsieh *et al.* presented algorithms to find a minimum weighted connected dominating set and a minimum weighted Steiner tree of a distance-hereditary graph in $O(\log n)$ time using $O(n + m)$ processors on a CRCW PRAM. A minimum connected γ-dominating set and a γ-dominating clique of a distance-hereditary graph can be found in $O(\log n \log\log n)$ time using $O((n + m)/ \log\log n)$ processors on a CRCW PRAM [21]. In [22], Hsieh *et al.* solved several subgraph optimization problems including the maximum independent set problem, the maximum clique problem, the vertex connectivity

Jieh Hsiang, Atsushi Ohori (Eds.): ASIAN'98, LNCS 1538, pp. 113–124, 1998.

problem, the edge connectivity problem, the dominating set problem and the independent dominating set problem in $O(\log^2 n)$ time using $O(n+m)$ processors on a CREW PRAM.

Given a simple graph $G = (V, E)$, a vertex $v \in V$ is said to *dominate* itself and all vertices $u \in V$ adjacent to v. A *perfect dominating set* of G is a subset D of V such that every vertex in $V \setminus D$ is dominated by exactly one vertex of D. The *perfect dominating set problem* is to find a perfect dominating set of G with the minimum cardinality [23]. In this paper, we show the perfect dominating problem can be solved in linear time on a distance-hereditary graph G. We also parallelize the sequential algorithm in $O(\log^2 n)$ time using $O(n+m)$ processors on a CREW PRAM, where n and m are the number of vertices and edges of G. If G is represented by a decomposition tree form, the perfect dominating set problem can be optimally solved in $O(\log n)$ time using $O(n/\log n)$ processors on an EREW PRAM. The complexities of the domination problem and its variants, including (a) the dominating set problem, (b) the independent dominating set problem, (c) the connected dominating set problem, (d) the connected γ-dominating set problem, and (e) the perfect dominating set problem on distance-hereditary graphs are summaried in Table 1.

Problem	Sequential	Parallel		
		Time	Processors	Model
(a)	$O(n+m)$[8]	$O(\log^2 n)$	$O(n+m)$	CREW[22]
(b)	$O(n+m)$[8]	$O(\log^2 n)$	$O(n+m)$	CREW[22]
(c)	$O(n+m)$[5]	$O(\log n)$	$O(n+m)$	CRCW[19]
(d)	$O(n+m)$[5]	$O(\log n \log\log n)$	$O((n+m)/\log\log n)$	CRCW[21]
(e)	$O(n+m)$	$O(\log^2 n)$	$O(n+m)$	CREW

Table 1. The complexities of various domination problems.

The computation model used here is the deterministic parallel random access machine (PRAM) which permits concurrent read and exclusive write (CREW), or exclusive read and write (EREW) in its shared memory. The rest of this paper is organized as follows. In Section 2, we review some previously known properties of distance-hereditary graphs and give some basic definitions. In Section 3, we first show the perfect domination problem can be recursively solved in $O(n+m)$ time on a distance-hereditary graph represented by its binary tree form, called a decomposition tree. We then show that our recursive scheme can be efficiently parallelized using the tree contraction technique. Conclusion is given in Section 4.

2 Preliminaries

This paper considers finite, simple, undirected graphs $G = (V, E)$, where V and E are the vertex and edge sets of G, respectively. Let $n = |V|$ and $m = |E|$. For standard graph-theoretic terminologies and notations, see [13]. Let $G[X]$ denote the subgraph of G induced by $X \subseteq V$. The *union* of two graphs $G_1 = (V_1, E_1)$ and $G_2 = (V_2, E_2)$ is the graph $G = (V_1 \cup V_2, E_1 \cup E_2)$.

The class of distance-hereditary graphs can be defined by the following recursive definition.

Definition 1. [8] (1) A graph consisting of a single vertex v is a *primitive* distance-hereditary graph with the twin set $\{v\}$.
(2) If G_1 and G_2 are distance-hereditary graphs with the twin sets S_1 and S_2, respectively, then the union of G_1 and G_2 is a distance-hereditary graph G with the twin set $S_1 \cup S_2$. In this case, we say G is formed from G_1 and G_2 by *the false twin operation* $\odot$.
(3) If G_1 and G_2 are distance-hereditary graphs with the twin sets S_1 and S_2, respectively, then the graph G obtained from G_1 and G_2 by connecting every vertex of S_1 to all vertices of S_2 is a distance-hereditary graph with the twin set $S_1 \cup S_2$. In this case, we say G is formed from G_1 and G_2 by the *true twin operation* $\otimes$.
(4) If G_1 and G_2 are distance-hereditary graphs with the twin sets S_1 and S_2, respectively, the graph G obtained from G_1 and G_2 by connecting every vertex of S_1 to all vertices of S_2 is a distance-hereditary graph with the twin set S_1. In this case, we say G is formed from G_1 and G_2 by the *attachment operation* $\oplus$.

The above definition implies that a distance-hereditary graph can be represented by a binary tree form, called a *decomposition tree*, which is defined as follows.

Definition 2. (1) The tree consisting of a single vertex labeled v is a decomposition tree of the primitive distance-hereditary graph $G = (\{v\}, \emptyset)$.
(2) Let $\mathcal{D}_1$ and $\mathcal{D}_2$ be the decomposition trees of distance-hereditary graphs G_1 and G_2, respectively.
(a) If G is a distance-hereditary graph formed from G_1 and G_2 by the true twin operation, then a tree $\mathcal{D}$ with the root r represented by $\otimes$ and with the roots of $\mathcal{D}_1$ and $\mathcal{D}_2$ being the two children of r is a decomposition tree of G.
(b) If G is a distance-hereditary graph formed from G_1 and G_2 by the attachment operation, then a tree $\mathcal{D}$ with the root r represented by $\oplus$ and with the root of $\mathcal{D}_1$ (respectively, $\mathcal{D}_2$) being the right (respectively, left) child of r is a decomposition tree of G.
(c) If G is a distance-hereditary graph formed from G_1 and G_2 by the false twin operation, then a tree $\mathcal{D}$ with the root r represented by $\odot$ and with the roots of $\mathcal{D}_1$ and $\mathcal{D}_2$ being the two children of r is a decomposition tree of G.

Figure 1 illustrates a decomposition tree of a distance-hereditary graph.

The sequential and parallel complexities for constructing a decomposition tree are given below.

Lemma 1. *[8,20] A decomposition tree of a distance-hereditary graph can be constructed in sequential $O(n+m)$ time, and in parallel $O(\log^2 n)$ time using $O(n+m)$ processors on a CREW PRAM.*

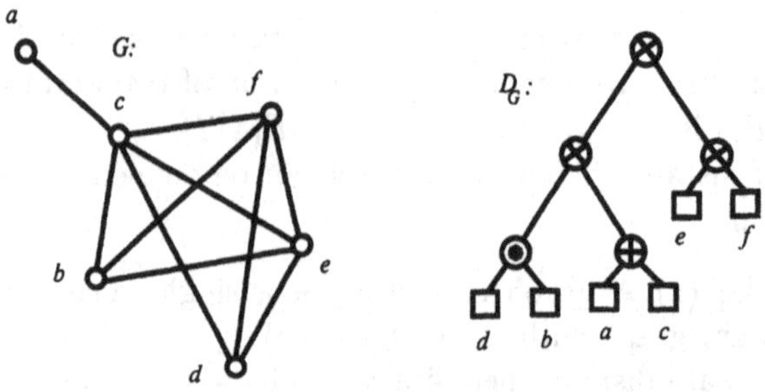

Fig. 1. A distance-hereditary graph G with its decomposition tree D_G.

For a vertex x in a decomposition tree D_G, let $D_G(x)$ be the subtree rooted at x and let G_x be the subgraph of G induced by the leaves of $D_G(x)$. Also let S_x be the twin set of G_x and let $V_x = V(G_x)$. For a node v in a binary tree T, let *child*(v), *sib*(v) and *par*(v) denote the children, the sibling and the parent of v, respectively.

3 The Perfect Dominating Set Problem

3.1 Recursive Formulas

Let $G = (V, E)$ be a distance-hereditary graph and S be its twin set. Let $D(G)$ denote a minimum perfect dominating set of G. An *S-type perfect dominating set* of G is a perfect dominating set of G which contains at least one vertex of S. An *$\overline{S}$-type perfect dominating set* of G is a perfect dominating set of G which contains no vertex of S. A *minimum S-type* (respectively, *$\overline{S}$-type*) *perfect dominating set* of G, denoted by $D_S(G)$ (respectively, $D_{\overline{S}}(G)$), is an S-type (respectively, $\overline{S}$-type) perfect dominating set of G with the minimum cardinality. A perfect dominating set Q of $G[V \setminus S]$ is called H-type if $Q \subseteq (V \setminus S)$ and no vertex in Q is adjacent to any vertex of S. Let $H(G)$ denote an H-type perfect dominating set of $G[V \setminus S]$ with the minimum cardinality.

We say that two disjoint vertex subsets X and Y of V *form a join* in a graph $G = (V, E)$ if every vertex of X is adjacent to all vertices of Y. For k (> 1) sets $S_1, S_2, \ldots, S_k$, the min operator on $\{S_i | \ 1 \le i \le k\}$ is used to select a set S_j such that $|S_j| = min\{|S_i| | \ 1 \le i \le k\}$.

Lemma 2. *Suppose G is a distance-hereditary graph formed from G_1 and G_2 with the twin sets S_1 and S_2, respectively, by the true twin operation and S is the twin set of G. Then,*
(1) $D(G) = min\{D_S(G), D_{\overline{S}}(G)\}$,
(2) $D_S(G) = min\{D_{S_1}(G_1) \cup H(G_2), H(G_1) \cup D_{S_2}(G_2)\}$,
(3) $D_{\overline{S}}(G) = D_{\overline{S_1}}(G_1) \cup D_{\overline{S_2}}(G_2)$,
(4) $H(G) = H(G_1) \cup H(G_2)$.

Proof. We first show (1) holds. By definition, S_1 and S_2 form a join and the twin set S is the union of S_1 and S_2. Besides, all vertices in $V(G_1) \setminus S_1$ are not adjacent to any vertex in $V(G_2) \setminus S_2$. Suppose D is a perfect dominating set of G. Let $D_1 = D \cap V(G_1)$ and $D_2 = D \cap V(G_2)$. There are two cases.
CASE 1. D does not contain any vertex of S. Thus D is an $\overline{S}$-type perfect dominating set.
CASE 2. D contains at least a vertex of S. Obviously, D is an S-type perfect dominating set of G.
On the other hand, if D' is an S-type perfect dominating set of G or an $\overline{S}$-type perfect domionating set of G, then D' is also a perfect dominating set of G. Therefore, (1) holds.

We next show (2) holds. Suppose D is an S-type perfect dominating set of G and let $D_1 = D \cap V(G_1)$ and $D_2 = D \cap V(G_2)$. By the definition of the perfect domination problem, it is impossible that $D \cap S_1 \neq \emptyset$ and $D \cap S_2 \neq \emptyset$. Thus we consider the following two cases.
CASE 1. D does not contain any vertex in S_1. By definition, D contains at least one vertex of S_2. Since no vertex of $V(G_2)$ is adjacent to any vertex of $V(G_1)\setminus S_1$, D_1 is an H-type perfect dominating set of $G[V(G_1) \setminus S_1]$ and D_2 is an S-type perfect dominating set of G_2.
CASE 2. D does not contain any vertex in S_2. By arguments similar to show the above case, D_1 is an S-type perfect dominating set of G_1 and D_2 is an H-type perfect dominating set of $G[V(G_2) \setminus S_2]$.
On the other hand, if
(a) P is an H-type perfect dominating set of $G[V(G_1) \setminus S_1]$ and Q is an S-type perfect dominating set of G_2 or
(b) P is an S-type perfect dominating set of G_1 and Q is an H-type perfect dominating set of $G[V(G_2) \setminus S_2]$,
then $P \cup Q$ is an S-type perfect dominating set of G. From the above discussion, (2) holds. Formulas (3) and (4) can be shown similarly. □

Lemma 3. *Suppose G is a distance-hereditary graph formed from G_1 and G_2 with the twin sets S_1 and S_2, respectively, by the attachment operation and S is the twin set of G. Then,*
(1) $D(G) = min\{D_{\overline{S}}(G), D_S(G)\}$,
(2) $D_S(G) = D_{S_1}(G_1) \cup H(G_2)$,
(3) $D_{\overline{S}}(G) = min\{H(G_1) \cup D_{S_2}(G_2), D_{\overline{S_1}}(G_1) \cup D_{\overline{S_2}}(G_2)\}$,
(4) $H(G) = H(G_1) \cup D_{\overline{S_2}}(G_2)$.

Proof. By definition, $S = S_1$. Besides, S_1 and S_2 form a join in G. Clearly, (1) and (2) hold. We next show (3) holds. Suppose D is an $\overline{S}$-type perfect dominating set of G and let $D_1 = D \cap V(G_1)$ and $D_2 = D \cap V(G_2)$. If $D \cap S_2 = \emptyset$, then $D \cap S_1 = \emptyset$ and $D \cap S_2 = \emptyset$. Therefore, D_1 (respectively, D_2) is an $\overline{S_1}$-type ($\overline{S_2}$-type) perfect dominating set of G_1 (respectively, G_2). If $D \cap S_2 \neq \emptyset$, then D_2 is an S-type perfect dominating set of G_2 and D_1 is clearly an H-type perfect dominating set of $G[V(G_1) \setminus S_1]$. Conversely, if $D' = P \cup Q$ satisfying that either (1) P (respectively, Q) is an $\overline{S_1}$-type (respectively, $\overline{S_2}$-type) perfect dominating sets or (2) P is an H-type perfect dominating set of $G[V(G_1) \setminus S_1]$ and Q is an S-type perfect dominating set of G_2, respectively, then D' is a perfect dominating set of G. Thus (3) holds. Formula (4) can be shown from the structural characteristics of G. □

Since no vertex of G_1 is adjacent to any vertex of G_2 if G is formed from G_1 and G_2 by the false twin operation, the following lemma can be obtained.

Lemma 4. *Suppose that G is a distance-hereditary graph formed from G_1 and G_2 with the twin sets S_1 and S_2, respectively, by the false twin operation, and S is the twin set of G. Then,*
(1) $D(G) = D(G_1) \cup D(G_2)$,
(2) $D_S(G) = min\{D_{S_1}(G_1) \cup D(G_2),\ D(G_1) \cup D_{S_2}(G_2)\}$,
(3) $D_{\overline{S}}(G) = D_{\overline{S_1}}(G_1) \cup D_{\overline{S_2}}(G_2)$,
(4) $H(G) = H(G_1) \cup H(G_2)$.

According to the recursive formulas generated in lemmas 2–4, we have the following theorem.

Theorem 1. *The perfect dominating set problem on a distance-hereditary graph G can be solved in $O(n+m)$ time.*

Proof. By Lemma 1, a decomposition tree D_G for the given distance-hereditary graph G can be constructed in $O(n+m)$ time. By Lemmas 2–4, $D(G)$ can be found using the dynamic programming technique and postorder traversal of $V(D_G) = O(n)$. □

3.2 Parallel Implementation

In this section, we show the sequential algorithm described in the previous section can be optimally parallelized using the binary tree contraction technique described in [1].

The *binary tree contraction technique* can be regarded as a general method for scheduling parallel computations on trees and has been applied to some problems on graphs and to evaluation of binary arithmetic computation trees [1,16]. This technique recursively applies two operations, *prune* and *bypass*, to a given binary tree. *Prune*(u) is an operation which removes a leaf node u from the current tree, and *bypass*(v) is an operation (following a prune operation) that removes a node v with exactly one child w and then lets the parent of v become the new parent of w. Figure 2 shows two procedures *prune*(u) and *bypass*(v).

The algorithm initially numbers the leaves in a left to right order and then repeat the following steps. In each step, *prune* and *bypass* work only on the leaves with odd index and their parents. Hence, these two operations can be performed independently and delete $\lfloor \frac{l}{2} \rfloor$ leaves together with their parents on the binary tree in each step, where l is the number of the current leaves. Therefore, the tree will be reduced to a three-node tree after repeating the steps in $\lceil \log n \rceil$ times, where n is the number of leaves of an input tree.

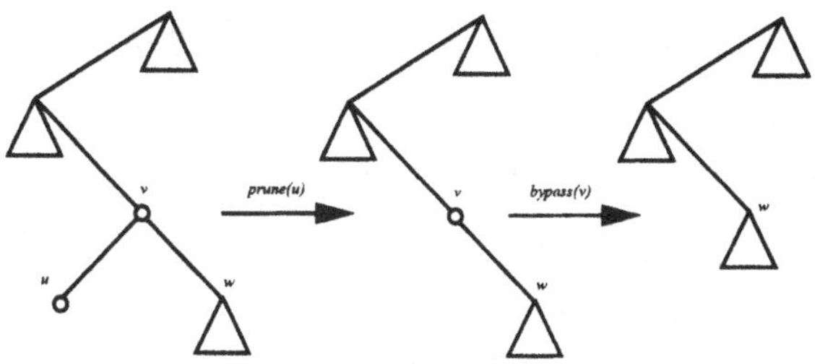

Fig. 2. Two procedures *prune*(u) and *bypass*(v).

Lemma 5. *[1] If the prune operation and bypass operation can be performed by one processor in constant time, the binary tree contraction algorithm can be implemented in $O(\log n)$ time using $O(n/\log n)$ processors on an EREW PRAM, where n is the number of nodes in an input binary tree.*

Definition 3. Let G be a distance-hereditary graph and let D_G be a decomposition tree. The *closed system on D_G* is defined as follows. Initially, each leaf l of D_G (representing a primitive distance-hereditary graph G_l) is associated with $D(G_l)$, $D_{S_l}(G_l)$, $D_{\overline{S_l}}(G_l)$ and $H(G_l)$. There are a constant number of min and $\cup$ operators associated with each internal node ($\otimes$ or $\oplus$ or $\odot$) of D_G. Let $C^u_{j,k} \in \{D(G_u), D_{S_u}(G_u), D_{\overline{S_u}}(G_u), H(G_u)\}$ and $C^w_{j,k} \in \{D(G_w), D_{S_w}(G_w), D_{\overline{S_w}}(G_w), H(G_w)\}$. For each internal node v with the left and right children u and w, respectively, the solutions of $D(G_v)$, $D_{S_v}(G_v)$, $D_{\overline{S_v}}(G_v)$ and $H(G_v)$ can be obtained by the following rule:

$$D(G_v) = min\{C^u_{1,1} \cup C^w_{1,1}, C^u_{1,2} \cup C^w_{1,2}, \ldots, C^u_{1,p} \cup C^w_{1,p}\}, \quad (1)$$
$$D_{S_v}(G_v) = min\{C^u_{2,1} \cup C^w_{2,1}, C^u_{2,2} \cup C^w_{2,2}, \ldots, C^u_{2,q} \cup C^w_{2,q}\}, \quad (2)$$
$$D_{\overline{S_v}}(G_v) = min\{C^u_{3,1} \cup C^w_{3,1}, C^u_{3,2} \cup C^w_{3,3}, \ldots, C^u_{3,r} \cup C^w_{3,r}\}, \quad (3)$$
$$H(G_v) = min\{C^u_{4,1} \cup C^w_{4,1}, C^u_{4,2} \cup C^w_{4,2}, \ldots, C^u_{4,s} \cup C^w_{4,s}\}, \quad (4)$$

where p, q, r, s are all constants. Let γ be the root of D_G. The goal is to find $D(G_\gamma) = D(G)$. □

In the following, we show the binary tree contraction can be used to optimally solve closed system. During the process of tree contraction, we construct four functions associated with each node $v \in V(D_G)$. Let X_1, X_2, X_3 and X_4 are indeterminate that stand for the possibly unknown solutions of $D(G_v), D_{S_v}(G_v), D_{\overline{S_v}}(G_v)$ and $H(G_v)$. The functions associated with v possess the following form:

(i) $F^v_1(X_1, X_2, X_3, X_4) = min\{X_{a_1} \cup \alpha_{a_1}, X_{a_2} \cup \alpha_{a_2}, \ldots, X_{a_p} \cup \alpha_{a_p}\}$;
(ii) $F^v_2(X_1, X_2, X_3, X_4) = min\{X_{b_1} \cup \alpha_{b_1}, X_{b_2} \cup \alpha_{b_2}, \ldots, X_{b_q} \cup \alpha_{b_q}\}$;
(iii) $F^v_3(X_1, X_2, X_3, X_4) = min\{X_{c_1} \cup \alpha_{c_1}, X_{c_2} \cup \alpha_{c_2}, \ldots, X_{c_r} \cup \alpha_{c_r}\}$;
(iv) $F^v_4(X_1, X_2, X_3, X_4) = min\{X_{d_1} \cup \alpha_{d_1}, X_{d_2} \cup \alpha_{d_2}, \ldots, X_{d_s} \cup \alpha_{d_s}\}$,

where $y_j \in \{1,2,3,4\}$, $X_{y_k} \neq X_{y_l}$ and each α_{y_j} is some vertex subset of G_v for all y in $\{a,b,c,d\}$.

We call the above functions *goal functions* and their common form as *closed form*. In the execution of the tree contraction, let v' be the child of $par(v)$ (in the original tree D_G) which is a ancestor of v or v itself. We let the functions F_1^v, F_2^v, F_3^v and F_4^v to represent $D(G_{v'})$,$D_{S_{v'}}(G_{v'})$, $D_{\overline{S_v}}(G_{v'})$ and $H(G_{v'})$, respectively.

During the process of executing the tree contraction, some nodes are removed and the functions of the remaining nodes are adjusted such that the functions remain closed and the following invariant is maintained.

Invariant (A): Let v be an internal node of the current tree such that v holds min and $\cup$ operators which generate the solutions of $D(G_v), D_{S_v}(G_v), D_{\overline{S_v}}(G_v)$, and $H(G_v)$ based on Equations (1)–(4). Let u (respectively, w) be the left (respectively, right) child of v in the current tree whose associated functions are $F_t^u(X_1,X_2,X_3,X_4)$ (respectively, $F_t^w(X_1,X_2,X_3,X_4)$) for all $1 \le t \le 4$. For each $C_{k,l}^u \in \{D(G_u), D_{S_u}(G_u), D_{\overline{S_u}}(G_u), H(G_u)\}$ (respectively, $C_{k,l}^w \in \{D(G_w), D_{S_w}(G_w), D_{\overline{S_w}}(G_w), H(G_w)\}$) in Equations (1)–(4), we replace it with $F_{k,l}^u \in \{F_1^u, F_2^u, F_3^u, F_4^u\}$ (respectively, $F_{k,l}^w \in \{F_1^w, F_2^w, F_3^w, F_4^w\}$) that represent $C_{k,l}^{u'}$ (respectively, $C_{k,l}^{w'}$), where u' (respectively, w') is the child of v in the original D_G which is an ancestor of u (respectively, w) or u (respectively, w) itself. Then,

- $D(G_v) = min\{F_{1,1}^u(D(G_u), D_{S_u}(G_u), D_{\overline{S_u}}(G_u), H(G_u)) \cup F_{1,1}^w(D(G_w), D_{S_w}(G_w), D_{\overline{S_w}}(G_w), H(G_w)), F_{1,2}^u(D(G_u), D_{S_u}(G_u), D_{\overline{S_u}}(G_u), H(G_u)) \cup F_{1,2}^w(D(G_w), D_{S_w}(G_w), D_{\overline{S_w}}(G_w), H(G_w)), \ldots, F_{1,p}^u(D(G_u), D_{S_u}(G_u), D_{\overline{S_u}}(G_u), H(G_u)) \cup F_{1,p}^w(D(G_w), D_{S_w}(G_w), D_{\overline{S_w}}(G_w), H(G_w))\}$.
- $D_{S_v}(G_v) = min\{F_{2,1}^u(D(G_u), D_{S_u}(G_u), D_{\overline{S_u}}(G_u), H(G_u)) \cup F_{2,1}^w(D(G_w), D_{S_w}(G_w), D_{\overline{S_w}}(G_w), H(G_w)), F_{2,2}^u(D(G_u), D_{S_u}(G_u), D_{\overline{S_u}}(G_u), H(G_u)) \cup F_{2,2}^w(D(G_w), D_{S_w}(G_w), D_{\overline{S_w}}(G_w), H(G_w)), \ldots, F_{2,q}^u(D(G_u), D_{S_u}(G_u), D_{\overline{S_u}}(G_u), H(G_u)) \cup F_{2,q}^w(D(G_w), D_{S_w}(G_w), D_{\overline{S_w}}(G_w), H(G_w))\}$.
- $D_{\overline{S_v}}(G_v) = min\{F_{3,1}^u(D(G_u), D_{S_u}(G_u), D_{\overline{S_u}}(G_u), H(G_u)) \cup F_{3,1}^w(D(G_w), D_{S_w}(G_w), D_{\overline{S_w}}(G_w), H(G_w)), F_{3,2}^u(D(G_u), D_{S_u}(G_u), D_{\overline{S_u}}(G_u), H(G_u)) \cup F_{3,2}^w(D(G_w), D_{S_w}(G_w), D_{\overline{S_w}}(G_w), H(G_w)), \ldots, F_{3,r}^u(D(G_u), D_{S_u}(G_u), D_{\overline{S_u}}(G_u), H(G_u)) \cup F_{3,r}^w(D(G_w), D_{S_w}(G_w), D_{\overline{S_w}}(G_w), H(G_w))\}$.
- $H(G_v) = min\{F_{4,1}^u(D(G_u), D_{S_u}(G_u), D_{\overline{S_u}}(G_u), H(G_u)) \cup F_{4,1}^w(D(G_w), D_{S_w}(G_w), D_{\overline{S_w}}(G_w), H(G_w)), F_{4,2}^u(D(G_u), D_{S_u}(G_u), D_{\overline{S_u}}(G_u), H(G_u)) \cup F_{4,2}^w(D(G_w), D_{S_w}(G_w), D_{\overline{S_w}}(G_w), H(G_w)), \ldots, F_{4,s}^u(D(G_u), D_{S_u}(G_u), D_{\overline{S_u}}(G_u), H(G_u)) \cup F_{4,s}^w(D(G_w), D_{S_w}(G_w), D_{\overline{S_w}}(G_w), H(G_w))\}$.

□

Initially, we define the functions for a node $v \in D_G$ to be

(i) $F_1^v(X_1,X_2,X_3,X_4) = min\{X_1 \cup \emptyset\}$,
(ii) $F_2^v(X_1,X_2,X_3,X_4) = min\{X_2 \cup \emptyset\}$,
(iii) $F_3^v(X_1,X_2,X_3,X_4) = min\{X_3 \cup \emptyset\}$,
(iv) $F_4^v(X_1,X_2,X_3,X_4) = min\{X_4 \cup \emptyset\}$.

The Invariant (A) holds trivially in this case. We use the tree contraction algorithm to reduce the given input tree D_G into a three-node tree T' such that solving closed system on D_G is equivalent to solving closed system on T'. We augment the prune and bypass operations by constructing corresponding functions so as to maintain the invariant (A).

In the execution of the tree contraction, assume $prune(u)$ and $bypass(par(u))$ are performed consecutively. Let $par(u) = v$ and $sib(u) = w$. Assume u is the left child of v (the case of u being the right child can be similarly computed). Note that u and v are removed; hence, their contributions to the four target solutions computed at node $par(v)$ have to be incorporated into the functions associated with w. Assume, without loss of generality, that v contains the operators min and $\cup$ which perform Equations (1)–(4). The four target solutions associated with node v is given by

- $D(G_v) = min\{F^u_{1,1}(D(G_u), D_{S_u}(G_u), D_{\overline{S_u}}(G_u), H(G_u)) \cup F^w_{1,1}(X_1, X_2, X_3, X_4), F^u_{1,2}(D(G_u), D_{S_u}(G_u), D_{\overline{S_u}}(G_u), H(G_u)) \cup F^w_{1,2}(X_1, X_2, X_3, X_4), \ldots, F^u_{1,p}(D(G_u), D_{S_u}(G_u), D_{\overline{S_u}}(G_u), H(G_u)) \cup F^w_{1,p}(X_1, X_2, X_3, X_4))\} = min\{Q_1 \cup min\{X_{a_1} \cup \alpha_{a_1}, X_{a_2} \cup \alpha_{a_2}, \ldots, X_{a_r} \cup \alpha_{a_r}\}, Q_2 \cup min\{X_{b_1} \cup \alpha_{b_1}, X_{b_2} \cup \alpha_{b_2}, \ldots, X_{b_s} \cup \alpha_{b_s}\}, \ldots, Q_p \cup min\{X_{c_1} \cup \alpha_{c_1}, X_{c_2} \cup \alpha_{c_2}, \ldots, X_{c_t} \cup \alpha_{c_t}\}\} = min\{min\{X_{a_1} \cup (Q_1 \cup \alpha_{a_1}), X_{a_2} \cup (Q_1 \cup \alpha_{a_2}), \ldots, X_{a_r} \cup (Q_1 \cup \alpha_{a_r})\}, min\{X_{b_1} \cup (Q_2 \cup \alpha_{b_1}), X_{b_2} \cup (Q_2 \cup \alpha_{b_2}), \ldots, X_{b_s} \cup (Q_2 \cup \alpha_{b_s})\}, \ldots, min\{X_{c_1} \cup (Q_p \cup \alpha_{c_1}), X_{c_2} \cup (Q_p \cup \alpha_{c_2}), \ldots, X_{c_t} \cup (Q_p \cup \alpha_{c_t})\},\}$ (distributive law)
  $= min\{min\{X_{a_1} \cup \alpha'_{a_1}, X_{a_2} \cup \alpha'_{a_2}, \ldots, X_{a_r} \cup \alpha'_{a_r}\}, min\{X_{b_1} \cup \alpha'_{b_1}, X_{b_2} \cup \alpha'_{b_2}, \ldots, X_{b_s} \cup \alpha'_{b_s}\}, \ldots, min\{X_{c_1} \cup \alpha'_{c_1}, X_{c_2} \cup \alpha'_{c_2}, \ldots, X_{c_t} \cup \alpha'_{c_t}\},\} = min\{X_{a_1} \cup \alpha'_{a_1}, X_{a_2} \cup \alpha'_{a_2}, \ldots, X_{a_r} \cup \alpha'_{a_r}, X_{b_1} \cup \alpha'_{b_1}, X_{b_2} \cup \alpha'_{b_2}, \ldots, X_{b_s} \cup \alpha'_{b_s}, \ldots, X_{c_1} \cup \alpha'_{c_1}, X_{c_2} \cup \alpha'_{c_2}, \ldots, X_{c_t} \cup \alpha'_{c_t}\}$ (associative law)
  $= min\{X_{d_1} \cup ((\cup_j \{\alpha'_{a_j} \mid a_j = d_1\}) \cup (\cup_j \{\alpha'_{b_j} \mid b_j = d_1\}) \ldots, (\cup_j \{\alpha'_{c_j} \mid c_j = d_1\})), X_{d_2} \cup ((\cup_j \{\alpha'_{a_j} \mid a_j = d_2\}) \cup (\cup_j \{\alpha'_{b_j} \mid b_j = d_2\}) \ldots, (\cup_j \{\alpha'_{c_j} \mid c_j = d_2\})), \ldots X_{d_k} \cup ((\cup_j \{\alpha'_{a_j} \mid a_j = d_k\}) \cup (\cup_j \{\alpha'_{b_j} \mid b_j = d_k\}) \ldots, (\cup_j \{\alpha'_{c_j} \mid c_j = d_k\}))\}$ (communicative and distributive laws)
  $= min\{X_{d_1} \cup \beta_{d_1}, X_{d_2} \cup \beta_{d_2}, \ldots, X_{d_k} \cup \beta_{d_k}\}$ (associative law), where X_i, $1 \leq i \leq 4$, are unknown target solutions of node w, assuming that the invariant (A) holds before the $prune(u)$ and $bypass(v)$ operation.
- $D_{S_v}(G_v) = min\{F^u_{2,1}(D(G_u), D_{S_u}(G_u), D_{\overline{S_u}}(G_u), H(G_u)) \cup F^w_{2,1}(X_1, X_2, X_3, X_4), F^u_{2,2}(D(G_u), D_{S_u}(G_u), D_{\overline{S_u}}(G_u), H(G_u)) \cup F^w_{2,2}(X_1, X_2, X_3, X_4), \ldots, F^u_{2,q}(D(G_u), D_{S_u}(G_u), D_{\overline{S_u}}(G_u), H(G_u)) \cup F^w_{2,q}(X_1, X_2, X_3, X_4\} = min\{X_{e_1} \cup \beta_{e_1}, X_{e_2} \cup \beta_{e_2}, \ldots, X_{e_l} \cup \beta_{e_l}\}$.
- $D_{\overline{S_v}}(G_v) = min\{F^u_{3,1}(D(G_u), D_{S_u}(G_u), D_{\overline{S_u}}(G_u), H(G_u)) \cup F^w_{3,1}(X_1, X_2, X_3, X_4), F^u_{3,2}(D(G_u), D_{S_u}(G_u), D_{\overline{S_u}}(G_u), H(G_u)) \cup F^w_{3,2}(X_1, X_2, X_3, X_4), \ldots, F^u_{3,r}(D(G_u), D_{S_u}(G_u), D_{\overline{S_u}}(G_u), H(G_u)) \cup F^w_{3,r}(X_1, X_2, X_3, X_4)\} = min\{X_{f_1} \cup \beta_{f_1}, X_{f_2} \cup \beta_{f_2}, \ldots, X_{f_y} \cup \beta_{f_y}\}$.
- $H(G_v) = min\{F^u_{4,1}(D(G_u), D_{S_u}(G_u), D_{\overline{S_u}}(G_u), H(G_u)) \cup F^w_{4,1}(X_1, X_2, X_3, X_4), F^u_{4,2}(D(G_u), D_{S_u}(G_u), D_{\overline{S_u}}(G_u), H(G_u)) \cup F^w_{4,2}(X_1, X_2, X_3, X_4), \ldots, F^u_{4,s}(D(G_u), D_{S_u}(G_u), D_{\overline{S_u}}(G_u), H(G_u)) \cup F^w_{4,s}(X_1, X_2, X_3, X_4)\} = min\{X_{g_1} \cup \beta_{g_1}, X_{g_2} \cup \beta_{g_2}, \ldots, X_{g_z} \cup \beta_{g_z}\}$.

Hence, the contribution of four target solutions to the node $par(v)$ is given by

(i) $F_1^w(X_1, X_2, X_3, X_4) = F_1^v(D(G_v), D_{S_v}(G_v), D_{\overline{S_v}}(G_v), H(G_v)) = min\{X_{h_1} \cup \alpha_{h_1}, X_{h_2} \cup \alpha_{h_2}, \ldots, X_{h_k} \cup \alpha_{h_k}\}$ (the process of simplifying is similar to simplify the function corresponding to $P_\emptyset^i(G_v)$ describe in last paragraph). The following functions can be further simplified as closed form similar to (i).
(ii) $F_2^w(X_1, X_2, X_3, X_4) = F_2^v(D(G_v), D_{S_v}(G_v), D_{\overline{S_v}}(G_v), H(G_v))$.
(iii) $F_3^w(X_1, X_2, X_3, X_4) = F_3^v(D(G_v), D_{S_v}(G_v), D_{\overline{S_v}}(G_v), H(G_v))$.
(iv) $F_4^w(X_1, X_2, X_3, X_4) = F_4^v(D(G_v), D_{S_v}(G_v), D_{\overline{S_v}}(G_v), H(G_v))$.

The invariant (A) is then clearly maintained.

Our algorithm for solving closed system consists of an initial assignment of four functions to each node of D_G, and an application of the tree contraction algorithm such that *prune*(u) and *bypass*$(par(u))$ operations are augmented as specified in the previous paragraph. Once the tree contraction algorithm terminates, we have a three-node tree T' with a root γ holding a constant number of *min* and $\cup$ operators and two leaves u and v. According to the functions associated with u and v, $D(G_u), D_{S_u}(G_u), D_{\overline{S_u}}(G_u), H(G_u)$ and $D(G_v), D_{S_v}(G_v), D_{\overline{S_v}}(G_v), H(G_v)$ can be obtained. According to the operators associated with γ, a solution $D(G_r) = D(G)$ can be found.

We now discuss the complexities of the above implementation.

Lemma 6. *The functions described in executing prune(u) and bypass$(par(u))$ can be constructed in $O(1)$ time using one processor.*

Proof. By the definition of the closed form and the process of the goal function composition. □

By Lemmas 5 and 6, we have the following result.

Lemma 7. *The closed system can be implemented in $O(\log n)$ time using $O(n/\log n)$ processors on an EREW PRAM.*

Since solving the perfect dominating set problem using a given decomposition tree can be reduced to the problem of solving the closed system, we have the following theorem.

Theorem 2. *Given a decomposition tree of a distance-hereditary graph G, the perfect dominating set problem on G can be solved in $O(\log n)$ time using $O(n/\log n)$ processors on an EREW PRAM.*

4 Conclusion

In this paper, we have solved the perfect domination problem on distance-hereditary graphs in $O(\log^2 n)$ time using $O(n + m)$ processors on a CREW PRAM. It leads to the result that the perfect domination problem on distance-hereditary graphs belongs to NC. The bottleneck of our algorithm is the decomposition tree construction. If such a tree can be optimally constructed on an EREW PRAM, the complexities of our algorithm can be further reduced to $O(\log n)$ time using $O(n/\log n)$ processors on an EREW PRAM.

The technique we utilize is the binary tree contraction technique. Previous parallel algorithm by using the tree contraction to solve a subgraph optimization problem consists of two phases. The first phase is to compute the value used to measure the weight of a target subgraph. The second phase is to actually find a target subgraph according to the information gathered in the first phase. In this paper, we develop a one-phase tree contraction scheme based on the properties of the tree contraction and the given problem. We hope the technique can be applied to more subgraph optimization problems on those graphs which are tree-representable.

References

1. K. Abrahamson, N. Dadoun, D. G. Kirkpatrick, and T. Przytycka, A simple parallel tree contraction algorithm. *Journal of Algorithms.*, 10, pp. 287-302, 1989.
2. H. J. Bandelt and H. M. Mulder. Distance-hereditary graphs. *Journal of Combinatorial Theory Series B*, 41(1):182-208, Augest 1989.
3. C. Berge. *Graphs and hypergraphs.* North-Holland, Amsterdam, 1973.
4. N. Biggs. Perfect codes in graphs. *J. Combin. Theory Ser. B*, 15:289-296, 1973.
5. A. Brandstädt and F. F. Dragan, A linear time algorithm for connected γ-domination and Steiner tree on distance-hereditary graphs, *Networks*, 31:177-182, 1998.
6. M. S. Chang and Y. C. Liu. Polynomial algorithm for the weighted perfect domination problems on chordal graphs and split graphs. *Information Processing Letters*, 48:205-210, 1993.
7. G. J. Chang, C. Pandu Rangan, and S. R. Coorg. Weighted independent perfect domination on cocomparability graphs. *Discrete Applied Mathematics*, 63:215-222, 1995.
8. M. S. Chang, S. Y. Hsieh, and G. H. Chen. Dynamic Programming on Distance-Hereditary Graphs. Proceedings of 7th International Symposium on Algorithms and Computation, ISAAC'97, LNCS 1350, pp. 344-353.
9. E. Dahlhaus, "Optimal (parallel) algorithms for the all-to-all vertices distance problem for certain graph classes," Lecture notes in computer science 726, pp. 60-69.
10. E. Dahlhaus. Efficient parallel recognition algorithms of cographs and distance-hereditary graphs. *Discrete applied mathematics*, 57(1):29-44, February 1995.
11. A. D'atri and M. Moscarini. Distance-hereditary graphs, steiner trees, and connected domination. *SIAM Journal on Computing*, 17(3):521-538, June, 1988.
12. F. F. Dragan, Dominating cliques in distance-hereditary graphs, *Algorithm Theory-SWAT'94 "4th Scandinavian Workshop on Algorithm Theory, LNCS 824, Springer, Berlin*, pp. 370-381, 1994.
13. M. C. Golumbic. *Algorithmic graph theory and perfect graphs*, Academic press, New York, 1980.
14. P. L. Hammer and F. Maffray. Complete separable graphs. *Discrete applied mathematics*, 27(1):85-99, May 1990.
15. X. He. Efficient parallel algorithms for solving some tree problems. *Proc. 24th Allerton Conference on Communication, Control, and Computing*, 777-786, 1986.
16. X. He. Efficient parallel algorithms for series-parallel graphs. *Journal of Algorithms*, 12:409-430, 1991.
17. X. He and Y. Yesha. Binary tree algebraic computation and parallel algorithms for simple graphs. *Journal of Algorithms*, 9:92-113, 1988.

18. E. Howorka. A characterization of distance-hereditary graphs. *Quarterly Journal of Mathematics (Oxford)*, 28(2):417-420. 1977.
19. S.-y. Hsieh, C. W. Ho, T.-s. Hsu, M. T. Ko, and G. H. Chen. Efficient parallel algorithms on distance-hereditary graphs. *Parallel Processing Letters*, to appear. A preliminary version of this paper is in *Proceedings of the International Conference on Parallel Processing*, pp. 20–23, 1997.
20. S.-y. Hsieh, Parallel decomposition of Distance-Hereditary Graphs with its application. Manuscript, 1998.
21. S.-y. Hsieh, C. W. Ho, T.-s. Hsu, M. T. Ko, and G. H. Chen. A new simple tree contraction scheme and its application on distance-hereditary graphs. *Proceedings of Irregular'98*, LNCS, Springer-Verlag, to appear.
22. S.-y. Hsieh, C. W. Ho, T.-s. Hsu, M. T. Ko, and G. H. Chen. Characterization of efficiently solvable problems on distance-hereditary Graphs. *Proceedings of 8th International Symposium on Algorithms and Computation, ISAAC'98*, Springer-Verlag, to appear.
23. M. Livingston and Q. F. Stout. Perfect dominating sets. *Congr. Numer.*, 79:187-203, 1990.
24. Falk Nicolai. Hamiltonian problems on distance-hereditary graphs. Technique report, Gerhard-Mercator University, Germany, 1994.

Taxonomy and Expressiveness of Preemption: A Syntactic Approach *

Sophie Pinchinat[1], Éric Rutten[1], and R.K. Shyamasundar[2]

[1] EP-ATR Group, IRISA, F-35042, Rennes, France,
{pinchina, rutten}@irisa.fr
[2] Computer Science Group, Tata Institute of Fundamental Research, Bombay 400 005, India, shyam@tcs.tifr.res.in

Abstract. We propose a taxonomy of preemptive (*suspensive* and *abortive*) operators capturing the intuition of such operators that exist in the various synchronous languages. Some of the main contributions of the paper are: a precise notion of *preemption* is established at a structural level ; we show that the class of *suspensive* operators is strictly more expressive than *abortive operators*, and we show that *suspension* is primitive while *abortion* is not.
The proof techniques relies on a syntactic approach, based on SOS-specification formats, to categorize the different preemption features ; also an equivalence criterion between operators specifications is proposed to provide us with expressive power measurement.

1 Introduction

Process preemption is the notion of controlling the life and death of an activity. Various forms of preemption such as *interrupts* have been in use in the context of operating systems for a long time. Well-known occurrences are suspension and abortion of processes (also known as, in the case of the UNIX operating system, respectively `^z` and `^c`). However, it is only recently that the vital role of preemption operators is coming to light in the context of synchronous programming languages. Berry [Ber93] has argued for the need and importance of *process preemption* operators for programming reactive and real-time systems that have inherently a time-dependent model. A variety of preemption operators can be seen in synchronous languages or formalisms such as ARGOS, ESTEREL, LUSTRE, STATECHARTS, SIGNAL etc, [pro91] (Some of these operators are described in Example 2 of this paper).

In spite of the wide usage of the notion of preemption, there have been no attempts in characterizing these operators at structural level or transformational level. The advantage of such a characterization is that it is possible to look at existing notions like expressiveness or completeness in the context of synchronous calculi such as Meije [Sim85] and SCCS [Mil83], this time, in the context of

* Work supported by IFCPAR (Indo-French Center for the Promotion of Advanced Research), New Delhi.

Jieh Hsiang, Atsushi Ohori (Eds.): ASIAN'98, LNCS 1538, pp. 125–141, 1998.

preemption. Such a characterization will also make it possible to characterize classes of operators with *good behaviors* based on syntactic formats such as *GSOS* [BIM95], *tyft* [GV92] etc. Furthermore such frameworks would also lead to the study of canonical models from the operational models.

In this paper, we provide a characterization of preemption operators within such a spirit. First, we propose an SOS-specification of preemption operators through a sub-fragment of the *tyft* format [GV92] called the *xyfg/xyfz* format. This framework leads to the natural categorization of the *suspensive* and *abortive* operators capturing the intuition of such operators that exist in the various synchronous languages. Some of the main contributions of the paper are:

- A precise notion of *preemption* at a structural level is established.
- It is shown that the class of *suspensive* operators is strictly more expressive than *abortive operators*, and
- From the class of operators we consider (see Section 2.2) it is further established that *suspension* is primitive while *abortion* is not.

The paper is organized as follows : Section 2.1 introduces the framework of SOS-specifications for describing operators and proposes a criterion of equivalence between operators (and specifications). Classes of preemption operators will be described in so-called *xyfg/xyfz* specifications, introduced in Section 2.2. In Section 3, the taxonomy of preemption operators is presented ; it uses syntactic criteria over the specification rules of the operators. Finally, Section 4 answers the expressiveness issues and Section 5 concludes this work.

2 Preliminary Notions

2.1 General Notions

Notation: We use set V to denote a denumerable set of *term variables*, whose typical elements denoted by $v, v_1, v_2...$ and X to denote a denumerable set of meta-variables, whose typical elements are denoted by $x, x_1, ..., y, y_1....$

The distinction between meta-variables and variables is made for pedagogical purposes: meta-variables like $x, x_1, ...$ will be used to describe clauses of the operational rules schemes, whereas variables $v, v_1, ...$ will be used to refer to contexts as open terms of the language.

Definition 1. (Signature) *A* signature *is a pair* $\Sigma = (F, \nabla)$ *where* $F = \{f, g, ...\}$ *is a denumerable set of* function names *disjoint from* $V \cup X$, *and* $\nabla : F \to \mathbb{N}$ *is the* arity function. *We write* $(f, n) \in \Sigma$ *to express that* $f \in F$ *and* $\nabla(f) = n$.

$T(\Sigma \cup V \cup X)$ *will denote the set of terms over* Σ *that might possibly contain variables in* $V \cup X$, *and will be ranged over by* $T, T_1, T_2, ..., S, U, ...$ *For* $T \in T(\Sigma \cup V \cup X)$, $Var(T) \subseteq V \cup X$ *denotes the set of variables occurring in* T. *If* $Var(T) \neq \emptyset$ *then* T *is called an* open term (over Σ)*; otherwise it is a* closed term. $T(\Sigma)$ *will denote the set of terms over* Σ, *with typical elements* $t, t', t_1, t_2, \cdots$.

The height *of a term* $T \in T(\Sigma \cup V \cup X)$, *written* $|T|$, *is defined by induction over the structure of* T *by* $|T|$ *is* 1 *if* T *is a variable, otherwise* T *is some* $f(T_1, ..., T_n)$, *then* $|T|$ *is* $1 + max\{0, |T_1|, ..., |T_n|\}$

A substitution *is any partial function* $V \cup X \rightarrow T(\Sigma \cup V \cup X)$. *Typical elements for substitutions will be written* $\sigma, \sigma', \rho, \xi, ...$ *Write* $Dom(\sigma)$ *the domain of partial functions* σ, *and* $v\sigma$ *the image of variable* v *by* σ.

Any substitution σ *can be extended to the domain of open terms over* Σ *by taking* $T\sigma$ *as the term obtained by replacing in* T *any* $v \in Dom(\sigma)$ *by* $v\sigma$.

Classically, given two open terms T, T' *over* Σ *and* $v \in Var(T)$, $T[T'/v]$ *is the term* $T\sigma$ *where* $Dom(\sigma) = \{v\}$ *and* $v\sigma = T'$.

Example 1. Consider signature Σ_0 composed of $\{(nil, 0), (a\supset, 1), (a>, 1), (a., 1), (b., 1), (>, 2), (||, 2), (\times, 2), (+, 2)\}$. Using infix notations for operators, examples of terms are $a.(nil), || \ (a.(nil), b.(nil)), a > (a.(nil)) \in T(\Sigma_0)$, and $a \supset (v), > (v_1, v_2) \in T(\Sigma_0 \cup V)$.

Classically (see [Plo81], [GV92]), a formal system is associated to the signature in order to define the operational semantics of closed terms. This system is composed of deductive rules that are used to prove (labeled) transitions between terms. Such a set of rules together with the signature, is called an *SOS specification.*

Throughout the paper, we assume a denumerable set of action names, A disjoint from $\Sigma \cup V \cup X$.

Definition 2. (SOS specification) *An* SOS specification *(over* A*) is a tuple* $P = (\Sigma, R)$ *where* Σ *is a signature and* R *is a set of rules of the form*

$$\frac{\{T_i \xrightarrow{a_i} T_i' \mid i \in I\}}{T \xrightarrow{a} T'} \qquad \text{where } I \text{ is finite, } T_i, T_i', T, T' \in T(\Sigma \cup X),\ a, a_i \in A.$$

Expressions $T_i \xrightarrow{a_i} T_i'$ *are called the* premises *of the rule.*

A specification (Σ, R) *is* elementary *if* $\nabla_\Sigma(f) = 0$ *for all* $f \in F_\Sigma$.

We assume the reader is familiar with the notion of *proof* of a transition in the formal system given by the set of rules. However, a formal definition is given in the Appendix. We write $\vdash_{\mathcal{P}}^{P} t \xrightarrow{a} t'$ if $\mathcal{P}$ is a proof of $t \xrightarrow{a} t'$ (in P), and $\vdash^{P} t \xrightarrow{a} t'$ if there is some proof of this transition.

We say that two specifications P_1 and P_2 *agree* if for all $f \in \Sigma_1 \cap \Sigma_2$, $\nabla_{\Sigma_1}(f) = \nabla_{\Sigma_2}(f)$. Given two agreeing specifications P_1 and we define the *union* of P_1 and P_2, $P_1 \oplus P_2$ by $(\Sigma_1 \cup \Sigma_2, R_1 \cup R_2)$, where $\Sigma_1 \cup \Sigma_2$ is standardly defined. Two specifications P_1 and P_2 are *disjoint* if $\Sigma_1 \cap \Sigma_2 = \emptyset$ (and therefore $R_1 \cap R_2 = \emptyset$).

Example 2. **(Typical SOS Rules)** Using Σ_0 defined above, SOS-specification P_0 over $\{a, b\}$ is given below; P_0 is based on several operators well known from the literature (with prefix notation instead of usual infix one).

Pure Esterel ("a suspend" operator)

$$\frac{}{a\supset(x_1) \xrightarrow{a} a\supset(x_1)} \quad (1) \qquad \frac{x_1 \xrightarrow{b} y_1}{a\supset(x_1) \xrightarrow{b} a\supset(y_1)} \quad (2)$$

Pure Esterel ("do watching a" operator)

$$\frac{x_1 \xrightarrow{a} y_1}{a{>}(x_1) \xrightarrow{a} nil} \quad (3) \qquad \frac{x_1 \xrightarrow{b} y_1}{a{>}(x_1) \xrightarrow{b} a{>}(y_1)} \quad (4)$$

Let $\mu \in \{a, b\}$,
Operator ∇ of [SP95]

$$\frac{x_2 \xrightarrow{\mu} y_2}{\nabla(x_1, x_2) \xrightarrow{\mu} y_2} \quad (5) \qquad \frac{x_1 \xrightarrow{\mu} y_1}{\nabla(x_1, x_2) \xrightarrow{\mu} \nabla(y_1, x_2)} \quad (6)$$

SCCS, Meije,...

$$\frac{}{\mu.(x_1) \xrightarrow{\mu} x_1} \quad (7) \qquad \frac{x_1 \xrightarrow{\mu} y_1}{+(x_1, x_2) \xrightarrow{\mu} y_1} \quad (8)$$

$$\frac{x_2 \xrightarrow{\mu} y_2}{+(x_1, x_2) \xrightarrow{\mu} y_2} \quad (9) \qquad \frac{x_1 \xrightarrow{\mu} y_1}{\|\,(x_1, x_2) \xrightarrow{\mu} \|\,(y_1, x_2)} \quad (10)$$

$$\frac{x_2 \xrightarrow{\mu} y_2}{\|\,(x_1, x_2) \xrightarrow{\mu} \|\,(x_1, y_2)} \quad (11) \qquad \frac{x_1 \xrightarrow{\mu} y_1 \;\; x_2 \xrightarrow{\mu} y_2}{\|\,(x_1, x_2) \xrightarrow{\mu} \|\,(y_1, y_2)} \quad (12)$$

$$\frac{x_1 \xrightarrow{\mu} y_1 \;\; x_2 \xrightarrow{\mu} y_2}{\times(x_1, x_2) \xrightarrow{\mu} \times(y_1, y_2)} \quad (13)$$

SOS-specifications naturally describe a set of programs defined by their operational semantics, i.e. their corresponding state-transitions graphs also called *Labeled Transition Systems.*

Definition 3. (Labeled Transition System, $TS(P)$, executions, traces)
A labeled transition system (over A) *is a structure* $S = (Q, \rightarrow)$ *where* Q *is a set of states, and* $\rightarrow \subseteq Q \times A \times Q$ *is the transition relation.* $(q, a, q') \in \rightarrow$ *will be written* $q \xrightarrow{a} q'$.

Given $q \in Q$, *we write* $Ex_S(q)$ *for the set of all* executions starting from *q and defined by all the maximal (finite or infinite) sequences of the form* $q =$

$q_0 \xrightarrow{a_0} q_1 \xrightarrow{a_1} q_2 \ldots$ *A* trace starting from q *is a word* $a_0 a_1 \ldots$ *s.t. there exists an execution from* q *of the form* $q = q_0 \xrightarrow{a_0} q_1 \xrightarrow{a_1} q_2 \ldots$ *We write* $Tr(q)$ *for the set of traces starting from* q.

Given a specification $P = (\Sigma, R)$ *(over* A*), we write* $TS(P)$ *for the labeled transition system over* A *associated to* P *and defined by* $TS(P) = (T(\Sigma), \rightarrow)$ *where* $t \xrightarrow{a} t'$ *whenever* $\vdash^P t \xrightarrow{a} t'$.

Definition 4. (Bisimulation over labeled transition systems) [Par81,Mil89] *Let* $S_1 = (Q_1, \rightarrow_1)$ *and* $S_2 = (Q_2, \rightarrow_2)$ *be two labeled transition systems over* A. *A* bisimulation *relation between* S_1 *and* S_2 *is a total*[1] *relation* $\varrho \subseteq Q_1 \times Q_2$ *s.t.* $(q_1, q_2) \in \varrho$ *implies for all* $q_1 \xrightarrow{a}_1 q_1'$ *there exists* $q_2 \xrightarrow{a}_2 q_2'$ *with* $(q_1', q_2') \in \varrho$, *and vice versa, for all* $q_2 \xrightarrow{a}_2 q_2'$ *there exists* $q_1 \xrightarrow{a}_1 q_1'$ *with* $(q_1', q_2') \in \varrho$.

Since bisimulation relations between S_1 *and* S_2 *are closed under arbitrary unions, there exists a greatest bisimulation, which we write* $\sim_{S_1,S_2}$. *We simply write* $\sim_S$ *whenever* $S_1 = S_2 = S$ *and we omit the subscripts when they are clear from the context.*

Specifications also describe program combinators, called *contexts* here; this is formalized in the following.

Definition 5. (Contexts) *Given a specification* $P = (\Sigma, R)$, *a* Σ-context *is an open term* $T \in T(\Sigma \cup V)$ *where all variables occurring in* T *are distinct. We write* $C(\Sigma)$ *the set of* Σ*-contexts, and* $C^h(\Sigma)$ *the set of contexts of height* $h \in \mathbb{N}$. *We call an* n-hole context *a context with* n *variables. Zero-hole contexts are closed terms; they represent programs.*

Among Σ*-contexts, those of the form* $f(v_1, \ldots, v_n)$, *with* $n > 0$ *and* $v_1, \ldots, v_n \in V$, *will be called* Σ-operators, *and we shall write* $O(\Sigma) \subseteq C(\Sigma)$ *for the set of* Σ*-operators.*

Clearly, any mapping ϕ *from* $O(\Sigma)$ *to some domain of terms (maybe based on another signature* Σ'*), can be structurally extended to* $C(\Sigma)$ *according to* $\phi(v) = v$ *for all* $v \in V$ *and* $\phi(f(T_1, \ldots, T_n)) = \phi(f(v_1, \ldots, v_n))[\phi(T_i)/v_i]$.

In order to compare the expressive power of operators, we need a notion of operational equivalence between specifications. To do so, we introduce a notion of *open bisimulation* over *contexts* which coincides with the standard notion of bisimulation over closed terms (see Definition 4) when equivalent contexts are applied to bisimilar programs. The "programs" will be given separately by an elementary specification (0-arity operators) describing their operational semantics.

Definition 6. (Open bisimulation) *Let* $P_i = (\Sigma_i, R_i)$ $(i = 1, 2)$ *be two specifications. An* open bisimulation *between* P_1 *and* P_2 *is a total relation* $\chi \subseteq C(\Sigma_1) \times C(\Sigma_2)$ *s.t. for any elementary specification* $B = (\Sigma, R)$ *(disjoint from* P_1 *and* P_2*)*

[1] $\forall q_1 \in Q_1, \exists q_2 \in Q_2, (q_1, q_2) \in \varrho$ and vice versa.

the relation $\{(T_1\sigma, T_2\sigma') \mid (T_1, T_2) \in \chi, \sigma, \sigma' : V \to T(\Sigma)$ *and* $v\sigma \sim_{TS(B)} v\sigma'\}$ *is a bisimulation between* $TS(P_1 \oplus B)$ *and* $TS(P_2 \oplus B)$*. In the following, we shall write* $T_1 \,\chi\, T_2$ *instead of* $(T_1, T_2) \in \chi$.

Definition 6 of *open bisimulation* can be related to proposals in the literature: it generalizes the *context bisimulation* of [Lar89] and coincides with the *instance closed bisimulation* of [Ren97]. However, we do not enter more details since an accurate comparison between the variants of "open bisimulations" is a topic in its own and would be out of the scope of this paper.

We say that two specifications P_1 and P_2 are *equivalent*, written $P_1 \equiv P_2$, if there exists an open bisimulation between P_1 and P_2; $\equiv$ is indeed an equivalence relation. Notice that we do not require any congruence property for $\equiv$: indeed, open bisimilar contexts do not necessarily remain equivalent when instantiated by bisimilar sub-contexts. The congruence property can be achieved by two-ways explicit syntactic mappings between contexts, leading to a notion of *effectively equivalent* specifications.

Definition 7. (Effectively equivalent specifications) *We say that* P_1 *and* P_2 *are* effectively equivalent *if there exist two mappings* $\phi_{12} : O(\Sigma_1) \to C(\Sigma_2)$ *and* $\phi_{21} : O(\Sigma_2) \to C(\Sigma_1)$ *such that the relation* $\chi = \{(T, \phi_{12}(T)) \mid T \in C(\Sigma_1)\} \cup \{(\phi_{21}(S), S) \mid S \in C(\Sigma_2)\}$ *is an open bisimulation between* P_1 *and* P_2

Effective equivalence of specifications is a strong notion with concrete applications as it provides us with a translation between programs (i.e. closed terms) in a compositional way.

2.2 The Format

Confining to particular rule formats enables to characterize precisely the class of operators we are able to treat. In this paper, we consider a subclass of so-called *tyft* format operators of [GV88,GV92]. This subclass is called the *xyfg/xyfz* format.

We assume given a specification $P = (\Sigma, R)$ whose rules have the general following form:

$$\frac{\{T_i \xrightarrow{a_i} y_i \mid i \in I\}}{f(x_1, ..., x_n) \xrightarrow{a} T} \tag{14}$$

where I is a finite set of indexes, $f \in \Sigma$, x_j $(1 \leq j \leq n)$ and y_i $(i \in I)$ are all different variables from X, $a_i, a \in A$, $T_i, T \in T(\Sigma \cup X)$. We then say that r is *a rule for* f, and we define *op*$(r) = f$, $lht(r) = f(x_1, ..., x_n)$ (for "left-hand term"), $rht(r) = T$ (for "right-hand term"). Also, we let $Var(r)$ denote the set of all variables occurring in $lht(r)$.

Definition 8. (xyfg/xyfz format) *An SOS rule is in the* xyfg/xyfz *format if it is of the form (15) or (16) below (where* $I \subseteq \{1, ..., n\}$*,* $(f, n) \in \Sigma$ *and the* x_j*'s and the* y_i*'s are distinct variables):*

Basic rules

$$\frac{\{x_i \xrightarrow{a_i} y_i \mid i \in I\}}{f(x_1, ..., x_n) \xrightarrow{a} g(z_1, ..., z_m)} \tag{15}$$

where $(g, m) \in \Sigma$, *and* $\{z_1, ..., z_m\} \subseteq \{x_j\}_{1 \leq j \leq n} \cup \{y_i\}_{i \in I}$ *are distinct variables s.t.* $\forall i \in I$, $\{x_i, y_i\} \not\subseteq \{z_1, ..., z_m\}$. *Therefore* $m \leq n$.

Projective rule

$$\frac{\{x_i \xrightarrow{a_i} y_i \mid i \in I\}}{f(x_1, ..., x_n) \xrightarrow{a} z} \tag{16}$$

where $z \in \{x_j\}_{1 \leq j \leq n} \cup \{y_i\}_{i \in I}$

All the rules of Example 2 are xyfg/xyfz : Rules (3), (5), (7), (8) and (9) are projective, the others are basic. In (3), operator $(nil, 0) \in \Sigma_0$ corresponds to (g, m) in (15).

The xyfg/xyfz format is at the crossing of several formats in the literature : first, it is a fragment of the pure tyft format of [GV92]. However, in tyft rules as in (14), term T can be any open term whereas in an xyfg/xyfz rule, term $T \in O(\Sigma)$. Also, our format respects the definition of [Pin91] referred to as "without copy" format. Copying allows several occurrences of the same variable x (or occurrences of derived variables y in the premises) to occur in the right hand side term of the rule. Finally, xyfg/xyfz format strictly generalizes the *basic* format of [BD92]. As far as we know, most of the well-known description languages of the literature (e.g. Meije, SCCS, Esterel, Signal, ...) bear an SOS-specification description in this format (see Example 2).

An operator of a given specification is an *xyfg/xyfz operator* if all the rules for it are xyfg/xyfz, and we call an *xyfg/xyfz specification* (or simply "specification" for short in the following) any SOS-specification $P = (\Sigma, R)$ s.t. every $f \in \Sigma$ is xyfg/xyfz.

3 A Taxonomy for Preemption

The notion *preemption* has been widely associated with interrupts, process scheduling and operating systems. For instance, killing and suspending processes (for example **^c** or **^z** in the UNIX operating systems) have been used widely in operating systems and hardware description languages. However, it is only in the works of G. Berry on ESTEREL, one finds the notion of *preemption* elevated to the status of an operator explicitly. In fact, [Ber93] argues the need of considering preemption and concurrency as orthogonal features in reactive language specifications. The two primary categories of preemptive operators are the *suspensive* and *abortive* operators. In fact, these operators can be seen in the new look-ahead architectures abundantly (look-ahead or IA-64 architecture). In terms of the evolution of the state processes, besides execution (transition from one state to the next, different one), we would have suspension (transition while remaining in the same state) and abortion (transition with loss of any state information about the process). From this point of view, operators intuitively considered not preemptive can nevertheless be regarded as performing suspension or abortion. For example, the sequence operator, as in `P1 ; P2`, can indeed be understood as an operator that "installs" both processes, P2 in a suspended state initially, suspends P2 as long as P1 executes, and aborts P1 when it terminates, while P2 is resumed. Of course it might not at all be implemented that way, and this point might be seen as counter-intuitive (in classical architectures). But if one considers a system where installing a process would take more time than resuming it, then this way of achieving sequence might be in favour of reaction fastness. And anyway our concern here is that the behaviour defined is the one where first that of P1 is observed, and then that of P2.

The intuition behind the use of a syntactic criteria lies in the consideration that abortion is characterized by the definitive loss of information

In this section, preemption is characterized in a syntactic way: this characterization is based on the syntax of the rule schemes describing the operators.

According to the intuition, a unary operator, like operator $a\supset(v)$ in Example 2, has a suspensive feature if there exists a rule for it, namely Rule (1), in which operator leaves its argument unchanged by the transition. This can be generalized to higher arity operators, see below. On the other hand, abortive operators would be characterized by SOS-rules in which no reference to the argument, or to any of its derivatives, will occur in the target term. Definitions below also introduce "relax" operators as a natural complementary notion of the suspensive and abortive ones.

Definition 9. (Suspensive, abortive and evolutive rules) *A rule is said to be* suspensive with respect to the j-th argument *(or* w.r.t. j *for short) if* $x_j \in Var(rht(r))$. *It is* abortive w.r.t. the j-th argument *(or* w.r.t. j*) if* $x_j \notin Var(rht(r))$ *and (if* y_j *is defined)* $y_j \notin rht(r)$. *Finally, it is* evolutive w.r.t. the j-th argument *(or* w.r.t. j*) if* $j \in I$ *and* $y_j \in rht(r)$. *A rule is* relax *if it is evolutive w.r.t. all its arguments.*

In Example (2), Rule(1) (resp. (2)) is suspensive (resp. evolutive) w.r.t. 1. Rule (3) is abortive w.r.t. 1, and Rule (4) is relax. Rule (5) is abortive w.r.t. 1 and evolutive w.r.t. 2, and Rule (6) is evolutive w.r.t. 1 and suspensive w.r.t. 2. Rule (7) is suspensive w.r.t. 1. Rule (8) (resp. (9)) is abortive w.r.t. 2 (resp. 1). Etc...

The taxonomy of Definition 9 extends to (Σ-)operators. We obtain definitions for *preemptive* (more precisely *suspensive* or *abortive*) and *non-preemptive* (also called *relax*) ones:

Definition 10. (Suspensive, (pure) abortive and relax operators) *Let* f *be an xyfg/xyfz operator. We say that* f *is*

- suspensive *if it has a suspensive rule w.r.t. some* j *and no abortive rule.*
- abortive *if there exists a rule for* f *abortive w.r.t. some* j
- relax *if all the rules for* f *are relax.*

We write $\mathcal{S}$ (resp. $\mathcal{A}$, $\mathcal{R}$) the sub-class of suspensive (resp. abortive, relax) operators. Sub-classes $\mathcal{S}$, $\mathcal{A}$ and $\mathcal{R}$ form a partition of xyfg/xyfz operators. An operator is *preemptive* if it is suspensive or abortive. Among abortive operators, we distinguish so-called *pure abortive* ones defined as abortive operators with no suspension feature, i.e. with no suspensive rule for it. In the following, let $\mathcal{A}_p$ denote the class of pure abortive operators.

Refering to our example: $a\supset$, $\mu.$ and $||$ are suspensive, $a>$ and $+$ are pure abortive. $>$ is abortive but not pure abortive as it possesses a suspensive rule (see Rule (6)). Finally, $\times$ is relax. The sequence operator mentioned above would have a suspensive rule, as well as an abortive rule, and hence, as an operator, it is to be considered abortive. In fact, such a flexibility allows the interpretation in various architectures (including, lookahead architectures).

In the literature, mostly classes $\mathcal{S}$ and $\mathcal{A}_p$ have been considered. In the Esterel language [Ber93], the "**a suspend**" operator belongs to $\mathcal{S}$. It describes the suspension of a process at a signal occurrence (here for signal **a**). The various versions of **do watching** as well as the **trap** belong to $\mathcal{A}_p$. However, non pure abortive operators arise very naturally : in [SP95], operator $\bigtriangledown$ describes the abortion of a process by the starting of another process.

4 Expressiveness Issues

We now address expressiveness issues for the classes of operators $\mathcal{S}$ and $\mathcal{A}$. The main result of this paper shows that the class $\mathcal{S}$ of suspensive operators is strictly more expressive than the class $\mathcal{A}$ of abortive ones.

Basically, we show how to replace abortive operators by suspensive ones. To do so, we replace every abortive rule by a suspensive one, by keeping track of the absorbed variables in the right hand term of the rule. Therefore, the arity of the right hand term operator has to be increased. However, increasing the arity cannot be made locally for each rule, but has to take into account all the rules in which the concerned operator is involved. To do so, we give the specification a canonical decomposition into sub-specifications, each of them being associated an increase of the arity for each operator. By transforming uniformly all the abortive operators into new suspensive ones with greater arity and new rules, we show that the obtained specification is effectively equivalent to the original one.

Let P be a specification. We first explain how to decompose P: define the *operators graph of* P, written $G(P)$, as the non-directed graph whose vertices are all the function names $f \in \Sigma_P$ and whose edges are the pairs (f, g) s.t. there exists a rule r with $lht(r)$ of the form $f(...)$ and $rht(r)$ of the form $g(...)$, or vice versa.

P is *connected* if $G(P)$ is connected. Otherwise, decompose $G(P)$ into connected components $\{\Sigma_1, ...\}$ (Note that there might be infinitely many Σ_k's.) and partition R according to the following equivalence relation: "*$op(r_1)$ and $op(r_2)$ belong to the same connected component*". Denote the partitions of the equivalence relations by $\{R_1, R_2, ...\}$ where the indices for R_k's have been chosen in a such way that $r \in R_k$ iff $op(r) \in \Sigma_k$. Clearly, $P = \bigoplus_k P_k$, where $P_k = (\Sigma_k, R_k)$. Such a decomposition is unique and is referred to as *the canonical decomposition of P*.

Let $\Sigma = (F, \nabla)$ be a signature with bounded arity function, and define N as the maximal element of the set $\{\nabla(f) \mid f \in \Sigma\}$. We define $\Sigma_{\uparrow N}$ by $F_{\Sigma_{\uparrow N}} = \{f_{\uparrow N} \mid f \in F_\Sigma\}$ and $\nabla_{\Sigma_{\uparrow N}} : F_{\Sigma_{\uparrow N}} \to \mathbb{N}$ delivering the constant value N.

Finally, for a rule r, we define $abs(r) \subseteq X$ the set of *absorbed variables* in r, to denote all the variables x_k that appear in $lht(r)$, s.t. neither x_k nor y_k (corresponding to a premise if any) occur in $rht(r)$. For example, in Rule (5), the set of absorbed variables is $\{x_1\}$.

We now define an extension of a connected specification:

Definition 11. **(The N-extension of P)** *let $P = (\Sigma, R)$ be a connected specification and assume the set $\{\nabla(f) \mid f \in \Sigma\}$ has a maximal element N.*
*We define the N-*extension of *P, written $P_{\uparrow N}$, by*

- **case (1)** *If for all $f \in F_\Sigma$, $\nabla_\Sigma(f) = N$ then $\Sigma_{P_{\uparrow N}} \stackrel{def}{=} \Sigma_{\uparrow N}$,*
  case (2) *otherwise, there exists $f \in F_\Sigma$ s.t. $\nabla_\Sigma(f) < N$ (and therefore $N \geq 1$), then $\Sigma_{P_{\uparrow N}} \stackrel{def}{=} \Sigma_{\uparrow N} \cup \{(\Pi, N)\}$, where Π is a new function name.*
- *$R_{P_{\uparrow N}}$ contains the rules (we write $\boldsymbol{abs(r)}$ to denote the tuple of variables in $abs(r)$ ordered by increasing indexes) :*
  Extended basic rules : *if r is like (15) then $r_{\uparrow N}$ is ($\mathbf{x_{n+1}}, ..., \mathbf{x_N}$ are fresh meta-variables)*

$$\frac{\{x_i \xrightarrow{a_i} y_i \mid i \in I\}}{f_{\uparrow N}(x_1, ..., x_n, \mathbf{x_{n+1}}, ..., \mathbf{x_N}) \xrightarrow{a} g_{\uparrow N}(z_1, ..., z_m, \boldsymbol{abs(r)}, \mathbf{x_{n+1}}, ..., \mathbf{x_N})} \quad (17)$$

  Extended projective rules : *if r is like (16) then $r_{\uparrow N}$ is ($\mathbf{x_{n+1}}, ..., \mathbf{x_N}$ are fresh meta-variables)*

$$\frac{\{x_i \xrightarrow{a_i} y_i \mid i \in I\}}{f_{\uparrow N}(x_1, ..., x_n, \mathbf{x_{n+1}}, ..., \mathbf{x_N}) \xrightarrow{a} \boldsymbol{\Pi}(z, \boldsymbol{abs(r)}, \mathbf{x_{n+1}}, ..., \mathbf{x_N})} \quad (18)$$

  *If R contains a projective rule, then also add the following rule (referred to as *-rule):*

$$\frac{\mathbf{x_1} \xrightarrow{a} \mathbf{y_1}}{\boldsymbol{\Pi}(\mathbf{x_1}, \mathbf{x_2}, ..., \mathbf{x_N}) \xrightarrow{a} \boldsymbol{\Pi}(\mathbf{y_1}, \mathbf{x_2}, ..., \mathbf{x_N})} \quad (19)$$

For example, consider P, composed of rules (5) and (6) for operator ∇. Then the maximal arity being 2, and Rule (5) being projective, $R_{\uparrow 2}$ is then

$$\frac{x_2 \xrightarrow{\mu} y_2}{\nabla(x_1, x_2) \xrightarrow{\mu} \Pi(y_2, y_1)} \quad (20) \qquad \frac{x_1 \xrightarrow{\mu} y_1}{\Pi(x_1, x_2) \xrightarrow{\mu} \Pi(y_1, x_2)} \quad (21)$$

$$\frac{x_1 \xrightarrow{\mu} y_1}{\nabla(x_1, x_2) \xrightarrow{\mu} \nabla(y_1, x_2)} \quad (22)$$

Extending connected specifications leads to only suspensive or relax operators (By construction $abs(r_{\uparrow N}) = \emptyset$ for all $r \in R$. Noting that $abs(r) = \emptyset$ iff for every j, r is suspensive or evolutive w.r.t. j, concludes the proof.). Also, P is connected and has no abortive rule entails that P and $P_{\uparrow N}$ are isomorphic (see definition in the Appendix).

Theorem 1. *Let P be a connected specification with bounded arity (call N the maximum), then P and $P_{\uparrow N}$ are effectively equivalent (See Appendix for the full proof.).*

Notice that specification $P_{\uparrow N}$ fits the basic format of [BD92]. Theorem 1, but mostly its generalization in Theorem 2, shows that, assuming the $\equiv$-equivalence criterion is accepted, the xyfg/xyfz format is not more expressive than the basic format. The translation from P to $P_{\uparrow N}$ would precisely deliver the same basic format presentation of CCS proposed in [BD92] with moreover a proof that it is correct with regard to the original specification of CCS in [Mil81,Mil89].

4.1 Abortion Can Be Simulated by "for Ever" Suspension

Let $\mathcal{SR}$*-specification* be a specification that contains only suspensive or relax operators. We show how to transform any specification into an equivalent $\mathcal{SR}$-specification. This is formalized by Theorem 2. Note that the result also holds for infinite specifications provided connected sub-specifications have bounded arity.

Theorem 2. *Let P be a specification (with bounded arity for each connected sub-specification of P). Then there exists an $\mathcal{SR}$-specification, $\hat{P}$, which is effectively equivalent to P.*

Proof (sketch): We use Theorem 1 for each component of the canonical decomposition of P; see Appendix for the full proof.

Theorem 2 is powerful because it delivers a constructive way to translate any abortive operator into suspensive and relax ones. Moreover, extending the arity of operators w.r.t. the connected sub-specification they belong to minimizes the arities in the extended specifications. This technique also applies to infinitely many connected specifications even if no global maximal arity in the signature exists.

4.2 Suspension Is Primitive

We prove here that class $\mathcal{S}$ is strictly more expressive than class $\mathcal{A}_p$ in the sense that it is not possible to express suspension by means of pure abortive and/or relax operators (the question for non pure abortive operators is irrelevant because non-pure abortive operators have necessarily some suspensive feature, which trivially can be used to encode suspension). We show the result in the framework of "terminating" programs, - i.e. programs with only finite executions. In this framework, we first prove that abortive and relax operators preserve termination.

Proposition 1. *Let $P = (\Sigma, R)$ be an $\mathcal{A}_p\mathcal{R}$-specification s.t. for any program δ, i.e. any $(\delta, 0) \in \Sigma$, all executions from δ are finite. Then, for all $t \in T(\Sigma)$, any execution $\pi \in Ex_{TS(P)}(t)$ is also finite (See Appendix for the proof.).*

We now build an $\mathcal{SR}$-specification P s.t. there is no $\mathcal{A}_p\mathcal{R}$-specification equivalent to P, not even "trace" equivalent: consider P_{susp} the $\mathcal{SR}$-specification which signature is $\{(nil, 0), (\supset, 1)\}$ and which rules are (1) and (2) of Example 2. Clearly, program $a\supset(nil)$ possesses an infinite trace, namely a^{ω}. Thanks to Proposition 1, no ending $\mathcal{A}_p\mathcal{R}$-specification can be used to build a program which is trace equivalent to $a\supset(nil)$, as all its executions would be finite. This concludes the proof.

5 Conclusion - Debate

In this paper, we have characterized the notion of preemption widely used in reactive and real-time programming languages in the context of SOS specifications. As far as our knowledge goes, this is the first attempt of characterization of preemption in a formal setting rather than invoking virtual/real operating system dependent intuitions. The proposed framework has led to the natural categorization of the *suspensive* and *abortive* operators that exist in the various synchronous languages.

An interesting improvement of this work would be to consider semantic arguments in between the intuition underlying the preemptive concepts and the syntactic categorization proposed here; we believe that a notion of control attached to processes can achieve this issue. Such solution would give a formal rationale to the Definition 10. The latter nevertheless already contains semantic motivations, briefly presented in the introduction of Section 3. We conjecture that any attempt in defining the preemption concepts at a more semantic level would agree with the syntactic taxonomy we defend here, when considered in an SOS setting.

At least, the syntactic categorization provide us with a clear mathematical framework to tackle expressiveness issues: we have shown that *suspensive* operators are strictly more expressive than *abortive operators*, and shown *suspensive* operators to be primitive and the *abortive* to be non-primitive.

The translation of abortive operators into suspensive ones has been made possible through the notion of *effective equivalence* between specifications. We argue that *effective equivalence* between specifications, see Definition 7, is the good notion to achieve both constructive and compositional translations of various operators. Indeed, this makes it possible to reason about operators independently of their context of use.

Finally, it should be remarked that we did not say anything about complexity issues, as only expressiveness aspects are treated here. It should be noted that the present contribution gives a clear comparisons between general infinite classes of operators but also between particular (finite) sets of operators. Theorem 2 is general enough to show first, that the xyfg/xyfz format is in fact not more expressive than the basic format of Badouel and Darondeau, by means of the transformation of a given specification P into $\hat{P}$.

Expressiveness questions still remain to be answered. For example, since suspensive (and relax) operators are now proved to be expressive enough, one can think of a strict minimal expressive complete sub-class of suspensive operators from which any kind of preemption could be derived. In particular, is there any "primitive" suspensive operator s.t. any other operator would be captured, using simple constructions? If so, then this would be another very strong argument in favor of Definition 10.

Acknowledgments The authors would like to thank Philippe Darondeau for the original idea of handling preemption syntactically, Vincent Schmitt for carefully reading the draft and Philippe Schnoebelen for helpful discussion, as well as the anonymous referees for their suggestions and critical remarks.

References

[BD92] E. Badouel and Ph. Darondeau. Structural operational specifications and trace automata. In *Proc. CONCUR'92, Stony Brook, NY, LNCS 630*, pages 302–316. Springer-Verlag, August 1992.

[Ber93] G. Berry. Preemption in concurrent systems. In *Proc. FSTTCS'93, Bombay, India, LNCS 761*, pages 72–93. Springer-Verlag, 1993.

[BIM95] B. Bloom, S. Istrail, and A. R. Meyer. Bisimulation can't be traced. *Journal of the ACM*, 42(1):232–268, January 1995.

[GV88] J. F. Groote and F. W. Vaandrager. Structured operational semantics and bisimulation as a congruence. Research Report CS-R8845, CWI, November 1988.

[GV92] J. F. Groote and F. W. Vaandrager. Structured operational semantics and bisimulation as a congruence. *Information and Computation*, 100(2):202–260, October 1992.

[Lar89] K. G. Larsen. Compositional theories based on an operational semantics of contexts. In *Stepwise Refinement of Distributed Systems. Models, Formalisms, Correctness, Mook, LNCS 430*, pages 487–518. Springer-Verlag, May 1989.

[Mil81] R. Milner. A modal characterisation of observable machine-behaviour. In *Proc. CAAP'81, Genoa, LNCS 112*, pages 25–34. Springer-Verlag, March 1981.

[Mil83] R. Milner. Calculi for synchrony and asynchrony. *Theoretical Computer Science*, 23(3):267–310, 1983.

[Mil89] R. Milner. A complete axiomatisation for observational congruence of finite-state behaviours. *Information and Computation*, 81(2):227–247, 1989.

[Par81] D. Park. Concurrency and automata on infinite sequences. In *Proc. 5th GI Conf. on Th. Comp. Sci., LNCS 104*, pages 167–183. Springer-Verlag, March 1981.

[Pin91] S. Pinchinat. Ordinal processes in comparative concurrency semantics. In *Proc. 5th Workshop on Computer Science Logic, Bern, LNCS 626*, pages 293–305. Springer-Verlag, October 1991.

[Plo81] G. D. Plotkin. A structural approach to operational semantics. Lect. Notes, Aarhus University, Aarhus, DK, 1981.

[pro91] Special issue on *Real-time systems designs and programming*, *Proceedings of the IEEE*, volume 79, September 1991.

[Ren97] A. Rensink. Bisimilarity of open terms. In Catuscia Palamidessi and Joachim Parrow, editors, *Proc. EXPRESS '97: Expressiveness in Concurrency (Santa Margherita Ligure, Italy, September 8–12, 1997)*, volume 7 of *entcs*. Elesevier Science Publishers, 1997.

[Sim85] R. De Simone. Higher-level synchronising devices in MEIJE-SCCS. *Theoretical Computer Science*, 37:245–267, 1985.

[SP95] R.K. Shyamasundar S. Pinchinat, E. Rutten. Preemption in reactive laguages (a preliminary report). In *In Algorithms, Concurrency and Knowledge, Proc. of the Asian Computing Science Conference, ACSC'95, Pathumthani, Thailand, LNCS 1023*, pages 111–125. Springer-Verlag, December 1995.

Appendix

Definition of Proofs

Let $P = (\Sigma, R)$ be a specification. We use $\Theta, \Theta_1, ...$ to denote transitions in P, and $\Upsilon, \Upsilon_1, ...$ to denote expressions in rules. A *proof* of a transition Θ *in* P is a finite tree, $\mathcal{P}$, whose edges are ordered and whose vertices are labeled by transitions in P s.t. :

- the root is labeled by Θ,
- if Θ' is the label of some vertex and $\Theta_1, ..., \Theta_m$ are the labels of its children (no children when $m = 0$), then there is a rule $r \in R$ of the form

  $$\frac{\Upsilon_1 \ldots \Upsilon_m}{\Upsilon}$$

  and a substitution σ s.t. $\Theta_i = \Upsilon_i\sigma$ and $\Theta' = \Upsilon\sigma$.

  We write $\vdash_{\mathcal{P}}^{P}\Theta$ if $\mathcal{P}$ is a proof of Θ (in P), and $\vdash^{P}\Theta$ if $\vdash_{\mathcal{P}}^{P}\Theta$ for some proof $\mathcal{P}$. We omit the subscripts when they are clear from the context. Sub-proofs are sub-proof-trees.

Isomorphic Specifications

Two specifications $P_i = (\Sigma_i, R_i)$ $(i = 1, 2)$ are said to be *isomorphic* if there exists a bijection $\theta : \Sigma_1 \to \Sigma_2$ s.t. for each rule $r_1 \in R_1$, the rule obtained by substituting every rule of R_1; that is, isomorphic specifications are the same modulo renaming of operators.

Proof of Theorem 1

If P contains no abortive rule the result is trivial since P and $P_{\uparrow N}$ are isomorphic. We can now assume that P has at least one abortive rule, entailing $N \geq 1$.

Let define ϕ and ϕ' by $\phi(v) = v$ for all $v \in V$, $\phi(f(v_1,...,v_n)) = f_{\uparrow N}(v_1,...,v_n,v_{n+1},...,v_n)$ for all $(f,n) \in \Sigma$ where $v_{n+1},...,v_N$ are new variables, and $\phi'(v) = v$ for all $v \in V$, $\phi'(f_{\uparrow N}(v_1,...,v_n,v_{n+1},...,v_N) = f(v_1,...,v_n)$ for all $(f,n) \in \Sigma$. Finally, define $\phi'(\Pi(v_1,...,v_N) = v_1$. Now extend ϕ (resp. ϕ') to $C(\Sigma)$ (resp. $C(\Sigma_{P_{\uparrow N}})$ by :

- $\phi(f(T_1,...,T_n) = \phi(f(v_1,...,v_N))[\phi(T_j)/v_j]_{1\leq j\leq\nabla(f)}$
- $\phi'(f_{\uparrow N}(S_1,...,S_N) = f(\phi'(S_1),...,\phi'(S_{\nabla(f)}))$

To prove that ϕ and ϕ' provide us with the desired result, we first establish the intermediate following result:

Proposition 2. *Let $\chi \subseteq C(\Sigma_P) \times C(\Sigma_{P_{\uparrow N}})$ be the least relation s.t.*

- *$v \;\chi\; v$ for all $v \in V$,*
- *$f(T_1,...,T_n) \;\chi\; f_{\uparrow N}(S_1,...,S_N)$, for all $(f,n) \in \Sigma$, all $T_j \;\chi\; S_j$ $(j = 1,...,n)$ and all $S_{n+1},...,S_N$,*
- *$T \;\chi\; \Pi(S,S_2,...,S_N)$ for all $T \;\chi\; S$ and all $S_2,...,S_N$.*

Then relation χ is an open bisimulation between P and $P_{\uparrow N}$.

Proof. Let B be an elementary specification, disjoint from P and $P_{\uparrow N}$.

We define $\sim\subseteq T(\Sigma_P \cup \Sigma_B) \times T(\Sigma_{P_{\uparrow N}} \cup \Sigma_B)$ as the least relation such that $\sim\supseteq\sim_{TS(B)}$, and $f(t_1,...,t_n) \sim f_{\uparrow N}(s_1,...,s_n,s_{n+1},...,s_N)$ whenever $(f,n) \in \Sigma_P$, $t_j \sim s_j$, for all $j = 1,...,n$, and $t \sim \Pi(s,s_2,...,s_N)$, whenever $t \sim s$.

It is enough to prove that $\sim$ is a bisimulation between $TS(P \oplus B)$ and $TS(P_{\uparrow N} \oplus B)$.

Let $t \sim s$, and let $\vdash_{\mathcal{P}}^{P\oplus B} t \xrightarrow{a} t'$. We show that there exists $\vdash_{\mathcal{P}'}^{P_{\uparrow N}\oplus B} s \xrightarrow{a} s'$ s.t. $t' \sim s'$. The proof is done by induction over the height of the proof $\mathcal{P}$, written $h(\mathcal{P})$.

$h(\mathcal{P}) = 0$: The only rule r in $\mathcal{P}$ is an axiom. If $r \in R_B$, then $t = \beta \in T(\Sigma_B)$ and $s = \beta' \in T(\Sigma_B)$ for some $\beta \sim_{TS(B)} \beta'$ and it is trivial. Otherwise, $r \in R_P$ is of the form

$$\frac{}{f(x_1,...,x_n) \xrightarrow{a} rht(r)}$$

and t is some $f(t_1,...,t_n)$ and s is some $f_{\uparrow N}(s_1,...,s_N)$ with all $t_j \sim s_j$ $(j = 1,...,n)$. $\mathcal{P}$ is obtained by applying rule r to t with substitution ν where $x_j\nu = t_j$ and $t' = rht(r)\nu$.
Define ν' by $x_k\nu' = s_k$ for all $k = 1,...,N$. Rule $r_{\uparrow N}$ together with ν' gives a proof $\vdash_{\mathcal{P}'}^{P_{\uparrow N}\oplus B} s \xrightarrow{a} rht(r_{\uparrow N})\nu'$. By construction of ν', $t' \sim rht(r_{\uparrow N})\nu'$ (Check the two cases when rule r is basic or projective, i.e. where $rht(r)$ is some $g(z_1,...,z_m)$ or some z).

$h(\mathcal{P}) > 0$: This case is very similar to the previous one, with an additional induction argument for sub-proofs in $\mathcal{P}$. We do not give the proof here.

Reciprocally, let $\vdash_{\mathcal{P}'}^{P_{\uparrow N} \oplus B} s \xrightarrow{a} s'$. We show that there exists some $\vdash_{\mathcal{P}}^{P \oplus B} t \xrightarrow{a} t'$ with $t' \sim s'$. Again we use an induction over the height of $\mathcal{P}'$, $h(\mathcal{P}')$.

$h(\mathcal{P}') = 0$: Proof $\mathcal{P}'$ is based on some axiom. If this axiom is in R_B then $s = \beta' \in T(\Sigma_B)$ and $t = \beta \in T(\Sigma_B)$ with $\beta \sim_{TS(B)} \beta'$ and it is trivial. Otherwise, the axiom belongs to R_P and is necessarily some $r_{\uparrow N}$ (because Rule(*) is not an axiom). Proof $\mathcal{P}'$ is obtained from $r_{\uparrow N}$ and a substitution ν'. W.l.o.g. assume s has the form $f_{\uparrow N}(s_1, ..., s_N)$. Define the substitution $\nu : X \rightarrow T(\Sigma_P \cup \Sigma_B)$ by $x_j \nu = t_j$ for all $j = 1, ..., n$. Applying ν to rule r gives a proof $\mathcal{P}$ s.t. $\vdash_{\mathcal{P}}^{P \oplus B} t \xrightarrow{a} t'$. By construction of ν, $t' \sim s'$ (consider the two cases where $r_{\uparrow N}$ is extended basic or extended projective).

$h(\mathcal{P}') > 0$: W.l.o.g. we can avoid the cases where s is some $\Pi(s_1, s_2, ..., s_N)$ since $\vdash_{\mathcal{P}'} \Pi(s_1, s_2, ..., s_N) \xrightarrow{a} s'$ iff $s' = \Pi(s_1', s_2, ..., s_N)$ and $\vdash_{\mathcal{P}''} s_1 \xrightarrow{a} s_1'$ with $h(\mathcal{P}'') < h(\mathcal{P}')$, and $t' \sim \Pi(s_1', s_2, ..., s_N)$ iff $t' \sim s_1'$.
The case $s = f_{\uparrow N}(s_1, ..., s_N)$ is very similar to the previous one, with an additional induction argument for sub-proofs in $\mathcal{P}'$. It is straight forward.

Now, we can build a proof by induction over the structure of open terms that $T \chi \phi(T)$ and $\phi'(S) \chi S$, for all $T \in C(\Sigma_P)$, $S \in C(\Sigma_{P_{\uparrow N}})$, which concludes.

Proof of Theorem 2

Let $P = (\Sigma, R)$ be a (xyfg/xyfz) specification with bounded arity and write $N \stackrel{\text{def}}{=} max\{\nabla_\Sigma(f) \mid f \in \Sigma\}$. Let $P = \bigoplus_k P_k$ be the canonical decomposition of P and let N_k be the maximal arity of P_k.

Definition 12. *We define* $\hat{P} \stackrel{def}{=} \bigoplus_k (P_{k\uparrow N_k})$, *where in each* $P_{k\uparrow N_k}$ *the possible additional symbol* Π *is indexed by* k.

Write $\bigoplus_k P_k$ for the canonical decomposition of P, each P_k with maximal arity N_k.

Call ϕ_k and ϕ_k' the mappings in the proof of Theorem 1 when applied to P_k and define $\phi : C(\Sigma_P) \rightarrow C(\Sigma_{\hat{P}})$ by $\phi(T) = T$ if $T \in V$ and $\phi(T) = \phi_k(f(v_1, ..., v_{N_k}))[\phi(T_j)/v_j]_{1 \leq j \leq n}$ if $(f, n) \in \Sigma_k$ and $T = f(T_1, ..., T_n)$.

Notice that ϕ and ϕ_k coincide over $C(\Sigma_k)$. (Also we can define a mapping ϕ' to come back from $P_{\uparrow N}$ in a similar way). It remains to prove that T and $\phi(T)$ are open bisimilar. We reason by induction over the maximal number of alternations of function names belonging to different Σ_k in T : for $T \in C(\Sigma)$, define $alt(T)$, the *maximal number of alternations* in T by (write $T(\epsilon)$ for the topmost symbol of T) as follows:

- $alt(T) = 0$ if $T \in C(\Sigma_k)$,
- $alt(f(T_1, ..., T_n)) = max\{alt(T_j) \mid 1 \leq j \leq n\}$ if $f, T_j(\epsilon) \in \Sigma_k$ for some k, otherwise $1 + max\{alt(T_j) | T_j(\epsilon) \in \Sigma_{k'}$ and $f \notin \Sigma_{k'}\}$

For example, $alt(|| \, (a.(nil), v)) = 2$, $alt(+(v_1, +(v_2, v_3)) = 0$.

If $alt(T) = 0$, then necessarily $T \in C(\Sigma_k)$ for some k and by Theorem 1 T and $\phi_k(T)$ are open bisimilar. Otherwise $alt(T) = h + 1$ with $h \geq 0$. Then T is some l-holes Σ_k-context (with, say, l variables $v_1, ..., v_l$) applied to contexts $T_1, ..., T_l$ with less number of alternations. Formally $T = T^k \rho$ where $T^k \in C(\Sigma_k)$ and $v_j \rho = T_j \in C^{h'}(\Sigma)$ with $h' < h$.

Then by definition of ϕ, $\phi(T) = \phi_k(T^k)[\phi(T_j)/v_j]$.

Let B be an elementary specification. To show that $T\sigma$ and $\phi(T)\sigma'$ are bisimilar for all substitution $\sigma, \sigma' : V \to T(\Sigma_B)$ with $v\sigma \sim_{TS(B)} v\sigma'$, we use the induction hypothesis over T_j and $\phi(T_j)$, that is T_j and $\phi(T_j)$ are open bisimilar. Then $T_j\sigma \sim \phi(T_j)\sigma'$.

Consider the new elementary specification B' composed of programs $T_j\sigma \in T(\Sigma \cup \Sigma_B)$ and $\phi(T_j)\sigma' \in T(\Sigma_{\hat{P}} \cup \Sigma_B)$. By applying Theorem 1 to T^k, we have $T^k\xi \sim \phi_k(T^k)\xi'$ for substitutions $\xi, \xi' : V \to T(\Sigma \cup \Sigma_B) \bigcup T(\Sigma_{\hat{P}} \cup \Sigma_B)$ s.t. $v_j\xi = T_j\sigma \sim \phi(T_j)\sigma' = v_j\xi'$.

Because $T^k\xi = T\sigma$ and $\phi_k(T^k)\xi = \phi(T)\sigma'$ we conclude that $T\sigma \sim \phi(T)\sigma'$.

For lack of space we do not give the proof that $\phi'(S)$ and S are open bisimilar for some suitable definition of mapping $\phi' : O(\Sigma_{P \uparrow N}) \to C(\Sigma_P)$.

Proof of Proposition 1

By induction over $|t|$, the height of t.

If $|t| = 1$, then t is a constant, and we are done by assumption.

Otherwise, let t be s.t. $|t| \geq 2$ and let $\pi \in Ex(t)$. Assume π is infinite, of the form $t = t_0 \xrightarrow{a_1} t_1 \xrightarrow{a_2} t_2 ....$ The xyfg/xyfz format ensures that $|t_j| \leq |t|$ for all $j \in \mathbb{N}$.

Now because P is an $\mathcal{A}_p\mathcal{R}$-specification, only abortive or relax rules apply along a proof of π, among which only a finite number of abortive ones (as we cannot infinitively decrease the height of (finite) terms.

Then there exists k s.t. a proof of $\pi' \stackrel{\text{def}}{=} t_k \xrightarrow{a_{k+1}} t_{k+1}..$ only uses relax rules. Clearly π' is an infinite execution if π is.

By assumption t_k cannot be a constant, it is then of the form $f_l(u_1^k, ..., u_n^k)$ with $n \geq 1$, and because only relax rules are applied, all the following t_l's are some $f_l(u_1^l, ..., u^n)$.

Now a proof of $t_k \xrightarrow{a_{k+1}} t_{k+1}$ relies on proofs that $u_i^k \xrightarrow{b_i^{k+1}} u_i^{k+1}$ (for all $i = 1, ..., n$ and some b_i^{k+1}), as well as a proof of $t_{k+1} \xrightarrow{a_{k+2}} t_{k+2}$ relies on proofs that $u_i^{k+1} \xrightarrow{b_i^{k+2}} u_i^{k+2}$ (for all $i = 1, ..., n$ and some b_i^{k+2}), and so on and so worth. Therefore we can build a proof of some infinite execution from, for example, u_1^k, but because $|u_1^k| \leq |t_k| < |t|$, it contradicts the induction hypothesis.

Exploring Regional Locality in Distributed Shared Memory

Zhiyi Huang*, Chengzheng Sun, and Abdul Sattar

School of Computing & Information Technology
Griffith University, Brisbane, Qld 4111, Australia
{hzy,scz,sattar}@cit.gu.edu.au

Abstract. Two most commonly used classifications of *reference locality* are: *temporal locality* and *spatial locality*. This paper introduces a new class of reference locality, called *Regional Locality*, which is the program behavior that a set of addresses which are accessed in one critical or non-critical region will be very likely accessed as a whole in the same critical region or other non-critical regions. We proposed three updates propagation protocols based on Regional Locality in Distributed Shared Memory systems. These protocols include: Selective Lazy/Eager Updates Propagation protocol, First Hit Updates Propagation protocol, and Second Hit Updates Propagation protocol. Our experimental results indicate that Regional Locality exists in executions of many Distributed Shared Memory concurrent programs. We have shown that the proposed protocols outperform the existing updates propagation protocols based on temporal locality. Exploring Regional Locality in other shared memory systems would be an interesting future research direction.

Key Words: Distributed Shared Memory, Temporal Locality, Regional Locality

1 Introduction

Reference locality [13] in program behavior has been studied and explored extensively in memory design, code optimization, multiprogramming, etc. There are two broad classifications of locality: *temporal locality*, which means an address accessed in the past is likely to be accessed in the near future; and *spatial locality*, which says an address nearby in memory space to the one just accessed is likely to be accessed in the near future. In addition to *temporal locality* and *spatial locality*, many Distributed Shared Memory (DSM) concurrent programs exhibit the third kind of reference locality – *Regional Locality* in their executions. Before explaining *Regional Locality*, we need to give a brief introduction of DSM systems and regions in executions of DSM programs.

A DSM system provides application programmers the illusion of shared memory on top of message passing distributed systems, which facilitates the task of

* The author's current address: Dept. of Computer Science, University of Otago, P.O. Box 56, Dunedin, New Zealand.

Jieh Hsiang, Atsushi Ohori (Eds.): ASIAN'98, LNCS 1538, pp. 142–156, 1998.

parallel programming in distributed systems. Many DSM systems require explicit synchronization primitives in DSM concurrent programs in order to optimize their performance. An execution of a DSM concurrent program can be viewed as a sequence of regions which are delimited by synchronization primitives, such as *acquire, release* and *barrier*, as shown in Fig 1. A critical region begins with an *acquire* and ends with a *release*, while a non-critical region begins with a *release* (out-most one in nested critical regions) or a *barrier* and ends with an *acquire* (out-most one in nested critical regions) or a *barrier*. We say two critical regions are the same if both of them are protected by the same lock.

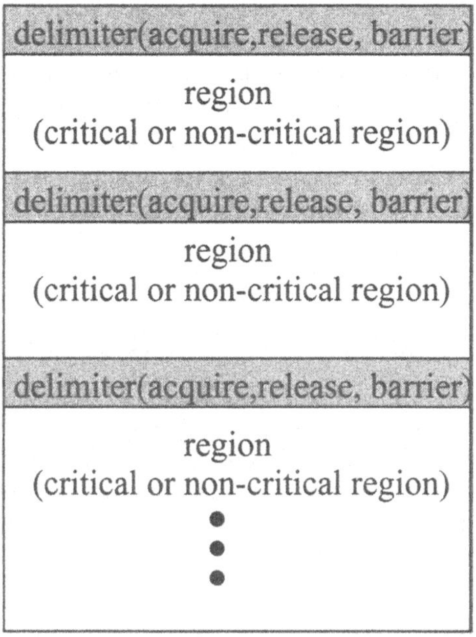

Fig. 1. Region-based view of program execution

Regional Locality is the program behavior that a set of addresses which are accessed in one critical or non-critical region will be very likely accessed as a whole in the same critical region or other non-critical regions. For instance, in a page-based DSM system, suppose processor P_1 enters a critical region and accesses pages $\{m_1, m_2, ..., m_n\}$ during the execution of the critical region, and processor P_2 enters the same critical region afterwards. P_2 will most likely access pages $\{m_1, m_2, ..., m_n\}$ during the execution of this critical region, since the same critical region usually protect the same set of data objects. The similar behavior also exists in non-critical regions of a DSM program. For example, suppose processor P_1 enters a non-critical region and accesses pages $\{m_1, m_2, ..., m_n\}$ during the execution of the non-critical region, and processor P_2 enters another non-critical region afterwards. Since data objects accessed in a non-critical region often migrate together from one processor to another processor, which is regulated by the programmer to avoid data race in non-critical regions, when P_2 accesses one or two members of the page set $\{m_1, m_2, ..., m_n\}$, it will very likely access every member of the set $\{m_1, m_2, ..., m_n\}$.

Regional Locality is similar to temporal locality in the aspect that it acquires the knowledge of locality from the past execution of the program. Their difference is that temporal locality uses all the addresses accessed by a processor in the past as one locality group for the processor itself, while *Regional Locality* divides into groups the addresses accessed by a processor in the past according to their occurring program regions and uses these groups as locality groups for all processors. Like other kinds of locality, *Regional Locality* can also be explored to improve performance of DSM programs. In this paper we focus on exploring *Regional Locality* in updates propagation in DSM systems.

The rest of this paper is organized as follows. In Section 2, we propose updates propagation protocols based on *Regional Locality*. Our proposed protocols are compared with related work in Section 3. Experimental results are analyzed and discussed in Section 4. Finally, the major contributions of this paper and future work are presented in Section 5.

2 Updates Propagation Based on Regional Locality

Many weaker sequential consistency models [6,8,3,11,10] have been proposed for DSM systems. The goal of these models is to achieve Sequential Consistency [12] on networks of workstations as efficient and convenient as possible. These models can take advantage of explicit synchronization primitives, such as *acquire*, *release*, and *barrier*, to select the *time*, the *processor*, and the *data* for making shared memory consistent [14].

Even though weaker sequential consistency models can improve performance by reducing messages for memory consistency, there are still a large number of messages for updates propagation, which significantly affect the performance of the DSM systems [9].

A DSM updates propagation protocol determines when and how updates on one copy of a page are propagated to other copies of the same page on other processors. Updates on a page can be represented by a *single-writer* scheme or by a *multiple-writer* scheme [5]. An updates propagation protocol can be integrated with either a single-writer scheme or a multiple-writer scheme.

There have existed a number of different protocols for propagating updates in DSM systems [9]. One protocol, adopted by the TreadMarks DSM system [1], works as follows: when an old copy of a page needs to be renewed, the old copy is invalidated first; only when the invalidated old copy is really accessed by a processor and a page fault occurs, are the updates of the page sent to the processor. We call this protocol as the *Lazy Updates Propagation* (LUP) protocol since it propagates updates lazily when updated pages are accessed.

In *Lazy Updates Propagation* each page fault involves an updates requesting message to a remote processor, and an updates propagating message from a remote processor. The large number of messages caused by page faults influence seriously the performance of DSM systems. If we can prefetch and apply the updates of several pages in a single page fault, we can reduce page faults and the messages caused by page faults. In this way the performance of the DSM system will be significantly improved. The challenge here is that we should prefetch as much useful updates as possible while avoiding prefetch of useless updates propagation. It is important to be aware that prefetch is a double-edged sword in the sense that prefetch of useful updates can improve performance while prefetch of useless updates may on the contrary seriously degrade the performance. However, it is non-trivial to detect which updates are useful and which ones are useless to a processor.

In the following sections we use *Regional Locality* as heuristics to detect which updates will be needed in the future execution of a processor. Based on this knowledge we prefetch useful updates in our novel updates propagation protocols. To make these protocols concrete, we describe them in the context of Lazy Release Consistency (LRC) model [11].

The LRC model is an improvement of the Eager Release Consistency (ERC) model [8]. Both ERC and LRC are called Release Consistency (RC) models. The RC models take advantage of explicit synchronization primitives, e.g., *acquire*, *release*, *barrier*, to optimize the memory consistency protocols. The ERC model requires that shared memory updates be propagated outward at *release* primitives, while the LRC model postpones updates propagation till another processor has successfully performed an *acquire* primitive. At successful *acquire* primitives, the DSM system is able to know precisely which processor is the next one to access the shared data, so updates can be propagated only to that particular processor (or no propagation at all if the next processor is the current processor). Therefore the LRC model can reduce more messages than ERC in the system.

It is worth pointing out that the ideas in the following proposed protocols are independent of any consistency models.

2.1 Updates Propagation in Critical Regions

In updates propagation we are only concerned about the updated pages whose updates need to be propagated. To explore *Regional Locality* in updates propagation in critical regions, every lock in a processor is associated with a *Critical Region Updated Pages Set (CRUPS)* which stores pages updated in a critical region. The CRUPSs actually keep the knowledge of *Regional Locality* in critical regions. A CRUPS is formed as follows. Before a processor enters a critical region by acquiring a lock, an empty CRUPS is created for the lock. If the processor updates a page during the execution of the critical region, the identifier of the page is recorded into the CRUPS of the corresponding lock. When the processor exits from the critical region, it stops recording in the CRUPS, but keeps the the contents of the CRUPS for use in the next acquisition of the same lock.

According to *Regional Locality*, we know when a processor enters a critical region it will very likely access the pages previously updated in the same critical region. So when a processor P_2 enters a critical region by acquiring a lock from another processor P_1, P_1 can assume that P_2 will access the pages in its CRUPS of the lock and thus piggy-backs the updates of these pages on the lock grant message. This idea is essentially a data prefetching technique based on the acquired knowledge of *Regional Locality*.

Based on the above idea we propose a hybrid updates propagation protocol, called the *Selective Lazy/Eager Updates Propagation (SLEUP)* [14]. This protocol can be precisely specified as follows.

Protocol 1 *The Selective Lazy/Eager Updates Propagation (SLEUP) protocol*

For any pair of processors P_1 and P_2 in a DSM system, suppose P_1 has left a critical region by releasing a lock L, with a *Critical Region Updated Pages Set* $CRUPS_L$ for lock L, and P_2 is the next processor to enter the same critical region by acquiring lock L. The updates made by P_1 are propagated to P_2 as follows:

1. At the entry of a critical region,
   (a) updates of these pages whose page identifiers are in $CRUPS_L$ are propagated from P_1 to P_2, and all corresponding copies at P_2 are updated;
   (b) invalidation notices of these updated pages whose page identifiers are not in $CRUPS_L$ are propagated from P_1 to P_2, and all corresponding copies at P_2 are invalidated.
2. During the execution of the critical region in P_2, when an invalidated page is accessed, a page fault triggers the propagation of the updates of the missing page from P_1 to P_2. □

To illustrate how SLEUP works, we give an example in Fig. 2. Suppose P_1 reads x and writes y, P_2 reads y and writes x, in the same critical region. For the first time when P_1 enters the critical region, its write on y is detected and therefore y is recorded into $CRUPS_1$. When P_2 acquires the lock, P_1 piggy-backs updates of y, whose identifier is in $CRUPS_1$, and invalidation notice of z, whose identifier is not in $CRUPS_1$, on the lock grant message. When P_2 receives updates of y and invalidation notice of z, it updates its copy of y and invalidates its copy of z. During the execution of this critical region at P_2, the write on x is detected and therefore x is recorded into $CRUPS_2$. When P_1 acquires the lock again, P_2 piggy-backs updates of x, whose identifier is in $CRUPS_2$, on the lock grant message. From this example, we know if the *Regional Locality* holds in critical regions, there is no page fault during the execution of critical regions and the number of messages is reduced by prefetching the updates of the to-be-accessed pages in SLEUP. The experimental results in Section 4 demonstrate the effectiveness of the SLEUP protocol.

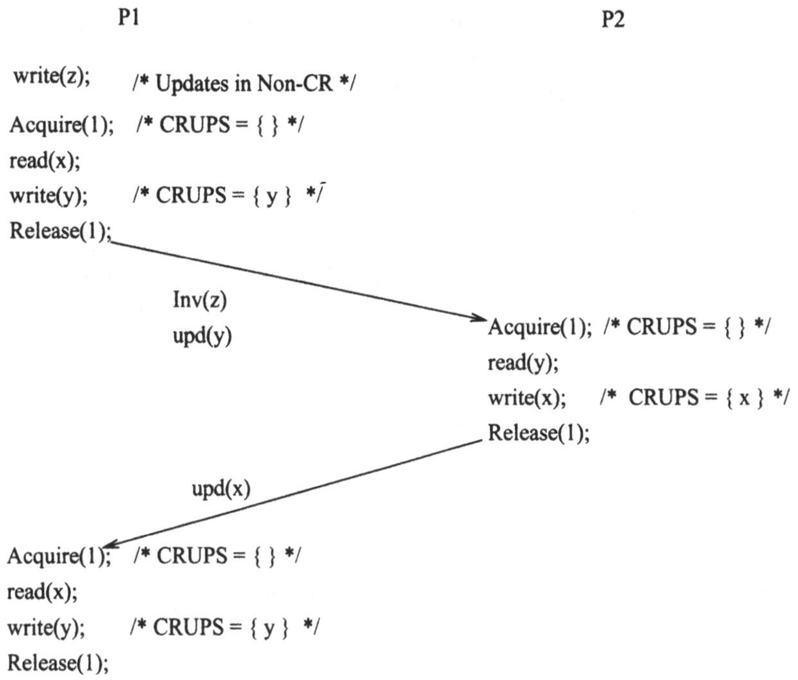

Fig. 2. An example for the SLEUP protocol

2.2 Updates Propagation in Non-critical Regions

To explore *Regional Locality* in updates propagation in non-critical regions, we detect the pages updated in non-critical regions and aggregate them together. We propose a *Non-Critical Region Updated Pages Set (NCRUPS)* scheme for grouping pages updated in non-critical regions. In every processor we associate every non-critical region with a NCRUPS. The NCRUPSs actually keep the knowledge of *Regional Locality* in non-critical regions. A NCRUPS is formed as follows. When a processor enters a non-critical region, a unique empty NCRUPS is created and assigned to the non-critical region; when a processor updates a page during the execution of a non-critical region, the identifier of the page is recorded into the corresponding NCRUPS; when a processor leaves a non-critical region, it stops recording into the corresponding NCRUPS but saves the NCRUPS for later use.

By using the NCRUPS scheme, we can group pages updated inside each non-critical region and optimally propagate updates of these pages to a processor when it is about to access them. We use some hints to decide whether a processor is about to access the pages in a NCRUPS so as to propagate all the updates of these pages to the processor. The first hint we use is the first page fault on any page in a NCRUPS. This hint suggests all the pages in the NCRUPS might be accessed soon by the processor according to *Regional Locality.* Therefore when a fault on a page in a NCRUPS occurs in a processor, we propagate the updates of all the pages in the NCRUPS to the processor.

Based on the above idea, we propose an updates propagation protocol called *First Hit Updates Propagation (FHUP)*. This protocol is precisely described as follows.

Protocol 2 *The First Hit Updates Propagation protocol*
For any pair of processors P_1 and P_2, suppose P_1 has left a non-critical region and stored a NCRUPS N_1 for the non-critical region, and P_2 is the processor which enters a non-critical region afterwards. The updates of the pages in N_1 are propagated as follows:

1. The invalidation notices of all pages in N_1 and N_1 itself are propagated from P_1 to P_2 at *acquire* or *barrier* accesses according to the Lazy Release Consistency model.
2. When P_2 receives the invalidation notices and N_1, it invalidates the corresponding pages and stores N_1 in its *remote NCRUPS list.*
3. During the execution of the non-critical region in P_2, if a page fault is caused by an invalidated page in N_1, the updates of all the pages in N_1 are requested from P_1 and propagated to P_2, and N_1 is removed from P_2's *remote NCRUPS list.* □

The FHUP protocol is a very concise protocol to optimize updates propagation in non-critical regions. It can effectively reduce the number of messages in some applications. For example, the *Integer Sort (IS)* application has the regular access pattern shown in Fig. 3. *IS* uses barriers to delimit different computation stages. At every stage, every processor has an independent set of working (read/write) pages. The processors shift their working pages with each other when changing stages. With this access pattern, the FHUP protocol works as follows: before the second barrier, the locality groups are formed and kept in the NCRUPSs {1,2,3,4}, {5,6,7,8}, {9,10,11,12}, and {13,14,15,16} in their respective processors; at the second barrier in P_1, the invalidation notices of pages in the NCRUPSs {5,6,7,8}, {9,10,11,12}, and {13,14,15,16} are propagated to P_1, and these NCRUPSs are stored in P_1's *remote NCRUPS list*; during the execution of the second non-critical region in P_1, once page 5 is accessed, P_1 checks if page 5 is a member of any NCRUPS in its *remote NCRUPS list* and finds the matched NCRUPS {5,6,7,8}; P_1 requests the updates of the pages {5,6,7,8} from P_2, applies these updates on these pages, and then removes the NCRUPS {5,6,7,8} from its *remote NCRUPS list.* For this access pattern, the FHUP protocol can reduce page faults by prefetching updates of several to-be-accessed pages in a single page fault.

However, the FHUP protocol may incur useless updates propagation for some other access patterns. For example, the *Successive Over-Relaxation (SOR)* application has the regular access pattern shown in Fig. 4. *SOR* uses barriers to delimit different computation stages. At every non-critical region, P_1 updates pages {1,2,3,4}, P_2 updates pages {5,6,7,8}, but P_1 and P_2 falsely share page 4 and 5 (False sharing means two processors update different data objects that

P1	P2	P3	P4
barrier	barrier	barrier	barrier
r.w. 1 2 3 4	r.w. 5 6 7 8	r.w. 9 10 11 12	r.w. 13 14 15 16
barrier	barrier	barrier	barrier
r.w. 5 6 7 8	r.w. 9 10 11 12	r.w. 13 14 15 16	r.w. 1 2 3 4
barrier	barrier	barrier	barrier
r.w. 9 10 11 12	r.w. 13 14 15 16	r.w. 1 2 3 4	r.w. 5 6 7 8
barrier	barrier	barrier	barrier
r.w. 13 14 15 16	r.w. 1 2 3 4	r.w. 5 6 7 8	r.w. 9 10 11 12
barrier	barrier	barrier	barrier

Fig. 3. Memory access pattern (1)

lie in the same page). In the second non-critical region, P_1 has the NCRUPS {5,6,7,8} in its *remote NCRUPS list*, and P_2 has the NCRUPS {1,2,3,4} in its *remote NCRUPS list. remote NCRUPS list.* When the FHUP protocol is applied, the updates of all the pages {1,2,3,4} are propagated to P_2 and the updates of all the pages {5,6,7,8} are propagated to P_1, though P_2 only reads page 4 and P_1 only reads page 5. Therefore, the FHUP protocol detects the incorrect knowledge of *Regional Locality* and thus propagates useless updates in *SOR*. The useless updates propagation in FHUP causes performance degradation (see Section 4).

	P1		P2
	barrier		barrier
r.	1 2 3 4 5	r.	4 5 6 7 8
w.	1 2 3 4	w.	5 6 7 8
	barrier		barrier
r.	1 2 3 4 5	r.	4 5 6 7 8
w.	1 2 3 4	w.	5 6 7 8
	barrier		barrier
	.		.
	.		.
	.		.

Fig. 4. Memory access pattern (2)

Another problem in the FHUP protocol is that if an invalid page is a member of two or more NCRUPSs in the *remote NCRUPS list*, the protocol will propagate updates of all pages in these NCRUPSs, while some of these pages may not be accessed by the processor in the following execution. For example, in Fig. 5 processors shift their working pages as in *IS*, but their working pages are overlapped because the size of data objects do not align with the size of pages (This is also a sort of false sharing). In the second non-critical region, P_1 has the NCRUPS {4,5,6,7}, {7,8,9,10} and {10,11,12,13} in its *remote NCRUPS list.* Suppose the first page fault is on page 7 in P_1. According to the FHUP protocol, the NCRUPS {4,5,6,7} and {7,8,9,10} will be selected, and P_1 will request updates of pages {4,5,6,7} and {7,8,9,10} from P_2 and P_3 respectively, though P_1 only accesses pages {7,8,9,10} at the second non-critical region. Again FHUP detects the incorrect knowledge of *Regional Locality* and thus propagates useless updates for the above access pattern.

P1	P2	P3	P4
barrier	barrier	barrier	barrier
r.w. 1 2 3 4	r.w. 4 5 6 7	r.w. 7 8 9 10	r.w. 10 11 12 13
barrier	barrier	barrier	barrier
r.w. 7 8 9 10	r.w. 10 11 12 13	r.w. 1 2 3 4	r.w. 4 5 6 7
barrier	barrier	barrier	barrier

Fig. 5. Memory access pattern (3)

From above examples we know that the FHUP protocol does not have sufficient hints to detect correct knowledge of *Regional Locality* for false sharing access patterns, and may cause useless updates propagation. To overcome this drawback, we use both the first and the second page faults on pages in a NCRUPS as hints. That is, if a page in a NCRUPS is accessed in a non-critical region by a processor, and later another page in the same NCRUPS is accessed in the same non-critical region by the same processor, then all the pages in the NCRUPS are believed to be very likely accessed by the processor and therefore the updates of all the pages in the NCRUPS are propagated to the processor.

Based on the above idea we propose an updates propagation protocol called *Second Hit Updates Propagation (SHUP).* This protocol is precisely specified as follows.

Protocol 3 *The Second Hit Updates Propagation protocol*

For any pair of processors P_1 and P_2, suppose P_1 has left a non-critical region and stored a NCRUPS N_1 for the non-critical region, and P_2 is the processor which enters a non-critical region afterwards. The updates of pages in N_1 are propagated as follows:

1. The invalidation notices of all pages in N_1 and N_1 itself are propagated from P_1 to P_2 at *acquire* or *barrier* accesses according to the Lazy Release Consistency model.
2. When P_2 receives the invalidation notices and N_1, it invalidates the corresponding pages and stores N_1 in its *remote NCRUPS list.*

3. During the execution of the non-critical region in P_2, if a page fault is caused by an invalidated page which is a member of N_1 in P_2's *remote NCRUPS list*, the condition if N_1 is labeled as *first-hit* in P_2's *remote NCRUPS list* is tested.
   - If N_1 is not labeled as *first-hit*, the updates of the fault page are requested from P_1 and propagated to P_2, and the fault page is removed from N_1 which is then labeled as *first-hit* in P_2's *remote NCRUPS list.*
   - If N_1 is labeled as *first-hit*, the updates of the pages in N_1, which have not yet sent to P_2, are requested from P_1 and propagated to P_2, and N_1 is removed from P_2's *remote NCRUPS list.*
4. When P_2 leaves the non-critical region, all the NCRUPSs labeled as *first-hit* in P_2's *remote NCRUPS list* are reset, and all the empty NCRUPSs are removed from the list. □

The advantage of the SHUP protocol is that the second page fault is used to correctly detect *Regional Locality* and avoid useless updates propagation. For example, for the access pattern in Fig. 4, since there is no second page fault, the SHUP protocol only propagates the updates of page 5 to P_1, rather than propagates the updates of all the pages {5,6,7,8} to P_1 as in the FHUP protocol. Also for the access pattern in Fig. 5, the SHUP protocol only propagates the updates of the pages {7,8,9,10} to P_1 because the second page fault on page 8 rejects the NCRUPS {4,5,6,7}.

3 Comparison with Related Work

There is no updates propagation protocol explicitly exploring *Regional Locality.*

A Lazy Hybrid (LH) protocol [7] is proposed based on temporal locality. The idea behind the LH protocol is that programs usually have significant temporal locality, and therefore any page accessed by a process in the past is likely to be accessed in the future. The LH protocol therefore selects updates of pages that have been accessed in the past (regardless whether or not in the same critical/non-critical region) by the processor acquiring a lock or arriving at a barrier, and piggy-backs the updates on grant messages. The similarity between LH and our protocols is that both of them use some kinds of locality heuristics to prefetch updates of pages. The major difference between LH and our protocols is the following: the former uses a heuristic without distinguishing the accessed pages which are in the same critical/non-critical region from these pages which are not, but the latter makes this distinction based on *Regional Locality* and hence can be more accurate in selecting the updates for prefetch. Since the heuristic in the LH protocol is very speculative, it can cause useless updates propagation, and thus degrades the performance of the underlying DSM system. This point has been verified by our experimental results.

Other updates propagation protocols based on data prefetching are proposed [2,4]. They are similar to our First Hit Updates Propagation in the aspect that they use the first page fault to trigger the prefetch of pages of a group in non-critical regions. But their criteria for grouping pages are different. In [2] page groups have fixed size which is decided by the user or by the system at run-time. Accessed pages are filled in sequence into a group until the group is full, and then another group is created. The Adaptive++ in [4] fills into a group those pages updated between two barriers. But FHUP fills into a group those pages updated inside a region.

No protocol uses the second page fault as our Second Hit Updates Propagation to avoid useless updates propagation.

4 Experimental Results

All our protocols are implemented in TreadMarks. The Lazy Hybrid protocol is also implemented in TreadMarks in order to compare *Regional Locality* with temporal locality in DSM. All these protocols are evaluated with the Lazy Updates Propagation (LUP) protocol adopted in TreadMarks, which does not explore any locality and is a benchmark for those exploring locality.

The experimental platform consists of 8 SGI workstations running IRIX Release 5.3. These workstations are connected by a 10 Mbps Ethernet. Each of them has a 100 MHz processor and 32 Mbytes memory. The page size in the virtual memory is 4 KB.

We used 8 applications in the experiment: *TSP, BT, QS, Water, FFT, SOR, Barnes, IS*, among which the source code of *TSP, QS, Water, FFT, SOR, Barnes, IS* are provided by TreadMarks research group. All the programs are written in C language. *TSP* (Travelling Salesman Problem) finds the minimum cost path that starts at a designated city, passes through every other city exactly once, and returns to the original city. *BT* (Binary Tree) is an algorithm that creates a fixed-depth binary tree. In the algorithm multiple processes explore a binary tree to search for unexpanded nodes. If a process finds an unexpanded node, it expands the node and creates new unexpanded nodes. The algorithm terminates when the fixed-depth binary tree is established. *QS* (Quick Sort) is a recursive sorting algorithm that operates by repeatedly partitioning an unsorted input list into a pair of unsorted sublists, such that all of the elements in one of the sublists are strictly greater than the elements of the other, and then recursively invoking itself on the two unsorted sublists. *Water* is a molecular dynamics simulation. Each time-step, the intra- and inter-molecular forces incident on a molecule are computed. *FFT* (3-D Fast Fourier Transform) numerically solves a partial differential equation using forward and inverse FFT's. *SOR* (Successive Over-Relaxation) uses a simple iterative relaxation algorithm. The input is a two-dimensional grid. During each iteration, every matrix element is updated to a function of the values of neighboring elements. *Barnes* (Barnes-Hut) simulates the evolution of a system of bodies under the influence of gravitational forces. It is a classical gravitational N-body simulation, in which every body is modeled as a point mass and exerts forces on all other bodies in the system. *IS* (Integer Sort) ranks an unsorted sequence of N keys. The rank of a key in a sequence is the index value i that the key would have if the sequence of keys were sorted.

All the keys are integers in the range $[0, B_{max}]$ and the method used is bucket sort.

Among these applications, *TSP* and *BT* only use locks for synchronization, and *QS* uses one lock to protect a task queue, Water uses both locks and barriers for synchronization, and *FFT, SOR, Barnes*, and *IS* only use barriers for synchronization. The FHUP and SHUP protocol are not applied to *TSP* and *BT* since there is no update on shared memory in non-critical regions in these two applications. Also since there is no critical regions in *FFT, SOR, Barnes*, and *IS*, the SLEUP protocol are not applied to them.

The experimental results are given in Table 1 In the table, the item *Time* is the total running time of an application program; the *Total Data* is the sum of total message data; the *Updates Data* is the sum of total propagated updates data; the *Page Fault* is the number of page faults; and the *Mesgs* is the total number of messages.

4.1 Regional Locality

From the experimental results we know *Regional Locality* exists in many DSM concurrent programs. Among the applications with *Regional Locality* are *TSP*, *BT*, *QS*, *Water*, *Barnes*, and *IS*. By applying SLEUP, FHUP and SHUP, which explore *Regional Locality*, the average improvement on the performance of these applications is 20.2% when compared with LUP in original TreadMarks system. The maximum improvement is up to 53.8% (*TSP*). Particularly, by exploring *Regional Locality*, the number of page faults and the number of messages are reduced to 46% and 66% respectively in average. There is no improvement on the performance of some applications, such as *FFT* and *SOR*, because they don't have any *Regional Locality*.

4.2 Regional Locality vs. Temporal Locality

Protocols based on *Regional Locality* outperform those based on temporal locality for all of our applications. Compared with LUP, LH degrades the performance of many programs, such as *Water*, *FFT*, *SOR*, *Barnes*, *IS*. (Because message buffer overflows at barriers, we have not provided running results of *Barnes* based on the LH protocol [1]). The average degradation is 34.4%, and the maximum degradation is up to 108.6% (*FFT*). The reason for the degradation is that LH propagates a large amount of useless updates. The average amount of useless updates propagated in LH is 27.8% of the total propagated updates. Even though LH can improve some applications, such as *TSP*, *BT*, and *QS*, but its performance is still not as good as SLEUP/SHUP/FHUP. The performance of SLEUP/SHUP/FHUP is 17.7% better than that of LH in average. The average amount of updates propagated in SLEUP/SHUP/FHUP is 29.7% less than that in LH. Even though in some applications, such as *FFT*,

[1] The buffer overflows because of too much (useless) updates propagation at barriers in LH, and therefore its performance will be further degraded at barriers.

SOR and *IS*, the number of page faults and the number of messages in LH are less than those in SLEUP/SHUP/FHUP, however, the overall performance of SLEUP/SHUP/FHUP is better than that of LH since LH propagates a large amount of useless updates.

application	protocol	Time (secs)	Total Data (bytes)	Updates Data (bytes)	Page Fault	Mesgs
TSP	LUP	15.86	1267683	448958	1029	2846
	LH	8.63	1287368	463437	355	1405
	SLEUP	7.33	1252737	443896	245	1209
BT	LUP	82.92	39511375	8921228	26478	96979
	LH	72.08	40964979	9390072	13918	68542
	SLEUP	69.71	39148835	8761972	6469	53925
QS	LUP	20.09	10153006	6100023	3046	10432
	LH	15.52	10844953	6962709	962	6095
	SLEUP	13.36	9165498	5354832	956	5936
	SLEUP+FHUP	14.96	11596416	7838800	829	5447
	SLEUP+SHUP	12.38	9282800	5430895	930	5886
Water	LUP	32.59	11717602	9980061	4314	24495
	LH	36.82	14535830	12590288	2137	21668
	SLEUP	31.07	11834142	9981561	3024	21920
	SLEUP+FHUP	31.92	13759521	11607920	1733	18906
	SLEUP+SHUP	30.63	12159638	9979899	1992	19764
FFT	LUP	4.44	3220826	2188032	557	2135
	LH	9.26	5540076	4487644	174	1735
	FHUP	4.87	3902122	2820048	291	1603
	SHUP	4.60	3306240	2188032	557	2136
SOR	LUP	13.70	7391113	14140	203	4301
	LH	15.10	7934204	473636	16	4992
	FHUP	14.53	7556048	134885	203	4302
	SHUP	13.84	7416629	14140	203	4303
Barnes	LUP	49.38	50943423	37198386	12791	75943
	LH	X	X	X	X	X
	FHUP	48.14	55534888	37687510	12640	74318
	SHUP	49.17	55136208	37199430	12763	75659
IS	LUP	113.42	71732008	69626536	4444	11305
	LH	120.15	75004402	73404180	192	8044
	FHUP	108.20	72100823	69626536	2774	7965
	SHUP	110.62	72223052	69623400	3998	10384

Table 1. Performance Statistics for applications

From the above discussion we know temporal locality is more speculative than *Regional Locality.* Temporal locality does not have the as accurate knowledge of the to-be-accessed data as *Regional Locality.* This inaccuracy of temporal locality causes the useless updates propagation and degrades the performance of DSM systems.

4.3 Detection of Regional Locality

We use the CRUPS scheme to detect *Regional Locality* in critical regions, and use the NCRUPS scheme and the first/second page fault to detect *Regional Locality* in non-critical regions. Accuracy of the detected *Regional Locality* affects the performance of the protocols based on *Regional Locality*. On one hand, incorrect knowledge of *Regional Locality* causes useless updates propagation. For example, for *FFT* and *SOR* the FHUP protocol detects the incorrect knowledge of *Regional Locality*. So FHUP propagates useless updates and degrades performance in these two applications. On the other hand, incomplete knowledge of *Regional Locality* hinders the improvement on performance. For instance, SHUP can not find complete *Regional Locality* as immediate as FHUP in *IS* and *Barnes*. So SHUP does not perform as well as the FHUP for these two applications.

From the above discussion we know, even though both FHUP and SHUP are based on *Regional Locality*, FHUP is more speculative while SHUP is more conservative in terms of detection of *Regional Locality*. Their merits become prominent in different applications.

The overhead of the CRUPS scheme is very small because it takes advantage of the write-protection mechanism provided in the TreadMarks system. There are some overhead for bookkeeping the *remote NCRUPS list* in the NCRUPS scheme. For example, for *FFT* and *SOR* where there is no *Regional Locality*, SHUP slightly degrades their performance (3.6% degradation for *FFT*, 1.0% degradation for *SOR*) because of this bookkeeping overhead.

5 Conclusions

In this paper, we have discussed the program behavior – *Regional Locality* and evaluated this new class of reference locality in updates propagation in DSM systems. We have proposed three novel updates propagation protocols, SLEUP, FHUP, and SHUP, which explore *Regional Locality* in DSM systems. The experimental results indicate:

1. *Regional Locality* exists in executions of many Distributed Shared Memory concurrent programs. Updates propagation protocols exploring *Regional Locality* significantly improve the performance of the DSM systems.
2. The protocols based on *Regional Locality* outperform those based on the more speculative temporal locality. Protocols exploring temporal locality causes performance degradation for many applications in our experiment.

Our future research is to explore *Regional Locality* in other shared memory systems.

Acknowledgments

This research is supported by an ARC (Australian Research Council) large grant (A49601731), and a NCGSS grant by Griffith University.

References

1. C. Amza, et al: "TreadMarks: Shared memory computing on networks of workstations," *IEEE Computer,* 29(2):18-28, February 1996.
2. C. Amza, A.L. Cox, K. Rajamani, and W. Zwaenepoel: "Tradeoffs between False Sharing and Aggregation in Software Distributed Shared Memory", *In Proc. of the Sixth Conference on Principles and Practice of Parallel Programming,* pp. 90-99, June 1997.
3. B.N. Bershad, et al: "The Midway Distributed Shared Memory System," *In Proc. of IEEE COMPCON Conference,* pp528-537, 1993.
4. R. Bianchini, R. Pinto, and C.L. Amorim: "Data prefetching for software DSMs", *In Proc. of the 12th ACM international Conference on Supercomputing,* July 1998.
5. J.B. Carter, J.K. Bennett, and W. Zwaenepoel: "Techniques for reducing consistency-related information in distributed shared memory systems," *ACM Transactions on Computer Systems,* 13(3):205-243, August 1995.
6. M. Dubois, C. Scheurich, and F.A. Briggs: "Memory access buffering in multiprocessors," *In Proc. of the 13th Annual International Symposium on Computer Architecture,* pp.434-442, June 1986.
7. S. Dwarkadas, et al: "Evaluation of Release Consistent Software Distributed Shared Memory on Emerging Network Technology", *In Proc. of the 20th Symposium on Computer Architecture,* pp.144-155, May 1993.
8. K. Gharachorloo, D. Lenoski, J. Laudon: "Memory consistency and event ordering in scalable shared memory multiprocessors," *In Proc. of the 17th Annual International Symposium on Computer Architecture,* pp15-26, May 1990.
9. Zhiyi Huang, Wan-Ju Lei, Chengzheng Sun, and Abdul Sattar: "Heuristic Diff Acquiring in Lazy Release Consistency Model," *In Proc. of 1997 Asian Computing Science Conference (ASIAN'97),* LNCS 1345, Springer-Verlag, pp98-109, Dec. 1997.
10. L. Iftode, J.P. Singh and K. Li: "Scope Consistency: A Bridge between Release Consistency and Entry Consistency," *In Proc. of the 8th Annual ACM Symposium on Parallel Algorithms and Architectures,* 1996.
11. P. Keleher: "Lazy Release Consistency for Distributed Shared Memory," *Ph.D. Thesis,* Rice Univ., 1995.
12. L. Lamport: "How to make a multiprocessor computer that correctly executes multiprocess programs," *IEEE Transactions on Computers,* 28(9):690-691, September 1979.
13. J.R. Spirn: "Program Locality and Dynamic Memory Management," *PhD thesis,* Princeton University, 1973.
14. Chengzheng Sun, Zhiyi Huang, Wan-Ju Lei, and Abdul Sattar: "Toward Transparent Selective Sequential Consistency in Distributed Shared Memory Systems," *In Proc. of the 18th IEEE International Conference on Distributed Computing Systems,* pp.572-581, Amsterdam, May 1998.

Guaranteed Mutually Consistent Checkpointing in Distributed Computations

Zhonghua Yang*, Chengzheng Sun, Abdul Sattar, and Yanyan Yang

School of Computing and Information Technology
Griffith University, Nathan
Qld 4111 Australia
{z.yang, c.sun, a.sattar, yyang}@cit.gu.edu.au

Abstract. In this paper, we emplore the isomorphism between vector time and causality to characterize consistency of a set of checkpoints in a distributed computing. A necessary and sufficient condition, to determine if a set of checkpoints can form a consistent global checkpoint, is presented and proved using the isomorphic power of vector time and causality. To the best of our knowledge, this is the first attempt to use the isomorphism for this purpose. This condition leads to a simple and straightforward algorithm for a guaranteed mutually consistent global checkpointing. In our approach, a process can take a checkpoint whenever and wherever it wants while other related process may be asked to take an additional checkpoint for ensuring the mutual consistency. We also show how this condition and the resulting algorithm can be used to obtain a maximum and minimum global checkpoints, another important paradigm for distributed applications.

1 Introduction

A large class of important problems in distributed systems can be cast as periodically taking a consistent global checkpoints and executing some reactions based on the checkpoints that have been taken. Examples of such problems include distributed debugging and monitoring, fault-tolerant and rollback-based recovery,detection of state properties such as a deadlock and termination. This paradigm requires consistently recording (often, periodically recording) the global state of a distributed computing. Informally, a global state is a collection (union) of the local states, one from each process of the computation, recorded by a process. The saved process state is called a checkpoint. A global state is also called a global checkpoint. Such a checkpoint is said to be consistent if it has been passed through, or if it could have been passed through, by the current computation [4, 19]. In a distributed system based on message-passing without shared memory, consistency means if an event of message *receive* is included in a checkpoint, the event of its corresponding message *send* should also be included. Obviously, there is no such distributed computation in which a message has been recorded

* Currently with Gintic Institute, Nanyang Technological University, Singapore

Jieh Hsiang, Atsushi Ohori (Eds.): ASIAN'98, LNCS 1538, pp. 157–168, 1998.

as being received but which has not been sent in the recording. Thus, a fundamental problem in distributed computing is to ensure that a global checkpoint obtained is consistent which is the focus of this paper.

In this paper, we first present a necessary and sufficient condition to determine if a set of local checkpoint can form some consistent global checkpoint. This condition use the *isomorphism* between the vector time and the causal partial order. In the literature, there are two published work that describe the necessary and sufficient condition [11, 1]. Netzer-Xu's [11] necessary and sufficient condition to characterize a consistent global state is expressed in terms of a *"zigzag"* relation defined on the set of local checkpoints. Baldoni *et al*'s [1] condition is based on the precedence relation defined on checkpoint *intervals*. While our condition and their conditions are equivalent from a theoretical point of view, our condition, derived from the isomorphism between the vector time and causal order, leads to a simple and straightforward algorithm that guarantees mutually consistent checkpoints as described later in this paper.

There have been many algorithms for obtaining distributed global checkpoints, for example, see [6] for a survey. Generally, there are two approaches to checkpointing:

- *Coordinated approach*: the processes coordinate their checkpointing actions such that the current instance of global checkpoint in the system is guaranteed to be consistent. Such a consistent set of checkpoints can then be used, for example, for recovery, When a failure occurs, the system restarts from these checkpoints. The disadvantages of this approach are that it requires a number of communication messages between processes for each checkpointing and introduces synchronization delays during normal operation.
- *Uncoordinated* or *independent approach*: In the second approach each process takes checkpoints independently (whenever and wherever it wants) and saves them on its stable storage [16], and when a consistent global checkpoint is required, it has to be constructed from the available set of local checkpoints. There is no guarantee that a consistent global checkpoint can actually be constructed. In fact, some of the local checkpoints might turn out to be useless as they belong to none of consistent global states. This approach, if used in a fault-tolerant system based on recovery, would lead to so called domino effect [12].

The algorithm we proposed in this paper is a combination of the above two approaches. Thus it is called *semi-coordinated* approach, that is, a process can *independently* take its local checkpoints (whenever and wherever it wants), and *only* if doing so results in an inconsistent checkpoint by checking against the necessary and sufficient condition. The *related* processes are forced to take *additional* local checkpoints, too. This guarantees the mutually-consistent checkpoints. In our algorithm, we use the vector time as an instrument to provide this guarantee.

The rest of this paper is organized as follows. Section 2 describes a system model on which this work is based. In Section 3, we review the vector time mechanism and isomorphism between it and causal precedence, and then derive the necessary and sufficient condition for obtaining a consistent global checkpoints.

Section 4 presents a vector-based checkpoint algorithm that guarantees mutually consistent checkpointing. Section 5 shows how our algorithm can be used to construct a maximum and minimum global consistent checkpoints. Finally, we conclude the paper in Section 6.

2 System Model

A distributed system consists of a finite set of n processes $\{P_1, ..., P_n\}$, each executing its own sequential program modeled by a sequence of *events*. These processes communicate with each other solely by message-passing. We assume that the communication channels between processes are FIFO and reliable. Events correspond to the state changes that take place in the process. Such a sequence of events, denoted by E_i, is called a local history of local computation P_i. The collection of local histories of processes participating in a distributed system forms the execution history of the system. For the notational purpose, e_i^x denotes the xth event ($x \geq 0$) executed by P_i, or simply e_i if the ordinarity is not important.

For our purpose, the events of interest in any distributed system are the *sending* and *receiving* of message, and internal events. The checkpointing events that correspond to the recording of local states by individual processes are the only internal events we consider in this paper. We assume that the first event in each process is an internal local checkpoint event. Also we do not explicitly consider messages in the execution history, rather, they are implied by the presence of message *send* and *receive* events. The global set of events appearing in the execution history cannot be placed naturally in a total order, whereas it is possible in the events of a single process. Instead, a partial order on the events can be defined using Lamport's *happen-before* relation: in the global event set, we say that event e_i *directly happens before* event e_j, denoted by $e_i \overset{d}{\rightarrow} e_j$, if

- e_i and e_j are events in the same process and e_i occurs immediately before e_j; or
- e_i is the sending of a message m and e_j is the receiving of m.

The transitive closure of the $\overset{d}{\rightarrow}$ relation is the *happen-before* relation [9], denoted by $\rightarrow$.

If for two distinct events e_i and e_j, $e_i \not\rightarrow e_j$ and $e_j \not\rightarrow e_i$, e_i and e_j are said to be concurrent, denoted by $e_i \parallel e_j$.

In the system of N processes, a global checkpoint is defined as a set of N local checkpoints, one from each process. A consistent global checkpoint is a global checkpoint in which no two constituent checkpoints are related by the happen-before relation [8], Formally.

Definition 1. *In a distributed computation of n processes, let CKPT denote a global checkpoint by* $\{ckpt_1, ckpt_2, \ldots, ckpt_n\}$. *CKPT is said to be consistent if for i, j = 1, ..., n,*

$$ckpt_i \parallel ckpt_j$$

Intuitively, if any two checkpoints are not causally related, i.e. pairwise concurrent, they clearly are consistent with each other, and can belong to some consistent global checkpoint.

3 Characterizing Consistency of Global Checkpoints

In this section, we state and prove a necessary and sufficient condition to determine if an arbitrary set of local checkpoints can form a consistent global checkpoint. Our characterization of consistency uses the isomorphic power of the structure of vector time and the causality structure of the underlying distributed computation. Before we present our condition, we will briefly review vector time and its properties, due to Matern [10].

3.1 Isomorphism between Vector Time and Causality

Both Mattern [10] and Fidge [7] introduced vector time as an operational instrument to represent causal dependency of events in a distributed computing. Suppose that a distributed computing consists of the set of processes $\{p_1, p_2, \ldots, p_n\}$. Each process, p_i, has a vector clock, V_i. Events occurring in a process are assigned a vector time, $V(e)$, obtained from the process' vector clock. This set of vector clocks in a distributed system advances by the following rules:

VT1 $V_i[1, \ldots, n]$ is initialized to all elements equal 0.
VT2 1. Whenever an event, e_i, occurs, $V_i[i] := V_i[i] + 1$.
2. If the event is a message send event, the reading of V_i is attached as a timestamp to the message being sent.
3. If the event is a message receive event, e_j, corresponding to the message send event, e_i, the process updates V_j and assigns its value to e_j by taking a pairwise maximum value between V_j and the timestamp of the message, that is, $V_j(e_j) = sup(V_i, V_j)$, where $sup(V_i, V_j) = max(V_i[k], V_j[k])$ for $1 \leq k \leq n$.

The comparison between vector time is defined using the relations $<$, $>$, and $\|$.

Definition 2. *For two vector time u, v,*

$$u = v \text{ iff } \forall i : u[i] = v[i]$$

$$u \leq v \text{ iff } \forall i : u[i] \leq v[i]$$

$$u < v \text{ iff } u \leq v \text{ and } u \neq v$$

$$u \parallel v \text{ iff } (u \not< v) \text{ and } (v \not< u)$$

It has been shown that a computationally very simple relation $<$ defined on vector time, i.e. $(V, <)$, characterizes causality [15]:

Theorem 1. *For two events e and e′ of a distributed computation, we have:*

$$e \rightarrow e' \text{ iff } V(e) < V(e')$$

$$e \parallel e' \text{ iff } V(e) \parallel V(e')$$

In other words, the structure of vector time is isomorphic to the causality structure of the underlying distributed computation.

In fact we can restrict the comparison to just two vector components in order to determine the precise causal relationship between two events (e_i and e_j) if their origin p_i and p_j are known.

Lemma 1. *For two distinct events e_i and e_j, we have*

$$e_i \rightarrow e_j \text{ iff } V(e_i)[i] \leq V(e_j)[i]$$

$$e_i \parallel e_j \text{ iff } (V(e_i)[i] > V(e_j)[i]) \text{ and } (V(e_j)[j] > V(e_i)[j])$$

The isomorphism as expressed in Theorem 1 and Lemma 1 is essential to our characterization of consistency and to the design of our algorithm. It is also a key feature to show correctness of this algorithm.

3.2 Necessary and Sufficient Consistency Condition

Now we are ready to present a necessary and sufficient condition to determine if a set of checkpoints are mutually consistent.

Theorem 2. *Let $CKPT = \{ckpt_i | V_i$ is a vector time assigned to $ckpt_i$ and $i = 1, ..., n\}$ be a set of checkpoint events in a distributed computation, one from each process, CKPT forms a consistent global checkpoint if and only if for each pair of local checkpoints $ckpt_i$ and $ckpt_j$:*

$$V_i(ckpt_i) \parallel V_j(ckpt_j)$$

Proof. Using vector time as an instrument, the theorem immediately follows from Theorem 1 and Lemma 1. □

4 Algorithm for Guaranteed Mutually Consistent Checkpointing

In our algorithm described in this section, processes take local checkpoints in an uncoordinated way, *whenever and wherever it wants.* While doing so, some other *related* processes may be forced to take *additional* checkpoint in order to guarantee the checkpoints that have been arbitrarily taken, are mutually consistent.

What are the *related* processes to be forced to take checkpoints? The answer is those *causally related* processes, and is based on the following observation: a local checkpoint that has been taken arbitrarily by a process may not belong to some consistent global checkpoints (and thus may be *useless!*). The only source for this possible inconsistency is the communication events: a local checkpoint might have recorded a message *receive* event but the communicating process has *not yet* recorded the corresponding message *send* event. In this case, unless the communicating process is forced to take an additional checkpoint as well to include the *send* event, the inconsistency results. This observation motivates our algorithm.

Each process maintains a boolean array, $recvd_i[1, \ldots, n]$ to record the fact that a message *receive* event has occurred since the last checkpoint. Initially and whenever a local checkpoint is being taken, $recved_i$ is set for components to *false* (0). The array component $recvd_i[j]$ is set to *true*(1) if it has received a message from process p_j since the last checkpoint. Thus $recvd_i$ records from whom the process p_i has received messages since the last checkpoint. These processes are potential candidates who will *possibly* be forced to take an additional checkpoint if it has not done so. In fact, the checkpointing process uses this information (in $recvd_i$) to inform the partner process by sending a *request timestamped with the vector time* of the checkpoint being taken that the message received has been recorded in a local checkpoint and if the partner process has not checkpointed the *send* event, please do so. Checkpointing by the partner process may trigger a further request to yet another process for (possibly) checkpointing. In order to properly terminate this checkpointing process, the process, while checkpointing, will stop sending any (new) application message and wait for acknowledgment.

Since each process independently takes its local checkpoints, it is possible that when a process records its local state including a message *receive*, the *sending* process had already checkpointed the *send* event. In this case, there is no need for the sending process to take an additional checkpoint. The sending process simply acknowledges with a vector time of the latest checkpoint that includes the *send* event. We call the checkpoint being taken by p_i and the checkpoint in p_j whose vector time is been returned as the *corresponding checkpoints.* According to Lemma 1, by comparing the vector time of the most recent checkpoint with the timestamped vector time of the *request* message, it is easy for the sending process to find out whether the additional checkpoint needs to be taken. In addition, each process p_i maintains a set of pair of the index and vector time of the checkpoints, $S_i = \{(l, V_i) | l \in N\}$, which can be used for constructing a *maximum/minimum* consistent global checkpoint as described in the next section.

The algorithm is formally described as the following procedure or rules:

Process p_i *record_local_state*

- As an internal event, record local state:
- $V_i[i] = V_i[i] + 1;$
- $S_i = S_i + \{(++l, V_i)\}$
- recvd = 0;

Process p_i *checkpointing rule*

- stop sending any new application message;
- if for all $k \neq i : \{1, \ldots, n\}$, $recvd_i[k] = 0$ *record_local_state.*
  else for all $k \neq i : \{1, \ldots, n\}$, $recvd_i[k] \neq 0$
  - *record_local_state.*
  - send $request\_for\_checkpointing(V_i(ckpt_i))$;
  - wait for ack messaage: $done(V_k(ckpt_k))$;
- resume sending application message (if any).

Process p_j **responding rule to** $request\_for\_checkpointing(V_i(ckpt_i))$

- if ($V_j[j]$ of the last checkpoint of process) $< V_i(ckpt_i)[j]$
  execute *checkpointing rule*; (* *the send event not yet checkpointed* *)
- acknowledge: $done(V_j(ckpt_j))$.

It is essential to note that since a checkpoint is an internal event within a process, every time a checkpoint is taken by p_i, the ith component of its vector time increases by 1, making its vector time incomparable to the vector time of events in other process from which p_i has received messages.

Lemma 2. *For two corresponding checkpoints, ckpt$_i$ and ckpt$_j$ caused by ckpt$_i$, we have*

$$V_i(ckpt_i) \parallel V_j(ckpt_j)$$

Proof. From the advance rules of vector time, after checkpointing, $V_i(ckpt_i)[i] > V_j(ckpt_j)[i]$, and similarly, $V_j(ckpt_j)[j] > V_i(ckpt_i[j]$. According to Lemma 1, $V_i(ckpt_i) \parallel V_j(ckpt_j)$ □

4.1 Example

We further explain the algorithm using an example (Fig. 1). The example distributed computation has three processes $\{p_1, p_2, p_3\}$ with initial checkpoints $ckpt_1^1, ckpt_2^1$, and $ckpt_3^1$. At some point, after p_2 received message $m1$, it decides to take a checkpoint $ckpt_2^2$ and finds that $recvd$ = [100] suggesting that it has received a message ($m1$) since the last checkpointing ($ckpt_2^1$), so it sends out a *request* timestamped with its vector time (now [230]). After receiving this request and from the incoming vector time stamp, it realizes a need to take a checkpoint as well (because $V_1(ckpt_1^1)[1] < V_2(ckpt_2^2)[1]$), and so takes the checkpoint which is $ckpt_1^2$ with its vector time [300]. From two vector times ([300] and [230]), they are concurrent. Later, p_1, after sending the message $m3$, its wants to take a checkpoint, since $recvd$ = [000], no other process is involved in its checkpointing. It is easy to check that $\{ckpt_1^3, ckpt_2^2, ckpt_3^1\}$ forms a consistent global checkpoint.

The checkpoint $ckpt_3^2$ demonstrates a more complex scenario. After receiving a message $m5$, p_3 wants to checkpoint its local state, since $recvd_3$ = [010], it sends a request timestamped with a vector time [473] to p_2 to ensure the consistency. After checking, p_2 needs to checkpoint, too. While doing so, p_2

requests p_1 with the timestamp [480] ($recvd_2 = [100]$). However, there is no need for p_1 to take a checkpoint because $V_1(ckpt_1^3)[1] > V_2(ckpt_2^3[1]$. As a result, p_3 has taken a checkpoint $ckpt_3^2$ as it wished and p_2 has also taken a checkpoint $ckpt_2^3$ as requested to ensure the consistency. Clearly, Checkpoints $\{ckpt_1^3, ckpt_2^3, ckpt_3^2\}$ form a consistent global checkpoint.

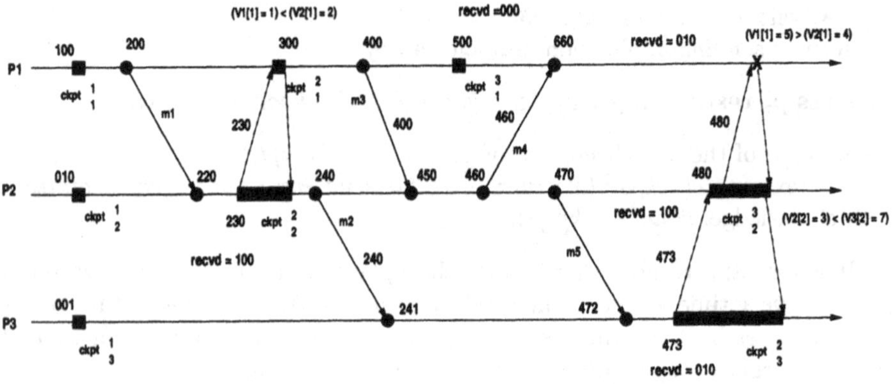

Fig. 1. An example distributed computation.

This example clearly shows that the algorithm provides a guaranteed mutually consistency between the checkpoints. Below we give a formal proof of this claim.

4.2 Correctness of the Algorithm

The key to the correctness of the algorithm is to properly advance the vector time of checkpoints. Note that in the algorithm this is achieved by (1) the checkpoint event as an internal event increments its own component of the vector time ($V_i[i] = V_i[i] + 1$), (2) the *request* for checkpointing per se does not advance the vector time. In essence, forcing a process to take an additional checkpoint is forcing the vector time to advance in such a way that two checkpoints are concurrent.

Lemma 3. *Let $ckpt_i$ be a checkpoint of process p_i, there always is a checkpoint in another process, p_j, of the computation, such that $ckpt_i \parallel ckpt_j$.*

Proof. Immediately from Lemma 2. □

Theorem 3. *In a distributed computation of n processes, let CKPT denote a set of checkpoints taken by the algorithm, one from each process, denoted by $\{ckpt_i | i = 1, \ldots, n\}$ such that $V_i(ckpt_i) \parallel V_j(ckpt_j)$, then the set CKPT forms a consistent global checkpoint.*

Proof. From Lemma 2, and Lemma 3, the $CKPT$ is a set of checkpoints that are pairwise concurrent. According to Definition 1, the set form a consistent global checkpoint. □

Corollary 1. *No checkpoint taken by the algorithm is useless.*

4.3 Discussion

Limited Coordination. In our algorithm, while processes enjoy independence in taking local checkpoints, they have an obligation to take additional checkpoints. This obligation is coercive, necessary for the consistency guarantee. Because of this obligation, we call it *semi-coordinated* approach. A question naturally arised here is to what extent a process would coercively undertake this obligation. To one extreme, if a checkpoint taken by one process would trigger all other processes to take checkpoints as well, this becomes a fully coordinated approach. Fortunately, in many distributed applications, and in most cases, the involvement of other processes in checkpointing is very limited in terms of scope and in terms of numbers of additional checkpoints. The scope is limited because only very few processes are likely to be involved. The number of additional checkpoints is limited because when a *request* comes in, it is likely that the expected checkpoints had already been taken. Our claim in this regards is supported by the following observation [15]:

Observation 1. *In a distributed computation, even if the number* n *of processes is large, only few of them are likely to interact frequently by direct message exchange.*

This observation reveals that distributed computing typically exhibits the nature of communication *locality*. Our approach explicitly explores the locality of distributed computing.

Inhibition. As can be noted (for example in Fig. 1), during checkpointing, the underlying application is delayed to ensure that the necessary and sufficient condition is satisfied. This delay (also called *inhibition*) is perhaps the price to be paid for the guaranteed consistency. For the discussion of the role and spectrum of inhibition in asynchronous consistent-cut protocols, see [17, 5].

Event Analysis Based on Vector Time. As pointed out earlier, there have been other published work giving the necessary and sufficient condition [11, 2]. Netzer *et al* derive their condition based on *zigzag* notion by analysing the interaction pattern in distributed computations. Baldoni *et al* base their work on the notion of *checkpoint intervals* and analyze the relationship between the intervals. Vector time was not used in their analysis. We have also based our work on event analysis and used vector time as a tool in the derivation. There exists a recent development in the theoretical framework based on logical vector time in which several meaningful timestamps of abstract events are derived [3].

5 Constructing Maximum and Minimum Consistent Global Checkpoints

In this section, we demonstrate how the technique developed in the preceding sections can be used to find the maximum and minimum consistent global checkpoints that contain a *target checkpoint* in one process. The concept of the maximum and minimum consistent global checkpoints is very important for many distributed applications [18]. For example, for software error recovery, a *target checkpoint* may be suggested by a diagnosis procedure to maximize the chance of bypassing the software bug that caused error; for debugging applications, the target checkpoint can be defined by user-specified breakpoint; yet another example is in the context of mobile distributed computing, periodic checkpoints of a process running on a mobile host may be stored in different locations, as the mobile host moves between cells [20], and the target checkpoint may be the available or easily accessible checkpoints. In rollback-based failure recovery, the maximum global checkpoint is the most recent consistent global checkpoint (called the *recovery line*), whereas the minimum global checkpoint corresponds to the notion of "move forward only if absolutely necessary during a normal execution" or "undo as much as possible during a rollback" [18].

The maximum and minimum consistent global checkpoints are formally defined below, which are based on partially ordered relations.

Definition 3. *Given a target checkpoint $ckpt_i$ of process p_i, let G denote the consistent global checkpoint, i.e. a set of checkpoints, each from a different process of the computation,*

1). G is the maximum consistent global checkpoint containing $ckpt_i$ if and only if for all $ckpt_j \in G$, $V_j(ckpt_j)[j]$ is the largest in process p_j such that $ckpt_j \parallel ckpt_i$.

2). G is the minimum consistent global checkpoint containing $ckpt_i$ if and only if for all $ckpt_j \in G$, $V_j(ckpt_j)[j]$ is the smallest in process p_j such that $ckpt_j \parallel ckpt_i$.

The algorithms for constructing the maximum and minimum consistent global checkpoints is straightforward after periodically checkpointing the application. Recall that during checkpointing, the process p_i has already maintained a set, S_j, of pair $(l, V_j(ckpt_j))$, i.e. $S_j = \{(l, V_j(ckpt_j) | l = 1, \ldots, last\}$ where *last* is the index for the most recent checkpoint. The construction of maximum consistent global checkpoint proceeds as follows:

1. Given a target checkpoint $ckpt_i$, let G be a global checkpoint, then $G = G + \{ckpt_i\}$.
2. For all $j \neq i$ and $j = 1, \ldots, n$ search S_j from the checkpoint index *last* for the first checkpoint $ckpt_j$ such that $V_j(ckpt_j) \parallel V_i(ckpt_i)$, then $G = G + \{ckpt_j\}$
3. After the search and comparison finish, G is the *maximum* consistent global checkpoint containing the target checkpoint $ckpt_i$ of p_i.

Similarly, if the search and comparison starts from reversing direction, i.e. from $l = 1$ rather than from $l = last$, the set G obtained is the *minimum* consistent global checkpoint containing the target checkpoint $ckpt_i$ of p_i.

6 Conclusion

Consistent global checkpoint is an important paradigm that can be found in many distributed application and was studied extensively [6]. This paper's contributions are :

- First, we presented a necessary and sufficient condition to characterize the consistency. Our characterization differs from the two previous work in that it employs the power of isomorphism between vector time and causality, which makes it simple and straightforward to derive the algorithm for guaranteed mutually consistent global checkpoint.
- Second, the algorithm has adopted a *semi-coordinated approach* towards checkpointing, a combination of *coordinated checkpointing* and *uncoordinated independent checkpointing*, which provides a guaranteed consistency for any checkpoint taken while keeping the coordination to the minimum. Further, our algorithm is vector-time based, this simple mechanism ensures the correctness of the algorithm and its implementation.
- Third, we have demonstrated how our algorithm can be used to find a maximum and minimum consistent global checkpoint, a very useful notion in many applications.

Since vector clock is a well-known mechanism and has been implemented in many distributed algorithms [14, 13], our work can be easily adapted and used in these systems with a little extra effort and cost.

Acknowledgments

We are grateful to the anonymous referees whose comments improved the presentation of this paper.

References

[1] R. Baldoni, J-M. Helary, and M. Raynal. Mutually Consistent Recording in Asynchronous Computation. Technical Report 981, IRISA, Campus de Beaulieu, 35042 Rennes Cedex, France, January 1996.

[2] R. Baldoni, Jean-Michel Helary, and Michel Raynal. About State Recording in Asynchronous Computations (Abstract). In *PODC'96*, page 55, 1996.

[3] Twan Basten, Thomas Kunz, James P. Black, Michael H. Coffin, and David J. Taylor. Vector Time and Causality Among Abstract Events in Distributed Computations. *Distributed Computing*, 11(1):21–39, 1997.

[4] K. Mani Chandy and Leslie Lamport. Distributed Snapshots: Determining Global States of Distributed Systems. *ACM Transactions on Computer Systems*, 3(1):63–75, February 1985.

[5] Carol Critchlow and Kim Taylor. The Inhibition Spectrum and the Achievement of Causal Consistency. *Distributed Computing*, 10(1):11–27, 1996.

[6] E. N. Elnozahy, D. B. Johnson, and Y-M. Wang. A Survey of Rollback-Recovery Protocols in Message-Passing Systems. Technical Report CMU-CS-96-181, CS, CMU, 3 October 1996. Submitted for Publication in *ACM Computing Survey.*

[7] C. J. Fidge. Timestamps in Message-Passing Systems that Preserve Partial Ordering. In *Proceedings of 11th Australian Computer Science Conference*, pages 56–66, February 1988.

[8] Richard Koo and Sam Toueg. Checkpointing and Rollback-Recovery for Distributed System. *IEEE Transactions on Software Engineering*, SE-13(1):23–31, January 1987.

[9] Leslie Lamport. Time, Clocks, and the Ordering of Events in a Distributed System. *Communications of the ACM*, 21(7):558–565, July 1978.

[10] Friedemann Mattern. Virtual Time and Global States of Distributed Systems. In M. Cosnard and P. Quinton, editors, *Proceedings of International Workshop on Parallel and Distributed Algorithms (Chateau de Bonas, France, October 1988)*, pages 215–226, Amsterdam, 1989. Elsevier Science Publishers B. V.

[11] Robert H. B. Netzer and Jian Xu. Necessary and Sufficient Conditions for Consistent Global Snapshots. *IEEE Transactions on Parallel and Distributed Systems*, 6(2):165–169, February 1995.

[12] B. Randell. System Structure for Software Fault Tolerance. *IEEE Transactions on Software Engineering*, SE-1(2):220–232, June 1975.

[13] Michel Raynal, André Schiper, and Sam Toueg. The Causal Ordering Abstraction and a Simple Way to Implement it. *Information Processing Letters*, 39:343–350, 27 September 1991.

[14] Andre Schiper, Jorge Eggli, and Alain Sandoz. A new algorithm to implement causal ordering. In *Distributed Algorithms, 3rd International Workshop Proceedings*, pages 219–232, 1989.

[15] R. Schwarz and F. Mattern. Detecting Causal Relationships in Distributed Computations: In Search of the Holy Grail. *Distributed Computing*, 7(3):149–174, 1994.

[16] R. E. Strom and S. Yemini. Optimistic Recovery in Distributed Systems. *ACM TOCS*, 3(3):204–226, August 1985.

[17] K. Taylor. The Role of Inhibition in Asynchronous Consistent-Cut Protocols. In J.-C. Bermond and M. Raynal, editors, *Distributed Algorithms: 3rd Int'l Workshop*, pages 280–291, Nice, France, September 1989. LNCS 392. Springer-Verlag. Also Tech Report TR 89-995, April 1989, Cornell University.

[18] Yi-Min Wang. Maximum and Minimum Consistenct Global Checkpoints and their Applications. In *Proc. of IEEE 14th Symposium on Reliable Distributed Systems*, pages 86–95, Bad Newenahr, Germany, September 1995. IEEE.

[19] Zhonghua Yang and T. Anthony Marsland. *Global states and time in distributed systems.* IEEE Computer Society Press, 1994. ISBN: 0-8186-5300-0.

[20] Zhonghua Yang, Chengzheng Sun, and Abdul Sattar. Consistent Global States of Mobile Distributed Computations. In *Proceedings of The 1998 International Conference on Parallel and Distributed Processing Techniques and Applications (PDPTA'98)*, Las Vegas, Nevada, USA, July 13-16 1998. To appear.

Type Inference for First-Class Messages with Feature Constraints

Martin Müller[1] and Susumu Nishimura[2]

[1] Universität des Saarlandes, 66041 Saarbrücken, Germany
mmueller@ps.uni-sb.de
[2] RIMS, Kyoto University, Sakyo-ku, Kyoto 606-8502, Japan
nisimura@kurims.kyoto-u.ac.jp

Abstract. We present a constraint system OF of feature trees that is appropriate to specify and implement type inference for first-class messages. OF extends traditional systems of feature constraints by a selection constraint $x\langle y\rangle z$ "by first-class feature tree" y, in contrast to the standard selection constraint $x[f]y$ "by fixed feature" f. We investigate the satisfiability problem of OF and show that it can be solved in polynomial time, and even in quadratic time in an important special case. We compare OF with Treinen's constraint system EF of feature constraints with first-class features, which has an NP-complete satisfiability problem. This comparison yields that the satisfiability problem for OF with negation is NP-hard. Based on OF we give a simple account of type inference for first-class messages in the spirit of Nishimura's recent proposal, and we show that it has polynomial time complexity: We also highlight an immediate extension that is desirable but makes type inference NP-hard.
Keywords: object-oriented programming; first-class messages; constraint-based type inference; complexity; feature constraints

1 Introduction

First-class messages add extra expressiveness to object-oriented programming. First-class messages are analogous to first-class functions in functional programming languages; a message refers to the computation triggered by the corresponding method call, while a functional argument represents the computation executed on application. For example, a **map** method can be defined by means of first-class messages as follows

method **map**(o,l) = *for each message* m *in* l: o ← m

where o is an object, l is a list of first-class messages, and o←m sends message m to o.

First-class messages are more common and crucial in distributed object-oriented programming. A typical use of first-class messages is the delegation of messages to other objects for execution. Such delegate objects are ubiquitous

Jieh Hsiang, Atsushi Ohori (Eds.): ASIAN'98, LNCS 1538, pp. 169–187, 1998.

in distributed systems: for example, proxy servers enable access to external services (*e. g.*, ftp) beyond a firewall. The following delegate object defines simple proxy server:

let ProxyServer = { **new**(o) = { **send**(m) = o ← m} };

This creates an object ProxyServer with a method **new** that receives an object o. The method returns a second object that, on receipt of a message labeled **send** and carrying a message m, forwards m to o. To create a proxy to an FTP server, we can execute

let FtpProxy = ProxyServer ← **new**(ftp);

where ftp refers to an FTP object. A typical use of this new proxy is the following one:

FtpProxy ← **send**(**get**('paper.ps.gz'))

Delegation cannot be easily expressed without first-class messages, since the requested messages are not known statically and must be abstracted over by a variable m.

In a programming language with records, abstraction over messages corresponds to abstraction over field names: For example, one might want to use a function let fn $x = y.x$; to select the field x from record y. Neither first-class messages nor first-class record fields can be type checked in languages from the ML family such as SML [14] or the objective ML dialect O'Caml [24].

Recently, the second author has proposed an extension to the ML type system that can deal with first-class messages [18]. He defines a type inference procedure in terms of kinded unification [20] and proves it correct. This procedure is, however, formally involved and not easily understandable or suitable for further analysis.

In this paper, we give a constraint-based formulation of type inference for first-class messages in the spirit of [18] that considerably simplifies the original formulation, and we settle its complexity. For this purpose, we define a new constraint system over feature trees [3] that we call OF (*objects* and *features*). This constraint system extends known systems of feature constraints [5,30,27,4] by a new tailor-made constraint: this new constraint is motivated by the type inference of a message sending statement o ← m, and pinpoints the key design idea underlying Nishimura's system.

We investigate the (incremental) satisfiability problem for OF and show that it can be solved in polynomial time, and in time $O(n^2)$ for an important special case. We also show that the satisfiability problem for positive and negative OF constraints is NP-hard, by comparing OF with Treinen's feature constraint system EF [30].

Based on OF, we define monomorphic type inference for first-class messages. Our formulation considerably simplifies the original one based on kinded unification. A key difference between both is that we strictly separate the types (semantics) from the type descriptions (syntax), whereas the original system confused syntax and semantics by allowing variables in the types themselves.

From our complexity analysis of OF we obtain that monomorphic type inference for first-class messages can be done in polynomial time. Incrementality is important for modular program analysis without loss of efficiency in comparison to global program analysis. Our constraint-based setup of type inference allows us to explain ML-style polymorphic type inference [10,13] as an instance HM(OF) of the HM(X) scheme [29]: Given a monomorphic type system based on constraint system X, the authors give a generic construction of HM(X), *i. e.*, type inference for ML-style polymorphic constrained types. Type inference for the polymorphic system remains DEXPTIME-complete, of course [11].

In the remainder of the introduction we summarize the main idea of the type system for first-class messages and of the constraint system OF.

1.1 The Type System

The type system contains types for objects and messages and explains what type of messages can be sent to a given object type. An object type is a labeled collection of method types (*i. e.*, a product of function types distinguished by labels) marked by obj. *E. g.*, the object

let o = { **pos**(x) = x>0, **neg**(p) = ¬ p}

implements two methods **pos** and **neg** that behave like functions from integer and boolean to boolean, respectively. Hence, it has an object type obj(**pos**:int → bool, **neg**:bool → bool).[1] When a message $f(M)$ is sent to an object, the corresponding method is selected according to the message label f and then applied to the message argument M. Since a message parameter may refer to a variety of specific messages at run-time, it has a message type marked by msg that collects the corresponding types (as a sum of types distinguished by labels). For example, the expression

m = if b then **pos**(42) else **neg**(true);

defines, depending on b, a message m of message type msg(**pos**:int, **neg**:bool). The expression o ← m is well-typed since two conditions hold:

1. For both labels that are possible for m, **pos** and **neg**, the object o implements a method that accepts the corresponding message arguments of type int or bool.
2. Both methods **pos** and **neg** have the same return type, here bool. Thus the type of o ← m is unique even though the message type is underspecified.

These are the crucial intuitions underlying Nishimura's type system [18]. Our type inferences captures these intuitions fully. Formally, however, our type inference implements a type system that does not exactly match the original one:

[1] Notice that the colons in the type obj(**pos**:int → bool, **neg**:bool → bool) do not separate items from the annotation of their types, but rather the field names from the associated type components. This notation is common in the literature on feature trees and record typing.

Ours is slightly weaker and hence accepts more programs than Nishimura's. This weakness is crucial in order to achieve polynomial time complexity of type inference. However, type inference for a stronger system that fills this gap would require both positive and negative OF constraints and thus make type inference NP-hard.

1.2 Constraint-Based Type Inference

It is well-known that many type inference problems have a natural and simple formulation as the satisfiability problem of an appropriate constraint system (*e. g.* [32,21]). Constraints were also instrumental in generalizing the ML-type system towards record polymorphism [20,23,33], overloading [19,6] and subtyping [1,8] (see also [29]).

Along this line, we adopt *feature trees* [3] as the semantic domain of the constraint system underlying our type system. A feature tree is a possibly infinite tree with unordered marked edges (called *features*) and with marked nodes (called *labels*), where the features at the same node must be pairwise different. For example, the picture on the right shows a feature tree with two features conf and year that is labeled with paper at the root and asian *resp.* 1998 at the leaves.

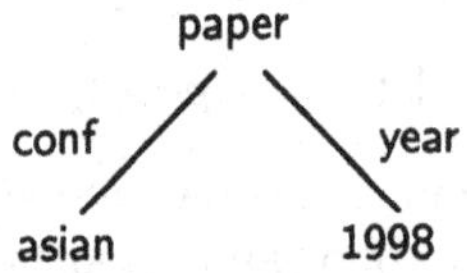

Feature trees can naturally model objects, records, and messages as compound data types with labeled components. A base type like int is a feature tree with label int and no features. A message type $\mathsf{msg}(f_1{:}\tau_1, \ldots, f_n{:}\tau_n)$ is a feature tree with label msg, features $\{f_1, \ldots, f_n\}$, and corresponding subtrees $\{\tau_1, \ldots, \tau_n\}$, and an object type $\mathsf{obj}(f_1{:}\tau_1 \to \tau_1', \ldots, f_n{:}\tau_n \to \tau_n')$ is a feature tree with label obj, features $\{f_1, \ldots, f_n\}$, and corresponding subtrees $\tau_1 \to \tau_1'$ through $\tau_n \to \tau_n'$; the arrow notation $\tau \to \tau'$ in turn is a notational convention for a feature tree with label $\to$ and subtrees τ, τ' at fixed and distinct features d and r, the names of which should remind of "domain" and "range".

Feature trees are the interpretation domain for a class of constraint languages called *feature constraints* [5,30,27,4,16]. These are a class of feature description logics, and, as such, have a long tradition in knowledge representation and in computational linguistics and *constraint-based grammars* [22,25]. More recently, they have been used to model record structures in constraint programming languages [2,27,26].

The constraint language of our system OF is this one:

$$\varphi \quad ::= \quad \varphi \wedge \varphi' \mid x = y \mid a(x) \mid x[f]y \mid F(x) \mid x\langle y \rangle z$$

The first three constraints are the usual ones: The symbol $=$ denotes equality on feature trees, $a(x)$ holds if x denotes a feature tree that is labeled with a at the root, and $x[f]y$ holds if the subtree of (the denotation of) x at feature f is defined and equal to y. For a set of features F, the constraint $F(x)$ holds if x has *at most* the features in F at the root; in contrast, the arity constraint of CFT [27] forces x to have *exactly* the features in F. The constraint $x\langle y \rangle z$ is new. It holds for three feature trees τ_x, τ_y, and τ_z if (i) τ_x has more features at the root than τ_y, and if (ii) for all root features f at τ_y, the subtree of τ_x at f equals $\tau_y.f \rightarrow \tau_z$ (where $\tau_y.f$ is the subtree of τ_y at f).

It is not difficult to see that $x\langle y\rangle z$ is tailored to type inference of message sending. For example the ProxyServer above gets the following polymorphic constrained type:

$$\forall\alpha\beta\gamma\ .\mathsf{obj}(\alpha) \wedge \mathsf{msg}(\beta) \wedge \alpha\langle\beta\rangle\gamma \Rightarrow \ \{\mathbf{new}{:}\alpha \rightarrow \{\mathbf{send}{:}\beta \rightarrow \gamma\}\}$$

Using notation from [29], this describes an object that accepts a message labeled **new** with argument type α, returning an object that accepts a message labeled **send** with argument type β and has return type γ; the type expresses the additional constraint that α be an object type, β be a message type appropriate for α, and the corresponding method type in α has return type γ.

Plan. Section 2 defines the constraint system OF, considers the complexity of its satisfiability problem, and compares OF with the feature constraint systems from the literature. Section 3 applies OF to recast the type inference for first-class messages and compares it with the original system [18]. Section 4 concludes the paper.

Some of the proofs in this paper are only sketched for lack of space. The complete proofs are found in an appendix of the full paper [17].

2 The Constraint System OF

2.1 Syntax and Semantics

The constraint system OF is defined as a class of constraints along with their interpretation over feature trees. We assume two infinite sets $\mathcal{V}$ of *variables* $x, y, z, \ldots$, and $\mathcal{F}$ of *features* $f, \ldots$, where $\mathcal{F}$ contains at least d and r, and a set $\mathcal{L}$ of *labels* $a, b, \ldots$ that contains at least $\rightarrow$: The meaning of constraints depends on this label. We write $\overline{x}$ for a sequence $x_1, \ldots, x_n$ of variables whose length n does not matter, and $\overline{x}{:}\overline{y}$ for a sequence of pairs $x_1{:}y_1, \ldots, x_n{:}y_n$. We use similar notation for other syntactic categories.

Feature Trees. A *path* π is a word over features. The *empty path* is denoted by ε and the free-monoid concatenation of paths π and π' as $\pi\pi'$; we have $\varepsilon\pi = \pi\varepsilon = \pi$. Given paths π and π', π' is called a *prefix of* π if $\pi = \pi'\pi''$ for some path π''. A *tree domain* is a non-empty prefix closed set of paths. A *feature tree* τ is a pair (D, L) consisting of a tree domain D and a *labeling function* $L : D \rightarrow \mathcal{L}$. Given a feature tree τ, we write D_τ for its tree domain and L_τ for its labeling function. The *arity* $\mathsf{ar}(\tau)$ of a feature tree τ is defined by $\mathsf{ar}(\tau) = D_\tau \cap \mathcal{F}$. If $\pi \in D_\tau$, we write as $\tau.\pi$ the subtree of τ at path π: formally $D_{\tau.\pi} = \{\pi' \mid \pi\pi' \in D_\tau\}$ and $L_{\tau.\pi} = \{(\pi', a) \mid (\pi\pi', a) \in L_\tau\}$. A feature tree is *finite* if its tree domain is finite, and *infinite* otherwise. The *cardinality* of a set S is denoted by $\#S$. Given feature trees $\tau_1, \ldots, \tau_n$, distinct features $f_1, \ldots, f_n$, and a label a, we write as

$a(f_1{:}\tau_1, \ldots, f_n{:}\tau_n)$ the feature tree whose domain is $\bigcup_{i=1}^n \{f_i\pi \mid \pi \in D_{\tau_i}\}$ and whose labeling is $\{(\varepsilon, a)\} \cup \bigcup_{i=1}^n \{(f_i\pi, b) \mid (\pi, b) \in L_{\tau_i}\}$. We use $\tau_1 \to \tau_2$ to denote the feature tree τ with $L_\tau = (\varepsilon, \to)$, $\mathsf{ar}(\tau) = \{d, r\}$, $\tau.d = \tau_1$, and $\tau.r = \tau_2$.

Syntax. An *OF constraint* φ is defined as a conjunction of the following *primitive* constraints:

$x = y$	(Equality)
$a(x)$	(Labeling)
$x[f]y$	(Selection)
$F(x)$	(Arity Bound)
$x\langle y\rangle z$	(Object Selection)

Conjunction is denoted by $\wedge$. We write $\varphi' \subseteq \varphi$ if all primitive constraints in φ' are also contained in φ, and we write $x = y \in \varphi$ [etc.] if $x = y$ is a primitive constraint in φ [etc.]. We denote with $F(\varphi)$, $L(\varphi)$, and $V(\varphi)$ the set of features, labels, and variables occurring in a constraint φ. The *size* $S(\varphi)$ of a constraint φ is the number of variable, feature, and label symbols in φ.

Semantics. We interpret OF constraints in the structure $\mathcal{FT}$ of feature trees. The signature of $\mathcal{FT}$ contains the symbol $=$, the ternary relation symbol $\cdot\langle\cdot\rangle\cdot$, for every $a \in \mathcal{L}$ a unary relation symbol $a(\cdot)$, and for every $f \in \mathcal{F}$ a binary relation symbol $\cdot[f]\cdot$. We interpret $=$ as equality on feature trees and the other relation symbols as follows.

$a(\tau)$	if	$(\varepsilon, a) \in L_\tau$
$\tau[f]\tau'$	if	$\tau.f = \tau'$
$F(\tau)$	if	$\mathsf{ar}(\tau) \subseteq F$
$\tau\langle\tau'\rangle\tau''$	if	$\forall f \in \mathsf{ar}(\tau') : f \in \mathsf{ar}(\tau)$ and $\tau.f = \tau'.f \to \tau''$

Let Φ and Φ' be first-order formulas built from OF constraints with the usual first-order connectives $\vee$, $\wedge$, $\neg$, $\to$, *etc.*, and quantifiers. We call Φ *satisfiable* (valid) if Φ is satisfiable (valid) in $\mathcal{FT}$. We say that Φ *entails* Φ', written $\Phi \models_{\mathrm{OF}} \Phi'$, if $\Phi \to \Phi'$ is valid, and that Φ is *equivalent* to Φ' if $\Phi \leftrightarrow \Phi'$ is valid.

A key difference between the selection constraints $x[f]y$ and $x\langle y\rangle z$ is that "selection by (fixed) feature" is functional, while "selection by (first-class) feature tree" is not:

$$x[f]y \wedge x[f]y' \to y = y' \tag{1}$$
$$x\langle y\rangle z \wedge x\langle y\rangle z' \not\to z = z' \tag{2}$$

The reason for the second equation not to hold is that y may have no subtrees: In this case, the constraint $x\langle y\rangle z$ does not constrain z at all. *I. e.*, this implication holds:

$$\{\}(y) \quad \to \quad \forall z\, x\langle y\rangle z \tag{3}$$

If, however, y is known to have at least one feature at the root, then selecting both z and z' by y from x implies equality of z and z':

$$y[f]y' \wedge x\langle y\rangle z \wedge x\langle y\rangle z' \quad \rightarrow \quad z = z' \tag{4}$$

OF cannot express that y has a non-empty arity; rather, to express that y has some feature it must provide a concrete witness. Using negation, this can be expressed as $\neg\{\}(x)$. However, while satisfiability for OF is polynomial, it becomes NP-hard if it is extended such that $\neg\{\}(x)$ can be expressed (see Section 2.3).

Feature Terms. For convenience, we will occasionally use feature terms [3] as a generalization of first-order terms: Feature terms t are built from variables by feature tree construction like $a(f_1{:}t_1, \ldots, f_n{:}t_n)$, where again the features $f_1, \ldots f_n$ are required to be pairwise distinct. Equations between feature terms can be straightforwardly expressed as a conjunction of OF constraints $x = y$, $a(x)$, $F(x)$, $x[f]y$, and existential quantification. For example, the equation $x = a(f{:}b)$ corresponds to the formula $\exists y\ (a(x) \wedge \{f\}(x) \wedge x[f]y \wedge b(y) \wedge \{\}(y))$. In analogy to the notation $\tau_1 \rightarrow \tau_2$, we use the abbreviation $x = y \rightarrow z$ for the equation $x = {\rightarrow}(d{:}y, r{:}z)$.

2.2 Constraint Solving

Theorem 1. *The satisfiability problem of OF constraints is decidable in incremental polynomial space and time.*

For the proof, we define constraint simplification as a rewriting system on constraints in Figure 1. The theorem follows from Propositions 1, 2 and 3 below. Rules (Substitution), (Selection), (Label Clash), and (Arity Clash) are standard. Rules (Arity Propagation I/II) reflect the fact that a constraint $x\langle y\rangle z$ implies the arity bound on x to subsume the one on y. (Arity Intersection) normalizes a constraint to contain at most one arity bound per variable. (Object Selection I) reflects that $x\langle y\rangle z$ implies all features necessary for y to be also necessary for x, and (Object Selection II) establishes the relation of x, y, and z at a joint feature f.

Notice that the number of fresh variables introduced in rule (Object Selection I) is bounded: This rule adds at most one fresh variable per constraint $x\langle y\rangle z$ and feature f and the number of both is constant during constraint simplification. For the subsequent analysis, it is convenient to think of the fresh variables as fixed in advance. Hence, we define the finite set : $V'(\varphi) =_{def} V(\varphi) \cup \{v_{x,f} \in \mathcal{V} \mid x \in V(\varphi), f \in F(\varphi), v_{x,f} \text{ fresh}\}$.

Remark 1. In addition to the rules in Figure 1, there are two additional rules justified by implications (3) and (4):

$$\frac{\varphi \wedge x\langle y\rangle z}{\varphi} \qquad \text{if } \{\}(y) \in \varphi \qquad \text{(Empty Message)}$$

$$\frac{\varphi \wedge x\langle y\rangle z \wedge x\langle y\rangle z'}{\varphi \wedge x\langle y\rangle z \wedge z = z'} \qquad \text{if } y[f]y' \in \varphi \qquad \text{(Non-empty Message)}$$

$$\frac{\varphi \wedge x = y}{\varphi[y/x] \wedge x = y} \quad \text{if } x \in fv(\varphi) \qquad \text{(Substitution)}$$

$$\frac{\varphi \wedge x[f]y \wedge x[f]z}{\varphi \wedge x[f]z \wedge y = z} \qquad \text{(Selection)}$$

$$\frac{\varphi \wedge x\langle y\rangle z \wedge F(x)}{\varphi \wedge x\langle y\rangle z \wedge F(x) \wedge F(y)} \quad \text{if not exists } F' : F'(y) \in \varphi \qquad \text{(Arity Propagation I)}$$

$$\frac{\varphi \wedge x\langle y\rangle z \wedge F(x) \wedge F'(y)}{\varphi \wedge x\langle y\rangle z \wedge F(x) \wedge F \cap F'(y)} \quad \text{if } F \cap F' \neq F' \qquad \text{(Arity Propagation II)}$$

$$\frac{\varphi \wedge F(x) \wedge F'(x)}{\varphi \wedge F \cap F'(x)} \qquad \text{(Arity Intersection)}$$

$$\frac{\varphi}{\varphi \wedge x[f]x'} \quad \text{if } x\langle y\rangle z \wedge y[f]y' \in \varphi \text{ and not exists } z : x[f]z \in \varphi,\ x' \text{ fresh} \qquad \text{(Object Selection I)}$$

$$\frac{\varphi}{\varphi \wedge x' = y' \to z} \quad \text{if } x\langle y\rangle z \wedge y[f]y' \wedge x[f]x' \in \varphi \text{ and } x' = y' \to z \notin \varphi \qquad \text{(Object Selection II)}$$

$$\frac{\varphi \wedge a(x) \wedge b(x)}{\text{fail}} \quad \text{if } a \neq b \qquad \text{(Label Clash)}$$

$$\frac{\varphi \wedge F(x) \wedge x[f]x'}{\text{fail}} \quad \text{if } f \notin F \qquad \text{(Arity Clash)}$$

Fig. 1. Constraint Solving Rules

The first one is just a simplification rule that does not have an impact on the satisfiability check. It helps reducing the size of a solved constraint and therefore saves space and time. Secondly, compact presentation of a solved constraint can be crucial in the type inference application where solved constraints must be understood by programmers. The second one is a derived rule that should be given priority over rule (Object Selection II).

Proposition 1. *The rewrite system in Figure 1 terminates on all OF constraints* φ.

Proof. Let φ be an arbitrary constraint. Obviously, $F(\varphi)$ is a finite set and the number of occurring features is fixed since no rule adds new feature symbols. Secondly, recall that the number of fresh variables introduced in rule (Object Selection I) is bounded. Call a variable x *eliminated* in a constraint $x = y \wedge \varphi$ if $x \notin V(\varphi)$. We use the constraint measure (O_1, O_2, A, E, S) defined by

(O_1) number of sextuples (x, y, z, x', y', f) of non-eliminated variables $x, y, z, x', y' \in V'(\varphi)$ and features $f \in F(\varphi)$ such that $x\langle y\rangle z \wedge x[f]x' \wedge y[f]y' \in \varphi$ but $x' = y' \to z \notin \varphi$.

(O_2) number of tuples (x, f) of non-eliminated variables $x \in V'(\varphi)$ and features $f \in F(\varphi)$ such that there exists y, y' and z with $x\langle y\rangle z \wedge y[f]y' \in \varphi$ but $x[f]x' \notin \varphi$ for any x'.

(A) number of non-eliminated variables $x \in V'(\varphi)$ for which no arity bound $F(x) \in \varphi$ exists.

(E) number of non-eliminated variables.

(S) size of constraint as defined above.

The measure of φ is bounded and strictly decreased by every rule application as the following table shows. this proves our claim.

	O_1	O_2	A	E	S
(Arity Propagation II)	$=$	$=$	$=$	$=$	$<$
(Arity Intersection)	$=$	$=$	$=$	$=$	$<$
(Selection)	$=$	$=$	$=$	$=$	$<$
(Substitution)	$\leq$	$\leq$	$\leq$	$<$	$=$
(Arity Propagation I)	$=$	$=$	$<$	$=$	$>$
(Object Selection I)	$=$	$<$	$>$	$>$	$>$
(Object Selection II)	$<$	$=$	$=$	$=$	$>$

□

Proposition 2. *We can implement the rewrite system in Figure 1 such that it uses space $O(n^3)$ and incremental time $O(n^5)$, or, if the number of features is bounded, such that it uses linear space and incremental time $O(n^2)$.*

Proof. We implement the constraint solver as a rewriting on pairs (P, S) where S is the store that flags failure or represents a satisfiable constraint in a solved form, and where P is the pool (multiset) of primitive constraints that still must be added to S. To decide satisfiability of φ we start the rewriting on the pool of primitive constraints in φ and the empty store and check the failure flag on termination.

For lack of space, we defer some involved parts of the proof to the full paper [17].

Define $n_i = \#V(\varphi)$, $n_v = n_i \cdot n_f = \#V'(\varphi)$, $n_l = \#L(\varphi)$, $n_f = \#F(\varphi)$. In the full paper, we define a data structure for the store that consists of a union-find data structure [12] for equations, tables for the constraints $a(x)$, $F(x)$, and $x[f]z$, a list for constraints $x\langle y\rangle z$, and two adjacency list representations of the graphs whose nodes are the initial variables, and whose edges (x, y) are given by the constraints $x\langle y\rangle z$ for the first one and $y\langle x\rangle z$ for the second one. (See appendix of the full paper [17] for details). This data structure has size

$$O(n_i \cdot n_f + n_i + n_v \cdot n_f + n_i \cdot n_f + n) \quad = \quad O(n_v \cdot n_f + n)$$

which is $O(n)$ if the number of features is assumed constant and $O(n^3)$ otherwise. It also allows to check in time $O(1)$ whether it contains a given primitive constraint; and to add it in quasi-constant time.[2] This is clear in the non-incremental

[2] All constraints except equations can be added in time $O(1)$, but addition of an equation costs amortized time $O(\alpha(n_v))$ where $\alpha(n_v)$ is the inverse of Ackermann's function. For all practical purposes, $\alpha(n_v)$ can be considered as constant.

(off-line) case where n_v, n_i, n_f,and n_s are fixed. In the incremental (on-line) case, where n_v, n_i, n_f, and n_s may grow, we can use dynamically extensible hash tables [7] to retain constant time check and update for primitive constraints.

Each step of the algorithm removes a primitive constraint from the pool P, adds it to the store S, and then derives all its immediate consequences under the simplification rules: Amongst them, equations $x = y$ and selections $x[f]y$ are put back into the pool, while selections $x\langle y\rangle z$ and arity bounds $F(x)$ are directly added to the store.

We show that every step can be implemented such that it costs time $O(n+n_i \cdot n_f)$.[3] (The complete analysis of this time bound can be found in appendix of the full paper [17]). We also show that every step may at most add $O(n)$ equations and $O(n_v)$ selection constraints of the form $x[f]y$. It remains to estimate the number of steps: There are at least $O(n)$ steps needed for touching all primitive constraints in φ.

- Amongst the new equations, there are at most $O(n_v)$ relevant ones, in the sense that one can at most execute n_v equations before all variables are equated. That is, all but $O(n_v)$ equations cost constant time.
- Amongst the new selection constraint, there are at most $O(n_v \cdot n_f)$ relevant ones since adding a selection constraint $x[f]y$ induces immediate work only if x has no selection constraint on f yet. The others will generate a new equation and terminate then. Hence, all but $O(n_v \cdot n_f)$ selection constraints cost constant time.

In summary, there are $O(n+n_v \cdot n_f)$ steps that cost $O(n+n_i \cdot n_f)$. Each of these steps may add $O(n)$ equations and $O(n_v)$ selections each of which may add a new equation itself. Hence we have $O((n + n_v \cdot n_f) \cdot (n + n_v))$ steps that cost $O(1)$. Overall, the algorithm has the complexity

$$O((n+n_v \cdot n_f) \cdot (n+n_i \cdot n_f) + (n+n_v \cdot n_f) \cdot (n+n_v) \cdot 1) \;=\; O((n+n_v \cdot n_f) \cdot (n+n_i \cdot n_f))$$

Since $O(n_f) = O(n)$ and $O(n_v) = O(n_i \cdot n_f) = O(n^2)$, this bound is $O(n^5)$. If the number of features is bounded, $O(n_v) = O(n_i) = O(n)$, so the bound is rather $O(n^2)$. □

Notice that a constraint system of records with first-class record labels is obtained as an obvious restriction of OF and the above result implies the same time complexity bound as OF.

Proposition 3. *Every OF constraint φ which is closed under the rules in Figure 1 (and hence is different from fail) is satisfiable.*

Proof. For the proof, we need to define a notion of path reachability similar to the one used in earlier work, such as [15,16]. For all paths π and constraints φ,

[3] To be precise, each step costs $O(n + n_i \cdot n_f + \alpha(n_v))$ which we sloppily simplify to $O(n + n_i \cdot n_f)$.

we define a binary relation $\overset{\varphi}{\rightsquigarrow}_\pi$, where $x \overset{\varphi}{\rightsquigarrow}_\pi y$ reads as "y is reachable from x over path π in φ":

$$\begin{array}{ll} x \overset{\varphi}{\rightsquigarrow}_\varepsilon x & \text{for every } x \\ x \overset{\varphi}{\rightsquigarrow}_\varepsilon y & \text{if} \quad y = x \in \varphi \text{ or } x = y \in \varphi \\ x \overset{\varphi}{\rightsquigarrow}_f y & \text{if} \quad x[f]y \in \varphi \\ x \overset{\varphi}{\rightsquigarrow}_{\pi\pi'} y & \text{if} \quad x \overset{\varphi}{\rightsquigarrow}_\pi z \text{ and } z \overset{\varphi}{\rightsquigarrow}_{\pi'} y. \end{array}$$

Define relations $x \overset{\varphi}{\rightsquigarrow}_\pi a$ meaning that "label a can be reached from x over path π in φ":

$$x \overset{\varphi}{\rightsquigarrow}_\pi a \quad \text{if} \quad x \overset{\varphi}{\rightsquigarrow}_\pi y \text{ and } a(y) \in \varphi$$

Fix an arbitrary label unit. For every closed constraint φ we define the mapping α from variables into feature trees defined as follows.

$$\begin{array}{rcl} D_{\alpha(x)} & = & \{\pi \mid \text{exists } y : \ x \overset{\varphi}{\rightsquigarrow}_\pi y\} \\ L_{\alpha(x)} & = & \{(\pi, a) \mid x \overset{\varphi}{\rightsquigarrow}_\pi a\} \cup \{(\pi, \mathsf{unit}) \mid \pi \in D_{\alpha(x)} \text{ but } \nexists a : x \overset{\varphi}{\rightsquigarrow}_\pi a\} \end{array}$$

It remains to be shown that α defines a mapping into feature trees for closed constraints φ, and that α indeed satisfies φ. This can be done by a straightforward induction over paths π. □

2.3 Relation to Feature Constraint Systems

We compare OF with feature constraint systems in the literature: Given a two-sorted signature with variables $x, y, z, \ldots$ and $u, v, w, \ldots$ ranging over feature trees and features, *resp.*, collections of feature constraints from the following list have, amongst others, been considered [3,27,30]:

$$\varphi \quad ::= \quad x = y \mid a(x) \mid x[f]y \mid Fx \mid u = f \mid x[u]y \mid \varphi \wedge \varphi'$$

The constraints $x = y$, $a(x)$, and $x[f]y$ are the ones of OF. The arity bound Fx (where F is a finite set of features) states that x has *exactly* the features in F at the root.

$$F\tau \quad \text{if} \quad \mathsf{ar}(\tau) = F$$

Apparently, both arity constraints are interreducible by means of disjunctions: $F(x) \leftrightarrow \bigvee_{F' \subseteq F} F'x$. The constraints of FT [3] contain $x = y$, $a(x)$, and $x[f]y$, CFT [27] extends FT by Fx, and EF [30] contains the constraints $x{=}y$, $a(x)$, $x = f$, Fx, and $x[u]y$.

The satisfiability problems for FT and CFT are quasi-linear [27]. In contrast, the satisfiability problem for EF is NP-hard, as Treinen shows by reducing the minimal cover problem to it [30,9]. Crucial in this proof is the following implication

$$\{f_1, \ldots, f_n\}x \wedge x[u]y \quad \rightarrow \quad \bigvee_{i=1}^{n} u = f_i$$

In order to express a corresponding disjunction in OF, we need existential quantification and constraints of the form $\neg\{\}(y)$

$$\{f_1,\ldots,f_n\}(x) \wedge x\langle y\rangle z \wedge \neg\{\}(y) \quad \rightarrow \quad \bigvee_{i=1}^{n} \exists z_i\; y[f_i]z_i$$

With this new constraint we reduce the satisfiability check for EF to the one for OF.

Proposition 4. *There is an embedding* $[\![\cdot]\!]$ *from EF constraints into OF with negative constraints of the form* $\neg\{\}(x)$ *such that every EF constraint* φ *is satisfiable iff* $[\![\varphi]\!]$ *is.*

Proof. Labeling $a(x)$ and equality $x = y$ translate trivially. Now assume two special labels unit and lab; we use these to represent labels f in EF by feature trees lab(f:unit).

$$\begin{array}{rcl} [\![u = f]\!] & = & \exists x\;(\mathsf{lab}(u) \wedge \{f\}(u) \wedge u[f]x \wedge \mathsf{unit}(x) \wedge \{\}(x)) \\ [\![x[u]y]\!] & = & x\langle u\rangle y \wedge \neg\{\}(u) \\ [\![\{f_1,\ldots,f_n\}x]\!] & = & \{f_1,\ldots,f_n\}(x) \wedge \bigwedge_{i=1}^{n} \exists y\; x[f_i]y \end{array}$$

To show that satisfiability of an EF constraint φ implies satisfiability of the OF constraint $[\![\varphi]\!]$ we map every EF solution of φ to an OF solution of $[\![\varphi]\!]$ by replacing every feature f by lab(f:unit) and every feature tree of the form $a(f{:}\tau\ldots)$ by $a(f{:}\mathsf{unit} \rightarrow \tau\ldots)$.

For the inverse, we take a satisfiable OF constraint $[\![\varphi]\!]$ and construct an OF solution of $[\![\varphi]\!]$ which maps all variables u in selector position in $x\langle u\rangle y$ to a feature tree with exactly one feature. From this solution we derive an EF solution of φ by replacing these singleton-feature trees by their unique feature. Notice that the solution constructed in the proof of Proposition 3 does not suffice since it may map u to a feature tree without any feature.

Formally, we extend the definition of path reachability by $x \overset{\varphi}{\rightsquigarrow}_\pi F$ meaning that "arity bound F can be reached from x over path π in φ":

$$x \overset{\varphi}{\rightsquigarrow}_\pi F \quad \text{if} \quad x \overset{\varphi}{\rightsquigarrow}_\pi y \text{ and } F(y) \in \varphi$$

We assume an order on $F(\varphi)$, and, for non-empty F, let $min(F)$ denote the smallest feature in F wrt. this order. We define α as follows:

$$\begin{array}{rcl} D_{\alpha(x)} & = & \{\pi \mid \text{exists } y : x \overset{\varphi}{\rightsquigarrow}_\pi y\} \cup \{\pi f \mid x \overset{\varphi}{\rightsquigarrow}_\pi F, f = min(F)\} \\ L_{\alpha(x)} & = & \{(\pi, a) \mid x \overset{\varphi}{\rightsquigarrow}_\pi a\} \cup \{(\pi, \mathsf{unit}) \mid \pi \in D_{\alpha(x)}, \nexists a : x \overset{\varphi}{\rightsquigarrow}_\pi a\} \end{array}$$

By the constraint $\neg\{\}(u)$ in the translation of $x\langle u\rangle y$ we know that, for closed and non-failed φ, the set F must be non-empty in the first line. Hence, α is a well-defined mapping into feature trees. It is easy to show that α satisfies φ and that α corresponds to an EF solution as sketched above. □

Corollary 1. *The satisfiability problem of every extension of OF that can express* $\neg\{\}(x)$ *is NP-hard.*

For example, the satisfiability problem of positive and negative OF constraints is NP-hard.

3 Type Inference

We reformulate the type inference of [18] in terms of OF constraints. As in that paper, we consider a tiny object-oriented programming language with this abstract syntax.[4]

$$\begin{array}{rcll} M & ::= & b & \text{(Constant)} \\ & | & x & \text{(Variable)} \\ & | & f(M) & \text{(Message)} \\ & | & \{f_1(x_1) = M_1, \ldots, f_n(x_n) = M_n\} & \text{(Object)} \\ & | & M \leftarrow N & \text{(Message Passing)} \\ & | & \mathsf{let}\ y = M\ \mathsf{in}\ N & \text{(Let Binding)} \end{array}$$

The operational semantics contains no surprise (see [18]). For the types, we assume additional distinct labels msg and obj to mark message and object types, and a set of distinct labels such as int, bool, *etc.*, to mark base types. Monomorphic *types* are all feature trees over this signature; monomorphic *type terms* are feature terms:

$$\begin{array}{rcll} t & ::= & \alpha & \text{(Type variable)} \\ & | & \mathsf{int} \mid \mathsf{bool} \mid \ldots & \text{(Base type)} \\ & | & \mathsf{msg}(f_1{:}t_1, \ldots, f_n{:}t_n) & \text{(Message type)} \\ & | & \mathsf{obj}(f_1{:}t_1 \to t'_1, \ldots, f_n{:}t_n \to t'_n) & \text{(Object type)} \end{array}$$

Somewhat sloppily, we allow for infinite (regular) feature terms such as to incorporate recursive types without an explicit μ notation. Recursive types are necessary for the analysis of recursive objects. We assume a mapping typeof from constants of base type to their corresponding types. We also use the *kinding* notation $x :: a(f_1{:}t_1, \ldots, f_n{:}t_n)$ to constrain x to a feature tree whose arity is underspecified, *e. g.*, $a(x) \wedge \bigwedge_{i=1}^{n} x[f_i]t_i$.

Monomorphic Type Inference. The monomorphic type system is given in Figure 2. As usual, Γ is a finite mapping from variables to type terms and $\Gamma; x : t$ extends Γ so that it maps variable x to t. The type system defines judgments $\varphi, \Gamma \vdash M : t$ which reads as "under the type assumptions in Γ subject to the constraint φ, the expression M has type t";[5] the constraint φ in well-formed judgements is required to be satisfiable. We do not comment further on the type system here but refer to [18] for intuitions and to [29,28] for notation. The corresponding type inference is given in Figure 3 as a mapping $\mathcal{I}$ from a variable x and a program expressions M to an OF constraint such that every solution of x in $\mathcal{I}(x, M)$ is a type of M. For ease of reading, we use the bound variables in program expressions as their corresponding type variables.

[4] In contrast to [18], we drop letobj and allow let to introduce recursively defined expressions.

[5] This terminology is slightly sloppy but common: Since t may contain type variables it is rather a type *term* than a type and it would be accurate to say that M has "some type matching t".

$$\frac{x : t \in \Gamma}{\varphi, \Gamma \vdash x : t}\ \textsc{Var} \qquad \frac{}{\varphi, \Gamma \vdash b : \mathsf{typeof}(b)}\ \textsc{Const} \qquad \frac{\varphi, \Gamma \vdash M : t' \quad \varphi \models_{\mathrm{OF}} t :: \mathsf{msg}(f : t')}{\varphi, \Gamma \vdash f(M) : t}\ \textsc{Msg}$$

$$\frac{\varphi, \Gamma; x_i : t_i \vdash M_i : t'_i \quad \text{for every } i = 1, \ldots, n}{\varphi, \Gamma \vdash \{f_1(x_1) = M_1, \ldots, f_n(x_n) = M_n\} : \mathsf{obj}(f_1{:}t_1{\to}t'_n, \ldots, f_n{:}t_n{\to}t'_n)}\ \textsc{Obj}$$

$$\frac{\varphi, \Gamma \vdash M : t_1 \quad \varphi, \Gamma \vdash N : t_2 \quad \varphi \models_{\mathrm{OF}} \mathsf{obj}(t_1) \wedge \mathsf{msg}(t_2) \wedge t_1 \langle t_2 \rangle t_3}{\varphi, \Gamma \vdash M \leftarrow N : t_3}\ \textsc{MsgPass}$$

$$\frac{\varphi, \Gamma; y : t_1 \vdash M : t_1 \quad \varphi, \Gamma; y : t_1 \vdash N : t_2}{\varphi, \Gamma \vdash \mathsf{let}\ y = M\ \mathsf{in}\ N : t_2}\ \textsc{Let}\ \text{(monomorphic)}$$

Fig. 2. The Monomorphic Type System

$$\begin{array}{lcll}
\mathcal{I}(x, b) & = & a(x) \wedge \{\}(x) & \text{if } a = \mathsf{typeof}(b) \\
\mathcal{I}(x, y) & = & x = y & \\
\mathcal{I}(x, f(M)) & = & \exists y\ (\mathsf{msg}(x) \wedge x[f]y \wedge \mathcal{I}(y, M)) & \\
\mathcal{I}(x, \{f_1(x_1) = M_1, \ldots, f_n(x_n) = M_n\}) & = & \mathsf{obj}(x) \wedge \{f_1, \ldots, f_n\}(x) \wedge & \\
 & & \bigwedge_{i=1}^{n} \exists x_i\ \exists x'\ \exists z\ (x[f_i]x' \wedge x' = x_i \to z \wedge \mathcal{I}(z, M_i)) & \\
\mathcal{I}(x, M \leftarrow N) & = & \exists y\ \exists z\ (y\langle z \rangle x \wedge \mathsf{obj}(y) \wedge \mathcal{I}(y, M) \wedge \mathsf{msg}(z) \wedge \mathcal{I}(z, N)) & \\
\mathcal{I}(x, \mathsf{let}\ y = M\ \mathsf{in}\ N) & = & \exists y\ (\mathcal{I}(y, M) \wedge \mathcal{I}(x, N)) &
\end{array}$$

Fig. 3. Monomorphic Type Inference for First-Class Messages with OF Constraints

Correctness of the type inference with respect to the type system is obvious, and it should be clear that soundness of the type system (with respect to the assumed operational semantics) can be shown along the lines given in [18]. The type inference generates a constraint whose size is proportional to the size of the given program expression. Hence, we know from Proposition 2 that type inference can be done in polynomial time and space.[6]

Let us give some examples. To reduce the verbosity of OF constraints, we shall freely use feature term equations as introduced above. First, the statement

let o1 = {**succ**(x)=x+1, **pos**(x)=x>0};

defines an object with two methods **succ** : int→int and **pos** : int→bool. Type inference gives the type of this object as an OF constraint on the type variable o_1 equivalent to

$$\varphi_1 \quad \equiv \quad o_1 = \mathsf{obj}(\mathbf{succ} : \mathsf{int}{\to}\mathsf{int}, \mathbf{pos} : \mathsf{int}{\to}\mathsf{bool}).$$

[6] To be precise, we have to show that every satisfiable OF constraint derived by type inference is satisfiable in the smaller domain of types; this is easy.

A delegate object for the object o1 is defined as follows:

let o2 = {**redirect**(m)= o1 ← m};

where m is a parameter that binds messages to be redirected to o1. Assuming the variable o_1 to be constrained by φ_1, the constraint φ_2 restricts o_2 to the type of o2:

$$\varphi_2 \quad \equiv \quad \exists m\, \exists z\, (o_2 = \mathsf{obj}(\mathbf{redirect} : m {\rightarrow} z) \wedge o_1\langle m\rangle z \wedge \mathsf{msg}(m)).$$

The return type of a message passing to this object, *e. g.*,

let w = o2← **redirect**(**succ**(1));

is described as the solution of $\varphi_1 \wedge \varphi_2 \wedge \varphi_3$ for the type variable w, where

$$\varphi_3 \quad \equiv \quad \exists z'\, (o_2\langle z'\rangle w \wedge z' :: \mathsf{msg}(\mathbf{redirect} : \mathsf{msg}(\mathbf{succ} : \mathsf{int}))),$$

The solved form of $\varphi_1 \wedge \varphi_2 \wedge \varphi_3$ contains the primitive constraint $\mathsf{int}(w)$, which tells the intended result type int.

If o1 does not respond to the message argument of **redirect**, for instance as in

let v = o2← **redirect**(**pred**(1)),

a type error is detected as inconsistency in the derived constraint. Here, the constraint

$$\varphi_4 \quad \equiv \quad \exists z'\, (o_2\langle z'\rangle w' \wedge z' :: \mathsf{msg}(\mathbf{redirect} : \mathsf{msg}(\mathbf{pred} : \mathsf{int})))$$

implies $\exists z'\, (o_1\langle z'\rangle w' \wedge z' :: \mathsf{msg}(\mathbf{pred} : \mathsf{int}))$, and hence that o_1 has a feature **pred** which contradicts φ_1 by an arity clash.

Now recall that in OF the implication $x\langle y\rangle z \wedge x\langle y\rangle z' \rightarrow z = z'$ does *not* hold. The following example demonstrates how this weakness affects typing and type inference.

let o1 = {**a**(x)=x+1, **b**(x)=x>0} in o2 = {**b**(x)=x=0,**c**(x)=x*2}
in o3 = {**foo**(m)= begin o1← m; o2←m end};

It is easy to see that the **foo** method always returns bool, since the argument message of **foo** must be accepted by both the objects o1 and o2, which share only the method name **b**. However, type inference for this program derives (essentially) the constraint

$$o_1 = \mathsf{obj}(\mathbf{a} : \mathsf{int}{\rightarrow}\mathsf{int}, \mathbf{b} : \mathsf{int}{\rightarrow}\mathsf{bool}) \wedge o_2 = \mathsf{obj}(\mathbf{b} : \mathsf{int}{\rightarrow}\mathsf{bool}, \mathbf{c} : \mathsf{int}{\rightarrow}\mathsf{int}) \wedge$$
$$o_3 = \mathsf{obj}(\mathbf{foo} : m{\rightarrow}z) \wedge o_1\langle m\rangle z_1 \wedge o_2\langle m\rangle z_2$$

Herein, the result type z of the method **foo** is neither entailed to equal z_1 nor z_2. This is reasonable since the message m in this program is not sent and hence may safely return anything. By a similar argument, the following program can be considered acceptable:

let o1 = {a(x)=x+1} in o2 = {c(x)=x*2}
in o3 = {**foo**(m)= **begin if** b **then** o1←m **else** o2←m **end**}

One may complain that this kind of methods should be detected as a type error. Manipulating the type system and the type inference to do this is easy: One just needs to exclude types msg(), *i. e.*, message types without any feature. However, recall that the polynomial time complexity of the analysis depends on this weakness: The corresponding clause in the type inference

$$\mathcal{I}(x, f(M)) = \exists y\,(\neg\{\}(x) \wedge \mathsf{msg}(x) \wedge x[f]y \wedge \mathcal{I}(y, M))$$

generates OF constraints with negation such that constraint solving (and hence, type inference) would become NP-hard.[7]

Polymorphic Type Inference. We can obtain the polymorphic type inference by applying the scheme HM(X) [29]. The constraint system OF is a viable parameter for HM(X) since it satisfies the two required properties, called coherence and soundness. Both rely on a notion of monomorphic types, in our case, given by feature trees; it does no harm that these may be infinite. The *coherence* property requires that the considered order on types is semantically well-behaved; this is trivial in our case since we only consider a trivial order on feature trees. The *soundness* property that a solved constraint indeed has a solution follows from Proposition 3.

Comparison with Nishimura. In Nishimura's original type system [18], abbreviated as $\mathcal{D}$ in the following, constraints are modeled as kinded type variables. The kindings have a straightforward syntactic correspondence with OF constraints: the message kinding $x :: \langle\!\langle f_1{:}t_1, \ldots, f_n{:}t_n \rangle\!\rangle_F$ corresponds to $x :: \mathsf{msg}(f_1{:}t_1, \ldots, f_n{:}t_n) \wedge F(x)$ and the object kinding $x :: \{\!|y_1 \to t_1, \ldots, y_n \to t_n|\!\}_F$ corresponds to $\mathsf{obj}(x) \wedge \bigwedge_{i=1}^{n} x\langle y_i \rangle t_i \wedge F(x)$.

Our reformulation HM(OF) of $\mathcal{D}$ is in the same spirit as the reformulation HM(REC) [29] of Ohori's type system for the polymorphic record calculus: Both recast the kinding system as a constraint system. One might thus expect the relation of $\mathcal{D}$ and HM(OF) to be as close as that between Ohori's system and HM(REC) which type exactly the same programs ("full and faithful"); this is, however, not the case.

There is a significant difference between the the kind system in $\mathcal{D}$ and OF. In $\mathcal{D}$, kinded types may contain variables, *e. g.*, an object returning integers as a response to messages of type y receives the kind $\{\!|y \to \mathsf{int}|\!\}_F$. On unifying two types with kindings $\{\!|y \to \mathsf{int}|\!\}_F$ and $\{\!|y \to z|\!\}_F$, the type inference for $\mathcal{D}$ unifies z and int since it is *syntactically* known that both z and int denote the type of the response of the same object to the same message. Thus in $\mathcal{D}$, the name of type variables is crucial. In this paper, variables only occur as part of type descriptions (*i. e.*,

[7] The altered type inference does still not exactly correspond to the original. For example, we would not accept message sending to an empty object as in {} ← m, while the original one does.

syntax) while the (semantic) domain of types does not contain variables. *E. g.*, we understand $\{\!|y\rightarrow\mathsf{int}|\!\}$ not as a *type* but as part of a *type description* which can be expressed by a constraint like $\mathsf{obj}(x) \wedge x\langle y\rangle\mathsf{int}$.

As a consequence, well-typedness in our system does not depend on the choice of variable names but only on the type of variables. This is usual for ML-style type systems but does not hold for $\mathcal{D}$. Consider the following example:

$$\{\mathbf{foo}(\mathsf{m}) = (\mathsf{o}\leftarrow\mathsf{m}) + 1;\ (\mathsf{o}\leftarrow\mathsf{m})\ \&\ \mathsf{true}\}$$

This program is accepted by the OF-based type system, since the constraint $o\langle m\rangle\mathsf{int} \wedge o\langle m\rangle\mathsf{bool}$ is satisfiable. The type system $\mathcal{D}$, however, rejects it after trying to unify int and bool during type inference. To insist that this is a syntactic argument notice that $\mathcal{D}$ accepts the following program, where o is replaced by the object constant {}:

$$\{\mathbf{baz}(\mathsf{m}) = (\{\}\leftarrow\mathsf{m}) + 1;\ (\{\}\leftarrow\mathsf{m})\ \&\ \mathsf{true}\}$$

4 Conclusion

We have presented a new constraint system OF over feature trees and investigated the complexity of its satisfiability problem. OF is designed for specification and implementation of type inference for first-class messages in the spirit of Nishimura's system [18]. We have given a type system for which monomorphic type inference with OF constraints can be done in polynomial time; this system is weaker than the original one, but the additional expressiveness would render monomorphic type inference NP-hard as we have shown. Given OF, we can add ML-style polymorphism by instantiating the recent HM(X) scheme to the constraint system OF.

Acknowledgements. We would like to thank the members of RIMS, Andreas Rossberg and Joachim Walser for careful proofreading and feedback, as well as Martin Sulzmann for extensive discussion on HM(X). We also acknowledge helpful remarks of the referees.

References

1. A. Aiken and E. Wimmers. Type inclusion constraints and type inference. In *Proceedings of the 6th ACM Conference on Functional Programming and Computer Architecture*, pp. 31–41. ACM Press, New York, June 1993.
2. H. Aït-Kaci and A. Podelski. Towards a meaning of life. *The Journal of Logic Programming*, 16(3 – 4):195–234, July, Aug. 1993.
3. H. Aït-Kaci, A. Podelski, and G. Smolka. A feature-based constraint system for logic programming with entailment. *Theoretical Computer Science*, 122(1–2):263–283, Jan. 1994.
4. R. Backofen. A complete axiomatization of a theory with feature and arity constraints. *The Journal of Logic Programming*, 24(1 – 2):37–71, 1995. Special Issue onComputational Linguistics and Logic Programming.

5. R. Backofen and G. Smolka. A complete and recursive feature theory. *Theoretical Computer Science*, 146(1–2):243–268, July 1995.
6. F. Bourdoncle and S. Merz. Type checking higher-order polymorphic multi-methods. In *Proceedings of the 24th ACM Symposium on Principles of Programming Languages*, pp. 302–315. ACM Press, New York, Jan. 1997.
7. M. Dietzfelbinger, A. Karlin, K. Mehlhorn, F. Meyer Auf Der Heide, H. Rohnert, and R. E. Tarjan. Dynamic perfect hashing: Upper and lower bounds. *SIAM Journal of Computing*, 23(4):738–761, Aug. 1994.
8. J. Eifrig, S. Smith, and V. Trifonow. Type inference for recursively constrained types and its application to object-oriented programming. *Electronic Notes in Theoretical Computer Science*, 1, 1995.
9. M. R. Garey and D. S. Johnson. *Computers and Intractability: A Guide to the Theory of NP-Completeness.* W.H. Freeman and Company, New York, 1979.
10. R. Hindley. The principal type scheme of an object in combinatory logic. *Transactions of the American Mathematical Society*, 146:29–60, Dec. 1969.
11. H. G. Mairson. Deciding ML typebility is complete for deterministic exponential time. In *Proceedings of the 17th ACM Symposium on Principles of Programming Languages*, pp. 382–401. ACM Press, New York, Jan. 1990.
12. K. Mehlhorn and P. Tsakalides. Data structures. In van Leeuwen [31], chapter 6, pp. 301–342.
13. R. Milner. A theory of type polymorphism in programming. *Journal of Computer and System Science*, 17(3):348–375, 1978.
14. R. Milner, M. Tofte, R. Harper, and D. MacQueen. *The Definition of Standard ML (Revised).* The MIT Press, Cambridge, MA, 1997.
15. M. Müller, J. Niehren, and A. Podelski. Inclusion constraints over non-empty sets of trees. In M. Bidoit and M. Dauchet, eds., *Proceedings of the Theory and Practice of Software Development*, vol. 1214 of *Lecture Notes in Computer Science*, pp. 345–356. Springer-Verlag, Berlin, Apr. 1997.
16. M. Müller, J. Niehren, and A. Podelski. Ordering constraints over feature trees. In G. Smolka, ed., *Proceedings of the 3rd International Conference on Principles and Practice of Constraint Programming*, vol. 1330 of *Lecture Notes in Computer Science*, pp. 297–311. Springer-Verlag, Berlin, 1997. Full version submitted to special journal issue of CP'97.
17. M. Müller and S. Nishimura. Type inference for first-class messages with feature constraints. Technical report, Programming Systems Lab, Universität des Saarlandes, 1998. `http://www.ps.uni-sb.de/Papers/abstracts/FirstClass98.html`.
18. S. Nishimura. Static typing for dynamic messages. In *Proceedings of the 25th ACM Symposium on Principles of Programming Languages*, pp. 266–278. ACM Press, New York, 1998.
19. M. Odersky, P. Wadler, and M. Wehr. A second look at overloading. In *Proceedings of the 7th ACM Conference on Functional Programming and Computer Architecture.* ACM Press, New York, 1995.
20. A. Ohori. A polymorphic record calculus and its compilation. *ACM Transactions on Programming Languages and Systems*, 17(6):844–895, 1995.
21. J. Palsberg. Efficient inference of object types. In *Proceedings of the 9th IEEE Symposium on Logic in Computer Science*, pp. 186–185. IEEE Computer Society Press, 1994.
22. C. Pollard and I. Sag. *Head-Driven Phrase Structure Grammar.* Studies in Contemporary Linguistics. Cambridge University Press, Cambridge, England, 1994.

23. D. Rémy. Type checking records and variants in a natural extension of ML. In *Proceedings of the* 16th *ACM Symposium on Principles of Programming Languages*, pp. 77–87. ACM Press, New York, 1989.
24. D. Rémy and J. Vouillon. Objective ML: A simple object-oriented extension of ML. In *Proceedings of the* 24th *ACM Symposium on Principles of Programming Languages*, pp. 40–53. ACM Press, New York, 1997.
25. W. C. Rounds. Feature logics. In J. v. Benthem and A. ter Meulen, eds., *Handbook of Logic and Language*, pp. 475–533. Elsevier Science Publishers B.V. (North Holland), 1997. Part 2: General Topics.
26. G. Smolka. The Oz Programming Model. In J. van Leeuwen, ed., *Computer Science Today*, vol. 1000 of *Lecture Notes in Computer Science*, pp. 324–343. Springer-Verlag, Berlin, 1995.
27. G. Smolka and R. Treinen. Records for logic programming. *The Journal of Logic Programming*, 18(3):229–258, Apr. 1994.
28. M. Sulzmann. Proofs of properties about HM(X). Technical Report YALEU/DCS/RR-1102, Yale University, 1998.
29. M. Sulzmann, M. Odersky, and M. Wehr. Type inference with constrained types (extended abstract). In B. Pierce, ed., *Proceedings of the* 4th *International Workshop on Foundations of Object-oriented Programming*, Jan. 1997. Full version to appear in TAPOS, 1998.
30. R. Treinen. Feature constraints with first-class features. In A. M. Borzyszkowski and S. Sokołowski, eds., *International Symposium on Mathematical Foundations of Computer Science*, vol. 711 of *Lecture Notes in Computer Science*, pp. 734–743. Springer-Verlag, Berlin, 30 August–3 September 1993.
31. J. van Leeuwen, ed. *Handbook of Theoretical Computer Science*, vol. A (Algorithms and Complexity). The MIT Press, Cambridge, MA, 1990.
32. M. Wand. Complete type inference for simple objects. In *Proceedings of the IEEE Symposium on Logic in Computer Science*, pp. 37–44. IEEE Computer Society Press, 1987. Corrigendum in LICS '88, p. 132.
33. M. Wand. Type inference for record concatenation and multiple inheritance. *Information and Computation*, 93:1–15, 1991.

Two Flavors of Offline Partial Evaluation

Simon Helsen[1] and Peter Thiemann[2]

[1] Universität Tübingen
Wilhelm-Schickard-Institut für Informatik
Sand 13, D-72076 Tübingen, Germany
helsen@informatik.uni-tuebingen.de
[2] University of Nottingham
Department of Computer Science
University Park
Nottingham NG7 2RD, England
pjt@cs.nott.ac.uk

Abstract. Type-directed partial evaluation is a new approach to program specialization for functional programming languages. Its merits with respect to the traditional offline partial evaluation approach have not yet been fully explored. We present a comparison of type-directed partial evaluation with standard offline partial evaluation in both a qualitative and quantitative way. For the latter we use implementations of both approaches in Scheme. Both approaches yield equivalent results in comparable time.

1 Introduction

Partial evaluation is a technique for automatically specializing programs. One approach is *offline* partial evaluation where specialization is entirely driven by the results of a program analysis. We consider two offline frameworks which are superficially quite different.

In the *traditional approach* the program analysis is a *binding-time analysis*, an abstraction of the semantics of specialization. A binding-time analysis determines for each program point whether the specializer should generate code or execute it.

An offline partial evaluator is then either an interpreter of annotated programs or it follows the approach of *writing cogen by hand* [34]. Self-application of the partial evaluator improves the performance of the interpreter-based alternative. It can transform the annotated program into a dedicated program generator. The *cogen-by-hand* alternative performs this step directly, thus avoiding any interpretive overheads. The latter alternative is the current state of the art in partial evaluation [1, 22, 5, 42, 13].

In the *type-directed approach* [15] it is only the type of the program (and its free variables) that drives the specialization. It avoids interpretation completely by applying to compiled programs without necessarily requiring access to their source, as long as their types are known. It guarantees that the specialized program is in normal form.

Jieh Hsiang, Atsushi Ohori (Eds.): ASIAN'98, LNCS 1538, pp. 188–205, 1998.

The aim of this work is to clarify the relationship between these two approaches. Some of the issues considered have already been touched upon in Danvy's article "Type-directed Partial Evaluation" [15], but some delicate issues were left implicit. Therefore, we have set out to clarify the principal differences and commonalities of the two approaches and we have performed some practical experiments using representative implementations of both approaches.

For the traditional partial evaluators, we have used the PGG system [46]. It is an implementation of the *cogen-by-hand* approach for the Scheme language.

For type-directed partial evaluation (TDPE), we have used Danvy's implementation for Scheme [15, 14] and our own reimplementation in Scheme to perform experiments with self-application of TDPE.

Although both systems are based on Scheme, the two approaches are applicable to other functional languages like ML and Haskell.

Our experiments concentrate on compilation, the flagship application of partial evaluation. Compiling with a partial evaluator means to specialize an interpreter for a programming language L with respect to an L-program. We call such an interpreter as well as any program submitted to a specializer the *subject program*. We have found that:

- both approaches to specialization require changes to the subject programs to specialize well;
- if the subject program has a simple type and polyvariant program point specialization is not required then TDPE can simulate traditional partial evaluation without change, otherwise if the subject program is untyped some transformations are required to hide the untyped parts from TDPE;
- in all cases, a traditional partial evaluator can achieve the result of a specialization with TDPE, subject to improving binding times using eta-expansion [19] and repeating the binding-time analysis;
- both specialization methods have comparable runtimes (excluding type inference, compilation, etc).

These observations hold for TDPE as originally defined [15]. Recently, Danvy and others [16, 41] have defined online variants of TDPE that are strictly more powerful and yield strictly better results than traditional methods. To match these results, a traditional partial evaluator must revert to multiple passes including aggressive post-processing [40].

The rest of the paper is structured as follows. In Sec. 2 we introduce traditional partial evaluation as well as TDPE. Section 3 formulates important aspects of specialization and puts them into perspective with respect to both approaches. Section 4 shows how both approaches relate to each other in terms of an eta-expanding binding-time analysis. Section 5 analyzes the run-time behavior of both approaches.

Throughout, we assume familiarity with basic notions of partial evaluation [12, 31].

$$
\begin{array}{lll}
\text{expressions} & \mathit{Expr} \ni & e ::= x \mid c \mid e@e \mid \lambda x.e \\
\text{types} & \mathit{Type} \ni & t ::= b \mid t \to t \\
\text{reduction} & & (\lambda x.e_1)@e_2 \mapsto e_1\{x := e_2\}
\end{array}
$$

Fig. 1. The simply-typed lambda calculus

$$
\begin{array}{lll}
\text{two-level expressions} & \mathit{TLT} \ni & e ::= x \mid e \,\overline{@}\, e \mid \overline{\lambda}\, x.e \mid e \,\underline{@}\, e \mid \underline{\lambda}\, x.e \\
\text{two-level types} & & t ::= \overline{b} \mid t \overline{\to} t \mid \underline{b} \mid t \underline{\to} t \\
\text{static reduction} & & (\overline{\lambda}\, x.e_1)\, \overline{@}\, e_2 \mapsto e_1\{x := e_2\}
\end{array}
$$

$$
\begin{array}{cc}
\vdash_{dyn} \underline{b} & \vdash_{dyn} t_2 \underline{\to} t_1 \\
\vdash_{wft} \overline{b} & \vdash_{wft} \underline{b}
\end{array}
$$

$$
\frac{\vdash_{wft} t_2 \quad \vdash_{wft} t_1}{\vdash_{wft} t_2 \overline{\to} t_1}
\qquad
\frac{\vdash_{wft} t_2 \quad \vdash_{wft} t_1 \quad \vdash_{dyn} t_2 \quad \vdash_{dyn} t_1}{\vdash_{wft} t_2 \underline{\to} t_1}
$$

$$
A\{x : t\} \vdash_{bta} x : t
$$

$$
\frac{A\{x : t_2\} \vdash_{bta} e : t_1 \quad \vdash_{wft} t_2 \overline{\to} t_1}{A \vdash_{bta} \overline{\lambda}\, x.e : t_2 \overline{\to} t_1}
\qquad
\frac{A \vdash_{bta} e_1 : t_2 \overline{\to} t_1 \quad A \vdash_{bta} e_2 : t_2}{A \vdash_{bta} e_1 \,\overline{@}\, e_2 : t_1}
$$

$$
\frac{A\{x : t_2\} \vdash_{bta} e : t_1 \quad \vdash_{wft} t_2 \underline{\to} t_1}{A \vdash_{bta} \underline{\lambda}\, x.e : t_2 \underline{\to} t_1}
\qquad
\frac{A \vdash_{bta} e_1 : t_2 \underline{\to} t_1 \quad A \vdash_{bta} e_2 : t_2}{A \vdash_{bta} e_1 \,\underline{@}\, e_2 : t_1}
$$

Fig. 2. The simply-typed two-level lambda calculus

2 Two Paradigms for Specialization

This section presents the kernels of the two paradigms for specialization. To simplify our later comparison, the formal presentation focuses on a simply-typed lambda calculus with full β reduction (see Fig. 1). We omit the typing rules since they are standard [36].

To discuss specialization, we employ the two-level call-by-name lambda calculus [37,24] defined in Fig. 2. Overlining denotes *static* specialization-time constructs and underlining denotes *dynamic* run-time constructs.

To discuss implementations of specialization, we augment the simply-typed lambda calculus with a datatype *Expr* for generated or specialized expressions. The operations on *Expr* are *mkLam* : $\mathit{Var} \times \mathit{Expr} \to \mathit{Expr}$, which constructs a lambda expression, and *mkApp* : $\mathit{Expr} \times \mathit{Expr} \to \mathit{Expr}$. In addition, the impure operator *gensym* : $\mathit{Unit} \to \mathit{Var}$ generates a new variable every time it is called. Most of the time we are using the derived operations shown in Fig. 3.

The specifications are for specializing a call-by-name lambda calculus. Specializing the call-by-value lambda calculus or the computational lambda calculus (call-by-value with certain side effects) requires identical changes to both specifications.

$$\hat{\lambda}\, f \equiv \mathit{let}\ y = \mathit{gensym}\ ()\ \mathit{in}\ \mathit{mkLam}(y, fy)$$
$$f \,\hat{@}\, a \equiv \mathit{mkApp}(f, a)$$

Fig. 3. Derived operations on *Expr*

$$\mathit{cogen} : \mathit{TLT} \rightarrow \mathit{Impl}$$

$$\mathit{cogen}(x) \equiv x$$

$$\mathit{cogen}(\overline{\lambda}\, x.e) \equiv \lambda\, x.\mathit{cogen}(e) \qquad \mathit{cogen}(\underline{\lambda}\, x.e) \equiv \hat{\lambda}\, \lambda\, x.\mathit{cogen}(e)$$

$$\mathit{cogen}(f\, \overline{@}\, a) \equiv (\mathit{cogen}(f))(\mathit{cogen}(a)) \qquad \mathit{cogen}(f\, \underline{@}\, a) \equiv (\mathit{cogen}(f))\, \hat{@}\, (\mathit{cogen}(a))$$

Fig. 4. Cogen-based offline partial evaluation [42]

2.1 Cogen-Based Offline Partial Evaluation

A natural approach to implementing a *cogen-by-hand* partial evaluation system is to provide an implementation of each of the constructs of the two-level lambda calculus [22, 42]. In this case, the generation of the dedicated specializer boils down to a trivial translation that replaces each construct in a term of the two-level calculus by its implementation.

Figure 4 shows such an implementation in terms of a mapping *cogen* from two-level expressions *TLT* to an implementation language *Impl*. The $\hat{\lambda}$ combinator interprets the dynamic lambda using a higher-order syntax representation, the $\hat{@}$ combinator interprets dynamic application. The static constructs map into the corresponding constructs of the implementation language.

2.2 Type-Directed Partial Evaluation

The heart of an implementation of TDPE is a pair of mutually recursive functions, *reify* and *reflect*, shown in Fig. 5. *Reify*, written as $\downarrow^t v$, accepts a type t and a value v of type t and converts it into an expression of type t. *Reflect*, written $\uparrow_t e$, accepts a type t and an expression e of type t and converts it into a value of type t. *Type* denotes simple types, *Value* stands for (compiled) values, *Expr* denotes (specialized) expressions and *TLT* are two-level expressions.

Reify at a function type constructs a lambda expression and applies the corresponding function v from the compiled program to the freshly generated variable. *Reflect* constructs an application expression and wraps it into a function to transport it to the correct place in the compiled program.

$$\downarrow : \mathit{Type} \to \mathit{Value} \to \mathit{Impl} \qquad \uparrow : \mathit{Type} \to \mathit{Expr} \to \mathit{Impl}$$

$$\begin{array}{lll} \mathit{reify} & \downarrow^{b} v & = v \\ & \downarrow^{t_1 \to t_2} v & = \mathit{let}\ y = \mathit{gensym}\ ()\ \mathit{in}\ \mathit{mkLam}(y, \downarrow^{t_2} (v(\uparrow_{t_1} y))) \\ \mathit{reflect} & \uparrow_{b} e & = e \\ & \uparrow_{t_1 \to t_2} e & = \lambda\, v.\ \uparrow_{t_2} (\mathit{mkApp}(e, \downarrow^{t_1} v)) \end{array}$$

Fig. 5. Specification of TDPE [15]

3 Aspects of Specialization Techniques

Each of the following subsections considers one aspect of offline specialization techniques and comments on its significance for the traditional as well as for the type-directed approach.

3.1 Types

Types play an important role for both approaches [15, p.247, sec.2]. TDPE specializes by normalizing a compiled object with respect to its simple type. In practice, the specialized code has a simple type while the computation at specialization time can be untyped. The source program has to be closed with respect to primitive operations and the dynamic values because that is the only way their types can be specified. In contrast to many traditional systems, TDPE does not admit recursive types since there is no general way to reflect dynamic values.

In many traditional systems, the binding-time analysis imposes a certain type discipline upon the language, mostly based on simple typing with partial types and recursion (Lambdamix [24], Henglein's analysis [27], Similix 5.0 [9], and in particular the PGG system [46]). The binding-time analysis defers untypable expressions to run-time. Furthermore, all expressions that depend on dynamic data are also made dynamic. In consequence, the specialization-time computation has a simple type with recursion whereas the specialized program is unconstrained: it can be arbitrarily untyped and/or impure.

In principle, a binding-time analysis could also be based on more powerful type systems. For example, systems with subtyping [44], soft typing [11], or dynamic typing [28] could provide a suitable basis.

While the type of the subject program is usually fixed in the traditional approach, this need not be the case for TDPE. This flexibility is due to the interpretive nature of the *reify*/*reflect* pair of functions, both of which interpret their type argument. In terms of the compilation paradigm, it means that *the type of the interpreter may depend on the type of its source program.* This has two consequences:

1. it is possible to perform "simple type specialization" [17] which can remove type tags in a typed interpreter during specialization;

2. it is no longer sufficient to know the type of the subject program (interpreter) before starting a specialization, but it is necessary to know the *type of the subject program applied to the static input*, that is, the type of the interpreter applied to its source program. Effectively, it boils down to perform type inference of the source program before being able to compile it. In general, this type inference cannot be done by the compiler which compiles the interpreter, but there must be a separate program to type check the source program.

3.2 Polyvariance and Program Point Specialization

Polyvariant specialization means:

> Any program point in the source program gives rise to zero or more program points in the specialized program [23, 10].

Both techniques, traditional partial evaluators and TDPE, perform polyvariant specialization in this sense.

A related, but different issue is concerned with *program point specialization*. This technique uses memoization points to avoid code duplication and potentially infinite specialization. The specialized programs are sets of mutually recursive function definitions.

Program point specialization is a standard feature of traditional partial evaluators [8, 6], which has not yet been achieved for TDPE. It gives raise to a number of problems, for example, traditional systems must use a closure-based representation for functions to be able to compare them.

3.3 Continuation-Based Reduction

Continuation-based reduction is a commonly used name for a contextual binding-time-improving transformation which takes place during specialization [7]. Continuations are one implementation technique for it. Its main use is the implementation of non-standard reductions in two-level calculi and of dynamic choice of static values [20]. Both systems make use of the same technique to guarantee sound specialization in the presence of computational effects [26, 35]. Both systems have options to switch this feature off for selected operators. For these operators, the systems perform a call-by-name transformation (i.e., the operator has no side effects).

3.4 Computational Effects

There are two dimensions of computational effects to consider: effects at specialization time and effects in the specialized program.

Since TDPE does not constrain the computation at specialization time, side effects during specialization are permitted as long as they respect the typing properties. Recent results enable traditional systems to perform impure computations at specialization time, too [43]. Two important problems here are side effects under dynamic control and polyvariant program point specialization, which are discussed elsewhere in this paper.

Both approaches handle computational effects in the specialized program in essentially the same way [35,26]. The necessary modifications to Figures 4 and 5 are almost identical [14,45].

3.5 Compilation vs. Interpretation

TDPE as described by Danvy [15] applies to a compiled program and hence performs specialization at full compiled speed. Indeed, this observation is one of Danvy's key contributions because the idea of normalization by evaluation has been developed in an interpretive setting [4].

A traditional partial evaluator accesses the source program to perform the binding-time analysis. Then it interprets the resulting annotated program. A cogen-based partial evaluator turns the annotated program into a program generator as indicated by the *cogen* function. The program generator has (assuming a monovariant binding-time analysis) about the same size as the original program and the static parts run at full compiled speed, since their translation is trivial.

Specialization with either system involves compilation:

- The source program must be compiled to be amenable to TDPE.
- In a cogen-based system, the *cogen* function maps a binding-time annotated program to a program generator. The generator is then compiled before it can perform specialization.

There is a difference in the kind of program that is compiled in the two systems. In the cogen-based system, the compiled program consists of the static part of the subject program interspersed with syntax constructors, which generate code during specialization. TDPE, on the other hand, uses the original program in compiled form. This may result in a more optimized compiled program.

3.6 Termination

Neither TDPE nor traditional systems can guarantee the termination of specialization if there are static fixpoints present in the subject program. However, if the subject program is restricted to the simply-typed lambda calculus (without recursion) then TDPE is sure to terminate, by the strong normalization property of the calculus. A traditional system can employ an extra program analysis which guarantees the termination of specialization [29,2].

3.7 Binding-Time Improvements

A *binding-time improvement* is a program transformation geared at improving the effectiveness of specialization. This goal is usually achieved by using special programming idioms to separate the binding times.

Traditional specializers require binding-time improvements [31] whereas TDPE does not [40, 15]. However, achieving satisfactory results is not trivial using TDPE, either. It is still necessary to address some issues.

Staging Discipline The subject program must obey a *staging discipline.* It means that the subject program must compute all values that we expect to see in the specialized programs. This is non-obvious so we illustrate it using an example.

Returning to the compilation application, consider the specialization of an environment lookup $\rho(v)$ in an interpreter. Obviously, the name v of the variable should disappear in the specialized (compiled) program. Instead, we expect something like `lookup store 5` as compiled code. But to this end the interpreter must actually compute the index/address `5` and perform the environment lookup in two stages: in the first (static) stage, compute the index using an additional (static) environment; in the second (dynamic) stage, perform `lookup store index`. This is quite similar to separating binding times, which is what binding-time improvements are about.

The work of Harrison and Kamin [25] provides some more evidence for this fact. For example, they must precompute some labels to compile conditional jumps. Their solution is to have the interpreter interpret the code in two passes: in the first pass, it computes the addresses, and then it "snaps back" to perform the actual computation in the second pass.

Dynamic Recursion A program contains dynamic recursion if there is at least one loop that is controlled by run-time (i.e., dynamic) data. This is a frequent phenomenon, since most non-trivial programs contain dynamic recursion. For instance, an interpreter will interpret loops or recursive functions in its source language by dynamic recursion. Traditional partial evaluation memoizes calls to the specializer at points that may give rise to dynamic recursion: dynamic conditionals and dynamic lambda abstractions [8]. Thus it creates a set of top-level mutually recursive functions, one for each memoized call to the specializer.

This approach is currently not possible with TDPE. Instead, the general idea to deal with dynamic recursion [15] is to provide a fixed-point combinator at a suitable type and abstract the subject program over the fixed-point operator. This may not be easy as demonstrated with the following example, again dealing with compilation.

Suppose we want to compile the language Mixwell [32] which provides mutually recursive of first-order functions. The typical semantics of such a language includes semantic equations $\mathcal{E} : \mathit{Exp} \rightarrow \mathit{FunctionEnv} \rightarrow \mathit{ValueEnv} \rightarrow \mathit{Value}$ for expressions and goes on to provide the meaning of a program $f_i(\overline{x_i}) = e_i$ as the environment

$$\mathit{fix}\ \lambda\, \psi \in \mathit{FunctionEnv}.[f_i \mapsto \lambda\, \overline{y_i}.\mathcal{E}[\![e_i]\!]\psi\emptyset[\overline{x_i \mapsto y_i}]]$$

It turns out that it is not straightforward to come up with a suitable fixed-point combinator *fix*.

One strategy (suggested by Danvy[1]) is to implement the function environment ψ as a function and use the fixed-point combinator at a different type for each program: this turns out to be problematic because the type of ψ must reflect the arity of each f_i. In other words, the type of the result of ψf_i depends on the particular argument f_i. Unfortunately, this kind of type is currently outside the scope of TDPE, unless we employ the trick to hide the actual arity of the functions inside of some kind of "dynamic" type. To do so, we have to rewrite the interpreter by including coercions into and out of the dynamic type. But still, the type of ψ—and hence of *fix*—depends on the number of functions f_i in the source program.

If we take this last idea to the extreme, we implement the function environment ψ as an abstract type with lookup and update functions. This works satisfactory for the Mixwell interpreter, but it is still necessary to insert coercions. In this case, the most natural implementation of ψ is a list and the implementation of the fixed-point combinator uses an impure update operation. Anyway, we must split the function environment in the interpreter into a compile-time and a run-time part to achieve a static lookup, just like explained above for the variable lookup.

Dynamic Conditional On a smaller scale, a similar problem exists for dynamic conditionals. In the traditional approach, the specializer inserts a memoization point at a dynamic conditional. This is not possible with TDPE.

In principle, there is no problem with handling dynamic conditionals in TDPE [15]. However, the solution can give raise to code duplication which is why most examples use a workaround. The trick is to hide the conditional inside a primitive function and abstract it. Clearly, to avoid changing the semantics in a call-by-value language, such a primitive must work at a functional type.

4 Qualitative Comparison

In this section, we investigate the exact relationship between TDPE and an aggressive binding-time analysis. Although TDPE does not perform an explicit binding-time analysis, it does so implicitly. We find that using eta-expansion [20] enables the traditional approach to achieve the same results as TDPE. We illustrate this with an example drawn from an applied lambda calculus.

Consider the expression given by

$$E \quad \equiv \quad (\lambda\, f.f \,@\, ((\mathit{if}\ \texttt{\#f}\ f\ g) \,@\, 0)) \,@\, (\lambda\, z.z). \qquad (1)$$

[1] in personal communication, March '98.

$$\Downarrow : \mathit{Type} \to \mathit{TLT} \to \mathit{TLT}$$
$$\Uparrow : \mathit{Type} \to \mathit{TLT} \to \mathit{TLT}$$

$$\begin{array}{lll} \mathit{reify} & \Downarrow^{b} e & = e \\ & \Downarrow^{t_1 \to t_2} e & = \underline{\lambda} x.\, \Downarrow^{t_2} (e \,\overline{@}\, (\Uparrow_{t_1} x)) \\ \mathit{reflect} & \Uparrow_{b} e & = e \\ & \Uparrow_{t_1 \to t_2} e & = \overline{\lambda} v.\, \Uparrow_{t_2} (e \,\underline{@}\, \Downarrow^{t_1} v) \end{array}$$

Fig. 6. TDPE using two-level eta-expansion [15]

Assuming that g is known to be a function, but otherwise unknown (dynamic), we explore three different binding-time annotation schemes. But first, we rephrase TDPE so that it maps two-level expressions to two-level expressions.

4.1 TDPE and Two-Level Eta-Expansion

If we rewrite TDPE to a syntactic transformation on two-level terms as in Fig. 6, it turns out that this new specification is related to the implementation in Fig. 5 via the *cogen* function.

Lemma 1. *Suppose* $e \in \mathit{TLT}$ *with all annotations static and* $\vdash_{bta} e : t$. *Then*

1. $\vdash_{bta} \Downarrow^{t} e : \underline{t}$ *where the underlying type of* $\underline{t}$ *is identical to* t, *but with all annotations dynamic;*
2. $\downarrow^{t} \mathit{cogen}(e) = \mathit{cogen}(\Downarrow^{t} e)$.

4.2 Standard Binding-Time Analysis

A standard binding-time analysis [27] (as implemented in PGG or in Similix) yields the two-level term

$$(\overline{\lambda} f.f \,\underline{@}\, ((\overline{\mathit{if}}\ \texttt{\#f}\ f\ g) \,\underline{@}\, 0))\ \overline{@}\ (\underline{\lambda}\, z.z) \tag{2}$$

which statically reduces to

$$(\lambda\, z.z) \,@\, (g \,@\, 0).$$

This result is not satisfactory because the dynamic g pollutes the surrounding binding times.

4.3 Eta-Expanding Binding-Time Analysis

Since the type of the free variable g is known to be $A \to A$ for some base type A, a prephase of the binding-time analysis could exploit this knowledge and eta-expand g to yield

$$(\lambda\, f.f \,@\, ((\mathit{if}\ \texttt{\#f}\ f\ (\lambda\, w.g \,@\, w)) \,@\, 0)) \,@\, (\lambda\, z.z). \tag{3}$$

The same could be done with the type of the result. However, in the present example the result has type A, a base type.

Applying the same binding-time analysis as before to the term (3) yields

$$(\overline{\lambda} f.f \,\overline{@}\, ((\overline{\mathit{if}}\ \texttt{\#f}\ f\ (\overline{\lambda} w.g \,\underline{@}\, w)) \,\overline{@}\, 0)) \,\overline{@}\, (\overline{\lambda} z.z) \tag{4}$$

and static reduction of this term results in

$$g \,@\, 0.$$

4.4 Type-Directed Partial Evaluation

To simulate a binding-time analysis for TDPE, we first have to construct a completely static variant of E (as we only have the compiled program at our disposal) and close it over g:

$$E' \quad \equiv \quad \overline{\lambda} g.(\overline{\lambda} f.f \,\overline{@}\, ((\overline{\mathit{if}}\ \texttt{\#f}\ f\ g) \,\overline{@}\, 0)) \,\overline{@}\, (\overline{\lambda} z.z) \tag{5}$$

The term E' has type $t = (A \to A) \to A$. Performing type-directed partial evaluation is the same as expanding $\Downarrow^t E'$ and then compiling and running the result. In this particular case, $\Downarrow^t [\,]$ corresponds to the context:

$$\underline{\lambda} g.[\,] \,\overline{@}\, \overline{\lambda} w.g \,\underline{@}\, w$$

The resulting term

$$\underline{\lambda} g.(\overline{\lambda} g.(\overline{\lambda} f.f \,\overline{@}\, ((\overline{\mathit{if}}\ \texttt{\#f}\ f\ g) \,\overline{@}\, 0)) \,\overline{@}\, (\overline{\lambda} z.z)) \,\overline{@}\, \overline{\lambda} w.g \,\underline{@}\, w \tag{6}$$

is statically convertible with the term (4) constructed by binding-time analysis after eta expansion. One static reduction step brings us to

$$\underline{\lambda} g.(\overline{\lambda} f.f \,\overline{@}\, ((\overline{\mathit{if}}\ \texttt{\#f}\ f\ (\overline{\lambda} w.g \,\underline{@}\, w)) \,\overline{@}\, 0)) \,\overline{@}\, (\overline{\lambda} z.z) \tag{7}$$

which is identical to (4), up to the outermost abstraction of g. It statically reduces to

$$\lambda g.g \,@\, 0. \tag{8}$$

It is easy to see that wrapping a free variable (or primitive operator) g whose type t is known into a bunch of eta-redexes corresponding to t enables the same reductions as TDPE.

Lemma 2. *Suppose $E[g]$ is an expression with free variable $g : t$. Then TDPE-style eta-expansion of $\lambda g.E[g]$ is statically convertible to $E[g']$ where each occurrence of g is replaced by $\Uparrow_t g$. That is*

$$\Downarrow^{t \to t'} \overline{\lambda} g.E[g] \text{ statically reduces to } \underline{\lambda} z. \Downarrow^{t'} E[\Uparrow_t z.$$

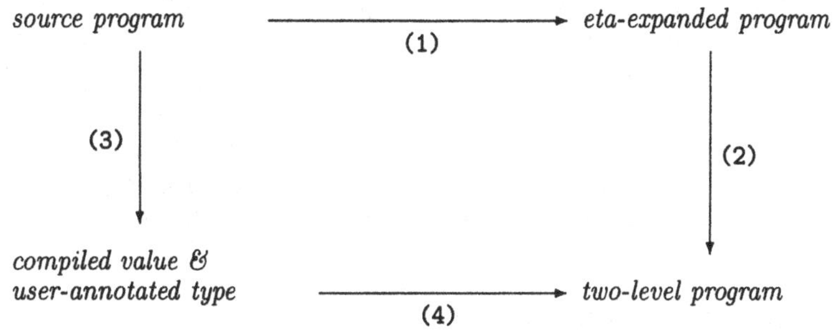

Fig. 7. TDPE and binding-time analysis

4.5 Assessment

Although it is possible to automate an eta-expanding prephase as in Sec. 4.3 to the binding-time analysis, current systems leave it to the programmer to perform the expansion manually as a binding-time improvement [19]. In contrast, TDPE *always* performs the eta-expansion because that is its fundamental working principle. If eta-expansion is not possible, e.g., if the top-level type has negative occurrences of recursive types, TDPE is not applicable, so manual workarounds have to be developed. In the traditional approach, eta-expansion is only required very rarely and it has to be done by hand, anyway.

A conclusion to draw from this example is that an eta-expanding binding-time analysis anticipates some static reduction steps that TDPE has to execute. This anticipation is possible because every binding-time analysis relies on a flow analysis. TDPE has to unveil this flow on the fly. However, its flow information is precise —in fact perfect— because it happens at run-time and exploits actual values (for example, TDPE ignores semantically dead code which may deteriorate the results of a static analysis), whereas a flow analysis can only provide conservative approximations.

The diagram in Fig. 7 summarizes this subsection. The arrow (1) signifies type-guided eta expansion, (2) is a binding-time analysis, (3) is compilation with user-annotated type information, and (4) is the reify/reflect phase of TDPE. The results of (2) and (4) are statically convertible.

4.6 Type Dependencies

In our opinion, the strength of TDPE lies in applications where the type for residualization depends on the particular static input. Simple type specialization [17] is such an application. In those cases, the traditional approach is still viable in the presence of an eta-expanding binding-time analysis. However, it would be forbiddingly expensive because we would have to perform the binding-time analysis for each combination of the subject program and static input. In addition, we would have to run *cogen* and to compile the resulting generating extension.

On the other hand, many applications keep the type argument of *reify* fixed, among them compilation. Here, the extra power provided by TDPE cannot be exploited and it seems more advantageous to use a traditional cogen-based system because it provides additional features like memoization for free.

If the type argument t is fixed, self-application of TDPE [15, sec.2.4] can produce a customized eta-expander which is specialized with respect to t. Of course, any other specialization mechanism could do the job, too.

5 Quantitative Comparison

In this section, we report on experiments that we conducted to examine the pragmatics of both systems more accurately. They are all concerned with compilation by specializing interpreters for various languages. These are:

Tiny [38] A simple imperative language with expressions, assignments, **if**, **while**, and sequence commands. We have examined one version in direct style and another in continuation-passing style. The same interpreters are considered in the TDPE papers [15, 14]. Since the interpreter already contained the proper combinators to handle dynamic recursion, no changes are required.

Mixwell [32] A first-order functional language with named procedures. The interpreter is written in direct style. As discussed in Sec. 3.7, a binding-time improvement is required to make the interpreter amenable to TDPE. The changes do not affect Mixwell's suitability for traditional specialization.

Mini-Scheme A large subset of Scheme. We have implemented this interpreter to be able to run realistic compilations. To this end, we have used the preprocessor of the PGG system to transform Scheme into Mini-Scheme. The implementation uses techniques similar to those developed for the Mixwell interpreter. Mini-Scheme is written in continuation-passing style.

5.1 Results of Specialization

We have used both systems to specialize the above interpreters with respect to various programs. Since all programs that are amenable to TDPE can be processed by traditional specialization without using memoization, we switched this feature off in the PGG system [46]. In all cases we were able to obtain specialized programs that were identical up to renaming of bound variables.

- The Tiny interpreter in direct style is directly amenable to specialization with PGG without any modification. The residual programs are identical to those produced by TDPE.
- The Tiny interpreter in continuation-passing style needs some binding-time improvements for specialization with the PGG system in the form of eta expansions as described in Sec. 4.3.
- The Mixwell interpreter—in its TDPE-ready version—is directly amenable to PGG specialization and yields identical results from both specializers.

– The Mini-Scheme interpreter is equally amenable to TDPE and PGG and produces identical residual programs. In this case, the interpreter requires no eta expansion although it is written in continuation-passing style. This is due to the use of dynamic primitives in direct style.

5.2 Compile Times

In the experiments, we have specialized the Mini-Scheme interpreter with respect to realistic programs taken from Andrew Wright's Scheme benchmark suite: **Boyer** a term-rewriting theorem prover, **Gpscheme** an implementation of genetic programming, and **Matrix** tests whether a random matrix $M \in \{+1,-1\}^{n \times n}$ is maximal under permutation and negation of rows and columns. **Append** is just a standard list appending program.

program	A: *TDPE*	B: *TDPE-cogen*	C: *PGG*	A/B	A/C	B/C
Append	0.16	0.15	0.12	1.07	1.33	1.25
Boyer	6.55	5.38	4.73	1.22	1.38	1.13
Gpscheme	10.13	8.85	8.87	1.14	1.14	0.99
Matrix	15.22	13.16	12.46	1.15	1.22	1.05
Compiler Generation		0.15	4.92			0.03

Table 1. Compile-time benchmarks (in sec.)

Table 1 shows compile times in seconds for these programs. The *TDPE* column indicates the times obtained with Danvy's TDPE system and with our own reimplementation of it. The *TDPE-cogen* column indicates the times obtained with self-applied TDPE [15, sec.2.4]. To obtain these figures, we used our reimplementation of TDPE. The *PGG* column lists the figures obtained using the PGG system. The remaining columns list ratios as indicated in their headers.

All experiments were performed on an IBM PowerPC Workstation with 128MB RAM using Scheme48, an implementation of Scheme based on a byte-code interpreter. Each column of data was obtained with a fresh Scheme48 session and an heap image of 12 MB. All figures are averages of 5 consecutively executed runs.

The *TDPE-cogen* column indicates that self-application does not play such a prominent role in achieving efficiency as in traditional partial evaluation. Although self-application removes the overhead of type interpretation, it only improves compile times by about 15%. Hence the interpretation of the type argument does not contribute essentially to the specialization time. In the traditional approach, self-application usually speeds up the specialization by a factor of 4–6.

Self-application at type t generates a term quite similar to $\Downarrow^t [\ ]$. It does not depend on a particular subject program, but is generally applicable to all programs of type t. This is in contrast to traditional generating extensions which are tailored to specialize one particular subject program.

We did not construct a TDPE compiler generator by hand. All it would do is construct the same term as the *TDPE-cogen*. It might do it faster, but we believe there is not much to improve on the compiler generation time in Table 1.

5.3 An Analytical Perspective

Let us consider the issue of compile time from an analytical perspective. Looking back at the core of both specialization algorithms in Figures 4 and 5, there is actually not so much difference between the way specialization proceeds.

Here is the case for PGG (see Fig. 4): For each lambda in the source program, the specializer produced by the PGG system processes one lambda and — in the dynamic case — it generates a fresh variable name, applies the function to it, and constructs a lambda expression. Static applications are just applications and a dynamic application just constructs an application expression.

For TDPE (see Fig. 5) it is quite similar: TDPE must process each lambda and each application in the source program. In addition to that, for each lambda that is deemed to be dynamic, it generates a fresh variable name, applies a function to it, and constructs a residual lambda. For each application that is deemed dynamic, it constructs a function that constructs the residual application.

From the above discussion, we extract the following facts:

- processing a static lambda, a dynamic lambda, a variable, or a static application involves exactly the same actions for cogen-based partial evaluation and TDPE;
- processing a dynamic application involves constructing the residual application in both cases, in addition TDPE has to construct a function to pass it to the compiled application.

The numbers in table 1, which are averages of several subsequent measurements, indicate that the extra lambda construction has no serious impact on compile times. Indeed, after removal of type interpretation, compilation with TDPE is about identical to compilation with PGG.

6 Related Work and Conclusion

Apart from Danvy's articles [15, 14, 21, 16] there are few investigations on the pragmatics of TDPE. In his M.Sc. thesis [40], Rhiger performs experiments with action semantics interpreters where he compares the space and time requirements in a TDPE system with those in Similix. He concludes that compilation with TDPE is considerably faster and uses less space.

In this paper, however, we compare TDPE with the technology used in the PGG system and obtain different results. This is because PGG is based on a hand written cogen which is faster than a self-applied partial evaluator.

We have found that TDPE delivers the same residual programs as traditional partial evaluation if the latter is coupled with an eta-expanding binding-time analysis. Even that was rarely necessary in the examples we considered. Disregarding program generator generation time, we illustrated that the time taken by a cogen-based partial evaluator is similar to the time taken by a TDPE system. However, TDPE allows for additional flexibility since it is possible to specify a different type for each static input.

The position of TDPE could be further strengthened if it were possible to integrate the unavoidable type inference phase into the system. The recent integration of TDPE into an ML programming system [3] is a promising step forward. It eliminates many of the problems in making a program "TDPE-ready". However, it is still insufficient for ambitious applications like simple type specialization [17] where the implementation of a type inference engine is left to the user.

The online extensions of TDPE [16] provide more flexibility for the user and achieve a certain degree of polyvariant specialization which is common in traditional specializers. They also enhance the transformational power of TDPE beyond the reach of traditional one-pass offline techniques.

References

[1] Lars Ole Andersen. *Program Analysis and Specialization for the C Programming Language.* PhD thesis, DIKU, University of Copenhagen, May 1994. (DIKU report 94/19).

[2] Peter Holst Andersen and Carsten Kehler Holst. Termination analysis for offline partial evaluation of a higher order functional language. In Radhia Cousot, editor, *Proc. International Static Analysis Symposium, SAS'96*, volume 1145 of *Lecture Notes in Computer Science*, pages 67–82, Aachen, Germany, September 1996. Springer-Verlag.

[3] Vincent Balat and Olivier Danvy. Strong normalization by type-directed partial evaluation and run-time code generation. In *Proceedings of the ACM SIGPLAN Workshop on Types in Compilation (TIC'98)*, Lecture Notes in Computer Science, Kyoto, Japan, March 1998.

[4] Ulrich Berger and Helmut Schwichtenberg. An inverse of the evaluation functional for typed λ-calculus. In *Proc. of the 6th Annual IEEE Symposium on Logic in Computer Science*, pages 203–211, Amsterdam, The Netherlands, July 1991. IEEE Computer Society Press.

[5] Lars Birkedal and Morten Welinder. Hand-writing program generator generators. In Manuel V. Hermenegildo and Jaan Penjam, editors, *International Symposium on Programming Languages, Implementations, Logics and Programs (PLILP '94)*, volume 844 of *Lecture Notes in Computer Science*, pages 198–214, Madrid, Spain, September 1994. Springer-Verlag.

[6] Anders Bondorf. Automatic autoprojection of higher order recursive equations. *Science of Computer Programming*, 17:3–34, 1991.

[7] Anders Bondorf. Improving binding times without explicit CPS-conversion. In *Proc. 1992 ACM Conference on Lisp and Functional Programming*, pages 1–10, San Francisco, California, USA, June 1992.

[8] Anders Bondorf and Olivier Danvy. Automatic autoprojection of recursive equations with global variables and abstract data types. *Science of Computer Programming*, 16(2):151–195, 1991.

[9] Anders Bondorf and Jesper Jørgensen. Efficient analyses for realistic off-line partial evaluation. *Journal of Functional Programming*, 3(3):315–346, July 1993.

[10] Mikhail A. Bulyonkov. Polyvariant mixed computation for analyzer programs. *Acta Informatica*, 21:473–484, 1984.
[11] Robert Cartwright and Mike Fagan. Soft typing. In *Proc. Conference on Programming Language Design and Implementation '91*, pages 278–292, Toronto, June 1991. ACM.
[12] Charles Consel and Olivier Danvy. Tutorial notes on partial evaluation. In *Proc. 20th Annual ACM Symposium on Principles of Programming Languages*, pages 493–501, Charleston, South Carolina, January 1993. ACM Press.
[13] Charles Consel and Francois Noël. A general approach for run-time specialization and its application to C. In POPL1996 [39], pages 145–156.
[14] Olivier Danvy. Pragmatics of type-directed partial evaluation. In Danvy et al. [18], pages 73–94.
[15] Olivier Danvy. Type-directed partial evaluation. In POPL1996 [39], pages 242–257.
[16] Olivier Danvy. Online type-directed partial evaluation. In *Proc. Third Fuji International Symposium on Functional and Logic Programming*, Kyoto, Japan, April 1998. World Scientific Press, Singapore.
[17] Olivier Danvy. A simple solution to type specialization. Technical Report RS-98-1, BRICS, University of Aarhus, Denmark, January 1998. To appear in ICALP98.
[18] Olivier Danvy, Robert Glück, and Peter Thiemann, editors. *Dagstuhl Seminar on Partial Evaluation 1996*, volume 1110 of *Lecture Notes in Computer Science*, Schloß Dagstuhl, Germany, February 1996. Springer-Verlag.
[19] Olivier Danvy, Karoline Malmkjær, and Jens Palsberg. The essence of eta-expansion in partial evaluation. *Lisp and Symbolic Computation*, 8(3):209–227, July 1995.
[20] Olivier Danvy, Karoline Malmkjær, and Jens Palsberg. Eta-expansion does The Trick. *ACM Transactions on Programming Languages and Systems*, 18(6):730–751, November 1996.
[21] Olivier Danvy and Rene Vestergaard. Semantics-based compiling: A case study in type-directed partial evaluation. In Kuchen and Swierstra [33], pages 182–197.
[22] Robert Glück and Jesper Jørgensen. An automatic program generator for multi-level specialization. *Lisp and Symbolic Computation*, 10(2):113–158, July 1997.
[23] Robert Glück and Morten Heine Sørensen. A roadmap to metacomputation by supercompilation. In Danvy et al. [18], pages 137–160.
[24] Carsten K. Gomard and Neil D. Jones. A partial evaluator for the untyped lambda-calculus. *Journal of Functional Programming*, 1(1):21–70, January 1991.
[25] William L. Harrison and Samuel N. Kamin. Modular compilers based on monad transformers. In *IEEE International Conference on Computer Languages, ICCL 1998*, Chicago, USA, May 1998. IEEE Computer Society Press.
[26] John Hatcliff and Olivier Danvy. A computational formalization for partial evaluation. *Mathematical Structures in Computer Science*, 7(5):507–542, 1997.
[27] Fritz Henglein. Efficient type inference for higher-order binding-time analysis. In Hughes [30], pages 448–472.
[28] Fritz Henglein. Dynamic typing: Syntax and proof theory. *Science of Computer Programming*, 22:197–230, 1994.
[29] Carsten Kehler Holst. Finiteness analysis. In Hughes [30], pages 473–495.
[30] John Hughes, editor. *Functional Programming Languages and Computer Architecture*, volume 523 of *Lecture Notes in Computer Science*, Cambridge, MA, 1991. Springer-Verlag.
[31] Neil D. Jones, Carsten K. Gomard, and Peter Sestoft. *Partial Evaluation and Automatic Program Generation*. Prentice-Hall, 1993.

[32] Neil D. Jones, Peter Sestoft, and Harald Søndergaard. An experiment in partial evaluation: The generation of a compiler generator. In J.-P. Jouannaud, editor, *Rewriting Techniques and Applications*, pages 124–140, Dijon, France, 1985. Springer-Verlag. LNCS 202.

[33] Herbert Kuchen and Doaitse Swierstra, editors. *International Symposium on Programming Languages, Implementations, Logics and Programs (PLILP '96)*, volume 1140 of *Lecture Notes in Computer Science*, Aachen, Germany, September 1996. Springer-Verlag.

[34] John Launchbury and Carsten Kehler Holst. Handwriting cogen to avoid problems with static typing. In *Draft Proceedings, Fourth Annual Glasgow Workshop on Functional Programming*, pages 210–218, Skye, Scotland, 1991. Glasgow University.

[35] Julia L. Lawall and Peter Thiemann. Sound specialization in the presence of computational effects. In *Proc. Theoretical Aspects of Computer Software*, volume 1281 of *Lecture Notes in Computer Science*, pages 165–190, Sendai, Japan, September 1997. Springer-Verlag.

[36] John C. Mitchell. *Foundations for Programming Languages.* MIT Press, 1996.

[37] Flemming Nielson and Hanne Riis Nielson. *Two-Level Functional Languages*, volume 34 of *Cambridge Tracts in Theoretical Computer Science.* Cambridge University Press, 1992.

[38] Larry C. Paulson. Compiler generation from denotational semantics. In Bernhard Lorho, editor, *Methods and Tools for Compiler Construction*, pages 219–250. Cambridge University Press, 1984.

[39] *Proc. 23rd Annual ACM Symposium on Principles of Programming Languages*, St. Petersburg, Fla., January 1996. ACM Press.

[40] Morten Rhiger. A study in higher-order programming languages. Master's thesis, University of Aarhus, Aarhus, Denmark, December 1997.

[41] Tim Sheard. A type-directed, on-line, partial evaluator for a polymorphic language. In Charles Consel, editor, *Proc. ACM SIGPLAN Symposium on Partial Evaluation and Semantics-Based Program Manipulation PEPM '97*, pages 22–35, Amsterdam, The Netherlands, June 1997. ACM Press.

[42] Peter Thiemann. Cogen in six lines. In R. Kent Dybvig, editor, *Proc. International Conference on Functional Programming 1996*, pages 180–189, Philadelphia, PA, May 1996. ACM Press, New York.

[43] Peter Thiemann. Correctness of a region-based binding-time analysis. In *Proc. Mathematical Foundations of Programming Semantics, Thirteenth Annual Conference*, volume 6 of *Electronic Notes in Theoretical Computer Science*, page 26, Pittsburgh, PA, March 1997. Carnegie Mellon University, Elsevier Science BV. URL: http://www.elsevier.nl/locate/entcs/volume6.html.

[44] Peter Thiemann. A unified framework for binding-time analysis. In Michel Bidoit and Max Dauchet, editors, *TAPSOFT '97: Theory and Practice of Software Development*, volume 1214 of *Lecture Notes in Computer Science*, pages 742–756, Lille, France, April 1997. Springer-Verlag.

[45] Peter Thiemann. Aspects of the pgg system: Specialization for standard scheme. In John Hatcliff, Torben Æ. Mogensen, and Peter Thiemann, editors, *Partial Evaluation—Practice and Theory. Proceedings of the 1998 DIKU International Summerschool*, Lecture Notes in Computer Science. Springer-Verlag, 1998.

[46] Peter Thiemann. *The PGG System—User Manual.* University of Nottingham, Nottingham, England, June 1998. Available from `ftp://ftp.informatik.uni-tuebingen.de/pub/PU/thiemann/software/pgg/`.

First-Class Contexts in ML

Masatomo Hashimoto

Research Institute for Mathematical Sciences,
Kyoto University, Sakyo-ku, Kyoto 606-8502, Japan
masatomo@kurims.kyoto-u.ac.jp
http://www.kurims.kyoto-u.ac.jp/~masatomo/

Abstract. This paper develops an ML-style programming language with first-class contexts i.e, expressions with holes. A programming language with first-class contexts can provide various advanced features such as macros, distributed programming and linking modules. A possibility of such a programming language was shown by the theory of simply typed context calculus developed by Hashimoto and Ohori. This paper extends the simply typed system of the context calculus to an ML-style polymorphic type system, and gives an operational semantics and a sound and complete type inference algorithm.

1 Introduction

A *context* is a term with holes in it. The basic operation for a context is to fill its holes with a term. For example, a term $(\lambda x.[\cdot])\ 5$ is a context where $[\cdot]$ indicates a hole. If its hole is filled with $f\ x$, we obtain $(\lambda x.f\ x)\ 5$. In this example, x in $f\ x$ is captured by λx in $(\lambda x.f\ x)\ 5$. That is, hole filling is essentially different from capture-avoiding substitution in the lambda calculus.

Contexts have so far been a meta-level tool and their applicability to programming languages has been limited to meta-level manipulation of programs. We believe that if a programming language is extended with first-class contexts, the resulting language will provide various advanced features. Let us briefly mention a few of them.

Type-safe macros. Holes can be regarded as some kind of meta variables ranging over a set of expressions. In this sense, a language extended with first-class contexts can naturally express macros based on token substitution seen in the C preprocessor. Such macros take arguments by hole filling. If the extended language is typed one, then we can obtain type-safe macros.

Distributed programming. In the setting of distributed programming, we send program pieces to remote sites which share common resources such as common runtime libraries, and then program pieces are executed there making bindings for necessary resources. We can regard such pieces as an open terms and such resources as contexts. In this sense, necessary bindings are made by hole filling.

Jieh Hsiang, Atsushi Ohori (Eds.): ASIAN'98, LNCS 1538, pp. 206–223, 1998.

Linking modules. A linking module which imports and exports some variables can naturally be regarded as a context containing free variables whose values will be supplied by some other contexts. One naive way of modeling a module exporting a set of functions $F_1, \ldots, F_n$ through identifiers $f_1, \ldots, f_n$ would be regarded as a context such as $(\lambda f_1. \cdots ((\lambda f_n.[\cdot])\ F_1) \cdots)\ F_n$. To link such a module and a program, hole filling will be performed. Since contexts are first-class, we can write programs which link program modules together in a dynamic manner.

In spite of potentially many benefits including those in the above, a programming language with first-class contexts has not been well investigated. A context-enriched calculus, called $\lambda\mathbf{C}$ was proposed in [11] by Lee and Friedman. However, $\lambda\mathbf{C}$ cannot represent contexts directly: in $\lambda\mathbf{C}$, contexts are clearly distinguished as "source code" from the ordinary lambda terms as "compiled code". The effect of hole filling is formulated as source code manipulation, and then compiled to lambda terms.

In [8], Hashimoto and Ohori have developed a simply typed lambda calculus with first-class contexts. In the calculus, contexts are truly first-class, and subject reduction and Church-Rosser have been proved with respect to the reduction which is the mixture of the ordinary β and fill reduction. In this paper, we establish a basis for a realistic programming language with first-class contexts based on the context calculus. For the purpose, we need more flexible type system and a concrete evaluation strategy. We chose ML [3] as a base language. A prominent feature of ML is the combination of polymorphism, robustness and compile-time error detection. We would like to extend ML with first-class contexts preserving all those benefits of ML. The followings are essential to achieve the goal.

- a polymorphic type deduction system,
- an operational semantics and the soundness of the type system, and
- a sound and complete type inference algorithm.

We give an operational semantics by extending the usual call-by-value evaluation strategy using closures. Developing a polymorphic type system and a type inference algorithm are more complex and challenging issue. In addition to the problem of discovering an appropriate typing for contexts, there are two technical difficulties to overcome. First, since contexts are first-class, we can define a function which receives contexts as its argument, and we can define a function which composes contexts. This indicates that the problem similar to the record concatenation will arise. Second, naive embedding of first-class contexts to ML type system makes types no longer first-order: the `let` construct introduces type schemes and then they may be provided through the hole in the scope of `let` binding. We solve the problems by using the techniques of typechecking record terms[12,13] for the former and by using the unification algorithm for polytypes [6] for the latter.

The rest of this paper is organized as follows. Section 2 introduces the target language informally. In Section 3, we define the types, terms and the semantics, and then prove type soundness. Section 4 defines the type inference algorithm. Finally, in Section 5, we discuss further investigation and conclude the paper.

2 Informal Discussion

In addition to the ordinary ML constructs, we introduce *labeled holes* ranged over by $X, Y, \ldots$, *hole abstraction* $\delta X.e$ and *context application* $e_1 \odot e_2$ as in [8]. For example, a simple context $(\lambda x.[\cdot])$ 5 appeared in the previous section is written as $\delta X.(\lambda x.X)$ 5. To represent the effect of hole filling, we write as $(\delta X.(\lambda x.X)\ 5) \odot (f\ x)$, and then this program will be evaluated to $(\lambda x.f\ x)$ 5.

To see what kind of type should be given to a context, let us examine the relationship between contexts and records. We can encode a record $\{l_1 = e_1, \ldots, l_n = e_n\}$ as

$$r \equiv \delta X.(\lambda l_1.\cdots.\lambda l_n.X)\ e_1 \cdots e_n$$

where field access is simulated as $r \odot l_i$. We can also define a function which composes two records as

$$comp \equiv \lambda r_1.\lambda r_2.\delta X.r_1 \odot (r_2 \odot X).$$

Since we would like to get the information about which variables to be captured through the context applications, our system essentially contains the same difficulty on typing as the one of calculi for record concatenation [16,7,12]. Especially, in [12], Rémy gives a record a type $\{\chi \Rightarrow \pi\}$ where χ and π denote row variables. The intuition is that a record of such type is formulated as if it is a function: given any input row of fields χ it returns the output row π. For example, the empty record has type $\{\chi \Rightarrow \chi\}$ since it does not change the input row, and one element record $\{a = 1\}$ has type $\{\chi; a : - \Rightarrow \chi; a : int\}$ which adds one more field which is not be previously defined, where "–" denotes that the field a is not present. This view of record types is quite compatible with the contexts, since contexts also have an aspect of function. Based on this observation, we give the following type for contexts.

$$[\rho_1 \triangleright \tau_1 /\!/ \rho_2 \triangleright \tau_2]$$

A context of the above type takes a term of type τ_1 as input which may have free variables indicated in ρ_1, and returns a term of type τ_2 with the variables in ρ_1 being consumed to yield ρ_2. For instance, a context $\delta X.(\lambda x.X)$ 5 has the type $[\chi; x : int \triangleright \alpha /\!/ \chi; x : - \triangleright \alpha]$. Note that the direction of increase of fields is inverted in the context. This form of context types is a generalization of simple context types given in [8], and is suitable for integrating them in a polymorphic type system.

Let us mention a point to notice when typing for contexts are integrated with ML-style polymorphism.

Since we have `let` construction from ML, the following context can be defined.

$$r' \equiv \delta X.\texttt{let}\ l_1 = e_1\ \texttt{in}\ \cdots \texttt{let}\ l_n = e_n\ \texttt{in}\ X$$

However, naive typing for the above expression introduces a higher-order type $[\chi; l_1 : \sigma_1; \ldots; l_n : \sigma_n \triangleright \alpha /\!/ \chi; l_1 : -; \ldots; l_n : - \triangleright \alpha]$ beyond type schemes of ML. In our system, the above expression is typed as follows.

$$r' : [\chi; l_1 : [\sigma_1]; \ldots; l_n : [\sigma_n] \triangleright \alpha /\!/ \chi; l_1 : -; \ldots; l_n : - \triangleright \alpha]$$

where type annotation $[\sigma_i]$ denotes "monomorphic" polytypes which locks instantiation of generic type variables of orignal type schemes σ_i as seen in [6]. We can use there polymorphic values in a context application $r' \odot_{\{l_1:[\sigma_1];\ldots;l_n:[\sigma_n]\}} e$ where $\{l_1 : [\sigma_1]; \ldots; l_n : [\sigma_n]\}$ is needed to keep the decidability of type inference. We call such an annotation associated to context application an *interface*. If unification for these locked polytypes is succeeded, they are unlocked and able to be used as usual type schemes in e.

With these preparations, let us show some examples of programming with first-class contexts.

Typed macros. We cannot write a function which manipulates programming text itself in the original ML. For example, given a conditional function *cond*, we can define $ifThenElse$ as follows.

$$ifThenElse \equiv \delta X.\delta Y.\delta Z.cond(X, Y, Z) \ : \ [\chi \triangleright bool /\!/ \chi \triangleright [\pi \triangleright \alpha /\!/ \pi \triangleright [\psi \triangleright \alpha /\!/ \psi \triangleright \alpha]]]$$

where the symbol $\odot$ associate to the left. If we use an usual function instead of the context, both *then* part and *else* part will be evaluated. The point here is that we can regard holes as meta variables. Another example is the following *or* operator which captures a variable v.

$$or \equiv \delta X.\delta Y.\mathtt{let}\ v = X\ \mathtt{in}\ (ifThenElse \odot v \odot v \odot Y) \\ : \ [\chi \triangleright bool /\!/ \chi \triangleright [\pi; v : bool \triangleright bool /\!/ \pi; v{-} \triangleright bool]]$$

The binding information that the above type provides will prevents the variable v from being unintentionally captured when programmers use this macro. We will be able to avoid automatically such unintended capture if we use the technique of hygienic macro expander[10] which avoids name conflicts by time-stamping all such variables.

Programs for distribution. We can treat programs which contain free variables in presence of first-class contexts. In the setting of distributed programming, one often wants to send a piece of "open" program to a remote site and execute it there. We can define such a program as

$$code \equiv \delta X.X \odot_{\mathcal{I}} e$$

where $\mathcal{I}$ denotes an interface. In this case, a remote site which receives such a program will prepare a program which at least provides bindings for variables in $\mathcal{I}$, for example, $\delta X.\mathtt{let}\ f_1 = e_1\ \mathtt{in}\ \cdots \mathtt{let}\ f_n = e_n\ \mathtt{in}\ X$ where $dom(\mathcal{I}) \subseteq \{f_i\}$ and apply *code* to it.

Linking modules. A module here is a program fragment which imports bindings for possibly free variables in the fragment, and exports some bindings. They are linked together to produce a complete program. We can represent a module which imports $f_1, \ldots, f_n$ and exports $g_1, \ldots, g_m$ as follows.

$$M \equiv \delta X.\delta Y.X \odot_{\{f_1:\tau_1,\ldots,f_n:\tau_n\}} (\mathtt{let}\ g_1 = e_1\ \mathtt{in}\ \cdots \mathtt{let}\ g_m = e_m\ \mathtt{in}\ Y) \\ : [\chi \triangleright [\pi; f_i : \tau_i; g_j; - \triangleright \alpha /\!/ \psi; f_i : - \triangleright \beta] /\!/ \chi \triangleright [\pi; f_i : \tau_i; g_j; \tau'_j \triangleright \alpha /\!/ \psi; f_i : - \triangleright \beta]]$$

The input of this context is any context which exports f_i and none of g_j, and the output is a context which exports both f_i and g_j. These modules are linked together using the following link operator $\bowtie$.

$$m_1 \bowtie m_2 \equiv \delta X.\delta Y.(m_1 \odot (m_2 \odot X)) \odot Y.$$

Note that $\bowtie$ is associative and the result of applying this operator to a pair of modules produces again a module. To construct a complete program, we must prepare other two kinds of module $main \equiv \delta X.X \odot_{\mathcal{I}} e$ which exports no bindings and $top \equiv \delta X.\mathtt{let}\ h_l = e_l\ \mathtt{in}\ X$ which imports no bindings. Then a complete program is produced by $main \odot ((M_1 \bowtie \ldots \bowtie M_k) \odot top)$.

3 The Language

3.1 Types, Terms, and the Static Semantics

We use the following notations for functions. The domain and the codomain of a function f is written as $dom(f)$ and $cod(f)$ respectively. We sometimes regard a function as a set of pairs and write $\emptyset$ for the empty function. Let f and g be functions. We write $f \uplus g$ for $f \cup g$ provided that $dom(f) \cap dom(g) = \emptyset$. The restriction of a function f to the domain D and to the domain $dom(f) \setminus D$ are written as $f|_D$ and $f\backslash_D$ respectively.

We let $\mathcal{V}$ be a finite set of term variables. The set of types is given by the syntax:

$\iota ::= \theta \mid - \mid \tau$	Fields
$\rho^{\mathcal{V}} ::= \chi^{\mathcal{V}} \mid -^{\mathcal{V}} \mid \rho^{\mathcal{V}\cup\{x\}}; x : \iota$	Rows defining all variables except those in $\mathcal{V}$
$\tau ::= \alpha \mid b \mid \tau \to \tau \mid [\rho^{\emptyset} \triangleright \tau /\!/ \rho^{\emptyset} \triangleright \tau] \mid [\sigma]$	Monotypes
$\xi ::= \alpha \mid \chi^{\mathcal{V}}$	Variables
$\sigma ::= \tau \mid \forall \xi.\tau$	Type schemes

where $x, y, \ldots$ range over an infinitely countable collection of term variables, α, β and γ range over an infinitely countable collection of type variables, χ, π and ψ range over an infinitely countable collection of row variables, θ ranges over an infinitely countable collection of field variables and b ranges over a given set of base types. The definitions of fields and rows are just as ones in [13] except for the fact that a field is tagged with a *variable* instead of a *label*. We omit superscripts in rows whenever we can complete them. We sometimes regard a ρ as a set of pairs of variables and monotypes, that is, $(x : \tau) \in \rho$ if and only if $\rho = \rho'; x : \tau \cdots$. In addition to the ordinary set of monotypes, $[\rho_1 \triangleright \tau_1 /\!/ \rho_2 \triangleright \tau_2]$ denotes a context type, and $[\sigma]$ denotes a polytype as mentioned before. We say a context type $[\rho_1 \triangleright \tau_1 /\!/ \rho_2 \triangleright \tau_2]$ is *legal* if $(x : -) \in \rho_1$ then $(x : \tau) \notin \rho_2$, and a type scheme σ is legal if $[\sigma']$ does not occur anywhere other than $\rho; x : [\sigma']$ in σ and if any context type in σ is legal.

The constructs $\forall \alpha.\sigma$ and $\forall \chi.\sigma$ bind type variable α and row variable χ in σ, respectively. The set of *free type variables* and *free row variables* of a type scheme σ is denoted as $FTV(\sigma)$ and $FRV(\sigma)$, respectively. The definition of FTV and FRV are usual. We write $FV(\sigma)$ for $FTV(\sigma) \cup FRV(\sigma)$. We identify type schemes up to α-conversion as usual.

We define some notations on types which will be needed when we define a type system. Let "$\bullet$" denote an unspecified part of types. We write $EI([\rho_1 \triangleright \bullet /\!\!/ \rho_2 \triangleright \bullet])$ for the *extracted interface from a context type* which is the maximum set of pairs of variables and monotypes satisfying the condition: if $(x : \tau) \in EI([\rho_1 \triangleright \bullet /\!\!/ \rho_2 \triangleright \bullet])$, then ρ_1 contains $(x : \tau)$ and ρ_2 contains $(x : -)$. We define the set of *prohibited variables*, denoted by $PV([\rho \triangleright \bullet /\!\!/ \rho' \triangleright \bullet])$, for the set of variables prohibited to be exported by a context having that type, by $PV([\rho \triangleright \bullet /\!\!/ \rho' \triangleright \bullet]) = \{x | (x : -) \in \rho \cap \rho'\}$.

A *type substitution* is a function from a finite set of type variables to the set of type schemes. We write $\{\sigma_1/\alpha_1, \ldots, \sigma_n/\alpha_n\}$ for the type substitution that maps each α_i to σ_i simultaneously. A type substitution φ is extended to the set of all type variables by defining $\varphi(\alpha) = \alpha$ for all $\alpha \notin dom(\varphi)$, and in turn it is extended to the set of any type schemes, as usual. However, we maintain that the domain of a type substitution always means the domain of the original finite function.

A *row substitution* is a function from a finite set of row variables to the set of rows. We use the notation $\{\rho_1^{\mathcal{V}_1}/\chi_1^{\mathcal{V}_1}, \ldots, \rho_n^{\mathcal{V}_n}/\chi_n^{\mathcal{V}_n}\}$ for the row substitution that simultaneously maps each $\chi_i^{\mathcal{V}_i}$ to $\rho_i^{\mathcal{V}_i}$. A row substitution is extended to the set of all row variables and in turn to the set of all type schemes as well as the type substitution mentioned above, and the domain of it is also treated similarly.

A *compound substitution*, or simply *substitution*, is a function from the set of type schemes to the set of type schemes. Let μ and φ be a row substitution and a type substitution, respectively. A substitution S, denoted by the sequence of type substitutions and row substitutions, is defined as a composition of extended type substitutions and row substitutions: if $S = S'\mu$ then $S(\sigma) = S'(\mu(\sigma))$ or if $S = S'\varphi$ then $S(\sigma) = S'(\varphi(\sigma))$, where S' possibly be an empty sequence. The domain of S is the set of variables defined as the union of all domains of the components. We write $S \circ S'$ for the composition of S and S', defined as $(S \circ S')(\sigma) = S(S'(\sigma))$. A *ground substitution* is a substitution S such that for any $\sigma \in cod(S)$, σ contains no free variables. We exclude any substitutions which collapse legal context types in the rest of the development.

The set of terms is given by the grammar:

$$\begin{array}{ll} \mathcal{I} ::= \{x_1 : \tau_1, \ldots, x_n : \tau_n\} & \text{Interfaces} \\ e ::= x \,|\, c^b \,|\, \lambda x.e \,|\, e\ e \,|\, \mathtt{let}_\sigma\ x = e\ \mathtt{in}\ e \,|\, X^{\mathcal{V}} \,|\, \delta X.e \,|\, e \odot_{\mathcal{I}} e & \text{Terms} \end{array}$$

c^b is a constant which has a base type b. $X^{\mathcal{V}}$ is a hole. $\mathcal{V}$ on the shoulder of hole X denotes the set of variables which does not exported i.e. those variables which will be used locally in the context containing X. $\delta X.e$ denotes a context built up by the hole abstraction. $e_1 \odot_{\mathcal{I}} e_2$ is a context application. $\mathcal{I}$ denotes the set of variables and their (closed) types which is exported by e_1 and imported by e_2 during the computation of the context application. Note that the variables in $dom(\mathcal{I})$ are regarded as bound in the term $e_1 \odot_{\mathcal{I}} e_2$.

$$\textsf{Var}\ \emptyset, \mathcal{T} \rhd x : \tau \quad \text{if } \mathcal{T}(x) \succeq \tau \qquad\qquad \textsf{Const}\ \emptyset, \mathcal{T} \rhd c^b : b$$

$$\textsf{Abs}\ \frac{\{X_i : [\rho_i \rhd \tau_i /\!/ \rho_i'; x : \iota_i \rhd \bullet]\}, \mathcal{T} \uplus \{x : \tau_a\} \rhd e : \tau_b}{\{X_i : [\rho_i \rhd \tau_i /\!/ \rho_i'; x : - \rhd \bullet]\}, \mathcal{T} \rhd \lambda x.e : \tau_a \to \tau_b} \quad \text{if } \iota_i = \tau_a \text{ or } \iota_i = -$$

$$\textsf{App}\ \frac{\mathcal{H}_1, \mathcal{T} \rhd e_1 : \tau_1 \to \tau_2 \quad \mathcal{H}_2, \mathcal{T} \rhd e_2 : \tau_1}{\mathcal{H}_1 \uplus \mathcal{H}_2, \mathcal{T} \rhd e_1\ e_2 : \tau_2}$$

$$\textsf{Let}\ \frac{\mathcal{H}, \mathcal{T} \rhd e_1 : \sigma \quad \{X_i : [\rho_i \rhd \tau_i /\!/ \rho_i'; x : \iota_i \rhd \bullet]\}, \mathcal{T} \uplus \{x : \sigma\} \rhd e_2 : \tau}{\mathcal{H} \uplus \{X_i : [\rho_i \rhd \tau_i /\!/ \rho_i'; x : - \rhd \bullet]\}, \mathcal{T} \rhd \mathtt{let}_{\sigma_0}\ x = e_1\ \mathtt{in}\ e_2 : \tau}$$

if $\iota_i = -$, or for some $\sigma_1 \preceq \sigma$ if there exists S such that $S(\sigma_0) = S(\sigma_1)$, $\iota_i = [\sigma_1]$

$$\textsf{Hole}\ \{X : [\rho; x_i : - \rhd \tau /\!/ \rho; x_i : - \rhd \bullet]\}, \mathcal{T} \rhd X^{\{x_i\}} : \tau$$

$$\textsf{HAbs}\ \frac{\mathcal{H} \uplus \{X : [\rho_1 \rhd \tau_1 /\!/ \rho_2 \rhd \bullet]\}, \mathcal{T} \rhd e : \tau_2}{\mathcal{H}, \mathcal{T} \rhd \delta X.e : [\rho_1 \rhd \tau_1 /\!/ \rho_2 \rhd \tau_2]}$$

$$\textsf{CApp}\ \frac{\mathcal{H}, \mathcal{T} \rhd e_1 : [\rho_a \rhd \tau_a /\!/ \rho_b \rhd \tau_b] \quad \{X_i : [\rho_i \rhd \tau_i /\!/ \rho_a \rhd \bullet]\}, \mathcal{T} \uplus \mathcal{T}' \rhd e_2 : \tau_a}{\mathcal{H} \uplus \{X_i : [\rho_i \rhd \tau_i /\!/ \rho_b \rhd \bullet]\}, \mathcal{T} \rhd e_1 \odot_{\mathcal{I}} e_2 : \tau_b}$$
$$\text{if } EI([\rho_a \rhd \bullet /\!/ \rho_b \rhd \bullet]) \supseteq [\mathcal{T}'] = \mathcal{I}$$

$$\textsf{Gen}\ \frac{\mathcal{H}, \mathcal{T} \rhd e : \tau}{\mathcal{H}, \mathcal{T} \rhd e : \sigma} \quad \text{if } \sigma = Gen(\mathcal{H}, \mathcal{T}, \tau)$$

Fig. 1. Typing rules

The type system is defined as a proof system deriving a typing of the form

$$\mathcal{H}, \mathcal{T} \rhd e : \sigma$$

which indicates that e has type scheme σ under a variable type assignment $\mathcal{T}$ and a hole type assignment $\mathcal{H}$ which is a function assigning types $[\rho \rhd \tau /\!/ \rho' \rhd \bullet]$ to labeled holes. We assume that any $\mathcal{T}$ and $\mathcal{H}$ do not contain illegal type schemes in the rest of the development. The set of typing rules is given in Figure 1.

The generalization $Gen(\mathcal{H}, \mathcal{T}, \sigma) = \forall \bar{\xi}.\sigma$ where $\bar{\xi}$ are all free variables of σ that do not occur in $\mathcal{H}$ and $\mathcal{T}$. We write $\sigma \preceq \sigma'$ when $\sigma = \forall \xi_1 \cdots \xi_n.\tau$, $\sigma' = \forall \xi_1' \cdots \xi_m'.\tau'$ such that each ξ_j is not free in $\forall \xi_1' \cdots \xi_m'.\tau'$ and $\tau = S(\tau')$ for some S such that $dom(S) = \{\xi_1', \ldots, \xi_m'\}$. Let $\mathcal{T} = \{x_i : \sigma_i\}$. We write $[\mathcal{T}]$ for $\{x_i : [\sigma_i]\}$.

Some explanations of the typing rules are in order.

- Rule Abs. We require that all rows in the right side of the context type of any hole in the hole type assignment contain x. Then the rule changes x-field to "–" and also discharges $\{x : \tau_a\}$ from the type assignment.
- Rule Let. The annotation σ_0 associated with `let` specifies the generality of the type of variable x which will be captured through the possible context application. We can omit this burden in the following cases:
  - e_2 has no hole,
  - σ is a monomorphic type, and

- σ itself is programmer's choice for the type of x exported through the holes in e_2.

  In other cases, this annotation is needed to keep principality of the type system of ML.
- Rule Hole. $X^{\{x_i\}}$ keeps row input unchanged when it is not surrounded by any binding constructs. x_i are excluded from the hole type assignment by assigning "–" to them.
- Rule CApp. e_2 expects that e_1 provides the bindings for the free variables in $dom(\mathcal{I})$, and $\mathcal{I}$ also provides the type informations for the variables which will be captured by e_1. Note that e_1 may export more bindings than e_2 requires.

In our system, each free hole occurs linearly as in [8]. If multiple occurrences of a hole are allowed, we must maintain the information of the bindings exported through each occurrence of a hole. The linearity condition is ensured by the rules App, Let, Hole and CApp.

The following lemma shows that typing judgments are stable under substitution.

Lemma 1. *If* $\mathcal{H}, \mathcal{T} \triangleright e : \sigma$, *then for any substitution* S, $S(\mathcal{H}), S(\mathcal{T}) \triangleright e : S(\sigma)$.

Proof. By simple induction on the derivation of $\mathcal{H}, \mathcal{T} \triangleright e : \sigma$. □

Note that S is not applied to the term e. We must consider variables occurring in the type annotations in e as closed ones quantified by existential quantifiers.

3.2 Dynamic Semantics

We give a call-by-value operational semantics of the system in the style of *natural semantics*[9] by giving a set of rules to derive a reduction relation of the form

$$\eta, \zeta \vdash e \Downarrow v$$

indicating that e evaluates to a value v under a *hole environment* η, which is a function from a finite set of holes to values, and a *variable environment* ζ, which is a function from a finite set of variables to values. The set of values is given below.

$$v ::= c^b \mid func(\eta, \zeta, x, e) \mid cont(\eta, \zeta, X, e) \mid clos(\eta, \zeta, \mathcal{V}, e) \mid wrong$$

$func(\eta, \zeta, x, e)$ and $cont(\eta, \zeta, X, e)$ indicate a *function closure* and a *context closure* representing a function value and a context value, respectively. $clos(\eta, \zeta, \mathcal{V}, e)$ indicates a *term closure* representing a value corresponding to an open term to be filled in the suitable contexts. This value can be regarded as a generalization of a function closure; if $\mathcal{V} = \{x_1, \ldots, x_n\}$, it takes a set of values one for each x_i, and evaluates e under the hole environment η and the variable environment obtained from ζ by extending with the bindings for $\{x_1, \ldots, x_n\}$. $wrong$ represents the runtime error.

$$\text{Var}\ \eta,\zeta \vdash x \Downarrow v \quad \text{if } \zeta(x) = v \qquad\qquad \text{Const}\ \eta,\zeta \vdash c^b \Downarrow c^b$$

$$\text{Func}\ \eta,\zeta \vdash \lambda x.e \Downarrow \mathit{func}(\eta,\zeta,x,e)$$

$$\text{App}\ \frac{\eta,\zeta \vdash e_1 \Downarrow \mathit{func}(\eta',\zeta',x,e') \quad \eta,\zeta \vdash e_2 \Downarrow v' \quad \eta',\zeta'\{x \mapsto v'\} \vdash e' \Downarrow v}{\eta,\zeta \vdash e_1\ e_2 \Downarrow v}$$

$$\text{Let}\ \frac{\eta,\zeta \vdash e_1 \Downarrow v' \quad \eta,\zeta\{x \mapsto v'\} \vdash e_2 \Downarrow v}{\eta,\zeta \vdash \mathbf{let}_\sigma\ x = e_1\ \mathbf{in}\ e_2 \Downarrow v}$$

$$\text{Hole}\ \frac{\eta',\zeta'\{x_i \mapsto \zeta(x_i)\} \vdash e \Downarrow v}{\eta,\zeta \vdash X^\nu \Downarrow v} \quad \text{if } \eta(X) = \mathit{clos}(\eta',\zeta',\{x_i\},e)$$

$$\text{Cont}\ \eta,\zeta \vdash \delta X.e \Downarrow \mathit{cont}(\eta,\zeta,X,e)$$

$$\text{CApp}\ \frac{\eta,\zeta \vdash e_1 \Downarrow \mathit{cont}(\eta',\zeta',X,e') \quad \eta'\{X \mapsto \mathit{clos}(\eta,\zeta,\mathit{dom}(\mathcal{I}),e_2)\},\zeta' \vdash e' \Downarrow v}{\eta,\zeta \vdash e_1 \odot_{\mathcal{I}} e_2 \Downarrow v}$$

Fig. 2. Evaluation rules

The set of rules for the call-by-value operational semantics is given in Figure 2. This set of rules should be taken with the following implicit rules yielding *wrong*: if the evaluation of any of its component specified in the rule yields *wrong* or does not satisfy the side condition of the rule then the entire term yields *wrong*. This operational semantics is readily implementable.

3.3 Type Soundness

We extend the set of types with auxiliary types of the form $[\mathcal{I} \rhd \tau]$ for term closures. A value v has a closed type scheme σ, denoted by $\models v : \sigma$, if it is derivable from the rules given in Figure 3.

Let $\mathcal{H},\mathcal{T} \rhd e : \sigma$ be a derivable typing judgment. A hole environment η and a variable environment ζ *satisfy* the typing judgment $\mathcal{H},\mathcal{T} \rhd e : \sigma$, denoted by $\langle\eta,\zeta\rangle \models \langle\mathcal{H},\mathcal{T} \rhd e : \sigma\rangle$, when the following conditions hold.

- For all $x \in \mathit{dom}(\mathcal{T})$, $\models \zeta(x) : \mathcal{T}(x)$.
- If the last rule which is used in the derivation of $\mathcal{H},\mathcal{T} \rhd e : \sigma$ is CApp, $\mathcal{H}_0 \uplus \{X_i : [\rho_i \rhd \tau_i /\!/ \rho_b \rhd \bullet]\},\mathcal{T} \rhd e_1 \odot_{\mathcal{I}} e_2 : \tau_b$ is derived from $\mathcal{H}_0,\mathcal{T} \rhd e_1 : [\rho_a \rhd \tau_a /\!/ \rho_b \rhd \tau_b]$ and $\{X_i : [\rho_i \rhd \tau_i /\!/ \rho_a \rhd \bullet]\},\mathcal{T} \uplus \mathcal{T}' \rhd e_2 : \tau_a$. Then,
  - for all $X \in \mathit{dom}(\mathcal{H}_0)$, if $\mathcal{H}_0(X) = [\bullet \rhd \tau /\!/ \bullet \rhd \bullet]$ then $\models \eta(X) : [\mathcal{I}' \rhd \tau]$, where $\mathcal{I}' \subseteq EI(\mathcal{H}_0(X)) \uplus [\mathcal{T}\backslash_{PV(\mathcal{H}_0(X))}]$.
  - And for all X_i, $\models \eta(X_i) : [\mathcal{I}_i \rhd \tau_i]$, where $\mathcal{I}_i \subseteq [\mathcal{T}'\backslash_{PV([\rho_i \rhd \tau_i /\!/ \rho_b \rhd \bullet])}] \uplus EI([\rho_i \rhd \tau_i /\!/ \rho_a \rhd \bullet]) \uplus [\mathcal{T}\backslash_{PV([\rho_i \rhd \tau_i /\!/ \rho_b \rhd \bullet])}]$.

  Otherwise, for all $X \in \mathit{dom}(\mathcal{H})$, if $\mathcal{H}(X) = [\bullet \rhd \tau /\!/ \bullet \rhd \bullet]$ then $\models \eta(X) : [\mathcal{I} \rhd \tau]$, where $\mathcal{I} \subseteq EI(\mathcal{H}(X)) \uplus [\mathcal{T}\backslash_{PV(\mathcal{H}(X))}]$.

$\models c^b : b$	
$\models v : [\sigma]$	$\Leftrightarrow \models v : \sigma$
$\models \mathit{func}(\eta, \zeta, x, e) : \tau_1 \to \tau_2$	$\Leftrightarrow$ for all v such that $\models v : \tau_1$, if $\eta, \zeta\{x \mapsto v\} \vdash e \Downarrow v'$ then $\models v' : \tau_2$
$\models \mathit{clos}(\eta, \zeta, \{x_i\}, e) : [\{x_i : \tau_i\} \triangleright \tau]$	$\Leftrightarrow$ for all v_i such that $\models v_i : \tau_i$, if $\eta, \zeta\{x_i \mapsto v_i\} \vdash e \Downarrow v'$ then $\models v' : \tau$
$\models \mathit{cont}(\eta, \zeta, X, e) : [\rho_1 \triangleright \tau_1 /\!/ \rho_2 \triangleright \tau_2]$	$\Leftrightarrow$ for all $\mathcal{I}$ such that $\mathcal{I} \subseteq EI([\rho_1 \triangleright \bullet /\!/ \rho_2 \triangleright \bullet])$, for all v such that $\models v : [\mathcal{I} \triangleright \tau_1]$, if $\eta\{X \mapsto v\}, \zeta \vdash e \Downarrow v'$ then $\models v' : \tau_2$
$\models v : \forall \xi_1 \cdots \xi_n . \tau$	$\Leftrightarrow$ for any ground substitution S such that $dom(S) = \{\xi_1, \ldots \xi_n\}, \models v : S(\tau)$.

Fig. 3. Definition of value typing

With these preparations, we prove the following soundness theorem which denotes that a well-typed program will not produce a runtime error. The proof is deferred to the appendix.

Theorem 1 (Type Soundness). *If $\mathcal{H}, \mathcal{T} \triangleright e : \sigma$ is derivable, then for any ground substitution S such that $dom(S)$ contains all the free variables in the derivation of $\mathcal{H}, \mathcal{T} \triangleright e : \sigma$, and for any η, ζ such that $\langle \eta, \zeta \rangle \models \langle S(\mathcal{H}, \mathcal{T} \triangleright e : \sigma) \rangle$, if $\eta, \zeta \vdash e \Downarrow v$ then $\models v : S(\sigma)$.*

4 Type Inference

In this section, we develop a type inference algorithm.

In the algebraic point of view, the definition of context types can be regarded as a combination of the record type appeared in [13], and locked polytype appeared in [6]. First, we define a first-order unification for our type system using these techniques.

Solving unification problems is formulated as the transformation of *unification problems* defined as follows.

$U ::= \bot \mid \top \mid U \wedge U \mid \exists \alpha . U \mid E \mid \sigma \doteq \sigma$	Unification problems
$E ::= E_\tau \mid E_\rho$	Multi-equations
$E_\tau ::= \tau \mid \tau \doteq E_\tau$	Multi-equations for types
$E_\rho ::= \rho \mid \rho \doteq E_\rho$	Multi-equations for rows

The symbol $\bot$ denotes a unification problem that has no solution, and $\top$ denotes a trivial unification problem. We treat them as a unit and a zero for $\wedge$. That is $U \wedge \top$ and $U \wedge \bot$ are equal to U and $\bot$, respectively. We also identify $\top$ with singleton multi-equations. That is, we can always assume that U contain at least one multi-equation $\alpha \doteq E$ for each type variable of U and at least one multi-equation $\chi \doteq E$ for each row variable of U. A complex formula is the conjunction of other formulas or the existential quantification of another formula. The symbol $\wedge$ is commutative and associative. The symbol $\exists$ acts as a binder. The symbol $\doteq$ is commutative and associative.

A substitution S is a solution of a multi-equation E for monotypes, if results of applying it to all terms of E coincide, and S is a solution of $\sigma \doteq \sigma'$ if $S(\sigma) \equiv S(\sigma')$ where $\equiv$ is modulo reordering and renaming of bound variables, and removal of redundant universally quantified variables. We can say $\forall\bar{\xi}.\tau \equiv \forall\bar{\xi}'.\tau'$ if and only if there exists a substitution S such that

1. $S(\tau) = S(\tau')$
2. $S|_{\bar{\xi}}$ and $S|_{\bar{\xi}'}$ are injective in $\bar{\xi} \cup \bar{\xi}'$
3. no variable of $\bar{\xi} \cup \bar{\xi}'$ appears in $S\backslash_{(\bar{\xi}\cup\bar{\xi}')}$.

We introduce another kind of unificands $\bar{\xi} \leftrightarrow \bar{\xi}'$ whose solutions are substitutions satisfying the above conditions 2 and 3. We assume $\bar{\xi} \cap \bar{\xi}' = \emptyset$ in order to avoid unnecessary complexity. The symbols $\doteq$ in polytype equations and $\leftrightarrow$ are commutative. Two unification problems are equivalent if they have the same set of solutions.

Given a unification problem U, we define the constraint ordering $\prec_U$ as the transitive closure of the immediate precedence ordering containing all pairs $\alpha \prec \alpha'$ such that there exists a multi-equation $\alpha \doteq \tau \doteq E$ in U where τ is a non-variable term that contains α'. A unification problem is strict if $\prec_U$ is strict.

A unification problem is in solved form if it is either $\top$ or $\bot$, or if it is strict and of the form $\exists\bar{\xi}. \bigvee_{i\in 1\ldots n} E_i$ where E_i contain at most one non-variable term, and if $i \neq j$ then E_i and E_j contain no variable term in common.

We write $U \Rightarrow \exists\bar{\xi}.S$ if S is a principal solution of U and variables $\bar{\xi}$ are not free in U, and $U \Rightarrow \bot$ if U is unsatisfiable. We write $|\sigma|$ for the size of σ: the number of occurrences of symbols $\_ \to \_$, $[\_]$, $\_;x:\_$, or $[\_ \triangleright \_ /\!/ \_ \triangleright \_]$ in σ. We use the notation $|\_|$ also for rows by abuse of notation.

The unification algorithm is given as a set of rewriting rules that preserves equivalence in Figure 4. There are implicit compatible rules that allow to rewrite complex formulas by rewriting any of sub-formula, and crash rules that yield $\bot$ when the top symbols in both sides of $\doteq$ are not the same symbol.

The rules Occur,Merge,Absorb and Decompose-Fun are for the ordinary first-order unification. The other part of the system includes the rules for polytypes Decompose-Poly,Polytypes,Renaming-True and Renaming-False which are originated from the first-order unification for polytypes in [6], and also includes the rules for rows Decompose-Row,Mutate-Absent and Mutate-Field which are from [15]. The rule Decompose-Cont naturally decomposes context types.

Theorem 2. *Given a unification problem U, the set of rules in Figure 4 computes a most general unifier S, or fails with computing $\bot$.*

Proof (Sketch). By showing the right and the left side of each rule have exactly the same set of solutions. The termination of the algorithm can be shown by the induction on the appropriate weight. □

Occur

if $\prec_U$ is not strict **then** $U \Rrightarrow \bot$

Merge

$\xi \doteq E \wedge \xi \doteq E' \Rrightarrow \xi \doteq E \doteq E'$

Absorb

$\xi \doteq \xi \doteq E \Rrightarrow \xi \doteq E$

Decompose-Fun

if $|\tau_1 \to \tau_2| \leq |\tau_1' \to \tau_2'|$ **then**

$\tau_1 \to \tau_2 \doteq \tau_1' \to \tau_2' \doteq E \Rrightarrow \tau_1 \to \tau_2 \doteq E \wedge \tau_1 \doteq \tau_1' \wedge \tau_2 \doteq \tau_2'$

Decompose-Poly

if $|\sigma| \leq |\sigma'|$ **then** $[\sigma] \doteq [\sigma'] \doteq E \Rrightarrow [\sigma'] \doteq E \wedge \sigma \doteq \sigma'$

Decompose-Cont

if $|[\rho_1 \triangleright \tau_1 /\!/ \rho_2 \triangleright \tau_2]| \leq |[\rho_1' \triangleright \tau_1' /\!/ \rho_2' \triangleright \tau_2']|$ **then**

$$[\rho_1 \triangleright \tau_1 /\!/ \rho_2 \triangleright \tau_2] \doteq [\rho_1' \triangleright \tau_1' /\!/ \rho_2' \triangleright \tau_2'] \doteq E \Rrightarrow [\rho_1 \triangleright \tau_1 /\!/ \rho_2 \triangleright \tau_2] \doteq E \wedge \bigwedge \begin{cases} \tau_1 \doteq \tau_1' \\ \tau_2 \doteq \tau_2' \\ \rho_1 \doteq \rho_1' \\ \rho_2 \doteq \rho_2' \end{cases}$$

Decompose-Row

if $|\rho_1; x : \iota_1| \leq |\rho_2; x : \iota_2|$ **then**

$\rho_1; x : \iota_1 \doteq \rho_2; x : \iota_2 \doteq E \Rrightarrow \rho_1; x : \iota_1 \doteq E \wedge \rho_1 \doteq \rho_2 \wedge \iota_1 \doteq \iota_2$

Polytypes

let $\bar\xi \cap \bar\xi' = \emptyset$ **and** $\bar\xi \cap FV(\tau') = \emptyset$ **and** $\bar\xi' \cap FV(\tau) = \emptyset$ **in**

$\forall\bar\xi.\tau \doteq \forall\bar\xi'.\tau' \Rrightarrow \exists\bar\xi\bar\xi'.\tau \doteq \tau' \wedge \bar\xi \leftrightarrow \bar\xi'$

Renaming-True

let $\bar\xi = (\xi_i)^{i \in 1 \ldots n+p}$ **and** $\bar\xi' = (\xi_i')^{i \in 1 \ldots n+q}$ **in** $\exists\bar\xi\bar\xi'.(\xi_i \doteq \xi_i')^{i \in 1 \ldots n} \wedge \bar\xi \leftrightarrow \bar\xi' \Rrightarrow \top$

Renaming-False

if $\beta \in \bar\xi$ **and** $\tau \notin \bar\xi' \cup \{\beta\}$ **then** $\beta \doteq \tau \doteq E \wedge \bar\xi \leftrightarrow \bar\xi' \Rrightarrow \bot$

if $\beta \in \bar\xi \cap FV(\tau)$ **and** $\tau \neq \beta$ **then** $\beta' \doteq \tau \doteq E \wedge \bar\xi \leftrightarrow \bar\xi' \Rrightarrow \bot$

Mutate-Absent

$\rho; x : \iota \doteq - \doteq E \Rrightarrow - \doteq E \wedge \iota \doteq - \wedge \rho \doteq -$

Mutate-Field

if $|\rho_1; x : \iota_1| \leq |\rho_2; x : \iota_2|$ **then**

$\rho_1; x : \iota_1 \doteq \rho_2; y : \iota_2 \doteq E \Rrightarrow \exists\chi.\rho_1; x : \iota_1 \doteq E \wedge \rho_1 \doteq \chi; y : \iota_2 \wedge \rho_2 \doteq \chi; x : \iota_1$

Fig. 4. Rules for first-order unification

A typing problem is formulated as a triple $\mathcal{H}, \mathcal{T} \dot{\triangleright} e : \tau$. A solution of a typing problem is a substitution S such that $S(\mathcal{H}), S(\mathcal{T}) \triangleright e : S(\tau)$. The set of solutions of a typing problem is stable under substitutions by Lemma 1. Therefore we can treat typing problems as unification problems. Uniform treatment of type inference and unification enables us to prove the theorems in the simpler way as described in [14].

We use the operator $\langle \_ \rangle$ to unlock monomorphic polytypes. Its effect is defined by $\langle [\sigma] \rangle \equiv \sigma$ and $\langle \tau \rangle \equiv \tau$ if τ is not $[\sigma]$. Let $\mathcal{I}$ be $\{x_1 : \tau_1, \ldots, x_n : \tau_n\}$. We write $(\rho; \mathcal{I})$ for $(\rho; x_1 : \tau_1; \ldots; x_n : \tau_n)$, $(\rho; \mathcal{I}^-)$ for $(\rho; x_1 : -; \ldots; x_n : -)$ and $\langle \mathcal{I} \rangle$ for $\{x_1 : \langle \tau_1 \rangle, \ldots, x_n : \langle \tau_n \rangle\}$ respectively. The rules for solving typing problems are given in Figure 5. The following theorem shows that the type inference algorithm is sound and complete. We can prove it in the similar way to Theorem 2 due to the uniform treatment of unification and type inference.

Theorem 3. *Given a typing problem $\mathcal{H}, \mathcal{T} \dot{\triangleright} e : \tau$, the set of rules in Figures 4 and 5 computes a principal solution S, or fails with computing $\bot$.*

5 Conclusion

In [8], Hashimoto and Ohori have extended the simply typed lambda calculus with the feature of first-class contexts. In such a calculus, binding effects originally introduced by function abstraction can be propagated through the holes. In this previous work, the type system can precisely describe such effects in the simply typed setting.

In the present paper, we have developed the basis for developing a practical programming language enjoying the benefit of first-class contexts by giving an ML-style polymorphic type deduction system, an operational semantics and soundness of the type system and a sound and complete type inference algorithm. Using this language we can represent various useful features such as simple type-safe macros, linking modules, programs for distribution, and so on. There are several interesting issues that merit further investigation. We briefly mention some of them.

Efficient implementation. Based on this work, we have implemented a experimental interpreter system on a Standard ML system. However, there is a plenty of room for improvements including the representation of closures and the type checking algorithm. We believe that a number of existing compilation techniques for records can be utilized for the purpose.

Extension to second-order system. In the present system, contexts are only able to export the bindings for the term variables. As seen in the module systems, however, the definitions of types are also exported in the realistic applications. If the system is extended to second-order system to be able to provide bindings for types, applicability of contexts for the applications in such areas will be increased.

Var

let $\forall\bar{\xi}.\tau' = \mathcal{T}(x)$ **and** $\bar{\xi} \cap FV(\tau) = \emptyset$ **in** $\mathcal{H}, \mathcal{T} \dot{\rhd} x : \tau \;\Rrightarrow\; \exists\bar{\xi}.(\tau \doteq \tau')$

Func

let $dom(\mathcal{H}) = \{X_i\}$ **and** $\alpha, \beta, \gamma_i, \chi_i, \pi_i, \psi \notin FV(\mathcal{H}) \cup FV(\mathcal{T}) \cup FV(\tau)$ **in**

$$\mathcal{H}, \mathcal{T} \dot{\rhd} \lambda x.e : \tau \;\Rrightarrow\; \exists \alpha\gamma_i\beta\chi_i\pi_i\psi. \bigwedge \begin{cases} \{X_i : [\chi_i \rhd \gamma_i /\!/ \pi_i \rhd \bullet]\}, \mathcal{T} \uplus \{x : \alpha\} \dot{\rhd} e : \beta \\ \tau \doteq \alpha \to \beta \\ \pi_i \doteq \psi; x : \alpha \\ \mathcal{H} \doteq \{X_i : [\chi_i \rhd \gamma_i /\!/ \psi; x : - \rhd \bullet]\} \end{cases}$$

App

let $\alpha \notin FV(\mathcal{H}) \cup FV(\mathcal{T}) \cup FV(\tau)$ **and** $\mathcal{H} = \mathcal{H}_1 \uplus \mathcal{H}_2$ **in**

$\mathcal{H}, \mathcal{T} \dot{\rhd} e_1\ e_2 : \tau \;\Rrightarrow\; \exists\alpha.(\mathcal{H}_1, \mathcal{T} \dot{\rhd} e_1 : \alpha \to \tau) \wedge (\mathcal{H}_2, \mathcal{T} \dot{\rhd} e_2 : \alpha)$

Let

let $\mathcal{H} = \mathcal{H}_1 \uplus \mathcal{H}_2$ **and** $dom(\mathcal{H}_2) = \{X_i\}$ **and** $\beta_i, \chi_i, \pi_i, \psi \notin FV(\mathcal{H}_2) \cup FV(\mathcal{T})$
and $\bar{\xi_0} = FV(\tau_0)$ **and** $\bar{\xi_1}$ be a copy of $\bar{\xi_1}$ outside of $\mathcal{H}$ and $\mathcal{T}$ **and** $\tau_1 = \{\bar{\xi_1}/\bar{\xi_0}\}\tau_0$
and $\sigma_0 = \forall\bar{\xi_0}.\tau_0$ **and** $\bar{\xi} \cap (FV(\mathcal{H}) \cup FV(\mathcal{T})) = \emptyset$ **in**
if $\mathcal{H}_1, \mathcal{T} \dot{\rhd} e_1 : \tau_1 \;\Rrightarrow\; \exists\bar{\xi}'.S$ **then let** $\sigma = Gen(S(\tau_1), S(\mathcal{H}), S(\mathcal{T}))$ **in**
if $\bar{\xi} \cap (dom(S) \cup FV(cod(S))) = \emptyset$ **then**
$\mathcal{H}, \mathcal{T} \dot{\rhd} \mathtt{let}_{\sigma_0}\ x = e_1$ **in** $e_2 : \tau$

$$\Rrightarrow\; \exists\bar{\xi}'\bar{\xi_1}\beta_i\chi_i\pi_i\psi. \bigwedge \begin{cases} S \\ \{X_i : [\chi_i \rhd \beta_i /\!/ \pi_i \rhd \bullet]\}, \mathcal{T} \uplus \{x : \sigma\} \dot{\rhd} e_2 : \tau \\ \pi_i \doteq \psi; x : [\forall\bar{\xi}.\tau_1] \\ \mathcal{H}_2 \doteq \{X_i : [\chi_i \rhd \beta_i /\!/ \psi; x : - \rhd \bullet]\} \end{cases}$$

else $\mathcal{H}, \mathcal{T} \dot{\rhd} \mathtt{let}_{\sigma_0}\ x = e_1$ **in** $e_2 : \tau \;\Rrightarrow\; \bot$

Hole

let $\mathcal{H} = \{X : [\rho_1 \rhd \tau' /\!/ \rho_2 \rhd \bullet]\}$ **and** $\chi \notin FV([\rho_1 \rhd \tau' /\!/ \rho_2 \rhd \bullet])$ **in**

$\mathcal{H}, \mathcal{T} \dot{\rhd} X^{\{x_i\}} : \tau \;\Rrightarrow\; \exists\chi.\tau \doteq \tau' \;\wedge\; \rho_1 \doteq \rho_2 \doteq \chi; x_i : -$

Cont

let $\alpha, \beta, \chi, \pi \notin FV(\mathcal{H}) \cup FV(\mathcal{T}) \cup FV(\tau)$ **in**

$\mathcal{H}, \mathcal{T} \dot{\rhd} \delta X.e : \tau \;\Rrightarrow\; \exists\alpha\beta\chi\pi.\mathcal{H} \uplus \{X : [\chi \rhd \alpha /\!/ \pi \rhd \bullet]\}, \mathcal{T} \dot{\rhd} e : \beta \;\wedge\; \tau \doteq [\chi \rhd \alpha /\!/ \pi \rhd \beta]$

CApp

let $\mathcal{H} = \mathcal{H}_1 \uplus \mathcal{H}_2$ **and** $dom(\mathcal{H}_2) = \{X_i\}$
and $\alpha, \beta_i, \chi, \pi, \chi_i, \pi_i \notin FV(\mathcal{H}) \cup FV(\mathcal{T}) \cup FV(\tau)$ **in**
if $\mathcal{H}_1, \mathcal{T} \dot{\rhd} e_1 : [\chi; \mathcal{I} \rhd \alpha /\!/ \pi; \mathcal{I}^- \rhd \tau] \;\Rrightarrow\; \exists\bar{\xi}.S$ **then**
let $\mathcal{I}' = EI([S(\chi; \mathcal{I}) \rhd \bullet /\!/ S(\pi; \mathcal{I}^-) \rhd \bullet])$ **in**

$$\mathcal{H}, \mathcal{T} \dot{\rhd} e_1 \odot_{\mathcal{I}} e_2 : \tau \;\Rrightarrow\; \exists\bar{\xi}\alpha\beta_i\chi\pi\chi_i\pi_i. \bigwedge \begin{cases} S \\ \{X_i : [\chi_i \rhd \beta_i /\!/ \pi_i \rhd \bullet]\}, \mathcal{T} \uplus \langle \mathcal{I}' \rangle \dot{\rhd} e_2 : \alpha \\ \pi_i \doteq \chi; \mathcal{I} \\ \mathcal{H}_2 \doteq \{X_i : [\chi_i \rhd \beta_i /\!/ \pi; \mathcal{I}^- \rhd \bullet]\} \end{cases}$$

Fig. 5. Type inference algorithm

Relationship with modal operators. In our system, first-class contexts can provide a simple macro system in a type-safe way. We can provide macro arguments by hole filling. However, simple hole filling causes generation of unefficient code in general. For the purpose of generating efficient code, we need a notion of computation stages. Integration of our system and the feature of explicit code generation using modal operators seen in ML with modality [5,17] will produce a more interesting system.

Relationship with other systems. There are several formal systems for manipulating names and bindings: Aït-Kaci and Garrigue's label-selective λ-calculus [2], Dami's $\lambda\mathcal{N}$ [4] and $\lambda\sigma$-calculus of Abadi et.al. [1]. Although none of them can directly represent the notion of first-class contexts, similar features appear to be representable in those system. The precise relationship between the context calculus and those calculi would be interesting further investigation.

Acknowledgments

The author would like to acknowledge helpful discussions with Jacques Garrigue and Yasuhiko Minamide, and would like to thank Masahito Hasegawa, Susumu Nisimura and Atsushi Ohori for useful suggestions and comments in polishing the manuscript. Thanks are also due to the anonymous reviewers for their helpful comments and suggestions.

References

1. Martín Abadi, Luca Cardelli, Pierre-Louis Curien, and Jean-Jacques Lèvy. Explicit substitutions. In *Conference Record of the Seventeenth Annual ACM Symposium on Principles of Programming Languages, San Francisco, California*, pages 31–46. ACM, January 1990. Also Digital Equipment Corporation, Systems Research Center, Research Report 54, February 1990.
2. Hassan Aït-Kaci and Jacques Garrigue. Label-selective λ-calculus syntax and confluence. In R. K. Shyamasundar, editor, *Foundations of Software Technology and Theoretical Computer Science*, volume 761 of *Lecture Notes in Computer Science*, pages 24–40. Springer-Verlag, October 1993.
3. L. Damas and R. Milner. Principal type-schemes for functional programs. In *Proc. ACM Symposium on Principles of Programming Languages*, pages 207–212, 1982.
4. Laurent Dami. A lambda-calculus for dynamic binding. *to appear in Theoretical Computer Science*, 192(2), February 1998. special issue on Coordination.
5. R. Davies and F. Pfenning. A modal analysis of staged computation. In *Conference Record of Symposium on Principles of Programming Languages*, pages 258–270, 1996.
6. Jacques Garrigue and Didier Rémy. Extending ML with semi-explicit higher order polymorphism. In *Proceedings of the International Symposium on Theoretical Aspects of Computer Software*, number 1281 in LNCS, pages 20–46, Sendai, Japan, September 1997. Springer-Verlag.
7. R. Harper and B. Pierce. A record calculus based on symmetric concatenation. In *Proc. ACM Symposium on Principles of Programming Languages*, 1991.

8. Masatomo Hashimoto and Atsushi Ohori. A typed Context Calculus. Preprint 1098, Research Institute for Mathematical Sciences, Kyoto, Japan, 1996. Also available from `http://www.kurims.kyoto-u.ac.jp/~masatomo/`.
9. G. Kahn. Natural semantics. In *Proc. Symposium on Theoretical Aspects of Computer Science*, pages 22–39. Springer Verlag, 1987.
10. E. Kohlbecker, D. P. Friedman, M. Felleisen, and B. Duba. Hygienic macro expansion. In *Proceedings of the 1986 ACM Conference on Lisp and Functional Programming*, pages 151–159, 1986.
11. Shin-Der Lee and Daniel Friedman. Enriching the Lambda Calculus with Contexts: Towards A Theory of Incremental Program Construction. In *Proceedings of International Conference on Functional Programming*, ACM SIGPLAN notices, pages 239–250, 1996.
12. D. Rémy. Typing Record Concatenation for Free. In *Proc. ACM Symposium on Principles of Programming Languages*, pages 166–176, 1992.
13. D. Rémy. Type Inference for Records in a Natural Extension of ML. In C.A Gunter and J.C. Mitchell, editors, *Theoretical Aspects of Object-Oriented Programming*, pages 67–96. MIT Press, 1994.
14. Didier Rémy. Extending ML type system with a sorted equational theory. Research Report 1766, Institut National de Recherche en Informatique et Automatisme, Rocquencourt, BP 105, 78 153 Le Chesnay Cedex, France, 1992.
15. Didier Rémy. Syntactic theories and the algebra of record terms. Research Report 1869, Institut National de Recherche en Informatique et Automatisme, Rocquencourt, BP 105, 78 153 Le Chesnay Cedex, France, 1992.
16. M. Wand. Type inference for records concatenation and simple objects. In *Proceedings of 4th IEEE Symposium on Logic in Computer Science*, pages 92–97, 1989.
17. Philip Wickline, Peter Lee, and Frank Pfenning. Run-time code generation and Modal-ML. In *Proceedings of the ACM SIGPLAN'98 Conference on Programming Language Design and Implementation (PLDI)*, pages 224–235, Montreal, Canada, 17–19 June 1998.

A Proof of the Main Theorem

Theorem 1 (Type Soundness) *If $\mathcal{H}, \mathcal{T} \rhd e : \sigma$ is derivable, then for any ground substitution S such that $dom(S)$ contains all the free variables in the derivation of $\mathcal{H}, \mathcal{T} \rhd e : \sigma$, and for any η, ζ such that $\langle \eta, \zeta \rangle \models \langle S(\mathcal{H}, \mathcal{T} \rhd e : \sigma) \rangle$, if $\eta, \zeta \vdash e \Downarrow v$ then $\models v : S(\sigma)$.*

Proof. Let S be a ground substitution which satisfies the condition in the theorem. We proceed by induction on the derivation of $\mathcal{H}, \mathcal{T} \rhd e : \sigma$. The case of Const is quite easy.

Case Var $\emptyset, \mathcal{T} \rhd x : \tau \quad (\mathcal{T}(x) \succeq \tau)$:

Suppose $\langle \eta, \zeta \rangle \models \langle S(\emptyset, \mathcal{T} \rhd x : \tau) \rangle$ and $\eta, \zeta \vdash x \Downarrow v$. Let $\mathcal{T}(x) = \forall \xi_1 \cdots \xi_n . \tau_0$. Then $\models v : S(\mathcal{T}(x)) = \forall \xi_1 \cdots \xi_n . S(\tau_0)$ by the definition of satisfying and the bound variable convention. Since $\mathcal{T}(x) \succeq \tau$, there is some S_0 such that $dom(S_0) = \{\xi_1, \ldots, \xi_n\}$ and $S_0(\tau_0) = \tau$. Then $S(\tau) = S(S_0(\tau_0)) = (S \circ S_0)(S(\tau_0))$ by the bound variable convention. Since $dom(S) \supseteq FV(\tau)$, $S \circ S_0$ is ground. Therefore $\models v : (S \circ S_0)(S(\tau_0))$ by the definition of value typing.

$$\textit{Case}\quad \mathsf{Abs}\ \frac{\{X_i : [\rho_i \triangleright \tau_i /\!/ \rho'_i; x : \iota_i \triangleright \bullet]\}, \mathcal{T} \uplus \{x : \tau_a\} \triangleright e : \tau_b}{\{X_i : [\rho_i \triangleright \tau_i /\!/ \rho'_i; x : - \triangleright \bullet]\}, \mathcal{T} \triangleright \lambda x.e : \tau_a \to \tau_b}$$

($\iota_i = \tau_a$ or $\iota_i = -$) :

Suppose $\langle \eta, \zeta \rangle \models \langle S(\{X_i : [\rho_i \triangleright \tau_i /\!/ \rho'_i; x : - \triangleright \bullet]\}, \mathcal{T} \triangleright \lambda x.e : \tau_a \to \tau_b) \rangle$. Then for all $x \in \mathit{dom}(\mathcal{T})$, $\models \zeta(x) : S(\mathcal{T}(x))$ and for all X_i, $\models \eta(X_i) : [\mathcal{I}_i \triangleright S(\tau_i)]$ where $\mathcal{I}_i \subseteq EI(S([\rho_i \triangleright \bullet /\!/ \rho'_i; x : - \triangleright \bullet])) \uplus [S(\mathcal{T}) |_{\mathit{dom}(\mathcal{T}) \setminus PV(S([\rho_i \triangleright \bullet /\!/ \rho'_i; x : - \triangleright \bullet]))}]$. Since for all X_i, the difference between $EI(S([\rho_i \triangleright \tau_i /\!/ \rho'_i; x : \iota_i \triangleright \bullet]))$ and $EI(S([\rho_i \triangleright \tau_i /\!/ \rho'_i; x : - \triangleright \bullet]))$ is at most $\{x : S(\tau_a)\}$, for any v' such that $\models v' : S(\tau_a)$, we can derive $\langle \eta, \zeta\{x \mapsto v\} \rangle \models \langle S(\{X_i : [\rho_i \triangleright \tau_i /\!/ \rho'_i; x : \iota_i \triangleright \bullet]\}, \mathcal{T} \uplus \{x : \tau_a\} \triangleright e : \tau_b) \rangle$ by the definition of satisfying. Hence, if $\eta, \zeta\{x \mapsto v\} \vdash e \Downarrow v'$, then $\models v' : S(\tau_b)$ by the induction hypothesis. By the definition of value typing, $\models \mathit{func}(\eta, \zeta, x, e) : S(\tau_a) \to S(\tau_b)$.

$$\textit{Case}\quad \mathsf{App}\ \frac{\mathcal{H}_1, \mathcal{T} \triangleright e_1 : \tau_1 \to \tau_2 \quad \mathcal{H}_2, \mathcal{T} \triangleright e_2 : \tau_1}{\mathcal{H}_1 \uplus \mathcal{H}_2, \mathcal{T} \triangleright e_1\ e_2 : \tau_2} :$$

Suppose $\langle \eta, \zeta \rangle \models \langle S(\mathcal{H}_1 \uplus \mathcal{H}_2, \mathcal{T} \triangleright e_1\ e_2 : \tau_2) \rangle$. By the definition of satisfying, $\langle \eta, \zeta \rangle \models \langle S(\mathcal{H}_1, \mathcal{T} \triangleright e_1 : \tau_1 \to \tau_2) \rangle$ and $\langle \eta, \zeta \rangle \models \langle S(\mathcal{H}_2, \mathcal{T} \triangleright e_2 : \tau_1) \rangle$. If $\eta, \zeta \vdash e_1\ e_2 \Downarrow v$ then for some η', ζ', e' and v', we have $\eta, \zeta \vdash e_1 \Downarrow \mathit{func}(\eta', \zeta', x, e')$, $\eta, \zeta \vdash e_2 \Downarrow v'$ and $\eta', \zeta'\{x : v'\} \vdash e' \Downarrow v$ by the evaluation rule App. Then by the induction hypothesis, $\models \mathit{func}(\eta', \zeta', x, e') : S(\tau_1 \to \tau_2)$ and $\models v' : S(\tau_1)$. The rest of this case is by the definition of value typing.

$$\textit{Case}\quad \mathsf{Let}\ \frac{\mathcal{H}, \mathcal{T} \triangleright e_1 : \sigma \quad \{X_i : [\rho_i \triangleright \tau_i /\!/ \rho'_i; x : \iota_i \triangleright \bullet]\}, \mathcal{T} \uplus \{x : \sigma\} \triangleright e_2 : \tau}{\mathcal{H} \uplus \{X_i : [\rho_i \triangleright \tau_i /\!/ \rho'_i; x : - \triangleright \bullet]\}, \mathcal{T} \triangleright \mathtt{let}_{\sigma_0}\ x = e_1\ \mathtt{in}\ e_2 : \tau}$$

($\iota_i = -$, or for some $\sigma_1 \preceq \sigma$ if there exists S_0 such that $S_0(\sigma_0) = S_0(\sigma_1)$, $\iota_i = [\sigma_1]$):

Suppose $\langle \eta, \zeta \rangle \models \langle S(\mathcal{H} \uplus \{X_i : [\rho_i \triangleright \tau_i /\!/ \rho'_i; x : - \triangleright \bullet]\}, \mathcal{T} \triangleright \mathtt{let}_{\sigma_0}\ x = e_1\ \mathtt{in}\ e_2 : \tau) \rangle$. Obviously, $\langle \eta, \zeta \rangle \models \langle S(\mathcal{H}, \mathcal{T} \triangleright e_1 : \sigma) \rangle$ by the definition. If $\eta, \zeta \vdash \mathtt{let}_{\sigma_0}\ x = e_1\ \mathtt{in}\ e_2 \Downarrow v$, then $\eta, \zeta \vdash e_1 \Downarrow v'$ and $\eta, \zeta\{x \mapsto v'\} \vdash e_2 \Downarrow v$ by the evaluation rule Let. By the induction hypothesis applied to $\eta, \zeta \vdash e_1 \Downarrow v'$ and $\langle \eta, \zeta \rangle \models \langle S(\mathcal{H}, \mathcal{T} \triangleright e_1 : \sigma) \rangle$, we have $\models v' : S(\sigma)$. Since for all X_i, the difference between $EI(S([\rho_i \triangleright \tau_i /\!/ \rho'_i; x : \iota_i \triangleright \bullet]))$ and $EI(S([\rho_i \triangleright \tau_i /\!/ \rho'_i; x : - \triangleright \bullet]))$ is at most $\{x : S([\sigma_1])\}$. By the definition of value typing, $\models v_0 : S(\sigma)$ if and only if $\models v_0 : S(\sigma_1)$ since S is ground. Therefore, for all X_i, if $\models \eta(X_i) : [\{\ldots, x : S([\sigma_1]), \ldots\} \triangleright \tau_i]$ then $\models \eta(X_i) : [\{\ldots, x : S([\sigma]), \ldots\} \triangleright \tau_i]$. Then, we can derive $\langle \eta, \zeta\{x \mapsto v'\} \rangle \models \langle S(\{X_i : [\rho_i \triangleright \tau_i /\!/ \rho'_i; x : \iota_i \triangleright \bullet]\}, \mathcal{T} \uplus \{x : \sigma\} \triangleright e_2 : \tau) \rangle$ by the definition of satisfying similarly to the case of Abs. Then $\models v : S(\tau)$ by the induction hypothesis.

$$\textit{Case}\quad \mathsf{Hole}\ \{X : [\rho; x_i : - \triangleright \tau /\!/ \rho; x_i : - \triangleright \bullet]\}, \mathcal{T} \triangleright X^{\{x_i\}} : \tau :$$

Suppose $\langle \eta, \zeta \rangle \models \langle S(\{X : [\rho; x_i : - \triangleright \tau /\!/ \rho; x_i : - \triangleright \bullet]\}, \mathcal{T} \triangleright X^{\{x_i\}} : \tau) \rangle$. Then for any $x \in \mathit{dom}(\mathcal{T})$, $\models \zeta(x) : S(\mathcal{T}(x))$, and $\models \eta(X) : [\mathcal{I} \triangleright S(\tau)]$ for some $\mathcal{I} \subseteq [\mathcal{T} |_{\mathit{dom}(\mathcal{T}) \setminus \{x_i\}}]$. Let $\{y_i\} = \mathit{dom}(\mathcal{I})$. If $\eta, \zeta \vdash X^{\{x_i\}} \Downarrow v$, then for some η', ζ' and e, we have $\eta(X) = \mathit{clos}(\eta', \zeta', \{y_i\}, e)$ and $\eta', \zeta'\{y_i \mapsto \zeta(y_i)\} \vdash e \Downarrow v$ by the evaluation rule Hole. Since $\{y_i\} \subseteq \mathit{dom}(\mathcal{T})$, we have $\models \zeta(y_i) : S(\mathcal{I}(y_i))$. Then by the definition of value typing, $\models v : S(\tau)$.

$$\textit{Case}\quad \mathsf{HAbs}\ \frac{\mathcal{H} \uplus \{X : [\rho_1 \triangleright \tau_1 /\!/ \rho_2 \triangleright \bullet]\}, \mathcal{T} \rhd e : \tau_2}{\mathcal{H}, \mathcal{T} \rhd \delta X.e : [\rho_1 \triangleright \tau_1 /\!/ \rho_2 \triangleright \tau_2]}:$$

Suppose $\langle \eta, \zeta \rangle \models \langle S(\mathcal{H}, \mathcal{T} \rhd \delta X.e : [\rho_1 \triangleright \tau_1 /\!/ \rho_2 \triangleright \tau_2]) \rangle$ and $\eta, \zeta \vdash \delta X.e \Downarrow cont(\eta, \zeta, X, e)$. Let $\mathcal{I} = EI(S([\rho_1 \triangleright \bullet /\!/ \rho_2 \triangleright \bullet]))$. For all v and $\mathcal{I}'$ such that $\mathcal{I}' \subseteq \mathcal{I}$ and $\models v : [\mathcal{I}' \triangleright S(\tau_1)]$, we have $\langle \eta\{X \mapsto v\}, \zeta \rangle \models \langle S(\mathcal{H} \uplus \{X : [\rho_1 \triangleright \tau_1 /\!/ \rho_2 \triangleright \bullet]\}, \mathcal{T} \rhd e : \tau_2) \rangle$ by the definition of satisfying. If $\eta\{X \mapsto v\} \vdash e \Downarrow v'$, we have $\models v' : S(\tau_2)$ by the induction hypothesis. Then $\models cont(\eta, \zeta, X, e) : [\rho_1 \triangleright S(\tau_1) /\!/ \rho_2 \triangleright S(\tau_2)]$ by the definition of value typing.

$$\textit{Case}\quad \mathsf{CApp}\ \frac{\begin{array}{l}\mathcal{H}, \mathcal{T} \rhd e_1 : [\rho_a \triangleright \tau_a /\!/ \rho_b \triangleright \tau_b] \\ \{X_i : [\rho_i \triangleright \tau_i /\!/ \rho_a \triangleright \bullet]\}, \mathcal{T} \uplus \mathcal{T}' \rhd e_2 : \tau_a\end{array}}{\mathcal{H} \uplus \{X_i : [\rho_i \triangleright \tau_i /\!/ \rho_b \triangleright \bullet]\}, \mathcal{T} \rhd e_1 \odot_{\mathcal{I}} e_2 : \tau_b}:$$
$$(EI([\rho_a \triangleright \bullet /\!/ \rho_b \triangleright \bullet]) \supseteq [\mathcal{T}'] = \mathcal{I})$$

Suppose $\langle \eta, \zeta \rangle \models \langle S(\mathcal{H} \uplus \{X_i : [\rho_i \triangleright \tau_i /\!/ \rho_b \triangleright \bullet]\}, \mathcal{T} \rhd e_1 \odot_{\mathcal{I}} e_2 : \tau_b) \rangle$. If $\eta, \zeta \vdash e_1 \odot_{\mathcal{I}} e_2 \Downarrow v$, then for some η', ζ' and e', we have $\eta, \zeta \vdash e_1 \Downarrow cont(\eta', \zeta', X, e')$ and $\eta'\{X \mapsto clos(\eta, \zeta, dom(\mathcal{I}), e_2)\}, \zeta' \vdash e' \Downarrow v$ by the evaluation rule CApp. Since $\langle \eta, \zeta \rangle \models \langle S(\mathcal{H}, \mathcal{T} \rhd e_1 : [\rho_a \triangleright \tau_a /\!/ \rho_b \triangleright \tau_b]) \rangle$ by the definition of satisfying, $\models cont(\eta', \zeta', X, e') : S([\rho_a \triangleright \tau_a /\!/ \rho_b \triangleright \tau_b])$ by the induction hypothesis. Therefore for all $\mathcal{I}'$ such that $\mathcal{I}' \subseteq EI([\rho_a \triangleright \tau_a /\!/ \rho_b \triangleright \tau_b])$, for all v' such that $\models v' : [\mathcal{I}' \triangleright \tau_a]$, if $\eta'\{X \mapsto v'\}, \zeta' \vdash e' \Downarrow v''$, then $\models v'' : \tau_b$ by the definition of value typing. Let v_i be values such that $\models v_i : S(\mathcal{T}'(x_i))$ where $dom(\mathcal{I}) = \{x_i\}$. Since for all X_i, $EI(S([\rho_i \triangleright \tau_i /\!/ \rho_b \triangleright \bullet])) \subseteq EI(S([\rho_i \triangleright \tau_i /\!/ \rho_a \triangleright \bullet])) \cup S([\mathcal{T}'])$ by the definition of satisfying, we have $\langle \eta, \zeta\{x_i \mapsto v_i\} \rangle \models \langle S(\{X_i : [\rho_i \triangleright \tau_i /\!/ \rho_a \triangleright \bullet]\}, \mathcal{T} \uplus \mathcal{T}' \rhd e_2 : \tau_a) \rangle$. Therefore by the induction hypothesis, if $\eta, \zeta\{x_i \mapsto v_i\} \vdash e_2 \Downarrow v'''$, then $\models v''' : S(\tau_a)$. Then $\models clos(\eta, \zeta, dom(\mathcal{I}), e_2) : [S([\mathcal{T}']) \triangleright S(\tau_a)]$ by the definition of value typing. By the definition of value typing, if $\eta'\{X \mapsto clos(\eta, \zeta, dom(\mathcal{I}), e_2)\}, \zeta' \vdash e' \Downarrow v$, then $\models v : S(\tau_b)$.

$$\textit{Case}\quad \mathsf{Gen}\ \frac{\mathcal{H}, \mathcal{T} \rhd e : \tau}{\mathcal{H}, \mathcal{T} \rhd e : \sigma}\quad (\sigma = Gen(\mathcal{H}, \mathcal{T}, \tau)):$$

Suppose $\langle \eta, \zeta \rangle \models \langle S(\mathcal{H}, \mathcal{T} \rhd e : \sigma) \rangle$. Then there are some $\xi_1, \ldots \xi_n$ such that $\sigma = \forall \xi_1 \cdots \xi_n.\tau$. By the bound variable convention, we can assume that none of $\{\xi_1, \ldots \xi_n\}$ appears in S. Then $S(\sigma) = \forall \xi_1 \cdots \xi_n.S(\tau)$. Let S' be any ground substitution such that $dom(S') = \{\xi_1, \ldots \xi_n\}$. $S' \circ S$ is ground. If $\eta, \zeta \vdash e \Downarrow v$, then $\models v : S'(S(\tau))$ by the induction hypothesis. □

Formal Methods: Past, Present, and Future

Jeannette M. Wing

Computer Science Department
Carnegie Mellon University
Pittsburgh, PA 15213-3890, USA

Abstract. A formal method is a mathematically-based technique used to describe properties of hardware and software systems. It provides a framework within which large, complex systems may be specified, designed, analyzed, and verified in a systematic rather than ad hoc manner. A method is formal if it has a sound mathematical basis, typically given by a formal specification language.

In my talk I will review the seeds and early development of formal methods. Citing notable case studies, I will survey the state of the art in the areas in which researchers and engineers most recently have made the greatest strides: software specification, model checking, and theorem proving. To close, I will suggest future research directions that should result in the most promising payoffs for practitioners.

Jieh Hsiang, Atsushi Ohori (Eds.): ASIAN'98, LNCS 1538, pp. 224–224, 1998.

A Comparison of Petri Net Semantics under the Collective Token Philosophy*

Roberto Bruni[1], José Meseguer[2], Ugo Montanari[3], and Vladimiro Sassone[4]**

[1] Dipartimento di Informatica, Università di Pisa
Corso Italia 40, I-56125 Pisa, Italia bruni@di.unipi.it
[2] Computer Science Laboratory, SRI International
Menlo Park, CA, USA meseguer@csl.sri.com
[3] Dipartimento di Informatica, Università di Pisa
Corso Italia 40, I-56125 Pisa, Italia ugo@di.unipi.it
[4] Queen Mary and Westfield College, University of London
London E1 4NS, UK vs@dcs.qmw.ac.uk

Abstract. In recent years, several semantics for *place/transition Petri nets* have been proposed that adopt the *collective token philosophy*. We investigate distinctions and similarities between three such models, namely *configuration structures*, *concurrent transition systems*, and *(strictly) symmetric (strict) monoidal categories*. We use the notion of adjunction to express each connection. We also present a purely logical description of the collective token interpretation of net behaviours in terms of theories and theory morphisms in *partial membership equational logic*.

Introduction

Petri nets, introduced by Petri in [17] (see also [18]), are one of the most widely used and representative *models for concurrency*, because of the simple formal

* 1991 *Mathematics Subject Classification.* Primary 68Q55, 68Q10, 68Q05.
Key words and phrases. Petri Nets, Transition Systems, Monoidal Categories.
** The first and fourth author thank the support by **BRICS** — **Basic Research in Computer Science**, *Centre of the Danish National Research Foundation.*
The first three authors have been partly supported by Office of Naval Research Contracts N00014-95-C-0225 and N00014-96-C-0114, by National Science Foundation Grant CCR-9633363, and by the Information Technology Promotion Agency, Japan, as part of the Industrial Science and Technology Frontier Program 'New Models for Software Architecture' sponsored by NEDO (New Energy and Industrial Technology Development Organization). Also research supported in part by US Army contract DABT63-96-C-0096 (DARPA); CNR Integrated Project *Metodi e Strumenti per la Progettazione e la Verifica di Sistemi Eterogenei Connessi mediante Reti di Comunicazione*; and Esprit Working Groups *CONFER2* and *COORDINA*. Research carried out in part while the first and the third authors were visiting at Computer Science Laboratory, SRI International, and the third author was visiting scholar at Stanford University

Jieh Hsiang, Atsushi Ohori (Eds.): ASIAN'98, LNCS 1538, pp. 225–244, 1998.

description of the net model, and of its natural characterisation of *concurrent* and *distributed systems*. The extensive use of Petri nets has given rise to different schools of thought concerning the semantical interpretation of nets, with each view justified either by the theoretical characterisation of different properties of the modelled systems, or by the architecture of possible implementations.

A real dichotomy runs on the distinction between *collective* and *individual token philosophies* noticed, e.g., in [6]. According to the collective token philosophy, net semantics should not distinguish among different instances of the idealised resources (the so-called 'tokens') that rule the basics of net behaviour. The rationale for this being, of course, that any such instance is *operationally* equivalent to all the others. As obvious as this is, it disregards that operationally equivalent resources may have different origins and histories, and may, therefore, carry different *causality* information. Selecting one instance of a resource rather than the other, may be as different as being or not being causally dependent on some previous event. And this may well be an information one is not ready to discard, which is the point of view of the individual token philosophy.

In this paper, however, we focus on the collective token interpretation as the first step of a wider programme aimed at investigating the two approaches and their mutual relationships in terms of the behavioural, algebraic, and logical structures that can give adequate semantics account of each of them.

Starting with the classical 'token-game' semantics, many behavioural models for Petri nets have been proposed that follow the collective token philosophy. In fact, too many to be systematically reviewed here. Among all these, however, a relatively recent proposal of van Glabbeek and Plotkin is that of *configuration structures* [6]. Clearly inspired by the domains of configurations of *event structures* [22], these are simply collections of (multi)sets that, at the same time, represent the legitimate system states and the system dynamics, i.e., the transitions between such states. One of the themes of this paper is to compare configuration structure with the algebraic model based on *monoidal categories* [11], which also adopts the collective token philosophy and which provides a precise algebraic reinterpretation [5] of yet another model, namely the *commutative processes* of Best and Devillers [1]. In particular, we shall observe that configuration structures are *too abstract* a model, i.e., that they make undesirable identifications of nets, and conclude that monoidal categories provide a superior model of net behaviour.

To illustrate better the differences between the two semantic frameworks above, we adopt *concurrent transition systems* as a bridge-model. These are a much simplified, deterministic version of *higher dimensional transition systems* [3] that we select as the simplest one able to convey our ideas. Concurrent transition systems resemble configuration structures, but are more expressive. They also draw on earlier very significant models, such as *distributed transition systems* [9], *step* and *PN transition systems* [16], and *local event structures* [8]. Moreover, the equivalence of the behavioural semantics of concurrent transition systems and the algebraic semantics of monoidal categories can be stated very concisely. As we explain also in this paper, the algebraic semantics is itself amenable to a purely logical description in terms of theories in *partial membership equational logic* [10].

The main result of this research is a new precise characterisation of the relationships between all these behavioural, algebraic, and logical models within the collective token philosophy. We show that Best-Devillers commutative processes, the algebraic monoidal category model, and the concurrent transition system behavioural model all coincide in the precise sense of being related by equivalences of categories. And we also show how the behavioural model afforded by configuration structures is too abstract, but is precisely related to all the above models by a natural transformation that characterises the identification of inequivalent nets and behaviours caused by configuration structures.

The structure of the paper is as follows. In Section 1 we recall the basic definitions about PT Petri nets, remarking the distinction between the collective and individual token philosophies, and we introduce the frameworks under comparison, i.e., configuration structures, concurrent transition systems, and monoidal categories (also in their membership equational logic characterisation), discussing for each of them the corresponding models that they associate to a Petri net. Section 2 and Section 3 compare concurrent transition systems with, respectively, monoidal categories and configuration structures. Finally, the concluding section describes related work on the individual token philosophy.

1 Background

1.1 Petri Nets and the Collective Token Philosophy

Place/transition nets, the most widespread flavour of Petri nets, are graphs with distributed states described by (finite) distributions of resources ('tokens') in 'places'. These are usually called *markings* and represented as multisets $u\colon S \to \mathbb{N}$, where $u(a)$ indicates the number of tokens that place a carries in u. We shall use $\mu(S)$ to indicate the set of *finite* multisets on S, i.e., multiset that yield a zero on all but finitely many $a \in S$. Multiset union makes $\mu(S)$ a free commutative monoid on S.

Definition 1. A *place/transition* (*PT* for short) *Petri net* N is a tuple $(\partial_0, \partial_1, S, T)$, where S is a set of *places*, T is a set of *transitions*, $\partial_0, \partial_1\colon T \to \mu(S)$ are functions assigning, respectively, source and target to each transition.

Informally, $\partial_0(t)$ prescribes the minimum amount of resources needed to enable t, whilst $\partial_1(t)$ describe the resources that the occurrence of t contributes to the global state. This is made explicit in the following definition, where we shall indicate multiset inclusion, union, and difference by, respectively, $\subseteq$, $+$, and $-$.

Definition 2. Let u and v be markings and X a finite multiset of transitions of a net N. We say that u evolves to v under the *step* X, in symbols $u\,[X\rangle\,v$, if

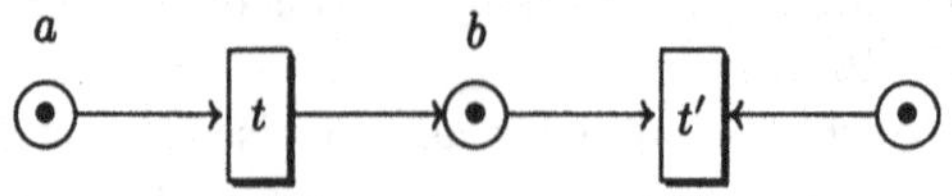

Fig. 1.

the transitions in X are concurrently enabled at u i.e., $\sum_{t \in T_N} X(t) \cdot \partial_0(t) \subseteq u$, and

$$v = u + \sum_{t \in T_N} X(t) \cdot (\partial_1(t) - \partial_0(t)).$$

A *step sequence* from u_0 to u_n is a sequence $u_0\ [X_1\rangle\ u_1 ... u_{n-1}\ [X_n\rangle\ u_n$.

PT nets are often considered together with a state: a *marked* PT net N is a PT net $(\partial_0, \partial_1, S, T)$ together with an *initial marking* $u_0 \in \mu(S)$. In order to equip PT nets with a natural notion of morphism, since that $\mu(S)$ is a monoid under $+$ with unit $\varnothing$, we consider maps of transition systems that preserve the additional structure.

Definition 3. A *morphism* of nets from $N = (\partial_0, \partial_1, S, T)$ to $N' = (\partial_0', \partial_1', S', T')$ is a pair $\langle f_t, f_p \rangle$ where $f_t : T \to T'$ is function, $f_p : \mu(S) \to \mu(S')$ is homomorphism of monoids such that $\partial_i' \circ f_t = f_p \circ \partial_i$, for $i = 0, 1$. A morphism of marked nets is a morphism of nets such that $f_p(u_0) = u_0'$.
We shall use **Petri** (respectively **Petri$_*$**) to indicate the category of (marked) PT nets and their morphisms with the obvious componentwise composition of arrows.

To compare the effects of the collective and of the individual token philosophy on observing causal relations between fired transitions, let us consider the example in Figure 1 that we adapt from [6]. (As usual, boxes stand for transitions, circles for places, dots for tokens, and oriented arcs represent ∂_0 and ∂_1.)

Observe that the firing of t produces a second token in place b. According to the individual token philosophy, it makes a difference whether t' consumes the token b originated from the firing of t, or the one coming from the initial marking. In the first case the occurrence of t' causally depends on that of t, and in the second the two firings are independent. In the collective token philosophy, instead, the two firings are always considered to be concurrent, because the firing of t does not change the enabling condition of t'.

1.2 Configuration Structures

In the same paper where they introduce the distinction between collective token and individual token philosophy, van Glabbeek and Plotkin propose *configuration structures* to represent the behaviour of nets according to the collective token philosophy. These are structures inspired by event structures [22] whose dynamics is uniquely determined by an explicitly-given set of possible configurations of the system. However, the structures they end up associating to nets are not exactly configuration structures. They enrich them in two ways: firstly, by considering *multi*sets instead of sets of occurrences, and secondly, by using an explicit transition relation between configurations. While the first point can be handled easily, as we do below, the second one seems to compromise the basic ideas underlying the framework and to show that configuration structures do not offer a faithful representation of the behaviour of nets under the collective token philosophy.

Definition 4. A *configuration structure* is given by a set E and a collection C of finite multisets over the set E. The elements of E are called *events*, and the elements of C *configurations*.

The idea is that an event is an occurrence of an action the system may perform, and that a configuration X represents a state of the system, which is determined by the collection X of occurred events. The set C of admissible configurations yields a relation representing how the system can evolve from one state to another.

Definition 5. Let (E, C) be a configuration structure. For X, Y in C we write $X \longrightarrow Y$ if

(1) $X \subset Y$,
(2) $Y - X$ is finite,
(3) for any multiset Z such that $X \subset Z \subset Y$, we have $Z \in C$.

The relation $\longrightarrow$ is called the *step transition relation.*

Intuitively, $X \longrightarrow Y$ means that the system can evolve from state X to state Y by performing the events in $Y - X$ *concurrently.* To stress this we shall occasionally write $X \xrightarrow{L} Y$, with $L = Y - X$. Observe that the last condition states that the events in $Y - X$ can be performed concurrently if and only if they can be performed in any order. In our opinion, this requirement embodies an *interleaving*-oriented view, as it reduces concurrency to nondeterminism. As we explain below, we view this as the main weakness of configuration structures.

In the following definition we slightly refine the notion of net configuration proposed in [6], as this may improperly include multisets of transitions that cannot be fired from the initial marking.

Definition 6 (From PT Nets to Config. Structures [6]). Let $N = (\partial_0, \partial_1, S, T, u_0)$, be a *marked* PT net. A finite multiset X of transitions is called *fireable* if there exists a partition $X_1, ..., X_n$ of X such that $u_0 \; [X_1\rangle \; u_1 ... u_{n-1} \; [X_n\rangle \; u_n$ is a step sequence. A *configuration* of N is a fireable multiset X of transitions. The configuration structure associated to N is $cs(N) = (T, C_N)$, where C_N is the set of configurations of N.

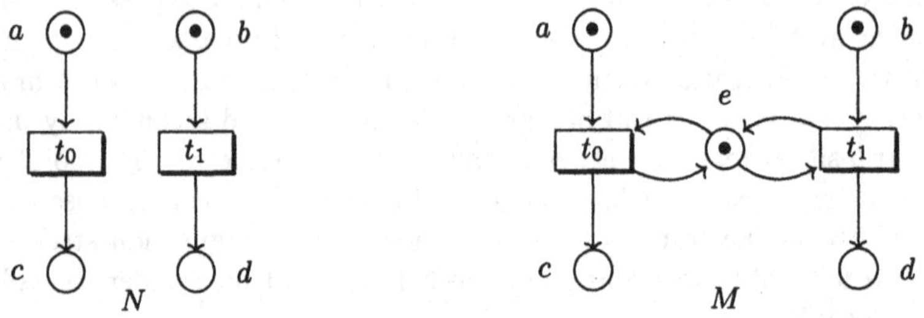

Fig. 2. The nets N and M of our running example.

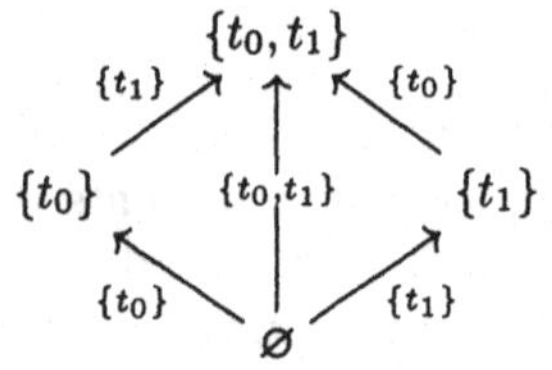

Fig. 3. The configuration structure $cs(N) = cs(M)$ for the nets N and M.

It follows that for each configuration X the function $u_X\colon S \to \mathbb{Z}$ given by

$$u_X = u_0 + \sum_{t \in T} X(t) \cdot (\partial_0(t) - \partial_1(t))$$

is a (reachable) marking, i.e., $0 \leq u_X(a)$ for all $a \in S$. Moreover, if X is a configuration and $u_X\ [U\rangle\ v$, then $X + U$ is also a configuration and $v = u_{X+U}$.

Generally speaking, if N is a *pure net*, i.e., a net with no *self-loops*, $cs(N)$ can be considered a reasonable semantics for N. Otherwise, as observed also in [6], it is not a good idea to reduce N to $cs(N)$. Consider for example, the marked nets N and M of Figure 2. They have very different behaviours, indeed: in N the actions t_0 and t_1 are concurrent, whereas in M they are mutually exclusive. However, since in M any interleaving of t_0 and t_1 is possible, the diagonal $\varnothing \longrightarrow \{t_0, t_1\}$ sneaks into the structure by definition. As a result, both N and M yield the configuration structure represented in Figure 3, even though $\{t_0, t_1\}$ is *not* an admissible step for M. The limit case is the marked net consisting of a single self-loop: the readers can check for themselves that, according to $cs(\_)$, it can fire arbitrarily large steps.

These problems have prompted us to look for a semantic framework that represents net behaviours more faithfully than configuration structures. The key observation is that there is nothing wrong with the assumption that if a step involving many parallel actions can occur in a certain state, then all the possible interleaving sequences of those action can also occur from that state. The problematic bit is assuming the inverse implication, because, as a matter of fact, it reduces concurrency to nondeterminism and makes the set of configurations determine uniquely the transition relation. Our proposed solution is concurrent transition systems.

1.3 Concurrent Transition Systems

The analysis of the previous section suggests seeking a model that enforces the existence of all appropriate interleavings of steps, without allowing this to determine the set of transitions completely. Several such models appear in the literature. Among those that inspired us most, we recall *distributed transition systems* [9], *step transition systems* [16], *PN transition systems* [16], and *higher dimensional transition systems* [3]. Also closely related are the *local event structures* of [8], a model that extends event structures (rather than transition systems) by allowing the firing of sets (but *not* multisets) of events. Drawing on all these, we have here chosen the simplest definition that suits our current aim.

Definition 7. A *concurrent transition system* (CTS for short) is a structure $H = (S, L, \mathit{trans}, s_0)$, where S is a set of *states*, L is a set of *actions*, $s_0 \in S$ is the initial state, and $\mathit{trans} \subseteq S \times (\mu(L) - \{\varnothing\}) \times S$ is a set of *transitions*, such that:

(1) if $(s, U, s_1), (s, U, s_2) \in \mathit{trans}$, then $s_1 = s_2$,
(2) if $(s, U, s') \in \mathit{trans}$ and U_1, U_2 is a partition of U, then there exist $v_1, v_2 \in S$ such that $(s, U_1, v_1), (s, U_2, v_2), (v_1, U_2, s'), (v_2, U_1, s') \in \mathit{trans}$.

Condition (1) above states that the execution of a multiset of labels U in a state s deterministically leads to a different state. The second condition guarantees that all the possible interleavings of the actions in U are possible paths from s to s' if $(s, U, s') \in \mathit{trans}$. Notice that, by (1), the states v_1 and v_2 of (2) are uniquely determined.

We formalise the idea that different paths which are different interleavings of the same concurrent step can be considered equivalent.

Definition 8. A *path* in a CTS is a sequence of contiguous transitions

$$(s, U_1, s_1)(s_1, U_2, s_2) \cdots (s_{n-1}, U_n, s_n).$$

A *run* is a path that originates from the initial state.

Definition 9. Given a CTS H, *adjacency* is the least reflexive, symmetric, binary relation $\leftrightarrow_H$ on the paths of H which is closed under path concatenation and such that

$$(s, U_1, s_1)(s_1, U_2, s_2) \leftrightarrow_H (s, U_1 + U_2, s_2).$$

Then, the *homotopy* relation $\leftrightharpoons_H$ on the paths of H is the transitive closure of $\leftrightarrow_H$. The equivalence classes of runs of H with respect to the homotopy relation are called *computations*.

In order to simplify our exposition, we now refine the notion of concurrent transition system so as to be able to associate to each path between two states the same multiset of actions. As we shall see, such transition systems enjoy interesting properties.

Definition 10. A CTS is *uniform* if all its states are *reachable* from the initial state, and the union of the actions along any two *cofinal* runs yield the same multiset, where cofinal means ending in the same state.

In a uniform CTS $H = (S, L, trans, s_0)$ each state s can be associated with the multiset of actions on any run to s. Precisely, we shall use ς_s to indicate $\sum_{i=1}^{n} U_i$, for $(s_0, U_1, s_1)(s_1, U_2, s_2)...(s_{n-1}, U_n, s)$ a run of H. Observe also that uniform CTS are necessarily acyclic, because any cycle $(s, U_0, s_1)\ldots(s_n, U_n, s)$ would imply the existence of runs to s carrying different actions. In the rest of the paper, we shall consider *only* uniform concurrent transition systems.

Introducing the natural notion of computation-preserving morphism for CTS, we define a category of uniform concurrent transition systems. In the following, for functions $f: A \to B$, we denote by $f^\mu: \mu(A) \to \mu(B)$ the obvious multiset extension of f, i.e., $f^\mu(X)(b) = \sum_{a \in f^{-1}(b)} X(a)$.

Definition 11. For H_1 and H_2 CTS, a *morphism* from H_1 to H_2 consists of a map $f: S_1 \to S_2$ that preserves the initial state and a function $\alpha: L_1 \to L_2$ and such that $(s, U, s') \in trans_1$ implies $(f(s), \alpha^\mu(U), f(s')) \in trans_2$.

We denote by **CTS** the category of uniform CTS and their morphisms.

Definition 12 (From PT Nets to CTS). Let $N = (\partial_0, \partial_1, S, T, u_0)$ be a marked PT Petri net. The concurrent transition system associated to N is

$$ct(N) = (M_N, T, trans_N, \varnothing),$$

where M_N is the set of *fireable* multisets of transitions of N, and $(X, U, X') \in trans_N$ if and only if $u_X\ [U\rangle\ u_{X'}$. (Recall that $u_X: S \to \mathbb{Z}$ is by definition a reachable marking.)

Although this construction is formally very close to that proposed for configuration structures, the difference is that CTS do not enforce diagonals to fill the squares: these are introduced if and only if the associated step is actually possible (see Figure 4). We shall give a precise categorical characterisation of the representations of nets in the CTS framework in Section 2. For the time being, we notice the following.

Proposition 1. *$ct(N)$ is a functor from* **Petri$_*$** *to* **CTS**.

Although all cofinal runs of a CTS carry the same multiset of actions, it is not the case that all such runs are homotopic, i.e., they do not necessarily represent the same computation. Enforcing this is the purpose of the next definition.

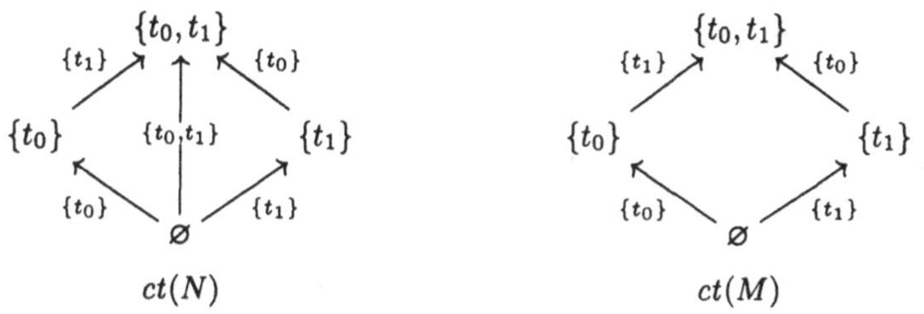

Fig. 4. The CTS $ct(N)$ and $ct(M)$ for the nets N and M of Figure 2.

Definition 13. An *occurrence* concurrent transition system is a concurrent transition system H in which all pairs of *cofinal* transitions $(s_1, U_1, s), (s_2, U_2, s) \in trans_H$ are the final steps of *homotopic* paths.

It can be shown that the previous definition implies the following property.

Proposition 2. *All cofinal paths of an occurrence CTS are homotopic.*

We shall use **oCTS** to indicate the full subcategory of **CTS** consisting of occurrence CTS. Clearly, a uniform CTS can be unfolded into an occurrence CTS.

Definition 14 (From CTS to Occurrence CTS). Let $H = (S, L, trans, s_0)$ be a concurrent transition system. Its *unfolding* is the occurrence concurrent transition system $\mathcal{O}(H) = (S', L, trans', \epsilon)$, where S' is the collection of computations of H, and

$$trans' = \big\{([\pi]_{\leftrightarrows}, U, [\pi']_{\leftrightarrows}) \;\big|\; \exists s, s' \in S,\ [\pi']_{\leftrightarrows} \in S',\ \pi' \leftrightarrows_H \pi(s, U, s')\big\}.$$

Proposition 3. $\mathcal{O}(\_)$ *extends to a right adjoint to the inclusion of* **oCTS** *in* **CTS**.

Proof. For H a concurrent transition system, consider $\varepsilon_H : \mathcal{O}(H) \to H$ that maps each $[\pi]_{\leftrightarrows} \in S_{\mathcal{O}(H)}$ to its final state $s \in S_H$. It is easy to verify that this forms the counit of the adjunction.

1.4 Monoidal Categories

Several interesting aspects of Petri net theory can be profitably developed within category theory, see e.g. [21, 11, 2]. Here we focus on the approach initiated in [11] (other relevant references are [5, 13, 19, 15, 20]) which exposes the monoidal structure of Petri nets under the operation of parallel composition. In [11, 5] it is shown that the sets of transitions can be endowed with appropriate algebraic structures in order to capture some basic constructions on nets. In particular, the *commutative processes* by Best and Devillers [1], which represent the natural behavioural model for PT nets under the collective token philosophy, can be characterised adding a functorial *sequential* composition on the *monoid* of steps, thus yielding a strictly symmetric strict monoidal category $\mathcal{T}(N)$.

Definition 15. For N a PT net, let $\mathcal{T}(N)$ be the strictly symmetric strict monoidal category freely generated by N.

Using **CMonCat** to denote the category of strictly symmetric strict monoidal categories and strict monoidal functors, $\mathcal{T}(\_)$ is a functor from **Petri** to **CMonCat**. The category $\mathcal{T}(N)$ can be inductively defined by the following inference rules and axioms.

$$\frac{u \in \mu(S_N)}{id_u : u \to u \in \mathcal{T}(N)} \qquad \frac{t \in T_N,\ \partial_0(t) = u,\ \partial_1(t) = v}{t : u \to v \in \mathcal{T}(N)}$$

$$\frac{\alpha : u \to v,\ \beta : u' \to v' \in \mathcal{T}(N)}{\alpha \oplus \beta : u + u' \to v + v' \in \mathcal{T}(N)} \qquad \frac{\alpha : u \to v,\ \beta : v \to w \in \mathcal{T}(N)}{\alpha ; \beta : u \to w \in \mathcal{T}(N)}$$

where the following equations, stating that $\mathcal{T}(N)$ is a strictly symmetric strict monoidal category, are satisfied by all arrows α, α', β, β', γ, δ and all multisets u and v:

neutral:	$id_\varnothing \oplus \alpha = \alpha,$	
commutativity:	$\alpha \oplus \beta = \beta \oplus \alpha,$	
associativity:	$(\alpha \oplus \beta) \oplus \delta = \alpha \oplus (\beta \oplus \delta),$	$(\alpha;\beta);\gamma = \alpha;(\beta;\gamma),$
identities:	$\alpha; id_u = \alpha = id_v; \alpha,$	$id_u \oplus id_v = id_{u+v},$
functoriality:	$(\alpha;\beta) \oplus (\alpha';\beta') = (\alpha \oplus \alpha');(\beta \oplus \beta').$	

The intuition here is that arrows are step sequences and arrow composition is their concatenation, whereas the monoidal operator $\oplus$ allows for parallel composition. It turns out that this algebraic structure describes precisely the processes à la Best and Devillers.

Proposition 4 (cf. [11]). *The presentation of $\mathcal{T}(N)$ given above provides a complete and sound axiomatisation of the algebra of the commutative processes of N.*

By analogy with **Petri**$_*$, we take a pointed category $(\mathbf{C}, c_0)$ to be a category $\mathbf{C}$ together with a distinguished object $c_0 \in \mathbf{C}$. Similarly, a pointed functor from $(\mathbf{C}, c_0)$ to $(\mathbf{D}, d_0)$ is a functor $F: \mathbf{C} \to \mathbf{D}$ that maps the distinguished object c_0 to the distinguished object d_0. Then, using **CMonCat**$_*$ to denote the category of pointed strictly symmetric strict monoidal categories and their pointed functors, the previous construction extends immediately to a functor $\mathcal{T}_*(N)$: **Petri**$_* \to$ **CMonCat**$_*$, such that for $N = (\partial_0, \partial_1, S, T, u_0)$ a marked PT net, then

$$\mathcal{T}_*(N) = (\mathcal{T}(\partial_0, \partial_1, S, T), u_0).$$

1.5 A Logical Characterisation of the Algebraic Model

The algebraic semantics of PT Petri nets can be expressed very compactly by means of a morphism between theories in *partial membership equational logic* (**PMEqtl**) [10], a logic of partial algebras with subsorts and subsort polymorphism whose *sentences* are Horn clauses on equations $t = t'$ and membership assertions $t : s$. Such a characterisation can have also practical applications, as there are tools available that support executable specifications in partial algebras. This section and the Appendix provide an informal introduction to the main ideas of **PMEqtl**. The interested reader is referred to [10, 12] for self-contained presentations.

A *theory* in **PMEqtl** is a pair $T = (\Omega, \Gamma)$, where Ω is a signature over a *poset* of sorts and Γ is a set of **PMEqtl**-sentences in the language of Ω. We denote by $\mathbf{PAlg}_\Omega$ the category of partial Ω-algebras, and by $\mathbf{PAlg}_T$ its full subcategory consisting of T-algebras, i.e., those partial Ω-algebras that satisfy all the sentences in Γ.

The features of **PMEqtl** (partiality, poset of sorts, membership assertions) offer a natural framework for the specification of categorical structures. For instance, a notion of *tensor product* for partial algebraic theories is used in [12] to obtain, among other things, a very elegant definition of the theory of monoidal categories that we recall in the Appendix. More precisely, we define the theories `PETRI` of PT nets and `CMONCAT` of strictly symmetric strict monoidal categories, using a self-explanatory Maude-like notation (Maude [4] is a language recently developed at SRI International; it is based on rewriting logic and supports the execution of membership equational logic specifications).

To study the relationships between `PETRI` and `CMONCAT`, the Appendix defines also an intermediate theory `CMON-AUT` of automata whose states form a commutative monoid. Our main result is then that the composition of the obvious inclusion functor of **Petri** into $\mathbf{PAlg}_{\mathtt{CMON-AUT}}$ and the free functor $\mathcal{F}_{\mathtt{V}}$ from $\mathbf{PAlg}_{\mathtt{CMON-AUT}}$ to $\mathbf{PAlg}_{\mathtt{CMONCAT}}$ associated to the theory morphism `V` from `CMON-AUT` to `CMONCAT` corresponds exactly to the functor $\mathcal{T}(\_)$: **Petri** → **CMonCat**.

Proposition 5. *The functor* $\mathcal{T}(\_)$: **Petri** → **CMonCat** *is the composition*

$$\mathbf{Petri} \hookrightarrow \mathbf{PAlg}_{\mathtt{CMON-AUT}} \xrightarrow{\mathcal{F}_V} \mathbf{PAlg}_{\mathtt{CMONCAT}}$$

2 Concurrent Transition Systems and Monoidal Categories

In this section we state the faithfulness of the CTS representation of nets, as given in Definition 12, with respect to the collective token philosophy. To accomplish this aim, we show that both the $ct(\_)$ and the $\mathcal{T}(\_)$ constructions yield two equivalent categories of net behaviours.

Regarding the monoidal approach, the obvious choice consists in taking the comma category of $\mathcal{T}(N)$ with respect to the initial marking, thus yielding a category whose objects are the commutative processes of N from its initial marking.

An arrow from process p to process q is then the *unique* commutative process r such that $p;r = q$ in $\mathcal{T}(N)$. We denote the resulting category by $(u_0 \downarrow \mathcal{T}(N))$.

An analogous construction can be defined starting from $ct(N)$. The first step is to observe that the paths of a generic CTS under the homotopy relation define a category.

Definition 16. For $H = (S, L, trans, s_0)$ a CTS, we define the *category of computations* of H to be the category $\mathcal{C}(H)$ whose

- ▷ *objects* are computations $[\pi]_{\leftrightarrows}$ of H,
- ▷ *arrows* are the homotopy equivalence classes of paths in H such that

$$[\psi]_{\leftrightarrows}\colon [\pi]_{\leftrightarrows} \to [\pi']_{\leftrightarrows} \quad \text{iff} \quad \pi' \leftrightarrows_H \pi\psi,$$

- ▷ *arrow composition* is defined as the homotopy class of path concatenation, i.e.,

$$[\psi]_{\leftrightarrows}; [\psi']_{\leftrightarrows} = [\psi\psi']_{\leftrightarrows},$$

- ▷ *identity arrow* at $[\pi]_{\leftrightarrows}$ is $\epsilon_{[\pi]_{\leftrightarrows}}$, the homotopy class of the empty path at the final state of π.

This construction extends easily to a functor $\mathcal{C}(\_)$ from **CTS** to **Cat**, the category of (small) categories and functors, yielding a functor $\mathcal{C}(ct(\_))$ from **Petri**$_*$ to **Cat**. Observe also that $\mathcal{C}(\_)$ factors through $\mathcal{O}\colon \mathbf{CTS} \to \mathbf{oCTS}$ via the obvious path construction.

Theorem 1. *Let N be marked PT net with initial marking u_0. Then, the categories $\mathcal{C}(ct(N))$ and $(u_0 \downarrow \mathcal{T}(N))$ are isomorphic.*

Proof. We sketch the definition of functors

$$\mathsf{F}\colon (u_0 \downarrow \mathcal{T}(N)) \to \mathcal{C}(ct(N)) \quad \text{and} \quad \mathsf{G}\colon \mathcal{C}(ct(N)) \to (u_0 \downarrow \mathcal{T}(N))$$

inverses to each other. The functor F maps an object of the comma category to the homotopy class of any of the object's interleaving (which is well-defined because of the diamond equivalence of [1]). Its action on morphisms is analogous.

On the other hand, for a computation $[\pi]_{\leftrightarrows}$ in $\mathcal{C}(ct(N))$, starting from the initial marking we can determine uniquely the corresponding arrow on $\mathcal{T}(N)$, and therefore define the action of G on both objects and arrows.

The categories of computations for the concurrent transition systems associated to nets N and M of Figure 2 are shown in Figure 5, where we use c_0 and c_1 to denote, respectively, the computations $[(\varnothing, \{t_0\}, \{t_0\})]_{\leftrightarrows}$, and $[(\varnothing, \{t_1\}, \{t_1\})]_{\leftrightarrows}$ in both of $ct(N)$ and $ct(M)$. Analogously, p_1 and p_0 indicate the homotopy classes of the paths $[(\{t_0\}, \{t_1\}, \{t_0, t_1\})]_{\leftrightarrows}$ and $[(\{t_1\}, \{t_0\}, \{t_0, t_1\})]_{\leftrightarrows}$, respectively. However, $c_0; p_1$ and $c_1; p_0$ yield the same result $c = [(\varnothing, \{t_0, t_1\}, \{t_0, t_1\})]_{\leftrightarrows}$ in $\mathcal{C}(ct(N))$, whereas in $\mathcal{C}(ct(M))$ they denote different objects: $c' = [(\varnothing, \{t_0\}, \{t_0\})(\{t_0\}, \{t_1\}, \{t_0, t_1\})]_{\leftrightarrows}$ and $c'' = [(\varnothing, \{t_1\}, \{t_1\})(\{t_1\}, \{t_0\}, \{t_0, t_1\})]_{\leftrightarrows}$.

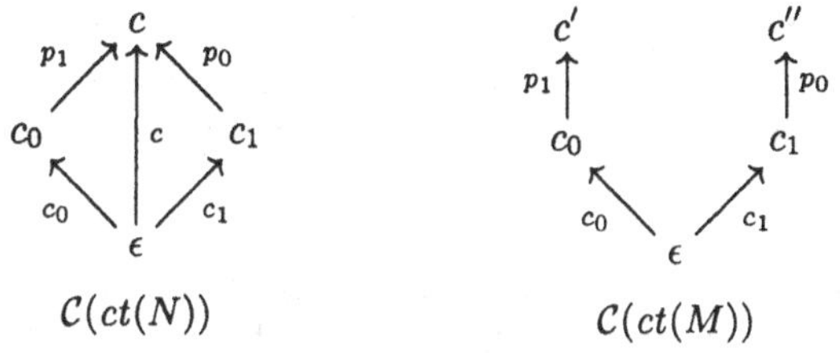

Fig. 5. The categories $\mathcal{C}(ct(N))$ and $\mathcal{C}(ct(M))$ for the nets of Figure 2.

3 Configuration Structures and Concurrent Transition Systems

In this section we first give a categorical structure to the class of configuration structures, and then show that the obvious injection of configuration structures into CTS yields a reflection.

Definition 17. For (E_1, C_1) and (E_2, C_2) configuration structures, a *cs-morphism* from (E_1, C_1) to (E_2, C_2) is a function $g: E_1 \to E_2$ such that for each configuration $X \in C_1$, then $g^\mu(X) \in C_2$. We denote by **CSCat** the category of configuration structures and cs-morphisms.

The obvious injection functor $\mathfrak{I}(\_)$ from **CSCat** to **CTS** maps a configuration structure $CS = (E, C)$ into the concurrent transition system

$$\mathfrak{I}(CS) = (C, E, trans_{CS}, s_0),$$

where $trans_{CS} = \{(X, L, Y) \mid X \xrightarrow{L} Y\}$, and maps a cs-morphism $g: E_1 \to E_2$ to the morphism (g', g), where $g': C_1 \to C_2$ is the obvious extension g^μ of g to multisets, with domain restricted to C_1.

Theorem 2. *The functor* $\mathfrak{I}(\_)$: **CSCat** $\to$ **CTS** *is the right adjoint of a functor* $\mathfrak{R}(\_)$: **CTS** $\to$ **CSCat**. *Moreover, since the counit of the adjunction is the identity,* $\mathfrak{I}(\_)$ *and* $\mathfrak{R}(\_)$ *define a full reflection.*

Proof. We sketch the proof, giving the precise definition of the reflection functor. The reflection functor $\mathfrak{R}(\_)$ maps a uniform CTS $H = (S, L, trans, s_0)$ into the configuration structure $\mathfrak{R}(H) = (L, C_S)$ such that $C_S = \{\varsigma_s \mid s \in S\}$ (recall that ς_s is the multiset union of the actions of any run leading to s).

We denote the component at H of the unit of the adjunction by $\rho_H: H \to \mathfrak{I}(\mathfrak{R}(H))$.

Theorem 3 (Configuration Structures via CTS). *Let N be a marked PT net. Then* $cs(N) = \mathfrak{R}(ct(N))$.

Proof. The events of $cs(N)$, the actions of $ct(N)$ and, therefore, the events of $\mathcal{R}(ct(N))$ are the transitions of N. The states S of the uniform CTS $ct(N)$ are exactly the configurations of $cs(N)$, and for each $s \in S$, we have $\varsigma_s = s$. This suffices, since a configuration structure is entirely determined by its set of configurations.

These results support our claim that configuration structures do not offer a faithful representation of net behaviours. In fact, $\mathcal{R}(\_)$ clearly collapses the structure excessively, as the natural transformation associated to the reflection map ρ can identify non homotopic runs (e.g., c' and c'' of Figure 5).

Concluding Remarks and Future Work

We have investigated the expressiveness of some 'collective-token' semantics for PT nets. In particular, to remedy the weakness of configuration structures, we have introduced *concurrent transition systems* — a version of higher dimensional transition system [3] more suited to the collective token philosophy, as they do not assign individual identities to multiple action occurrences in a multiset — and have shown that they can provide a faithful description of net behaviours.

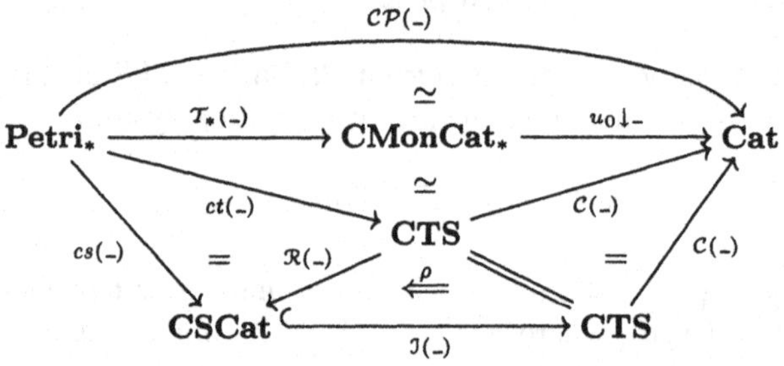

Fig. 6.

The diagram of functors, equivalences and natural transformations in Figure 6 summarises the relationships between all these models. In the diagram, commutation on the nose (resp. natural equivalence) is represented by $=$ (resp. $\simeq$), and ρ denotes the unit of the reflection into the subcategory of configuration structures. The functor $\mathcal{CP}(\_)$ gives the category of Best-Devillers commutative processes. The functor $ct(\_)$ corresponds to the construction of the CTS for a given net, as defined in Section 1.3. The functor $\mathcal{C}(\_)$ yields the construction of the category of computations (i.e., homotopy equivalence classes of paths beginning in the initial state) of a CTS. The equivalence $\simeq$ between $\mathcal{C}(ct(\_))$ and $(u_{\text{in}} \downarrow \mathcal{T}(\_))$ is shown in Section 2, providing the faithfulness of the construction.

The functor $cs(\_)$ represents the abstraction from nets to configuration structure, defined in Section 1.2. Unfortunately, **CSCat** is a reflective subcategory of **CTS**, as shown in Section 3 via the adjunction $\mathcal{R}(\_) \dashv \mathcal{I}(\_)$. The reflection functor $\mathcal{R}(\_)$ identifies too many things, so that the natural transformation associated to the reflection map ρ can identify non homotopic runs. Our running example shows that causality informations can get lost when using configuration structures, because homotopic paths are mapped into the same equivalence class.

	Structures		
Computation Model	**Behavioural**	**Algebraic**	**Logical**
Nets and Collective Token Philosophy	Conf. structures, CTS, Commutative processes	$\mathcal{T}(N)$	CAT ⊗ CMON
Nets and Individual Token Philosophy	Conc. Pomsets, Event Struct., Processes	$\mathcal{P}(N), \mathcal{Q}(N)$ $\mathcal{Z}(N)$?	CAT ⊗ MON + SYM

Table 1.

The conceptual framework of this paper is summarised in Table 1, which makes explicit our research programme on the *behavioural*, *algebraic* and *logical* aspects of the two computational interpretations of PT nets, namely the *collective token* and the *individual token* philosophies, from the viewpoints of the structures suited to each of them and their mutual relationships.

The first row of Table 1 has been treated in this paper. As for the individual token interpretation, obvious candidates for suitable behavioural structures are *event structures*, *concatenable pomsets* and, especially, various kinds of *concatenable processes* [5, 20]. From the logical viewpoint, it is not difficult to formulate a theory SYM of permutations and symmetries (cf. [19]) bridging the gap from strictly symmetric categories to categories symmetric only up to coherent isomorphism. On the other hand, the investigation of suitable algebraic models is still open, as our current best candidates, the symmetric strict monoidal categories $\mathcal{P}(N)$ of *concatenable processes* [5] and $\mathcal{Q}(N)$ of *strongly concatenable processes* [20], are both somehow unsatisfactory: $\mathcal{P}(\_)$ is a *non*-functorial construction, a drawback that inhibits many of the applications we have in mind, whilst $\mathcal{Q}(\_)$ solves the problem at the price of complicating the construction and relying on a non commutative monoid of objects.

We are currently searching for a better categorical construction, say $\mathcal{Z}(N)$, based on a suitable notion of *pre-net* that may subsume and underly the theory of PT nets and allow us to complete our programme.

Also, the complete analysis and comparison of bisimulation related issues in the various models considered in the paper (as in [6] for configuration structures) deserve further work that we leave for a future paper.

References

[1] E. Best and R. Devillers (1987), Sequential and Concurrent Behaviour in Petri Net Theory. *Theoretical Computer Science* **55**, 87–136, Elsevier.

[2] C. Brown and D. Gurr (1990), A Categorical Linear Framework for Petri Nets, in *Proceedings of the 5th Symposium on Logics in Computer Science*, 208–218, IEEE Press.

[3] G.L. Cattani and V. Sassone (1996), Higher Dimensional Transition Systems, in *Proceedings of the 11th Symposium on Logics in Computer Science*, 55–62, IEEE Press.

[4] M. Clavel, S. Eker, P. Lincoln, and J. Meseguer (1996), Principles of Maude, in *Proceedings First Intl. Workshop on Rewriting Logic and its Applications*, J. Meseguer (Ed.), *Electronic Notes in Theoretical Computer Science* **4**, `http://www.elsevier.nl/locate/tcs`, Elsevier.

[5] P. Degano, J. Meseguer, and U. Montanari (1996), Axiomatizing the Algebra of Net Computations and Processes. *Acta Informatica* **33**(7), 641–667, Springer-Verlag.

[6] R.J. van Glabbeek and G.D. Plotkin (1995), Configuration Structures, in *Proceedings of the 10th Symposium on Logics in Computer Science*, 199–209, IEEE Press.

[7] U. Goltz and W. Reisig (1983), The Non-Sequential Behaviour of Petri Nets. *Information and Computation* **57**, 125–147, Academic Press.

[8] P.W. Hoogers, H.C.M. Kleijn, and P.S. Thiagarajan (1996), An Event Structure Semantics for General Petri Nets. *Theoretical Computer Science* **153**(1-2), 129–170, Elsevier.

[9] K. Lodaya, R. Ramanujam, and P.S. Thiagarajan (1989), A Logic for Distributed Transition Systems, in *Linear time, branching time, and partial order in logics and models for concurrency*, J.W. de Bakker *et al.* (Eds.), *Lecture Notes in Computer Science* **354**, 508–522, Springer-Verlag.

[10] J. Meseguer (1998), Membership Equational Logic as a Logical Framework for Equational Specification, in *Proceedings of the 12th WADT Workshop on Algebraic Development Techniques*, F. Parisi-Presicce (Ed.), *Lecture Notes in Computer Science* **1376**, 18–61, Springer-Verlag.

[11] J. Meseguer and U. Montanari (1990), Petri Nets are Monoids. *Information and Computation* **88**(2), 105–155, Academic Press.

[12] J. Meseguer and U. Montanari (1998), Mapping Tile Logic into Rewriting Logic. in *Proceedings of the 12th WADT Workshop on Algebraic Development Techniques*, F. Parisi-Presicce (Ed.), *Lecture Notes in Computer Science* **1376**, 62–91, Springer-Verlag.

[13] J. Meseguer, U. Montanari, and V. Sassone (1996), Process versus Unfolding Semantics for Place/Transition Petri Nets. *Theoretical Computer Science* **153**(1-2), 171–210, Elsevier.

[14] J. Meseguer, U. Montanari, and V. Sassone (1997), On the Semantics of Place/Transition Petri Nets. *Mathematical Structures in Computer Science* **7**, 359–397, Cambridge University Press.

[15] J. Meseguer, U. Montanari, and V. Sassone (1997), Representation Theorems for Petri Nets, in *Foundations of Computer Science*, C. Freska *et al.* (Eds.), *Lecture Notes in Computer Science* **1337**, 239–249, Springer-Verlag.

[16] M. Mukund (1992), Petri Nets and Step Transition Systems. *International Journal of Foundations of Computer Science*, **3**(4), 443–478, World Scientific.

[17] C.A. Petri (1962), *Kommunikation mit Automaten.* PhD thesis, Institut für Instrumentelle Mathematik, Bonn.

[18] W. Reisig (1985), *Petri Nets (an Introduction).* EATCS Monographs on Theoretical Computer Science **4**, Springer-Verlag.

[19] V. Sassone (1996), An Axiomatization of the Algebra of Petri Net Concatenable Processes. *Theoretical Computer Science* **170**, 277–296, Elsevier.

[20] V. Sassone (1998), An Axiomatization of the Category of Petri Net Computations. *Mathematical Structures in Computer Science* **8**, 117–151, Cambridge University Press.

[21] G. Winskel (1987), Petri Nets, Algebras, Morphisms and Compositionality. *Information and Computation* **72**, 197- 238, Academic Press.

[22] G. Winskel (1988), An Introduction to Event Structures, in *Linear time, branching time, and partial order in logics and models for concurrency*, J.W. de Bakker *et al.* (Eds.), *Lecture Notes in Computer Science* **354**, 365–397, Springer-Verlag.

Appendix. Recovering the Algebraic Semantics of Nets via Theory Morphisms

In order to define the theory of strictly symmetric strict monoidal categories, we first recall the definition of the theory of categories from [12].

The poset of sorts of the **PMEqtl**-theory of categories is `Object` $\leq$ `Arrow`. There are two unary operations `d(_)` and `c(_)`, for *domain* and *codomain*, and a binary composition operation `_;_` defined if and only if the codomain of the first argument is equal to the domain of the second argument. Functions with explicitly given domain and codomain are always *total*.

```
fth CAT is
 sorts Object Arrow.
 subsort Object < Arrow.
 ops d(_) c(_) : Arrow -> Object.
 op _;_.
 var a : Object.
 vars f g h : Arrow.
 eq d(a) = a.
 eq c(a) = a.
 ceq a;f = f if d(f) == a.
 ceq f;a = f if c(f) == a.
 cmb f;g : Arrow iff c(f) == d(g).
 ceq d(f;g) = d(f) if c(f) == d(g).
 ceq c(f;g) = c(g) if c(f) == d(g).
 ceq (f;g);h = f;(g;h) if c(f) == d(g) and c(g) == d(h).
endfth
```

The extension of the theory `CAT` to the theory of monoidal categories is almost effortless thanks to the tensor product construction of theories, which is informally defined as follows.

Let $T = (\Omega, \Gamma)$ and $T' = (\Omega', \Gamma')$ be theories in partial membership equational logic, with $\Omega = (S, \leq, \Sigma)$ and $\Omega' = (S', \leq', \Sigma')$. Their *tensor product* $T \otimes T'$ is the theory with signature $\Omega \otimes \Omega'$ having: poset of sorts $(S, \leq) \times (S', \leq')$, and signature $\Sigma \otimes \Sigma'$, with operators $f_l \in (\Sigma \otimes \Sigma')_n$ and $g_r \in (\Sigma \otimes \Sigma')_m$ for each $f \in \Sigma_n$ and $g \in \Sigma'_m$ (indices l and r stand respectively for `left` and `right` and witness whether the operator is inherited from the left or from the right component). The axioms of $T \otimes T'$ are the determined from those of T and T' as explained in [12].

The essential property of the tensor product of theories is expressed in the following theorem, where $\mathbf{PAlg}_T(\mathbf{C})$ indicates the category of T-algebras taken over the base category $\mathbf{C}$ rather than over **Set**, the category of small sets and function.

Theorem 4. *Let T, T' be theories in partial membership equational logic. Then, we have the following isomorphisms of categories:*

$$\mathbf{PAlg}_T(\mathbf{PAlg}_{T'}) \simeq \mathbf{PAlg}_{T \otimes T'} \simeq \mathbf{PAlg}_{T'}(\mathbf{PAlg}_T).$$

To define the theory of monoidal categories, we introduce a theory `CMON` of commutative monoids and apply the tensor product construction. Here we exploit the possibility given by Maude of declaring the associativity, commutativity and unit element as attributes of the monoidal operator.

```
fth CMON is
 sort Monoid.
 op 0 : -> Monoid.
 op _⊕_ : Monoid Monoid -> Monoid [assoc comm id: 0].
endfth
```

The theory of strictly symmetric strict monoidal categories is then defined as follows. Notice also the use of `left` and `right` corresponding to the indices l and r discussed above.

```
fth CMONCAT is CMON ⊗ CAT renamed by (
 sort (Monoid,Object) to Object.
 sort (Monoid,Arrow) to Arrow.
 op  0 left to 0.
 op _⊕_ left to _⊕_.
 op _;_ right to _;_.
 op d(_) right to d(_).
 op c(_) right to c(_).).
endfth
```

In order to define a theory in **PMEqtl** that represents PT Petri nets and their morphisms, we first introduce a theory whose models are automata whose states form a commutative monoid.

```
fth CMON-AUT is
 sorts State Transition.
 op 0 : -> State.
 op _⊗_ : State State -> State [assoc comm id: 0].
 ops origin(_) destination(_) : Transition -> State.
endfth
```

Proposition 6. *The category* **Petri** *is a full subcategory of* $\mathbf{PAlg}_{\texttt{CMON-AUT}}$.

Proof. It is immediate to check that each PT net is just a model of CMON-AUT whose states are the object of the commutative monoid freely generated by the set of places.

Exploiting the modularity features of Maude, we can characterise **Petri** as a subcategory of $\mathbf{PAlg}_{\texttt{CMON-AUT}}$. We import a functional module MSET[E :: TRIV] of multisets, parametrised on a functional theory of TRIV of elements, whose models are sets corresponding to the places of the net.

```
fth TRIV is sort Element.
endfth

fmod MSET[E :: TRIV] is
 sort MSet.
 subsort Element < MSet.
 op ∅ : -> MSet.
 op _+_ : MSet MSet -> MSet [assoc comm id: ∅].
endfm

fth PETRI[S :: TRIV] is
 protecting MSET[S] renamed by (sort MSet to Marking.).
 sort Transition.
 ops pre(_) post(_) : Transition -> Marking.
endfth
```

A theory morphism H from T to T', also called a *view* in Maude, is a mapping of the operators and sorts of T into T', preserving domain, codomain and subsorting, and such that the translation of the axioms of T are entailed by those of T'. It originates a forgetful functor $\mathcal{U}_H : \mathbf{PAlg}_{T'} \to \mathbf{PAlg}_T$ that — for T and T' theories without freeness constraints, such as those required in PETRI[S] — admits a left adjoint $\mathcal{F}_H : \mathbf{PAlg}_T \to \mathbf{PAlg}_{T'}$ whose effect is to lift H to a free model construction in $\mathbf{PAlg}_{T'}$. The inclusion functor from **Petri** to $\mathbf{PAlg}_{\texttt{CMON-AUT}}$ is induced as the forgetful functor of a theory morphism I specified as a view in Maude as follows.

```
view I from CMON-AUT to PETRI[S :: TRIV] is
 sort Marking to MSet.
 op origin(_) to pre(_).
```

```
 op destination(_) to post(_).
 op 0 to ∅.
 op _⊗_ to _+_.
endview
```

Finally, the algebraic semantics of PT nets under the collective token philosophy, i.e., the construction $\mathcal{T}(\_)$, can be easily recovered via a simple theory morphism specified in Maude-like notation as

```
view V from CMON-AUT to CMONCAT is
 sort State to Object.
 sort Transition to Arrow.
 op origin(_) to d(_).
 op destination(_) to c(_).
endview
```

As stated in Proposition 5, the construction $\mathcal{T}(\_)$: **Petri** → **CMonCat** is then the following functor composition.

$$\mathbf{Petri} \hookrightarrow \mathbf{PAlg}_{\mathtt{CMON-AUT}} \xrightarrow{\mathcal{F}_V} \mathbf{PAlg}_{\mathtt{CMONCAT}}$$

Bisimulation Lattice of Chi Processes

Yuxi Fu*

Department of Computer Science
Shanghai Jiaotong University, Shanghai 200030, China

Abstract. Chi calculus was proposed as a process algebra that has a uniform treatment of names. The paper carries out a systematic study of bisimilarities for chi processes. The notion of L-bisimilarity is introduced to give a possible classification of bisimilarities on chi processes. It is shown that the set of L-bisimilarities forms a four element lattice and that well-known bisimilarities for chi processes fit into the lattice hierarchy. The four distinct L-bisimilarities give rise to four congruence relations. Complete axiomatization system is given for each of the four relations. The bisimulation lattice of asynchronous chi processes and that of asymmetric chi processes are also investigated. It turns out that the former consists of two elements while the latter twelve elements. Finally it is pointed out that the asynchronous asymmetric chi calculus has a bisimulation lattice of eight elements.

The χ-calculus ([4]) was introduced with two motivations in mind. One is to remove the *ad hoc* nature of prefix operation in π-calculus ([11]) by having a uniform treatment of names ([3]), thus arriving at a conceptually simpler language. The second is to materialize a communication-as-cut-elimination viewpoint ([5]), therefore taking up a proof theoretical approach to concurrency theory, an approach that has been proved very fruitful in the functional world. Independently Parrow and Victor have come up with essentially the same language, Update Calculus as they term it ([13]). They share, we believe, the first motivation but have quite a different second one originated from concurrent constraint programming. The difference between π and χ lies mainly in the way communications happen. The former adopts the familiar value-passing mechanism whereas the latter takes an information exchange or information update viewpoint. The algebraic theory of the language has been investigated in the above mentioned papers. Parrow and Victor have looked into strong bisimilarity and axiomatization of it for Update Calculus, while Fu has examined an observational bisimilarity for χ-processes. More recently, Parrow and Victor have proposed Fusion Calculus ([14,17]), which is a polyadic version of χ-calculus. The authors have also studied an observational equivalence called weak hyperbisimilarity. What we know about the language, albeit little, tells us that it can practically do everything π can do and its algebraic properties are just as satisfactory. The studies carried out so far are however preliminary.

* Supported by the National Nature Science Foundation of China.

Jieh Hsiang, Atsushi Ohori (Eds.): ASIAN'98, LNCS 1538, pp. 245–262, 1998.

The objective of this paper is to continue our examination of the algebraic theory of χ-calculus. Section 1 reviews the operational semantics of χ. Section 2 defines L-bisimilarities and investigates their relationship. Section 3 gives alternative characterizations of L-bisimilarities. Section 4 presents a complete axiomatization system for each of the congruence relations induced by the four L-bisimilarities. The next three sections look into the L-bisimilarities of asynchronous, asymmetric, asynchronous asymmetric χ-calculi respectively.

1 Operational Semantics

In π-calculus there are two kinds of closed names, one has dummy names as x in $m(x).P$ and local names as x in $(x)\overline{m}x.P$. In simple words, the χ-calculus is obtained from π-calculus by unifying these names. This identification forces a unification of input and output prefix operations. The two π-processes just mentioned then turn into $(x)m[x].P$ and $(x)\overline{m}[x].P$ respectively. In the resulting calculus communications are completely symmetric as exemplified by the following reductions:

$$\overline{m}[x].P|m[x].Q \xrightarrow{\tau} P|Q$$
$$(x)(R|(\overline{m}[y].P|m[x].Q)) \xrightarrow{\tau} R[y/x]|(P[y/x]|Q[y/x]), \text{ where } y \neq x$$
$$(x)\overline{m}[x].P|(y)m[y].Q \xrightarrow{\tau} (z)(P[z/x]|Q[z/y]), \text{ where } z \text{ is fresh}$$

The reader is referred to [3,4,5,6,13,14,17] for more explanations and examples.

Let $\mathcal{N}$ be a set of names, ranged over by lower case letters. $\overline{\mathcal{N}}$, the set of conames, denotes $\{\overline{x} \mid x \in \mathcal{N}\}$. The following conventions will be used: α ranges over $\mathcal{N} \cup \overline{\mathcal{N}}$, μ over $\{\tau\} \cup \{\alpha[x], \alpha x \mid x \in \mathcal{N}\}$, and δ over $\{\tau\} \cup \{\alpha[x], \alpha x, [y/x] \mid x, y \in \mathcal{N}\}$. The set $\mathcal{C}$ of χ-processes are defined by BNF as follows:

$$P := \mathbf{0} \mid \alpha[x].P \mid P|P \mid (x)P \mid [x{=}y]P \mid P{+}P$$

The process $\alpha[x].P$ is in prefix form. Here α or $\overline{\alpha}$ is the subject name, and x the object name, of the prefix. The composition operator "|" is standard. In $(x)P$ the name x is declared local; it cannot be seen from outside. The set of global names, or nonlocal names, in P is denoted by $gn(P)$. We will adopt the α-convention saying that a local name in a process can be replaced by a fresh name without changing the syntax of the process. The choice combinator '+' is well-known. The process $P{+}Q$ acts either as P or as Q exclusively. In this paper we leave out the replication operator. The result of this paper would not be affected had it been included.

The operational semantics can be defined either by reduction semantics ([4]) or in terms of a labeled transition system ([3]). Here we opt for a pure transition semantics as it helps to present our results with clear-cut proofs. The labeled transition system given below defines an early semantics. The reason to use an early semantics is that the definition of weak bisimulation is more succinct in early semantics than in late semantics. In the following formulation, symmetric rules are systematically omitted:

$$\frac{}{\alpha[x].P \xrightarrow{\alpha[x]} P}\mathsf{Sqn} \qquad \frac{P \xrightarrow{\delta} P'}{[x{=}x]P \xrightarrow{\delta} P'}\mathsf{Cnd} \qquad \frac{P \xrightarrow{\delta} P'}{P{+}Q \xrightarrow{\delta} P'}\mathsf{Sum}$$

$$\frac{P \xrightarrow{\mu} P'}{P|Q \xrightarrow{\mu} P'|Q}\mathsf{Cmp}_0 \qquad \frac{P \xrightarrow{[y/x]} P'}{P|Q \xrightarrow{[y/x]} P'|Q[y/x]}\mathsf{Cmp}_1$$

$$\frac{P \xrightarrow{\alpha x} P' \quad Q \xrightarrow{\overline{\alpha}[x]} Q'}{P|Q \xrightarrow{\tau} P'|Q'}\mathsf{Cmm}_0 \qquad \frac{P \xrightarrow{\alpha x} P' \quad Q \xrightarrow{\overline{\alpha} x} Q' \quad x \notin gn(P|Q)}{P|Q \xrightarrow{\tau} (x)(P'|Q')}\mathsf{Cmm}_1$$

$$\frac{P \xrightarrow{\alpha[x]} P' \quad Q \xrightarrow{\overline{\alpha}[x]} Q'}{P|Q \xrightarrow{\tau} P'|Q'}\mathsf{Cmm}_2 \qquad \frac{P \xrightarrow{\alpha[x]} P' \quad Q \xrightarrow{\overline{\alpha}[y]} Q' \quad x \neq y}{P|Q \xrightarrow{[y/x]} P'[y/x]|Q'[y/x]}\mathsf{Cmm}_3$$

$$\frac{P \xrightarrow{\delta} P' \quad x \notin n(\delta)}{(x)P \xrightarrow{\delta} (x)P'}\mathsf{Loc}_0 \qquad \frac{P \xrightarrow{\alpha[x]} P' \quad x \notin \{\alpha, \overline{\alpha}\}}{(x)P \xrightarrow{\alpha y} P'[y/x]}\mathsf{Loc}_1 \qquad \frac{P \xrightarrow{[y/x]} P'}{(x)P \xrightarrow{\tau} P'}\mathsf{Loc}_2$$

Labeled transitions of the form $\xrightarrow{[y/x]}$, called update transitions, are first introduced in [3,13] to help define communications in a transition semantics. In applying Loc_1 local names need be renamed if necessary to prevent y from being captured. In Loc_0, $n(\delta)$ denotes the set of names appeared in δ. The notation $[y/x]$ occurred in $P[y/x]$ for example is an atomic substitution of y for x. A general substitution σ is the composition of atomic substitutions, whose effect is defined by $P[y_1/x_1]\ldots[y_n/x_n] \stackrel{\text{def}}{=} (P[y_1/x_1]\ldots[y_{n-1}/x_{n-1}])[y_n/x_n]$. The composition of zero atomic substitution is an empty substitution $[]$ whose effect is vacuous.

The next lemma collects some technical results whose proofs are simple inductions on derivation.

Lemma 1. *(i) If $P \xrightarrow{\mu} P'$ then $P\sigma \xrightarrow{\mu\sigma} P'\sigma$.*
(ii) If $P \xrightarrow{[y/x]} P'$ and $x\sigma \neq y\sigma$ then $P\sigma \xrightarrow{[y\sigma/x\sigma]} P'\sigma[y\sigma/x\sigma]$.
(iii) If $P \xrightarrow{[y/x]} P'$ and $x\sigma = y\sigma$ then $P\sigma \xrightarrow{\tau} P'\sigma$.
(iv) If $P \stackrel{[y/x]}{\Longrightarrow} P'$ then $P \stackrel{[x/y]}{\Longrightarrow} P'[x/y]$.
(v) $P \xrightarrow{\alpha x} P'$ if and only if $P \xrightarrow{\alpha z} P_1$ for some fresh z such that $P' \equiv P_1[x/z]$.
(vi) Suppose $a \notin gn(P)$. If $(x)(P|a[x]) \xrightarrow{\tau}\xrightarrow{ay} P'$ then $(x)(P|a[x]) \xrightarrow{ay}\xrightarrow{\tau} P'$.
(vii) Suppose $a \notin gn(P)$. If $(x)(P|a[x]) \xrightarrow{\tau} P'|a[y]$ then $P \xrightarrow{[y/x]} P'$.

Let $\Longrightarrow$ be the reflexive and transitive closure of $\xrightarrow{\tau}$. We will write $\stackrel{\mu}{\Longrightarrow}$ ($\stackrel{\delta}{\Longrightarrow}$) for $\Longrightarrow\xrightarrow{\mu}\Longrightarrow$ ($\Longrightarrow\xrightarrow{\delta}\Longrightarrow$). We will also write $\stackrel{\widehat{\mu}}{\Longrightarrow}$ ($\stackrel{\widehat{\delta}}{\Longrightarrow}$) for $\stackrel{\mu}{\Longrightarrow}$ ($\stackrel{\delta}{\Longrightarrow}$) if $\mu \neq \tau$ ($\delta \neq \tau$) and for $\Longrightarrow$ otherwise. A sequence of names $x_1, \ldots, x_n$ will be abbreviated to $\boldsymbol{x}$; and consequently $(x_1)\ldots(x_n)P$ will be abbreviated to $(\boldsymbol{x})P$. When the length of $\boldsymbol{x}$ is zero, $(\boldsymbol{x})P$ is just P.

2 Bisimulation Lattice

We introduce in this section L-bisimilarities, which are refinement of the local bisimilarity of [4]. The reason to study L-bisimilarities is that they provide a framework to understand bisimilarity relations of interest.

In a symmetric calculus such as χ, it does not make much sense to say that an action with positive, respectively negative, subject name is an input, respectively output, action. An action is an input or output, depending on if the object name is being received or being sent out. Let o denote the set $\{a[x] \mid a, x \in \mathcal{N}\}$ of output actions, $\bar{o}$ the set $\{\bar{a}[x] \mid a, x \in \mathcal{N}\}$ of co-output actions, i the set $\{ax \mid a, x \in \mathcal{N}\}$ of input actions, $\bar{i}$ the set $\{\bar{a}x \mid a, x \in \mathcal{N}\}$ of co-input actions and u the set $\{[y/x] \mid x, y \in \mathcal{N}\}$ of updates. Let $\mathcal{L}$ stand for $\{\cup S \mid S \subseteq \{o, \bar{o}, i, \bar{i}, u\} \wedge S \neq \emptyset\}$.

Definition 1. *Let $\mathcal{R}$ be a binary symmetric relation on $\mathcal{C}$ and let L be an element of $\mathcal{L}$. The relation $\mathcal{R}$ is an L-bisimulation if whenever $P\mathcal{R}Q$ then for any process R and any sequence $\boldsymbol{x}$ of names it holds that if $(\boldsymbol{x})(P|R) \xrightarrow{\phi} P'$ for $\phi \in L \cup \{\tau\}$ then there exists some Q' such that $(\boldsymbol{x})(Q|R) \stackrel{\widehat{\phi}}{\Longrightarrow} Q'$ and $P'\mathcal{R}Q'$. The L-bisimilarity $\approx_L$ is the largest L-bisimulation.*

This is a uniform definition of 31 L-bisimilarities. The intuition behind is that $\approx_L$ is what an observer recognizes if he/she is capable of observing actions in L and only in L. We will show that the L-bisimilarities collapse to four distinct relations. In the rest of this section let L be an arbitrarily fixed element of $\mathcal{L}$. First we establish a few technical lemmas. The next one follows directly from definition.

Lemma 2. *If $P \Longrightarrow P_1 \approx_L Q$ and $Q \Longrightarrow Q_1 \approx_L P$ then $P \approx_L Q$.*

For $\phi \in L$, let $\langle\phi\rangle$ be a process such that (i) $\langle\phi\rangle \xrightarrow{\phi} \mathbf{0}$ and (ii) if $\langle\phi\rangle \xrightarrow{\phi} A$ then $A \equiv \mathbf{0}$.

Lemma 3. *Suppose $a \notin gn(P|Q)$. Then (i) $(x)(P|a[x]) \approx_L (x)(Q|a[x])$ implies $P \approx_L Q$; and (ii) $P|a[x] \approx_L Q|a[x]$ implies $P \approx_L Q$.*

Proof. (i) Suppose $\phi \in L$ and $n(\phi) \cap gn(P|Q) = \emptyset$. As $(x)(P|a[x])|\bar{a}[x].\langle\phi\rangle \stackrel{\phi}{\Longrightarrow} (P|\mathbf{0})|\mathbf{0}$, Q_1 exists such that $(x)(Q|a[x])|\bar{a}[x].\langle\phi\rangle \stackrel{\phi}{\Longrightarrow} (Q_1|\mathbf{0})|\mathbf{0} \approx_L (P|\mathbf{0})|\mathbf{0}$, which implies $(x)(Q|a[x]) \stackrel{ax}{\Longrightarrow} Q_1|\mathbf{0} \approx_L P|\mathbf{0}$, which in turn implies $Q \Longrightarrow Q_1$. Similarly P_1 exists such that $P \Longrightarrow P_1 \approx_L Q$. By Lemma 2, $P \approx_L Q$. (ii) can be proved similarly. □

Lemma 4. *If $P \approx_L Q$ then $P\sigma \approx_L Q\sigma$ for an arbitrary substitution σ.*

Proof. Suppose $P \approx_L Q$. We only have to show that for $x \in gn(P|Q)$ and $y \neq x$ one has that $P[y/x] \approx_L Q[y/x]$. Let b be a distinct fresh name. Suppose $\phi \in L$

and $n(\phi) \cap gn(P|Q) = \emptyset$. By definition the actions $(x)(P|(\bar{b}[y]|b[x].\langle\phi\rangle)) \stackrel{\phi}{\Longrightarrow} P[y/x]|(\mathbf{0}|\mathbf{0})$ must be matched up by

$$(x)(Q|(\bar{b}[y]|b[x].\langle\phi\rangle)) \stackrel{\phi}{\Longrightarrow} Q_1|(\mathbf{0}|\mathbf{0}). \tag{1}$$

If $(x)(Q|(\bar{b}[y]|b[x].\langle\phi\rangle)) \stackrel{\tau}{\longrightarrow} (x')(Q_2|(\bar{b}[y]|b[x'].\langle\phi\rangle))$ then by symmetry and α-convention the reduction is the same as

$$(x)(Q|(\bar{b}[y]|b[x].\langle\phi\rangle)) \stackrel{\tau}{\longrightarrow} (x)(Q_3|(\bar{b}[y]|b[x].\langle\phi\rangle))$$

such that $Q \stackrel{\tau}{\longrightarrow} Q_3$. It follows that (1) can be factorized as follows

$$\begin{aligned}(x)(Q|(\bar{b}[y]|b[x].\langle\phi\rangle)) &\Longrightarrow (x)(Q'|(\bar{b}[y]|b[x].\langle\phi\rangle))\\ &\stackrel{\tau}{\longrightarrow} Q'[y/x]|(\mathbf{0}|\langle\phi\rangle)\\ &\stackrel{\phi}{\Longrightarrow} Q_1|(\mathbf{0}|\mathbf{0})\end{aligned}$$

for some Q' and Q_1 such that $Q \Longrightarrow Q'$ and $Q'[y/x] \Longrightarrow Q_1 \approx_L P[y/x]$. By Lemma 1, $Q[y/x] \Longrightarrow Q'[y/x]$. Similarly P_1 exists such that $P[y/x] \Longrightarrow P_1 \approx_L Q[y/x]$. By Lemma 2, $P[y/x] \approx_L Q[y/x]$. □

By definition the L-bisimilarity is closed under localization and composition. Using Lemma 4 it can be easily seen that $\approx_L$ is closed under prefix operation.

Theorem 1. *If $P \approx_L Q$ and $O \in \mathcal{C}$ then (i) $\alpha[x].P \approx_L \alpha[x].Q$; (ii) $P|O \approx_L Q|O$; (iii) $(x)P \approx_L (x)Q$; and (iv) $[x{=}y]P \approx_L [x{=}y]Q$.*

We investigate next the order structure of L-bisimilarities.

Theorem 2. *The following properties hold of the L-bisimilarities:*
(i) $\approx_o \not\subseteq \approx_{\bar{o}}$; $\approx_{\bar{o}} \not\subseteq \approx_o$. (ii) $\approx_L \subseteq \approx_u$. (iii) $\approx_L \subseteq \approx_i = \approx_{\bar{i}}$.

Proof. (i) It is obvious that $(x)a[x].(b)(\bar{b}[x]|b[z]) \not\approx_o a[z]+(x)a[x].(b)(\bar{b}[x]|b[z])$. It takes a while to see that $(x)a[x].(b)(\bar{b}[x]|b[z]) \approx_{\bar{o}} a[z]+(x)a[x].(b)(\bar{b}[x]|b[z])$.

(ii) To prove $\approx_L \subseteq \approx_u$, one only has to show that if $P \approx_L Q$ and $P \stackrel{[y/x]}{\longrightarrow} P'$ then Q' exists such that $Q \stackrel{[y/x]}{\Longrightarrow} Q'$ and $P' \approx_L Q'$. Now $P \stackrel{[y/x]}{\longrightarrow} P'$ implies that $(x)(P|a[x]) \stackrel{\tau}{\longrightarrow} P'|a[y]$ for a fresh a. So $(x)(Q|a[x]) \Longrightarrow Q'|a[y]$ for some Q' such that $P'|a[y] \approx_L Q'|a[y]$. It follows from Lemma 3 that $P' \approx_L Q'$. Clearly $(x)(Q|a[x]) \Longrightarrow Q'|a[y]$ can be factorized as

$$(x)(Q|a[x]) \Longrightarrow (x)(Q_1|a[x]) \stackrel{\tau}{\longrightarrow} Q_2|a[y] \Longrightarrow Q'|a[y],$$

where $Q \Longrightarrow Q_1$. By (vii) of Lemma 1, $(x)(Q_1|a[x]) \stackrel{\tau}{\longrightarrow} Q_2|a[y]$ implies $Q_1 \stackrel{[y/x]}{\longrightarrow} Q_2$. Hence $Q \stackrel{[y/x]}{\Longrightarrow} Q'$.

(iii) Assume $P \approx_L Q$ and $P \stackrel{\alpha x}{\longrightarrow} P'$. Suppose $\phi \in L$ and $n(\phi) \cap gn(P|Q) = \emptyset$. Now $P|(\bar{\alpha}[z]+\langle\phi\rangle) \stackrel{\tau}{\longrightarrow} P_1|\mathbf{0}$ for some fresh z such that $P' \equiv P_1[x/z]$. There has to be some Q_1 such that $Q|(\bar{\alpha}[z]+\langle\phi\rangle) \Longrightarrow Q_1|\mathbf{0} \approx_L P_1|\mathbf{0}$. So $Q \stackrel{\alpha z}{\Longrightarrow} Q_1 \approx_L P_1$. Therefore $Q \stackrel{\alpha x}{\Longrightarrow} Q_1[x/z] \approx_L P_1[x/z] \equiv P'$ by Lemma 1 and Lemma 4. Hence $\approx_L \subseteq \approx_i = \approx_{\bar{i}}$. □

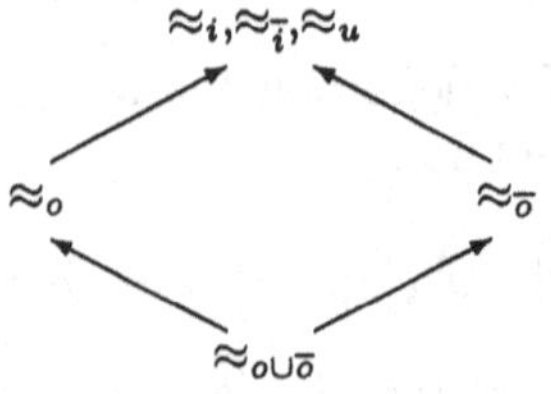

Fig. 1. The Bisimulation Lattice of Chi Processes

In the proof of (iii) of the above theorem, we need to use a fresh name z because we cannot conclude $R \xrightarrow{\alpha x} R'$ from $R|\overline{\alpha}[x] \xrightarrow{\tau} R'|\mathbf{0}$. It may well be that R participates in the communication by performing $R \xrightarrow{\alpha[x]} R'$.

Let $\mathcal{L}(\chi)$ be $\{\approx_L | \ L \in \mathcal{L}\}$, the set of all L-bisimilarities. $\mathcal{L}(\chi)$ is a partial order when equipped with $\subseteq$. For $\approx_{L_1}, \approx_{L_2} \in \mathcal{L}(\chi)$, $\approx_{L_1 \cup L_2}$ is the infimum. Theorem 2 says that $\mathcal{L}(\chi)$ is a four element lattice. The diagram in Fig. 1 is a pictorial representation of the lattice. In the diagram each node is the principal representative of a number of L-bisimilarities that boil down to a same relation. An arrow indicates a strict inclusion. The bottom element is represented by $\approx_{o\cup\bar{o}}$ while the top element is by $\approx_i = \approx_{\bar{i}} = \approx_u$. We will call $(\mathcal{L}(\chi), \subseteq)$ the bisimulation lattice of χ-processes. The lattice structure suggests that the ability to observe output actions is stronger than that to observe input actions. One way to understand this is that the effect of an output action is unknown whereas that of an input action has already been delimited.

3 Alternative Characterization

The definition of L-bisimilarity is natural but intractable. It contains universal quantifications over both processes and names. In this section alternative characterizations of the four distinct L-bisimilarities are presented. For each of the relations, an open style bisimilarity is shown to coincide with it. In the alternative definitions, one still has a universal quantification over substitutions. But it is clear that one only has to consider a finite number of them at each step. First we will see how barbed bisimilarity fits into the lattice hierarchy.

3.1 Barbed Bisimilarity

Barbed bisimilarity ([12]) seems to be the weakest bisimulation equivalence proposed so far. It applies to a whole range of process calculi and therefore acts as a convenient tool to study relationships between different calculi. The relationship of barbed bisimilarity to other bisimilarities is itself an interesting question. Usually it is easy to show that a given bisimilarity is included in the barbed one. The difficulty is in deciding if the inclusion is strict. This section answers the question for χ-processes.

Definition 2. *A process P is strongly barbed at a, notation $P{\downarrow}a$, if $P \xrightarrow{\alpha x} P'$ or $P \xrightarrow{\alpha[x]} P'$ for some P' such that $a \in \{\alpha, \overline{\alpha}\}$. P is barbed at a, notation $P{\Downarrow}a$, if some P' exists such that $P \Longrightarrow P'{\downarrow}a$. A binary relation $\mathcal{R}$ is barbed if $\forall a \in \mathcal{N}.P{\Downarrow}a \Leftrightarrow Q{\Downarrow}a$ whenever $P\mathcal{R}Q$.*

Definition 3. *Let $\mathcal{R}$ be a barbed symmetric relation on $\mathcal{C}$. It is called a barbed bisimulation if whenever $P\mathcal{R}Q$ then for any R and any sequence $\boldsymbol{x}$ of names it holds that if $(\boldsymbol{x})(P|R) \xrightarrow{\tau} P'$ then Q' exists such that $(\boldsymbol{x})(Q|R) \Longrightarrow Q'$ and $P'\mathcal{R}Q'$. The barbed bisimilarity $\approx_b$ is the largest barbed bisimulation.*

The next result locates $\approx_b$ in the bisimulation lattice.

Theorem 3. *$\approx_b$ is the same as $\approx_i$.*

Proof. As $\approx_i$ is clearly barbed, $\approx_i \subseteq \approx_b$. To prove the reverse inclusion, first notice that $\approx_b$ is closed under substitution, the proof of which is similar to that of Lemma 4. Now suppose $P \approx_b Q$ and $P \xrightarrow{\alpha x} P'$. By (v) of Lemma 1 $P \xrightarrow{\alpha z} P_1$ for some fresh z such that $P' \equiv P_1[x/z]$. Let a be fresh. Now $P|(\overline{\alpha}[z].a[a]|\overline{a}[a]) \xrightarrow{\tau}\xrightarrow{\tau} P_1|(\mathbf{0}|\mathbf{0})$. This sequence of reductions must be matched up by $Q|(\overline{\alpha}[z].a[a]|\overline{a}[a]) \Longrightarrow Q_1|(\mathbf{0}|\mathbf{0}) \approx_b P_1|(\mathbf{0}|\mathbf{0})$. There are only two ways for Q to evolve into Q_1: either $Q \overset{\alpha[z]}{\Longrightarrow} Q_1$ or $Q \overset{\alpha z}{\Longrightarrow} Q_1$. The former is impossible because z is fresh. Hence $Q \overset{\alpha z}{\Longrightarrow} Q_1 \approx_b P_1$. It follows from Lemma 1 that $Q \overset{\alpha x}{\Longrightarrow} Q_1[x/z] \approx_b P_1[x/z] \equiv P'$. Conclude that $\approx_b \subseteq \approx_i$. □

3.2 Open Bisimilarity

Open bisimilarity is proposed by Sangiorgi in [16] for π-processes as a "correction of late bisimulation". This section defines open bisimilarity for χ-processes and relates it to one of the L-bisimilarities.

Definition 4. *Let $\mathcal{R}$ be a binary symmetric relation on $\mathcal{C}$. It is called an open bisimulation if whenever $P\mathcal{R}Q$ then for any substitution σ it holds that if $P\sigma \xrightarrow{\delta} P'$ then Q' exists such that $Q\sigma \overset{\widehat{\delta}}{\Longrightarrow} Q'$ and $P'\mathcal{R}Q'$. The open bisimilarity $\approx_{open}$ is the largest open bisimulation.*

It is clear from the definition that $\approx_{open}$ is closed under substitution.

Lemma 5. *$\approx_{open}$ is closed under localization and composition.*

This easy lemma can be proved by constructing appropriate bisimulations.

Theorem 4. *$\approx_{open}$ coincides with $\approx_{o\cup\overline{o}}$.*

Proof. By Lemma 4 and the proof of Theorem 2, $(o \cup \overline{o})$-bisimilarity is an open bisimulation. By Lemma 5, open bisimilarity is an $(o \cup \overline{o})$-bisimulation. □

The definition of open bisimilarity makes it easy to give axiomatization system for finite χ-processes. Theorem 4 enables us to axiomatize the bottom element of the bisimulation lattice $\mathcal{L}(\chi)$. In order to do the same for the other three elements of the bisimulation lattice, one would like to characterize these three L-bisimilarities in an 'open' style, so to speak. This is precisely what we are going to do next. The intuition for the following definition comes from the example given in the proof of (i) of Theorem 2.

Definition 5. *Let $\mathcal{R}$ be a binary symmetric relation on $\mathcal{C}$. It is called an open i-bisimulation (open o-bisimulation, open $\bar{o}$-bisimulation) if whenever $P\mathcal{R}Q$ then for any substitution σ it holds that*
(i) if $P\sigma \xrightarrow{\phi} P'$ for $\phi \in i \cup \bar{i} \cup u \cup \{\tau\}$ ($\phi \in o \cup i \cup \bar{i} \cup u \cup \{\tau\}$, $\phi \in \bar{o} \cup i \cup \bar{i} \cup u \cup \{\tau\}$) then Q' exists such that $Q\sigma \stackrel{\widehat{\phi}}{\Longrightarrow} Q'$ and $P'\mathcal{R}Q'$; and
(ii) if $P\sigma \xrightarrow{\alpha[x]} P'$ ($P\sigma \xrightarrow{\overline{a}[x]} P'$, $P\sigma \xrightarrow{a[x]} P'$) then some Q' exists such that $P'\mathcal{R}Q'$ and either $Q\sigma \stackrel{\alpha[x]}{\Longrightarrow} Q'$ ($Q\sigma \stackrel{\overline{a}[x]}{\Longrightarrow} Q'$, $Q\sigma \stackrel{a[x]}{\Longrightarrow} Q'$) or $Q\sigma \stackrel{\alpha z}{\Longrightarrow}\stackrel{[x/z]}{\Longrightarrow} Q'$ ($Q\sigma \stackrel{\overline{a}z}{\Longrightarrow}\stackrel{[x/z]}{\Longrightarrow} Q'$, $Q\sigma \stackrel{az}{\Longrightarrow}\stackrel{[x/z]}{\Longrightarrow} Q'$) for some fresh z.
The open i-bisimilarity (open o-bisimilarity, open $\bar{o}$-bisimilarity), denoted by $\approx^{i}_{open}$ ($\approx^{o}_{open}$, $\approx^{\bar{o}}_{open}$), is the largest open i-bisimulation (open o-bisimulation, open $\bar{o}$-bisimulation).

The next theorem explains the reason to have Definition 5.

Theorem 5. *(i) $\approx^{o}_{open} = \approx_{o}$; (ii) $\approx^{\bar{o}}_{open} = \approx_{\bar{o}}$; (iii) $\approx^{i}_{open} = \approx_{i}$.*

Proof. It is enough to see how to establish (iii). Suppose $P \approx_i Q$ and $P \xrightarrow{\alpha[x]} P'$. For a fresh name z one has $P|\overline{\alpha}[z] \xrightarrow{[x/z]} P'|\mathbf{0}$. As $\approx_i = \approx_u$, Q' exists such that $Q|\overline{\alpha}[z] \stackrel{[x/z]}{\Longrightarrow} Q'|\mathbf{0} \approx_i P'|\mathbf{0}$. There are only two possibilities: either $Q \stackrel{\alpha[x]}{\Longrightarrow} Q' \approx_i P'$ or $Q \stackrel{\alpha z}{\Longrightarrow}\stackrel{[x/z]}{\Longrightarrow} Q' \approx_i P'$. Hence $\approx_i \subseteq \approx^{i}_{open}$ by Lemma 4.

To prove the reverse inclusion we use the fact that $\approx^{i}_{open}$ is by definition closed under substitution. We only have to show that the composition and localization operators preserve the relation $\approx^{i}_{open}$. To prove that $\{((\boldsymbol{v})(P|R), (\boldsymbol{v})(Q|R)) \mid P \approx^{i}_{open} Q\}$ is an open i-bisimulation, it is sufficient to examine the cases where P performs an output action. We consider only one case:

- Suppose that $(\boldsymbol{v})(P|R) \xrightarrow{\alpha z} (\boldsymbol{u})(P'[z/y]|R[z/y])$, where $y \in \{\boldsymbol{v}\}$, is derived from $P \xrightarrow{\alpha[y]} P'$ by applying rule Loc_1. Suppose $P \xrightarrow{\alpha[y]} P'$ is matched up by $Q \stackrel{\alpha w}{\Longrightarrow} Q_1 \stackrel{[y/w]}{\Longrightarrow} Q'$ for some Q_1, Q' and fresh w. By Lemma 1, $Q \stackrel{\alpha z}{\Longrightarrow} Q_1[z/w] \stackrel{[y/z]}{\Longrightarrow} Q'[z/w][y/z] \equiv Q'[y/z]$ as $w \notin gn(Q')$. By (iv) of Lemma 1, $Q \stackrel{\alpha z}{\Longrightarrow} Q_1[z/w] \stackrel{[z/y]}{\Longrightarrow} Q'[y/z][z/y] \equiv Q'[z/y]$. It follows that
$$(\boldsymbol{v})(Q|R) \stackrel{\alpha z}{\Longrightarrow} (\boldsymbol{v})(Q_1[z/w]|R) \Longrightarrow (\boldsymbol{u})(Q'[z/y]|R[z/y])$$
matches up $(\boldsymbol{v})(P|R) \xrightarrow{\alpha z} (\boldsymbol{u})(P'[z/y]|R[z/y])$.

The closure property enables us to conclude that $\approx^{i}_{open}$ is an i-bisimulation. □

The open style bisimilarities are particularly suitable for χ-like process calculi in which names are uniform.

4 Axiomatization

The L-bisimilarities are not congruence relations. To get a congruence relation from $\approx_L$ we use the standard approach.

Definition 6. *$P =_L Q$ if and only if $P \approx_L Q$ and whenever $P \xrightarrow{\tau} P'$ ($Q \xrightarrow{\tau} Q'$) then Q' (P') exists such that $Q \stackrel{\tau}{\Longrightarrow} Q'$ ($P \stackrel{\tau}{\Longrightarrow} P'$) and $P' \approx_L Q'$.*

We will call $=_L$ the L-congruence on χ-processes. According to the bisimulation lattice, there are only four distinct L-congruence relations. The aim of this section is to give complete axiomatization systems for all the four distinct L-congruence relations. In this section we omit most of the proofs since they are very much similar to the corresponding proofs in [7,10]. In the axiomatization we need a prefix operation that generalizes the standard τ-operation. It is defined as follows:

$$[y|x].P \stackrel{\text{def}}{=} (a)(\overline{a}[y]|a[x].P) \quad \text{where } a \text{ is fresh.}$$

The next result is known as Hennessy Lemma. It is very useful in the study of axiomatization systems.

Lemma 6. *$P \approx_L Q$ if and only if either $[x|x].P =_L Q$ or $P =_L Q$ or $P =_L [x|x].Q$.*

For purpose of axiomatization, let π and γ range over $\{\alpha[x], [y|x] \mid x, y \in \mathcal{N}\}$. In the rest of this section M and N denote finite lists of match equalities $x{=}y$. Suppose M is $x_1{=}y_1, \ldots, x_n{=}y_n$. Then $[M]P$ denotes $[x_1{=}y_1]\ldots[x_n{=}y_n]P$. If M logically implies N, we write $M \Rightarrow N$; and if both $M \Rightarrow N$ and $N \Rightarrow M$ we write $M \Leftrightarrow N$. If M is an empty list, it plays the role of logical truth, in which case $[M]P$ is just P. Clearly a list M of match equalities defines an equivalence relation on the set $n(M)$ of names appeared in M. We use σ_M to denote an arbitrary substitution that replaces all members of an equivalence class by a representative of that class.

In [16] Sangiorgi presents a complete system for strong open congruence on π-processes. Parrow and Victor consider in their paper ([13]) two axiomatization systems for strong hyperbisimilarity, one with match operator and one without match operator. In Fig. 2 a conditional equational system AS is defined together with some derived rules and their justifications. The expansion law is the following equation:

$$P|Q = \begin{array}{l} \sum_i [M_i](\boldsymbol{x})\pi_i.(P_i|Q) + \sum^{\pi_i=a_i[x_i]}_{\gamma_j=\overline{b_j}[y_j]} [M_i][N_j](\boldsymbol{x})(\boldsymbol{y})[a_i{=}b_j][x_i|y_j].(P_i|Q_j) + \\ \sum_j [N_j](\boldsymbol{y})\gamma_j.(P|Q_j) + \sum^{\pi_i=\overline{a_i}[x_i]}_{\gamma_j=b_j[y_j]} [M_i][N_j](\boldsymbol{x})(\boldsymbol{y})[a_i{=}b_j][x_i|y_j].(P_i|Q_j) \end{array}$$

where P is $\sum_i [M_i](\boldsymbol{x})\pi_i.P_i$ and Q is $\sum_j [N_j](\boldsymbol{y})\gamma_j.Q_j$. Rules concerning equivalence and congruence relations have been omitted. This is Victor and Parrow's

L1	$(x)\mathbf{0} = \mathbf{0}$	
L2	$(x)\alpha[y].P = \mathbf{0}$	$x \in \{\alpha, \overline{\alpha}\}$
L3	$(x)\alpha[y].P = \alpha[y].(x)P$	$x \notin \{y, \alpha, \overline{\alpha}\}$
L4	$(x)(y)P = (y)(x)P$	
L5	$(x)[y{=}z]P = [y{=}z](x)P$	$x \notin \{y, z\}$
L6	$(x)(P{+}Q) = (x)P{+}(x)Q$	
L7	$(x)[x{=}y]P = \mathbf{0}$	
L8	$(x)[y\|x].P = [y\|y].P[y/x]$	$x \neq y$
L9	$(x)[y\|z].P = [y\|z].(x)P$	$x \notin \{y, z\}$
M1	$[M]P = [N]P$	if $M \Leftrightarrow N$
M2	$[x{=}y]P = [x{=}y]P[y/x]$	
M3	$[x{=}y](P{+}Q) = [x{=}y]P{+}[x{=}y]Q$	
S1	$P{+}\mathbf{0} = P$	
S2	$P{+}Q = Q{+}P$	
S3	$P{+}(Q{+}R) = (P{+}Q){+}R$	
S4	$[x{=}y]P{+}P = P$	
U1	$[y\|x].P = [x\|y].P$	
U2	$[x\|x].P = [y\|y].P$	
U3	$[y\|x].P = [y\|x].[x{=}y]P$	
Expansion Law		
LD1	$(x)[x\|x].P = [y\|y].(x)P$	U2 and L9
MD1	$[x{=}y].\mathbf{0} = \mathbf{0}$	S1 and S4
MD2	$[x{=}x].P = P$	M1
MD3	$[M]P = [M](P\sigma_M)$	M2
SD1	$P{+}P = P$	MD2 and S4
SD2	$[M]P{+}P = P$	S-rules
UD1	$[y\|x].P = [y\|x].P[y/x]$	U3 and M2

Fig. 2. Axiom System AS and its Derived Rules

system without mismatch. The only difference is that we use a symmetric update prefix operator.

We will write $AS \cup \{R_1, \ldots, R_n\} \vdash P = Q$ to mean that the equality $P = Q$ is derivable from the rules and axioms of AS together with rules $R_1, \ldots, R_n$. When no confusion arises, we simply write $P = Q$. We will also write $P \stackrel{R}{=} Q$ to indicate that R is the major axiom applied to derive $P = Q$.

Definition 7. *A process P is in normal form if $P \equiv \sum_{i\in I_1}[M_i]\alpha_i[x_i].P_i + \sum_{i\in I_2}[M_i](x)\alpha_i[x].P_i + \sum_{i\in I_3}[M_i][z_i|y_i].P_i$ such that x does not appear in P and P_i is in normal form for each $i \in I_1 \cup I_2 \cup I_3$. Here I_1, I_2 and I_3 are pairwise disjoint finite indexing sets.*

Notice that if P is in normal form and σ is a substitution then $P\sigma$ is in normal form. The depth of a process measures the maximal length of nested prefixes in the process. The structural definition goes as follows: (i) $d(\mathbf{0}) = 0$; (ii) $d(\alpha[x].P) = 1 + d(P)$; (iii) $d(P|Q) = d(P) + d(Q)$; (iv) $d((x)P) = d(P)$; (v) $d([x{=}y]P) = d(P)$; (vi) $d(P{+}Q) = max\{d(P), d(Q)\}$; (vii) $d([x|y].P) = 1{+}d(P)$.

T1	$\alpha[x].[y\|y].P = \alpha[x].P$
T2	$P + [y\|y].P = [y\|y].P$
T3	$\alpha[x].(P + [y\|y].Q) = \alpha[x].(P + [y\|y].Q) + \alpha[x].Q$
TD1	$[x\|z].[y\|y].P = [x\|z].P$
TD2	$[x\|z].(P + [y\|y].Q) = [x\|z].(P + [y\|y].Q) + [x\|z].Q$
O1	$(z)m[z].(P + [x\|z].Q) = (z)m[z].(P + [x\|z].Q) + m[x].Q \quad x \neq z$
O2	$(z)\overline{m}[z].(P + [x\|z].Q) = (z)\overline{m}[z].(P + [x\|z].Q) + \overline{m}[x].Q \quad x \neq z$
O3	$(z)\alpha[z].(P + [x\|z].Q) = (z)\alpha[z].(P + [x\|z].Q) + \alpha[x].Q \quad x \neq z$

Fig. 3. The Tau Laws and the Output Laws

Lemma 7. *In AS each process P is provably equal to some P′ in normal form such that* $d(P') \leq d(P)$.

We need the χ-version of the well-known tau laws as given in Fig. 3. TD1 and TD2 are derivable from T1 and T3 respectively.

The tau laws are enough to characterize $=_{o\cup\bar{o}}$. To get complete systems for the other three L-congruence relations, we need what we call output laws $O1$, $O2$ and $O3$ given in Fig. 3.

The following lemma is crucial to the proof of the completeness theorem.

Lemma 8. *Suppose Q is in normal form. Then*
(i) if $Q\sigma_M \stackrel{\tau}{\Longrightarrow} Q'$ *then* $AS \cup \{T1, T2, T3\} \vdash Q = Q + [M][x|x].Q'$ *for each* x;
(ii) if $Q\sigma_M \stackrel{\alpha[x]}{\Longrightarrow} Q'$ *then* $AS \cup \{T1, T2, T3\} \vdash Q = Q + [M]\alpha[x].Q'$;
(iii) if $z \notin gn(Q) \cup n(M)$ *and* $Q\sigma_M \stackrel{\alpha z}{\Longrightarrow} Q'$ *then* $AS \cup \{T1, T2, T3\} \vdash Q = Q + [M](z)\alpha[z].Q'$;
(iv) if $Q\sigma_M \stackrel{[x/y]}{\Longrightarrow} Q'$ *then* $AS \cup \{T1, T2, T3\} \vdash Q = Q + [M][x|y].Q'$;
(v) if $z \notin gn(Q) \cup n(M)$ *and* $Q\sigma_M \stackrel{mz}{\Longrightarrow}\stackrel{[x/z]}{\Longrightarrow} Q'$ *then* $AS \cup \{T1, T2, T3\} \cup \{O1\} \vdash Q = Q + [M]m[x].Q'$;
(vi) if $z \notin gn(Q) \cup n(M)$ *and* $Q\sigma_M \stackrel{\overline{m}z}{\Longrightarrow}\stackrel{[x/z]}{\Longrightarrow} Q'$ *then* $AS \cup \{T1, T2, T3\} \cup \{O2\} \vdash Q = Q + [M]\overline{m}[x].Q'$;
(vii) if $z \notin gn(Q) \cup n(M)$ *and* $Q\sigma_M \stackrel{\alpha z}{\Longrightarrow}\stackrel{[x/z]}{\Longrightarrow} Q'$ *then* $AS \cup \{T1, T2, T3\} \cup \{O3\} \vdash Q = Q + [M]\alpha[x].Q'$.

Proof. (i) through (iv) are proved by inductions on derivation. (v) through (vii) are proved using (iii) and (iv). □

Theorem 6. *We have the following completeness results:*
(i) $AS \cup \{T1, T2, T3\}$ *is sound and complete for* $=_{o\cup\bar{o}}$;
(ii) $AS \cup \{T1, T2, T3\} \cup \{O1\}$ *is sound and complete for* $=_{\bar{o}}$;
(iii) $AS \cup \{T1, T2, T3\} \cup \{O2\}$ *is sound and complete for* $=_{o}$;
(iv) $AS \cup \{T1, T2, T3\} \cup \{O3\}$ *is sound and complete for* $=_{i}$.

Proof. The soundness part is clear.

(i) Suppose P and Q are in normal form and $P =_{o\cup\bar{o}} Q$. We prove the completeness by induction on the sum of the depths of P and Q. Let $[M_i](x)\alpha_i[x].P_i$ be a summand of P. Now $([M_i](x)\alpha_i[x].P_i)\sigma_{M_i} \stackrel{\alpha_i\sigma_{M_i}x}{\longrightarrow} P_i\sigma_{M_i}$ must be matched up by $Q\sigma_{M_i} \stackrel{\alpha_i\sigma_{M_i}x}{\Longrightarrow} Q'$ such that $P_i\sigma_{M_i} \approx_{o\cup\bar{o}} Q'$. By Lemma 6, we know that either $[y|y].P_i\sigma_{M_i} =_{o\cup\bar{o}} Q'$ or $P_i\sigma_{M_i} =_{o\cup\bar{o}} Q'$ or $P_i\sigma_{M_i} =_{o\cup\bar{o}} [x|x].Q'$. Suppose $P_i\sigma_{M_i} =_{o\cup\bar{o}} [y|y].Q'$ is the case. Both $P_i\sigma_{M_i}$ and $[y|y].Q'$ are in normal form and $d(P_i\sigma_{M_i}) + d([y|y].Q') < d(P) + d(Q)$. So by induction hypothesis $P_i\sigma_{M_i} = [y|y].Q'$. It follows that

$$\begin{aligned}[M_i](x)\alpha_i[x].P_i &\stackrel{MD3}{=} [M_i](x)\alpha_i\sigma_{M_i}[x].P_i\sigma_{M_i}\\ &\stackrel{I.H.}{=} [M_i](x)\alpha_i\sigma_{M_i}[x].[y|y].Q'\\ &\stackrel{T1}{=} [M_i](x)\alpha_i\sigma_{M_i}[x].Q'.\end{aligned}$$

Hence $[M_i](x)\alpha_i[x].P_i + Q = [M_i](x)\alpha_i\sigma_{M_i}[x].Q' + Q = Q$ by (iii) of Lemma 8. The situation is the same when $P' =_{o\cup\bar{o}} Q'$ or $P' =_{o\cup\bar{o}} [x|x].Q'$. It can be similarly proved that $[M_i]\alpha_i[x_i].P_i + Q = Q$, respectively $[M_i][x_i|y_i].P_i + Q = Q$, whenever $[M_i]\alpha_i[x_i].P_i$, respectively $[M_i][x_i|y_i].P_i$, is a summand of P. Conclude that $P + Q = Q$. Symmetrically $P + Q = P$. Hence $P = Q$.

(iv) Let P and Q be in normal form and $P =_i Q$. Suppose

$$([M_i]\alpha_i[x_i].P_i)\sigma_{M_i} \stackrel{\alpha_i\sigma_{M_i}[x_i\sigma_{M_i}]}{\longrightarrow} P_i\sigma_{M_i}$$

is matched up by $Q\sigma_{M_i} \stackrel{\alpha_i\sigma_{M_i}z}{\Longrightarrow} Q_1 \stackrel{[x_i\sigma_{M_i}/z]}{\Longrightarrow} Q'$ such that $P_i\sigma_{M_i} \approx_i Q'$. By Theorem 4 this is the only situation not covered by the proof of (i). By Lemma 6, either $[x|x].P_i\sigma_{M_i} =_i Q'$ or $P_i\sigma_{M_i} =_i Q'$ or $P_i\sigma_{M_i} =_i [x|x].Q'$. Now suppose $[x|x].P_i\sigma_{M_i} =_i Q'$ is the case. Both $[x|x].P_i\sigma_{M_i}$ and Q' are in normal form. So by induction hypothesis $[x|x].P_i\sigma_{M_i} = Q'$. Therefore

$$\begin{aligned}[M_i]\alpha_i[x_i].P_i &= [M_i]\alpha_i\sigma_{M_i}[x_i\sigma_{M_i}].P_i\sigma_{M_i}\\ &= [M_i]\alpha_i\sigma_{M_i}[x_i\sigma_{M_i}].Q'.\end{aligned}$$

Thus $[M_i]\alpha_i[x_i].P_i + Q = [M_i]\alpha_i\sigma_{M_i}[x_i\sigma_{M_i}].Q' + Q = Q$ by (vii) of Lemma 8. The rest of the proof can be safely omitted. □

5 Asynchronous Chi Calculus

In the world of π-calculus, attention has been paid to an asynchronous version of the language ([8,2,1]). It has been argued that it has the same expressive power as the synchronous one. There is also a case for asynchronous χ-calculus. Merro has recently given a fully abstract translation from the asynchronous χ to the asynchronous π ([9]). One hopes to establish that χ and π have the same expressive power by relating χ to its asynchronous cosine. As one would expect the asynchronous χ is defined as follows:

$$P := \mathbf{0} \mid a[x].P \mid \bar{a}[x] \mid P|P \mid (x)P \mid [x{=}y]P \mid P{+}P$$

The operational semantics remains unchanged. So does the definition of L-bisimilarity. Lemma 4 and Theorem 1 still hold. But the bisimulation lattice shrinks.

Theorem 7. $\approx_o \subset \approx_{\overline{o}} = \approx_u = \approx_i = \approx_{\overline{i}}$. *The inclusion is strict.*

Proof. The proofs of the equivalence $\approx_u = \approx_i = \approx_{\overline{i}}$ and the strictness of the inclusion are as before. It remains to show that $\approx_L \subseteq \approx_{\overline{o}}$ for all L-bisimilarities $\approx_L$. Now suppose $P \approx_L Q$ and $P \stackrel{\overline{a}[x]}{\longrightarrow} P'$. Let R be $a[x]+\langle\phi\rangle$ such that $\phi \in L$ and $n(\phi) \cap gn(P|Q) = \emptyset$. Then $P|R \stackrel{\tau}{\longrightarrow} P'|\mathbf{0}$. It follows that Q' exists such that $Q|R \stackrel{\tau}{\longrightarrow} Q|\mathbf{0}$ and $P' \approx_L Q'$. There are two cases: Either $Q \stackrel{\overline{a}[x]}{\Longrightarrow} Q'$ or $Q \stackrel{\overline{a}z}{\Longrightarrow} Q_2 \stackrel{[x/z]}{\Longrightarrow} Q'$ for some fresh z. In the latter case, notice that no action is causally dependent on the action $\overline{a}z$. So all the rest of the actions can be performed before the action at that particular $\overline{a}$ happens. But then the update $\stackrel{[x/z]}{\longrightarrow}$ becomes a communication in which a local name is substantiated by x. It follows that the delayed action at that particular $\overline{a}$ must be $\overline{a}[x]$. That is $Q \stackrel{\overline{a}z}{\Longrightarrow} Q_2 \stackrel{[x/z]}{\Longrightarrow} Q'$ can be rearranged as $Q \stackrel{\overline{a}[x]}{\Longrightarrow} Q'$. So in either case $P \stackrel{\overline{a}[x]}{\longrightarrow} P'$ is matchable by $Q \stackrel{\overline{a}[x]}{\Longrightarrow} Q'$. □

Consequently the bisimulation lattice of the asynchronous χ contains only two elements.

6 Asymmetric Chi Calculus

The simplicity of the lattice $\mathcal{L}(\chi)$ is due essentially to the symmetry of the language. If we insist that there is a difference between an action with a positive subject name and an action with a negative subject name then an asymmetric version of χ-calculus results. This is the Update Calculus of Parrow and Victor.

The operational semantics of the asymmetric χ-calculus is defined similarly as is for symmetric χ. The rule Sqn, Cnd and Sum remain unchanged. Other rules are given below:

$$\frac{P \stackrel{\mu}{\longrightarrow} P' \quad \text{if } \mu = \overline{m}(x) \text{ then } x \notin gn(Q)}{P|Q \stackrel{\mu}{\longrightarrow} P'|Q}\,\mathsf{Cmp}_0$$

$$\frac{P \stackrel{[y/x]}{\longrightarrow} P'}{P|Q \stackrel{[y/x]}{\longrightarrow} P'|Q[y/x]}\,\mathsf{Cmp}_1 \qquad \frac{P \stackrel{(y/x]}{\longrightarrow} P' \quad y \notin gn(Q)}{P|Q \stackrel{(y/x]}{\longrightarrow} P'|Q[y/x]}\,\mathsf{Cmp}_2$$

$$\frac{P \stackrel{mx}{\longrightarrow} P' \quad Q \stackrel{\overline{m}[x]}{\longrightarrow} Q'}{P|Q \stackrel{\tau}{\longrightarrow} P'|Q'}\,\mathsf{Cmm}_0 \qquad \frac{P \stackrel{mx}{\longrightarrow} P' \quad Q \stackrel{\overline{m}(x)}{\longrightarrow} Q' \quad x \notin gn(P)}{P|Q \stackrel{\tau}{\longrightarrow} (x)(P'|Q')}\,\mathsf{Cmm}_1$$

$$\frac{P \stackrel{m[x]}{\longrightarrow} P' \quad Q \stackrel{\overline{m}[x]}{\longrightarrow} Q'}{P|Q \stackrel{\tau}{\longrightarrow} P'|Q'}\,\mathsf{Cmm}_2 \qquad \frac{P \stackrel{m[x]}{\longrightarrow} P' \quad Q \stackrel{\overline{m}[y]}{\longrightarrow} Q' \quad x \neq y}{P|Q \stackrel{[y/x]}{\longrightarrow} P'[y/x]|Q'[y/x]}\,\mathsf{Cmm}_3$$

$$\frac{P \xrightarrow{m[x]} P' \quad Q \xrightarrow{\overline{m}(y)} Q' \quad y \notin gn(P)}{P|Q \xrightarrow{(y/x]} P'[y/x]|Q'[y/x]} \mathsf{Cmm}_4$$

$$\frac{P \xrightarrow{\delta} P' \quad x \notin n(\delta)}{(x)P \xrightarrow{\delta} (x)P'} \mathsf{Loc}_0 \quad \frac{P \xrightarrow{m[x]} P' \quad x \neq m}{(x)P \xrightarrow{my} P'[y/x]} \mathsf{Loc}_1 \quad \frac{P \xrightarrow{\overline{m}[x]} P' \quad x \neq m}{(x)P \xrightarrow{\overline{m}(x)} P'} \mathsf{Loc}_2$$

$$\frac{P \xrightarrow{[y/x]} P'}{(x)P \xrightarrow{\tau} P'} \mathsf{Loc}_3 \quad \frac{P \xrightarrow{[y/x]} P'}{(y)P \xrightarrow{(y/x]} P'} \mathsf{Loc}_4 \quad \frac{P \xrightarrow{(y/x]} P'}{(x)P \xrightarrow{\tau} (y)P'} \mathsf{Loc}_5$$

In the rules, μ ranges over $\{\tau\} \cup \{m[x], \overline{m}[x], mx, \overline{m}(x) \mid m, x \in \mathcal{N}\}$ and δ ranges over $\{\tau\} \cup \{m[x], \overline{m}[x], mx, \overline{m}(x), [y/x], (y/x] \mid m, x, y \in \mathcal{N}\}$.

The localization operator in asymmetric χ-calculus is fundamentally different from the restriction combinator in π-calculus. The next example is quite illuminating: $(x)([x{=}y]\overline{a}[a]|\overline{b}[x]) \approx (x)\overline{b}[x]$ in π-calculus but $(x)([x{=}y]\overline{a}[a]|\overline{b}[x]) \not\approx (x)\overline{b}[x]$ in the asymmetric χ-calculus. In asymmetric χ-calculus the effect of the consecutive communications

$$(z)(a[z].(b)(b[z]|\overline{b}[y]))|(x)\overline{a}[x].Q \stackrel{\tau}{\Longrightarrow} (b)(\mathbf{0}|\mathbf{0})|Q[y/x] \approx Q[y/x]$$

is the same as the χ-communication

$$a[y]|(x)\overline{a}[x].Q \xrightarrow{\tau} \mathbf{0}|Q[y/x] \approx Q[y/x].$$

The asymmetric χ-calculus can be investigated in completely the same way as the χ-calculus has been. The proofs of the corresponding results are more or less the same. In this language, we think of an action with positive subject name as an input action whereas that with a negative subject name as an output action. Let fo denote the set $\{\overline{a}[x] \mid a, x \in \mathcal{N}\}$ of free output, fi the set $\{a[x] \mid x \in \mathcal{N}\}$ of free input, i the set $\{ax \mid x \in \mathcal{N}\}$ of input, ro the set $\{\overline{a}(x) \mid a, x \in \mathcal{N}\}$ of restricted output, u the set $\{[y/x] \mid x, y \in \mathcal{N}\}$ of updates and ru the set $\{(y/x] \mid x, y \in \mathcal{N}\}$ of restricted updates. We can define L-bisimilarities $\approx_L$, open bisimilarity and barbed bisimilarity for asymmetric χ-processes as we have for χ-processes. There are altogether 63 L-bisimilarities for the asymmetric χ-processes. The next theorem conveys all the necessary information to construct the bisimulation lattice of the asymmetric χ-calculus.

Theorem 8. *The following properties hold for asymmetric χ-calculus:*
(i) $\approx_{ru \cup fi \cup u}$ *and* $\approx_i$ *coincide respectively with open and barbed bisimilarities.*
(ii) $\approx_L \subseteq \approx_i$.
(iii) $\approx_L \subseteq \approx_{fo}$.
(iv) $\approx_{L_1} \not\subseteq \approx_{L_2}$ *if* $fi \cap L_1 = \emptyset$ *and* $fi \subseteq L_2$.
(v) $\approx_{L_1} \not\subseteq \approx_{L_2}$ *if* $ru \cap L_1 = \emptyset$ *and* $ru \subseteq L_2$.
(vi) $\approx_{L_1} \not\subseteq \approx_{L_2}$ *if* $(ru \cup ro) \cap L_1 = \emptyset$ *and* $ro \subseteq L_2$.
(vii) $\approx_{L_1} \not\subseteq \approx_{L_2}$ *if* $u \cap L_1 = \emptyset$ *and* $u \subseteq L_2$.
(viii) If $L \cap i = \emptyset$ *then the inclusion* $\approx_L \subset \approx_i$ *is strict.*
(ix) $\approx_{ru} \subset \approx_{ro}$. *The inclusion is strict.*

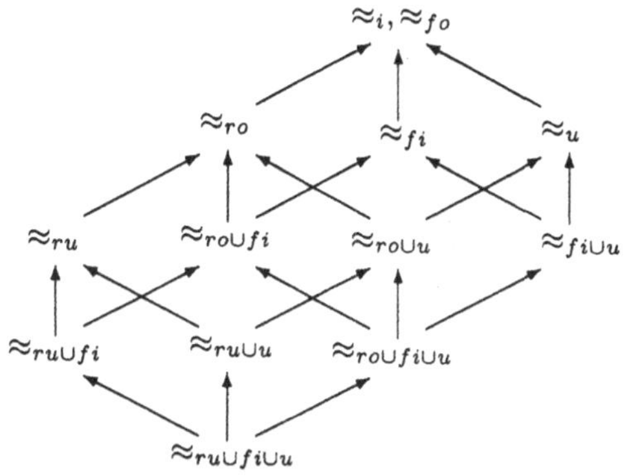

Fig. 4. The Bisimulation Lattice of Asymmetric Chi Processes

Proof. (i,ii) The proofs are similar to those in χ-calculus.

(iii) Suppose $P \approx_L Q$ and $P \xrightarrow{\overline{a}[x]} P'$. Let R be $a[x]+\langle\phi\rangle$ such that $\phi \in L$ and $n(\phi) \cap gn(P|Q) = \emptyset$. Then $P|R \xrightarrow{\tau} P'|\mathbf{0}$. It follows that Q' exists such that $Q|R \Longrightarrow Q'|\mathbf{0}$ and $P' \approx_L Q'$. Due to asymmetry, it must be the case that $Q \stackrel{\overline{a}[x]}{\Longrightarrow} Q'$.

(iv) Assume $fi \cap L_1 = \emptyset$ and $fi \subseteq L_2$. Then $(x)a[x].(b)(b[z]|\overline{b}[x]) \approx_{L_1} a[z] + (x)a[x].(b)(b[z]|\overline{b}[x])$ but $(x)a[x].(b)(b[z]|\overline{b}[x]) \not\approx_{L_2} a[z] + (x)a[x].(b)(b[z]|\overline{b}[x])$.

(v) One has $(a)((x)\overline{a}[x]|a[y])) \not\approx_{ru} \mathbf{0}$ but $(a)((x)\overline{a}[x]|a[y])) \approx_{L_1} \mathbf{0}$ whenever $ru \cap L_1 = \emptyset$.

(vi) Let R be $(x)\overline{a}[x].(b)(b[x]|(y)\overline{b}[y].(w)c[w])$. Suppose $(ru \cup ro) \cap L_1 = \emptyset$ and $ro \subseteq L_2$. Then $R \approx_{L_1} (x)\overline{a}[x].(w)c[w] + R$ but $R \not\approx_{L_2} (x)\overline{a}[x].(w)c[w] + R$.

(vii) Let R be $(b)(z)(\overline{b}[z]|b[x].(a)(a[z]|\overline{a}[y] + a[y]|\overline{a}[z]))$. Suppose $u \cap L_1 = \emptyset$ and $u \subseteq L_2$. Then $R \approx_{L_1} (a)(a[x]|\overline{a}[y]) + R$ but $R \not\approx_{L_2} (a)(a[x]|\overline{a}[y]) + R$.

(viii) By (ii) through (vii) the inclusion $\approx_L \subset \approx_i$ is strict whenever $L \cap i = \emptyset$.

(ix) Suppose $P \approx_{ru} Q$ and $P \xrightarrow{\overline{a}(x)} P'$. Then $P|a[z] \xrightarrow{(x/z)} P'|\mathbf{0}$ for fresh z. So $Q|a[z] \stackrel{(x/z)}{\Longrightarrow} Q'|\mathbf{0}$ for some Q'. Hence $Q \stackrel{\overline{a}(x)}{\Longrightarrow} Q'$. Therefore $\approx_{ru} \subseteq \approx_{ro}$. The strictness follows from (v). □

According to Theorem 8 the L-bisimilarities $\approx_{fi}$, $\approx_i$, $\approx_{ro}$, $\approx_u$ and $\approx_{ru}$ are all pairwise distinct. Using these five relations, the bisimulation lattice of asymmetric χ-processes can be generated. The pictorial description of the lattice is given by the diagram in Fig. 4. There are altogether 12 elements in the lattice. The bottom element is $\approx_{ru\cup fi\cup u}$, which characterizes the open bisimilarity. The top element is $\approx_i$, which coincides with the barbed bisimilarity.

7 The Asynchronous Asymmetric Chi

It seems reasonable to remove the symmetry of communications in asynchronous χ-calculus. The resulting language has the same grammar as the asynchronous χ

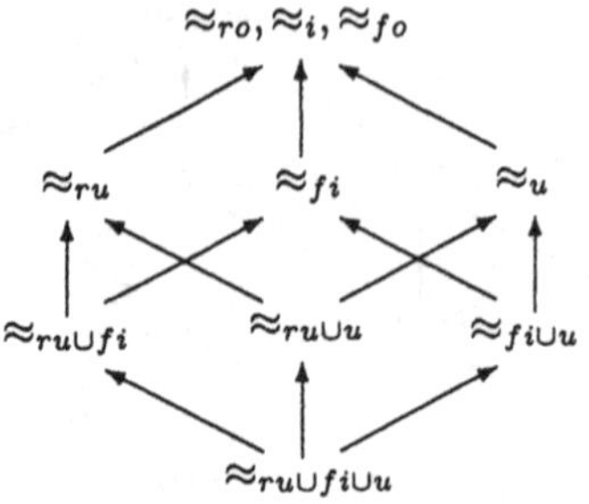

Fig. 5. The Bisimulation Lattice of Asynchronous Asymmetric Chi Processes

and the same operational semantics as the asymmetric χ. Without further ado, we come to describe the bisimulation lattice of the language.

Theorem 9. *In the asynchronous asymmetric χ-calculus, one has:*
(i) $\approx_{fi}, \approx_{ru}, \approx_u \subseteq \approx_{ro} = \approx_i = \approx_{fo}$;
(ii) $\approx_{fi}, \approx_{ru}, \approx_u$ *are pairwise distinct.*

Proof. Apart from the part to establish (vi), the proof of Theorem 8 works fine. The only extra work is to prove that $\approx_L \subseteq \approx_{ro}$ for all L-bisimilarities $\approx_L$. Suppose $P \approx_L Q$ and $P \stackrel{\overline{a}(x)}{\longrightarrow} P'$. Let R be $(y)a[y].b[y]$ for some fresh b. Then $P|R \stackrel{bx}{\Longrightarrow} P'|\mathbf{0}$. It follows that Q' exists such that $Q|R \stackrel{bx}{\Longrightarrow} Q'|\mathbf{0}$ and $P' \approx_L Q'$. The rest of the argument is similar to that given in the proof of Theorem 7. In $Q|R \stackrel{bx}{\Longrightarrow} Q'|\mathbf{0}$ only the reduction $\stackrel{bx}{\longrightarrow}$ causally depends on the communication involving R. So this particular communication can be delayed to happen just before the action involving b. It can then be easily seen that $Q \stackrel{\overline{a}(x)}{\Longrightarrow} Q'$. To help understand the idea. Let's see an example. Suppose Q is $(x)(\overline{a}[x]|Q_1)$. Then

$$\begin{aligned}(x)(\overline{a}[x]|Q_1)|(y)a[y].b[y] &\Longrightarrow (x)(\overline{a}[x]|Q_2)|(y)a[y].b[y]\\ &\longrightarrow (x)((\mathbf{0}|Q_2)|b[x])\\ &\stackrel{bx}{\Longrightarrow} (\mathbf{0}|Q_3)|\mathbf{0} \equiv Q'|\mathbf{0}.\end{aligned}$$

Clearly $(x)(\overline{a}[x]|Q_1) \Longrightarrow (x)(\overline{a}[x]|Q_3) \stackrel{\overline{a}(x)}{\longrightarrow} \mathbf{0}|Q_3 \equiv Q'$. □

The bisimulation lattice of the asynchronous asymmetric χ-calculus is pictured by the diagram in Fig. 5.

8 Final Remark

The χ-calculus is meant to be a concurrent generalization of λ-calculus. In the latter the variables are uniform in the sense that both free and closed variables can be instantiated by any term. Free and closed variables become global and local names in our model. In this way the names in χ-calculus behave very much like logical variables. This is not at all surprising as the calculus is designed with proof theory in mind. At the level of operational semantics, the computation-as-cut-elimination is a well accepted approach in the world of λ-calculus and its descendants but has attracted far less attention in process algebra. The χ-calculus advocates this approach and invites further study of it.

The L-bisimilarities are introduced as possible classification of bisimilarities on χ-processes. In both χ and its asymmetric version, open bisimilarity and barbed bisimilarity are respectively the bottom and the top elements of the bisimulation lattices. Other well-known bisimilarities also fit into the lattice hierarchy. For instance, ground bisimilarity coincides with $\approx_{o\cup\bar{o}}$.

The fact that the barbed bisimilarity on χ-processes is different from the obvious bisimilarity called open bisimilarity in this paper was first discovered in [6]. In present paper the difference is recast in the framework of L-bisimilarity. The barbed bisimilarity on χ-processes has some very interesting and unusual properties unknown from the study of π-processes. Our result implies that weak barbed congruence and weak hyperequivalence on Fusion processes are different.

The operational semantics of χ defined in this paper is slightly different from that given in [4]. In that paper the reduction

$$a[x].P|\overline{a}[x].Q \xrightarrow{\tau} P|Q$$

is not admissible although

$$(x)(a[x].P|\overline{a}[x].Q) \xrightarrow{\tau} (x)(P|Q)$$

is legal. It should be pointed out that if this restricted communication mechanism is adopted, the elements of the bisimulation lattices discussed in this paper would proliferate. For instance the bisimulation lattice of asymmetric χ-processes would have eighteen elements, the reason being that $\approx_{fo}$ is different from $\approx_i$ in this variant for the same reason that $\approx_{fi}$ is different from $\approx_i$.

In our definition of L-bisimilarities, an update transition $P \xrightarrow{[y/x]} P'$ is required to be matched up by $Q \stackrel{[y/x]}{\Longrightarrow} Q'$ such that $P' \approx_L Q'$. This is correct because we use an early semantics. In late semantics we must replace $P' \approx_L Q'$ by $P'[y/x] \approx_L Q'[y/x]$. A simple example suffices to explain the situation. Let R be $[y|x].(x[x]|\overline{y}[y].c[c])$ where all names are assumed to be distinct. Then $[y|x].c[c]+R \approx_L R$. In late semantics there is no R' such that $R \stackrel{[y/x]}{\Longrightarrow} R' \approx_L c[c]$.

In a sense, axiomatization is internalization. Usually a meta-operation is internalized as choice operator and a meta-judgement is internalized as match combinator in calculi of mobile processes. The simplicity of the axiomatization systems for χ-processes is due to the fact that, unlike in π-calculus, one does not have the trouble of having to treat localization operator separately by resorting to distinction. In χ-calculus, if a local name can be 'opened up' it is open for all instantiations. The work reported in this paper was carried out independently with [15]. As far as axiomatization is concerned, the novelty of our result is a complete system for barbed congruence. We believe that by adding a modified version of the output law O3 to Parrow and Victor's axiom system for weak hyperequivalence we get a complete system for the weak barbed congruence on finite Fusion processes.

An interesting avenue for further investigation is axiomatization of asymmetric χ-processes. We have already obtained complete systems for some of the twelve L-congruence relations. The rest appears more subtle.

References

1. Amadio, R., Castellani, I., Sangiorgi, D.: On Bisimulation for the Asynchronous π-Calculus. CONCUR'96, Lecture Notes in Computer Science 1119 (1996)
2. Boudol, G.: Asynchrony and the π-Calculus. Research Report 1702, INRIA, Sophia-Antipolis (1992)
3. Fu, Y.: The χ-Calculus. Proceedings of the International Conference on Advances in Parallel and Distributed Computing, March 19th-21th, Shanghai, IEEE Computer Society Press (1997) 74-81
4. Fu, Y.: A Proof Theoretical Approach to Communications. ICALP'97, July 7th-11th, Bologna, Italy, Lecture Notes in Computer Science 1256 (1997) 325–335
5. Fu, Y.: Reaction Graph. To appear in Journal of Computer Science and Technology (1998)
6. Fu, Y.: Variations on Mobile Processes. To appear in Theoretical Computer Science, Elsevier Science Publisher
7. Hennessy, M., Milner, R.: Algebraic Laws for Nondeterminism and Concurrency. Journal of ACM **67** (1985) 137–161
8. Honda, K., Tokoro, M.: An Object Calculus for Asynchronous Communication. ECOOP '91, Geneve, Lecture Notes in Computer Science (1991)
9. Merro, M.: On the Expressiveness of Chi, Update and Fusion Calculus. Express'98 (1998)
10. Milner, R.: Communication and Concurrency. Prentice Hall (1989)
11. Milner, R., Parrow, J., Walker, D.: A Calculus of Mobile Processes. Information and Computation **100** (1992) Part I:1–40, Part II:41–77
12. Milner, R., Sangiorgi, D.: Barbed Bisimulation. ICALP'92, Lecture Notes in Computer Science 623 (1992) 685–695
13. Parrow, J., Victor, B.: The Update Calculus. Proceedings of AMAST'97, Sydney, December 13-17 (1997)
14. Parrow, J., Victor, B.: The Fusion Calculus: Expressiveness and Symmetry in Mobile Processes. To appear in LICS'98 (1998)
15. Parrow, J., Victor, B.: The Tau-Laws of Fusion. To appear in CONCUR'98 (1998)
16. Sangiorgi, D.: A Theory of Bisimulation for π-Calculus. CONCUR'93, Lecture Notes in Computer Science 715 (1993)
17. Victor, B., Parrow, J.: Concurrent Constraints in the Fusion Calculus. To appear in ICALP'98 (1998)

Eventuality in LOTOS with a Disjunction Operator

Yoshinao Isobe, Yutaka Sato, and Kazuhito Ohmaki

Electrotechnical Laboratory
1-1-4 Umezono, Tsukuba, Ibaraki 305-8568, Japan
{isobe|ysato|ohmaki}@etl.go.jp

Abstract. *LOTOS* is a formal specification language, designed for the precise description of open distributed systems and protocols. Our purpose is to introduce the operators of logics (for example, disjunction, conjunction, greatest fixpoint, least fixpoint in μ-calculus) into (basic) LOTOS, in order to describe *flexible* specifications. *Disjunction operators* $\vee$ have been already proposed for expressing two or more implementations in a flexible pecification. In this paper, we propose an extended LOTOS with *two state operators*. They can control recursive behavior, in order to express *eventuality*. The eventuality is useful for *liveness properties* that something good *must* eventually happen. Then, we present a method for checking the consistency of a number of flexible specifications, and a method for producing a *conjunction specification* of them.

1 Introduction

The design of large scale distributed systems is known to be a complex task. In order to support the design, formal description techniques (FDTs) are used for verifying that a realized system conforms to its specification. Process algebra such as CCS[12], CSP[4], and LOTOS[17] is one of FDTs, and especially LOTOS is standardized by ISO.

In practise, *flexible specifications* are often given to a system instead of its complete specification in the first design step, and the flexible specifications are refined step by step, for reducing the number of possible implementations. In this case, a flexible specification represents two or more various implementations, however a specification described in process algebra usually represents only one implementation except equivalent implementations with it.

In order to describe such flexible specifications, disjunction operators $\vee$ have been proposed by Steen et al.[14] for LOTOS and independently by us[5] for Basic CCS. These operators are similar to a disjunction operator in logic, and if P_1 is an implementation of a specification S_1 and P_2 is an implementation of a specification S_2, then the specification $S_1 \vee S_2$ can be implemented by either P_1 or P_2, where an implementation is formally an specification expression which does not contain disjunction operators (i.e. it is executable). It is important to note that non-determinism of CSP can not always play the disjunction instead

Jieh Hsiang, Atsushi Ohori (Eds.): ASIAN'98, LNCS 1538, pp. 263–281, 1998.

of $\vee$, because specifications can contain non-determinism, such as for gambling machines or timeout (see [14]).

For example, the following specification AB represents implementations which can iteratively perform the action a or can stop after the action b.

$$AB := a; AB \vee b; \mathbf{stop}$$

where ; is a prefix operator, thus $a; AB$ requires its implementations that they can perform a and thereafter conform to the specification AB. The symbol := is used for defining the left *Constant* AB as the right specification, thus it is a recursive definition. In this case, the disjunction $\vee$ is recursively resolved. Therefore, all the following implementations satisfy the specification AB.

$$A_\infty := a; A_\infty, \qquad AB_0 := b; \mathbf{stop}, \qquad AB_2 := a; a; b; \mathbf{stop}$$

In the above example, the action b can not be always performed in implementations satisfying AB, because A_∞ satisfies AB.

Designers often require that something good *must* eventually happen, namely a *liveness property*. For example, if the above action b must eventually happen, then how is AB modified? An answer is to use an *infinite* disjunction (intuitively, like $\bigvee_{(n>0)} a^n; b; \mathbf{stop}$), but the infinity complicates integration, verification, et al. of flexible specifications.

In this paper, we propose to use two kinds of stats, called *stable states* and *unstable states*, in order to express eventuality. Intuitively, disjunction operators must be resolved so that a stable state is eventually selected. For example, the following specification AB' represents implementations which can perform finite a and *must eventually* stop after b.

$$AB' := \triangleleft a; AB' \vee \circ b; \mathbf{stop}$$

where $\triangleleft$ and $\circ$ are called an *un-stabilizer* and a *stabilizer*, and they make an unstable stable sate ($\triangleleft a; AB$) and a stable state ($\circ b; \mathbf{stop}$), respectively. Thus, ($\triangleleft a; AB$) makes it impossible to infinitely select the action a. Consequently, the above AB_0 and AB_2 satisfy AB', but A_∞ does not satisfy AB'.

The outline of this paper is as follows. In Section 2, we propose an extended labelled transition system called μLTS, by introducing unstable states into the ALTS[14]. The ALTS is an labelled transition system (LTS) extended by adding *unlabeled transitions* for disjunction operators. Then, we define a specification language called μLOTOS based on the μLTS. In Section 3, a satisfaction relation between an implementation and a specification is defined, and the properties of unstable states are shown. In Section 4, we present a method for checking the consistency of a number of specifications, and a method for producing a conjunction specification of them. In Section 5, we discuss related works. In Appendix, a table of the notations used in this paper is given.

2 Definition of Specifications

In this section, we present a specification language called μLOTOS for describing flexible specifications. In order to concisely explain our main ideas, we will only consider a small subset of the operators of LOTOS in this paper, but it is not difficult to introduce the other operators into μLOTOS.

In Subsection 2.1, the syntax of μLOTOS is defined. In Subsection 2.2, a μLTS is given, and then the semantics of μLOTOS is defined.

2.1 Syntax

We assume that a finite set of *names* $\mathcal{N}$ is given. The set of actions *Act* is defined as $Act = \mathcal{N} \cup \{i\}$ and $\alpha, \beta, \cdots$ are used to range over *Act*, where i is a special action called an *internal action* ($i \notin \mathcal{N}$). We give a set of *state operators* $\Psi = \{\circ, \triangleleft\}$, where $\circ$ is called a *stabilizer* and $\triangleleft$ is called an *un-stabilizer*. The set Ψ is ranged over by $\psi, \phi, \cdots$.

We also assume that a set of *specification constants* (also called *Constants*) $\mathcal{K}$ and a set of *specification variables* (also called *Variables*) $\mathcal{X}$ are given. The set $\mathcal{K}$ is ranged over by $A, B, \cdots$, and the set $\mathcal{X}$ is ranged over by $X, Y, \cdots$.

Then, the syntax of μLOTOS is defined.

Definition 21 *We define* specification expressions M *with the following syntax:*

$$M ::= A \mid X \mid \textbf{stop} \mid \psi\alpha; M \mid M \,[]\, M \mid M \,|[G]|\, M \mid M \vee M$$

where $A \in \mathcal{K}$, $X \in \mathcal{X}$, $\psi \in \Psi$, $\alpha \in Act$, *and* $G \subseteq \mathcal{N}$. *The set of all the specification expressions is denoted by* $\mathcal{M}$ *and* $M, N, \cdots$ *range over* $\mathcal{M}$. *The operators* ; , $[]$, $|[G]|$, *and* $\vee$ *are called a* Prefix, *a* Choice, *a* Parallel, *and a* Disjunction, *respectively.* □

The difference between the Choice operator $[]$ and the Disjunction operator $\vee$ is intuitively explained as follows. For the Choice, users decide whether $M \,[]\, N$ behaves like either M or N at run time, i.e. a dynamic choice. For the Disjunction, designers decide whether $M \vee N$ is implemented by either M or N in specification phase, i.e. a static choice. Thus, Disjunctions are used only in specifications and does not remain in implementations.

The Parallel operator $|[G]|$ of LOTOS synchronizes actions included in G and independently performs the other actions. This can synchronize three or more specifications.

We write $Var(M)$ for the set of Variables occurring in the specification expression M, and it is inductively defined as follows :

$$\begin{array}{ll} Var(A) = \emptyset, & Var(\psi\alpha; M) = Var(M), \\ Var(\textbf{stop}) = \emptyset, & Var(M \; op \; N) = Var(M) \cup Var(N), \\ Var(X) = \{X\}, & \end{array}$$

where *op* is $[]$ or $|[G]|$ or $\vee$. A specification expression M is called a *specification*, if it contains no Variables (i.e. $Var(M) = \emptyset$). The set of specifications is denoted by $\mathcal{S}$, and it is ranged over by $S, T, U, \cdots$.

A Constant is a specification whose meaning is given by a defining equation. We assume that for every Constant $A \in \mathcal{K}$, there is a defining equation of the form $A := S$, where S is a specification which can contain Constants again. Thus, it is a recursive definition. We assume that recursion must be guarded by Prefixes, such as $A := \circ a; A$. For example, we do not consider $A := A \,[\!]\, \circ a.\mathbf{stop}$.

The state operators $\circ$ and $\triangleleft$ make stable states and unstable states. A stable state corresponds to a state in standard LOTOS. If every un-stabilizer $\triangleleft$ is replaced with a stabilizer $\circ$, then μLOTOS is the same as the language of [14]. Note that stabilizer $\circ$ is often omitted. For example, $\circ\alpha; M$ is written as $\alpha; M$.

A specification which neither contains Disjunctions nor un-stabilizers, is called a *process* or an *implementation*. Thus, the set of processes $\mathcal{P}$ is a subset of $\mathcal{S}$, and the syntax is defined in terms of the following BNF expression:

$$P ::= A \mid \mathbf{stop} \mid \circ\alpha; P \mid P \,[\!]\, P \mid P|[G]|P$$

where $A \in \mathcal{K}_P \subseteq \mathcal{K}$, $\alpha \in Act$, and $G \subseteq \mathcal{N}$. We assume that for every Constant $A \in \mathcal{K}_P$, there is a defining equation of the form $A := P$, where $P \in \mathcal{P}$. The set $\mathcal{P}$ is ranged over by $P, Q, \cdots$.

In order to avoid too many parentheses, operators have binding power in the following order: Prefix > Parallel > Choice > Disjunction. We also use the following short notations:

$$\sum \mathcal{C} \equiv \begin{cases} \mathbf{stop} & (\mathcal{C} = \emptyset) \\ M_1 \,[\!]\, M_2 \,[\!]\, \cdots \,[\!]\, M_n & (\mathcal{C} = \{M_1, \cdots, M_n\}) \end{cases}$$

$$\bigvee \mathcal{C} \equiv \begin{cases} \mathbf{F} & (\mathcal{C} = \emptyset) \\ M_1 \vee M_2 \vee \cdots \vee M_n & (\mathcal{C} = \{M_1, \cdots, M_n\}) \end{cases}$$

where $\mathcal{C}$ is a finite subset of specifications and the relation $\equiv$ represents syntactic identity. $\mathbf{F}$ is a specification constant defined as follows:

$$\mathbf{F} := \triangleleft i; \mathbf{F}$$

where i is an internal action. Intuitively, no process satisfies $\mathbf{F}$, because $\mathbf{F}$ has only one unstable state. On the other hand, a specification constant $\mathbf{T}$ which is satisfied by all the processes is defined as follows:

$$\mathbf{T} := \bigvee \{ \sum \{\circ\alpha; \mathbf{T} \;:\; \alpha \in \mathcal{A}\} \;:\; \mathcal{A} \subseteq Act\}$$

The formal properties of $\mathbf{F}$ and $\mathbf{T}$ are shown in Proposition 32 in Section 3.

2.2 Semantics

At first, we propose an extended labelled transition system called μLTS, by introducing unstable states into the ALTS[14]. The ALTS is a labelled transition system (LTS) with unlabeled transitions. The difference between the μLTS and the ALTS is that the μLTS has the set $\bigcirc$ of stable states. In other words, if $\bigcirc$ is the set of all the states, then the μLTS is the same as the ALTS.

Definition 22 *A* μLTS *is a structure* $\langle ST, L, \rightarrow, \mapsto, \bigcirc \rangle$, *where* ST *is a set of states,* L *is a set of labels,* $\rightarrow \subseteq ST \times L \times ST$ *is a set of labelled transitions,* $\mapsto \subseteq ST \times ST$ *is a set of unlabelled transitions, and* $\bigcirc \subseteq ST$ *is a* set of stable states. *As a notational convention, we write* $s \xrightarrow{\alpha} s'$ *for* $(s, \alpha, s') \in \rightarrow$ *and* $s \mapsto s'$ *for* $(s, s') \in \mapsto$. □

In μLTS, stable states are defined as follows: a state $s \in \mathcal{ST}$ is *stable* if and only if either $s \in \bigcirc$ or $s \mapsto s' \not\rightarrow$ for all s', where $s \not\rightarrow$ means that there is no pair (α, s') such that $s \xrightarrow{\alpha} s'$. So, a stop $s \mapsto s' \not\rightarrow$ is stable, even if $s \notin \bigcirc$.

The semantics of μLOTOS is given by the μLTS $\langle \mathcal{M}, Act, \rightarrow, \mapsto, \bigcirc \rangle$, where $\rightarrow$ is defined in Definition 23, $\mapsto$ is defined in Definition 24, and $\bigcirc$ is defined in Definition 25. *In this paper, we consider only specification expressions with finite states.*

Definition 23 *The labelled transition relation* $\rightarrow \subseteq \mathcal{M} \times Act \times \mathcal{M}$ *is the smallest relation satisfying the following inference rules.*

Name	*Hypothesis*	$\vdash$	*Conclusion*
Act		$\vdash$	$\psi\alpha; M \xrightarrow{\alpha} M$
Con	$S \xrightarrow{\alpha} S'$, $A := S$	$\vdash$	$A \xrightarrow{\alpha} S'$
$\mathbf{Ch}_1$	$M \xrightarrow{\alpha} M'$	$\vdash$	$M \,[\,]\, N \xrightarrow{\alpha} M'$
$\mathbf{Ch}_2$	$N \xrightarrow{\alpha} N'$	$\vdash$	$M \,[\,]\, N \xrightarrow{\alpha} N'$
$\mathbf{Par}_1$	$M \xrightarrow{\alpha} M'$, $\alpha \notin G$	$\vdash$	$M \,\lvert[G]\rvert\, N \xrightarrow{\alpha} M' \,\lvert[G]\rvert\, N$
$\mathbf{Par}_2$	$N \xrightarrow{\alpha} N'$, $\alpha \notin G$	$\vdash$	$M \,\lvert[G]\rvert\, N \xrightarrow{\alpha} M \,\lvert[G]\rvert\, N'$
$\mathbf{Par}_3$	$M \xrightarrow{\alpha} M'$, $N \xrightarrow{\alpha} N'$, $\alpha \in G$	$\vdash$	$M \,\lvert[G]\rvert\, N \xrightarrow{\alpha} M' \,\lvert[G]\rvert\, N'$

□

Definition 24 *The unlabelled transition relation* $\mapsto\ \subseteq \mathcal{M} \times \mathcal{M}$ *is the smallest relation satisfying the following inference rules.*

Name	*Hypothesis*	$\vdash$	*Conclusion*
$\mathbf{Act}_\vee$		$\vdash$	$\psi\alpha; M \mapsto \psi\alpha; M$
$\mathbf{Stop}_\vee$		$\vdash$	$\mathbf{stop} \mapsto \mathbf{stop}$
$\mathbf{Con}_\vee$	$S \mapsto S'$, $A := S$	$\vdash$	$A \mapsto S'$
$\mathbf{Ch}_\vee$	$M \mapsto M'$, $N \mapsto N'$	$\vdash$	$M \,[\,]\, N \mapsto M' \,[\,]\, N'$
$\mathbf{Par}_\vee$	$M \mapsto M'$, $N \mapsto N'$	$\vdash$	$M \,\lvert[G]\rvert\, N \mapsto M' \,\lvert[G]\rvert\, N'$
$\mathbf{Dis}_1$	$M \mapsto M'$	$\vdash$	$M \vee N \mapsto M'$
$\mathbf{Dis}_2$	$N \mapsto N'$	$\vdash$	$M \vee N \mapsto N'$

□

Definition 25 *The set of stable states* $\bigcirc \subseteq \mathcal{M}$ *is the smallest relation satisfying the following inference rules.*

Name	*Hypothesis*	$\vdash$	*Conclusion*
$\mathbf{Act}_\circ$		$\vdash$	$\circ\alpha; M \in \bigcirc$
$\mathbf{Stop}_\circ$		$\vdash$	$\mathbf{stop} \in \bigcirc$
$\mathbf{Con}_\circ$	$S \in \bigcirc$, $A := S$	$\vdash$	$A \in \bigcirc$
$\mathbf{Ch}_\circ$	$M \in \bigcirc$, $N \in \bigcirc$	$\vdash$	$M \,[\,]\, N \in \bigcirc$
$\mathbf{Par}_\circ$	$M \in \bigcirc$, $N \in \bigcirc$	$\vdash$	$M \,\lvert[G]\rvert\, N \in \bigcirc$
$\mathbf{Dis}_\circ$	$M \in \bigcirc$, $N \in \bigcirc$	$\vdash$	$M \vee N \in \bigcirc$

□

The rules for labelled transitions $\longrightarrow$ is exactly same as the rules in standard LOTOS, except ψ in **Act**. The state operator ψ does not affect $\longrightarrow$.

Unstable states can be made from un-stabilizers $\triangleleft$, because there is no rule for $\triangleleft\alpha; M$ in Definition 25. It is noted that there are stable state M, even if $M \notin \bigcirc$. For example, the specification $S \equiv (\triangleleft a; S_1 \,|[a,b]|\, \circ b; S_2)$ is stable, because $S \mapsto S' \not\mapsto$ for all S', although $S \notin \bigcirc$.

Unlabelled transitions $\mapsto$ [14,5] are used for resolving disjunction operators, as shown in the rules $\mathbf{Dis}_{1,2}$. Intuitively, a process P satisfies a specification S, if and only if $S \mapsto S'$ and P satisfies S' for some specification S'. For example, the following specification VM of a vending machine can be implemented by either $(coin; coffee; \mathbf{stop})$ or $(coin; tea; \mathbf{stop})$,

$$VM := (coin; coffee; \mathbf{stop}) \vee (coin; tea; \mathbf{stop})$$

because $VM \mapsto (coin; coffee; \mathbf{stop})$ and $VM \mapsto (coin; tea; \mathbf{stop})$.

The definition of $\mapsto$ is slightly changed from [14]. In our definition, all the specification can perform unlabelled transitions, and it is not necessary to *successively* perform unlabelled transitions twice. Formally, the following proposition holds, where $\mathcal{M}_0$ is the set of specification expressions which do not change states by unlabelled transitions, thus $\mathcal{M}_0 = \{M : \{M' : M \mapsto M'\} = \{M\}\}$.

Proposition 21 *If $M \mapsto M'$, then $M' \in \mathcal{M}_0$.*

Proof By induction on the length of the inference of $M \mapsto M'$. We show only one case by $\mathbf{Par}_\vee$, here. By $\mathbf{Par}_\vee$, $M \mapsto M'$ implies that for some M_1, M_2, M_1', M_2', and G, $M \equiv M_1 \,|[G]|\, M_2$, $M' \equiv M_1' \,|[G]|\, M_2'$, $M_1 \mapsto M_1'$, and $M_2 \mapsto M_2'$. Thus, by induction, $M_1' \in \mathcal{M}_0$ and $M_2' \in \mathcal{M}_0$. These imply that if $M' \equiv M_1' \,|[G]|\, M_2' \mapsto M''$, then $M'' \equiv M_1' \,|[G]|\, M_2'$ by $\mathbf{Par}_\vee$. Hence, $M' \in \mathcal{M}_0$. □

In the rest of this paper, $\mathcal{M}_0$ (which is a subset of $\mathcal{M}$) is ranged over by $M_0, N_0, \cdots$. And also, we use $\mathcal{S}_0$ to denote the set of M_0 which contain no Variables, thus $\mathcal{S}_0 = \mathcal{S} \cap \mathcal{M}_0$, and $\mathcal{S}_0$ is ranged over by $S_0, T_0, \cdots$.

3 Satisfaction

In this section, we define a satisfaction $P \models S$ of a process P for a specification S as an extension of the satisfaction $P \models_{[14]} S$ in [14]. The definition of $\models_{[14]}$ has been given as follows: the satisfaction $\models_{[14]}$ is the largest relation such that, $P \models_{[14]} S$ implies that for some S_0, $S \mapsto S_0$ and for all $\alpha \in Act$ the following two conditions hold:

(*i*.[14]) if $P \xrightarrow{\alpha} P'$ then, for some S', $S_0 \xrightarrow{\alpha} S'$ and $P' \models_{[14]} S'$,
(*ii*.[14]) if $S_0 \xrightarrow{\alpha} S'$ then, for some P', $P \xrightarrow{\alpha} P'$ and $P' \models_{[14]} S'$.

This requires that there exists an S_0 which satisfies (*i*.[14]) and (*ii*.[14]). This makes it possible that a specification can be satisfied by two or more various processes. As shown in Proposition 21, S_0 can not be resolved any more by

$\mapsto$, but it may be resolved again after an labelled transition $S_0 \xrightarrow{\alpha} S'$. Therefore, the definition of the satisfaction is inductive. For example, the specification $(a; (b; \mathbf{stop} \vee c; \mathbf{stop}) \vee d; \mathbf{stop})$ can be implemented by either $(a; b; \mathbf{stop})$, or $(a; c; \mathbf{stop})$, or $(a; b; \mathbf{stop} \,[]\, a; c; \mathbf{stop})$, or $(d; \mathbf{stop})$.

In the definition of $\models_{[14]}$, the specification S_0 can be freely selected from $\{S_0 : S \mapsto S_0\}$. On the other hand, we can control the selection by state operators $\circ$ and $\triangleleft$. The key point is that S must eventually reach a stable state. Then, our satisfaction is defined as follows.

Definition 31 *A relation* $\mathcal{R} \subseteq \mathcal{P} \times \mathcal{S}$ *is a* satisfaction relation, *if* $(P, S) \in \mathcal{R}$ *implies* $(P, S) \in \theta(\mathcal{R})$, *where* $\theta(\mathcal{R}) \subseteq \mathcal{P} \times \mathcal{S}$ *is inductively defined for any relation* $\mathcal{R}$, *as follows:*

- $(P, S) \in \theta^{(0)}(\mathcal{R})$ *iff for some* S_0, $S \mapsto S_0$, $S_0 \in \bigcirc$, *and for all* $\alpha \in Act$,

  (*i*) *if* $P \xrightarrow{\alpha} P'$ *then, for some* S', $S_0 \xrightarrow{\alpha} S'$ *and* $(P', S') \in \mathcal{R}$,
  (*ii*) *if* $S_0 \xrightarrow{\alpha} S'$ *then, for some* P', $P \xrightarrow{\alpha} P'$ *and* $(P', S') \in \mathcal{R}$,

- $(P, S) \in \theta^{(n+1)}(\mathcal{R})$ *iff for some* S_0, $S \mapsto S_0$ *and for all* $\alpha \in Act$,

(*i*) *if* $P \xrightarrow{\alpha} P'$ *then, for some* (m, S'), $S_0 \xrightarrow{\alpha} S'$, $(P', S') \in \theta^{(m)}(\mathcal{R})$, $m \leq n$,
(*ii*) *if* $S_0 \xrightarrow{\alpha} S'$ *then, for some* (m, P'), $P \xrightarrow{\alpha} P'$, $(P', S') \in \theta^{(m)}(\mathcal{R})$, $m \leq n$,

- $(P, S) \in \theta(\mathcal{R})$ *iff* $(P, S) \in \theta^{(n)}(\mathcal{R})$, *for some* n. □

Definition 32 P satisfies S, *written* $P \models S$, *if* $(P, S) \in \mathcal{R}$, *for some satisfaction relation* $\mathcal{R}$. (i.e. $\models$ is the relation $\bigcup\{\mathcal{R} : \mathcal{R}$ is a satisfaction relation$\}$). *We use the notation* $Proc(S)$ *for the set of all the processes which satisfy the specification* S (i.e. $Proc(S) = \{P : P \models S\}$). □

The relation $\models$ is the largest satisfaction relation, and we can prove that $P \models S$ if and only if $(P, S) \in \theta(\models)$. $P \models S$ requires that S must reach a stable state S_0 after finite transitions, where P and S must keep the relation $\models$. It is noted that if $P \not\rightarrow$ and $S \mapsto S_0 \not\rightarrow$ for some S_0, then $(P, S) \in \theta^{(1)}(\models)$, even if $S_0 \notin \bigcirc$, because S_0 is stable. For example, $(\mathbf{stop}, \triangleleft a; S_1 \,|[a, b]|\, \circ b; S_2) \in \theta^{(1)}(\models)$.

The following relations between $\models$ and $\models_{[14]}$ can be easily shown.

- if $P \models S$, then $P \models_{[14]} S$.
- if $P \models_{[14]} S$ and S has only stable states, then $P \models S$

The important proposition for the Disjunction $\vee$ shown in [14] holds also for our satisfaction.

Proposition 31 *Let* $S, T \in \mathcal{S}$. *Then* $Proc(S \vee T) = Proc(S) \cup Proc(T)$.
Proof This is similar to the proof of Proposition 7 in [14]. □

In Subsection 2.1, we defined two special specifications **T** and **F**. Two propositions for **T** and **F** are given: Proposition 32 shows that all the processes satisfy **T** and no process satisfies **F**. Proposition 33 shows the properties for substitution, where the notation $M\{N/X\}$ indicates the substitution of N for every occurrence of the Variable X in M, and the notation $\tilde{M}$ is an indexed set $M_1, \cdots, M_n$. For example, $\{\tilde{S}/\tilde{X}\}$ represents $\{S_1/X_1, S_2/X_2, \cdots, S_n/X_n\}$, and $\{\mathbf{T}/\tilde{X}\}$ represents $\{\mathbf{T}/X_1, \mathbf{T}/X_2, \cdots, \mathbf{T}/X_n\}$.

Proposition 32 (1) *Proc*(**T**) $= \mathcal{S}$ *and* (2) *Proc*(**F**) $= \emptyset$.
Proof (1) **T** has only stable states and any combination of actions ($\mathcal{A} \subseteq Act$) can be selected by $\mapsto$ from **T**. (2) **F** has only one unstable state, because $\triangleleft i; \mathbf{F} \notin \bigcirc$ and **F** has always a transition by i. □

Proposition 33 *Let M contain Variables $\tilde{X}$ at most. For any $\tilde{S} \in \mathcal{S}$, the following relations hold.*

1. $Proc(M\{\tilde{S}/\tilde{X}\}) \subseteq Proc(M\{\mathbf{T}/\tilde{X}\})$.
2. $Proc(M\{\mathbf{F}/\tilde{X}\}) \subseteq Proc(M\{\tilde{S}/\tilde{X}\})$.

Proof (outline)

1. We can show that the following $\mathcal{R}$ is a satisfaction relation.
$$\mathcal{R} = \{(P,T) : \exists S, P \models S, T \in TR(S), P \in \mathcal{P}, S \in \mathcal{S}\} \cup \models$$
where $TR(S)$ is the set of all the specifications obtained from the specification S by replacing some subexpressions of S by **T**.
2. We can show that the following $\mathcal{R}$ is a satisfaction relation.
$$\mathcal{R} = \{(P, M\{\tilde{S}/\tilde{X}\}) : P \models M\{\mathbf{F}/\tilde{X}\}, P \in \mathcal{P}, S \in \mathcal{S}\} \cup \models$$
For this proof, the following property is used : If $M\{\mathbf{F}/\tilde{X}\} \mapsto T_0$ and $P \models T_0$, then for some M_0, $M \mapsto M_0$, $T_0 \equiv M_0\{\mathbf{F}/\tilde{X}\}$, M_0 is guarded, and for any $\tilde{S}$, $M\{\tilde{S}/\tilde{X}\} \mapsto M_0\{\tilde{S}/\tilde{X}\}$ □

Next, we show examples of $P \models S$. At first, consider the following process *PAB* and the specification *SAB*:

$$PAB := a; a; b; PAB \qquad SAB := \triangleleft a; SAB \vee \circ b; SAB$$

In the specification *SAB*, only ($\circ b$; *SAB*) is stable. Thus, *SAB* requires that the action b must always eventually be performed, although the action a may be performed zero or more times before b. In this case, we can show that $PAB \models SAB$, because the following $\mathcal{R}$ is a satisfaction relation,

$$\mathcal{R} = \{(PAB, SAB), (a; b; PAB, SAB), (b; PAB, SAB)\}$$

because $(PAB, SAB) \in \theta^{(2)}(\mathcal{R})$, $(a; b; PAB, SAB) \in \theta^{(1)}(\mathcal{R})$, and $(b; PAB, SAB) \in \theta^{(0)}(\mathcal{R})$.

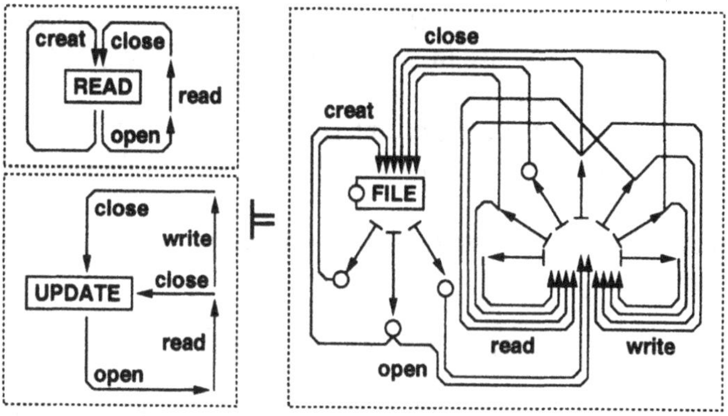

Fig. 1. The transition graphs of *READ*, *UPDATE*, and *FILE* (∘ : a stable state)

Secondly, the following specification *FILE* is considered.

$$FILE := open; OPENED \times creat; FILE$$
$$OPENED := \lhd write; OPENED \times \lhd read; OPENED \times close; FILE$$

where $M \times N$ is the short notation defined as follows.

$$M \times N \equiv M \vee N \vee (M \,[\,]\, N)$$

The specification *OPENED* requires that the action *close* must be eventually performed, because of the un-stabilizers of $\lhd write$ and $\lhd read$. Thus, this specification *FILE* requires that a file must be eventually closed by the action *close* after opened by the action *open*, and/or that a file can be created by the action *creat*. The subexpression ($\lhd write; OPENED \times \lhd read; OPENED$) permits that actions *write* and *read* are inserted after *open* and before *close*. For example, *FILE* can be implemented by the following processes *READ* or *UPDATE* (i.e. $READ \models FILE$ and $UPDATE \models FILE$).

$$READ := open; read; close; READ \,[\,]\, creat; READ$$
$$UPDATE := open; read; (close; UPDATE \,[\,]\, write; close; UPDATE)$$

The transition graphs of *READ*, *UPDATE*, and *FILE* are shown in Fig. 1, where each circle in *FILE* means a stable state, and unlabelled transitions which do not change states are omitted.

The un-stabilizers $\lhd$ in *OPENED* guarantee that the action *close* must be eventually performed. If the un-stabilizer of $\lhd read$ in *OPENED* is replaced by a stabilizer ∘, then *FILE* can be also implemented by the following unexpected process *READLOOP*.

$$READLOOP := open; LOOP, \qquad \text{where } LOOP := read; LOOP$$

As another example, a special case $I_S := \lhd i; I_S \vee S$ is interesting, where i is an internal action. This means that zero or more finite internal actions can be performed before S. Although the internal action is not distinguished from any other actions in Definition 31 like *strong bisimilarity*[12], it is possible by I_S to ignore finite internal actions like in *weak branching bisimilarity*[3] for convergent specifications (no internal action cycles (p.148 in [12])).

In the rest of this section, important properties of state operators $\circ$ and $\triangleleft$ are shown. At first, we define two subsets $\mathcal{M}_\nu$ and $\mathcal{M}_\mu$ of $\mathcal{M}$ as follows.

Definition 33 *The specification expressions M in $\mathcal{M}_\nu$ are defined with the following syntax:*

$$M ::= A \mid X \mid \mathbf{stop} \mid \circ\alpha; M \mid M \,[\!]\, M \mid M |[G]| M \mid M \vee M$$

where $A \in \mathcal{K}_\nu \subseteq \mathcal{K}$, $X \in \mathcal{X}$, $\alpha \in Act$, and $G \subseteq \mathcal{N}$. We assume that for every $A \in \mathcal{K}_\nu$, there is a defining equation of the form $A := P$ and $P \in \mathcal{M}_\nu$. □

Definition 34 *The specification expressions M in $\mathcal{M}_\mu$ are defined with the following syntax:*

$$M ::= X \mid S \mid \triangleleft\alpha; M \mid M \,[\!]\, M \mid M |[G]| M \mid M \vee M$$

where $S \in \mathcal{S}$, $\alpha \in Act$, and $G \subseteq \mathcal{N}$. □

It is important to note that differences between $\mathcal{M}_\nu$ and $\mathcal{M}_\mu$ are not only $\circ\alpha; M$ and $\triangleleft\alpha; M$. Every specification in $\mathcal{M}_\nu$ contains no unstable states, and $\mathcal{M}_\nu$ is the same as the language in [14]. On the other hand, $\mathcal{M}_\mu$ can contain the specification $\circ\alpha; M$, if M contains no Variable, because $\mathcal{M}_\mu$ contains $S \in \mathcal{S}$.

Then, Theorem 1 holds, where the indexed definition $\tilde{A} := \tilde{M}\{\tilde{A}/\tilde{X}\}$ represents $A_i := M_i\{A_1/X_1, \cdots, A_n/X_n\}$ for each $i \in \{1, \cdots, n\}$.

Theorem 1. *Let $\tilde{M}$ be guarded by Prefixes and contain Variables $\tilde{X}$ at most, and let $\tilde{A} := \tilde{M}\{\tilde{A}/\tilde{X}\}$.*

1. *Let $\tilde{M} \in \mathcal{M}_\nu$. $P \models M_i\{\tilde{A}/\tilde{X}\}$ if and only if $P \models M_i^{\langle n\rangle}\{\mathbf{T}/\tilde{X}\}$ for any n.*
2. *Let $\tilde{M} \in \mathcal{M}_\mu$. $P \models M_i\{\tilde{A}/\tilde{X}\}$ if and only if $P \models M_i^{\langle n\rangle}\{\mathbf{F}/\tilde{X}\}$ for some n.*

where $M_i^{\langle n\rangle}$ is the specification expression defined inductively as follows:

$$M_i^{\langle 0\rangle} \equiv X_i, \quad M_i^{\langle n+1\rangle} \equiv M_i\{\tilde{M}^{\langle n\rangle}/\tilde{X}\}$$

Proof (outline)

1. The 'only if part' is directly shown by Proposition 33(1). For the 'if part', we use another inductive definition $\bigcap_{i\geq 0} \models_{(i)}$ of $\models$, where $\models_{(0)} = \mathcal{P} \times \mathcal{S}$ and $\models_{(n+1)} = \theta(\models_{(n)})$. Then we can show that for any n, if $P \models_{(n)} N\{\tilde{M}^{\langle n\rangle}/\tilde{X}\}\{\mathbf{T}/\tilde{X}\}$, then $P \models_{(n)} N\{\tilde{M}^{\langle n\rangle}/\tilde{X}\}\{\tilde{A}/\tilde{X}\}$, where $N \in \mathcal{M}_\nu$ and N contain Variables $\tilde{X}$ at most. This is not difficult, because N and $\tilde{M}$ have no unstable states. Finally, we can set $N \equiv X_i$, then the result follows.

2. The 'if part' is directly shown by Proposition 33(2). For the 'only if part', we show that the following $\mathcal{R}$ is a satisfaction relation.

$$\begin{aligned}\mathcal{R} = \{(P, N\{\tilde{M}^{\langle n\rangle}/\tilde{X}\}\{\mathbf{F}/\tilde{X}\}) : \tilde{A} := \tilde{M}\{\tilde{A}/\tilde{X}\}, (P, N\{\tilde{A}/\tilde{X}\}) \in \theta^{(m)}(\models),\\ n \geq m, N \text{ and } \tilde{M} \text{ are guarded and contain Variables } \tilde{X} \text{ at most},\\ N \in \mathcal{M}_\mu, \tilde{M} \in \mathcal{M}_\mu\} \cup \models\end{aligned}$$

The key points are that (1) $N\{\tilde{M}^{\langle n\rangle}/\tilde{X}\}$ is still guarded after n transitions, (2) $N\{\tilde{A}/\tilde{X}\}$ must reach a stable state after m' transitions for some $m' \leq m$, because $(P, N\{\tilde{A}/\tilde{X}\}) \in \theta^{(m)}(\models)$, and (3) if $N'\{\mathbf{F}/\tilde{X}\}$ is stable and $N' \in \mathcal{M}_\mu$, then N' contains no Variables (i.e. $N'\{\mathbf{F}/\tilde{X}\} \equiv N'\{\tilde{A}/\tilde{X}\}$). □

Since we consider only finite state specifications, Theorem 1 shows that if $\tilde{M} \in \mathcal{M}_\nu$ then $\tilde{A}$ is the greatest fixpoint of recursive equations $\tilde{X} = \tilde{M}$, and if $\tilde{M} \in \mathcal{M}_\mu$ then $\tilde{A}$ is the least fixpoint of them. For example, if $M \equiv a; X \vee b; \mathbf{T}$, $A := M\{A/X\}$, and $P \models A$, then P may not perform b (i.e. may infinitely perform a), because $M \in \mathcal{M}_\nu$. On the other hand, if $M \equiv \lhd a; X \vee b; \mathbf{T}$, $A := M\{A/X\}$, and $P \models A$, then P must eventually perform b, because $M \in \mathcal{M}_\mu$.

4 Integration of Specifications

A number of flexible specifications are sometimes given to a large system instead of its complete specification, because many designers work on the same system design in parallel, and it is not easy for each designer to know the whole system. Such design method decreases responsibility of each designer, but it raises two important issues: *consistency check* of the flexible specifications and *integration* of them. In general, since the integrated specification satisfies all of them, it corresponds to a *conjunction specification* of them. The consistency and the conjunction specification are defined as follows.

Definition 41 *Let $S_i \in \mathcal{S}$. The specifications $S_1, \cdots, S_n$ are* consistent *with each other, if $\bigcap_{1\leq i\leq n} Proc(S_i) \neq \emptyset$. And the specification S is a* conjunction specification *of $S_1, \cdots, S_n$, if $Proc(S) = \bigcap_{1\leq i\leq n} Proc(S_i) \neq \emptyset$.* □

In Subsection 4.1, a relation $\sim$ is given for checking the consistency between two specifications. In Subsection 4.2, a method called the $\wedge$-method is given for producing a conjunction specification of two specifications. A conjunction specification of three or more specifications can be produced by iteratively using $\sim$ and the $\wedge$-method.

4.1 Consistency Check

In this subsection, we consider the consistency of *two* specifications. At first, a relation $\sim$ is defined as a generalized relation from the satisfaction $\models$.

Definition 42 *A relation $\mathcal{R} \subseteq \mathcal{S} \times \mathcal{S}$ is a* consistent relation, *if $(S, T) \in \mathcal{R}$ implies $(S, T) \in \Theta(\mathcal{R})$, where $\Theta(\mathcal{R}) \subseteq \mathcal{S} \times \mathcal{S}$ is inductively defined for any relation $\mathcal{R}$, as follows:*

- $(S,T) \in \Theta^{(0)}(\mathcal{R})$ *iff for some* S_0 *and* T_0, $S \mapsto S_0$, $T \mapsto T_0$, $S_0 \in \bigcirc$, $T_0 \in \bigcirc$,

  (i) *if* $S_0 \xrightarrow{\alpha} S'$ *then, for some* T', $T_0 \xrightarrow{\alpha} T'$ *and* $(S',T') \in \mathcal{R}$,
  (ii) *if* $T_0 \xrightarrow{\alpha} T'$ *then, for some* S', $S_0 \xrightarrow{\alpha} S'$ *and* $(S',T') \in \mathcal{R}$,

- $(S,T) \in \Theta^{(n+1)}(\mathcal{R})$ *iff for some* S_0 *and* T_0, $S \mapsto S_0$, $T \mapsto T_0$,

  (i) *if* $S_0 \xrightarrow{\alpha} S'$ *then, for some* (m,T'), $T_0 \xrightarrow{\alpha} T'$, $(S',T') \in \Theta^{(m)}(\mathcal{R})$, $m \leq n$,
  (ii) *if* $T_0 \xrightarrow{\alpha} T'$ *then, for some* (m,S'), $S_0 \xrightarrow{\alpha} S'$, $(S',T') \in \Theta^{(m)}(\mathcal{R})$, $m \leq n$,

- $(S,T) \in \Theta(\mathcal{R})$ *iff* $(S,T) \in \Theta^{(n)}(\mathcal{R})$, *for some* n. □

Definition 43 $S \sim T$, *if* $(S,T) \in \mathcal{R}$ *for some consistent relation* $\mathcal{R}$. □

The relation $\Theta(\mathcal{R})$ is an extension of $\theta(\mathcal{R})$ in Definition 32 to over $\mathcal{S} \times \mathcal{S}$, and we can show that $S \sim T$ if and only if $(S,T) \in \Theta(\sim)$. The relation $S \sim T$ requires that S and T must eventually reach stable states at the same time.

It is important to note that the relation $\sim$ is too strong to check the consistency between two specifications. For example, the following two specifications *SAB* and *SBA* (*SAB* was also used in Section 3) are consistent with each other,

$$SAB := \lhd a; SAB \vee \circ b; SAB, \qquad SBA := \circ a; SBA \vee \lhd b; SBA$$

because there exist processes P such that $P \models SAB$ and $P \models SBA$, for example $PAB := a; a; b; PAB$. On the other hand, $S \not\sim T$, because *SAB* and *SBA* can not reach stable states *at the same time*.

In this paper, we present a method for checking the consistency after transforming a specification into a *standard form*. At first, the following set is defined in order to define the standard form, where $Dri(S_0) = \{S' : \exists \alpha, S_0 \xrightarrow{\alpha} S'\}$.

Definition 44 *Let* $\mathcal{U} \subseteq \mathcal{S}$. *A set* $\mathcal{V} \subseteq \mathcal{S}$ *is a* pre-$\mathcal{U}$ set, *if* $S \in \mathcal{V}$ *implies that,*

(*pre*1) *if* $S \mapsto S_0 \notin \bigcirc$, *then* $Dri(S_0) \subseteq \mathcal{V}$,
(*pre*2) *if* $S \mapsto S_0 \in \bigcirc$, *then* $Dri(S_0) \subseteq \mathcal{U}$.

Then, $Pre(\mathcal{U}) = \bigcup\{\mathcal{V} : \mathcal{V}$ *is a pre-*$\mathcal{U}$ *set*$\}$. □

Then, the standard form is defined as follows, where $S \simeq T$ represents $Proc(S) = Proc(T)$.

Definition 45 *A set* $\mathcal{U} \subseteq \mathcal{S}$ *is a* standard set, *if* $S \in \mathcal{U}$ *implies that,*

(1) *if* $S \mapsto S_0 \notin \bigcirc$, *then for some* $S_0' \in \bigcirc$, $S \mapsto S_0' \simeq S_0$, $Dri(S_0') \subseteq Pre(\mathcal{U})$,
(2) *if* $S \mapsto S_0$, *then for some* S_0', $S \mapsto S_0' \simeq S_0$, $Dri(S_0') \subseteq \mathcal{U}$,
(3) *if* $S \mapsto S_0$, *then either* $Dri(S_0) \subseteq \mathcal{U}$ *or* $Dri(S_0) \subseteq Pre(\mathcal{U})$.

Then, $STD = \bigcup\{\mathcal{U} : \mathcal{U}$ *is a standard set*$\}$. □

Definition 46 *Let* $S \in \mathcal{S}$.

1. S *is in* standard form, *if* $S \in STD$.
2. S *is in* pre-standard form, *if* $S \in Pre(STD)$. □

As shown in Definition 45, if $S \in \mathit{STD}$ then for any S_0 such that $S \mapsto S_0$, for some $S_0' \in \bigcirc$ such that $S \mapsto S_0'$, $\mathit{Proc}(S_0) = \mathit{Proc}(S_0')$. And furthermore, for every derivation S' such that $S_0 \xrightarrow{\alpha} S'$, $S' \in \mathit{Pre}(\mathit{STD})$. This condition (1) makes it possible to *immediately* reach a stable state if S is in standard form, and thereafter S' must be in pre-standard form. In order to return to be in standard form, S' must eventually reach a stable state. The condition (2) requires that S *can* keep in standard form, and (3) requires that S *must* keep in either standard form or pre-standard form.

Then, a specification $\mathbf{ST}(S)$ produced form S is defined as follows.

Definition 47 *Let $S \in \mathcal{S}$. The specification $\mathbf{ST}(S)$ is defined as follows.*

$$\begin{aligned}
\mathbf{ST}(S) &:= \bigvee\{\mathit{ST}_0(S_0) : S \mapsto S_0\} \vee \{\mathit{SS}_0(S_0) : S \mapsto S_0 \notin \bigcirc\}\\
\mathbf{PST}(S) &:= \bigvee\{\mathit{ST}_0(S_0) : S \mapsto S_0 \in \bigcirc\} \vee \{\mathit{PST}_0(S_0) : S \mapsto S_0 \notin \bigcirc\}\\
\mathit{ST}_0(S_0) &\equiv \sum\{\psi\alpha; \mathbf{ST}(S') : S_0 \xrightarrow{\alpha} S', \mathit{St}(S_0) = \psi\}\\
\mathit{PST}_0(S_0) &\equiv \sum\{\psi\alpha; \mathbf{PST}(S') : S_0 \xrightarrow{\alpha} S', \mathit{St}(S_0) = \psi\}\\
\mathit{SS}_0(S_0) &\equiv \sum\{\circ\alpha; \mathbf{PST}(S') : S_0 \xrightarrow{\alpha} S'\}
\end{aligned}$$

where $\mathit{St} : \mathcal{S}_0 \to \Psi$ is a state function defined as : if $S_0 \in \bigcirc$ then $\mathit{St}(S_0) = \circ$, otherwise $\mathit{St}(S_0) = \triangleleft$. □

The specifications $\mathbf{ST}(S)$ and $\mathbf{PST}(S)$ are Constants. Since we consider only specifications S with finite states, the number of states of $\mathbf{ST}(S)$ is also finite. The key point is that $\mathbf{ST}(S)$ contains a stable state $\mathit{SS}_0(S_0)$ if $S \mapsto S_0 \notin \bigcirc$. It is important to note that the derivation of $\mathit{SS}_0(S_0)$ is $\mathbf{PST}(S')$ instead of $\mathbf{ST}(S')$. In order to return $\mathbf{ST}$, S' must eventually reach a stable state (This is similar to the requirement of STD).

Proposition 41 shows that the set of processes which satisfy S is not changed by the transformation $\mathbf{ST}$. And Proposition 42 shows that $\mathbf{ST}(S)$ is in standard form for any S. Therefore, for any specification S, we can transform S into a standard form S' such that $S \simeq S'$ by $\mathbf{ST}$.

Proposition 41 *Let $S \in \mathcal{S}$ and $S_0 \in \mathcal{S}_0$. Then*

$$\begin{aligned}
&S \simeq \mathbf{ST}(S) \simeq \mathbf{PST}(S),\\
&S_0 \simeq \mathit{ST}_0(S_0) \simeq \mathit{PST}_0(S_0) \simeq \mathit{SS}_0(S_0)
\end{aligned}$$

Proof (outline) For $S \simeq \mathbf{ST}(S) \simeq \mathbf{PST}(S)$, we can show that the following $\mathcal{R}_{1,2}$ are satisfaction relations.

$$\begin{aligned}
\mathcal{R}_1 &= \{(P, \mathbf{ST}(S)) \ : \ P \models S\} \cup \{(P, \mathbf{PST}(S)) \ : \ P \models S\}\\
\mathcal{R}_2 &= \{(P, S) \ : \ P \models \mathbf{ST}(S)\} \cup \{(P, S) \ : \ P \models \mathbf{PST}(S)\}
\end{aligned}$$

The relation $S_0 \simeq \mathit{ST}_0(S_0) \simeq \mathit{PST}_0(S_0) \simeq \mathit{SS}_0(S_0)$ can be shown by similar satisfaction relations. □

Proposition 42 *Let $S \in \mathcal{S}$. Then $\mathbf{ST}(S) \in \mathit{STD}$ and $\mathbf{PST}(S) \in \mathit{Pre}(\mathit{STD})$.*
Proof (outline) We can show that the following $\mathcal{V}$ and $\mathcal{U}$ are a pre-$\mathcal{U}$ set and a standard set, respectively : $\mathcal{V} = \{\mathbf{PST}(S) : S \in \mathcal{S}\}$ and $\mathcal{U} = \{\mathbf{ST}(S) : S \in \mathcal{S}\}$. □

The above examples *SAB* and *SBA* are used, again. The specification *SAB* is transformed by **ST** into the following specification:

$$\mathbf{ST}(SAB) := \lhd a; \mathbf{ST}(SAB) \vee \circ b; \mathbf{ST}(SAB) \vee \circ a; \mathbf{PST}(SAB)$$
$$\mathbf{PST}(SAB) := \lhd a; \mathbf{PST}(SAB) \vee \circ b; \mathbf{ST}(SAB)$$

The specification $\mathbf{ST}(SBA)$ is symmetrical with $\mathbf{ST}(SAB)$ for a and b. The state $(\circ a; \mathbf{PST}(SAB))$ is important, thus $\mathbf{ST}(SAB)$ contains a stable state which can perform the action a. This implies that $\mathbf{ST}(SAB)$ and $\mathbf{ST}(SBA)$ can reach stable states at the same time. In fact, we can prove that $\mathbf{ST}(SAB) \sim \mathbf{ST}(SBA)$.

Now, the relation $\sim$ can be used for checking the consistency of two specifications as shown in Proposition 43. The relation $\sim$ can be automatically checked by a similar algorithm to one for bisimilarity [6].

Proposition 43 *Let $S, T \in STD$. Then $S \sim T$ iff $Proc(S) \cap Proc(T) \neq \emptyset$.*
Proof ('if' part) We show that the following $\mathcal{R}$ is a consistent relation.

$$\mathcal{R} = \{(S,T) : P \models S, P \models T, S \in STD \cup Pre(STD), T \in STD \cup Pre(STD)\}$$

Let $P \models S$, $P \models T$, $S \in STD$, and $T \in STD$. Since $P \models S$, there exists S_0 such that $S \mapsto S_0$ and $P \models S_0$. Here, by Definition 45, for some $S'_0 \in \bigcirc$, $S \mapsto S'_0$ and $P \models S'_0$. Similarly, for some $T'_0 \in \bigcirc$, $T \mapsto T'_0$ and $P \models T'_0$.

For (i), let $S'_0 \xrightarrow{\alpha} S'$. Since $P \models S'_0 \in S_0$, for some P', $P \xrightarrow{\alpha} P'$ and $P' \models S'$. Furthermore, since $P \models T'_0$, for some T', $T'_0 \xrightarrow{\alpha} T'$ and $P' \models T'$. Here, by Definition 45, $S' \in STD \cup Pre(STD)$ and $T' \in STD \cup Pre(STD)$. Thus, $(S', T') \in \mathcal{R}$. For (ii), it is symmetrical. Consequently, $(S,T) \in \Theta^{(0)}(\mathcal{R})$.

For the other cases such that $S \in Pre(STD)$ and $T \in STD$, S can reach either a state $S' \in STD$ or a stop, because $P \models S$ (i.e. S must reach a stable state). Hence, these cases can be shown by induction on n of $(P,S) \in \Theta^{(n)}(\models)$.

('only if' part) Assume that $S \sim T$. By the definition of $\sim$, there exist S_0 and T_0 such that $S_0 \sim T_0$, $S \mapsto S_0$, and $T \mapsto T_0$. Then, it can be proven that the following process $\mathbf{CP}^{(n)}(S_0, T_0)$ satisfies both S_0 and T_0, where $n = |S_0, T_0| = \min\{n : (S_0, T_0) \in \Theta^{(n)}(\sim)\}$. The detail is omitted.

$$\begin{aligned}\mathbf{CP}^{(n)}(S_0,T_0) := \textstyle\sum\{\circ\alpha; \mathbf{CP}^{(n')}(S'_0,T'_0) : \exists(S',T'), |S'_0,T'_0| = n', n = 0,\\ S_0 \xrightarrow{\alpha} S' \mapsto S'_0, T_0 \xrightarrow{\alpha} T' \mapsto T'_0, S'_0 \sim T'_0\} \,[\!]\\ \textstyle\sum\{\circ\alpha; \mathbf{CP}^{(n')}(S'_0,T'_0) : \exists(S',T'), |S'_0,T'_0| = n' \leq n-1,\\ S_0 \xrightarrow{\alpha} S' \mapsto S'_0, T_0 \xrightarrow{\alpha} T' \mapsto T'_0, S'_0 \sim T'_0\}\end{aligned}$$ □

By Proposition 43, the above relation $\mathbf{ST}(SAB) \sim \mathbf{ST}(SBA)$ implies that $\mathbf{ST}(SAB)$ and $\mathbf{ST}(SBA)$ have common processes. Furthermore, this implies *SAB* and *SBA* have common processes by Proposition 41, thus they are consistent.

Proposition 43 shows a method to produce a common process $\mathbf{CP}^{(n)}(S_0, T_0)$ of two specifications S and T (i.e. $\mathbf{CP}^{(n)}(S_0, T_0) \in Proc(S) \cap Proc(T)$). We can also use $\mathbf{CP}^{(n)}(S_0, S_0)$ for producing an executable process P from a specification S such that $P \models S$, where $S \mapsto S_0$.

In the rest of this section, we give a relation $\cong$ which implies $\simeq$.

Definition 48 *A relation $\mathcal{R} \subseteq \mathcal{S} \times \mathcal{S}$ is a* full consistent relation, *if $(S,T) \in \mathcal{R}$ implies that the following conditions (1) and (2) hold:*

(1) *for all S_0 such that $S \mapsto S_0$, for some T_0, $T \mapsto T_0$, and (i), (ii), (iii) hold,*
(2) *for all T_0 such that $T \mapsto T_0$, for some S_0, $S \mapsto S_0$, and (i), (ii), (iii) hold,*
(i) *for all α and S', if $S_0 \xrightarrow{\alpha} S'$ then, for some T', $T_0 \xrightarrow{\alpha} T'$, and $(S',T') \in \mathcal{R}$,*
(ii) *for all α and T', if $T_0 \xrightarrow{\alpha} T'$ then, for some S', $S_0 \xrightarrow{\alpha} S'$, and $(S',T') \in \mathcal{R}$,*
(iii) *either $S_0 \not\rightarrow$ or $S_0 \in \bigcirc$ if and only if either $T_0 \not\rightarrow$ or $T_0 \in \bigcirc$* □

Definition 49 *S and T are* fully consistent, *written $S \cong T$, if $(S,T) \in \mathcal{R}$ for some full consistent relation $\mathcal{R}$.* □

The condition (*iii*) requires that S_0 is stable if and only if T_0 is stable. For example, $(S_1 \equiv \triangleleft a; S \,[]\, a; S)$ and $(S_2 \equiv \triangleleft a; S)$ are fully consistent, because both S_1 and S_2 are unstable.

The full consistency is an equivalence relation. And the full consistency implies that two specifications have the same processes as follows.

Proposition 44 *Let $S,T \in \mathcal{S}$. If $S \cong T$, then $S \simeq T$ (i.e. $Proc(S) = Proc(T)$).*
Proof It can be shown that the relation $\{(P,T) : \exists S, P \models S, S \cong T\}$ is a satisfaction relation. This proof is not difficult. □

The opposite direction of Proposition 44 (i.e. if $S \simeq T$, then $S \cong T$) does not always hold. For example, $A_1 := a; A_1$ and $A_2 := \triangleleft a; a; A_2$ have the same processes, but $A_1 \not\cong A_2$. The relation $\cong$ is a simple sufficient condition for $\simeq$.

4.2 Conjunction Specification

In this subsection, we present a method for producing a conjunction specification from two specifications. The pair of this method and the relation $\sim$ allows to check the consistency of three or more specifications, and to produce a conjunction specification of them.

The key idea for producing conjunction specifications is the standard form defined in Definition 46. If two specifications are not in standard form, then *eventualities* of them will be confused with each other. Another important point of our method is that *non-determinism* of Choices $[]$ and Disjunctions $\vee$ is considered. By this non-determinism, each state in a specification can consist with a number of various states in another specification. By considering the non-determinism, we present the $\wedge$-*method* which produces a specification constant $S \wedge T$ from two specifications S and T. Since we consider only finite state specifications S and T, the number of states of $S \wedge T$ is also finite.

Definition 410 *Let $S,T \in \mathcal{S}$. The specification $S \wedge T$ is defined as follows.*

$$
\begin{aligned}
S \wedge T &:= \bigvee\{S_0 \triangle T_0 : S \mapsto S_0, T \mapsto T_0, S_0 \sim T_0\} \\
S_0 \triangle T_0 &\equiv \textstyle\sum\{\psi\alpha; \bigvee\{S' \wedge T' : T_0 \xrightarrow{\alpha} T', S' \sim T'\} : S_0 \xrightarrow{\alpha} S', St(S_0) = \psi\} \,[] \\
&\quad\ \textstyle\sum\{\psi\alpha; \bigvee\{S' \wedge T' : S_0 \xrightarrow{\alpha} S', S' \sim T'\} : T_0 \xrightarrow{\alpha} T', St(T_0) = \psi\}
\end{aligned}
$$
□

The specification $S \wedge T$ performs common actions of S and T, like $S\,|[G]|\,T$. The main difference from $S\,|[G]|\,T$ is that $S \wedge T$ keeps the relation $\sim$ between S and T. For example, compare the following $S_{ab} \wedge S_{ac}$ and $S_{ab}\,|[a,b,c]|\,S_{ac}$.

$$S_{ab} \wedge S_{ac} \cong a;\mathbf{stop} \quad , \qquad S_{ab}\,|[a,b,c]|\,S_{ac} \cong a;\mathbf{stop} \vee \mathbf{stop}$$

where $S_{ab} \equiv a;\mathbf{stop} \vee b;\mathbf{stop}$ and $S_{ac} \equiv a;\mathbf{stop} \vee c;\mathbf{stop}$. $S_{ab} \wedge S_{ac}$ is rightly the common specification $a;\mathbf{stop}$ of S_{ab} and S_{ac}. On the other hand, $S_{ab}\,|[a,b,c]|\,S_{ac}$ contains also the specification **stop**. The **stop** arises from non-determinism of Disjunctions $\vee$, for example, by unlabelled transitions $S_{ab} \mapsto b;\mathbf{stop}$ and $S_{ac} \mapsto c;\mathbf{stop}$, where $b;\mathbf{stop}\,|[a,b,c]|\,c;\mathbf{stop} \not\longrightarrow$. The condition $S_0 \sim T_0$ in Definition 410 avoids mismatches by non-determinism, such as $b;\mathbf{stop}$ and $c;\mathbf{stop}$.

Furthermore, by non-determinism of Choices $[]$, there may exist two or more specifications T_i' such that $T_0 \xrightarrow{\alpha} T_i'$, $S' \sim T_i'$, and $T_i' \not\sim T_j'$, for each $S_0 \xrightarrow{\alpha} S'$. For example, if $S_0 \equiv a;(b;\mathbf{stop} \vee c;\mathbf{stop})$ and $T_0 \equiv a;b;\mathbf{stop}\,[]\,a;c;\mathbf{stop}$, then $S_0 \xrightarrow{a} S' \equiv b;\mathbf{stop} \vee c;\mathbf{stop}$, $T_0 \xrightarrow{a} T_1' \equiv b;\mathbf{stop}$, $T_0 \xrightarrow{a} T_2' \equiv c;\mathbf{stop}$, $S' \sim T_1'$, $S' \sim T_2'$, and $T_1' \not\sim T_2'$. In this case, a consistent pair such as (S', T_i') can not be uniquely decided. Therefore, all the consistent pairs are flexibly combined by Disjunctions, as shown in the part $\bigvee\{S' \wedge T' \mid T_0 \xrightarrow{\alpha} T', S' \sim T'\}$ in Definition 410.

Then, we give an expected proposition for the $\wedge$-method.

Proposition 45 *Let $S, T \in STD$. If $S \sim T$, then $S \wedge T$ is a conjunction specification of the specifications S and T, thus $Proc(S \wedge T) = Proc(S) \cap Proc(T)$.*
Proof We can show that the following $\mathcal{R}_1$ and $\mathcal{R}_2$ are satisfaction relations.

$$\begin{aligned}\mathcal{R}_1 &= \{(P,S) : \exists(S_0,T_0), S \mapsto S_0, S_0 \sim T_0, P \models S_0 \bigtriangleup T_0\}\\ \mathcal{R}_2 &= \{(P,U) : \exists(S_0,T_0), U \mapsto S_0 \bigtriangleup T_0, P \models S_0, P \models T_0,\\ &\qquad (Dri(S_0), Dri(T_0) \subseteq \text{either } STD \text{ or } Pre(STD))\}\end{aligned}$$

For $\mathcal{R}_2$, the key point is that S_0 and T_0 can reach stable states at the same time, because all the derivations of them are in (pre-)standard form. This means that $S_0 \bigtriangleup T_0$ can also reach a stable state. The detail is omitted. □

The two specifications $\mathbf{ST}(SAB)$ and $\mathbf{ST}(SBA)$ in Subsection 4.1 are used, again. By the $\wedge$-method, the following specifications are produced.

$$\begin{aligned}C_1 &\equiv \mathbf{ST}(SAB) \wedge \mathbf{ST}(SBA) := \lhd a;C_1 \vee \lhd b;C_1 \vee \circ a;C_2 \vee \circ b;C_3\\ C_2 &\equiv \mathbf{PST}(SAB) \wedge \mathbf{ST}(SBA) := \lhd b;C_1 \vee \lhd a;C_2 \vee \circ b;C_3\\ C_3 &\equiv \mathbf{ST}(SAB) \wedge \mathbf{PST}(SBA) := \lhd a;C_1 \vee \circ a;C_2 \vee \lhd b;C_3\end{aligned}$$

Then, By Proposition 41 and Proposition 45,

$$Proc(C_1) = Proc(\mathbf{ST}(SAB)) \cap Proc(\mathbf{ST}(SAB)) = Proc(SAB) \cap Proc(SAB).$$

In order to reach a stable state from C_1, either $(\circ a;C_2)$ or $(\circ b;C_3)$ must be eventually selected. If $(\circ a;C_2)$ is selected, then C_2 requires that b must be eventually performed. Thus, C_1 requires that a and b must be always eventually performed.

Finally, we give a theorem to produce a conjunction specification of three or more specifications by iteratively using $\sim$ and the $\wedge$-method (and the transformation by $\mathbf{ST}(S)$). This theorem also shows how to check their consistency.

Theorem 2. *Let $T_1, T_2 \in STD$, T_1 be a conjunction specification of $S_1, \cdots, S_m$, and T_2 be a conjunction specification of $S_{m+1}, \cdots, S_n$.*

(1) *If $T_1 \sim T_2$, then $T_1 \wedge T_2$ is a conjunction specification of $S_1, \cdots, S_n$.*

(2) *If $T_1 \not\sim T_2$, then $S_1, \cdots, S_n$ are not consistent.*

Proof This is easily proven by Proposition 43, Proposition 45, and the properties of intersection of sets. □

5 Conclusion and Related Work

In this paper, we have considered how to introduce least fixpoint and conjunction of μ-calculus[1,7,15] into LOTOS. In order to express the least fixpoint in a Labelled Transition System, we have proposed an extended LTS called μLTS, and have defined a language μLOTOS based on the μLTS. Then, the $\wedge$-method has been presented for producing a conjunction specification. In general, the conjunction specification S is not executable, because it may contain Disjunctions, but an executable process can be produced from S by $\mathbf{CP}$ in Proposition 43.

As a related work on flexible specifications, Larsen presented Modal Specifications to express loose specifications by required transitions $\longrightarrow_{\Box}$ and allowed transitions $\longrightarrow_{\Diamond}$ in [8] and a language called *modal CCS* based on the transitions in [9,10]. The difference between modal CCS and μLOTOS is explained by the following specifications S_1 in modal CCS and S_2 in μLOTOS.

$$S_1 := a_{\Diamond}; S_1 \,[\!]\, b_{\Box}; \mathbf{stop}, \qquad S_2 := \lhd a; S_2 \vee b; \mathbf{stop},$$

where $a_{\Diamond}$ represents an allowed action and $b_{\Box}$ represents a required action (LOTOS syntax is used also for S_1). The following process P_1 satisfies both S_1 and S_2, while the process P_2 satisfies only S_1, because the action a must not be infinitely performed in S_2, and the process P_3 satisfies only S_2, because the action b can not be postponed in S_1.

$$P_1 := b; \mathbf{stop}, \quad P_2 := a; P_2 \,[\!]\, b; \mathbf{stop}, \quad P_3 := a; b; \mathbf{stop}$$

The basic idea of the μLTS arose from the notion of divergence [16] (p.148 in [12]) which can avoid infinite loop by internal actions in the notion of divergence. An unstable state in μLTS is intuitively considered as a state which can perform internal actions. But internal actions are needed for expressing dynamic behavior such as timeout, and they should not be used for controlling resolution of Disjunction operators. Therefore, we have introduced an un-stabilizer $\lhd$.

For integration or refinement of specifications, a number of approaches were proposed, for example [2] [13] [10]. Brinksma[2] proposed a refined parallel operator for multiple labels. This operator is used to implement conjunction of LOTOS specifications. Steen et al.[13] proposed a conjunction operator $\otimes$ and a join operator $\bowtie$ in order to yield a common reduction and a common extension, respectively, in LOTOS. Larsen et al.[10] defined a conjunction operator $\wedge$ for loose specifications in modal CCS. However, these approaches do not consider the non-determinism of Disjunction operators $\vee$. Therefore, they can not be directly applied to μLOTOS.

For logical requirements, synthesis algorithms of processes were proposed in [7] and [11]. Kimura et al.[7] presented a synthesis algorithm for recursive processes by subcalculus of μ-calculus, but the subcalculus does not contain the disjunction $\vee$. Manna et al.[11] presented an algorithm for synthesizing a graph from requirements described in Propositional Temporal Logic (PTL). In PTL, eventualities can be expressed by an operator $\diamond$, but the synthesized graph from PTLs does *not* always represent *all* the common processes of them.

References

1. R.Barbuti : Selective mu-calculus: New Modal Operators for Proving Properties on Reduced Transition Systems, Formal Description Techniques and Protocol Specification, Testing and Verification, FORTE X/PSTV XVII, pp.519-534, 1997.
2. E.Brinksma : Constraint-oriented specification in a constructive formal description technique, LNCS 430, Springer-Verlag, pp.130-152, 1989.
3. P.J.B.Glabbeek and W.P.Weijland: Branching Time and Abstraction in Bisimulation Semantics, *Journal of the ACM*, Vol.43, No.3, pp.555-600, 1996.
4. C.A.R.Hoare :*Communicating Sequential Processes*, Prentice-Hall, 1985.
5. Y.Isobe, H.Nakada, Y.Sato, and K.Ohmaki : Stepwise Synthesis of Multi-Specifications using Static Choice Actions (in Japanese). Foundation of Software Engineering IV (FOSE'97), Lecture Notes 19, Kindaikagaku-sha, pp.12-19, 1997.
6. P.C.Kanellakis and S.A.Smolka: CCS Expressions, Finite State Processes, and Three Problems of Equivalence, *Information and Computation*, Vol.86, pp.43-68, 1990.
7. S.Kimura, A.Togashi and N.Shiratori : Synthesis Algorithm for Recursive Processes by μ-calculus, Algorithmic Learning Theory, LNCS 872,Springer-Verlag, pp.379-394, 1994.
8. K.G.Larsen : Modal Specifications, Automatic Verification Methods for Finite State Systems, LNCS 407, Springer-Verlag, pp.232-246, 1989.
9. K.G.Larsen : The expressive Power of Implicit Specifications, Automata, Languages and Programming, LNCS 510, Springer-Verlag, pp.204-216, 1991.
10. K.G.Larsen, B.Steffen, and C.Weise : A Constraint Oriented Proof Methodology Based on Modal Transition Systems, Tools and Algorithms for the Construction and Analysis of Systems, LNCS 1019, Springer-Verlag, pp.17-40, 1995.
11. Z.Manna and P.Wolper : Synthesis of Communicating Processes from Temporal Logic Specifications, *ACM Trans. on Programming Languages and Systems*, Vol.6, No.1, pp.67-93, 1984.
12. R.Milner : *Communication and Concurrency*, Prentice-Hall, 1989.
13. M.W.A.Steen, H.Bowman, and J.Derrick : Composition of LOTOS specification, Protocol Specification, Testing and Verification, XV, pp.73-88, 1995
14. M.W.A.Steen, H.Bowman, J.Derrick, and E.A.Boiten, : Disjunction of LOTOS specification, Formal Description Techniques and Protocol Specification, Testing and Verification, FORTE X/PSTV XVII, pp.177-192, 1997.
15. Colin Stirling : An Introduction to Modal and Temporal Logics for CCS, Concurrency: Theory, Language, and Architecture, LNCS 491, Springer-Verlag, pp.2-20, 1989.
16. D.J.Walker : Bisimulations and Divergence, Proc. of third annual IEEE symposium on Logic in Computer Science, pp.186 - 192, 1988.
17. ISO 8807: Information Processing Systems–Open System Interconnection–LOTOS–A formal description technique based on the temporal ordering of observational behavior, 1989.

A Appendix

Table 1. The notations used in this paper

Notation	Meaning
$\mathcal{N}$	the set of names $a, b, \cdots$
Act	the set of actions $\alpha, \beta, \cdots$, $(Act = \mathcal{N} \cup \{i\})$
Ψ	the set of state operators $\psi, \phi, \cdots$, $(\Psi = \{\circ, \triangleleft\})$
$\mathcal{K}$	the set of specification constants (Constants) $A, B, \cdots$
$\mathcal{X}$	the set of specification variables (Variables) $X, Y, \cdots$
$\mathcal{M}$	the set of specification expressions $M, N, \cdots$
$\mathcal{M}_0$	the set of specification expressions such that if $M_0 \mapsto M_0'$ then $M_0 \equiv M_0'$
$\mathcal{M}_\nu, \mathcal{M}_\mu$	subsets of $\mathcal{M}$, Definition 33 and 34
$\mathcal{S}$	the set of specifications $S, T, U, \cdots$
$\mathcal{S}_0$	the set of specifications such that if $S_0 \mapsto S_0'$ then $S_0 \equiv S_0'$
$\mathcal{P}$	the set of processes $P, Q, \cdots$
STD	the set of specifications in standard form, Definition 46
$Pre(STD)$	the set of specifications in pre-standard form
$Var(M)$	the set of Variables in M
$Proc(S)$	the set of all the processes to satisfy S, $(Proc(S) = \{P : P \models S\})$
$Dri(S_0)$	the set of derivations of S_0 $(Dri(S_0) = \{S' : \exists\alpha, S_0 \xrightarrow{\alpha} S'\})$
$\models$	satisfaction
$\sim$	a relation for checking consistency
$\simeq$	the relation $\{(S, T) : Proc(S) = Proc(T)\}$
$\cong$	full consistency, Definition 49
$:=$	definition of specification constants
$\equiv$	syntactic identity
$\theta(\mathcal{R})$	a relation to define $\models$, Definition 31
$\Theta(\mathcal{R})$	a relation to define $\sim$, Definition 42
St	a state function (if $S_0 \in \bigcirc$ then $St(S_0) = \circ$, otherwise $St(S_0) = \triangleleft$
$\mathbf{ST}(S)$	a specification in standard form, transformed from S

Towards a Characterisation of Finite-State Message-Passing Systems

Madhavan Mukund[1*], K Narayan Kumar[1**],
Jaikumar Radhakrishnan[2], and Milind Sohoni[3]

[1] SPIC Mathematical Institute, 92 G.N. Chetty Road, Madras 600 017, India.
{madhavan,kumar}@smi.ernet.in

[2] Computer Science Group, Tata Institute of Fundamental Research, Homi Bhabha Road, Bombay 400 005, India. jaikumar@tcs.tifr.res.in

[3] Department of Computer Science and Engineering, Indian Institute of Technology, Bombay 400 076, India. sohoni@cse.iitb.ernet.in

Abstract. We investigate an automata-theoretic model of distributed systems which communicate via message-passing. Each node in the system is a finite-state device. Channels are assumed to be reliable but may deliver messages out of order. Hence, each channel is modelled as a set of counters, one for each type of message. These counters may *not* be tested for zero.

Though each node in the network is finite-state, the overall system is potentially infinite-state because the counters are unbounded. We work in an interleaved setting where the interactions of the system with the environment are described as sequences. The behaviour of a system is described in terms of the language which it accepts—that is, the set of valid interactions with the environment that are permitted by the system.

Our aim is to characterise the class of message-passing systems whose behaviour is finite-state. Our main result is that the language accepted by a message-passing system is regular if and only if both the language and its complement are accepted by message-passing systems. We also exhibit an alternative characterisation of regular message-passing languages in terms of deterministic automata.

1 Introduction

Today, distributed systems which use asynchronous communication are ubiquitous—the Internet is a prime example. However, there has been very little work on studying the finite-state behaviour of such systems. In particular, this area lacks a satisfactory automata-theoretic framework. In contrast, automata theory for systems with synchronous communication is well developed via Zielonka's

* Partly supported by IFCPAR Project 1502-1.

** Currently on leave at Department of Computer Science, State University of New York at Stony Brook, NY 11794-4400, USA. kumar@cs.sunysb.edu.

Jieh Hsiang, Atsushi Ohori (Eds.): ASIAN'98, LNCS 1538, pp. 282–299, 1998.

asynchronous automata [Z87] and the connections to Mazurkiewicz trace theory [M78].

In [MNRS98], we introduce *networks of message-passing automata* as a model for distributed systems which communicate via message-passing. Each node in the network is a finite-state process. The number of different types of messages used by the system is assumed to be finite. This is not unreasonable if we distinguish "control" messages from "data" messages.

In our model, channels may reorder or delay messages, though messages are never lost. Since messages may be reordered, the state of each channel can be represented by a finite set of counters which record the number of messages of each type that have been sent along the channel but are as yet undelivered. The nodes cannot test if a counter's value is zero—this restriction captures the intuition that it is not practical for a node to decide that another process has *not* sent a message, since messages may be delayed arbitrarily.

Though each node in the network is finite-state, the overall system is potentially infinite-state since counter values are unbounded. Our goal is to characterise when such a network is "effectively finite-state". This is important because finite-state networks are amenable to verification using automated tools [H91].

To make precise the notion of a network being "effectively finite-state", we use formal language theory. The behaviour of the network is described in terms of its interaction with the environment. This can be represented as a formal language over a finite alphabet of possible interactions. Our goal then is to characterise when the language accepted by a network is regular.

In [MNRS98], we assume that each node interacts independently with its environment. Thus, the behaviour of the overall network is described as a language consisting of tuples of strings. The main result is that the language accepted by a *robust* message-passing network, whose behaviour is insensitive to message delays and differences in speed between nodes, can be "represented" by a sequential regular language.

Here, we adopt an interleaved approach and record the interactions of a network with its environment from the point of view of a sequential observer. In this framework, it is sufficient to concentrate on the global states of the system and regard the entire network as a single automaton equipped with a set of counters. Our main result is that a language L accepted by a message-passing automaton is regular if and only if the complement of L is also accepted by a message-passing automaton. *This is more general than requiring that L be robust in the sense of [MNRS98]—see Section 5.1.* We also demonstrate an alternative characterisation in terms of deterministic message-passing automata. Along the way, we describe a variety of results about message-passing automata, including pumping lemmas which are useful for showing when languages are *not* recognisable by these automata.

The paper is organised as follows. In the next section we define message-passing automata and establish some basic results about them. In Section 3 we prove a Contraction Lemma which leads to the decidability of the emptiness problem and the fact that the languages accepted by message-passing automata are not closed under complementation. Section 4 describes a family of pumping lemmas which are exploited in Section 5 to prove our main results concerning the regularity of languages accepted by message-passing automata. In the final section, we discuss in detail the connection between our results and those in Petri net theory and point out directions for future work. We have had to omit many proofs in this extended abstract. Full proofs and related results can be found in [MNRS97,MNRS98].

2 Message-Passing Automata

Natural numbers and tuples As usual, $\mathbb{N}$ denotes the set $\{0,1,2,\ldots\}$ of natural numbers. For $i,j \in \mathbb{N}$, $[i..j]$ denotes the set $\{i, i+1, \ldots, j\}$, where $[i..j] = \emptyset$ if $i > j$. We compare k-tuples of natural numbers component-wise. Let $\overline{m} = \langle m_1, m_2, \ldots, m_k \rangle$ and $\overline{n} = \langle n_1, n_2, \ldots, n_k \rangle$. Then $\overline{m} \leq \overline{n}$ iff $m_i \leq n_i$ for each $i \in [1..k]$.

Message-passing automata A *message-passing automaton* $\mathcal{A}$ is a tuple $(Q, \Sigma, \Gamma, T, q_{\text{in}}, F)$, where:

- Q is a finite set of *states*, with *initial state* q_{in} and *accepting states* $F \subseteq Q$.
- Σ is a finite *input alphabet.*
- Γ is a finite set of *counters.* We use $C, C', \ldots$ to denote counters. With each counter C, we associate two symbols, C^+ and C^-. We write $\Gamma^{\pm}$ to denote the set $\{C^+ | C \in \Gamma\} \cup \{C^- | C \in \Gamma\}$.
- $T \subseteq Q \times (\Sigma \cup \Gamma^{\pm}) \times Q$ is the *transition relation.*

Configurations A *configuration* of $\mathcal{A}$ is a pair (q, f) where $q \in Q$ and $f : \Gamma \to \mathbb{N}$ is a function which records the values stored in the counters. If the counters are $C_1, C_2, \ldots, C_k$ then we represent f by an element $\langle f(C_1), f(C_2), \ldots, f(C_k) \rangle$ of $\mathbb{N}^k$. By abuse of notation, the k-tuple $\langle 0, 0, \ldots, 0 \rangle$ is uniformly denoted $\overline{0}$, for all values of k.

We use χ to denote configurations. If $\chi = (q, f)$, $Q(\chi)$ denotes q and $F(\chi)$ denotes f. Further, for each counter C, $C(\chi)$ denotes the value $f(C)$.

Moves Each move of a message-passing automaton consists of either reading a letter from its input or manipulating a counter. Reading from the input represents interaction with the environment. Incrementing and decrementing counters correspond to sending and reading messages, respectively.

Formally, a message-passing automaton *moves* from configuration χ to configuration χ' on $d \in \Sigma \cup \Gamma^{\pm}$ if $(Q(\chi), d, Q(\chi')) \in T$ and one of the following holds:

- $d \in \Sigma$ and $F(\chi) = F(\chi')$.
- $d = C^+$, $C(\chi') = C(\chi) + 1$ and $C'(\chi) = C'(\chi')$ for every $C' \neq C$.
- $d = C^-$, $C(\chi') = C(\chi) - 1 \geq 0$ and $C'(\chi) = C'(\chi')$ for every $C' \neq C$.

Such a move is denoted $\chi \xrightarrow{(q,d,q')} \chi'$—that is, transitions are labelled by elements of T. Given a sequence of transitions $t_1 t_2 \ldots t_n = (q_1, d_1, q_2)(q_2, d_2, q_3) \ldots (q_n, d_n, q_{n+1})$, the corresponding sequence $d_1 d_2 \ldots d_n$ over $\Sigma \cup \Gamma^{\pm}$ is denoted $\alpha(t_1 t_2 \ldots t_n)$.

Computations, runs and languages A *computation* of $\mathcal{A}$ is a sequence $\chi_0 \xrightarrow{t_1} \chi_1 \xrightarrow{t_2} \ldots \xrightarrow{t_n} \chi_n$. We also write $\chi_0 \xRightarrow{t_1 t_2 \ldots t_n} \chi_n$ to indicate that there is a computation labelled $t_1 t_2 \ldots t_n$ from χ_0 to χ_n. Notice that χ_0 and $t_1 t_2 \ldots t_n$ uniquely determine all the intermediate configurations $\chi_1, \chi_2, \ldots, \chi_n$. If the transition sequence is not relevant, we just write $\chi_0 \Longrightarrow \chi_n$. As usual, $\chi \xRightarrow{t_1 t_2 \ldots t_n}$ denotes that there exists χ' such that $\chi \xRightarrow{t_1 t_2 \ldots t_n} \chi'$ and $\chi \Longrightarrow$ denotes that there exists χ' such that $\chi \Longrightarrow \chi'$.

For $K \in \mathbb{N}$, a *K-run* of $\mathcal{A}$ is a computation $\chi_0 \Longrightarrow \chi_n$ where $C(\chi_0) \leq K$ for each $C \in \Gamma$.

If δ is a string over $\Sigma \cup \Gamma^{\pm}$, $\delta\restriction_{\Sigma}$ denotes the subsequence of letters from Σ in δ. Let $w = a_1 a_2 \ldots a_k$ be a string over Σ. A *run of $\mathcal{A}$ over w* is a 0-run $\chi_0 \xRightarrow{t_1 t_2 \ldots t_n} \chi_n$ where $Q(\chi_0) = q_{\text{in}}$ and $\alpha(t_1 t_2 \ldots t_n)\restriction_{\Sigma} = w$. The run is said to be *accepting* if $Q(\chi_n) \in F$. The string w is *accepted* by $\mathcal{A}$ if $\mathcal{A}$ has an accepting run over w. The *language accepted* by $\mathcal{A}$, denoted $L(\mathcal{A})$, is the set of all strings over Σ accepted by $\mathcal{A}$.

A language over Σ is said to be *message-passing recognisable* if there is a message-passing automaton with input alphabet Σ that accepts this language.

Example 2.1. Let $L_{\text{ge}} \subseteq \{a, b\}^*$ be given by $\{a^m b^n \mid m \geq n\}$. This language is message-passing recognisable. Here is an automaton for L_{ge}. The initial state is indicated by $\Downarrow$ and the final states have an extra circle around them.

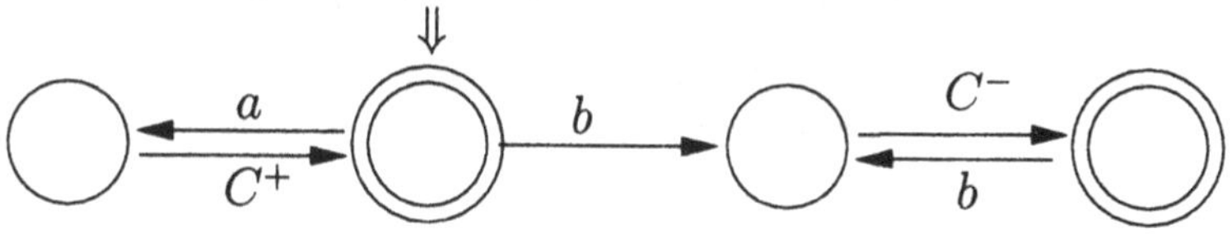

The following result is basic to analysing the behaviour of message-passing automata. It follows from the fact that any infinite sequence of N-tuples of natural numbers contains an infinite increasing subsequence. We omit the proof.

Lemma 2.2. *Let X be a set with M elements and $\langle x_1, f_1\rangle, \langle x_2, f_2\rangle, \ldots, \langle x_m, f_m\rangle$ be a sequence over $X \times \mathbb{N}^N$ such that each coordinate of f_1 is bounded by K and for $i \in [1..m-1]$, f_i and f_{i+1} differ on at most one coordinate and this difference is at most 1. There is a constant ℓ which depends only on M, N and K such that if $m \geq \ell$, then there exist $i, j \in [1..m]$ with $i < j$, $x_i = x_j$ and $f_i \leq f_j$.*

Weak pumping constant We call the bound ℓ for M, N and K from the preceding lemma the *weak pumping constant* for (M, N, K), denoted $\pi_{M,N,K}$.

It is easy to see that if $\langle M', N', K\rangle \leq \langle M, N, K\rangle$, then $\pi_{M',N',K'} \leq \pi_{M,N,K}$.

3 A Contraction Lemma

Lemma 3.1 (Contraction). *For every message-passing automaton $\mathcal{A}$, there is a constant k such that if $\chi_0 \stackrel{t_1t_2\ldots t_m}{\Longrightarrow} \chi_m$ is a computation of $\mathcal{A}$, with $m > k$, then there exist i and j, $m-k \leq i < j \leq m$, such that $\chi'_0 \stackrel{t_1\ldots t_i t_{j+1}\ldots t_m}{\Longrightarrow} \chi'_{m-(j-i)}$ is also a computation of $\mathcal{A}$, with with $\chi'_\ell = \chi_\ell$ for $\ell \in [0..i]$ and $Q(\chi_\ell) = Q(\chi'_{\ell-(j-i)})$ for all $\ell \in [j..m]$.*

Proof Sketch. Let $\mathcal{A}$ have M states and N counters. We show that k can be chosen to be $\pi_{M,N,0}$. Let $\chi_0 \stackrel{t_1t_2\ldots t_m}{\Longrightarrow} \chi_m$ be a computation of $\mathcal{A}$, with $m > \pi_{M,N,0}$. We define a sequence $f_m, f_{m-1}, \ldots, f_0$ of functions from Γ to $\mathbb{N}$ as follows:

$$f_m(C) = 0, \text{for all } C \in \Gamma$$

$$\text{For } i \in [0..m-1],\ f_i(C) = \begin{cases} f_{i+1}(C) & \text{if } \alpha(t_{i+1}) \notin \{C^+, C^-\} \\ f_{i+1}(C)+1 & \text{if } \alpha(t_{i+1}) = C^- \\ \max(0, f_{i+1}(C)-1) & \text{if } \alpha(t_{i+1}) = C^+ \end{cases}$$

We claim, without proof, that for each i, the function f_i represents the minimum counter values required to execute the transition sequence $t_{i+1}t_{i+2}\ldots t_m$.

Claim: $\forall i \in [1..m]$, $(Q(\chi_i), f) \stackrel{t_{i+1}t_{i+2}\ldots t_m}{\Longrightarrow}$ iff $f \geq f_i$.

Corollary to Claim: For each counter C and for each position $i \in [1..m]$, $C(\chi_i) \geq f_i(C)$.

Consider the sequence of N-tuples $f_m, f_{m-1}, \ldots f_0$. Since its length exceeds $\pi_{M,N,0}$, by Lemma 2.2 there exist positions i and j, $m \geq j > i \geq m-\pi_{M,N,0}$ such that $f_j \leq f_i$ and $Q(\chi_j) = Q(\chi_i)$. By the Corollary to Claim, for each counter C, $C(\chi_i) \geq f_i(C) \geq f_j(C)$. Thus, $\chi_i \stackrel{t_{j+1}t_{j+2}\ldots t_m}{\Longrightarrow}$ whereby $\chi_0 \stackrel{t_1t_2\ldots t_i}{\Longrightarrow} \chi_i \stackrel{t_{j+1}t_{j+2}\ldots t_m}{\Longrightarrow} \chi'_{m-(j-i)}$ is a valid computation of $\mathcal{A}$ for some configuration $\chi'_{m-(j-i)}$. Since $Q(\chi_j) = Q(\chi_i)$ and the computations $\chi_j \stackrel{t_{j+1}t_{j+2}\ldots t_m}{\Longrightarrow} \chi_m$ and $\chi_i \stackrel{t_{j+1}t_{j+2}\ldots t_m}{\Longrightarrow} \chi'_{m-(j-i)}$ are labelled by the same sequence of transitions, it follows that $Q(\chi_\ell) = Q(\chi'_{\ell-(j-i)})$ for each $\ell \in [j..m]$, as required. □

Corollary 3.2. *A message-passing automaton $\mathcal{A}$ with M states and N counters has an accepting computation iff it has an accepting computation whose length is bounded by $\pi_{M,N,0}$.*

It is possible to provide an explicit upper bound for $\pi_{M,N,K}$ for all values of M, N, and K. This fact, coupled with the preceding observation, yields the following result (which can also be derived from the decidability of the reachability problem for Petri nets).

Corollary 3.3. *The emptiness problem for message-passing automata is decidable.*

Corollary 3.4. *Message-passing recognisable languages are not closed under complementation.*

Proof Sketch. We saw earlier that $L_{\text{ge}} = \{a^m b^n \mid m \geq n\}$ is message-passing recognisable. We show that the language $L_{\text{lt}} = \{a^m b^n \mid m < n\}$ is not message-passing recognisable. Suppose that L_{lt} is accepted by an automaton $\mathcal{A}_{\text{lt}}$ with M states and N counters. Consider the string $w = a^J b^{J+1}$ where $J = \pi_{M,N,0}$ and let $\rho : \chi_0 \overset{t_1 t_2 \ldots t_n}{\Longrightarrow} \chi_n$ be an accepting run of $\mathcal{A}_{\text{lt}}$ on w. By applying the Contraction Lemma (repeatedly, if necessary) to ρ, we can obtain an accepting run ρ' of $\mathcal{A}_{\text{lt}}$ over a word of the form $a^J b^K$, where $K \leq J$, thus contradicting the assumption that $L(\mathcal{A}_{\text{lt}}) = L_{\text{lt}}$. □

4 A Collection of Pumping Lemmas

Our main result is based on a series of pumping lemmas, which we present in this section. For reasons of space, we do not provide some of the proofs. More details may be found in [MNRS97,MNRS98]. Some of the results of this section were used in [MNRS98] to show that *robust asynchronous protocols* are necessarily finite state.

Change vectors For a string w and a symbol x, let $\#_x(w)$ denote the number of times x occurs in w. Let v be a sequence of transitions. Recall that $\alpha(v)$ denotes the corresponding sequence of letters. For each counter C, define $\Delta_C(v)$ to be $\#_{C^+}(\alpha(v)) - \#_{C^-}(\alpha(v))$. The *change vector* associated with v, denoted Δv, is given by $\langle \Delta_C(v) \rangle_{C \in \Gamma}$.

Proposition 4.1. *Let $\mathcal{A} = (Q, \Sigma, \Gamma, T, q_{\text{in}}, F)$ be a message-passing automaton.*

(i) For any computation $\chi \overset{v}{\Longrightarrow} \chi'$ of $\mathcal{A}$ and any counter $C \in \Gamma$, $|\Delta_C(v)| \leq |v|$.

(ii) For any configuration χ and sequence of transitions v, $\chi \overset{v}{\Longrightarrow}$ iff for each prefix u of v and each counter $C \in \Gamma$, $C(\chi) + \Delta_C(u) \geq 0$.

(iii) Let $\chi \overset{u}{\Longrightarrow} \chi' \overset{v}{\Longrightarrow}$ with $Q(\chi) = Q(\chi')$ and $n \in \mathbb{N}$ such that, for every counter $C \in \Gamma$, either $\Delta_C(u) \geq 0$ or $C(\chi) \geq n|u| + |v|$. Then, $\chi \overset{u^n v}{\Longrightarrow}$.

Proof.

(i) This follows from the fact that each move can change a counter value by at most 1.

(ii) This follows immediately from the definition of a computation.

(iii) The proof is by induction on n.

Basis: For $n = 0$, there is nothing to prove.

Induction step: Let $n > 0$ and assume the result holds for $n-1$. We will show that $\chi \overset{u}{\Longrightarrow} \chi' \overset{u^{n-1} v}{\Longrightarrow}$.

From the assumption, we know that $\chi \stackrel{u}{\Longrightarrow} \chi'$. To show that $\chi' \stackrel{u^{n-1}v}{\Longrightarrow}$, we examine the value of each counter C at χ'. If $\Delta_C(u) < 0$, then $C(\chi) \geq n|u| + v$. Since $C(\chi') = C(\chi') + \Delta_C(u)$ and $|\Delta_C(u)| \leq |u|$, it follows that $C(\chi') \geq (n-1)|u| + v$. From the induction hypothesis, we can then conclude that $\chi' \stackrel{u^{n-1}v}{\Longrightarrow}$.

□

Pumpable decomposition Let $\mathcal{A}$ be a message-passing automaton with N counters and let $\rho : \chi_0 \stackrel{t_1 t_2 \ldots t_m}{\Longrightarrow} \chi_m$ be a computation of $\mathcal{A}$. A decomposition $\chi_0 \stackrel{u_1}{\Longrightarrow} \chi_{i_1} \stackrel{v_1}{\Longrightarrow} \chi_{j_1} \stackrel{u_2}{\Longrightarrow} \chi_{i_2} \stackrel{v_2}{\Longrightarrow} \chi_{j_2} \stackrel{u_3}{\Longrightarrow} \cdots \stackrel{u_n}{\Longrightarrow} \chi_{i_n} \stackrel{v_n}{\Longrightarrow} \chi_{j_n} \stackrel{u_{n+1}}{\Longrightarrow} \chi_m$ of ρ is said to be *pumpable* if it satisfies the following conditions:

(i) $n \leq N$.
(ii) For each $k \in [1..n]$, $Q(\chi_{i_k}) = Q(\chi_{j_k})$.
(iii) For each v_k, $k \in [1..n]$, Δv_k is non-zero and has at least one positive entry.
(iv) Let C be a counter and $k \in [1..n]$ such that $\Delta_C(v_k)$ is negative. Then, there exists $\ell < k$ such that $\Delta_C(v_\ell)$ is positive.

We refer to $v_1, v_2, \ldots, v_n$ as the *pumpable blocks* of the decomposition. We say that a counter C is *pumpable* if $\Delta_C(v_i) > 0$ for some pumpable block v_i. The following lemma shows that all the pumpable counters of a pumpable decomposition are simultaneously unbounded. We omit the proof. (This is similar to a well-known result of Karp and Miller in the theory of vector addition systems [KM69].)

Lemma 4.2 (Counter Pumping). *Let $\mathcal{A}$ be a message-passing automaton and ρ a K-run of $\mathcal{A}$, $K \in \mathbb{N}$, with a pumpable decomposition of the form* $\chi_0 \stackrel{u_1}{\Longrightarrow} \chi_{i_1} \stackrel{v_1}{\Longrightarrow} \chi_{j_1} \stackrel{u_2}{\Longrightarrow} \chi_{i_2} \stackrel{v_2}{\Longrightarrow} \chi_{j_2} \cdots \stackrel{u_n}{\Longrightarrow} \chi_{i_n} \stackrel{v_n}{\Longrightarrow} \chi_{j_n} \stackrel{u_{n+1}}{\Longrightarrow} \chi_m$. *Then, for any $I, J \in \mathbb{N}$, with $I \geq 1$, there exist $\ell_1, \ell_2, \ldots, \ell_n \in \mathbb{N}$ and a K-run ρ' of $\mathcal{A}$ of the form* $\chi'_0 \stackrel{u_1}{\Longrightarrow} \chi'_{i'_1} \stackrel{v_1^{\ell_1}}{\Longrightarrow} \chi'_{j'_1} \stackrel{u_2}{\Longrightarrow} \chi'_{i'_2} \stackrel{v_2^{\ell_2}}{\Longrightarrow} \chi'_{j'_2} \cdots \stackrel{u_n}{\Longrightarrow} \chi'_{i'_n} \stackrel{v_n^{\ell_n}}{\Longrightarrow} \chi'_{j'_n} \stackrel{u_{n+1}}{\Longrightarrow} \chi'_p$ *such that ρ' satisfies the following properties:*

(i) $\chi_0 = \chi'_0$.
(ii) $Q(\chi'_p) = Q(\chi_m)$.
(iii) For $i \in [1..n]$, $\ell_i \geq I$.
(iv) For every counter C, $C(\chi'_p) \geq C(\chi_m)$.
(v) Let Γ_{pump} *be the set of pumpable counters in the pumpable decomposition of* ρ. *For each counter* $C \in \Gamma_{\text{pump}}$, $C(\chi'_p) \geq J$.

Proof. The proof is by induction on n, the number of pumpable blocks in the decomposition.

Basis: If $n = 0$, there is nothing to prove.

Induction step: Let $n > 0$ and assume the lemma holds for all decompositions with $n-1$ pumpable blocks. For each counter C, let $J_C = \max(J, C(\chi_m))$.

By the induction hypothesis, for all $I', J' \in \mathbb{N}$, $I' \geq 1$, we can transform the prefix $\sigma : \chi_0 \stackrel{u_1}{\Longrightarrow} \chi_{i_1} \stackrel{v_1}{\Longrightarrow} \chi_{j_1} \stackrel{u_2}{\Longrightarrow} \cdots \stackrel{v_{n-1}}{\Longrightarrow} \chi_{j_{n-1}} \stackrel{u_n}{\Longrightarrow} \chi_{i_n}$ of ρ into a K-run $\sigma' : \chi'_0 \stackrel{u_1}{\Longrightarrow} \chi'_{i'_1} \stackrel{v_1^{\ell_1}}{\Longrightarrow} \chi'_{j'_1} \stackrel{u_2}{\Longrightarrow} \cdots \stackrel{v_{n-1}^{\ell_{n-1}}}{\Longrightarrow} \chi'_{j'_{n-1}} \stackrel{u_n}{\Longrightarrow} \chi'_{i'_n}$ satisfying the conditions of the lemma. We shall choose I' and J' so that the transition sequence $v_n^{\ell_n} u_{n+1}$ can be appended to σ' to yield the run claimed by the lemma.

To fix values for I' and J', we first estimate the value of ℓ_n, the number of times we need to pump v_n to satisfy all the conditions of the lemma. Let $\Gamma_{\mathrm{pos}}^n = \{C \mid \Delta_C(v_n) > 0\}$. It is sufficient if the number ℓ_n is large enough for each counter $C \in \Gamma_{\mathrm{pos}}^n$ to exceed J_C at the end of the new computation. For a counter $C \in \Gamma_{\mathrm{pos}}^n$ to be above J_C at the end of the computation, it is sufficient for C to have the value $J_C + |u_{n+1}|$ after $v_n^{\ell_n}$. By the induction hypothesis, the value of C before $v_n^{\ell_n}$ is at least $C(\chi_{i_n})$. Hence, it would take $\lceil \frac{J_C + |u_{n+1}| - C(\chi_{i_n})}{\Delta_C(v_n)} \rceil$ iterations of v_n for C to reach the required value after $v_n^{\ell_n}$. On the other hand, we should also ensure that $\ell_n \geq I$. Thus, it is safe to set ℓ_n to be the maximum of I and $\max_{C \in \Gamma_{\mathrm{pos}}^n} \lceil \frac{J_C + |u_{n+1}| - C(\chi_{i_n})}{\Delta_C(v_n)} \rceil$.

We set $I' = I$ and estimate a value for J' such that $\chi'_{i'_n} \stackrel{v_n^{\ell_n} u_{n+1}}{\Longrightarrow} \chi'_p$ with each counter $C \in (\Gamma \setminus \Gamma_{\mathrm{pos}}^n)$ achieving a value of at least $C(\chi_m)$ at χ'_p and each counter $C \in (\Gamma_{\mathrm{pos}} \setminus \Gamma_{\mathrm{pos}}^n)$ achieving a value of at least J_C at χ'_p.

By the induction hypothesis, $Q(\chi'_{i'_n}) = Q(\chi_{i_n})$ and $F(\chi'_{i'_n}) \geq F(\chi_{i_n})$. Since $\chi_{i_n} \stackrel{v_n u_{n+1}}{\Longrightarrow}$, it follows that $\chi'_{i'_n} \stackrel{v_n u_{n+1}}{\Longrightarrow}$. By Proposition 4.1 (iii), to ensure that $\chi'_{i'_n} \stackrel{v_n^{\ell_n} u_{n+1}}{\Longrightarrow} \chi'_p$, it is sufficient to raise each counter C with $\Delta_C(v_n) < 0$ to a value of at least $\ell_n|v_n| + |u_{n+1}|$ at $\chi'_{i'_n}$. If $\Delta_C(v_n) < 0$ then, by the definition of pumpable decompositions, $\Delta_C(v_i) > 0$ for some $i \in [1..n-1]$, so C gets pumped above J' in σ'.

Any counter C such that $\Delta_C(v_n) \geq 0$ will surely exceed $C(\chi_m)$ at χ'_p. On the other hand, a counter C such that $\Delta_C(v_n) < 0$ can decrease by at most $\ell_n|v_n| + |u_{n+1}|$ after $\chi'_{i'_n}$.

Putting these two facts together, it suffices to set J' to $\ell_n|v_n| + |u_{n+1}| + \max_{\{C \mid \Delta_C(v_n) < 0\}} J_C$.

Let $\rho' : \chi'_0 \stackrel{u_1}{\Longrightarrow} \chi'_{i'_1} \stackrel{v_1^{\ell_1}}{\Longrightarrow} \chi'_{j'_1} \stackrel{u_2}{\Longrightarrow} \cdots \stackrel{u_n}{\Longrightarrow} \chi'_{i'_n} \stackrel{v_n^{\ell_n}}{\Longrightarrow} \chi'_{j'_n} \stackrel{u_{n+1}}{\Longrightarrow} \chi'_p$. By the induction hypothesis, we know that $\chi'_0 = \chi_0$ and for $i \in [1..n-1]$, $\ell_i \geq I$. By construction, $\ell_n \geq I$ as well. We have also ensured that for every counter C, $C(\chi'_p) \geq C(\chi_m)$ and for every counter $C \in \Gamma_{\mathrm{pos}}$, $C(\chi'_p) \geq J$. The fact that $Q(\chi'_p) = Q(\chi_m)$ follows from the fact that each v_n loop brings the automaton back to $Q(\chi'_{i'_n}) = Q(\chi_{i_n})$, and the fact that both ρ and ρ' go through the same sequence of transitions u_{n+1} at the end of the computation. □

Having shown that all pumpable counters of a pumpable decomposition can be simultaneously raised to arbitrarily high values, we describe a sufficient condition for a K-run to admit a non-trivial pumpable decomposition.

Strong pumping constant For each $M, N, K \in \mathbb{N}$, we define the *strong pumping constant* $\Pi_{M,N,K}$ by induction on N as follows (recall that $\pi_{M,N,K}$ denotes the weak pumping constant for (M, N, K)):

$$\forall M, K \in \mathbb{N}. \quad \Pi_{M,0,K} = 1$$
$$\forall M, N, K \in \mathbb{N}. \; \Pi_{M,N+1,K} = \Pi_{M,N,\pi_{M,N+1,K}+K} + \pi_{M,N+1,K} + K$$

Lemma 4.3 (Decomposition). *Let $\mathcal{A}$ be a message-passing automaton with M states and N counters and let $K \in \mathbb{N}$. Let $\rho : \chi_0 \overset{t_1 t_2 \ldots t_m}{\Longrightarrow} \chi_m$ be any K-run of $\mathcal{A}$. Then, there is a pumpable decomposition $\chi_0 \overset{u_1}{\Longrightarrow} \chi_{i_1} \overset{v_1}{\Longrightarrow} \chi_{j_1} \overset{u_2}{\Longrightarrow} \chi_{i_2} \overset{v_2}{\Longrightarrow} \chi_{j_2} \cdots \overset{u_n}{\Longrightarrow} \chi_{i_n} \overset{v_n}{\Longrightarrow} \chi_{j_n} \overset{u_{n+1}}{\Longrightarrow} \chi_m$ of ρ such that for every counter C, if $C(\chi_j) > \Pi_{M,N,K}$ for some $j \in [0..m]$, then there exists $k \in [1..n]$, such that $\Delta_C(v_k)$ is positive.*

To prove this lemma, we need the following result.

Proposition 4.4. *Let $\mathcal{A}$ be a message-passing automaton with M states and N counters and let $\rho : \chi_0 \Longrightarrow \chi_n$ be a K-run of $\mathcal{A}$ in which some counter value exceeds $\pi_{M,N,K} + K$. Then, there is a prefix $\sigma : \chi_0 \Longrightarrow \chi_s$ of ρ such that:*

- *For each $m \in [0..s]$ and every counter C, $C(\chi_m) < \pi_{M,N,K} + K$.*
- *There exists $r \in [0..s-1]$, such that $\sigma : \chi_0 \Longrightarrow \chi_r \Longrightarrow \chi_s$, $Q(\chi_r) = Q(\chi_s)$ and $F(\chi_r) < F(\chi_s)$.*

Proof. Suppose that the lemma does not hold. Let $\rho : \chi_0 \overset{t_1 t_2 \ldots t_n}{\Longrightarrow} \chi_n$ be a computation of minimum length which fails to satisfy the lemma. Since the initial counter values in ρ are bounded by K and some counter value exceeds $\pi_{M,N,K} + K$ in ρ, it must be the case that the length of ρ is at least $\pi_{M,N,K}$.

By the definition of $\pi_{M,N,K}$, there exist i and j, $i < j \leq \pi_{M,N,K}$ such that $Q(\chi_i) = Q(\chi_j)$ and $F(\chi_i) \leq F(\chi_j)$. Since ρ is a K-run and $j \leq \pi_{M,N,K}$, all counter values at the configurations $\chi_0, \chi_1, \ldots, \chi_j$ must be bounded by $\pi_{M,N,K} + K$. If $F(\chi_i) < F(\chi_j)$, ρ would satisfy the lemma with $r = i$ and $s = j$, so it must be the case $F(\chi_i) = F(\chi_j)$.

Since $\chi_i = \chi_j$, we can construct a shorter computation $\rho' = \chi_0 \overset{t_1 t_2 \ldots t_i}{\Longrightarrow} \chi_i \overset{t_{j+1}}{\longrightarrow} \chi_{j+1} \overset{t_{j+2}}{\longrightarrow} \cdots \overset{t_n}{\longrightarrow} \chi_n$. It is easy to see that the same counter whose value exceeded $\pi_{M,N,K} + K$ in ρ must also exceed $\pi_{M,N,K} + K$ in ρ'—the only configurations visited by ρ which are not visited by ρ' are those in the interval $\chi_{i+1}, \chi_{i+2}, \ldots \chi_j$. However, we have already seen that all counter values in $\chi_0, \chi_1, \ldots, \chi_j$ are bounded by $\pi_{M,N,K} + K$.

It is clear that if ρ' satisfies the lemma, then so does ρ. On the other hand, if ρ' does not satisfy the lemma, then ρ is not a minimum length counterexample to the lemma. In either case we obtain a contradiction. □

We now return to the proof of the Decomposition Lemma.

Proof. (of Lemma 4.3) The proof is by induction on N, the number of counters.

Basis: If $N = 0$, set $n = 0$ and $u_1 = \rho$.

Induction step: Let Γ_{gt} denote the set of counters whose values exceed $\Pi_{M,N,K}$ in the K-run ρ.

If $\Gamma_{\text{gt}} = \emptyset$, we set $n = 0$ and $u_1 = \rho$.

Otherwise, by Proposition 4.4, we can find positions r and s in ρ such that $\chi_0 \overset{u'}{\Longrightarrow} \chi_r \overset{v'}{\Longrightarrow} \chi_s \Longrightarrow \chi_m$, with $Q(\chi_r) = Q(\chi_s)$, $F(\chi_r) < F(\chi_s)$ and all counter values at $\chi_0, \chi_1, \ldots, \chi_s$ bounded by $\pi_{M,N,K} + K$.

Let Σ be the input alphabet of $\mathcal{A}$ and Γ its set of counters. Fix a counter C' in which increases strictly between χ_r and χ_s—that is, $C'(\chi_s) > C'(\chi_r)$. By our choice of χ_r and χ_s, such a counter must exist. Construct an automaton $\mathcal{A}'$ with input alphabet $\Sigma \cup \{C'^+, C'^-\}$ and counters $\Gamma \setminus \{C'\}$. The states and transitions of $\mathcal{A}'$ are the same as those of $\mathcal{A}$. In other words, $\mathcal{A}'$ behaves like $\mathcal{A}$ except that it treats moves involving the counter C' as input letters.

Consider the computation $\chi_s \overset{t_{s+1}t_{s+2}\ldots t_m}{\Longrightarrow} \chi_m$ of $\mathcal{A}$. It is easy to see that there is a corresponding computation $\rho' : \chi'_s \overset{t_{s+1}t_{s+2}\ldots t_m}{\Longrightarrow} \chi'_m$ of $\mathcal{A}'$ such that for each $k \in [s..m]$, $Q(\chi_k) = Q(\chi'_k)$ and for each counter $C \neq C'$, $C(\chi_k) = C(\chi'_k)$.

From Proposition 4.4, we know that ρ' is in fact a $(\pi_{M,N,K}+K)$-run of $\mathcal{A}'$. Further, for every counter C in $\Gamma_{\text{gt}} \setminus \{C'\}$, there exists a $j \in [s..m]$, such that $C(\chi'_j) = C(\chi_j) > \Pi_{M,N,K} > \Pi_{M,N-1,\pi_{M,N,K}+K}$. (In the K-run ρ, no counter could have exceeded $\Pi_{M,N,K}$ before χ_s because Proposition 4.4 guarantees that all counter values at $\chi_0, \chi_1, \ldots, \chi_s$ are bounded by $\pi_{M,N,K}+K$.) By the induction hypothesis, we can find a pumpable decompostion

$$\chi'_s \overset{u'_1}{\Longrightarrow} \chi'_{i'_1} \overset{v'_1}{\Longrightarrow} \chi'_{j'_1} \overset{u'_2}{\Longrightarrow} \chi'_{i'_2} \overset{v'_2}{\Longrightarrow} \chi'_{j'_2} \overset{u'_3}{\Longrightarrow} \cdots \overset{u'_p}{\Longrightarrow} \chi'_{i'_p} \overset{v'_p}{\Longrightarrow} \chi'_{j'_p} \overset{u'_{p+1}}{\Longrightarrow} \chi_m$$

of ρ' such that if C is a counter with $C(\chi'_j) > \Pi_{M,N-1,\pi_{M,N,K}+K}$ for some $j \in [s..m]$, then there exists $k \in [1..p]$ such that $\Delta_C(v'_k)$ is positive.

Consider the corresponding computation

$$\chi_s \overset{u'_1}{\Longrightarrow} \chi_{i'_1} \overset{v'_1}{\Longrightarrow} \chi_{j'_1} \overset{u'_2}{\Longrightarrow} \chi_{i'_2} \overset{v'_2}{\Longrightarrow} \chi_{j'_2} \cdots \overset{u'_p}{\Longrightarrow} \chi_{i'_p} \overset{v'_p}{\Longrightarrow} \chi_{j'_p} \overset{u'_{p+1}}{\Longrightarrow} \chi_m$$

of $\mathcal{A}$. In this computation, for each $k \in [1..p]$, $Q(\chi_{i'_k}) = Q(\chi'_{i'_k}) = Q(\chi'_{j'_k}) = Q(\chi_{j'_k})$. Further, for each $C \in \Gamma_{\text{gt}} \setminus \{C'\}$, $C(\chi_{i'_k}) = C(\chi'_{i'_k})$ and $C(\chi_{j'_k}) = C(\chi'_{j'_k})$.

We prefix the computation $\chi_s \overset{u'_1 v'_1 \ldots u'_{p+1}}{\Longrightarrow} \chi_m$ with the K-run $\chi_0 \overset{u'}{\Longrightarrow} \chi_r \overset{v'}{\Longrightarrow} \chi_s$ which we used to identify χ_s and χ_r. We then assert that the composite K-run

$$\chi_0 \overset{u'}{\Longrightarrow} \chi_r \overset{v'}{\Longrightarrow} \chi_s \overset{u'_1}{\Longrightarrow} \chi_{i''_1} \overset{v'_1}{\Longrightarrow} \chi_{j''_1} \overset{u'_2}{\Longrightarrow} \chi_{i''_2} \overset{v'_2}{\Longrightarrow} \chi_{j''_2} \cdots \overset{u'_p}{\Longrightarrow} \chi_{i''_p} \overset{v'_p}{\Longrightarrow} \chi_{j''_p} \overset{u'_{p+1}}{\Longrightarrow} \chi_m.$$

provides the decomposition

$$\chi_0 \overset{u_1}{\Longrightarrow} \chi_{i_1} \overset{v_1}{\Longrightarrow} \chi_{j_1} \overset{u_2}{\Longrightarrow} \chi_{i_2} \overset{v_2}{\Longrightarrow} \chi_{j_2} \cdots \overset{u_n}{\Longrightarrow} \chi_{i_n} \overset{v_n}{\Longrightarrow} \chi_{j_n} \overset{u_{n+1}}{\Longrightarrow} \chi_m$$

of ρ claimed in the statement of the lemma. In other words, $u_1 = u'$, $v_1 = v'$, $\chi_{i_1} = \chi_r$ and $\chi_{j_1} = \chi_s$, while for $k \in [2..n]$, $u_k = u'_{k-1}$, $v_k = v'_{k-1}$, $\chi_{i_k} = \chi_{i'_{k-1}}$ and $\chi_{j_k} = \chi_{j'_{k-1}}$.

Let us verify that this decomposition satisfies all the conditions required by the lemma.

First we verify that this decomposition is pumpable.

- Since $p \leq N-1$, it is clear than $n = p+1 \leq N$.
- By construction $Q(\chi_{i_1}) = Q(\chi_r) = Q(\chi_s) = Q(\chi_{j_1})$. For $k \in [2..n]$, $Q(\chi_{i_k}) = Q(\chi_{i'_{k-1}}) = Q(\chi_{j'_{k-1}}) = Q(\chi_{j_k})$.
- We know that $\Delta v_1 = \Delta v'$ is non-zero and strictly positive by the choice of v'. For $k \in [2..n]$, we know that $\Delta_C(v_k) = \Delta_C(v'_{k-1})$ for $C \neq C'$. Since we have already established that $\Delta v'_{k-1}$ is non-zero and has at least one positive entry for $k \in [2..n]$, it follows that the corresponding change vectors Δv_k are also non-zero and have at least one positive entry.
- Let C be a counter and $k \in [1..n]$ such that $\Delta_C(v_k)$ is negative. Since $\Delta v_1 = \Delta v'$ is positive by the choice of v, it must be that $k \in [2..n]$. If $C \neq C'$, then $\Delta_C(v'_{k-1}) = \Delta_C(v_k)$ is negative. In this case, we already know that there exists $\ell \in [2..k-1]$, such that $\Delta_C(v'_{\ell-1}) = \Delta_C(v_\ell)$ is positive. On the other hand, if $C = C'$, it could be that $\Delta_{C'}(v'_z)$ is negative for all $z \in [1..p]$, since C' is treated as an input letter rather than as a counter in the automaton $\mathcal{A}'$. However, we know that $\Delta_{C'}(v_1) = \Delta_{C'}(v')$ is positive by the choice of v' and C', so C' also satisfies the condition of the lemma.

Finally, let C be a counter such that $C(\chi_j) > \Pi_{M,N,K}$ for some $j \in [1..m]$. If $C \neq C'$, then $C(\chi_j) > \Pi_{M,N-1,\pi_{M,N,K}+K}$ for some $j \in [s..m]$, so we already know that $\Delta_C(v'_{k-1}) = \Delta_C(v_k)$ is positive for some $k \in [2..n]$. On the other hand, if $C = C'$, we know that $\Delta_C(v_1) = \Delta_C(v')$ is positive by the choice of v' and C'.

□

The Counter Pumping Lemma allows us to pump blocks of transitions in a computation. However, it is possible for a pumpable block to consist solely of invisible transitions which increment and decrement counters. Using the Decomposition Lemma, we can prove a more traditional kind of pumping lemma, stated in terms of input strings. We omit the proof.

Lemma 4.5 (Visible Pumping). *Let L be a message-passing recognisable language. There exists $n \in \mathbb{N}$ such that for all input strings w, if $w \in L$ and $|w| \geq n$ then w can be written as $w_1 w_2 w_3$ such that $|w_1 w_2| \leq n$, $|w_2| \geq 1$ and $w_1 w_2^i w_3 \in L$ for all $i \geq 1$.*

Another consequence of Lemmas 4.2 and 4.3 is a strict hierarchy theorem for message-passing automata, whose proof we omit.

Lemma 4.6 (Counter Hierarchy). *For $k \in \mathbb{N}$, let $\mathcal{L}_k$ be the set of languages recognisable by message-passing automata with k counters. Then, for all k, $\mathcal{L}_k \subsetneq \mathcal{L}_{k+1}$.*

5 Regularity of Message-Passing Recognisable Languages

Automata with Bounded Counters

Let $\mathcal{A} = (Q, \Sigma, \Gamma, T, q_{in}, F)$ be a message-passing automaton. For $K \in \mathbb{N}$, define $\mathcal{A}[K] = (Q[K], T[K], Q[K]_{in}, F[K])$ to be the finite-state automaton over the alphabet $\Sigma \cup \Gamma^{\pm}$ given by:

- $Q[K] = Q \times \{f \mid f : \Gamma \longrightarrow [0..K]\}$, with $Q[K]_{in} = (q_{in}, \overline{0})$.
- $F[K] = F \times \{f \mid f : \Gamma \longrightarrow [0..K]\}$.
- If $(q, d, q') \in T$, then $((q, f), d, (q', f')) \in T[K]$ where:
  - If $d \in \Sigma$, $f' = f$.
  - If $d = C^+$, $f'(C') = f(C')$ for all $C' \neq C$ and
  $$f'(C) = \begin{cases} f(C)+1 & \text{if } f(C) < K \\ K & \text{otherwise.} \end{cases}$$
  - If $d = C^-$, $f'(C') = f(C')$ for all $C' \neq C$, $f(C) \geq 1$ and
  $$f'(C) = \begin{cases} f(C)-1 & \text{if } f(C) < K \\ K & \text{otherwise.} \end{cases}$$

Each transition $t = ((q, f), d, (q', f')) \in T[K]$ corresponds to a unique transition $(q, d, q') \in T$, which we denote t^{-1}. For a sequence of transitions $t_1 t_2 \dots t_n$, we write $(t_1 t_2 \dots t_n)^{-1}$ for $t_1^{-1} t_2^{-1} \dots t_n^{-1}$. For any sequence $t_1 t_2 \dots t_n$ of transitions in $T[K]$, $\alpha(t_1 t_2 \dots t_n) = \alpha((t_1 t_2 \dots t_n)^{-1})$. Moreover, if $(q_0, f'_0) \stackrel{t_1 t_2 \dots t_n}{\Longrightarrow} (q_n, f'_n)$ and $(q_0, f_0) \stackrel{(t_1 t_2 \dots t_n)^{-1}}{\Longrightarrow} \chi_n$, then $Q(\chi_n) = q_n$.

Thus, the finite-state automaton $\mathcal{A}[K]$ behaves like a message-passing automaton except that it deems any counter whose value attains a value K to be "full" . Once a counter is declared to be full, it can be decremented as many times as desired. The following observations are immediate.

Proposition 5.1. *(i) If* $(q_0, f'_0) \stackrel{t'_1}{\longrightarrow} (q_1, f'_1) \stackrel{t'_2}{\longrightarrow} \cdots \stackrel{t'_n}{\longrightarrow} (q_n, f'_n)$ *is a computation of* $\mathcal{A}$ *then,* $(q_0, f_0) \stackrel{t_1}{\longrightarrow} (q_1, f_1) \stackrel{t_2}{\longrightarrow} \cdots \stackrel{t_n}{\longrightarrow} (q_n, f_n)$ *is a computation of* $\mathcal{A}[K]$ *where*

- $t'_1 t'_2 \dots t'_n = (t_1 t_2 \dots t_n)^{-1}$.
- $\forall C \in \Gamma.\ \forall i \in [1..n].\ f_i(C) = \begin{cases} f'_i(C) & \text{if } f'_j(C) < K \text{ for all } j \leq i \\ K & \text{otherwise} \end{cases}$

(ii) Let $(q_0, f_0) \stackrel{t_1}{\longrightarrow} (q_1, f_1) \stackrel{t_2}{\longrightarrow} \cdots \stackrel{t_n}{\longrightarrow} (q_n, f_n)$ *be a computation of* $\mathcal{A}[K]$. *Then there is a maximal prefix* $t_1 t_2 \dots t_\ell$ *of* $t_1 t_2 \dots t_n$ *such that there is a computation* $(q_0, f'_0) \stackrel{t_1^{-1}}{\longrightarrow} (q_1, f'_1) \stackrel{t_2^{-1}}{\longrightarrow} \cdots \stackrel{t_\ell^{-1}}{\longrightarrow} (q_\ell, f'_\ell)$ *of* $\mathcal{A}$ *with* $f_0 = f'_0$. *Moreover, if* $\ell < n$, *then for some counter* C, $\alpha(t'_{\ell+1}) = C^-$, $f'_\ell(C) = 0$ *and there is a* $j < \ell$ *such that* $f'_j(C) = K$.

(iii) Let $L(\mathcal{A}[K])$ *be the language over* $\Sigma \cup \Gamma^{\pm}$ *accepted by* $\mathcal{A}[K]$. *Let* $L_\Sigma(\mathcal{A}[K]) = \{w{\restriction_\Sigma} \mid w \in L(\mathcal{A}[K])\}$. *Then,* $L(\mathcal{A}) \subseteq L_\Sigma(\mathcal{A}[K])$.

Synchronised Products of Message-Passing Automata

Product automata Let $\mathcal{A}_i = (Q_i, \Sigma_i, \Gamma_i, T_i, q^i_{\text{in}}, F_i)$, $i = 1, 2$, be a pair of message-passing automata. The *product automaton* $\mathcal{A}_1 \times \mathcal{A}_2$ is the structure $(Q_1 \times Q_2, \Sigma_1 \cup \Sigma_2, \Gamma_1 \cup \Gamma_2, T_1 \times T_2, (q^1_{\text{in}}, q^2_{\text{in}}), F_1 \times F_2)$, where $((q_1, q_2), d, (q'_1, q'_2)) \in T_1 \times T_2$ iff one of the following holds:

- $d \in (\Sigma_1 \cup \Gamma_1) \cap (\Sigma_2 \cup \Gamma_2)$ and $(q_i, d, q'_i) \in T_i$ for $i \in \{1, 2\}$.
- $d \in (\Sigma_1 \cup \Gamma_1) \setminus (\Sigma_2 \cup \Gamma_2)$, $(q_1, d, q'_1) \in T_1$ and $q_2 = q'_2$.
- $d \in (\Sigma_2 \cup \Gamma_2) \setminus (\Sigma_1 \cup \Gamma_1)$, $(q_2, d, q'_2) \in T_2$ and $q_1 = q'_1$.

For $t = ((q_1, q_2), d, (q'_1, q'_2)) \in T$ and $i \in \{1, 2\}$, let $\pi_i(t)$ denote (q_i, d, q'_i) if $d \in (\Sigma_i \cup \Gamma_i)$ and the empty string ε otherwise. As usual, $\pi_i(t_1 t_2 \ldots t_n)$ is just $\pi_i(t_1)\pi_i(t_2)\ldots\pi_i(t_n)$. Thus, for a sequence of transitions $\rho = t_1 t_2 \ldots t_n$ over $T_1 \times T_2$, $\pi_1(\rho)$ and $\pi_2(\rho)$ denote the projections of ρ onto the transitions of $\mathcal{A}_1$ and $\mathcal{A}_2$ respectively. Clearly, $\alpha(t_1 t_2 \ldots t_n)\lceil_{(\Sigma_i \cup \Gamma_i)} = \alpha(\pi_i(t_1 t_2 \ldots t_n))$ for $i \in \{1, 2\}$.

We shall often write a configuration $((q_1, q_2), f)$ of $\mathcal{A}_1 \times \mathcal{A}_2$ as a pair of configurations $((q_1, f_1), (q_2, f_2))$ of $\mathcal{A}_1$ and $\mathcal{A}_2$, where f_1 and f_2 are restrictions of f to Γ_1 and Γ_2 respectively.

The following observations are easy consequences of the definition of product automata.

Proposition 5.2. *(i)* $((q^1_{\text{in}}, \overline{0}), (q^2_{\text{in}}, \overline{0})) \stackrel{t_1 t_2 \ldots t_n}{\Longrightarrow} ((q_1, f_1), (q_2, f_2))$ *is a computation of* $\mathcal{A}_1 \times \mathcal{A}_2$ *if and only if* $(q^1_{\text{in}}, \overline{0}) \stackrel{\pi_1(t_1 t_2 \ldots t_n)}{\Longrightarrow} (q_1, f_1)$ *and* $(q^2_{\text{in}}, \overline{0}) \stackrel{\pi_2(t_1 t_2 \ldots t_n)}{\Longrightarrow} (q_2, f_2)$ *are computations of* $\mathcal{A}_1$ *and* $\mathcal{A}_2$ *respectively.*
(ii) If $\Sigma_1 = \Sigma_2$ *and* $\Gamma_1 \cap \Gamma_2 = \emptyset$, *then* $L(\mathcal{A}_1 \times \mathcal{A}_2) = L(\mathcal{A}_1) \cap L(\mathcal{A}_2)$.

5.1 Regularity and Closure under Complementation

Our first characterisation of regular message-passing recognisable languages is the following.

Theorem 5.3. *Let L be a language over Σ. L and $\overline{L}$ are message-passing recognisable iff L is regular.*

This result is related to the main result of [MNRS98] which states that if we record the behaviour of message-passing systems as tuples of sequences, every *robust* system is effectively finite-state. In the sequential setting, a language L would be robust in the sense of [MNRS98] if there were a single automaton $\mathcal{A}$ with accept and reject states such that for each word $w \in L$, *every* run of $\mathcal{A}$ on w leads to an accept state and for each word $w \notin L$, *every* run of $\mathcal{A}$ on w leads to a reject state. Here, the requirement on L is much weaker—all we demand is that both L and $\overline{L}$ be accepted independently by message-passing automata, possibly with very different state spaces.

To prove the theorem, we need an auxiliary result. Let $L \subseteq \Sigma^*$ be such that both L and its complement $\overline{L}$ are message-passing recognisable. Let $L = L(\mathcal{A})$ and $\overline{L} = L(\overline{\mathcal{A}})$, where we may assume that $\mathcal{A}$ and $\overline{\mathcal{A}}$ use disjoint sets of counters.

The language accepted by $\mathcal{A} \times \overline{\mathcal{A}}$ must be empty. Let M be the number of states of $\mathcal{A} \times \overline{\mathcal{A}}$ and N be the number of counters that it uses. Let K be a number greater than $\Pi_{M,N,0}$, the strong pumping constant for $(M, N, 0)$. Recall that $\mathcal{A}[K] = (Q[K], T[K], Q[K]_{\text{in}}, F[K])$ is a finite-state automaton *without* counters working on the input alphabet $\Sigma \cup \Gamma^{\pm}$.

Lemma 5.4. $L(\mathcal{A}[K] \times \overline{\mathcal{A}}) = \emptyset$.

Proof. Let $\mathcal{A}[K] = (Q[K], T[K], Q[K]_{\text{in}}, F[K])$ and $\overline{\mathcal{A}} = (\overline{Q}, \Sigma, \overline{\Gamma}, \overline{T}, \overline{q}_{\text{in}} \overline{F})$. Each computation ρ of $\mathcal{A}[K] \times \overline{\mathcal{A}}$ is of the form $((q_0, \overline{0}), (\overline{q}_0, \overline{0})) \xrightarrow{u_1} ((q_1, f_1), (\overline{q}_1, \overline{f}_1)) \xrightarrow{u_2} \cdots \xrightarrow{u_n} ((q_n, f_n), (\overline{q}_n, \overline{f}_n))$, where, for $i \in [0..n]$, $u_i \in T[K] \times \overline{T}$.

By Propositions 5.1 and 5.2, corresponding to the sequence $u_1 u_2 \ldots u_n$ there exists a maximal sequence of transitions $v_1 v_2 \ldots v_m$ of $\mathcal{A} \times \overline{\mathcal{A}}$ where:

- Each v_i belongs to $T \times \overline{T}$.
- For each $i \in [1..m]$, $\pi_2(v_i) = \pi_2(u_i)$.
- For each $i \in [1..m]$, $\pi_1(v_i) = \begin{cases} (\pi_1(u_i))^{-1} & \text{if } \pi_1(u_i) \neq \varepsilon \\ \varepsilon & \text{otherwise} \end{cases}$
- $\rho' : ((q_0, \overline{0}), (\overline{q}_0, \overline{0})) \xrightarrow{v_1} ((q_1, f_1'), (\overline{q}_1, \overline{f}_1)) \xrightarrow{v_2} \cdots \xrightarrow{v_m} ((q_m, f_m'), (\overline{q}_m, \overline{f}_m))$ is a computation of $\mathcal{A} \times \overline{\mathcal{A}}$.
- If $m < n$, then for some $\hat{C} \in \Gamma$, $\alpha(u_{m+1}) = \hat{C}^-$, $f_m'(\hat{C}) = 0$ and $f_j'(\hat{C}) = K$ for some $j \in [0..m]$.

Let us define the *residue length* of ρ to be $n - m$.

Suppose that $L(\mathcal{A}[K] \times \overline{\mathcal{A}})$ is non-empty. Since $L(\mathcal{A} \times \overline{\mathcal{A}})$ is empty, it is easy to see that any accepting run of $\mathcal{A}[K] \times \overline{\mathcal{A}}$ has a non-zero residue length. Without loss of generality, assume that the run ρ considered earlier is an accepting run of $\mathcal{A}[K] \times \overline{\mathcal{A}}$ whose residue length is minimal. Then, in the corresponding run ρ' of $\mathcal{A} \times \overline{\mathcal{A}}$, the counter $\hat{C} \in \Gamma$ attains the value K along ρ' and then goes to 0 at the end of the run so that the move labelled $\hat{C}^-$ is not enabled at $((q_m, f_m'), (\overline{q}_m, \overline{f}_m))$.

Since K exceeds the strong pumping constant for $\mathcal{A} \times \overline{\mathcal{A}}$, by Lemma 4.2 we can find an alternative run $\hat{\rho}' : ((q_0, \overline{0}), (\overline{q}_0, \overline{0})) \stackrel{v_1' v_2' \ldots v_\ell'}{\Longrightarrow} ((q_\ell', f_\ell'), (\overline{q}_\ell', \overline{f}_\ell'))$ with $(q_\ell', \overline{q}_\ell') = (q_m, \overline{q}_m)$, $f_\ell'(\hat{C}) \geq K$, and all other counter values at $(f_\ell', \overline{f}_\ell')$ at least as large as at $(f_m, \overline{f}_m')$. In particular, *every* counter which exceeded the cutoff value K along ρ' is pumpable and thus exceeds K along $\hat{\rho}'$ as well.

By Propositions 5.1 and 5.2, we can construct a corresponding sequence of transitions $u_1' u_2' \ldots u_\ell'$ over $T[K] \times \overline{T}$ such that $\pi_1(v_1' v_2' \ldots v_\ell') = (\pi_1(u_1' u_2' \ldots u_\ell'))^{-1}$ and $\pi_2(v_1' v_2' \ldots v_\ell') = \pi_2(u_1' u_2' \ldots u_\ell')$, where $\hat{\rho} : ((q_0, \overline{0}), (\overline{q}_0, \overline{0})) \stackrel{u_1' u_2' \ldots u_\ell'}{\Longrightarrow} ((q_\ell'', f_\ell''), (\overline{q}_\ell', \overline{f}_\ell'))$ is a run of $\mathcal{A}[K] \times \overline{\mathcal{A}}$ with $(q_\ell'', \overline{q}_\ell') = (q_m, \overline{q}_m)$ and $f_\ell''(C) \geq f_m(C)$ for each $C \in \Gamma$.

We already know that $\overline{f}_\ell'(C) \geq \overline{f}_m(C)$ for each $C \in \overline{\Gamma}$. Further, since every counter which exceeded the cutoff value K along ρ' also exceeds K along $\hat{\rho}'$, we know that any counter which has become full along ρ would also have saturated along $\hat{\rho}$. Thus, we can extend $\hat{\rho}$ to an accepting run σ by appending the sequence of transitions $u_{m+1}u_{m+2}\ldots u_n$ which occur at the end of the accepting run ρ.

Recall that $\alpha(u_{m+1}) = \hat{C}^-$ and $f'_\ell(\hat{C}) \geq 1$ by our choice of $\hat{\rho}'$. From this, it follows that the residue length of the newly constructed accepting run σ is at least one less than the residue length of ρ, which is a contradiction, since ρ was assumed to be an accepting run of minimal residue length. □

We can now prove Theorem 5.3.

Proof. (of Theorem 5.3)
Let $L = L(\mathcal{A})$ and $\overline{L} = L(\overline{\mathcal{A}})$. Define $\mathcal{A}[K]$ as above. We claim that $L_\Sigma(\mathcal{A}[K]) = L(\mathcal{A})$. By Proposition 5.1, we know that $L(\mathcal{A}) \subseteq L_\Sigma(\mathcal{A}[K])$. On the other hand, from the previous lemma it follows that $L_\Sigma(\mathcal{A}[K]) \cap L(\overline{\mathcal{A}}) = \emptyset$. This implies that $L_\Sigma(\mathcal{A}[K]) \subseteq \overline{L(\overline{\mathcal{A}})}$, which means that $L_\Sigma(\mathcal{A}[K]) \subseteq L(\mathcal{A})$. So $L(\mathcal{A}) = L_\Sigma(\mathcal{A}[K])$. Since $\mathcal{A}[K]$ is a finite-state automaton, it follows that $L(\mathcal{A})$ is regular. Therefore, if a language and its complement are message-passing recognisable then the language is regular.

The converse is obvious. □

Observe that our construction is effective—given message-passing automata $\mathcal{A}$ and $\overline{\mathcal{A}}$ for L and $\overline{L}$ respectively, we can construct a finite-state automaton $\mathcal{A}[K]$ for L.

5.2 Regularity and Determinacy

Our next characterisation of regularity is in terms of deterministic message-passing automata.

Deterministic Message-Passing Automata A message-passing automaton $\mathcal{A} = (Q, \Sigma, \Gamma, T, q_{\text{in}}, F)$ is said to be *deterministic* if the following two conditions hold:

- If $(q, d_1, q_1), (q, d_2, q_2) \in T$, with $d_1, d_2 \in \Sigma$, then $d_1 = d_2$ implies $q_1 = q_2$.
- If $(q, d_1, q_1), (q, d_2, q_2) \in T$, with $d_1 \in \Gamma^\pm$, then $d_1 = d_2$ and $q_1 = q_2$.

Though this notion of determinism seems rather strong, any relaxation of the definition will allow deterministic automata to simulate non-deterministic automata in a trivial manner. If we permit the automaton to choose between a counter move and another transition (which may or may not be a counter move), we can add a spurious counter C and replace any non-deterministic choice between transitions $t_1 = (q, d, q_1)$ and $t_2 = (q, d, q_2)$ by a choice between t_1 and a move (q, C^+, q_C) involving C which leads to a new state where $t'_2 = (q_C, d, q_2)$ is enabled.

The following result characterises languages accepted by deterministic message-passing automata. Similar results have been demonstrated for deterministic Petri net languages [Pel87,V82].

Proposition 5.5. *Let $\mathcal{A}$ be a deterministic message-passing automaton. Then, either $L(\mathcal{A})$ is regular or there is a word $w \notin L(\mathcal{A})$ such that every extension of w also does not belong to $L(\mathcal{A})$.*

Proof Sketch. Let $\mathcal{A}$ be a deterministic message-passing automaton. We say that $\mathcal{A}$ is *Γ-blocked on a word* w if, while reading w, $\mathcal{A}$ gets stuck at a state with a single outgoing edge labelled C^-, for some counter C. If $\mathcal{A}$ is Γ-blocked on w, it is easy to see $\mathcal{A}$ is also Γ-blocked on w' for any extension w' of w, so every extension of w is outside $L(\mathcal{A})$.

If $\mathcal{A}$ is not Γ-blocked for any word w, we construct a finite-state automaton $\mathcal{A}'$ with ε-moves over Σ with the same state space as $\mathcal{A}$. In $\mathcal{A}'$, each counter move (q, d, q'), $d \in \Gamma^{\pm}$, is replaced by a ε-move (q, ε, q'). There is a natural correspondence between computations of $\mathcal{A}$ and runs of $\mathcal{A}'$. It is easy to see that $L(\mathcal{A}) \subseteq L(\mathcal{A}')$. Using the fact that $\mathcal{A}$ is not Γ-blocked for any word w, we can show that any accepting run of $\mathcal{A}'$ can be mapped back to an accepting run of $\mathcal{A}$. Thus $L(\mathcal{A}') \subseteq L(\mathcal{A})$. In other words, $L(\mathcal{A}') = L(\mathcal{A})$, so $L(\mathcal{A})$ is regular. □

The preceding characterisation implies that non-deterministic message-passing automata are strictly more powerful than deterministic message-passing automata. Consider the language $L = \{w \mid w = w_1 a^m b^n a w_2\}$ where $w_1, w_2 \in \{a, b\}^*$ and $m \geq n \geq 1$. This language is message-passing recognisable but violates the condition of Proposition 5.5: L is not regular and for any word $w \notin L$, we can always find an extension of w in L—for instance, $waba \in L$ for all $w \in \{a, b\}^*$.

Observe, however, that even deterministic message-passing automata are strictly more powerful than normal finite-state automata. For instance, the language L_{ge} of Example 2.1 is not regular but the automaton accepting the language is deterministic.

With these observations about deterministic automata behind us, we can now state our alternative characterisation of regularity. First, we need some notation. For a string w, let w^R denote the string obtained by reading w from right to left. For a language L, let L^R be the set of strings $\{w^R \mid w \in L\}$.

Theorem 5.6. *Let L be a message-passing recognisable language such that L^R is recognised by a deterministic message-passing automaton. Then, L is regular.*

The idea is to compute a constant τ which depends on the number of states M and the number of counters N of $\mathcal{A}$ and to then show that L is recognised by the finite-state automaton $L[\tau]$. The proof is quite involved and we omit it due to lack of space.

6 Discussion

Other models for asynchronous commmunication Many earlier attempts to model asynchronous systems focus on the infinite-state case—for instance, the port automaton model of Panangaden and Stark [PS88] and the I/O automaton model of Lynch and Tuttle [LT87]. Also, earlier work has looked at issues far removed from those which are traditionally considered in the study of finite-state systems.

Recently, Abdulla and Jonsson have studied decision problems for distributed systems with asynchronous communication [AJ93]. However, they model channels as unbounded, fifo buffers, a framework in which most interesting questions become undecidable. The results of [AJ93] show that the fifo model becomes tractable if messages may be lost in transit: questions such as reachability of configurations become decidable. While their results are, in general, incomparable to ours, we remark that their positive results hold for our model as well.

Petri net languages Our model is closely related to Petri nets [G78,J86]. We can go back and forth between labelled Petri nets and message-passing networks while maintaining a bijection between the firing sequences of a net N and the computations of the corresponding automaton $\mathcal{A}$.

There are several ways to associate a language with a Petri net [H75,J86,Pet81]. The first is to examine all firing sequences of the net. The second is to look at firing sequences which lead to a set of *final markings*. The third is to identify firing sequences which reach markings which *dominate* some final marking. The third class corresponds to message-passing recognisable languages.

A number of positive results have been established for the first class of languages—for instance, regularity is decidable [GY80,VV80]. On the other hand, a number of negative results have been established for the second class of languages—for instance, it is undecidable whether such a language contains *all* strings [VV80]. However, none of these results, positive or negative, carry over to the third class—ours is one of the few tangible results for this class of Petri net languages.

Directions for future work We believe that Theorem 5.6 holds even without the determinacy requirement on L^R. An interesting question is to develop a method for transforming sequential specifications in terms of message-passing automata into equivalent distributed specifications in terms of the message-passing network model of [MNRS98]. Another challenging question is the decidability of regularity for message-passing recognisable languages.

References

[AJ93] P.A. Abdulla and B. Jonsson: Verifying programs with unreliable channels, in *Proc. 8th IEEE Symp. Logic in Computer Science*, Montreal, Canada (1993).

[GY80] A. Ginzburg and M. Yoeli: Vector Addition Systems and Regular Languages, *J. Comput. System. Sci.* **20** (1980) 277–284

[G78] S.A. Greibach: Remarks on Blind and Partially Blind One-Way Multicounter Machines, *Theoret. Comput. Sci* **7** (1978) 311–324.

[H75] M. Hack: Petri Net Languages, *C.S.G. Memo 124*, Project MAC, MIT (1975).

[H91] G.J. Holzmann: *Design and validation of computer protocols*, Prentice Hall (1991).

[J86] M. Jantzen: Language Theory of Petri Nets, in W. Brauer, W. Reisig, G. Rozenberg (eds.), *Petri Nets: Central Models and Their Properties, Advances in Petri Nets, 1986, Vol 1*, Springer LNCS **254** (1986) 397–412.

[KM69] R.M. Karp and R.E. Miller: Parallel Program Schemata, *J. Comput. System Sci.*, **3** (4) (1969) 167–195.

[LT87] N.A. Lynch and M. Tuttle: Hierarchical Correctness Proofs for Distributed Algorithms, *Technical Report MIT/LCS/TR-387*, Laboratory for Computer Science, MIT (1987).

[M78] A. Mazurkiewicz: Concurrent Program Schemes and their Interpretations, *Report DAIMI-PB-78*, Computer Science Department, Aarhus University, Denmark (1978).

[MNRS97] M. Mukund, K. Narayan Kumar, J. Radhakrishnan and M. Sohoni: Message-Passing Automata and Asynchronous Communication, *Report TCS-97-4*, SPIC Mathematical Institute, Madras, India (1997).

[MNRS98] M. Mukund, K. Narayan Kumar, J. Radhakrishnan and M. Sohoni: Robust Asynchronous Protocols are Finite-State, *Proc. ICALP 98*, Springer LNCS (1998) *(to appear)*.

[PS88] P. Panangaden and E.W. Stark: Computations, Residuals, and the Power of Indeterminacy, in T. Lepisto and A. Salomaa (eds.), *Proc. ICALP '88*, Springer LNCS **317** (1988) 439–454.

[Pel87] E. Pelz: Closure Properties of Deterministic Petri Nets, *Proc. STACS 87*, Springer LNCS **247**, (1987) 371-382.

[Pet81] J.L. Peterson: *Petri net theory and the modelling of systems*, Prentice Hall (1981).

[VV80] R. Valk and G. Vidal-Naquet: Petri Nets and Regular Languages, *J. Comput. System. Sci.* **20** (1980) 299–325.

[V82] G. Vidal-Naquet: Deterministic languages for Petri nets, *Application and Theory of Petri Nets*, Informatik-Fachberichte **52**, Springer-Verlag (1982).

[Z87] W. Zielonka: Notes on Finite Asynchronous Automata, *R.A.I.R.O.—Inf. Théor. et Appl.*, **21** (1987) 99–135.

Mobile Computation: Calculus and Languages (A Tutorial)

N. Raja and R.K. Shyamasundar

School of Technology & Computer Science
Tata Institute of Fundamental Research
Mumbai 400 005, India
{raja, shyam}@tcs.tifr.res.in

Abstract. This paper provides a brief overview of a tutorial on current research directions in mobile computation. In particular we provide an overview of the various abstract calculi for mobility, an overview of the programming languages that have been developed for mobile computation, and provide a comparative study of the language abstractions via the calculi and discuss the underlying challenges.

1 Introduction

Mobility denotes the physical or virtual movement of computational resources (comprising hardware and software) across a local or global network. The term *mobile computing* is used for environments where the hardware is mobile, while the term *mobile computation* is used in situations where software is mobile. In this survey we shall focus on mobile computation. With rapid advances in Internet technology, and the availability of powerful laptop and palmtop computers, the concept of mobility is undergoing a metamorphosis from a mere theoretical curiosity to become one of the essential requirements of every computing environment. The phenomenon of mobility on a global scale has the potential of causing wide ranging effects on the practice of computing and programming. Further, by providing a completely new paradigm for understanding the nature of computation, it forces us to reconsider our conceptual understanding of the notion of computation as well.

In this tutorial, we shall provide an overview of the calculi for mobility, an overview of the programming languages that have been developed for mobile computation, and provide a comparative study of the language abstractions via the calculi and discuss the underlying challenges. Following sections provide a brief overview of the various calculi for mobility & their evolution, and the widely used programming languages for mobile computation purposes.

2 Calculi for Mobility

What is an appropriate abstract model for mobile computation? Traditional research has focussed along three independent strands – functional, concurrent,

Jieh Hsiang, Atsushi Ohori (Eds.): ASIAN'98, LNCS 1538, pp. 300–304, 1998.

and distributed computing. However none of these models adequately captures the significant features of mobile computation [7]. Mobile computation demands an entirely new paradigm.

A number of calculi have been proposed over the years to study concurrent computation. New calculi are being evolved from these, with the addition of notions to capture features associated with mobile computation.

One of the earliest abstract framework for concurrent computing was provided by Actors [2]. Though the framework had an intuitive appeal to model massively parallel computation, it was not amenable to formal reasoning. Recent proposals have sought to rectify this situation with notions of nested structures of arbitrary depth, which mirrors the nesting of administrative domains on the web [25]. The earliest proposals of formal calculi for concurrent computing could deal only with static connectivity among processes, and in certain cases even the total number of processes had to be fixed in advance. Among these are Petrinets [26], CSP [18], and CCS [21]. In the setting of the Internet, communication links appear and disappear frequently. This is due to wide fluctuations in bandwidth of links, unpredictable failures and recovery of links giving rise to connections through alternative routes. So calculi which are restricted to static connectivity are clearly inadequate. The next generation of process calculi could model networks of processes with dynamic connectivity. Among these π-calculus [22], and Asynchronous π-calculus [17] directly modeled channel mobility, while Linda [10] and CHOCS [29] modeled process mobility. These calculi lack the notion of distributed locations of processes, which cannot be ignored in mobile computation over the web. These calculi have in turn been extended with primitives to capture distributed concurrent computing. LLinda [11] extends Linda, while Join-calculus [13] extends π-calculus. The next logical step towards developing a calculus for mobile computation was to incorporate explicit notions of locality in these calculi [4]. The notion of locations is important in modeling barriers caused due to administrative domains which impose their own restrictions on the movement of messages across them. Such extensions gave rise to the Distributed Join-calculus [14] and the Ambient calculus [6,7]. The Ambient calculus can also model mobility of active computations.

Apart from these calculi, a number of others have been proposed to study various orthogonal issues in mobile computation. The Spi calculus [1] is a preliminary attempt to model security aspects, while Mobile Unity [27] incorporates techniques for reasoning and specification of mobile computations.

There are a number of issues that need further exploration, such as refined notions of structured data, typing, and correctness proofs in a concurrent distributed mobile context. These notions need to be unified in a coherent semantic framework. Such an enterprise will lead to fundamental insights into the phenomenon of computation itself.

3 Programming Languages for Mobile Computation

One of the most fascinating outcomes of the development of mobile computation is the concrete realization of *mobile software*. Mobile software is programming language code which is shipped across a network from a source to a destination site, and is executed at the destination computer. The results (if any) are then returned to the source computer. The presence of mobile software in a framework where the source and destination computers are themselves mobile (due to hardware mobility) gives rise to a rich set of possibilities, and also gives raise to a number of issues that need to be addressed.

The desirability of mobile software arises primarily from the fact that it can vastly reduce the communication overheads while implementing services between servers and clients across a network. The savings are particularly enhanced if the service happens to be an interactive one. Reduction in the messages exchanged between server and client is particularly meaningful in an environment where communication links experience unpredictable fluctuations in their effective bandwidth, are susceptible to frequent failures, and the messages have to traverse a number of distinct administrative domains which erect barriers to the flow of messages across them. Secondly, mobile software provides a great degree of flexibility to the server computers, wherein the kind and number of services offered by them need not be static and determined in advance. Third, the maintenance of networks of mobile computers is rendered easier when the clients can themselves control the installation of latest software updates as and when required. Finally, as a valuable side effect, mobile software also leads to savings in storage space since programs can be fetched and executed on demand.

The possibility of mobile software gives rise to at least three kinds of situations depending on the entity which takes the initiative of moving the software – the provider, the execution site, or the software itself.

A number of issues crop up in the design and implementation of mobile software. First among these is the obvious requirement of portability. The same software should be capable of being executed across a variety of architectures and computing environments. The second requirement is that of safety. Safety demands that errors in the mobile software should not affect the environment of the execution site. Third, the myriad security issues such as secrecy, message integrity, authentication of servers and clients, and non-repudiation of messages transmitted assume great significance. Finally, the need for efficiency is omnipresent. Various programming languages have been designed for mobile software including those for agent-oriented programming. A few prominent ones among these are Obliq [9], Telescript [15], Limbo [20], O'Caml [19], Safe-Tcl [24], and Java [3]. A comparative study of these languages is contained in [30].

In spite of the availability of a number of languages for developing mobile software, there remains a wide scope for further improvements. For instance, transfer of active computations needs to be supported [7]. In the context of mobility, it is not sufficient to allow only the transfer of passive program code across computers; effective and efficient ways of transferring computation in progress, along with their environments (and proofs!) needs to be given careful consideration. The development of such programming paradigms could provide a positive feedback to the architecture of the Internet itself.

4 Discussion

The phenomenon of mobility represents a major revolution in the discipline of computing and programming. Research on calculi for mobility is seeking to address the challenges arising from mobile computation by unifying various traditional computation models; while research on programming languages seeks to create tools which will translate theoretical possibilities to realistic systems which would comprise computational environments in the decades to come.

In order to fully translate the potential benefits of mobility to a computerized society, research is needed on a whole spectrum of issues ranging from the formulation of a formal logical basis for computation in a mobile world, to the development of cost-effective and user friendly software tools which translate theoretical possibilities to practical and realistic computational environments.

The scenario of autonomous entities freely traversing globally distributed networks, requires the development of entirely new proof systems, behavioral theories, and software development methodologies in order to specify and establish properties of such computational entities [23]. Software tools which comprise implementations of verification systems, and specification languages would result on the basis provided by such proof methodologies.

The area of network security acquires a prominent place when mobility is prevalent. Traditional research on security has focussed mostly on secrecy issues, which have been handled through cryptology. More recent work on security has dealt with ways of reasoning about authentication mechanisms using logics of belief [5]. However, other aspects of security in mobile computation are yet to be addressed in a satisfactory manner [12].

References

1. Abadi, M., Gordon, A.D.: A calculus for Cryptographic Protocols: the SPI Calculus. Proc. ACM Conference on Computer and Communications Security, ACM Press (1997) 36–47.
2. Agha, G.: Actors: A Model of Concurrent Computing in Distributed Systems. MIT Press (1986).
3. Arnold, K., Gosling, J.: The Java Programming Language. Sun Microsystems (1996).
4. Boudol, G., Castellani, I., Hennessy, M., Kiehn, A.: A Theory of Processes with Localities. Formal Aspects of Computing, **6** (1994) 165–200.
5. Burrows, M., Abadi, M., Needham, R.: A Logic of Authentication. ACM Transactions on Computer Systems, **8** (1990) 18–36.
6. Cardelli, L., Gordon, A.D.: Mobile Ambients. Foundations of Software Science and Computational Structures, Lecture Notes in Computer Science, Vol. 1378, Springer-Verlag (1998) 140–155.
7. Cardelli, L.: Abstractions for Mobile Computation. Manuscript (1998).

8. Cardelli, L., Davies, R.: Service Combinators for Web Computing. DEC Research Report (1997).
9. Cardelli, L.: A Language with Distributed Scope. Computing Systems **8** (1995) 27–59.
10. Carriero, N., Gelernter, D.: Linda in Context. Communications of the ACM **32** (1989) 444–458.
11. Carriero, N., Gelernter, D., Zuck, L.: Bauhaus Linda. Proc. Object-Based Models and Languages for Concurrent Systems, Lecture Notes in Computer Science, Vol. 924. Springer-Verlag (1995) 66–76.
12. Chess, D.M.: Security Issues in Mobile Code Systems. Mobile Agents and Security, Lecture Notes in Computer Science, Vol 1419. Springer-Verlag (1998).
13. Fournet, C, Gonthier G.: The Reflexive CHAM and the Join Calculus. Proc. POPL, ACM Press (1996) 372–385.
14. Fournet, C, Gonthier G., Lévy, J-J., Maranget, L., Rémy, D.: A Calculus of Mobile Agents. Proc. CONCUR'96, Lecture Notes in Computer Science, Springer-Verlag (1996) 406–421.
15. General Magic: The Telescript Home Page. Available at http://www.genmagic.com/Telescript.
16. General Magic: Mobile Agents White Paper.
17. Honda, K., Tokoro, M.: An Object Calculus for Asynchronous Communication. Proc. ECOOP'91, Lecture Notes in Computer Science, Vol. 521. Springer-Verlag (1991) 133–147.
18. Hoare, C.A.R.: Communicating Sequential Processes. Prentice-Hall (1988).
19. Leroy, X.: Objective Caml. Available at http://pauillac.inria.fr/ocaml/.
20. Lucent Technologies: The Inferno Home Page. Available at http://inferno.bell-labs.com/inferno/index.html.
21. Milner, R.: Communication and Concurrency. Prentice-Hall (1988).
22. Milner, R., Parrow, J., Walker, D.: A Calculus of Mobile Processes, Parts 1–2. Information and Computation **100** (1992) 1–77.
23. Necula, G.C., Lee P.: Safe, Untrusted Agents Using Proof-Carrying Code. Mobile Agents and Security, Lecture Notes in Computer Science, Vol 1419. Springer-Verlag (1998).
24. Ousterhout, J.K.: Tcl and the Tk Toolkit. Addison-Wesley (1994).
25. Raja, N., Shyamasundar, R.K.: Actors as a Coordinating Model of Computation. Perspectives of System Informatics, Lecture Notes in Computer Science, Vol 1181. Springer-Verlag (1996) 191–202.
26. Reisig, W.: Petrinets. EATCS Monographs on Theoretical Computer Science (1990).
27. Roman, G-C., McCann, P.J., Plun, J.Y.: Mobile UNITY: reasoning and Specification in Mobile Computing. ACM Transactions on Software Engineering and Methodology, **6** (1997) 250–282.
28. Stamos, J.W., Gifford, D.K.: Remote Evaluation. ACM Transactions on Programming Languages and Systems **12** (1990) 537–565.
29. Thomsen, B.: Calculi for higher-order communicating systems, Ph.D. thesis, Imperial College, London University (1990).
30. Thorn, T.: Programming Languages for Mobile Code. ACM Computing Surveys, **29** (1997) (213–239).

Author Index

Springer and the environment

Lecture Notes in Computer Science

For information about Vols. 1–1454
please contact your bookseller or Springer-Verlag

Vol. 1455: A. Hunter, S. Parsons (Eds.), Applications of Uncertainty Formalisms. VIII, 474 pages. 1998. (Subseries LNAI).

Vol. 1456: A. Drogoul, M. Tambe, T. Fukuda (Eds.), Collective Robotics. Proceedings, 1998. VII, 161 pages. 1998. (Subseries LNAI).

Vol. 1457: A. Ferreira, J. Rolim, H. Simon, S.-H. Teng (Eds.), Solving Irregularly Structured Problems in Prallel. Proceedings, 1998. X, 408 pages. 1998.

Vol. 1458: V.O. Mittal, H.A. Yanco, J. Aronis, R-. Simpson (Eds.), Assistive Technology in Artificial Intelligence. X, 273 pages. 1998. (Subseries LNAI).

Vol. 1459: D.G. Feitelson, L. Rudolph (Eds.), Job Scheduling Strategies for Parallel Processing. Proceedings, 1998. VII, 257 pages. 1998.

Vol. 1460: G. Quirchmayr, E. Schweighofer, T.J.M. Bench-Capon (Eds.), Database and Expert Systems Applications. Proceedings, 1998. XVI, 905 pages. 1998.

Vol. 1461: G. Bilardi, G.F. Italiano, A. Pietracaprina, G. Pucci (Eds.), Algorithms – ESA'98. Proceedings, 1998. XII, 516 pages. 1998.

Vol. 1462: H. Krawczyk (Ed.), Advances in Cryptology - CRYPTO '98. Proceedings, 1998. XII, 519 pages. 1998.

Vol. 1463: N.E. Fuchs (Ed.), Logic Program Synthesis and Transformation. Proceedings, 1997. X, 343 pages. 1998.

Vol. 1464: H.H.S. Ip, A.W.M. Smeulders (Eds.), Multimedia Information Analysis and Retrieval. Proceedings, 1998. VIII, 264 pages. 1998.

Vol. 1465: R. Hirschfeld (Ed.), Financial Cryptography. Proceedings, 1998. VIII, 311 pages. 1998.

Vol. 1466: D. Sangiorgi, R. de Simone (Eds.), CONCUR'98: Concurrency Theory. Proceedings, 1998. XI, 657 pages. 1998.

Vol. 1467: C. Clack, K. Hammond, T. Davie (Eds.), Implementation of Functional Languages. Proceedings, 1997. X, 375 pages. 1998.

Vol. 1468: P. Husbands, J.-A. Meyer (Eds.), Evolutionary Robotics. Proceedings, 1998. VIII, 247 pages. 1998.

Vol. 1469: R. Puigjaner, N.N. Savino, B. Serra (Eds.), Computer Performance Evaluation. Proceedings, 1998. XIII, 376 pages. 1998.

Vol. 1470: D. Pritchard, J. Reeve (Eds.), Euro-Par'98: Parallel Processing. Proceedings, 1998. XXII, 1157 pages. 1998.

Vol. 1471: J. Dix, L. Moniz Pereira, T.C. Przymusinski (Eds.), Logic Programming and Knowledge Representation. Proceedings, 1997. IX, 246 pages. 1998. (Subseries LNAI).

Vol. 1472: B. Freitag, H. Decker, M. Kifer, A. Voronkov (Eds.), Transactions and Change in Logic Databases. Proceedings, 1996, 1997. X, 396 pages. 1998.

Vol. 1473: X. Leroy, A. Ohori (Eds.), Types in Compilation. Proceedings, 1998. VIII, 299 pages. 1998.

Vol. 1474: F. Mueller, A. Bestavros (Eds.), Languages, Compilers, and Tools for Embedded Systems. Proceedings, 1998. XIV, 261 pages. 1998.

Vol. 1475: W. Litwin, T. Morzy, G. Vossen (Eds.), Advances in Databases and Information Systems. Proceedings, 1998. XIV, 369 pages. 1998.

Vol. 1476: J. Calmet, J. Plaza (Eds.), Artificial Intelligence and Symbolic Computation. Proceedings, 1998. XI, 309 pages. 1998. (Subseries LNAI).

Vol. 1477: K. Rothermel, F. Hohl (Eds.), Mobile Agents. Proceedings, 1998. VIII, 285 pages. 1998.

Vol. 1478: M. Sipper, D. Mange, A. Pérez-Uribe (Eds.), Evolvable Systems: From Biology to Hardware. Proceedings, 1998. IX, 382 pages. 1998.

Vol. 1479: J. Grundy, M. Newey (Eds.), Theorem Proving in Higher Order Logics. Proceedings, 1998. VIII, 497 pages. 1998.

Vol. 1480: F. Giunchiglia (Ed.), Artificial Intelligence: Methodology, Systems, and Applications. Proceedings, 1998. IX, 502 pages. 1998. (Subseries LNAI).

Vol. 1481: E.V. Munson, C. Nicholas, D. Wood (Eds.), Principles of Digital Document Processing. Proceedings, 1998. VII, 152 pages. 1998.

Vol. 1482: R.W. Hartenstein, A. Keevallik (Eds.), Field-Programmable Logic and Applications. Proceedings, 1998. XI, 533 pages. 1998.

Vol. 1483: T. Plagemann, V. Goebel (Eds.), Interactive Distributed Multimedia Systems and Telecommunication Services. Proceedings, 1998. XV, 326 pages. 1998.

Vol. 1484: H. Coelho (Ed.), Progress in Artificial Intelligence – IBERAMIA 98. Proceedings, 1998. XIII, 421 pages. 1998. (Subseries LNAI).

Vol. 1485: J.-J. Quisquater, Y. Deswarte, C. Meadows, D. Gollmann (Eds.), Computer Security – ESORICS 98. Proceedings, 1998. X, 377 pages. 1998.

Vol. 1486: A.P. Ravn, H. Rischel (Eds.), Formal Techniques in Real-Time and Fault-Tolerant Systems. Proceedings, 1998. VIII, 339 pages. 1998.

Vol. 1487: V. Gruhn (Ed.), Software Process Technology. Proceedings, 1998. VIII, 157 pages. 1998.

Vol. 1488: B. Smyth, P. Cunningham (Eds.), Advances in Case-Based Reasoning. Proceedings, 1998. XI, 482 pages. 1998. (Subseries LNAI).

Vol. 1489: J. Dix, L. Fariñas del Cerro, U. Furbach (Eds.), Logics in Artificial Intelligence. Proceedings, 1998. X, 391 pages. 1998. (Subseries LNAI).

Vol. 1490: C. Palamidessi, H. Glaser, K. Meinke (Eds.), Principles of Declarative Programming. Proceedings, 1998. XI, 497 pages. 1998.

Vol. 1491: W. Reisig, G. Rozenberg (Eds.), Lectures on Petri Nets I: Basic Models. XII, 683 pages. 1998.

Vol. 1492: W. Reisig, G. Rozenberg (Eds.), Lectures on Petri Nets II: Applications. XII, 479 pages. 1998.

Vol. 1493: J.P. Bowen, A. Fett, M.G. Hinchey (Eds.), ZUM '98: The Z Formal Specification Notation. Proceedings, 1998. XV, 417 pages. 1998.

Vol. 1494: G. Rozenberg, F. Vaandrager (Eds.), Lectures on Embedded Systems. Proceedings, 1996. VIII, 423 pages. 1998.

Vol. 1495: T. Andreasen, H. Christiansen, H.L. Larsen (Eds.), Flexible Query Answering Systems. IX, 393 pages. 1998. (Subseries LNAI).

Vol. 1496: W.M. Wells, A. Colchester, S. Delp (Eds.), Medical Image Computing and Computer-Assisted Intervention – MICCAI'98. Proceedings, 1998. XXII, 1256 pages. 1998.

Vol. 1497: V. Alexandrov, J. Dongarra (Eds.), Recent Advances in Parallel Virtual Machine and Message Passing Interface. Proceedings, 1998. XII, 412 pages. 1998.

Vol. 1498: A.E. Eiben, T. Bäck, M. Schoenauer, H.-P. Schwefel (Eds.), Parallel Problem Solving from Nature – PPSN V. Proceedings, 1998. XXIII, 1041 pages. 1998.

Vol. 1499: S. Kutten (Ed.), Distributed Computing. Proceedings, 1998. XII, 419 pages. 1998.

Vol. 1501: M.M. Richter, C.H. Smith, R. Wiehagen, T. Zeugmann (Eds.), Algorithmic Learning Theory. Proceedings, 1998. XI, 439 pages. 1998. (Subseries LNAI).

Vol. 1502: G. Antoniou, J. Slaney (Eds.), Advanced Topics in Artificial Intelligence. Proceedings, 1998. XI, 333 pages. 1998. (Subseries LNAI).

Vol. 1503: G. Levi (Ed.), Static Analysis. Proceedings, 1998. IX, 383 pages. 1998.

Vol. 1504: O. Herzog, A. Günter (Eds.), KI-98: Advances in Artificial Intelligence. Proceedings, 1998. XI, 355 pages. 1998. (Subseries LNAI).

Vol. 1505: D. Caromel, R.R. Oldehoeft, M. Tholburn (Eds.), Computing in Object-Oriented Parallel Environments. Proceedings, 1998. XI, 243 pages. 1998.

Vol. 1506: R. Koch, L. Van Gool (Eds.), 3D Structure from Multiple Images of Large-Scale Environments. Proceedings, 1998. VIII, 347 pages. 1998.

Vol. 1507: T.W. Ling, S. Ram, M.L. Lee (Eds.), Conceptual Modeling – ER '98. Proceedings, 1998. XVI, 482 pages. 1998.

Vol. 1508: S. Jajodia, M.T. Özsu, A. Dogac (Eds.), Advances in Multimedia Information Systems. Proceedings, 1998. VIII, 207 pages. 1998.

Vol. 1510: J.M. Zytkow, M. Quafafou (Eds.), Principles of Data Mining and Knowledge Discovery. Proceedings, 1998. XI, 482 pages. 1998. (Subseries LNAI).

Vol. 1511: D. O'Hallaron (Ed.), Languages, Compilers, and Run-Time Systems for Scalable Computers. Proceedings, 1998. IX, 412 pages. 1998.

Vol. 1512: E. Giménez, C. Paulin-Mohring (Eds.), Types for Proofs and Programs. Proceedings, 1996. VIII, 373 pages. 1998.

Vol. 1513: C. Nikolaou, C. Stephanidis (Eds.), Research and Advanced Technology for Digital Libraries. Proceedings, 1998. XV, 912 pages. 1998.

Vol. 1514: K. Ohta, D. Pei (Eds.), Advances in Cryptology – ASIACRYPT'98. Proceedings, 1998. XII, 436 pages. 1998.

Vol. 1515: F. Moreira de Oliveira (Ed.), Advances in Artificial Intelligence. Proceedings, 1998. X, 259 pages. 1998. (Subseries LNAI).

Vol. 1516: W. Ehrenberger (Ed.), Computer Safety, Reliability and Security. Proceedings, 1998. XVI, 392 pages. 1998.

Vol. 1517: J. Hromkovič, O. Sýkora (Eds.), Graph-Theoretic Concepts in Computer Science. Proceedings, 1998. X, 385 pages. 1998.

Vol. 1518: M. Luby, J. Rolim, M. Serna (Eds.), Randomization and Approximation Techniques in Computer Science. Proceedings, 1998. IX, 385 pages. 1998.

Vol. 1520: M. Maher, J.-F. Puget (Eds.), Principles and Practice of Constraint Programming - CP98. Proceedings, 1998. XI, 482 pages. 1998.

Vol. 1521: B. Rovan (Ed.), SOFSEM'98: Theory and Practice of Informatics. Proceedings, 1998. XI, 453 pages. 1998.

Vol. 1522: G. Gopalakrishnan, P. Windley (Eds.), Formal Methods in Computer-Aided Design. Proceedings, 1998. IX, 529 pages. 1998.

Vol. 1524: G.B. Orr, K.-R. Müller (Eds.), Neural Networks: Tricks of the Trade. VI, 432 pages. 1998.

Vol. 1525: D. Aucsmith (Ed.), Information Hiding. Proceedings, 1998. IX, 369 pages. 1998.

Vol. 1526: M. Broy, B. Rumpe (Eds.), Requirements Targeting Software and Systems Engineering. Proceedings, 1997. VIII, 357 pages. 1998.

Vol. 1529: D. Farwell, L. Gerber, E. Hovy (Eds.), Machine Translation and the Information Soup. Proceedings, 1998. XIX, 532 pages. 1998. (Subseries LNAI).

Vol. 1530: V. Arvind, R. Ramanujam (Eds.), Foundations of Software Technology and Theoretical Computer Science. XII, 369 pages. 1998.

Vol. 1531: H.-Y. Lee, H. Motoda (Eds.), PRICAI'98: Topics in Artificial Intelligence. XIX, 646 pages. 1998. (Subseries LNAI).

Vol. 1096: T. Schael, Workflow Management Systems for Process Organisations. Second Edition. XII, 229 pages. 1998.

Vol. 1532: S. Arikawa, H. Motoda (Eds.), Discovery Science. Proceedings, 1998. XI, 456 pages. 1998. (Subseries LNAI).

Vol. 1533: K.-Y. Chwa, O.H. Ibarra (Eds.), Algorithms and Computation. Proceedings, 1998. XIII, 478 pages. 1998.

Vol. 1538: J. Hsiang, A. Ohori (Eds.), Advances in Computing Science – ASIAN'98. Proceedings, 1998. X, 305 pages. 1998.